THERMONUCLEAR MONARCHY

Also by Elaine Scarry

THERMONUCLEAR MONARCHY

CHOOSING BETWEEN DEMOCRACY AND DOOM

Elaine Scarry

W. W. NORTON & COMPANY

NEW YORK   LONDON

Grateful acknowledgement is made for permission to quote from the following: From *On the Citizen* by Thomas Hobbes, translated and edited by Richard Tuck and Michael Silverthorne (1998). Reprinted with permission of Cambridge University Press. From *The Iliad* by Homer, translated by Robert Fagles, translation copyright © 1990. Used by permission of Viking Penguin, a division of Penguin Group (USA) Inc. From poem "Psychiatrists (for my brother in the 21 century)" by Grandin Conover. Four-line epigraph reprinted from *Ten Years* (1972) by permission of the Estate of Grandin Conover. From "Sakharov on Gorbachev and Bush," by Andrei Sakharov, *Washington Post*, December 3, 1989; "Presidents' Answers Don't Always Answer," *International Herald Tribune*, December 4, 1989. Epigraph to Chapter 1 reprinted by permission of the Estate of Andrei Dmitrievich Sakharov. From "The Declaration of War: Constitutional and Unconstitutional Violence" by Elaine Scarry, in *Law's Violence*, edited by Austin Sarat and Thomas R. Kearns (1993). Material incorporated with revision and expansion into Chapter 1 used with permission of publisher, University of Michigan Press. From "War and the Social Contract: Nuclear Policy, Distribution, and the Rights to Bear Arms" by Elaine Scarry (1991) in *University of Pennsylvania Law Review*, vol. 139, no. 5. Material incorporated with revision and expansion into Chapter 2 used with permission of publisher. From "Consent and the Body: Injury, Departure, and Desire," by Elaine Scarry with copyright © 1990 by *New Literary History*, University of Virginia. Material incorporated with revision and expansion into Chapter 6 used with permission of Johns Hopkins University Press.

For information about permission to reproduce selections
from this book, write to Permissions, W. W. Norton & Company, Inc.,
500 Fifth Avenue, New York, NY 10110

For information about special discounts for bulk
purchases, please contact W. W. Norton Special Sales at
specialsales@wwnorton.com or 800-233-4830

Manufacturing by Courier Westford
Book design by Daniel Lagin
Production manager: Julia Druskin

Library of Congress Cataloging-in-Publication Data

Scarry, Elaine.
    Thermonuclear monarchy : choosing between democracy and doom / Elaine Scarry. — First Edition.
        p. cm.
    Includes bibliographical references and index.
    ISBN 978-0-393-08008-7 (hardcover)
    1. Nuclear disarmament—United States. 2. Nuclear weapons—Political aspects—United States. 3. Nuclear weapons—Moral and ethical aspects—United States. 4. Nuclear weapons—Government policy—United States. 5. Civil society—United States. 6. Democracy—United States. 7. Constitutional law—United States. I. Title.
    JX1974.7.S2177 2014
    327.1'7470973—dc23
                                        2013037713

W. W. Norton & Company, Inc.
500 Fifth Avenue, New York, N.Y. 10110
www.wwnorton.com

W. W. Norton & Company Ltd.
Castle House, 75/76 Wells Street, London W1T 3QT

1 2 3 4 5 6 7 8 9 0

When you hear the clams calling
     to the moon
To change the tides
I'd be interested in that kind of underworld.

Grandin Conover

CONTENTS

PART THREE
EVERYDAY CONSENT AND EMERGENCY DELIBERATION

THERMONUCLEAR MONARCHY

INTRODUCTION
THE FLOOR OF THE WORLD

I magine that there one day came to exist on earth—sometime in the future—a solitary country with a new technology. The technology has let this solitary country station a door (or more precisely, a series of doors) under the floor of every other country in the world.

If the leader of the solitary country ever feels imperiled or impeded by another country, he can open the trap door and, in a single day, eliminate the population of that rival country. Because the arrangement of doors beneath each national floor is sectioned, the leader can alternatively choose to eliminate just part of the enemy country, a fourth of it, or a third of it; he might choose to open the doors beneath the floor of the opponent's military installations only, thereby eliminating those installations and, say, one-thirtieth of the country's population.

As a shorthand, this ingenious technology and the policies that enable its use might be called the Flexible Floor Doctrine, for it enables the leader not simply to make rapid decisions about the portion of floor to be dropped beneath the feet of any single enemy population but beneath a whole series of enemies. Reciting a few codes and performing a few stark hand gestures, the leader can open the trap doors beneath one-quarter of the population in one nation, beneath one-half of the population in an adjacent nation, and beneath the entire population of a third allied nation located on the other side of the globe. Remarkably, he can do all this in a single hour of a single day.

It is easy to see that the Flexible Floor Doctrine has hideous disadvantages for all countries on earth other than the one controlling the floor levers. Even if the technology is used only once or twice in each century, it will be kept in a state of steady readiness (the levers, latches, and hinges will be kept fully lubricated; their mechanisms will undergo constant innovation and redesign; indeed, if the technology is not kept in a perfect state of repair, the floor doors might accidentally swing open even without any intentional act). The steady readiness of the polished technology means that the subject populations must stay always on their toes. Given the colossal asymmetry in the power to injure between the solitary leaders with access to the floor levers and the millions of inhabitants standing on those imperiling floors, the inhabitants will find themselves, whenever possible, trying to remain on good terms with those foreign leaders, their political acts, their economic decisions, even their moral descriptions.

Though it is hard to conceive of an international arrangement with greater asymmetry and therefore greater unfairness, the advanced country might come to think of itself as fair, even as the fairest of nations, for it each day has the power to annihilate millions of people and each day (or almost each day) abstains from doing so. (Other countries, in its view, seem to hit each other with sticks and stones every chance they get.) The inhabitants of earth will find it in their interest to agree with the lever country's description of its own generosity: they cannot influence whether the flexible floor is absent or present but only whether it stays closed or suddenly drops open beneath them, and they can diminish the chance of its dropping open beneath them by smiling, waving, and, in general, being cooperative and quiet. Those people who see the flexible floor as a moral outrage will have a hard time finding an effective way to protest it. Their complaints will go unheard; or if heard, will sound like unharmonious eruptions motivated by small-minded envy of the lever country's power, freedom, and fairness.

It might at first seem that, just as the Flexible Floor Doctrine confers overwhelming disadvantages on all the populations who reside on the flexible floor, so it confers profound *advantages* on the population who resides on sturdy ground and whose scientists, engineers, and leaders have put the flexible floor plan into place beneath other peoples' feet. While those other nervous populations must remain always aware of the flexible floor (sometimes acutely, sometimes peripherally), the people in the lever country need not think about it much at all. Sometimes they will be genuinely startled when they suddenly remember that there is such a thing! They have no power over whether their leader pulls the lever, nor any information about whether he contemplates doing so; so it is pointless to think about it, and pleasurable to have one's mind free for other matters.

But despite such apparent advantages, the population in the lever country is itself in mighty peril. The first peril is the possibility that once this technology is invented, another country (or two other countries, or three other countries) will obtain it and install a framework of doors under the original country's formerly secure floors. Second, because the central feature of the technology is that it allows One Person (the leader) to single-handedly retract life from beneath the feet of millions of people, some other One Person (a terrorist, a teenager, a criminal, a floor hacker) may gain access to the levers and so annihilate millions of people. Third, the original lever country can enter into economic competition with its opponent to deprive the opponent of the wherewithal to maintain the expensive flexible floor technology; but now that rusting technology of the former rival will be almost as dangerous as when used by the solitary state leader or stateless terrorist.

Even if the country that invented the original flexible floor technology remains the sole possessor of it (closely monitoring the rest of the world, interrupting any attempts to duplicate the technology, threatening annihilation if the offending country does not desist), a fourth and fifth peril remain. The fourth peril comes from what was originally set forth as an advantage. The inhabitants of the lever country need not be mindful of the flexible floor technology since they are not on the receiving end of the injury, are not themselves the ones controlling the levers, do not have visual access to the subterranean apparatus, do not have access to information about its contemplated use by their leader, do not hear the complaints of foreign populations, or hear those complaints only as alarmist envy. Ignorant of the profound moral harm that has been set in place—an arrangement for the annihilation of tens of millions of people against which there can be no act of self-defense—how can the inhabitants of the lever country discover the way to undo or redress it?

The fifth peril re-enacts and compounds the fourth, magnifying the passivity of the home population, ensuring that they cannot take action against the unprecedented moral harm in which they are themselves steeped. The essential feature of the flexible floor technology—it locates in the hands of a solitary person the power to kill millions of persons—carries with it a momentous shift in the nature of government, for it means that the home population's power of, and responsibility for, self-defense, has been lifted away from them and condensed into the head of government. Just as the flexible floor technology strips all foreign populations of the capacity for self-defense, so it has stripped the home population of the capacity for self-defense. Given the difference in the level of physical injury to which each is subject, one might justly worry that this must be a play on words. But we will eventually see the deep continuity in the two outcomes. For the moment, it is enough to note that the home country has unknowingly reverted to an archaic form of government. It has become what centuries earlier had been called a monarchy, though monarchies of the past were comparatively harmless because the executive had only the ceremonial pretense of omnipotence (crowns, gowns, and odd forms of bowing) rather than the literal technology for killing entire populations at will.

Out-of-ratio weapons—any form of weapon that allows a tiny number of people to kill many millions of people—bring about the fourth and fifth perils simultaneously, an unprecedented moral harm and an atavistic and infantilizing form of government; both entail the elimination of the right of self-defense. The foreign population's right of self-defense is eliminated by the sheer mass-killing power *located at the injuring end of the weapon*; the home population's right of self-defense is eliminated by the technological requirement for a small number of persons *at the firing end of the weapon*. So closely yoked are the two perils that eliminating one of the two harms would simultaneously eliminate the other.

If the home population could (as seems unlikely) burrow their way underground and dismantle the flexible floor technology, they would by that very act reacquire their own self-governing powers. Conversely, if they were to insist on the restoration of self-government, it could only be brought about by making the flexible floor disappear. The yoking of the two forms of repair is the subject of the many pages that follow.

This book is about weaponry that enables a tiny number of people (one, fifty-three, or two hundred twelve) to annihilate millions of people. These can be called out-of-ratio weapons, or weapons of mass destruction; and the most extreme form of them at present is nuclear weapons. Whenever the term *nuclear weapon* is used in this book, it is intended to address the problems raised by any out-of-ratio weapon, whether nuclear, biological, chemical, electromagnetic, or some future technology, such as the flexible floor. If a leader one day comes to have the technology to initiate earthquakes and control their severity and direction so that the earth opens up with controlled precision, the argument holds; if a leader were instead to acquire a wand to capture and redirect the energy of the 8 million lightning bolts that take place each day on earth, the argument would hold. The term *weapons of mass destruction* reminds us that the weapon is designed to kill millions of people. The term *out-of-ratio weapons* reminds us that such weapons always have two (not one) key features: they are designed to kill millions of people and they are designed to be fired by a small number of persons.

NUCLEAR WEAPONS AND THE FLEXIBLE FLOOR MODEL

Nuclear weapons conform to the flexible floor model in four ways. One: They exist in a state of steady readiness to retract life from beneath the feet of many millions of people. Two: Their use is monarchic. The country that deploys the most powerful nuclear arsenal—a country formerly dependent on its population, its legislature, and its executive acting in concert for any act of defense—has now largely eliminated its population and its legislature from the sphere of defense, and relies exclusively on its executive.

Of these two features, the first concerns the foreign populations at the receiving end of the injury, the second concerns the home population at the inflicting end of the injury, and each contains a corollary that carries us to the third and fourth points. Three: The foreign populations, having lost the capacity for self-preservation (traditionally identified as the most inalienable of natural rights and the ground of all other rights) have ceased to be, with respect to their own survival, rights-bearing persons and therefore have no standing to voice what from their perspective looks like a large-scale injustice. Four: The home population, having lost their responsibility for their own defense, have become unmindful that the weapons even exist, and can therefore secure neither their own safety (rescuing themselves from monarchy) nor the safety of any foreign people (as they could in the past by declining to go to war against a given country).

While these four points will strike many readers as self-evidently true, they will strike other readers as odd or unfamiliar, so it will be useful to provide a brief illustration of each. First, then, the technological readiness of the United States to retract life from beneath the floor of the world's inhabitants. The country's nuclear arsenal includes, but is by no means limited to, fourteen Ohio-class submarines, each carrying the equivalent in injuring power to 4000 Hiroshima blasts.[1] Each one of the fourteen ships carries enough power to destroy the people of an entire continent, to do this as a solo performance, without the assistance of its thirteen fellow ships. The precise arithmetic of this blast power can be hard to keep in mind. But one pair of numbers is easy to grasp: the earth has seven continents; the United States has fourteen Ohio-class submarines.

The United States population often imagines that the arsenal came into being during the Cold War with Russia and that its importance ended with the fall of the Berlin Wall in 1989. But of the fourteen Ohio-class ships, eight were built, christened, and commissioned after the fall of the Berlin Wall. Here are their names and birth dates. SSBN USS *West Virginia* was launched in 1989 and commissioned in October 1990 with the words, "Man this ship and bring her to life." SSBN USS *Kentucky* followed. Then, USS *Maryland* was launched in June of 1991 and commissioned on June 13, 1992. Then came SSBN USS *Nebraska*. Then, SSBN USS *Rhode Island* ("Man this ship and bring her to life"). Then came SSBN USS *Maine*, launched in July 1994 and commissioned in July 1995; followed by USS *Wyoming*, launched in July 1995 and commissioned in July 1996. Finally, USS *Louisiana* was launched in 1996 and commissioned on September 6, 1997: "Man this ship and bring her to life."

These eight ships—just the eight built since the fall of the Berlin Wall—carry the equivalent of 32,000 Hiroshima bombs. Each holds within its sleek contours eight times the full-blast power expended by Allied and Axis countries in World War II (this includes, in addition to the nuclear weapons dropped on Hiroshima and Nagasaki, the firebombing of sixty-seven other Japanese cities, the firebombing of Leipzig and Dresden, the bombing of Pearl Harbor, the nightly bombing of London, and six years of artillery fire on beaches, woodlands, hillsides, and cities). Together, the eight ships built since the fall of the Berlin Wall carry sixty-four times the total blast power expended by all sides in World War II.[2] The launching, christening, and commissioning of these ships was not covered in news reports, not even in the states whose names are borne on the ships along with their heavy cargo.

Also unreported during this same period were the voices of foreign populations—an illustration of the corollary cited above: the people who stand to be injured have no standing to make their words audible to the nuclear country. In 1995, seventy-eight countries from the U.N. General Assembly asked the International Court of Justice to provide a judgment about the illegality and inhumanity of nuclear weapons.

Among the petitioners were countries that had signed the nonproliferation treaties on the assumption that countries owning nuclear weapons would soon begin to give them up. The Fourth Review Conference of the Parties to the Treaty on the Non-Proliferation of Nuclear Weapons had written, in its final document in 1990, that "insufficient progress has been made towards the complete elimination of nuclear weapons" by those states in possession of them. Individual nations— including Islamic countries such as Qatar—explicitly cited the dismay of the nonproliferation treaty signers in their formal written statements to the International Court.[3] North Korea and India, neither of which yet possessed nuclear weapons in 1995, both wrote to the International Court of Justice urging the court to judge such weapons illegal.[4]

Many countries addressing the International Court expressed their conviction that international covenants, treaties, and protocols are violated by the possession, threatened use, or use of nuclear weapons. Sweden, Iran, and Egypt each noted that weapons that inflict disproportionate suffering are prohibited by the 1868 Declaration of St. Petersburg and the Geneva Protocols of 1925, 1949, and 1977.[5] The Republic of the Marshall Islands—reminding the court that atolls such as Bikini are still contaminated by the sixty-six atomic bombs the United States tested there—argued that nuclear weapons also violate the 1907 Hague Conventions prohibiting weapons whose effects trespass across the borders of neutral countries.[6] India focused on the many ways in which nuclear weapons fail to follow "rules of proportionality" in international warfare, and argued that nuclear weapons violate the United Nations Charter itself, whose fundamental purpose is to restrict force.[7] Japan—describing itself as "the only nation that has suffered nuclear attack"—argued that nuclear weapons contradict the philosophic foundations underlying international law.[8]

The United States argued the opposite. Its executive branch filed a formal statement, coauthored by the Department of State and the Department of Defense, defending the legality of nuclear weapons. It argued that *owning* nuclear weapons was not illegal. It argued that *threatening* to use nuclear weapons was not illegal. It argued that *using* those nuclear weapons—even *using* them *first*—was not illegal. It enumerated and rejected as inapplicable to nuclear weapons each and every international protocol, treaty, declaration, and human rights instrument intended to diminish suffering, as well as covenants intended to protect the earth, such as the 1985 Vienna Convention for the Protection of the Ozone Layer, and the 1992 Rio Declaration on Environment.[9]

The U.N. Charter restricting force was also quickly set aside. The U.S. executive branch acknowledged that the U.N. General Assembly had passed many resolutions declaring nuclear weapons "contrary to the U.N. Charter." But it then dismissed these resolutions, telling the court that "the General Assembly does not have the authority to 'legislate' or create legally binding obligations on its members." Finally, the U.S. executive rejected the 1948 U.N. Convention on the Prevention and Punishment of the Crime of Genocide. In its written statement to the court, the United States argued that "the deliberate killing of large numbers of people is not sufficient to establish this offense" of genocide; genocide only takes place if the aggressor sets out to destroy "in whole or in part, a national, ethnical, racial or religious group, as such."[10]

The court case went on for many days.[11] On none of these days was it front-page news in the United States; on almost none of these days was it page-fifteen news, or even page-twenty-three news, in the United States. Like the always invisible submarines and like the almost invisible land and air missiles—that are concentrated in states with sparse populations (Wyoming, Montana, North Dakota)—the foreign populations who stand to be injured remain invisible and inaudible, even when mounting a major case at the International Court of Justice.

Although the U.S. postal system is designed to receive foreign mail, any letter from abroad containing a message about nuclear weapons seems to become a dead letter. If the message is sent by telephone, the line goes dead. Maybe somewhere there is a giant storage silo into which—day by day over six decades—there has steadily fallen the layer upon layer of unread letters, petitions, and prayers from foreign voices describing injuries suffered and future injuries feared, the aspiration for international rules of symmetry, and the sense of symmetry betrayed. There, muffled in the thick residue of paper, will be found the echoing dismay of the people who once lived on Bikini island (who began calling out to us in 1946 and have called out to us every year since); the eloquent legal briefs from India and Iran and many other countries; the unopened and unread pages of Masuji Ibuse's exquisite and excruciating *Black Rain*, its parasols and cherry blossom petals drifting between thousands of other paper layers. Maybe the sheer weight of unread mail will one day press the paper into wood and create a giant ark, the ark of unheard voices. The ark of unheard voices is on a collision course with the ark that cannot hear voices, our nuclear submarines.

One of the persistent features of nuclear technology is that it constantly reenacts at one location any weakness that occurs at another location. The supersentient American population prides itself on its alertness—rightly, for many people receive and answer 300 e-mails a day while talking on a cell phone, listening to the radio, and driving a car. Yet this supersentient population cannot hear voices coming from outside the circle of its own horizon. As foreign voices do not reach the home population, so the voices of the home population, in their occasional lonely protest against our nuclear weapons, fall outside the perimeter of what their own government leaders can hear. This inability to receive incoming signals is literalized in the weapons themselves.

Take the USS *Rhode Island* (or any one of the other thirteen Ohio-class submarines). Empowered to destroy a continent, the Trident submarine is an Olympian feat of technological ingenuity. Yet when it is deeply submerged (and in wartime or any time of great political tension it must remain deeply submerged) it can o-n-l-y-r-e-c-e-i-v-e-t-i-n-y-a-m-o-u-n-t-s-o-f-i-n-f-o-r-m-a-t-i-o-n-v-e-r-y-v-e-r-y-s-l-o-w-l-y. In fact, the first three letters of the hyphenated passage would have taken fifteen minutes to arrive, and the submarine would have had no way to confirm its receipt of the letters.

The information is carried in Extremely Low Frequency (or ELF) waves, giant radio waves each 2500 miles in length that can (unlike any other band of the electromagnetic spectrum) penetrate the ocean depths. Until 2004, ELF waves were launched by a giant antenna in Michigan and Wisconsin that is eighteen square acres in size.[12] As ELF waves begin their circuit around the earth, they travel between the surface of the earth and the lower edge of the ionosphere, which together act as wave guides or rails. An ELF signal is often officially described as "a bell ringer": it tells the submarine to come up closer to the surface where it can receive a large volume of data quickly. (The rich data are relayed by the TACAMO system: TACAMO stands for Take Charge and Move Out; it involves a plane hovering over the ocean swirling its antenna, a two-mile-long wire, as though it were a lasso; it is not without its own extravagant communication problems.)[13] But this means that added to the fifteen minutes it takes to receive the ELF message is the time it takes the submarine to reach the new location, the upper layers of water it had been cautiously avoiding. Furthermore, evidence suggests that the ELF signals, in addition to serving as a bell ringer, are also relied on for the transmission of primary commands (the order to fire a weapon, the order to interrupt the firing of a weapon). The actual situation is still more meager than the fifteen-minute three-letter-long message suggests. So possible is it that even this message will not get through that standing Navy weapons procedure has during certain periods been premised on the absence of any outside message at all. The commander of a ship during those periods had the ability to launch nuclear weapons without an order from the civilian government.

In its capacity to receive signals, the Trident submarine exists in a pretechnological realm. The men on the ship are like the inhabitants of a tiny medieval village on a remote mountainside. With luck, the villagers receive light flashes from a lantern on a faraway peak. On many nights they see no flashes at all. The signal can only contain a syntactically simple message ("yes" or "no") whose context the villagers may or may not correctly guess. Yet despite its primitive level of communication, this encapsulated village has enough power to destroy a continent.

Both the United States as a country and any one of its Trident submarines are characterized by a vast capacity to injure and a low capacity to receive information that may bear on the question of whether those who will receive the injury have done something so deserving. A message to the submarine that says, "Ignore the previous order; we just learned our enemy has *not* committed any injustice against us" can perhaps be folded into a three-letter code. But it can be transmitted only very slowly and without certainty that it will reach its destination.

If our technological ability to receive information were as spectacular as our technogical abilty to injure is spectacular, would the use of nuclear weapons seem better? More justified? More accurate? More likely to be targeted at 100 million people truly deserving of this death? Probably not. Calling attention to our low level of comprehension may therefore seem beside the point since even with the most full and most accurate information in the world, the use of a massive killing weapon would be unjustified. But that is just the point: with the most complete and most accurate information in the world it would soon become self-evident that maintaining an arrangement for killing the world's people is an abomination; the contraction of information at the firing end of a nuclear weapon is therefore an essential part of its design; without it, the weapon would cease to exist. It is not, then, that full perceptual acuity would make genocidal power tolerable—just the reverse: it is that full perceptual acuity would make immediately legible the scale of the moral error in our weapons arrangements. Lacking full comprehension, we must learn to appreciate the depth of the moral error with our eyes half closed and our ears not yet able to hear.

This coupling of maximum power to injure and minimum power to hear outside voices leads us once again to the observation that the weapon has two ends (as does the weapons system designed around the weapon, and the form of government designed around the weapon system). Millions of people reside at the receiving end of the injury; only a handful of people reside at the end where the injury is authorized: the voices of millions—both foreign and domestic—are excluded from this zone.[14] Imagine if this structure were reversed: imagine a system of defense whose target of injury was the smallest number of people possible and where information gathering and authorization were distributed to the largest number of people.[15] Does that sentence have an odd ring? Let us hope not, for what it describes is democracy.

We have claimed that nuclear weapons approximate the flexible floor model in four respects, and have set out to illustrate each of the four. So far we have illustrated two: the readiness of our nuclear weapons to retract life from beneath the feet of the world's people on all seven continents; and the corollary to this, the fact that by depriving foreign people of any power of self-defense, we deprive them of any standing that might make their voices audible to us—whether by letter, poem, novel, resolution, or court plea. Two further points remain to be briefly illustrated, the conversion of the home country's government to a monarchic form of rule that places all defense in the executive branch of the government; and the corollary incapacitation of the population, which—now largely oblivious to all questions of defense—cannot rescue themselves from monarchy and cannot rescue foreign people from the abiding threat of the horrifying injury, or from the actual infliction of that injury.

Forms of government based on symmetry and distribution of power require weapons that entail symmetry and distribution of power. If an out-of-ratio weapon comes into being in the midst of a symmetrical form of government, one of the two must give way to accommodate the other. Either the out-of-ratio weapon must be renounced and dissolved, enabling the symmetrical government to survive; or the symmetrical form of government must be renounced and dissolved, replaced with an out-of-ratio government whose shape can accommodate the shape of the new out-of-ratio weapon. The second outcome has taken place in the United States following the invention of atomic weapons.

During his 1974 impeachment proceedings, President Richard Nixon told reporters, "I can go into my office and pick up the telephone, and in 25 minutes 70 million people will be dead."[16] His statement was a stark—but completely accurate—description of presidential power. Since the invention of atomic weapons, the United States has had a presidential first-use policy: it was in place, but not yet codified into a single, formal written doctrine, during the presidencies of Harry Truman, Dwight Eisenhower, John F. Kennedy, Lyndon Johnson, Richard Nixon, and Gerald Ford, and then became codified during the presidency of Jimmy Carter in Presidential Directive 59, which has continued in force through the presidencies of Ronald Reagan, George H. W. Bush, Bill Clinton, George W. Bush, and is in place today. Many people in the United States think of the country's nuclear weapons as retaliatory "defense" weapons. But the first-use policy presumes what its name states, that the United States will use them first. The effort that a president would have to exert to execute a first-use strike is minimal, as President Nixon's statement accurately records. The "nuclear briefcase" that contains the communication codes for the presidential launch of nuclear weapons has been kept since 1963 within arm's reach of each successive president.[17] It at all times resides in one of two places: either in the same room with the president or in the immediately adjacent room. When the president travels, the nuclear briefcase travels too: when President Carter went camping with his family in Idaho, their raft was accompanied by a neighboring raft carrying the "black bag"; after President Reagan was shot on March 30, 1981, he was carried to George Washington Hospital in a motorcade that also carried the nuclear briefcase and its military attendant.[18]

The American population tends to assume that its own level of worry about nuclear war corresponds to the president's contemplated use of the weapons: if we are thinking about nuclear war, he too must be thinking about it; if it has not so much as crossed our minds, it has probably not crossed his. The first of these two "if" clauses is certainly right; the second is just as certainly wrong.

The United States population and President Kennedy were both acutely conscious of the proximity of nuclear war during the Cuban Missile Crisis (though it is only over many decades that the population learned how gravely close we came). But most people would have a hard time naming a crisis other than the Cuban Missile Crisis where one of our presidents has carried us to the verge of nuclear war because in no instance other than the Cuban Missile Crisis has a president openly addressed his population during the crisis. Just as the population is not needed for carrying out the injury, so we are not privy to the president's deliberations on the matter. An out-of-ratio weapon requires that anything that might get in the way be gotten out of the way; an out-of-ratio weapon makes the presence of the population at the authorization end a structural impossibility.

Following President Harry Truman's use of an atomic weapon in Hiroshima and Nagasaki, a sequence of presidents considered using it again. President Eisenhower seriously contemplated using an atomic weapon in the 1954 Taiwan Straits as he did again in the 1959 Berlin crisis.[19] (We know this not because during the conflict the president discussed the matter with the full Congress or the population but because thirty years after Eisenhower's death his presidential papers were released to a library archive.) President Kennedy three times—once in Cuba; twice in lands unspecified—came very close to using nuclear weapons against the Soviet Union. (We know this not because the president addressed the population in all three periods but because forty years after his death, his Secretary of Defense, Robert McNamara, has stated that during the Kennedy administration, the country came "three times within a hair's breadth of nuclear war with the Soviet Union.")[20]

President Lyndon Johnson contemplated a preemptive nuclear strike against China to prevent that country from developing nuclear weapons; the U.S. population was informed of this event thirty-four years later. President Nixon contemplated using nuclear weapons three times other than in Vietnam, as he stated in an interview thirteen years after he left office; he did not specify time and place. The White House tape that records Nixon's conversation with his secretary of defense, Henry Kissinger, about the possibility of using a nuclear weapon in North Vietnam was released to the public twenty-eight years after he left office.

The crises just enumerated fall between 1954 and 1974; with the exception of the Cuban Missile Crisis, the dates on which the public first received small shreds of information about these nuclear crises go from 1985 to 2004. The fragments of information we may eventually receive about the contemplated use of nuclear weapons by later presidents—Gerald Ford, Jimmy Carter, Ronald Reagan, George H. W. Bush, Bill Clinton, George W. Bush, and Barack Obama—are likely to arrive only haphazardly and slowly over the next thirty years. None of these later presidents has stated that he did *not*, during his time in office, consider using a nuclear weapon. None of these presidents has asked that the military officer carrying the nuclear briefcase stop following him around. None of these presidents has directed the fleet of Ohio-class submarines to return to their Atlantic homeport in Kings Bay, Georgia, or their Pacific homeport in Bangor, Washington; day and night the ships move under waters all over the world. Eight of the fourteen ships were completed while presidents Bush and Clinton were in office; the overall number is fourteen rather than what was for a time eighteen because the four oldest have now been phased out of ballistic missile service and instead carry nuclear-armed cruise missiles. President George W. Bush directed nuclear engineers to complete a next-generation submarine by 2030, a next-generation Intercontinental Ballistic Missile by 2020, and a next-generation heavy bomber by 2040.[21] There is no indication that President Obama has interrupted the ongoing work on these new sea-based, land-based, and air-based delivery systems.[22] They are scheduled to arrive at just about the time we will begin to learn what nuclear catastrophes were contemplated in the early years of the twenty-first century—unless, of course, the catastrophe takes place, in which case we will already know.

In some of the nuclear crises, the thirty-years-out-of-date archive lets us begin to gauge how close the president came to initiating nuclear war; in other instances, we continue to reside in the region of speculative conversation, clearing our throats and trading uninformed guesses about—what was the subject again?—oh yes, about whether our country did or did not take steps to annihilate millions of people on a region of earth we cannot even name. Our two "if" clauses—if we are thinking about nuclear war, the president must also be thinking about it; if it does not cross our minds, it must not be crossing his—lead to a kind of magical thinking whereby we hope to keep foreign populations safe by not thinking about our own weapons, or thinking about them only three decades after the crisis is over.

Documentary evidence of our population's collective, nearly tour-de-force ability to abstain from mentioning aloud our own nuclear weapons exists in the period leading up to and through the 2003–5 phase of the war in Iraq.[23] Day by day over 400 days, American newspapers and journals were laden with statements about whether Saddam Hussein's Iraq *certainly did, probably did, probably did not, or certainly did not* own a nuclear weapon, but among these tens of thousands of articles, one looks in vain for even a solitary allusion to our own vast nuclear arsenal, to the fact that we own in addition to 3100 Trident I and Trident II warheads designed for our Ohio-class submarines (with a total blast power of 273,000,000 tons of TNT), land-based ICBM nuclear warheads with a total blast power of 503,000,000 tons of TNT, and air-based nuclear warheads for the B-2 and B-52 bombers equaling 410,000,000 tons of TNT.[24]

It is tempting to think that a country with monarchic arrangements in the realm of nuclear war can maintain a more attractive form of government throughout the rest of its civil fabric. That would be a mistake. A country *is* its arrangements for national defense; or in the words of Patrick Henry at the Virginia Ratification Debates, "It has been repeatedly said that the great object of national government [is] national defense."[25] The structures imposed on us by thermonuclear monarchy are structures that penetrate all the way down to the deepest details of civil life, as we will eventually see. For the moment, it may be enough to recall how the arrangements for nuclear war have in turn reshaped the arrangements for conventional war.

Because nuclear war has been placed in the solitary hands of presidents, presidents have assumed that conventional wars can also be fought on their own authority and have repeatedly taken the country to war without a constitutionally mandated congressional declaration of war. Since the invention of nuclear weapons, each new war—the Korean War, the Vietnam War, the Gulf War,[26] the war in former Yugoslavia,[27] the Iraq War—has been carried out without a congressional declaration, as have the invasions of Panama, Grenada, and Haiti. Since the president has such genocidal injuring power at his personal disposal through nuclear weapons, obtaining Congress's permission for much lesser acts of injuring (as in conventional wars) has often struck presidents as a needless bother: referring to the 1991 Gulf War, for example, President Bush boasted, "I didn't have to get permission from some old goat in the United States Congress to kick [Iraqi President] Saddam Hussein out of Kuwait."[28] This sense that the military serves at the pleasure of the president was candidly expressed by President Nixon during the Watergate aftermath: he said that the executive, legislative, and judiciary are not equal branches, because, unlike the executive, neither the legislative nor the judiciary has an army.[29]

Of all the presidents who have held office since the invention of nuclear weapons, Richard Nixon has been the most open about the shift in the form of government they impose. His lawyer before the federal court during the Watergate Hearings opened with the following words: "The President, my client, wants me to argue that he is as absolute a monarch as Louis XIV, and only four years at a time, and is not subject to the processes of any court in the land."[30] Nixon's sense that his country had endowed the executive branch with monarchic powers was also visible in his attempt to dress the White House guards in elaborate royal uniforms, described by Paul Fussell:

> First, the hat: a black plastic semi-shako with visor. It rose a full seven inches, and Washington hadn't seen its like since the British and Germans fought us in the 1770s. Then there was the tunic: high-collared, cream-colored, double-breasted, with a heavy gold fourragère...hanging from the right shoulder. Belt and pistol holsters were of shiny black, apparently "patent" leather.[31]

Thomas Paine had written in 1776 that if you ask anyone in America if he believes in monarchy, he'll just start laughing.[32] Ask anyone today in the United States if he believes in monarchy and he will also laugh. Paul Fussell precedes his factual description of the uniforms with the statement, "The new uniforms are hard to describe without laughing." Indeed, the uniforms were subjected to such immediate and widespread derision that they quickly vanished from the White House.[33]

But one of the reasons why the country has been tardy in addressing the severe problem of thermonuclear monarchy is precisely that the struggle against monarchy seems like a struggle won long ago and in no need of being debated today. (Isn't monarchy something we laugh at?) Can it really be the case that we need to start all over and rewrite Locke's *Second Treatise of Government* or Paine's *Common Sense*? Do we need to reawaken our scorn for patriarchy, a scorn already in full bloom by the seventeenth and eighteenth centuries, a scorn that has surely grown stronger and more self-assured with each passing century, decade, and year? How might we even debate the matter? Such a debate would require the recitation of principles to which we have already achieved such widespread agreement that anyone beginning to reannounce the basic principles of constitutions or social contract would appear to have lost his or her mind and would be scolded for platitude.

How, then, have we arrived at a thermonuclear monarchy whose ludicrous nature only becomes visible to us if a president—out of a lucky convergence of candor and bad taste—makes the lineaments of the ludicrous monarchy (let us call it a "ludocracy") visible? No one faults Richard Nixon for contemplating using nuclear weapons on four occasions, only for comparing himself to Louis XIV, for dressing White House police in the lavish insignia of royal subjugation, for spying on the rivals to his throne, and for lying to Congress. As moral errors, we will someday see, these acts are incomparable with the error of accepting a post that involves firing nuclear weapons, an assignment not only Nixon but each of our post-atom-bomb presidents has accepted: Truman, Eisenhower, Kennedy, Johnson, Nixon, Ford, Carter, Reagan, Bush, Clinton, Bush, Obama. Louis XIV was powerless compared to each of these men. That insight is Nixon's gift to us; it is precious; let us not (once we recover from our laughter) set it aside cavalierly.

Far from feeling angry with a succession of presidents for their unblinking willingness to step up into the post of thermonuclear monarch, the population has often been asked to feel sympathetic with their terrible burden. Nixon did not often appear to be worried by his power to inflict global harm (indeed, he sometimes seems to have boasted of it). But the portrait that survives from the Kennedy era—and that has come to be generalized to the presidential office irrespective of occupant—is of a president weighed down by the gravity of his nuclear decision-making. It is difficult to decouple the words "Cuban Missile Crisis" from the photograph of Kennedy in dark silhouette, seen from the back, looking out a large White House window, its etched black-and-white lines evocative of the gravity of his decisions.

The distress of presidential deliberation—not the distress of hundreds of thousands who stand to be annihilated or so badly burned they only half survive—becomes the focus of sympathy. The tragic lineaments of the nuclear arrangements, like their comic lineaments, are all spent on, absorbed into, the personal narrative of the president.

In part, this reflects the nature of compassion: public health scholars differentiate between our ready ability to feel "compassion" for a solitary person and our inability to feel "statistical compassion" when a large multitude undergoes far more excruciating forms of suffering.[34] But this odd short-circuiting of our compassion—our willingness to direct it toward the agent of the injury rather than to those potentially injured— also follows from the structural features of an out-of-ratio government that has arranged itself around an out-of-ratio weapon. Just as foreign peoples, by losing their capacity for self-preservation, have lost their standing to have their protests heard, so too they have ceased to have any interior psychological content for us vis-à-vis the weapons; it is as though they have ceased to be a center of suffering or a center of gravity. The single individual at the authorizing end precisely does, in contrast, have a psyche, a psyche whose great magnitude is apparent to us as in the very scale of the millions of lives he can contemplate killing.[35]

The willingness to speak with reverential hushed tones of the "awful" responsibilities of being president in a nuclear age is apparent in Theodore Sorensen's book about John Kennedy, *Decision-Making in the White House*:

> [The] breadth and scope of presidential decisions cannot be matched in any large corporation or Cabinet department, or even in the halls of Congress. For the President alone is ultimately accountable for the lives of more than 2.5 million American servicemen, for the deeds of 2.5 million federal employees, and he alone is ultimately held accountable to 190 million citizens, to more than 40 foreign allies *and, in a very real sense—as custodian of the nuclear trigger—to all men and to all mankind*."[36]

Once the romance and thrill of picturing such a colossus fades away and we recover our senses, we may ask how it can be that a man of Sorensen's reading and understanding—or more to the point, a man of John Kennedy's vast reading and understanding—could not be revolted by, not revolt against, a situation that allows one man "alone" to be "ultimately held accountable . . . to all men and to all mankind."

John Kennedy's attorney general and brother, Robert Kennedy, wrote an account of the Cuban Missile Crisis—*Thirteen Days*—that he left unfinished. A note at the end of the book tells us what has been left undone:

> It was Senator Kennedy's intention to add a discussion of the basic ethical question involved: what, if any, circumstance or justification gives this government or any government the moral right to bring its people and possibly all people under the shadow of nuclear destruction. He wrote this book in the summer and fall of 1967 on the basis of his personal diaries and recollections, but never had an opportunity to rewrite or complete it.[37]

Is the missing chapter missing because (as the author of the note believes) Robert Kennedy died prematurely? Or is it missing because, even had Robert Kennedy been graced with a hundred years of life, no positive answer could ever be intelligently provided. To the question, "What, if any, circumstance or justification gives this government or any government the moral right to bring its people and possibly all people under the shadow of nuclear destruction?" the only reasonable answer is: *There can be no circumstances or justification* that give this government or any government the moral right to bring its people and possibly all people under the shadow of nuclear destruction. It is easy to hear, in one's imagination, such a sentence being spoken aloud with John Kennedy's cadences and pronunciation. Would that he—or any of our presidents—had spoken it.

It would take a president of the stature of Lincoln to straighten out our current military arrangements. Because the population has been disempowered, disabled, for the last sixty years—because we, like foreign populations, have been frozen in structures of thermonuclear subjugation—we might think we must wait for a president to undertake the work of repair. The needed repairs *are*, in fact, ones that can be carried out by a president, a Congress, or a Supreme Court, and it does not seem unreasonable to hope that one, two, or all three branches of government will eventually assist us. In the meantime, however, the population must reacquire its own powers of self-government and carry out the repairs. Amazingly, a set of tools exists to let us undertake, and even complete, the repair.

If one were to view the current position of the United States population from a great distance, as though one were hearing our story told 300 years from now, it might seem as though we are today in an unsolvable situation. The foreign peoples of earth (as surely as if there were a flexible floor under their feet) stand in danger of being gravely harmed by our country's weapons and we ourselves have no power to intervene, to reach into the mechanism to disable it. Indeed, we do not even know the location of our Ohio-class submarines in any given season; we do not know which particular foreign population is being targeted by our ICBMs in any given year. Unable to exercise any power over the fate of other people, we have also lost our powers of self-protection and self-government. Yet, though it might seem too good to be true, a concrete object exists that enables us to reacquire our powers of self-government and to dismantle the nuclear arsenal simultaneously.

It is as if there had suddenly fallen from the skies into our midst an object—a dazzlingly beautiful object, like shards of many-colored glass—that would let us undertake the needed repair, requiring only that we bend over and pick it up. The object that lies on the ground at our feet is the United States Constitution and the way it outlaws nuclear weapons (or any out-of-ratio weapon that decouples the military might of the country from the population) is the subject of Part One of this book. To reacquire our democratic country and to release us from an unspeakable moral error we need only take this object in our hands and use it. It seems breathtaking that such a device could be ready at hand. At the same time, the fact that it is already in existence, and so readily available for use, increases the obligation of the population to repair the present situation. If we fail to do so, people in the future will say of us, "Though the vast nuclear arsenal was imposed on them, yet every citizen of the country had within easy reach—lying beside the front doorway, resting inside a hallway drawer, sitting in a vest pocket—the tool that would have enabled them to dismantle it."

As we look at the constitutional provisions for war making in Part One (The United States Constitution Outlaws Nuclear Weapons), we will gradually see that the requirement for government "by the people" means government by an *embodied* people, government by a people who have *bodily presence* to their governors. We cannot exist in the sphere of national defense as an *eviscerated* or *virtual* or *nominal* or *polled* population. (Lincoln once described such a substanceless population with derision as "*do nothing Sovereignty*" or "pigeon shadow soup.")[38] If this book makes a new contribution to social contract theory, it is in giving voice to this material requirement: present from the outset, it surfaces with increasing regularity as we proceed through the first four chapters and becomes the exclusive focus of Chapter 5, "Consent and the Body." Because physical presence is a major subject of this book, the book might end with the verbal genre that takes its form from physical presence, a calling of the roll—a recitation of the many people on whose shoulders there now rests the obligation to bring about a constitutional repair and to eliminate out-of-ratio weapons. But by the time we have traveled across all six chapters, we will understand why individualized enumeration is impossible. Thermonuclear monarchy is, as the conclusion states, "Against Us All." It must be redressed by all.

Thermonuclear monarchy is a specific and severe form of monarchy because it places national defense wholly outside the social contract. Therefore the charges against thermonuclear monarchy are not intended to be, and cannot be, generalized to benign forms of monarchy in countries that possess no out-of-ratio weapons. The United Kingdom is, like the United States, a thermonuclear monarchy because it has a prime minister empowered to fire nuclear weapons, not because it has a queen: as we will see in a later chapter, when the British government arranged a secure fallout shelter for 200 leading officials, it neglected to include the queen in its plans. There may be a reader of this book who lives in a country where there is a monarch, but a monarch who resides securely within the architecture of the country's constitution, a monarch who acts in concert with the country's legislature and population. The constitution of Norway, for example, prohibits Norway's king from extending his acts of war making beyond the boundary of the country without the authorization of the Storting or legislature: the king can act defensively *inside the borders* to repel an attack, but cannot act offensively—literally, cannot act one foot beyond the borders—without the legislature's declaration.[39] Furthermore, the Norwegian Constitution not only requires that the executive think and act within the constitution, but requires any member of the Council of State who perceives the monarch to be thinking or acting outside the constitution to state that judgment in writing:

> If any Member of the Council of State is of the opinion that the King's decision conflicts with the form of government or the laws of the Realm, it is his duty to make strong remonstrances against it, as well as to enter his opinion in the records. A member who has not thus protested is deemed to have been in agreement with the King, and is answerable in such manner as may be subsequently decided, and may be impeached by the Parliament [Storting] before the Court of Impeachment.[40]

Like monarchs of the present, monarchs of the past risked losing the throne by acting outside the constitution. When England's James II was deposed, he was charged with "breaking the original contract between king and people," and with having "abdicated the government and . . . the throne is thereby become vacant."[41] Following his deposition, King William and Queen Mary were elected monarchs. During their reign Parliament was transformed from a body that served "largely at the whim" of the throne to an independent institution that

has, since 1689, met every year without fail; the enfranchised population (more than one-quarter of adult males) participated in elections
approximately every two years—more often than at any time before or
since.[42] (When William and Mary traveled from Holland to England
to unseat James, their fleet carried, in addition to 15,000 soldiers and a
printing press, a returning British exile named John Locke, and a sheaf
of manuscript pages that once published would come to be known as
the *Second Treatise of Government*; it identifies the legislature as the
soul of any contractual country.)

War-making, more than any other activity, turned kings into
tyrants by permitting them to inflict their personal will on foreign
populations. But only modern weapons have allowed vast injuring
power to be folded inside the weapon and placed at the *personal disposal of the executive*. In the past, a king could not act in monolithic
solitude because (like American presidents in the preatomic age) he
had to convince men to carry the weapons onto the battlefield and convince them to pay for his wars. The historical record shows that in some
countries, such as medieval France, England, and Spain, the legislature
or assembly, far from being destroyed by war-making, *first came into
being* because a king wanted to go to war; to secure money and soldiers
from his territory, he had to establish a forum for debate and obtain
consent, which then eventually began to address many other matters as
well.[43] Kings sometimes formed executive armies or "standing armies"
that permitted the monarch to act without consulting the population;
far from being tolerated, such standing armies sometimes (as in early
America) became the occasion for getting rid not just of a particular
monarch but of the monarchic form of government altogether.

The oppressive features of monarchy will sometimes be cited in
these pages as we try to recall exactly why it was we wanted our country
to be a democracy and in indicting the present thermonuclear monarchy under which we now suffer. But the opposite is not the case: it is
not the case that the full horror and deformation of government existing in thermonuclear monarchy is descriptive of monarchies that lack

out-of-ratio weapons, whether of the present or past. Thermonuclear monarchy is far more atavistic than the term "monarchy" alone can ever imply. It carries us back to a territory that is not just anterior to democracy but anterior to social contract altogether. At the International Court of Justice, where seventy-eight countries asked for a decision on the illegality of nuclear weapons, Judge Christopher Gregory Weeramantry stated that "the use or threat of use of the weapon is unlawful *in all circumstances without exception*" and observed that to permit any threatened use of nuclear weapons is to erase all international and national law: "a world order dependent upon terror would take us back to the state of nature described by Hobbes in *The Leviathan.*"[44] Thermonuclear monarchy is more grave, more dark, more dangerous than any tyranny that has ever operated on earth.

Two staggering inventions exist side by side. One is the social contract: most elaborately known to us through the seventeenth- and eighteenth-century writings of Hobbes, Locke, and Rousseau, it ricochets forward and backward across the centuries; it has rich antecedents in medieval Europe, in ancient Greece, and still further back in Hebrew culture; just as it has an array of forward-moving descendants in the ceaselessly proliferating democratic constitutions that emerge throughout the eighteenth, nineteenth, twentieth, and twenty-first centuries. The other giant artifact on which almost as much human ingenuity has been spent is the nuclear array, all land-based, sea-based, sky-based missiles that carry the warheads to their destination, all orbiting, rotating, and fixed antennas and aerials that link the warheads to the small number of men who control and direct them. Though much younger than the social contract, this second artifact is spreading throughout the world almost as rapidly, reappearing in ever-new, seemingly insuppressible forms. Each of the two artifacts, left to itself, will proliferate. Each brought to bear on the other, will bring that other to a dead halt.

The two artifacts, the social contract and the nuclear array, are mutually exclusive. To exist each requires that the other be destroyed. Which one will it be?

PART ONE

THE UNITED STATES CONSTITUTION OUTLAWS NUCLEAR WEAPONS

A Prelude and Summary

Two provisions of the United States Constitution are radically incompatible with nuclear weapons. The first is the constitutional requirement for a Congressional declaration of war. The second is the constitutional requirement that distributes to the entire adult population shared responsibility for use of the country's arsenal—the provision we know as "the right to bear arms."

Both constitutional provisions are distributional requirements. The first gives the war-authorizing power to the largest body in the national government—not the president, or the Supreme Court, or the House acting alone, or the Senate acting alone, but the full Congress. The second gives the war-making power to a far larger group, the full adult population. At the time the Second Amendment was being formulated, great stress was placed on the importance of including in the military people from all regions of the country, all age groups, and all economic levels: although the provision at first included only white men across these ample categories, it eventually came to include people of both genders and all races. No war could be fought unless it was formally declared by the national legislature and then carried out by the population. By their participation in the fighting, the population ratified the congressional act.

The two chapters in Part One each describe in detail how one of the two constitutional provisions works. What will gradually become visible is the brilliant design of the Constitution: the two provisions are not abstract formulas or bare regulations but processes that have astonishing weight and gravity. They ensure that the country cannot go to war—cannot begin to injure a foreign population or our own population—without first undergoing a profound sequence of validating tests. The two provisions also ensure that the military can never be the path back to monarchy—crucial guarantees since recent history shows how easily the fog of war can destroy democracy and spawn single-leader rule.

While the democratic design of the two provisions will be unfolded in the chapters that follow, it may be useful to set forth four key points. First, the only way to bring nuclear weapons into line with the Constitution is to eliminate them. Those who endorse presidential use of nuclear weapons often defend the bypassing of the constitutional requirement for a congressional declaration of war by pointing out that the picture of Congress deliberating about whether to launch a nuclear weapon is ludicrous. They are right; it is ludicrous. Confronted with the legitimate recognition that a national legislature and nuclear weapons are irreconcilable, our country took the wholly illegitimate step of simply eliminating the national assembly. We ought, instead, to have kept our legislature and discarded the weapons—an alternative that still lies open to us today.

Second, once Congress was stripped of its responsibility for overseeing war—as happened the moment atomic weapons were invented—it was, in effect, infantilized. Deprived of its most weighty and arduous burden, it lost the very work that had given it its gravity as an institution. Though its members still convened in an august building, their capacity to deliberate about military and nonmilitary matters gradually deteriorated, as did their sense of obligation to the people of the nation. Now, six decades later, book after book has appeared describing Congress as "dysfunctional" or "dead."[1] Once Congress regains its authority over war, however, there is every reason to believe that it will travel back along the reverse path, reacquiring the stature, intelligence, eloquence, and commitment to the population it once had. In the chapter ahead, we look at the nature of congressional debate in the country's five constitutionally declared wars—the War of 1812, the Mexican-American War of 1846, the Spanish-American War of 1898, World War I, World War II—deliberations in which the full stature of the assembly comes clearly into view. The high quality of congressional analysis contrasts sharply with the low quality of debate carried out in secret presidential deliberations about whether to drop the atomic bomb in the Taiwan straits in 1954 and on East Germany in 1959.

Third, the same argument holds for the country's population. The picture of a full population participating in the launch of a nuclear weapon is ludicrous; thus the population has simply been eliminated from the sphere of military responsibility and oversight. We ought, instead, to have kept our population and discarded the weapons—an alternative still open to us.

Whether our population, by being stripped of its military responsibilities, has—like our Congress—suffered a diminution in civic stature is a question important to ask. The chapter on the Second Amendment reveals that in the past, civic stature and military stature went hand in hand. The Fifteenth Amendment extending the voting right to African Americans was won primarily on the argument that 180,000 blacks had fought in the Civil War and could not be deprived of the right to vote. The passage of the Nineteenth Amendment extending the voting right to women was linked in suffrage pageants and plays to the capacity of women to defend themselves and others. The Twenty-Sixth Amendment lowering the voting age from twenty-one to eighteen was argued on the basis that the Vietnam generation—both the soldiers who fought in Vietnam and the students who debated the war on university campuses—was the most mature generation the country had ever had; they had therefore, according to congressional testimony, earned for themselves and all future generations the right to vote at a younger age.

It is hard for the same population to maintain its civic stature as a great and noble people when it no longer has any voice in whether we invade former Yugoslavia, or Iraq, or Afghanistan, or Iran—let alone whether we possess nuclear weapons. Because such weapons are shrouded in secrecy, most Americans do not realize the country has a first-use policy. We are even uninformed about the numbers: a 2004 poll revealed that most Americans estimate that the United States possesses 200 nuclear weapons rather than the actual figure, 10,000.[2] When asked whether they want the total elimination of nuclear arms, 73 percent of Americans say yes, as do a similar portion of Russians and Canadians.[3] But since the weapons do not require the population's authorization or participation, their disapproval of them is inconsequential. When thirteen protestors objected to the christening of the SSBN *West Virginia*, the only news report was a two-sentence article, one sentence describing their arrest and the other noting that "an estimated 3,700 guests" attended the launch party.[4] There is no record of any other protest prompted by the eight newest Ohio-class ships.[5] Invisible at sea, the weapons are almost equally invisible beneath the land, as is most of the dissent they instigate. Of the original 1000 Minuteman ICBMs buried three-stories deep in fields and farms across the Great Plains, all ready for immediate launch, 450 are today still in place.[6] When one Montana rancher objected to the appropriation of his field, the Army Corps of Engineers "simply filed a condemnation proceeding against the plot of land in question."[7] That single ICBM, which can reach a foreign city in less time than it takes to read this brief chapter, contains a force twenty-seven times as great as the bomb dropped on Hiroshima.

There is no possibility of simply "repairing" our nuclear weapons by "redesigning them" so Congress and the population can exercise a voice over their use. By their very nature, nuclear weapons eliminate Congress and the population. Embedded in the fundamental design of nuclear weapons is a "delete" button—delete the legislature, delete the population. That delete button sits next to, and must itself be depressed before, the button is pushed that launches the missiles themselves.

Fourth, the purpose of nuclear weapons is to annihilate many millions of people in a few minutes: that outcome is not a "by-product"; it is the outcome they exist to bring about. That purpose can only be accomplished if we first annihilate the national legislature (what Locke called "the soul" of a contractual society) and the home population. A legislature and a population would so hopelessly encumber the use of such weapons that they must simply be gotten out of the way. The two forms of annihilation, as we saw in "The Floor of the World," are very different: those foreign people who are targeted by nuclear weapons will be vaporized if they are in the direct line of fire and will suffer death or grievous physical injury if they are in an outer circle. Neither Congress nor the home population, in contrast, is at first subject to physical injury. Their "annihilation" or "disappearance" is instead moral and political. It is their civic stature and their positions as guardians of democracy that have been vaporized. But because our own vast arsenal has incited (and every day continues to incite) other countries to acquire nuclear weapons, we do now stand to suffer direct physical injury and annihilation—a possibility that could never have come into being had we worked to eliminate them from our own ground and the territories of earth.

It may seem that the point of Part One is to grieve for the loss of our elected assembly and our population, to lament the fact that both have abandoned their posts. Such lamentation is warranted: as we will see in the chapters ahead, a population and a legislature cannot maintain their civic stature if they have forfeited their military responsibilities. The capacity for self-governance is premised on the capacity for self-defense. But the purpose of Part One is not to lament the lost constitutional provisions but to find them again, to show that they lie within our reach. Once we take them in our hands, they will enable us to eliminate our nuclear weapons (and, with the help of other populations and their own laws, both national and international, eliminate nuclear weapons worldwide).

In *The Rights of Man*, Thomas Paine wrote that the American and French revolutions had caused a way of thinking about governments that could never be undone; democracy would spread from country to country, he predicted, and undo monarchy and aristocracy. For Paine, the American Constitution provided the essential primer: "The American constitutions were to liberty what a grammar is to language: they define its parts of speech, and practically construct them into a syntax."[8] In creating this syntax of liberty, no part of the U.S. Constitution was more key than its arrangements for the military.

The two distributional sites for military decision-making—the congressional assembly and the population at large—give to war making the same importance as constitution making itself. To make the Constitution or to alter it through amendment requires a full congressional act followed by the population's ratification: this gives constitutional law a much greater gravity and weight than any other legislative act or federal law. Remarkably, the single other constitutionally mandated act that requires this same double location is war making. A democratic exercise of military power requires a full congressional act followed by the population's ratification, a ratification they enact by their consent to bear arms. Without these safeguards, the syntax of liberty and the grammar of democracy disappear.

Future generations—and, over millennia, future civilizations—will look back with astonishment at the seventy-year period during which the people of earth stood by while a tiny number of men (we could even say, a number of tiny men) held in their hands the power to destroy the earth. By taking these two constitutional provisions in our own hands we can remove that power from their hands. We can ensure that thermonuclear monarchy ends after seventy years and thereby ensure that our shared world does not end. What is at stake in democracy is something much greater than democracy: the future of earth and the thousands of species who share its ground.

CHAPTER 1

THE CONSTITUTION REQUIRES A CONGRESSIONAL DECLARATION OF WAR

Bush took a photograph out of his pocket—a family group, people of various generations on some cliffs by the sea. He said, "Here's the guarantee that we will never use nuclear weapons first. This is my family, my wife, children and grandchildren. I don't want them to die. No one on earth wants that."

—Andrei Sakharov

Shortly before he died, Andrei Sakharov urged the president of the United States to formally renounce the strategic policy of presidential first use of nuclear weapons. Although the president—drawing a photograph from his wallet—gave his personal assurance, what Sakharov wanted was not this act, but an official announcement. "[I]f," said Sakharov to Bush, "you insist that you will not strike first, you must make an official announcement of that, put it into the law." Mr. Bush was silent.[1] This opposition—a restraint imposed by personal goodwill or instead one imposed by a framework of laws—is as old as the idea of a republic. The distance between the two can be measured by assessing how the act of "representation" works in each. In articulating his reluctance to use nuclear weapons offensively, the president introduced into the visual space a "representation," a photograph, a fragile slip of paper. Both aesthetic representation and political representation were entailed—as they must always be entailed in the question of how other persons come before the mind in the moment one considers inflicting great injury upon them.

As Sakharov may or may not have been aware, a formal legal prohibition of presidential first use of nuclear weapons already exists. Article I, Section 8, Clause 11, of the U.S. Constitution requires a congressional declaration of war: it stipulates that the full House and Senate together (the full assembly of Representatives) are obligated to oversee the country's entry into war. The stark incompatibility of this constitutionally required declaration with the longstanding strategic policy of presidential first use has, since 1984, been repeatedly observed in both foreign policy and law journals.[2] It has also been addressed through law cases. In 1987, for example, two congressmen challenged presidential first use in court. The judge held that the plaintiffs' claims were not yet ripe for decision (not because the country was not close enough to nuclear war but because—in his view—more congressional plaintiffs were needed). He acknowledged that the "[plaintiffs] may have raised a new question that will require the attention of the United States Supreme Court, because of the uniqueness of the fact situation here."[3]

The observation that presidential first use violates the constitutional requirement for a congressional declaration of war has been made not only by scholars, religious leaders, congressional plaintiffs, and dissident intellectuals, but also by those at the center of executive power. At least where formerly classified presidential and National Security Council Memoranda have been made available, the severity of the constitutional breach has been acknowledged. President Eisenhower, for example, was prepared to use nuclear weapons during both the 1954–55 Taiwan Straits Crisis and the 1959 Berlin Crisis, but he repeatedly acknowledged that, without congressional authorization, his action (whether conventional or atomic) would be unconstitutional. "If Congressional authorization were not obtained," a memorandum records him as saying, "there would be logical grounds for impeachment. Whatever we do must be done in a Constitutional manner."[4]

The specter of a constitutional violation so grave it warrants impeachment has not, over the last six decades, stopped the progressive naturalization of a presidential first-use policy. Nor is it necessarily the case that the threat of impeachment, even if in force, would inhibit a president if longstanding strategic habits were in place, especially where the structure of technology itself appeared to require presidential action. Four months after Eisenhower made the previously cited statements, he changes from saying he will avoid initiating a strike because it is an impeachable act, to saying he will initiate a strike, if necessary, even though it is an impeachable act. The National Security Council Record for January 21, 1955, reads, "The President said that all might be sure of one thing—namely, that he would do in an emergency whatever had to be done to protect the vital interests of the United States. He would do this even if his actions should be interpreted as acts of war. He would rather be impeached than fail to do his duty."[5]

Just as the threat of impeachment may fail to inhibit, so, far from inhibiting, it may actually prompt or invite the act. As Eisenhower's vice president, Nixon was present at the National Security Council meetings just described and reinforced Eisenhower's own belief that solitary action would make him impeachable.[6] But as was noted earlier, during his own impeachment proceedings, Richard Nixon said to a group of Congressmen, "I can go into my office and pick up the telephone and in 25 minutes 70 million people will be dead." Impeachment—by being the path from the chief public officer to a private citizen (a demotion to the purely personal)—makes manifest the kinship between the personal concerns in looking at a family photo and worrying about getting fired. In some way, Nixon's boast and Bush's good-natured gesture of reaching into a wallet to produce a treasured photograph are strangely alike: the basic arrangements of a contractual society are designed to prevent the situation in which a personal decision is made. If the fate of 500 galley slaves is dependent on the personal decision of a ship's tyrant, no one can lightly dismiss the issue of that individual's goodwill, kindness, or humanism. One does not only *not* dismiss it. One actually wishes for it, urges it—and must be grateful to the wife or partner whose *picture in the mind* prevents his cruelty, and that, like the fear of losing office, acts to brake rather than incite fatal actions.

But how in a contractual republic should we have so abased ourselves as to be in a state of petition or gratitude for humanism that stays the hand (rather than eliminating the arrangements that keep us frozen in this posture of petition)? And if it is not we who are the galley slaves but the citizens of other republics—that is, if it is other populations and not we ourselves who will be injured—the same question arises: how did we so lose sight of ourselves as active citizens of a democracy that we left the fate of other populations up to a small number of individuals and the accident of how they feel about a photograph in a pocket? The grant of power by the population to the executive government was never a grant of power to give or retract the lives of millions of people, our own or other populations'. Not even the most benign and generous leader can make contractually tolerable a national arms policy that holds out to other populations this kind of threat—the threat of annihilation to be restrained by purely personal (rather than transpersonal and legal) inhibitions on violence.

This chapter looks at the way language works, the way "representation" works—the way pictures come before the mind—in the congressional declarations of war in the five wars in which the United States has had such a declaration: the War of 1812, Mexican War, Spanish-American War, World War I, and World War II.[7] It then contrasts these declarations with the way language, representation, and picture making work in a presidentially executed war. The deliberations of Congress and the deliberations of presidential council are so diametrically opposed that it is hard to see how the word "deliberation" can be used in the case of the president. Those proceedings are as solitary and personal as the Sakharov incident.

On one level, the photograph Sakharov invites us to contemplate—especially if seen at a distance and pushed out of focus so that individual features (the Bush genetics) were blurred, vastly multiplied, generalized—might seem an appropriate address from the populations of the earth to the handful of world political and military leaders empowered to annihilate them. The transgenerational faces would seem like small shells, lining the cliffs and coastlines of the world, traces of a life-form found on one of Darwin's journeys, that cannot be effaced, and, if they disappear from mind, are in the next crash of the wave uncovered once more, looking out from the ground of photograph and cliff, urging nothing, but bearing in their act of looking an absolute claim on our attention.

But this is not the photograph that the U.S. president showed the Soviet dissident; and its transgenerational content was framed by an excruciatingly personal gesture, the opening of the wallet, the accompanying narration, "This is my family, my wife, children, grandchildren. I don't want them to die. No one on earth wants that." The final sentence—which seems for a moment to say that the populations of the world are united in their shared concern that the Bush family not die—must be understood to assert this only by a grammatical accident: surely the speaker means that no one wants his or her own family to die. But most people's concern about nuclear weapons is not restricted to family love. The grammatical accident is made possible by the unrelentingly personal framework. The president speaks not as a representative of the earth, not even as a representative of the population of the country over which he presides, but as the representative of the family to which he belongs and which he has sired. Although family love is very great and very noble, it is not the basis for political obligation, whether that obligation is to one's own country or to an international community.[8] Locke's central project in the *Second Treatise*, for example, was to decouple political and paternal power. Contract theory, in general, assumes the unknowability, rather than the familial intimacy, of the persons with whose fate one aligns one's own. Bush offered his photograph as "a guarantee," but, as Sakharov's question and the president's silence made clear, it was precisely not a guarantee.

This chapter identifies three structural attributes of the congressional declaration of war that enable it to function as a guarantee, both to its own and to foreign populations. Those attributes entail linguistic representation and validation; they also help answer puzzles about the phenomena of linguistic "substitution" and "substitutability."

But the analysis must begin where the congressional declaration of war itself begins, with the designation of the speaker of the declaration.

Be it enacted by the Senate and House of Representatives of the United States of America, in Congress assembled, That war be and the same is hereby declared to exist.[9]

The italicized phrasing that opens the 1812 Declaration of War recurs in the later declarations of war, as well as in many other genres of congressional action. The most striking feature of the designated speaker is its resistance to any act of substitution. The consequences of this nonsubstitutability (both for issues of nuclear arms and for a general theory of linguistic representation)[10] will be unfolded in subsequent sections of this chapter.

Key throughout is an important distinction, most familiar to us through the philosophy of J. L. Austin, between descriptive sentences and speech acts. A descriptive sentence portrays the material world as it already exists; when its content matches the world, we say that the sentence is true; when it fails to match the world, we say that it is false. The truth of such a sentence is independent of the speaker; an extreme example is the conclusion arrived at by a scientific experiment; if it is true, it should be reproducible by any and all experimenters. In contrast, a speech act, far from mirroring already existing features of the world, creates a new reality. While the descriptive sentence is independent of its speaker, the speech act cannot be separated from its speaker since only certain persons are authorized to utter the speech act. That is why it is often true of speech acts that, as in the opening of the 1812 declaration, the designation of who is speaking is directly announced inside the sentence itself. So, too, the two people exchanging marriage vows begin their promise by announcing their own names. Since the speech act brings a new reality into being (for example, a marriage, or a war) it does not make sense to speak of it as true or false; instead it is regarded as valid or invalid.

THE WRONG SPEAKER OF THE SPEECH ACT

The first-use policy entails a presidential appropriation of the performative declaration by the Congress. The declaration of war is Congress's constitutionally stipulated obligation. It is therefore illegal for any institution or person to seize it, just as it is illegal for Congress to give it away. Legally, it can be neither appropriated nor delegated. But it also cannot be appropriated in the sense that, on some very literal level, it cannot be performed by the incorrect speaker. In *How to Do Things with Words*, Austin talks about the "necessary conditions" enfolded into a performative speech act, conditions that, if not met, do not merely impair or mar or make imperfect the speech act but, rather, disable it altogether so that it never occurs. That is, of the "unhappy" or "infelicitous" circumstances and features, some merely damage it, some prevent it from happening at all.[11] The enunciation of the performative act by the wrong speaker is in the latter group; when the wrong person speaks, the sentence (in Austin's oddly appropriate phrase) "misfires." Austin's concept of "necessary conditions" is close to what Howard Warrender, in his work on Hobbes, calls the "validating conditions" of an obligation, a contract, or a covenant. For Warrender, too, an inappropriate speaker makes the contract invalid or inoperative.[12]

If, in Austin's well-known sequence of examples, a person already married utters the marriage vow, the speech act simply does not take;[13] no marriage occurs. If a spectator at a cricket game cries "out," it is not a good call or a bad call but not a call at all.[14] Each of these (the marriage vow, the game call) is, like the declaration of war, a contractual act: it is what the philosopher Jürgen Habermas summarizes as an "institutionally bound speech act."[15] In each of these instances, the speech act is inoperative; it misfires.

Speech acts can involve sentences that are momentous for individuals. For many individuals, the marriage vow is the single most consequential sentence they will speak in a lifetime of sentences. For a defendant in a law case, the verdict spoken by the jurors—"Guilty" or "Not guilty"—is a sentence pregnant with consequence. Yet far more momentous is the sentence in a declaration of war: it brings into being a new reality in which tens of thousands of people, possibly millions, stand to be killed. It is unimaginable that a U.S. president would presume to appropriate the marriage vow and start pairing people he met coming through the White House or on the street. (The cult leader Jim Jones who paired members of his congregation in marriage eventually led 900 of them into group suicide.)[16] So, too, it is unimaginable that a president would simply dictate the front page of the *Washington Post* (as self-declared Ugandan president Idi Amin is known to have done in his country's paper). Only the leader of a totalitarian regime would presume to substitute his own "judgment" about the guilt or innocence of an alleged felon for the jurors' verdict. It is even unimaginable, except in jest, that a president would presume to telephone Wimbledon and announce whether the ball in a given volley was in or out. It seems almost disrespectful to the office of president even to picture a president arrogating to himself or herself the sacrament of marriage or announcing in a State of the Union Address the "verdict" of a criminal trial the entire country had been following.

The inappropriate usurpation of the performative could be said to be *the very sign of a tyrant; the flag of a noncontractual society.* Yet (remarkably) the most momentous performative act within our democratic, contractual society, the declaration of war, has for six decades been appropriated by the president in our formal strategic doctrines of flexible response and presidential first use almost without protest.

It is "invalid" in Warrender's sense, and "unhappy" in Austin's sense, as well as in the sense of the many millions of people who have never heard of J. L. Austin.

We have seen that a performative sentence spoken by the wrong person is not simply invalid but does not take place: no marriage is "achieved" if the vows are not taken by the couple themselves (even if they are held at gunpoint and made to live together for a year); no alleged murderer is "guilty" if the jurors have not themselves announced that verdict; no "call" has occurred at a game (even if the entire stadium of spectators complies with the celebrity phone call by remaining decorously in their seats). But if a president launches a nuclear weapon, millions of people die quickly and many millions more in the weeks following. Some act has certainly taken place. But what is that act?

What has taken place is not an act of governance. The impossibility of "governing" nuclear weapons emerges across many pages of this book. For now it is useful to recall that even those people who firmly endorse the United States' possession of nuclear weapons, acknowledge—almost to a person—that there is a terrifying chance of accidental launch or appropriation by a terrorist. The omnipresent part played by "accident" and "terrorism" in daily conversations about nuclear weapons is an unintentional acknowledgement—an open, omnipresent, unending announcement—that nuclear weapons are "ungovernable." What we need to see is that even, or especially, when used by a country's duly elected leader (whether of the United States or Pakistan or China) they are "ungovernable," a nullification of everything that is meant by the word "governance."

Nuclear weapons cannot be fired. They can only be misfired.

AUTHORITY IN A DECLARATION OF WAR IS TRANSMISSIBLE BUT NOT DELEGABLE

It is precisely to permit others to act—hence to permit transmission— that the law of nations, according to Hugo Grotius, requires that a just war be "duly and formally declared, and declared in such a manner, as to be known to each of the belligerent powers." What makes the declaration necessary is not the need to eliminate "clandestine dealings" (though that may be a secondary effect), but the need to identify the source of actions: "the necessity that it should be known for CERTAIN, that a war is not the PRIVATE undertaking of bold ADVENTURERS, but made and sanctioned by the PUBLIC and SOVEREIGN authority on both sides; so that it is attended with the effects of binding all the subjects of the respective states."[17]

In my earlier illustrations, the invalidation of the speech act occurred because one person "took" or "appropriated" the position of the authentic speaker. It becomes equally invalid if it is voluntarily given away by the authentic speaker to someone else.

The arguments that follow often speak of "transmissible authority" and this must be kept wholly distinct from "delegability." We can say that an action is *delegable* if it can itself be validly passed on to other persons so that the body originally obligated to carry out the action instead carries out the very different action of choosing the person(s) who will perform it. In *transmissible authority*, in contrast, the designated actors perform the action, which then radiates outward in its consequence, because transmission permits and creates the conditions under which many other actions can take place. There is no transfer or delegation of the original act, except that, as Grotius makes clear, its performance enables others to act on it (performing parallel, duplicate, or derivative actions that give it a wider materialization).[18] Everything therefore depends on the *point of origin* remaining stable. The distinction is important because the declaration of war (as well as many other performative speech acts) precisely *does* entail transmissible authority and precisely *does not* permit delegability.

In the case of the declaration of war, the lines of transmissible authority move in three directions. The declaration is addressed *to a first-person we* (the population of the home country who now perceive themselves in a fundamentally different way and collectively take hundreds of thousands of actions that reflect that change), *to a second-person you* (the foreign country now formally designated "the enemy" and whose government and population now collectively undertake hundreds of thousands of small actions including those of self-defense), and *to a third-person they* (third-party countries that are not at present on either side of the conflict but must take many actions, such as avoiding waters that have ceased to be neutral as well as actions to ensure their own continuing neutrality or that instead break that neutrality, replacing it with an alliance).[19]

The Constitution distributes different performative speech acts to different branches of the government, and the designated office cannot (or at least ought not to be able to) replace the verbal act with a verbal act of delegation.[20] The president cannot, at the moment he is empowered and required (by Article II, Section 1, Clause 8) to take the oath of office, instead announce, "I choose my brother to take the oath" or "I hereby designate Justice Sotomayor to speak my words.[21] Nor can he replace his State of the Union address with the verbal action of designating his daughter (who never got the break she deserved) or even his speechwriter the one to deliver the address.

Under one extreme circumstance—namely the president's death or grave impairment—his verbal acts can transfer to another person, but so serious is this shift that the Constitution designates the permissible sequence of replacements ahead of time. Crucially, the arrangements for first use of nuclear weapons form a line of succession that is not the same line of presidential succession the Constitution requires. Not surprisingly, it bypasses the Congress. Following the shooting of President Reagan, Alexander Haig's astonishing announcement, "I am in control here," was treated as a personal blunder. But, in fact, it exposed before the eyes of the nation—had we only understood what we were seeing—the extraordinary shift in the line of presidential succession that has come about through nonconstitutional means. The Twenty-Fifth Amendment to the Constitution requires that presidential authority move from the president, to the vice president, to the speaker of the House, to the president pro tem of the Senate, and then to the secretary of state. But the Reagan administration had also arranged for a military line of succession—or what Haig and others repeatedly referred to on the day of the shooting as a "crisis management" line of succession, renamed the "national command authority" a day later—that went from the president to vice president to (skipping the House and Senate, and even the civil cabinet member, secretary of state) the secretary of defense. In fact, some accounts of this new line of national command succession indicate that the line goes directly from the president to the secretary of defense. Hence, there was a consciously designed split between constitutional or civilian lines of authority and military lines of authority. Evidence suggests a third line of succession for controlling the nuclear codes and, therefore, firing atomic weapons.

As secretary of state, Alexander Haig was not "in control here" according to *any* of the three lines of succession; but the existence of three contradictory lines makes explicable Haig's own confusion about the matter. Press attention to Haig's "blunder" (and to his personal conflict with Secretary of Defense Caspar Weinberger) deflected attention from the far more astonishing and damaging revelation that secret, nonconstitutional lines of succession had been created that preempted the constitutional, popularly endorsed, and publicly recognized sequence.[22]

It is not only the executive branch that may not delegate authority to another part of the government. The Supreme Court may not, in a difficult decision about school integration, announce, instead of its "decision," its "designation" of the president as the agent of the decision. So, too, with Congress. Imagine that, at the moment of the roll call vote on a declaration of war, a member of Congress stepped to the microphone and, rather than performing the verbal action of "voting," instead announced that he or she was giving the vote to a neighbor who was particularly knowledgeable about Iraq-Iran relations (the neighbor might fairly influence the member's vote, but cannot himself or herself perform the vote). Neither can that same member of Congress step to the microphone and announce, "Mr. Speaker, I'm going to refrain from voting on this difficult matter and instead give my vote to the president, who has shown himself particularly knowledgeable." But now imagine that forty different members of Congress, as their turns arose in the roll call vote, all gave their votes away to their hometown neighbors. Or all gave their votes away to the president. That act, were it to occur, would surely be reported on national and international news as a disgraceful exhibition of subversion, an odd genre of revolution.

In fact, by the nation's acceptance of the flexible response and first-use doctrines, we have watched not one member of Congress, or 40, but all 535 give their vote away to the president. The gravity of this collective abdication is apprehensible if we recall that Congress is required to continue functioning—without interruption—even when there is a vacancy caused by the death or disablement of one of its members. Unlike the office of the presidency (where a predetermined successor is installed within hours), there is no constitutional presumption of immediate succession. The constitutional substitute for a dead or disabled congressional representative is another, newly elected representative.[23] Comprised of multiple members, Congress (like the Supreme Court) is treated by the Constitution as eternal and self-renewing and, therefore, unabsolvable from its obligations.

Finally, the mistaken sense that constitutionally designated acts of verbal performance can be shifted among branches is perhaps heightened by the belief that such shifts are reciprocal—that an action by the Congress might be given to the president, but so the president can let the Supreme Court do his or her work. But a transfer from one branch to the next is not made more appropriate by reciprocity. This is no more plausible than believing that a referee at Wimbledon on a Sunday afternoon can permit a priest in the audience to make a call, providing the priest in turn, permits the referee to administer the Eucharist on Sunday morning. The "misfires" in speech do not cancel out: they continue and are compounded.

There sometimes exists a startling belief that although powers of the government cannot be *taken*, they can be *given* away. Here are two brief examples. The first is the lawsuit we encountered earlier by two Congressmen alleging that Article I, Section 8, is incompatible with the presidential first-use doctrine. The case was turned down by a federal court in California on the grounds that Congress as a whole has not yet expressed collective alarm about the presidential appropriation. The judge's opinion that an executive appropriation of Articles I, Section 8, is constitutionally permissible if only 2 members of Congress protest (but might well be impermissible if 535 members of Congress one day protest) expresses an erroneous idea that Congress has the option of abdicating its obligation to oversee our entry into war.

The historical record reveals that even a member of Congress may make this error. During the Taiwan Straits Crisis, for example, President Eisenhower's conviction that conventional invasion, air strike, or use of nuclear weapons would be unconstitutional if not authorized by Congress was verbally reinforced by his secretary of state,[24] by the vice president,[25] by the attorney general,[26] and by a representative of the British cabinet (the British are described in these memoranda as "always very sensitive" about the subject of atomic weapons).[27] Remarkably, it is a member of Congress who appears in these records as disavowing congressional authorization. At this point in the record, Secretary of State John Foster Dulles has just been describing the British insistence that the president obtain the consent of Congress. Then, Eisenhower reports a phone conversation he has had with Speaker of the House Sam Rayburn:

> [Mr. Rayburn] had said that the President had all the powers he needed to deal with the situation, and that whatever the President decided to do would be unequivocally backed by the House of Representatives. He believed, however, that a joint resolution [i.e., a declaration of war] at this particular moment would be unwise because the President would be saying in effect that he did not have the power to act instantly, and a filibuster could start in the Congress, causing dissension both in the Congress and throughout the country. Accordingly, it was the Speaker's advice that the

President take whatever action he deemed necessary, and thereafter ask for Congressional approval of such action. Speaker Rayburn guaranteed that this approval would go through the House
in 45 minutes, without a word of criticism of the President.[28]

Speaker Rayburn's private phone conversation with President Eisenhower turns governance on its head. The life-saving constitutional
arrangements—a congressional debate or even filibuster that would block
either conventional assault or the firing of an atomic weapon, a growing
protest among the population (in response to the publicly audible congressional debate) that would also act to block conventional assault or the
firing of an atomic weapon—are here treated as unwanted impediments
on the executive will. It is, of course, the precise point of Article I, Section 8, to allow dissension to arise in Congress and from there to spread
throughout the country. This does not mean the country cannot go to
war. But it means that only when the reasons for war are fully persuasive
will a declaration be possible. The imperative to go to war must be so great
that it overrides the purposely impeding gates of dissent.

In fact, the Formosa Resolution—by which Congress on January 29,
1955, authorized (without a declaration of war) the use of armed forces—
was an extraordinary act of delegation and abdication, as opponents,
particularly in the Senate, vigorously argued. The resolution opened by
authorizing the president to use the military "as he deems necessary"
and closed by empowering him to dissolve the resolution which "shall
expire when the President shall determine that the peace and security
of the area is assured." Most dangerous was an open-ended clause in
the center of the resolution licensing "the taking of other measures as
he judges to be required or appropriate."[29] Thus, as various senators
pointed out, "we are authorizing the President to do anything he wants
to do with the approval of the Senate, and we are authorizing him to do
it in advance."[30] Senator Wayne Morse summarized the import of the
resolution: (1) it is an act of "predelegation"; (2) it means the president,
not the Congress, declares war; (3) it is "unconstitutional"; (4) with its

passage, the government ceases to be "a government by law"; (5) it is an act of establishing "personal government" in the White House; and (6) it is being passed without, on the population's part, any awareness of its grave import. Morse argued that, at the very least, Congress should openly announce to the people that they were currently performing a predelegatory, unconstitutional act that dissolved the government and replaced it with a personal regime.[31]

It may appear that (unlike Rayburn's pointed conversation with Eisenhower, and unlike the presidential first-use policy that has come securely into place since the 1950s) the Formosa Resolution, however much it predelegated the act of war, did not predelegate authority for *atomic* war. But the congressional record registers evidence of precisely this understanding. At one moment, for example, an amendment was introduced that would eliminate the resolution's open-ended phrasing. One senator worried that if the amendment were defeated (which it eventually was), the Joint Resolution might be seen as carrying "a directive to the President to make a preventive strike, using atomic weapons."[32] Several months after the passage of the Formosa Resolution, a new resolution was introduced in the Senate that would have called back from the president the military powers accorded to him in January: it explicitly prohibited the president from "construing" the Formosa Resolution as a license to use armed forces in dealing with Quemoy and Matsu. The preamble to this new resolution attributed the retraction in part to the danger of nuclear war: "Whereas there now is danger of United States involvement in atomic war with the Chinese Communists in the defense of the Matsu and Quemoy Islands."[33]

There are, to summarize, people who believe the president can seize congressional powers if he chooses: these believers support our current nuclear arrangements. A second group of persons decisively reject this presidentially initiated appropriation but accept the idea that Congress can delegate its powers to the president. A third group rejects both presidential appropriation and congressional delegation, but might entertain the plausibility of a conditional declaration of war. During the deliberations for a declaration of war preceding both the Spanish-American War[34] and World War I,[35] the formulations on the floor at some point took the form of a declaration stating that if event X should happen, the president was empowered without further word from Congress to begin military actions. In both instances, the conditional wording was quickly rejected as an inauthentic speech act and replaced with an actual declaration. The 1991 congressional authorization of force in Iraq was, even in its final form, a conditional declaration of war.[36] Because there was no declaration preceding either the Korean War or the Vietnam War, Congress's act preceding the Gulf War can be seen as a reclamation of much of the power it had formerly abdicated; nevertheless, the conditional phrasing was dangerous, since it enabled members of Congress to license the infliction of injury without full acknowledgement of their responsibility for that act.

Sometimes people argue that congressional funding for nuclear weapons licenses the president to use them *if* certain events arise. In other words, Congress appears to have made a conditional declaration. The Congress has explicitly prohibited interpreting an act of funding as an act of declaration: from the deliberations on the War of 1812 up through the 1974 War Power Act, Congress has periodically reiterated that in no case can its military spending ever be taken for a declaration of war or even an authorization of force. This explicit prohibition makes overt what should be visible even without direct statement.

We have seen that in its deep structure, "delegation" is only a slightly disguised form of shifting the speaker in a way that nullifies the speech act. In turn, a "conditional declaration" is a disguised form of "delegation," hence a delayed nullification of the speech act. If one sees the three verbal acts—the declaration, the delegation, and the conditional declaration—lined up, it becomes clear that no feature in the first permits it to be replaced by the other two:

"Be it enacted by the Senate and House of Representatives of the United States of America, in Congress assembled, That war be and is hereby declared to exist ..."

does not imply

Be it enacted by the Senate and the House in Congress assembled, That the president is hereby named the person to declare War ...

or

Be it enacted by the Senate and the House in Congress assembled, that should event X happen, our own obligation to declare war will be null and void and will be transferred to the president.

The constitutional grant of power obligates Congress to declare war, but nowhere empowers Congress to determine *who* shall declare war.[37] That is an arrogation of the Constitution's own power of distributing performative acts among the three branches of government.

The argument so far has focused exclusively on *who is speaking* the declaration rather than (as in the sections that follow below) on the linguistic features of the declaration itself. The identity of the speaker is critically important on both concrete and theoretical grounds. Concretely, it matters whether Congress or the president issues the declaration because of the scale of annihilating military power eventually released; and because, in the meantime, the sheer existence of a presidential first-use policy (even prior to its actualization) dissolves Article I, Section 8, the section that Joseph Story described as the cornerstone of the Constitution. Thus, we have a deformation of our social contract in the present and the possibility of actual annihilation of humankind in the future.

The arguments that follow turn from the speaker of the declaration to the language of the declaration to identify three major structural attributes.[38] The three are: the exact repeatability of the declarative sentence that thickens and gives substance to the verbal performative; the pressure to dismantle the performative act by deconstructing "the enemy"; and the inlaying of material persons and objects into the verbal act that anchors the performative to the material world.[39] The Congress has linguistic features that make its process of deliberation far more appropriate than the president's for overseeing our entry into war. Though it is the constitutionality of Article 1, Section 8, and not a demonstration of its brilliant features that legally protects us, it was clearly an apprehension of those brilliant features that made Congress the site chosen by the founders, and that should now dissuade us from ignoring this crucial section of the Constitution.

EXACT REPEATABILITY

The constitutional requirement that not the House acting alone, nor the Senate acting alone, but the total assembly oversee war means that the sentence

> *Be it enacted by the Senate and House of Representatives of the*
> *United States America, in Congress assembled, That war be and*
> the same is hereby declared to exist . . .

must, to become a declaration, have more than 500 voices enfolded into it.[40] Each person is required, in the presence of all others assembled, to agree to the sentence, to disagree, or abstain and so withhold his or her voice.[41] This enfolding of hundreds of voices within a sentence or a set of sentences is crucial on two overlapping grounds—exact repeatability and the coinhabitation of multiple voices—that (to use a term that emerges from the deliberations themselves)[42] *thicken* the performance.

The declaration goes from the proposal stage to the enactment stage by the sequential enfolding of voices; in the midst of what in some instances is hundreds of pages of sustained debate, this small set of sentences remains poised in front of the assembled group. Each by a positive vote says, "Be it enacted by the Senate and House," or perhaps more accurately, "Let it be enacted by the Senate and House." Although in the debate leading up to the vote, elaborate arguments, complications, and qualifications will have been brought before the members, at the moment of the vote each person who says yes gives (not a personally inflected version of the sentence but) an exact repetition of the proposed sentence.[43]

This inlaying of voices is a remarkable phenomenon. In ancient times, exactly repeatable sentences were associated with permanent, powerful, and sacred forms of commitment.[44] The phenomenon is ordinarily reserved for theological moments such as chant or prayer; in a political situation, it would be dangerously hypnotic if not accompanied by, or steeped in, a surrounding argument that radically changes it. Each congressman or congresswoman lays his or her voice into the declaration by means of a *conspicuously staged* vote. This means that one's own entry into the communal voice is marked by a highly formal, registered act. Although the individual voice only matters because it speaks in concert with the cumulative weight of the others, it remains, in terms of responsibility, always uniquely recoverable. Thus, for example, the single vote of no in the World War II declaration against Japan—that of Jeannette Rankin—remains recoverable not only for her contemporaries but for all subsequent history, as do, name by name, all the yes votes.[45] Not even unanimity would jeopardize the recoverability of individual votes, just as a unanimous jury verdict is often followed by a formal, person-by-person polling of each juror.

The presidential deliberations in the two cases where President Eisenhower contemplated using atomic weapons do not, in contrast, have any sentence or set of sentences on the table that those present understand themselves to be assessing. Nor is there any vote, let alone a roll call vote, that requires standing before peers and public for that day and for all subsequent history. The president's goal is not fully and straightforwardly legible even to this small circle of insiders with whom he deliberates. This lack of transparency in the inner chamber is a miniature version of the overall secrecy. Congressional deliberations on war are either open to the public as they are occurring or, in other instances, are made available to the public as soon as the declaration has been voted upon. In contrast, the presidential deliberations have been consistently withheld from contemporary eyes (as the "top secret" designation still visible in the Eisenhower papers makes clear) and are only made available to the population decades later.

The act of withholding the documents is consistent with the attitude toward "public knowledge" recorded inside the documents. Eisenhower, for example, expressed anger that the European press had reports of our "Honest John Missiles" going to Europe in 1954. The record includes a key sentence: "The President commented that if the people who were responsible for publicity could not better control the situation, they should be replaced by people who could better handle it."[46] During the period when Eisenhower contemplated using atomic weapons in Germany, the record indicates how important it was to withhold our thinking from West Berliners as well as from East Berliners: "Senator Johnson's volunteered statement that Senator Javits had proposed a resolution for a seven-man committee to tell our story to the Berliners brought an unpleasant reaction from the President."[47] As both examples suggest, presidential deliberations are not considered the business even of those populations directly put at risk by those deliberations. Not only enemies but allies and even, of course, the American people themselves are considered unworthy to overhear, let alone participate in, the deliberative process.

The first feature of congressional deliberation—exact repeatability—leads to a second major characteristic of any formal declaration of war. While exact repeatability pushes the process toward verbal thickening, there is simultaneously a relentless attempt to question and dispute the declaration, to thin it out, to dissipate it and make it disappear. This second feature provides a countermomentum to exact repeatability; only if the assembly overcomes that countermomentum does the declaration take place. While, then, the first feature can be said to "thicken the declaration" and the second to "thin it out," the second (like the first) contributes to the declaration's gradual acquisition of substance, since it constitutes a process of testing that anchors and makes responsible the attribution of otherwise highly volatile words such as *enemy*.

DISSENT AND TESTING: AN ETHICAL EXERCISE

The antiwar arguments made by members of Congress during the deliberations for the country's five declared wars take many different forms. Yet underlying their many variations is a single, coherent structure of dismantlement. The prowar arguments inevitably entail the charge that country X has inflicted injury on the United States. This framing coupling—country X and the action of injuring—is denied in almost all variations of the brake-on-war speech.

The attempted decoupling takes place through one of two genres of argument. One: *country X did not perform action A*. This form occurs only rarely; it may entail, for example, the argument that actions performed by particular persons within a foreign country cannot be understood as actions performed by the foreign country itself. Two: *country X did perform action A but action A is not grounds for war*. This second genre is far more frequent than the first. It ordinarily entails the argument that *injury does not give grounds for war*. The major way to show this is to introduce the name of a second country that has also performed injuring action A but toward whom there are no war feelings. In the War of 1812, for example, the motivation for declaring war against Great Britain was weakened by the fact that the major action held to be grounds for war—the infringement on the maritime rights of neutral countries during the Napoleonic Wars—was equally descriptive of France. Those opposing a declaration of war detached the given action A (blockade of ships, impressing of seamen) from country X (here Britain) and then reattached it to country Y (here France). This genre of argument—decoupling the action from country X and reattaching it to country Y—resembles an ethical practice advocated by Bertrand Russell who recommended that when reading or hearing the daily news, we ought routinely to substitute the names of other countries to the reported actions to test whether our response to the event arises from a moral assessment of the action or instead from a set of prejudices about the country.[48] This form of testing, introduced into the War of 1812, recurs throughout later congressional debates. The World War I deliberations against Germany, for example, contain brilliant attempts to detach given actions from Germany and to reattach them to Britain.

A variant is that country Y, the country to which the attributed action will be reattached, is in some cases not a third-party nation but the United States itself. This is true of the Mexican War, where the repeated charge that by crossing the Rio Grande, Mexico had invaded the United States was countered with parallel descriptions of U.S. troop movements. It is again true of the World War I deliberations: the charge that Germany, in going to war, had violated its contract with its own population was occasionally countered with the charge that a U.S. war declaration without the explicit authorization of the population would subvert our own contract. Remarkably, it recurs even in the deliberations for the World War II declaration against Germany, despite the rapidity and rabidity of that declaration: descriptions of unmotivated attacks by German submarines are redescribed as provoked attacks, and the U.S. status as a neutral country is redefined as a covert allied status with Britain achieved through Roosevelt's lend-lease arrangements.

The two linguistic features of the congressional declaration—the thickening of the sentences (through exact repeatability and the inlaying of voices) and the countermomentum to thin it out (by decoupling actions from one "enemy" country and reattaching it to a second, "friendly" country, whether a third party or even the United States itself)—are not features characteristic of the presidential deliberations about war.[49] There is no attempt to dismantle the designation of "enemy" by relocating it to an alternative geography; *hence there is no dissent*. Nor does the process of deliberation and decision making entail any enfolding of voices, nor even any clearly stated set of sentences to which everyone understands they are agreeing; *hence there is no explicit and self-conscious procedure for consent.* The absence of these two features from presidential deliberation can be assessed by looking at a moment of conversation that has the greatest claim to resembling one of those features, and then observing its distance from its counterpart in the congressional record.

The memoranda for the Taiwan Straits Crisis do not record any debate about the status of "enemy," nor even any debate about the nature of "enemy action" or "injurable action." One brief query about U.S. interest in the region, however, approximates an act of dissent:

> Secretary [of the Treasury] Humphrey replied that it was still going to be hard to explain to the American people why we were finding it necessary to hold on to Quemoy. In some exasperation, the President said to Secretary Humphrey that he sat in this room time after time with the maps all around him, and a look at the geography of the area would explain why we have to hold Quemoy.[50]

Unlike congressional debate, where skeptical speakers develop their uncertainty or opposition at length, Humphrey's query is quickly silenced by the hierarchical pressures of presidential consultation.

Despite its brevity, George Humphrey's expressed hesitation is striking because it is so rare. Ordinarily only the president himself introduces uncertainties; others tend to do so only if explicitly invited by the president. President Eisenhower's query about his own impeachability is an example. Observers of the Kennedy presidency have reported the same inhibitions on disagreement. Robert Kennedy wrote that the office "creates such respect and awe that it has almost a cowering effect on men. Frequently I saw advisers adapt their opinions to what they believed President Kennedy and, later, President Johnson wished to hear."[51] The problem is compounded by the fact that those holding opinions contrary to the president's are sometimes excluded in advance from meetings by well-intentioned participants or advisors.[52] According to both Robert Kennedy and Theodore Sorensen, President Kennedy consciously created situations—such as periodically leaving the room—designed to promote open discussion.[53]

Had anyone chosen to support Secretary of the Treasury Humphrey following his humiliating reprimand (no one did), the person could have pointed to the fact that in the September meetings Eisenhower himself had said almost the same thing:

> [The President] thought that Quemoy was not really important except psychologically.[54]

> The President said that he did not believe that we could put the proposition of going to war over with the American people at this time…It will be a big job to explain to the American people the importance of these islands to U.S. security.[55]

> The President said that we must recognize that Quemoy is not our ship. Letters to him constantly say what do we care what happens to those yellow people out there.[56]

Humphrey's brief dissent, though genuinely admirable, may actually have been prompted by his belief that he would be voicing aloud a worry that Eisenhower himself shared. Unfortunately, neither the president nor the other counselors appear to have remembered their earlier discussion.

Again, the memoranda for the 1959 Berlin Crisis do not contain attempts to dismantle the attributes of the word *enemy*, or to detach the designation from one country and reattach it to another; nor does anyone appear to question whether the status of "enemy," however incontestable, itself warrants the use of nuclear weapons. At one moment, however, a senator invited to the presidential conversation introduces a query. (Whereas in 1954 the president worried that without congressional authorization he may be impeached, by 1959 he appears to think that the inclusion of several senators might count as congressional authorization.) The senator confesses that he is having a hard time following the implications of their discussion, and he wonders how trivial an action will license our use of such weapons. As in the Taiwan straits example, the question swerves precariously close to the neighborhood of dissent, then quickly disappears. A situation is imagined in which the German Democratic Republic destroys the bridges and autobahn routes to West Germany; West Germany then begins to rebuild the routes; some German Democratic Republic soldiers then fire rifles at the bridge repairmen. At this point, the record reads:

> Senator Fulbright continued with his example. If the GDR fires rifles at this engineer company, do we then respond with the use of atomic weapons? The Senator admitted that he was somewhat lost on our sequence of actions. The President here admitted that our course of action is not entirely clear. What we do will depend on the actual events as they occur. He pointed out, however, that once a contingency of this type occurs, it is too late to approach the United Nations.[57]

Astonishingly, the president has responded to the senator's imagined scenario with the answer, "Maybe." Far from anyone challenging the use of nuclear weapons under the most extreme provocation, the record instead shows a contemplation of their use under the most modest circumstances with no one expressing disapproval. Perhaps someone present was dismayed, disturbed, or angered to learn that atomic weapons might well be used in retaliation for rifle fire but, if so, the person did not voice those reactions.

Just as these presidential papers show almost no act of dissent, neither is there any easily identifiable act of consent. Nothing in the record provides a counterpart to the feature of exact repeatability in the congressional record. There is no process of voting or voicing agreement to a decision,[58] in part because there is not, overarching the discussions, a set of sentences that everyone understands to be centrally at issue. Although, as in the preceding discussion of dissent, an "absent attribute" is difficult to illustrate, the vacancy can be summarized by President Eisenhower's own observation to the Supreme Allied Commander that the meetings on Taiwan never entailed disagreements on substance ("there have never been any great differences within the Administration on fundamentals") only disagreements on language ("Most of the talks centered around the question of 'what can we say and how can we say it' so as to retain the greatest possible confidence of our friends and at the same time put our enemies on notice"). In fact, as Eisenhower goes on to correct himself, there have been no real disagreements even about language ("I suppose that many of those around me would protest that even in this field I am sometimes something of an autocrat and insist upon the employment of my own phraseology when I consider the issue important").[59]

The autonomy and solitude of other presidents during the act of decision making has also been acknowledged. Often presidential decisions are admiringly described as *inscrutable*, a word that suggests not only that the decisions were made in isolation but that, even after the fact, they cannot be penetrated from the outside. Theodore Sorensen recounts assessments of both Roosevelt's and Truman's inscrutability. He cites Arthur Schlesinger, Jr.'s, summary of Roosevelt—"Once the opportunity for decision came safely into his orbit, the actual process of deciding was involved and inscrutable"—as well as Rexford Tugwell's sense that Roosevelt "allowed no one to discover the governing principle" of his decisions. He also quotes Truman's self-description: "No one can know all the processes and stages of [the President's] thinking in making important decisions. Even those closest to him ... never know all the reasons why he does certain things and why he comes to certain conclusions."[60] George W. Bush describes indecipherability as a presidential right: "I'm the commander—see, I don't need to explain—I do not need to explain why I say things. That's the interesting thing about being the president."[61] The inscrutability, hence unaccountability, of presidential decisions is one of the reasons that war making must occur in Congress, where the deliberative process is each day exposed and transcribed and where the participants feel obligated to articulate their reasons so that they can be scrutinized and subjected to testing.

The comparison between congressional and presidential deliberation is presented here not to say that the president's meetings should have a clear sentence to which they know they are all agreeing, that the agreement should be made explicit by a vote or clear sign, and that someone has the obligation to attempt to dismantle the deliberations to see whether the arguments can hold up under the strongest counterarguments. It is instead to say that although the secret, solitary, nondivisive form of meeting may be precisely appropriate to the hierarchical business of presidents, it is also precisely the reason the presidency is not the arena in which the country's decisions about going to war can be made.

The nature of the congressional declaration will be further clarified once we encounter the third major structural attribute below, the inlaying of persons and objects. It is there that the declaration's acquisition of a material form and the operations of political and aesthetic representation become most overt, though these phenomena are already at work in the two features already examined. The weighting of the declaration, easily apprehensible in "exact repeatability," is also at work in "dismantlement." Although dismantlement is an attempt to thin out or dissipate the declaration, it directly contributes, as noted earlier, to the declaration's acquisition of substance by testing the accuracy of the assumptions on which it is based and by necessitating stronger arguments on its behalf. We will return to the process by which the declaration gains material substance after first looking at one way in which it does *not* gain material substance.

This section below shows how difficult it is to achieve actual materiality. The true forms—two of which we have seen and a third we will come to after an interruption—confirm the gravity, substantiveness, and validity of the declaration. But now we see the temptations the members of Congress suffer to take a shortcut to materiality—to a false form of materiality.

THE FALSE FORM OF MATERIALITY

The declaration of war, as the rubric implies, declares that war exists. The phrasing can, and ultimately must, be understood as a self-conscious performative sentence, a sentence that initiates the state of reciprocal injuring it linguistically registers. The verbal act slightly precedes and is responsible for bringing into being the often vast material acts and consequences of war. It is possible to hear the sentence, however, not as a performative but as a descriptive sentence, seeming only to register a state of affairs that "already" exists. The country's first declaration reads:

> *Be it enacted by the Senate and House of Representatives of the United States of America, in Congress assembled,* That war be and the same is hereby declared to exist between the United Kingdom of Great Britain and Ireland and the dependencies thereof, and the United States of America and their Territories.[62]

The World War I resolution reads:

> *Resolved [by the Senate and House of Representatives of the United States of America, in Congress assembled,]* That the state of war between the United States and the Imperial German Government *which has thus been thrust upon the United States* is hereby formally declared.[63]

And the wording for World War II is:

> *Resolved [by the Senate and House of Representatives of the United States of America, in Congress assembled,]* That the state of war . . . ,

which has thus been thrust upon the United States is hereby formally declared.[64]

The "which" clause in both the World War I and the World War II declarations works to separate the physical act of war and the verbal act of the declaration and make the physical precede the verbal. The declaration presents itself as a replication of an already existing material reality.[65]

The self-camouflage as a description of an already existing reality rather than a performative intervention (a creation for which the speaker's own responsibility must be acknowledged) is even more emphatic in the grammatical structure of the declaration for the Mexican War in 1846 and the Spanish-American War in 1898. In the first of these, the usual announcement that the performative act is about to come—"Be it enacted by the Senate and House of Representatives of the United States of America in Congress assembled"—is (quite remarkably) preceded by a "whereas" clause. "Whereas, by the act of the Republic of Mexico, a state of war exists between that Government and the United States: *Be it [therefore] enacted by the Senate and House of Representatives of the United States of America in Congress assembled.*"[66] The declaration has a preamble asserting that war exists; the assertion is given a temporal location in the space prior to the verbal action of the bill.[67]

The declaration for the Spanish-American War is even more remarkable. If each of the other four asserts that the material form of war exists at least one second prior to itself (so that the declaration is merely a verbal replication of what already exists), the Spanish-American declaration engages in an act of actual backdating.[68] It takes place on April 25, and reads:

> *Be it enacted by the Senate and House of Representatives of the United States of America, in Congress assembled,* First. That war be, and the same is hereby, declared to exist, and that war has

existed since the 21st day of April, A.D. 1898, including said day, between the United States of America and the Kingdom of Spain.[69]

Another version was introduced (and rejected) in both the House and the Senate that would have backdated the war to February 15,[70] backdating not by four days (at which time Spain had broken diplomatic relations) but by more than two months. In the case of World War II, Roosevelt's request to Congress for a declaration of war entailed the same act of backdating: "I ask that the Congress declare that, since ... December 7, a state of war has existed between the United States and the Japanese Empire."[71]

In all these instances, the inherent ambiguity of the three-word declaration "that war exists" (an act of origination or instead only a description of what already exists) is pushed toward the descriptive by *grammatical structures* (the "which" clause in World War II), by a *preamble* that places the war in an antecedent linguistic space (in the Mexican War), or by a *stark act of backdating* (as in the Spanish-American War). The last of these—the action of backdating[72]—is a subgenre that overtly exposes what actually occurs in all the other subgenres and thus it provides an overarching description: a performative sentence that masquerades as a descriptive sentence backdates the material reality that it is itself bringing into being.

All these variants seek to make the declaration appear merely a verbal replication of an already existing state of affairs. The explanation for this is partially provided by the genre of "performatives" rather than the specific case of war declarations. Austin's discussion of performatives moves almost at once to the observation that performatives habitually sound like constatives or statements of fact: their "humdrum" verbs and their "masquerade" or "disguise" or "aping" of the descriptive is, Austin argues, what explains the failure of grammarians and philosophers to see that they are "operative" rather than "recitative" sentences. However characteristic of performatives in general, the inhibition on acknowledging the fact of origination is likely to be especially marked in war, where what is being originated is injury and bloodshed.

The original model for disguising the performative as the descriptive may well be Patrick Henry's speech in the Virginia Assembly urging that Virginia support the militia (and by doing so, assist states farther north) on the eve of the War of Independence. His "Give Me Liberty or Give Me Death" speech, the most remembered speech on liberty in the United States, is a brilliant feat of moving language from the performative (speech that originates a not-yet-existing material fact) to the descriptive (speech that merely registers an already existing material fact). This act of linguistic relocation occurs across three stages by which Henry makes the war come closer and closer: the distant future (hence, a stoppable war); the immediate future (hence, an unstoppable war); and the present (hence, a war already happening). The Revolutionary War was not yet happening; Patrick Henry's speech on March 23, 1775, occurred several weeks before the gunfire at Lexington and Concord on April 19, 1775.

The transition from the first stage to the second is marked by the words: "The war is inevitable—and let it come! I repeat, sir, let it come!" At this moment, war has changed from something deliberative and preventable to something inevitable. What is wholly unexpected is that, precisely at this moment, Henry shifts the war from something undesirable to something desirable. While the war's inevitability should bring with it a damaged or suppressed sense of agency, the shift to the optative ("let it come") and the strong assertive repetition ("I repeat, sir, let it come") restores agency, attaching it to the heroic energy of national self-defense. It is the rhapsody of energetic defense that follows in the transition from the second to the third stage, as Henry moves from the optative ("let it come!") to the descriptive ("The war is actually begun!") and, hence, to the complete erasure of the performative:

Gentlemen may cry, peace, peace,—but there is no peace. The war is actually begun! The next gale that sweeps from the north will bring to our ears the clash of resounding arms! Our brethren are already in the field! Why stand we here idle?

This then leads to the climactic set of sentences known to, and passed down across, successive generations of the country's population, beginning "I know not what course others may take; but as for me..."

Patrick Henry's cadence is audible in every subsequent war assembly: "The war is upon us; we simply declare it," says Senator Hardwick in the World War I deliberations;[73] the congressional agents are here only the object of a preposition, the recipient of an event placed cumbersomely on top of them. Or again, "War is here, if it is here, by the act of Spain," announces Senator Lodge in the deliberations for the Spanish-American declaration.[74] "War is a fact, sir," announces Senator Cass in the Mexican War.[75] "We behold..., on the side of Great Britain, a state of war against the United States, and on the side of the United States, a state of peace towards Great Britain," says President Madison in the deliberations for the 1812 Declaration.[76]

One might argue that the assertion that "the war has already begun" occurs in some wars because—as in World War II—the United States has been subjected to an actual attack that incontestably precedes the declaration. The shift from the performative to the descriptive in the formal World War II declaration—"Resolved, that the state of war... which has thus been thrust upon the United States is hereby formally declared"[77]—is improvisationally echoed throughout the congressional deliberation leading to that declaration. Repeatedly and appropriately, the war is described as "thrust upon us," "hurled into our very teeth," "thrown down to us," "forced upon us."[78] The declaration does "nothing more than recognize the existence of a situation thrust upon us"; it is "merely the statement of an obvious and patent fact."[79] Thus even before the vote on the declaration, there occurs the repeated phrase "We are at war"; "We are at war."[80]

But two factors make it clear that this is not an accurate explanation for the language. First, the trope "the war is actually begun" or "war is a fact, sir, we merely declare it" occurs universally in these assemblies, if less insistently and less heatedly. It is not confined to World War II, the one war where the country was directly and unequivocally attacked.

Second and more crucial, even where (as in World War II) hostilities or severe levels of injury exist, the infliction of injury is radically distinct from constitutionally authorized war. Though the five deliberations have crudities here and there, the level of debate is high. All five of the assemblies affirm the fact that physical hostilities cannot themselves constitute war, that injurability does not equal warability, that "war" in a contractual state means and can only mean a constitutionally authorized congressional declaration. No act of an enemy, no act of one's own soldiers, no act of a president on either side places the United States at war. Only the declaration of war can do that.[81]

Ultimately, as the argument that follows shows, the assembly does indeed acknowledge the full weight of its responsibility for the war it is itself creating, does acknowledge that if there is a separation between verbal proclamations and material enactments, the second follows rather than precedes the first. But along the way, it is by demoting the verbal action that it becomes possible to perform that verbal action. On a second level, the backdating of material reality can be seen not as a falsification or diminution but as an amplification of the powers of the performative. The performative has the ability not only to bring wars into being but to bring them into being retroactively, before its own announcement.

The argument below shows the way the declaration creates a material replication of its own already existing verbal action. It predicts the reality that it then brings into being; it issues a prophecy of war that it then fulfills. Insofar as it works "descriptively," it does so in the temporal direction opposite from what we originally thought. It precedes material reality while also identifying its point of origination after the fact. It therefore takes open responsibility for the fatal events it tried to disown. By leaving a clear signature, it identifies the agent, establishes and stabilizes the referent. The handprint of the national assembly is then recognizable in the actions of soldiers, the swerving of ships, the movement of troops, the speeches of the president. Without the congressional signature, these events remain ambiguously and fatally poised between the spheres of individual and national action.

THE INLAYING OF THE WEIGHT OF THE WORLD

The linguistic space between the proposing of the declaration and the final passage of the declaration is occupied by arguments for and against the declaration. But, a constant inclusion of persons and material objects, seemingly incidentally and parenthetically, also occurs there. In the days between April 2, 1917 (when the declaration of war against Germany was proposed) and the April 6, 1917, vote (when both senators and representatives inlaid their own voices into those sentences), Congress begins to dig a thirty-five-foot deep channel in the East River and Long Island Sound for the passage of ships moving in and out of the Navy yard;[82] it votes appropriations to clear back military debts, thereby reestablishing the country's credit;[83] it debates the relative merits of the universal draft and voluntary enlistment and the ability of each version of conscription to meet the distributional requirements of a democracy;[84] it spends $210,000 for the making and transporting of artificial limbs, as well as for "appliances" and "trusses" for disabled soldiers;[85] it reviews the country's lighthouses;[86] it acknowledges that it will soon "provide for an Army" of between 190,000 and 500,000 men,[87] as well as provide the equipment and training so that those men will not be butchered;[88] and it prints Field Regulations.[89]

Like the act of declaring war, the acts arranging for artificial limbs and the digging of channels for Naval ships are themselves verbal acts, awaiting successive levels of enactment and material realization. In some cases, the bill is voted upon; in others, it is only introduced or referred to a committee. But in the specificity of these details, the monolithically unitary act of "making war" begins to be broken down into what eventually becomes its hundreds of thousands of component parts; in this sense the enactment is already underway. Further, in the very particularity, the concreteness of the object world it introduces—East River, Upper Bay, Hell Gate, trusses, appliances, artificial limbs, field regulations—and in its obligation to begin to count (the number of men, the number of dollars, the number of limbs, the number of days and weeks for training), the verbal declaration begins to *thicken*. These objects are rhythmically enfolded, inlaid, into what might otherwise be hours of unanchored debate. This continual "enfolding of persons and things"[90] is a structural feature common to all the declarations.

Its occurrence is not, of course, strictly confined to the space between the proposed declaration and the accepted declaration; it spills outside the frame in either direction. In the days preceding the country's 1898 declaration of war, for example, the House of Representatives passed a bill for pensions for soldiers from earlier wars, another bill "to encourage enlistments by veterans of the late war during the coming war with Spain," and another providing for a "better organization of the line of the Army."[91] The final frame, too, can be passed over: in the day immediately following the 1812 declaration, President Madison transmitted to the Senate "the first copy of an edition of 'Regulations for the field exercise, manoeuvres, and conduct, of the Infantry of the United States'";[92] in close by days, John Dickey's "newly invented shell was taken up, and referred to the Secretary of the Navy";[93] and Congress held deliberations on the First Meridian, "an appendage, if not an attribute, of sovereignty."[94] How much of the enfolding of persons and things occurs inside the frame of the declaration is usually determined by the length of that interval. The declaration for World War II, for example, took only hours, but the enfolding of persons and objects took place throughout the two years preceding the deliberations and again in the months following.

Certainly on one level, the enfolding of persons and objects makes visible the way the declaration seeks its own enactment, begins to produce the very war it is about to declare. Simultaneously, a very different account holds true. As argued below, the inclusion of specific persons and objects *stabilizes and constrains* the performative by placing material limits on this form of speech.[95]

The many related acts that include objects and persons give weight to the declaration because they populate it. They imaginatively situate the country's population in the interval between the proposal and the passing. When, immediately following President Polk's address to Congress in 1846 or again President Wilson's address to Congress in 1917, a senator arranges for the printing of 20,000 copies of the speech,[96] the act acknowledges the existence of other minds, other minds who are, if only as readers, enlisted into the Congress's own verbal and auditory acts of speaking and listening. To picture a population that reads is to picture a population that needs to be addressed and persuaded.

The fact of acknowledging a people's existence is therefore only a half step away from acknowledging its capacity to resist. The material details credit the possibility of the population's resistance, the possibility of their psychological or moral hesitance, or more generally the simple cumbersomeness of moving embodied persons around. The instances cited above, for example, acknowledge the capacity of today's soldier to notice that the pension of yesterday's soldier has not yet been paid; they also acknowledge the fact that sailors, even if they are willing to fight (that is, even if they are not disgruntled by the unpaid pensions of yesterday's sailor) cannot move in and out of the Navy yard if there is no river channel that is as deep as their ship is thick. Ships and soldiers and citizens are thick. By acknowledging their thickness, the declaration reproduces that attribute, if only mimetically. "A soldier is not made in a day," argued a brilliant rhetorician, Senator Bayard, in 1812;[97] it takes, according to his reckoning, fourteen months "to form a soldier of a recruit." Incorrigible civilians become corrigible only in five seasons. So, too, as Bayard continued, it takes time to establish a numerical aggregate: "These are not the days of Cadmus. It will require great patience and industry, and a considerable length of time, to collect twenty-five thousand men."[98] It may be the 25,000 of the 1812 army, or the 200,000 of the 1917 army,[99] or the 100,000,000 of the 1917 citizenry, or the 130,000,000 of the 1941 citizenry, since it is alternatively the population as army and the population as citizenry whose approval in these declarations is needed and whose numerical aggregate is recited: "We know full well that if the 100,000,000 people constituting this great Republic act in unison of mind and heart..."[100]

The attention to numerical aggregates, the congressional act of census taking to which this intermediate space is devoted, is key. The war does not have an existence antecedent to the declaration, but the population does. It provides the anchoring material reality that diminishes the chances of unanchored performative intervention. A foolish or reckless war is less likely to be declared if, at every moment during the deliberations, Congress contemplates the actual population who must soon be convinced by that declaration—an act of contemplation that has no counterpart in secret presidential deliberations.

Numbers and names—not narratives, not anecdotes—become the main form of populating the declaration. When the members of Congress introduce numerical aggregates, they do so either by very exact registrations or instead by mystifying adjectives. The deliberations for the War of 1812, for example, alternate between numerically specific phrases ("997 citizens of Vermont" or "a memorial of three hundred and ten of his constituents")[101] and diffuse numerical adjectives ("sundry inhabitants of Vermont," "a petition of sundry inhabitants of New Bedford").[102] At one moment in the Spanish-American War, a member of Congress describes a petition as "signed by a large number of solid citizens of Milwaukee"; a reading of the letter specifies the actual number as twenty-four persons.[103] Although both genres of numbers occur in the five declarations, the pressure over successive declarations appears to move in the direction of both precision and inclusion. In the World War I deliberations, at least 50,000 persons are included by direct letters, petitions, or votes introduced into the congressional record. Because the people named and counted often originate the sending of the letters, they can be said to authorize their own appearance in the congressional deliberations.

The acts of naming and numbering are reflections of one another. Naming petitioners or signers is a way of establishing a count and, conversely, the count is a count of persons all of whom, by having names, can be presumed to have personal histories even though those histories are absent from the record. Numbering and naming will be returned to after briefly contemplating two exceptional, nonnumerical ways in which the population enters the record. Both are more overtly embodied: the one is imagistic (and therefore, though still verbal, has more explicit sensory content than do numbers); the other entails the population's actual bodily presence in the galleries of Congress. Although each form of inclusion is itself nonnumerical, each enables us to see more clearly precisely how the numbers function.

The first, the imagistic, is the phrase "blood and treasure." It occurs in the *Federalist Papers*, in the deliberations for the War of 1812, the Civil War, World War I, and World War II.[104] Because the phrase is so resonant, it sounds, when uttered, as though it must have a prehistory in European wars or in the language of pirate life. In fact, the terms "blood and treasure of the People" and "blood and treasure of the Nation" occur obsessively in the early eighteenth-century political and economic tracts of Daniel Defoe,[105] a writer who is partially responsible for the idea that constitutions need to be in writing.[106] Almost this same logic explains the numerical recitation of names throughout the postrevolutionary war deliberations: attention to "how many" signatures a petition or letter has reveals a commitment to democracy.[107] Though "blood and treasure" originates before the French and American revolutions, the phrase is used with a postrevolutionary meaning in U.S. deliberations. It expresses both the weight and the waste of war making, the heavy freight of bodies that will attend either victory or defeat. In *The Federalist No. 6,* Hamilton places the "blood and treasure" of the nation in opposition to the personal motives of leaders in going to war.[108] Those deliberating the War of 1812 pronounce the phrase frequently, often attaching it to the casualties and costs borne by their "Fathers" in the War of Independence.[109] Although in the World War I deliberation it sometimes has the jaunty bravado of a pirate idiom, it is usually invoked to announce the Kantian principle that only the people who "pay" for war should determine whether it will be fought. "That matter I prefer to let the people determine. If they want war, ... if they feel that the offense justifies war, since they must pay the price in *blood and treasure*, in the name of God let them settle that question for themselves."[110] The context is always democratic. The phrase—in its continual reappearance in U.S. war deliberations—expresses not simply the fact that war is bloody and costly but that it is the population's (not the government's) blood that bleeds, the population's (not the government's) money that will soon be spent.

The population—bodied forth in names, numbers, and the imagery of blood and treasure—has actual bodily presence in one literal way. People occupied the galleries of Congress in the deliberations for both the Spanish-American intervention and the World War I declaration.[111] Those assembled in the galleries may appear to resemble a theater audience: on April 4, 1917, for example, the House was concerned about the fair distribution of tickets to the relatives of congressional representatives for the following day, the day on which they knew the declaration was likely to occur.[112] A theatrical audience, however, can express its consent or dissent through the auditory means of clapping. In contrast, a formal rule makes it "a breach of order for any manifestation of approval or disapproval to be given by the galleries" (as the assembly on April 5, 1917, was reminded). A public recitation of the sentence prohibiting "manifestations of approval or disapproval" is repeated whenever applause occurs.[113]

The logic underlying this curious prohibition is worth unfolding. A "sample" of the population is present in the galleries. But the rule repressing their consent or dissent precisely works to prohibit them from acting as a "sample." It prevents them from "standing for" the population. Given the extraordinary efforts that the members of Congress make to record the voiced judgments of the population (long hours may be devoted to reading petitions that, even if unread, are formally entered into the record), this suppression of people in the galleries may at first seem strange. But the underlying logic is coherent. The sense that the congressional deliberations are a kind of theatrical performance is heightened by the spatial split between performers and watchers, and by the fact that the watchers are ticket holders. It is not, however, the members of Congress, but the people in the galleries, who are in danger of functioning like a theatrical illusion. The members of Congress do not merely seem to be the representatives of the people (as in a play, a particular actor seems to represent Othello). They actually do, by having been elected, represent the population. They are their constitutionally designated selves; and (unlike the actor playing Othello) their representation outlasts the meeting in the assembly. The gallery of live persons, in contrast, is in actual danger of functioning like illusionistic theater. In the charged atmosphere of debate, the accident of their preferences may seem to stand for the entire population's preferences. The hall is divided into the space of congressional members and the space of the population. Those present in the second space may appear to exhaust the category of population. Paradoxically, the members of Congress are representatives of the people; the people in the galleries are not representative of the people, though they are themselves people.[114] Put another way, the hall appears to be split between the representatives of the population (the members of Congress) and the population represented (the gallery occupants). The first actually are what they seem, whereas the second are not. Only if it were clear that the gallery occupants merely *represent* the population represented rather than *are* the population represented could their "manifestations of approval and disapproval" be safe.

In contrast to the dangerous illusion of popular confirmation potentially enacted by the people in the galleries, no one petition or letter on the floor is ever in danger of seeming to exhaust the category of "the people": each is framed by scores of other letters and petitions articulating other positions; further, most petitions specify the extent of, and conditions for, their own representativeness. The number of signatures in letters or petitions introduced into the midst of the World War I deliberations was at least 50,000. This count consists only of people who actually signed their names or who directly voted in a town meeting; a much larger figure, at least 100,000, occurs if one accepts the representational claims of the signers. Many of the letter writers identify themselves as a citizen of X, where X is a county, a congregation, a state assembly, a gender category, or a club. In some cases, they (like the members of Congress) have been explicitly authorized by the group to represent them; more often, they claim a bond of allegiance or residential identification with the group and, on that basis, generalize from their own position on the war to the position of the group. Because the letters are addressed to persons who are themselves representatives, and because a major ongoing issue on the floor of the debate concerns the obligation toward representation, the population's claims about, or theories on, slippages in representation are of particular interest.

The descriptions conform to four categories. The first entails a one-to-one correspondence between the number of persons signing and the size of the group represented: the signers of the letters or petitions claim to speak only for themselves. A telegram signed by 451 women, a letter signed by 10 persons, another by 35 persons, another by 71 persons, another by 23, another by 21, by 10, by 13, a unanimous town meeting of 2000, another in Wisconsin of 4000, a petition signed by 7555 persons in California, and so forth.[115] The majority of the letters have this stabilizing precision.

The remaining letters illustrate lapses from this one-to-one correspondence and can be seen as falling into three genres of representational slippage. Though less precise (and therefore less admirable) than the first category of letters, they (like those in the first group) register individual citizens' urgent sense that their counsel is needed and appropriate. Occasionally the letter entails an act of unanchored, or unexplained, self-magnification: I stand for 3000 people. No context, no narrative, no explanation is specified. What underlies the leap from "me" to "the many I represent" seems to be the speaker's confident assessment of his or her own normality. The tone of this genre, there-fore, alternates between modesty and swagger. A letter from a man in Mississippi instructs his representative to give the president the decla-ration he has requested and adds: "I feel safe in saying that 95 per cent of the people are with him."[116] In a second, more common genre of slippage, the magnification is achieved across a sequence of two num-bers. Rather than saying, "I stand for 3000 people," the person says, "I am part of a church of 300 in a community of 3000 worshippers." For example, "Delegates [we are not told how many] from 51 clubs repre-senting 300,000 automobile owners of Ohio" presented a "unanimous" resolution.[117] Or again, three signers of a letter provide a title under their names indicating they are themselves members of a "Committee [whose size is unspecified] Representing 90 percent of the Voters."[118] The double act of belonging (in the first example, 51 clubs, 300,000 car owners; in the second example, a committee, 90 percent of voters) allows a rapid upward leveraging of numbers. A third, closely related genre of slippage comes about by an apposition structure, which permits the number of signers to become conflated with the size of the member group:

> Dear Sir: At the annual meeting, held March 21, 1917, of the Har-vard Club of Boston, Mass., an organization of 4,500 members, the following resolutions were unanimously adopted.[119]

Unanimity seems achieved by 4500 persons rather than by the unspeci-fied number present. Or again,

> Vancouver Lodge, No. 823, with membership of 650 patriotic Americans, have passed today the following resolutions.[120]

But the majority of letters conform to the one-to-one model. The concern to include the population is evident throughout each of the war assem-blies; but it becomes especially explicit in the World War I deliberations because a major grievance against Germany (introduced in Wilson's presidential address and returned to throughout the debate) was Germany's entry into war without any consultation of her population. The constant enumeration of persons becomes a way of certifying the contractual vitality of the United States.[121] To include narratives—rather than names or numbers—would wrongly deflect concern away from the population's collective fate onto an inappropriately individual fatality.

In World War I, constant attempts were made to assess what the constituents thought about going to war, and to document what they thought. The senators and representatives present themselves as second-order beings who must speak and act on behalf of others to whom they are responsible. Wilson, too, is repeatedly described as elected by a population who did not want war. The reverse form of representation occurs in World War II. The members of Congress feel at liberty to speak authoritatively on behalf of the 130 million Americans who stand united in wanting to go to war. The direct attack on the United States preempts the issue of whether to put the country at risk. "[N]othing else will be enough except an answer from 130,000,000 united people that will tell this whole round earth";[122] "Just as I felt for the past 2 years that over 80 percent of our people were opposed to being involved ...I feel at this very hour that the same 80 percent of our people are united in full support of war resolution";[123] "the Japanese have aroused 130,000,000 Americans to a resolute determination to crush forever these arrogant Asiatic assassins";[124] "By this declaration we place behind our armed forces on sea, on land, and in the air the marshaled might of our 132,000,000 people."[125]

The representatives feel empowered not only to speak on behalf of the population's judgments and sentiments, but to give away the lives of that population. The second is perhaps always entailed in the first since, by committing the country to a path of war, Congress puts lives at risk. While this genre of speech often sounds high-handed, it accurately acknowledges that terrible costs lie ahead if the declaration passes—an acknowledgement absent in presidential meetings about nuclear strikes. A primary model is that of giving the lives of one's children. One representative gives her sons: "I am willing to give my sons to their country's defense. I am 100 percent in favor of avenging the wrong."[126] A representative from Pennsylvania gives his only son; then the constituents in his Pennsylvania district; then all the people of Pennsylvania as a whole.[127] Often the representative offers his or her entire community without going through the intermediate step of children: "I want to be on record before this great body, on behalf of 2,000,000 American citizens living in the American Territory of Puerto Rico.... On Behalf of these 2,000,000 American citizens of Puerto Rico I can pledge the fortunes, the lives, and the honor of my people to fight and to die for this great country."[128] Perhaps the most uncomfortably magisterial gesture of all occurs when a representative presumes to compensate one sacrificial group with the promise that another group will also be sacrificed. "Those who don the uniform on the field of battle or on the high seas may rest assured that full and supreme sacrifice of those at home, in the fields, in the factories, the mills, the mines, the forests, the offices, from town, country, and city.[129]

Sometimes this verbal form is genuinely magisterial, as in the contractual exchange of military sacrifice for political and civil rights by blacks and other groups not yet fully enfranchised. Representative Arthur W. Mitchell of Illinois pledged:

> the unbroken and continued loyalty not only of the First Congressional District, which I represent, but that of the 15,000,000 Negroes in America.... [T]he Negro proposes to give and will give all he has, including his life.... In view of the sacrifices which my group has always made and in view of the sacrifices which we are bound to make in this struggle, let me remind the Congress and the Government that the Negro expects the same treatment under our so-called democratic form of government that is accorded all other citizens.[130]

The repeated fusion of military and civil rights in the United States is described more fully in the next chapter on the right to bear arms, which shows the way the voting rights accorded in the constitution's Fifteenth, Nineteenth, and Twenty-Sixth amendments were achieved through the exercise of military rights.

The final weight of the declaration comes from three sources: the thickening that comes about through the enfolding of voices and the exact repeatability of sentences, the testing that comes by overcoming the attempt to dismantle the enemy object against whom the declaration is spoken, and, finally, the inlaying of persons, objects, and geography in the space between the declaration's introduction and its final acceptance, between the preliminary sketch and the final engraving. The vote is repeatedly weighed by the members of the war assemblies. Not all, but many, of the representatives become emptied of their individuality and attempt to body forth the scale of population they represent: "[W]e are intrusted with and are holding the power vested in 100,000,000 of American people.... The members of this Congress and the President of the United States are holding in their hands the destiny of 100,000,000 of people."[131] "[The member] may possibly be signing the death warrant of hundreds of thousands of his fellow citizens, bringing sorrow and distress to hundreds of now happy homes, and burdening posterity with a debt which will sap the moral and mental" life.[132]

One additional manifestation of the weight of the vote becomes visible in inverted form. Those who, for some reason, miss the vote feel compelled to give detailed narratives of their movements to account for their absence. One speaker explains, "I then proceeded via American Airlines to Washington, reaching the Capital Airport at 1:28 Monday afternoon, five minutes ahead of the plane's regularly scheduled arrival."[133] Another begins his narration at 7:10 on the morning of December 8 and continues, "After calling Speaker Rayburn twice from Knoxville I chartered a plane but could not get it off the ground because of Civil Aeronautics Authority orders to ground all civilian pilots. At

10:05 we got clearance, and although we made it in less than 3 hours the vote on the declaration of war against Japan was completed before I could get to the House Chamber. That is how fast democracy works once it is severely shaken."[134] He wired the clerk, we then learn, to say he would vote yes if he were there. A member of the House in the World War I deliberation gives an inappropriately long story about his wife's need for an operation and her refusal to be operated on without him, thereby necessitating his absence from Congress.[135] These autobiographies seem awkward and starkly out of place, yet their very ungainliness, their tone-deaf quality, itself becomes a sign of the weight of the vote, which must occasion such inappropriately individual, hence self-abasing, personal narratives in the midst of debates whose idiom is nonpersonal, whose diction is impersonal and politically inclusive.[136]

But this odd little genre of travel narratives reminds us that personal narratives and autobiographies are often prompted by failure. It is failure that is also signaled by the autobiographical narratives of presidents rehearsing the possibility of impeachment or looking at family photos. No solitary person can, like a full assembly, conjure forth the full weight of the population it is about to put at risk. With nuclear weapons, our government has lost the ability to imagine both its own and other populations—has lost even the inclination to imagine them. The shutting out of the population from top secret presidential war deliberations (revealed to the public only thirty or forty years later) inevitably means that the population also drops out of both executive language and the executive imagination. Only the nearly total disappearance of human beings—foreign and domestic—can explain how Eisenhower could fail to see the appalling asymmetry between a German soldier's rifle shot and a U.S. atom bomb, or how Nixon, ten years later, could contemplate nuclear missiles as a response to North Korea's shooting down of a U.S. reconnaissance plane.[137]

The bypassing of the constitutional requirement for a congressional declaration of war has called attention to a general set of differences between performative and descriptive speech. Descriptive speech achieves its responsibility to the world by the constraints on it to "represent" the materially given world. Performative speech, in contrast, achieves its responsibility to the material world by constraints on the speaker. Although its content originates rather than replicates events in the world, the requirement for "representation," far from disappearing, has simply been relocated from what is spoken to who is speaking. In description, the sentence represents; in a speech act, the speaker represents.

As we saw throughout this chapter, a descriptive sentence tolerates and sometimes even, as in science, requires a substitutable speaker, while a performative sentence requires a nonsubstitutable speaker.[138] A descriptive sentence replicates material reality, while a performative sentence, on one level free of the constraint of material replication, achieves crucial forms of materiality through the representational requirements on the speaker (Congress in the case of the declaration) that are then transferred to the linguistic center of the sentence (in the case of the declaration, exact repeatability, dismantlement of the object, and the inlaying of persons and objects).

Because so many descriptive sentences spoken by our government have failed to represent the world accurately and because so many performative sentences have been spoken by the wrong speaker, it sometimes seems that a general skepticism has arisen so that we no longer aspire to have descriptive sentences that are true and performative sentences constrained by the authorization to speak. But to lose this aspiration imperils our world. It takes away the ground from which we can criticize language that has ceased to be true and resist speakers who oblige us to live outside the rule of law.

CHAPTER 2

NUCLEAR WEAPONS VIOLATE THE SECOND AMENDMENT REQUIREMENT FOR AUTHORIZATION BY THE CITIZENRY

"Every nation," wrote Immanuel Kant, "must be so organized internally that not the head of the nation—for whom, properly speaking, war has no cost (since he puts the expense off on others, namely the people)—but rather the people who pay for it have the decisive voice as to whether or not there should be war."[1] He then added in parenthesis: "Of course, this necessarily presupposes the realization of the idea of that original contract."[2] This exercise of the population's voice, and with it, the affirmation of the social contract, is partly ensured in conventional war by the fact that the population carries the guns. If the population is not persuaded of the wisdom of going to war, it will decline to carry the guns and no war will be fought. Hobbes identifies the military as the final test point of consent when, in *Behemoth*, he writes: "[I]f men know not their duty, what is there that can force them to obey the laws? An army, you will say. But what shall force the army?"[3]

As we saw in Chapter 1, the longstanding United States strategic policy of presidential first use of nuclear weapons[4] is starkly incompatible with the country's constitutionally mandated requirement for a congressional declaration of war. But the deep illegality of nuclear weapons and the arrangements for their use emerges more fully into view when that congressional requirement is seen in relation to a second constitutional requirement: the Second Amendment, the right to bear arms. As we will see over the course of this chapter, the Second Amendment guarantees that no war can be fought unless it has received the authorization of its population.

Even if a society should go to war without first getting the consent of its Congress or Parliament, the act of calling upon the population, the call to arms, itself requires—as Hobbes reminds us—a direct courting of the population's consent. The population tests the claims that the president and Congress have made about the necessity of going to war; only if they are convinced of the validity of these claims do they fight. But what if a nation invents a form of weapons that does not require the population to carry them? Government then becomes severed from its population. Fortunately, the constitution has a provision that, if adhered to, would make this decoupling of the people from the governors impossible.

It is often wrongly said that soldiers simply obey orders, that they do not have the option of dissent and therefore do not exercise any consent over war. If this were really true, there would be no difference between soldiers and automated drones. In fact, because drones cannot be injured, they might seem preferable. But soldiers exercise judgments about whether what they are being directed to do is right or wrong. Inflicting an injury on other people is not an ethically neutral act and requires continual assessment to make sure the reasons for carrying out the act outweigh the many reasons for abstaining. A drone does not refuse to be launched; nor does it confer with other drones and start a collective rebellion. Soldiers often do this. This does not mean that soldiers regularly impede the government's desire to go to war (ordinarily, a government knows what its population thinks and would not presume to carry out an unwanted war); it means that if and when a country goes to war, it has only done so with the consent of its soldiers.

We begin here by noticing how crucial the consent or dissent of soldiers is in eras when conventional weapons are used; soldiers continually test the validity of presidential and congressional claims about war. We will then look at the constitutional location that guarantees this second source of braking power, the Second Amendment, the right to bear arms. While some law cases have already begun to show the way nuclear weapons violate the constitutional requirement for a congressional declaration of war, no legal case has yet been formulated that shows how nuclear weapons disenfranchise the entire population and thereby violate the Second Amendment. Such a case is urgently needed. This chapter shows the grounds for such a case. Even if no such case is brought, every person in the country should know that nuclear weapons, though targeted to hit foreign populations, are also a desecration of our own citizenry. If the United States population comes to hold a strong view on this matter, the court will eventually act.

THE SOLDIER'S DISSENT

In conventional war, a population's authorization of war is ongoing. Soldiers exercise their power of authorization both at *the threshold* and at *the interior* of war.

The soldiers' consent at the threshold becomes visible by inversion in eras when those drafted have refused to cross over the entryway. "The waging of war," legal scholar Alexander Bickel reminds us, "needs continuous political support [and] it is subject to a continuous round of informal referenda."[5] During the Vietnam War, the reflexes of consent were exercised and steadily sharpened. The antiwar movement succeeded in "toppling a sitting president, in the midst of war, in 1968, before a single national vote had been cast."[6] For Bickel, it is the very quality of constraint in the draft that insures ongoing scrutiny of the war:

> A democratic state which fights with a conscripted popular army,
> as most states like ours have done since the French Revolution,
> will do so effectively with difficulty when a large and intense body
> of opinion, particularly among those of fighting age, resolutely

opposes the war on moral and political grounds. A conscripted
army requires more than majority political decision to fight a war.[7]

After the invention of nuclear arms, U.S. presidents began to ignore the
constitutional requirement for a Congressional declaration of war even
when entering conventional war; thus, both the Korean War and the
Vietnam War were undeclared. Yet precisely because these wars were
fought with conventional weapons, the second species of consent still
protected the country: the drafting of soldiers meant the population
took responsibility for scrutinizing the war and made sure their own
voices would be heard.

That display of consensual powers at the threshold has also been
visible in other eras. The first federal conscription bill, issued by Abraham Lincoln, at once gave rise to the 1863 Draft Riots in New York
City, and similar, if much less fully documented, outbreaks of draft
resistance, riot, or near-rebellion occurred in Boston and smaller towns
in New York, Pennsylvania, Illinois, Indiana, and Ohio.[8] Still earlier,
toward the end of the War of 1812, the draft had been proposed by
the secretary of war. It never left the proposal stage because it was so
strongly resisted.[9]

As the exercise of the population's authorization can be seen at
the threshold, so it can be seen in the interior of war as well. The Vietnam War has been introduced here as the model of threshold consent
because of the well-known refusal by many of draft age to enter. But
the exercise of consent and dissent continued to be practiced by those
soldiers who had initially agreed to go: in one year alone, 1971, the
number of American soldiers who deserted reached 33,094.[10]

Dissent was also practiced by civilian advisors serving inside
the country and by the South Vietnamese population with whom the
United States was allied. In a "top-secret" cable to President Kennedy
on September 19, 1963, Ambassador Henry Cabot Lodge summarized
General Minh's litany of the factors weakening the Saigon-American
side. This list began with the greater allegiance of the Vietnamese

population and university students to the Viet Cong, proceeded to the problem of graft in the Vietnamese distribution of U.S. aid, and climaxed with the observation that the "'Heart of the Army is not in the war.'"[11] Neil Sheehan's biography of John Paul Vann, who headed the civilian pacification program in Vietnam, chronicles the way Vann's acute criticisms of the U.S. actions in Vietnam influenced journalists who in turn communicated this picture to Americans at home.[12] The book simultaneously provides a portrait of the influence of Vietnamese civilians throughout the countryside.[13] In effect, the United States armed a large portion of the population, many of whom chose to use their arms on behalf of the Viet Cong. Between November of 1962 and the early months of 1964, according to Sheehan, "with the exception of the heavy weapons specialists, the U.S. government armed virtually every fighter–right down to the local hamlet guerrillas—on the Communist side."[14]

So, too, the other U.S. wars that display the phenomenon of threshold consent also illustrate the ongoing exercise of consent or dissent as the war continues. The relative speed with which the United States extricated itself from the War of 1812 is conventionally attributed to the war's unpopularity with the country's population. The part played in the Civil War by the "collapse" of the Confederate army has also been documented: "Nearly 250,000 eligible whites are estimated to have deserted or to have avoided conscription altogether."[15]

Desertions during the Civil War were extremely high both on the side of the North and the side of the South, as the remarkable early twentieth-century historian Ella Lonn has documented. What determined the outcome of the war, and the fate of the nation, was the changing proportions, the number of defections steadily mounting in the South until, in the end, the army simply "melted away." Numbers that were counted "by the score" after Gettysburg in 1863 were counted "by the hundreds" in the winter of 1865. Huge numbers defected to the North: for example, in January and February of 1864, 1905 former Confederate soldiers took the northern oath of allegiance at Chattanooga;

a year later, 5203 took the northern oath in Chattanooga and Nashville between January and May.[16] Even larger numbers simply went home.

Each time Robert E. Lee looked back over his shoulder, the number of men following him had grown smaller, as his dispatches to President Davis record:

> November 18, 1864: "Desertion is increasing in the army not withstanding all my efforts to stop it."

> January 27, 1865: "I have the honor to call your attention to the alarming frequency of desertion from this army. You will perceive from the accompanying papers, that 56 deserted Hill's corps in three days."

> February 25, 1865: "Hundreds of men are deserting nightly and I cannot keep the army together unless examples are made of such cases."

> February 28, 1865 (a dispatch reporting 1094 desertions in ten days): "I am convinced . . . that it proceeds from the discouraging sentiment out of the army, which, unless it can be changed, will bring us calamity."[17]

The reasons for the desertions range from physical conditions (6000 men marching barefoot fifty miles a day or wearing on their feet skins still "warm and slippery" from the slaughterhouse) to moral autonomy (as when Lee after Gettysburg writes, "[I]t is difficult to get them to follow any course not in accordance with their inclination").[18] The desperate and varied attempts of generals to reverse the defections ranged from the granting of amnesties to executions to forming smaller (hence more easily controllable) companies to reading aloud the Articles of War "once a day for three days."[19]

Reading through the accounts of those desertions and the desperate attempts to stop them, we see why a U.S. (or Confederate) president might prefer to eliminate the draft altogether and have an arsenal of automated weapons that needed nothing from the population. But should the population agree to that? Again, the photographic negative has been placed here to make vividly legible what is more difficult to chronicle but no less real, the soldiers' political awareness during ongoing acts of consent. We know, for example, that throughout the winter of 1863–64, regiments near Vicksburg and along the Potomac "established debating societies" that addressed sophisticated political and constitutional issues;[20] as we also know Wisconsin regiments took straw votes, prior to the 1864 presidential election and published the results in newspapers "to bolster support for Lincoln back home."[21]

What has just been described—the dependence of a nation on the decisions of its soldiers—is not a peculiarity of American wars; any war that cannot be similarly characterized is the exception. Those who enter the war continue to exercise, on a day-by-day basis, their power to give or to withhold consent. Again the photographic negative—the withdrawal of consent in the actions of mutiny or rebellion—bestows clarity on the soldiers' more ordinary acts of cooperation and participation. Here is one such photographic negative, an irregularity in the rhythm of artillery fire in World War I France:

> Promptly at ten the next morning the artillery bombardment resumed—only to be checked immediately by a peculiar incident. In the fields surrounding the barracks were nearly a thousand horses which had not been fed for twenty-four hours. Now the rebels herded them together and drove them riderless down the road to the town of La Courtine.[22]

For a few hours, the road necessary for all communication and travel was clogged with the thousand newly wild horses, before they could be "collected and put out to pasture by the French. [Then t]he artillery began again."[23] The interruption of the guns, the irregularity in the rhythm of the noise, is the acoustical signature of the soldiers' will, the audible registration of the sheer materiality of men and horses running beneath and controlling the gunshot fire above. It is one of many volatile events from the 1917 mutinies in France, a narrative of "avalanching" soldiers' strikes reconstructed in the diaries and speeches of military and political leaders: "The troops refuse to go into the trenches," reported Colonel Herbillon, a military-liaison officer to the government, "order is menaced everywhere. [The] fever is extending itself."[24] According to historian B. H. Liddel Hart, "Cases of desertion in the French Army rose from 509 in 1914 to 21,174 in 1917." There were mutinies in sixteen different corps, "and in places the trenches were scarcely even guarded."[25]

Germany had an analogue in the naval rebellion of 1918 and the sailors' mutinies in Kiel and in Wilhelmshaven.[26] What began with the refusal of the German fleet to be ordered out against the British quickly spread and became, according to Liddell Hart, "the uprising of the German people against the leaders who had led them into disaster."[27] And among British troops, strikes, resistance, and marches of protest occurred in 1919 in Folkestone, Dover, Kent, London, Sussex, Hampshire, West Country, Salisbury Plain, Wales, Scotland, Canada, France, and (more mildly) India.[28] The soldiers, wanting to be demobilized, refused to carry out what they correctly perceived to be Churchill's next plan, the invasion of Russia to support the Whites against the Bolsheviks.[29]

Like the wild horses on the La Courtine road, civilians and soldiers periodically obstruct the road to war, interrupt it, clog it, even bring it to a close. Because "clogging" is here being treated sympathetically, and will continue to be celebrated in later sections of this chapter, it is useful to pause and remember a key principle that will be reiterated many times in this book. The clogging—the interruption—whether by Congress (as in Chapter 1) or by soldiers (in this chapter)—is *not* an impediment to acts of lovemaking or friendship; it is *not* an impediment to the music played by an orchestra; it is *not* an act of blocking traffic in a peaceful metropolitan city; it is *not* an interruption in the service provided by local libraries or hospitals or universities. It is an interruption of one thing: the action of injuring. It may be that, as happened at La Courtine, the injuring resumes after a pause. But the pause itself is not sinister: if sustained and multiplied it would lead to the end of war. Conversely, if all congressional and citizen brakes are bypassed, the inevitable momentum is toward total war.

Military leaders, by their constant insistence on the strategic primacy of "morale," have always acknowledged their absolute dependence on the consent of the soldiers.[30] Civilian leaders, too, have recorded that dependence. Churchill, writing to Lloyd George of his desire to carry out the 1919 "intervention" in Russia, continued: "[B]ut unfortunately we have not the power—our orders would not be obeyed, I regret to say."[31] Similarly, in response to the French mutinies in 1917, the leadership of France acknowledged that the war was becoming unfightable: "[T]here had never been anything like May 20! We seemed absolutely powerless. From every section of the front the news arrived of regiments refusing to man the trenches."[32] The war memoirs of Lloyd George record the early May conference between Pétain and himself during which Lloyd George expressed his recognition that French fighting power had become stalled not by a disability but by a refusal: "No, General . . . with your record I could not make this mistake [of thinking you can't fight], but I am certain that for some reason or other you won't fight."[33] Military leaders, civilian leaders, recruits, and soldiers thus share the recognition that conventional wars are fought only with the authorization of the population.

The power of dissenting soldiers at the interior of war is equally visible in wars of the late twentieth century. The defeat of Iran in a series of battles in the 1980–88 Iran-Iraq War, for example, has been partially attributed to the disenchantment of Iranian soldiers:

> According to numerous observers, it is this demoralization of the pasdarans and the bassidjis (volunteers) that is responsible for the defeats, otherwise inexplicable, at Fao, Chalamcheh and Majnoun, more than the Iraqis' now systematic use of chemical warfare. The latter in any case constituted an additional subject of recrimination against those in power, who "*had taken no precautions to protect us from these deadly weapons*". . . . Little by little, the

fronts came undone, despite the appeals of the authorities, which now fell on deaf ears. A campaign for the enlisting of volunteers, launched with great media support after the loss of Chalamcheh, managed, it is said, only to recruit . . . 250 volunteers in Tehran.[34]

Soldiers' strikes, acts of desertion, and disobedience also played a stunning role in the 1989–90 revolutions in Europe. The East Germany Army, once renowned for its discipline and training, was drastically reduced by desertions between November and March. Its size fell by almost half, from 173,000 to 90,000; remaining soldiers sometimes expressed reluctance to participate in ordinary activities such as the military exercises carried out by Soviet troops.[35] In late December, Romanian soldiers took the side of the population it had been ordered to suppress and in doing so brought about the fall of Ceauşescu. At the end of March, after the Soviet Army in Lithuania had received "permission to use violence" against the population, almost 2000 Lithuanian soldiers deserted, formally registering their names at the parliament building in Vilnius.[36]

Acts of dissent continue in the twenty-first century: among Americans serving in the army in Iraq, 2357 deserted in 2004 and 2543 in 2005; in 2006 the number jumped to 3196,[37] and in just six months of 2007, the number reached 4698,[38] after which the army's reporting on the phenomenon disappeared. Desertion rates have been part of the ongoing White House deliberations about its planned withdrawal from the war;[39] and Iraq Veterans Against the War have remained in the foreground of public dissent.

Finally, it should be noticed that the way a nation responds to a specific occasion of dissent may change over time. In the Korean War, ninety-five soldiers from the Puerto Rican 65th Regiment—one of the most valiant and decorated regiments serving there—were court-martialed for "refusing to attack the enemy as ordered" in what they perceived (and what any sensible observer would perceive) to be a suicide mission. Ninety-one were found guilty, dishonorably discharged, deprived of future pay, and sentenced to between one and eighteen years of hard labor. The events took place in the fall of 1952. By July of 1954, Secretary of the Army Robert Stevens had overturned the sentence of fifty-six of the soldiers and by 1954 all ninety-one had been pardoned.[40] Reversing a sentence took much longer for soldiers fighting in World War I. France executed 500 soldiers for desertion and then pardoned them in the 1930s. Britain executed 306 soldiers (some of whom, like their French counterparts, were suffering from shell shock); an act of Parliament pardoned them in 2006.[41] For those who dissent, the cost is likely to be extremely high; yet as the foregoing pages suggest, every war documents the indefatigable and incorrigible exercise of consent and dissent by soldiers.

These historical instances of obstruction, both at the threshold of war and at the interior of war are recited here not to portray conventional troops as primarily mutinous. On the contrary, the United States did pass over the threshold into the War of 1812, the Civil War, and the Vietnam War. France, Germany, and Britain, along with other countries, did over countless weeks, days, and years sustain the interior of World War I. Iraq and Iran did carry out a war. But they did so only with the assistance of their populations.

The kind of consensual act Kant imagined—the deliberate assembling of the representatives of the people for a voiced affirmation of war—is provided for in the country's social contract in Article I, Section 8, which stipulates unequivocally that Congress, not the president, has the obligation to declare war. It might appear that the second, Hobbesian form of consent, in contrast, would have no specifiable doctrinal location in the Constitution. This second species of consent appears to depend on the technical attributes of the guns themselves: because they must be carried onto the field by live persons, the leaders must address the population and persuade them to carry those guns. With out-of-ratio weapons (which enable a tiny number of people to kill millions) this requirement disappears: because there is no longer any need for the population to carry the arms, there ceases to be the need to elicit the population's consent, either at the opening of war or throughout its duration. Thus, the ordinary features of argument and citizenry are no longer needed or available.

It could easily have happened that this second pathway of consent would be left unprotected by the Constitution. The framers might well have assumed that it would be forever guaranteed by the material attributes of the guns themselves and therefore in need of no doctrinal protection. Both Hamilton and Madison, in fact, argued that the unqualified concentration of military power in the hands of the executive (of the kind we now have in the nuclear arsenal) was impossible because the need to amass that level of power also required the amassing of persons who certainly would not permit it. Hamilton, in *The Federalist No. 26* argued: "An army, so large as seriously to menace those liberties, could only be formed by progressive augmentations."[42] Then follows a cascade of rhetorical questions:

> Is it probable that such a [conspiracy between the legislature and executive to permit such a menace] would exist at all? Is it probable that it would be persevered in, and transmitted along through all the successive variations in a representative body . . . ? Is it presumable . . . ? Can it be supposed that there would not be found one man discerning enough to detect so atrocious a conspiracy, or bold or honest enough?[43]

Were the executive to concentrate this kind of power, wrote Hamilton, the people would retract their consent and turn their backs on the state created; the union would be dissolved, and a federalism would emerge so diverse it would give way to anarchy. Then, at the end, he returns once more to the impossibility of it: "But the question again recurs, upon what pretense could [the president] be put in possession of a force of that magnitude in time of peace?"[44]

Madison, like Hamilton, believed that this form of consent would be permanently protected by the technical attributes of the arms themselves. His formulation of this argument in *The Federalist No. 46* is perhaps even more evocative of the present nuclear circumstances than is Hamilton's: to imagine the endangering of government by a concentration of military power in the executive means imagining an executive with a "fixed plan for the extension of the military establishment; that the governments and the people of the States should silently and patiently behold the gathering storm and continue to supply the materials until it should be prepared to burst on their own heads."[45]

Given the assumption that the technology of war itself would permanently guarantee the continuous monitoring of executive claims by the citizenry, it is astonishing that the founders of the United States emblazoned the principle in writing, emblazoned it in the most permanent written record the country has. Although the principle is no longer protected by technology, it is protected and enshrined in the Second Amendment. Both Article I, Section 8, and the Second Amendment ensure the integrity of the social contract at the moment of entering war; both protect against the concentration of military power in the executive; both are radically incompatible with our standing arrangements for presidential use of nuclear weapons. The right to bear arms ensures that the population, along with Congress, serve as brakes on the reckless executive wish to go to war; simultaneously it enables the population to test and validate the claims Congress makes about war in its deliberations and declarations.

THE RIGHT TO BEAR ARMS: AN ARGUMENT ABOUT DISTRIBUTION

In the United States today, one large portion of the population is indifferent to the Second Amendment and sees it as unworthy of their attention. Another large portion of the population is passionate on its behalf. The two groups seem seldom to speak to one another in a way that would lead to collective enlightenment. The Second Amendment tends to enter our consciousness through seemingly random claims about why criminals should be allowed to walk around with pistols.[46] Alternatively, it emerges there through arguments made by gun clubs or even neighborhood watch groups who urge that there should be no state laws preventing us from carrying guns for hunting, for recreation, or for self-protection against the criminals carrying pistols.

But the Second Amendment is a very great amendment, and coming to know it only through criminals, personal protection against criminals, and the disputed claims of gun clubs seems the equivalent of our coming to know the First Amendment only through pornography. Freedom of speech may or may not protect pornography, and it is reasonable, even important, to look into that issue. But it would be difficult, probably impossible, to infer the monumental scale and solidity of that amendment from this one solitary inflection in its surface. The same is true of the right to bear arms. We have allowed ourselves to be preoccupied by subsidiary issues embedded in the amendment that have wholly distracted us from keeping the major issue in clear view. The history of its formulation and invocation makes clear that whatever its relation to the realm of individuals and the private uses they have devised for guns,[47] the amendment came into being primarily as a way of dispersing military power across the entire population. Like voting, like reapportionment, like taxation, what is at stake in the right to bear arms is a just distribution of political power.

When I speak here about a *distribution of arms*, what I mean is *a distribution of authorization over our nation's arms*. It is crucial to understand that the argument that follows about distributing arms does not express a hope that we can all have guns. It is rather to say that *if* as a nation-state we are to have injuring power, the authorization over the action of injuring (as well as over the risk of receiving injury in return) must be dispersed throughout the population in the widest possible way. *How much* injuring power the country should have is a wholly separate subject. Some believe we should have none; many believe we should have a great deal. The argument here does not touch that question; it is prior to it. However much injuring power we have, like all other forms of political access, it must be spread throughout our entire numerical expanse.

Because the right to bear arms is prior to such questions, revolutionaries have made it their first demand *whether they were militarist or pacifist.* During the first General Assembly in the French Revolution, Mirabeau argued that "it is impossible to imagine an aristocracy more frightening than that which is established in a state by the mere fact that one group of citizens would be armed and the other would not be."[48] Prior to achieving independence, India presented a list of eleven demands to Great Britain, the eleventh requiring the rearming of the population. Gandhi argued that the population would decide whether to use its weapons only after those weapons had been restored.[49] He wrote: "Among the many misdeeds of the British rule in India, history will look upon the Act depriving a whole nation of arms as the blackest."[50] The issue of arms distribution also became a focus in the pacific revolution in East Germany when on December 14, 1989, the parliament "decided to do away with the right of communist party authorities to possess or carry firearms," thereby ending the formal inequality of arms that had given the SED leadership access to the weapons from which the population itself was legally barred.[51]

Only five Supreme Court rulings in the United States have centered upon the Second Amendment, three in the nineteenth century, one in the twentieth, and one in the twenty-first.[52] Those five rulings are compatible with an interpretation emphasizing distributive justice, since they together stress collective rather than exclusively individual rights, and military responsibilities rather than recreational uses.[53] The most recent and most "in-depth" Supreme Court ruling—*District of Columbia v. Heller*—held by a 5-4 vote that the individual right of self-defense in the home is included among the protections afforded by the Second Amendment.[54] The formal opinions of both the majority and the minority acknowledged that the distributive and military protections of the amendment are its major emphases (emphases not directly relevant to the questions posed by *Heller*),[55] with the court dividing over whether (as the minority argued) the amendment is limited to those military protections or (as the majority argued) also includes the individual right.

Perhaps as important as the substantive debates in *Heller*—with unanimity about the military-related right, and disagreement about regulating the right of self-preservation against criminals—was the remarkable method of argument. The case, as legal theorist Cass Sunstein points out, "is the most explicitly and self-consciously originalist opinion in the history of the Supreme Court."[56] Sunstein here compares *Heller* not to the other right to bear arms cases but to *all cases* that have ever been argued by the Court across three centuries. The Court's act of submerging itself in historical details taking place at the time of the Constitution's founding cannot be explained by the amendment's lack of relevance today: 40 million Americans own guns and a much larger number—in fact, a majority of the U.S. population—support the individual right of gun ownership.[57] Nor does the extremely sparse case history intervening between the writing of the Constitution and the 2008 case sufficiently explain it.[58]

Over the course of this chapter—which itself of necessity is submerged in historical details—we will increasingly understand why coming to terms with the Second Amendment requires this originalist methodology. If the Constitution is the bare bones of our democracy, the war provisions are the marrow of those bones: getting into the inside of the inside requires this relocation back to the beginning.

If the Court is someday asked to bring the Second Amendment to bear on the problem of executive access to nuclear weapons, a distributive reading will be supported by the key attributes of the right to bear arms. Each of these basic attributes will be looked at below. Each in isolation illuminates the contemporary problem of arms. Together, they display an unexpected portrait of the deep structure underlying "contract" and "force." By the end of this chapter, it will become clear why the existence of nuclear weapons, their threatened use, and their use are not simply constitutional misdemeanors, but constitutional deformations of the most serious kind. Whether or not the legality of nuclear weapons is tested in the courts, all citizens working to abolish nuclear weapons should regard the right to bear arms as a constitutional amendment that supports their position, a right they should claim and act on.

DISTRIBUTION, RATIFICATION, AND THE BILL OF RIGHTS

The first argument centers on the form rather than content of the right to bear arms. The first ten amendments came into being through the agency of distribution. They came into being not at the Federal Constitutional Convention itself, but out of the ratification proceedings, the centrifugal period during which the proposed constitution was dispersed out to the population for confirmation. Until that confirmation, the document was merely a "proposal," a recommendation, or (as it was called during the Virginia Convention) "that paper on the desk over there."[59] Only the votes of the state-by-state ratification assemblies could transform the piece of paper into the solid foundation of the new country.

In the records of the ratification debates, the participants often make explicit arguments about what it means "to consent," "to contract," "to compact," or "to make a social contract."[60] Most important, the ratification itself is the performative action of consent. It is a speech act designed to bring a new reality—a new country—into being. The Virginia instruments of ratification sweep through a two-paragraph preamble asserting the knowledge, freedom, and deliberation with which the action of the third paragraph is performed, that third paragraph reading:

> We, the said delegates, in the name and behalf of the people of Virginia, do, by these presents, *assent to* and *ratify the Constitution*, recommended on the seventeenth day of September, one thousand seven hundred and eighty-seven, by the federal Convention, for the government of the United States; hereby announcing to all

those whom it may concern, that the said Constitution is binding upon the said people, according to an authentic copy hereto
annexed, in the words following.[61]

The resolution of South Carolina, shorn of all preambles, reads more
simply: "Resolved, That this Convention do assent to and ratify the
Constitution agreed to on the 17th day of September last, by the Convention of the United States of America, held at Philadelphia."[62]

In everyday life, the verbal act of consent can have a tonal range
that extends from reluctant acquiescence (as when one signs a medical
consent form for an operation) to eager affirmation (as when one utters
a marriage vow or agrees to make love). The latter, the complete merging
of obligation and desire, becomes audible in the reaction to the South
Carolina vote. According to a contemporary history of the event, there
had been a motion to delay the South Carolina vote until Virginia came
in with its vote, but the motion was rejected: "The rejection of it was
considered as decisive in favor of the constitution. When the result of
the vote was announced, an event unexampled in the annals of Carolina took place. Strong and involuntary expressions of applause and
joy burst forth from the numerous transported spectators."[63] Similar
exhilaration was audible in other states. When news of the successful
Virginia ratification reached New York, Antifederalists joined "jubi-
lant" Federalists in taverns to celebrate. According to John Jay, "[T]he
two parties mingled at each table, and the toasts (of which each had
copies) were communicated by the sound of drum and accompanied
by the discharge of cannon."[64]

But despite this jubilance, the ratifiers did not simply rubber stamp
the proposal the Federal Assembly had given them. On the contrary: they
required a huge change in it. If you ask most Americans today—or for that
matter people in foreign countries—to recite some part of the United States
Constitution, what they will probably recite is one or more of the amendments. These most familiar and most revered sections of the Constitution

were the result of deliberations carried out by the ratification assemblies, not by the Federal Assembly.

The most eloquent testimony to the distributive element in the right to bear arms is the fact that it came into being, along with the other nine amendments that together constitute the Bill of Rights, during the ratification process. In effect, the ratifiers endorsed the contract in exchange for an alteration in the contract—the promise of appended amendments. Roy Weatherup writes:

> There might never have been a federal Bill of Rights had it not been for one alarming event that is almost forgotten today. As part of the price of ratification in New York, it was agreed unanimously that a second federal convention should be called by the states, in accordance with Article V of the Constitution, to revise the document. [New York's] Governor Clinton wrote a circular letter making this proposal to the governors of all the states.[65]

Rather than put the entire Constitution at risk by a full reconsideration, Madison and the Federalists agreed to the addition of the sought-after amendments.

New York was successful because other state assemblies had already voiced strong reservations by attaching proposed "rights" amendments to their articles of ratification.[66] But New York's role was decisive and had been foreseen (even in the midst of the federal convention) by Elbridge Gerry of Massachusetts. Gerry, a tireless opponent of a central-ized military, warned in August of 1787 that the proposed Constitution lacked a sufficient "check" against a standing army in time of peace, and that there would be great opposition on this basis.[67] "He suspected," Madison wrote of Gerry in his convention notes,

> that preparations of force were now making against it. (He seemed to allude to the activity of the governor of New York at this crisis in

disciplining the militia of that state.) He thought an army dangerous in time of peace, and could never consent to a power to keep
up an indefinite number.[68]

During the New York convention in the summer months of 1788, Madison wrote letters to Edmund Randolph expressing his anxiety about the
outcome, and on July 16, acknowledging that ratification was uncertain,
added, "The best informed apprehend some clog that will amount to
a condition."[69] That "clog" or "condition" became the Bill of Rights. In
the end, New York changed the wording from "on condition" that an
amendment convention be called to the words "in full confidence" that
an amendment convention will be called.[70] Their confidence proved
justified; they had, in combination with other states, created a situation
that guaranteed the responsiveness of the Federal Assembly.

The fact that the ratifiers are in the position to clog or impede a
proposed contract goes hand in hand with the fact that they are in the
position to confer validation on that contract: their power to clog and
their power to validate are both expressions of materiality. On the one
hand, as we have seen, the transformation of a speculative recommendation into binding law can only occur through the instrumentation of
ratification; it is only this that gives it the weight and authority of the
material world. As Akhil Amar has written, "The Constitution is our
supreme law, superior to ordinary legislation, simply because its *source*
was the supreme lawmaker, superior to ordinary legislatures: 'We the
People of the United States.'"[71] In endorsing the proposed Constitution,
the population bestowed on it the solidity of their own embodiedness.
But their own embodiedness meant they had the power to get in the
way of its passage unless it could be given a form they regarded as
deserving of ratification.

The fact that the right to bear arms gained constitutional standing
through the agency of the ratification debates is critically important
because the amendment replicates three attributes of the ratification
process: first, its function as a distributional mechanism; second, the

immediacy and self-consciousness of the contracting action; third, the role played in the work of validation by the phenomenon of "materiality" or (in Madison's idiom) "clogging." The first of the three will be quickly sketched here, then elaborated along with the other two in the analysis of the Second Amendment that follows.

It may seem only a pleasurable coincidence that a distributional mechanism (the Second Amendment) should arise out of a distributional process (the ratification debates). But the gravity of this circularity soon becomes apparent. As a group, the first ten amendments are increasingly recognized as sponsoring collective rather than narrowly individual rights, not only because they ensure the population's ongoing access to procedural gates of consent such as assembly, jury, and open press, but because they in turn sponsor later revisions in the Constitution (such as the Thirteenth, Fourteenth, and Fifteenth amendments). These revisions in turn sponsor still later revisions: large parts of twentieth-century law, various legal commentators have observed, can be seen as elaborations of the Reconstruction amendments.[72] The gradual extension of the original contract to those large parts of the population (blacks and women) not included in its 1789 provisions occurs through the mediation of the amendments. The distributional work of the first ten amendments is, then, twofold: they multiply the number of consensual gates (assembly, jury, free press, arms) available to the limited population (white male) already included within the 1789 Constitution; they also vastly multiply over time the scale and diversity of the population that eventually has access to those multiplied consensual gates.

Underlying contract theory is a persistent question about the temporal duration of the act of consent: should consent be imagined as a single event that, once having occurred, cannot be retracted in the future? Or is it instead the case that consent is ongoing and can be withdrawn at any time, at once dissolving the contract? This distinction between what can be called "threshold consent" and "perpetual consent" is fundamental to all species of contract: social contract, medical contract, marital contract, etc.[73] It provides the language for appreciating what was at stake in the apparently circular phenomenon in which the ratification (the moment of distributing the contract to the population for its approval) gave rise to the amendments (themselves the agents of the Constitution's eventual distribution to the entire population).

In effect, the participants in the ratification debates settled the question of whether the parties to this contract would exercise "threshold consent" or instead "perpetual consent" by using the great, solitary threshold moment to revise the Constitution in such a way that the gateways become perpetual. The Federal Assembly had already built into the Constitution the possibility of perpetual consent in the Article V provisions for amendment. But the ratifiers made the immediate application of Article V a precondition for their own validation of Article V as well as all the contract's other articles. By specifying a series of materialized loci, they gave the practice of perpetual consent a material shape and a locatable form—newspapers, jury box, assembly hall, and (as will become clear) arms.

If the amendments as a group are "distributive" in their general character,[74] the Second Amendment is so specifically.[75] The repeated call for the decentering of military power at the ratification conventions was, in its overt phrasing, consciously poised against the centrist habits of the Constitutional Assembly. But in fact the amendment works to amplify, rather than to contradict, the dispersal of military power that had already occurred at the center. What is remarkable is that the two sites of contract making—the Federal Assembly and the ratification assemblies—each in their separate decisions on the military, chose the largest possible unit of people to oversee questions of war. During the Federal Assembly's deliberations on Article I, Section 8, the power to declare war—what Joseph Story would one day call "the highest act of legislation"[76]—was explicitly withheld from the president as well as from either the House or the Senate acting alone; it was given instead to the full Congress, the largest pool of persons among the three federal branches.[77] Again, during the deliberations of the ratification assemblies, the insistent call for a "right to bear arms" amendment envisioned military responsibility dispersed across the entire population.

At each site, a decision was made that war must be overseen by a group whose size was the largest possible and, perhaps even more striking, whose size was coterminous with the size of the deliberative body making the decision. The Constitutional Congress made the full Congress the arbiters of war; the Popular Assemblies made the population the arbiters of war. None disarmed themselves. To have done so would have been to dissolve the capacity even to enter into the act of contract making.

INEQUALITY OF ARMS DISSOLVES THE CONTRACT

We have seen that the right to bear arms seeks to ensure that however much injuring power the country has (whether very large or very small) it will be equally divided among its citizens. This provision transforms force by breaking it up into thousands upon thousands of small pieces: each person in a republic keeps watch over his or her small share. This ability to hold military power within the frame of the citizenry is synonymous with social contract; that is why ratifying the contract was conditional on the right to bear arms being accepted.

If, then, an equality of arms is essential to the social contract, an inequality of arms is potentially fatal to it. Throughout the ratification period, inequities of distribution in the nation's arms are described in the idiom of military defeat. Because social contract and armed coercion are understood as two antagonistic models, what is being perceived in this inequity is not some local species of unfairness, but a dissolution of the basic social contract itself. The fundamental logic of John Locke's social contract theory was to differentiate societies brought about by contract from those brought about by force of arms.[78] At the moment of going to war, only the population's explicit consent can keep the society from shifting back into the very blur of coercion that the contract replaced and from which it sought to distinguish itself.

The right to bear arms is widely recognized as going hand in hand with the long-standing distress over standing armies. The pre–Revolutionary American arguments against the standing army—as well as the longer tradition of British arguments—had as a single goal their opposition to the concentration of the military power in the hands of a monarch, president, or any other occupant of an executive site. They were thus themselves distributive arguments, urging a decentralization of the military by means of the militia.

While "standing army" and "militia" are terms from the past, their meanings—an executive army and a popular army—are painfully relevant in the twenty-first century since the concentration of military power in the hands of the executive is today far beyond what the eighteenth century dreaded. Their insistence on a constitutional provision that keeps the military authority in the hands of the people may prove decisive to us today. At least seven of the states[79] had constitutional provisions protecting the militia and prohibiting or advising against a standing army. When during the federal convention Madison identified "large standing armies" as "the greatest danger to liberty,"[80] he was echoing a long tradition that saw *not foreign armies but inequities in one's own military* as subverting the social contract because they slide the society back into the blur of precontractual coercion.

That backward slide is registered in the two recurring constructs of "invasion" and "disarming." An inequality of arms is described repeatedly in Anglo-American history as a military defeat or "invasion." For example, a 1769 resolution of the Massachusetts House of Representatives holds:

> That the establishment of a standing army, in this colony, in a time of peace, *without the consent* of the General Assembly of the same, is an INVASION of the natural rights of the people, as well as of those which they claim as free born Englishmen, confirmed by magna charta, the bill of rights, as settled at the revolution, and the charter of this province.[81]

Benjamin Franklin one year later writes to Samuel Cooper about the possibility that the King will raise and quarter his army:

> And while we continue so many distinct and separate States, our having the same Head... will not justify such an *Invasion* of the Separate Right of each State to be consulted on the Establishment of whatever Force is proposed to be kept up within its Limits, and *to give or refuse its Consent*, as shall appear most for the Public Good of that State.[82]

The inequalities that give rise to the conceptual geography of invasion are not themselves always inequalities of physical force or physical arms. One postrevolutionary tract arguing against inheritable military titles—Cassius's 1783 *Considerations on the Society or Order of Cincinnati*[83]—perceived the unequal distribution of military honor among the revolutionary soldiers as leading to two groups of citizens, the titled and the untitled (and implicitly, the entitled and the unentitled). Can anyone believe, Cassius asked, "that the remaining rights of the people which are yet left untouched, will not be invaded and violated, by men, who [disdain] the condition of private citizens?"[84]

The prerevolutionary and postrevolutionary charge of invasion resurfaces continually during the ratification period. Agrippa's 1788 letters in *The Massachusetts Gazette*, for example, include among their proposed conditions for accepting the Constitution an amendment ensuring each state's control of its own militia and an amendment prohibiting invasion: "[N]o continental army shall come within the limits of any state, other than garrison to guard the publick stores, *without the consent* of such states in times of peace."[85] Luther Martin's letters to *The Maryland Journal* argue that if the central government's call to the militia is unmediated by the authorizing "consent" of the states, the country will enter the condition of "martial law" and freemen will enter the situation of "slaves."[86] The palpable apprehension of "invasiveness"—the trespass over the physical boundaries of the state, over the nation-state, or instead over the physical boundaries of persons—is itself memorialized in the progression of the amendments in the Bill of Rights. After the Second Amendment's prohibition of an unequal distribution of arms comes the Third Amendment's prohibition of the nonconsensual entry of soldiers into houses, followed by the Fourth Amendment's prohibition of "unreasonable searches and seizures" of "persons, houses, papers, and effects."[87]

The insistent appearance of the invasion idiom in both the revolutionary and the ratification periods underscores the fact that the invading army may belong to another nation or to one's own. The unequal dispersal of military power—rather than the overt spectacle of incoming soldiers—instigates the vision of contractual collapse.

As defeat follows invasion, so the spectre of "disarming"[88] follows that of "invasion." The invocation of this second idiom displays the same clash of the literal and the metaphorical, the same apprehensive conflation of foreign and domestic agents of contractual subversion. The 1689 Declaration of Rights presented to William and Mary, which later became the British Bill of Rights, contained as its fifth and sixth charges against James II the assertion that he had attempted "to subvert" the "[l]aws and [l]iberties" by "raising and keeping a Standing army... in Time of Peace without Consent of Parliament" and "[b]y causing several good Subjects, being Protestants, to be disarmed at the same Time when Papists were both armed and employed contrary to Law."[89] The British king, as Roy Weatherup stresses, "did not disarm Protestants in any literal sense; the reference is to his desire to abandon the militia in favor of a standing army and his replacement of Protestants by Catholics at important military posts."[90] During the American Constitutional Convention, Elbridge Gerry opposed the standing army and national control of the militia on the grounds that they approximated a "disarm[ing]" of the state citizenry and a shifting of national structures toward a "system of Despotism."[91]

The charge of disarming recurs constantly during the ratification debates. The enslavement of the population that Luther Martin envisioned in Maryland would come about, he argued, through the standing army's attempts "to disarm" the militia.[92] At the Pennsylvania Ratification Committee, the minority report counseling against ratification attributed its dissent in part to the need for a constitutional provision stipulating "no law shall be passed for disarming the people."[93] The fact that Pennsylvania muskets were called in for repair during the period of debate led those opposing ratification to suspect military suppression of their dissent. In an address entitled "To the People of Pennsylvania," Centinel asked, "What otherwise is the meaning of disarming the militia, for the purpose as it is said of repairing their musquets at such a particular period? Does not the timing of the measure determine the intention?"[94] Aristocrotis, too, charged that a recall of the public arms "upon the pretence of having them cleaned" was a way of "disarm[ing]" the militia to discredit and disempower all objections to ratification.[95]

The often repeated words "invasion" and "disarming" reveal that a hoarding of military power by one individual or group is perceived not as a secondary or tertiary attribute of a given contractual society, but as something so profoundly incompatible with it that the form of the government itself dissolves: contract disappears, and it is replaced by latent despotism. Conversely, "militia" is understood to mean "a fair distribution of military power," and this "distribution of military power" is recognized as essential to the preservation of the social contract itself. It is for this reason that nineteenth-century legal philosophers like William Rawle identified the militia "as the palladium of the country"[96] and political leaders like Governor Brooks of Massachusetts called it "the palladium of . . . civil rights."[97] Joseph Story, explaining why the right to bear arms is "justly" considered "the palladium of the liberties of a republic," said that the militia provides a free country with a defense "against sudden foreign invasions, domestic insurrections, and domestic usurpations of power by rulers."[98] At the opening of this triad, physical invasiveness is attributed to the foreign power, but by the end it has migrated to home ground, as standing armies "afford [a facile means] to ambitious and unprincipled rulers to subvert the government or trample upon the rights of the people."[99]

Across several centuries of Anglo-American political and legal thinking, the basic conception is consistent. In the language of "invasion of rights" and "disarming," metaphor and material reality ride close to one another. Sometimes, as when the American colonists speak of the British standing army, what is pictured is the arrival onto the shore and entry into the country of an army referred to as though it were foreign, even though the speakers were themselves British subjects. The "foreignness," the invasiveness, and the capacity to disarm arise not from the fact that the army comes from another shore but from the fact that the army is independent of the population. The idiom of invasion and disarming occurs equally if the speaker is referring to an internal standing army, as when people on the island of Great Britain speak of the standing army there, or when people in the United States prohibit a standing army attached to its own central government.

One is invaded if there is an inequality of arms in the population group to which one belongs. If half the people in the space of a room were armed, and the other half not, the second group would by this language be disarmed, though the first intended the other no harm. If women were permitted to have arms and men were not, the men would be disarmed. If women were given weapons that were thousands of times more powerful than the ones men were permitted to possess, again the men would be disarmed. The same outcomes would hold wherever there occurred an asymmetry between any two groups: poor and rich, white and black, young and old, government officers and populace. It is this last pairing that we face today; and like Gandhi we might say, Give us back our arms and then we will tell you whether and when we will use them.

A free-standing missile is the realization of everything that ever was feared in a standing army. It permits the concentration of a military force in a central location. It is attached to executive will rather than to the will of the people. Its structures are permanently in place

and depend little on historical situations, leaving no room for impro-
visations and debate. It is inanimate and depends on the population
for nothing. One recalls Madison's two hypothetical governments, the
first dependent on its population and therefore permitted to stand,
and the second independent and therefore obliged to be eliminated.[100]
In the vocabulary of both the pre-Revolutionaries and the Federalists,
free-standing missiles have disarmed and invaded us. We have lost our
power of authorization over the arms. The contractual society has fallen
back into the blur of precontractual coercion.

Like Locke, the founders understood contract and coercion as
oppositional. Thus, the articles of ratification in Massachusetts and in
New Hampshire preface their assent with a prayer of thanks that they
can make a compact by assent rather than by fraud or surprise:

> The Convention ... acknowledging, with grateful hearts, the good-
> ness of the Supreme Ruler of the universe in affording the people
> of the United States, in the course of his providence, an oppor-
> tunity, deliberately and peaceably, without fraud or surprise, of
> entering into an explicit and solemn compact with each other, *by
> assenting to and ratifying a new Constitution* ... DO ... assent to
> and ratify the said Constitution.[101]

Like those ratifying the Constitution, those writing it also understood the opposition between "contract" and "force" to be elemental.
In *The Federalist No. 39*, Madison stressed that "[e]ach State ... [is] only
to be bound by its own voluntary act,"[102] just as during the Virginia
ratification debate, he contrasted the peaceable formation of the American government, which has "excited so much wonder and applause,"
with the coercive formation of other countries: "How was the imperfect
union of the Swiss cantons formed? By danger. How was the confed-
eracy of the United Netherlands formed? By the same. ... How was the
Germanic system formed? By danger."[103]

The Federalist Papers as a whole both open and close with Hamilton's climatic reiteration of this fundamental distinction between contract and force. "[I]t seems to have been reserved to the people of this country," he writes in the first paragraph of the first number, "to decide the important question, whether societies of men are really capable or not of establishing good government from reflection and choice, or whether they are forever destined to depend for their political constitutions on accident and force."[104] The final paragraph of the final number returns to the same ground: "The establishment of a Constitution, in time of profound peace, by the voluntary consent of a whole people, is a PRODIGY, to the completion of which I look forward with trembling anxiety."[105] Subsequent legal commentaries continued to perceive the Constitution within this basic framing opposition. So, for example, in 1825, William Rawle opens A View of the Constitution by placing the country's founding in the framework of contract, in contradistinction to political structures that emerge "under compulsion, or by artifice, or chance."[106] The repeated placement of the opposition in a terminal position—the beginning and the end of The Federalist Papers and the opening of Rawle's commentary—underscores its primacy.

The opposition between contract and coercion does not logically mean that the social contract must be empty of military provisions or war-making powers. On the contrary, it is precisely war making that must be overseen with explicit constitutional provisions and guarded over with the greatest possible care. It must be given a level of rigorous scrutiny and must be subjected to explicit consent procedures warranted by nothing else within the polis except the basic contract itself. This necessity accounts for the rigor and persistence with which the phrase "without consent" is attached to phrases about the standing army. With almost unswerving regularity, each of the sentences about "invasion" or "disarming" cited earlier—in the Massachusetts Resolution, in Franklin's letter, in Gerry's protest on the floor of the Assembly, and in Agrippa's letters to the Gazette—posits the gateway of explicit consent as a threshold that must be passed through. The terms army and consent are inseparable. Other than the Instruments of Ratification themselves, there is no issue to which the word *consent* is so relentlessly attached. Only by widely distributed and explicit consent can "force" be brought into, and made compatible with, the social contract.

SEALING THE SOCIAL CONTRACT THROUGH DISTRIBUTIVE UNIFORMITY

Defeat is, as the previous section suggested, the perceived outcome of the failure to distribute. But what is the material form of distribution? The only way one can have coercive power within a contractual society without sabotaging the social contract itself is by distribution. As a result, categories that appear to be ethically neutral, such as sheer material uniformity and sheer numerical spread, inevitably lead to the ethically charged language of political equality, representation, citizenship, "civilian power," and self-authorizing models such as voting. An asymmetrical hoarding of weapons by one sector is envisioned (even during peacetime) as a military conquest of the country from within; conversely, fair distribution of arms is perceived as the realization and guardian of the social contract, its greatest defense.

SOLID AND SENTIENT

The intolerable division between a government and the population in the case where the government has military power and the population has not is the most extreme form of military inequality, but only the most extreme. Those writing at the time of the Constitution's founding were also on guard against any form of military asymmetry even *within* the population itself.

In part, the desired uniformity is thought of as *geographical spread.* During the Virginia ratification debates, Mr. Grayson, worrying about centralization of the military, invoked as a warning the model of Britain, where there were admirable laws about the militia itself but where the militia had been permitted to atrophy in Scotland and Ireland.[107] In part, the uniformity is conceived in terms of a *class spread.* In the same

Virginia ratification debates, George Mason imagined the militia of a future day in which "the higher classes of people," as he put it, are gradually eliminated from the obligation of duty.[108] In part, the uniformity is also understood as a distribution *across age and property*. During the ratification period, Richard Henry Lee's pamphlet, *Letters from the Federal Farmer*, went within a few months through "four editions (and several thousands) of the pamphlet."[109] Asserting like Mason a present equity, Lee proceeded to imagine hypothetical inequities of the future when there would be a reversion from contract to the model of coercion, with the young and landless lording over the old and propertied:

> Should one fifth or one eighth part of the men capable of bearing arms, be made a select militia, as has been proposed, and those the young and ardent part of the community, possessed of but little or no property, and all the others put upon a plan that will render them of no importance, the former will answer all the purposes of an army, while the latter will be *defenceless*.[110]

The young and landless, by means of an inequality of arms, would suddenly rule over the older and landed. Universalizing provisions, Lee acknowledged, must be made and lodged somewhere, "but still we ought not so to lodge them, as evidently to give one order of men in the community, undue advantages over others; or commit the many to the mercy, prudence, and moderation of the few."[111]

Mason's and Lee's statements together make it clear that when there is an inequality of arms, one may be disadvantaged by being included in the militia or may instead be disadvantaged by being excluded. Both arguments agree only that the nonuniform model is coercive. Almost any distinguishing feature—whether an irregularity in guns, titles, military exercise, or service—sets off the contractual alarm.[112] Aristocrotis, for example, sees the constitutional division of the militia into two parts—active and nonactive—as prelude to subjugation on the basis of class and age.[113] Concerning one class made up of the young and landless (here the apprehensions of Aristocrotis and Richard Henry Lee coincide), Aristocrotis writes:

> [By their] daring of spirit [they] may gain an ascendancy over the minds of the vulgar. . . . The second class or inactive militia, comprehends all the rest of the peasants; viz. the farmers, mechanics, labourers, etc. which good policy will prompt the government to disarm. It would be dangerous to trust such a rabble as this with arms in their hands.[114]

Aristocrotis is not recommending that the second class be disarmed; he is ventriloquizing a future argument he fears a government might make.

Two unexpected features emerge across these various claims for uniformity. The constancy of their appearance underscores their importance. The first is materiality. The reversion to the coercive model is pictured as stripping people of their physical solidity, their very substance. Richard Henry Lee writes:

> It is true, the yeomanry of the country [at the present time] possess the lands, the weight of property, possess arms, and are too strong a body of men to be openly offended—and, therefore, it is urged, they will take care of themselves, that men who shall govern will not dare pay any disrespect to their opinions.[115]

But he goes on to imagine that a central power, Congress as it happens, could "by modeling the militia" gradually over "twenty or thirty years . . . by means imperceptible" divest men "of that boasted weight and strength."[116] The same apprehension of material divestiture is pictured where arms themselves are evenly dispersed but the insignia of military authority are not. In his 1783 tract against the Order of Cincinnati, Cassius predicted a race of hereditary patricians with access to centers of civil and military power "[a]nd the whole country besides themselves, a mere mob of plebeians without weight or estimation."[117] The non-uniform dispersal of guns present in the displacement of a militia by a standing army disarms and severs parts of the body. Sometimes a specified part of the body is removed, as when John DeWitt, in his essays in the *American Herald*, describes the new government's discomfort with putting "arms in the hands of a nervous people" as the necessity of "catching Samson asleep to trim him of his locks."[118] More frequent are the steady stream of references to a generalized form of bodily materiality—"weight" "burden," "firmness," or "ruggedness"[119]—that is in danger of being lost.

Though our focus here is necessarily on the period during which the Constitution was founded, the vocabulary of embodied solidity to express "resistance" is by no means unique to that period: it occurs across centuries, is voiced by pacifist as often as by military speakers,[120] and by women as often as men.[121]

In all these instances, the material nonuniformity of persons (geographical location, class, age, land) must be compensated for and irregularities eliminated by the strict material uniformity of guns, insignia, and degree of participatory service. In fact, in the federal convention, in the ratification conventions, and in most subsequent discussions of the right to bear arms, it is startling how often the discussion takes place across the specified material attributes of the weapons themselves. The members of the Constitutional Convention, for example, debated whether there could be geographical variations of arms—rifles in one local, muskets in another[122]—and disagreed about the degree of specificity required by words like "arming" and "organizing": "[Then Mr. King] by way of explanation said that by 'organizing,' the committee [he] meant proportioning the officers and men—by 'arming,' specifying the kind, size and caliber of arms—and by 'disciplining,' prescribing the manual exercise, evolutions, etc."[123]

The same surprising attention to materiality surfaces in William H. Sumner's brilliant 1823 analysis of the militia, *An Inquiry into the Importance of the Militia to a Free Commonwealth*.[124] For Sumner the civil nature of the military depends on its being distributive in the most concrete sense. Irregularities in material form strike him as alarming evidence of the country's growing indifference to the importance of keeping an army within a contractual frame:

> This is to be apprehended from the distribution of mutilated com-pilations, and what are called amended editions of the United States System of Infantry Tactics … for the militia, in several of the states, the tendency of which, will be to defeat the great design of [C]ongress for establishing [a] uniform system of discipline and field exercise for the army and militia, throughout the United States.[125]

The 1939 Supreme Court case *United States v. Miller*[126] might be criticized for the extraordinary emphasis the Court put on the physical attributes of the weapon. The ruling appeared to be stuck to the physi-cal surfaces of the particular gun in the case:

> In the absence of any evidence tending to show that possession or use of a "shotgun having a barrel of less than eighteen inches in length" at this time has some reasonable relationship to the preservation or efficiency of a well regulated militia, we cannot say that the Second Amendment guarantees the right to keep and bear such an instrument.[127]

But that odd emphasis on material attributes, whether or not appropri-ate to the Court's ruling,[128] belongs to a long tradition of attention to the physical properties of military equipment, as the Court's own citations from earlier provisions showed:

> [a citizen must] provide himself, at his own Expense, with a good Musket or Firelock, a sufficient Bayonet and Belt, a Pouch with a Box therein to contain not less than Twenty-four Cartridges suited to the Bore of his Musket or Firelock, each Cartridge containing

a proper Quantity of Powder and Ball, two spare Flints, a Blanket and Knapsack.[129]

Graphic material details are also prominent at every level of the recent Supreme Court decision in *District of Columbia v. Heller*. The case was not about the generic category of "arms," or even "guns," but a specific kind of gun—a handgun or pistol—as it was also about "trigger locks." Even hypothetical arguments during oral argument took an insistently concrete form, as occurred when Mr. Dellinger argued on behalf of District of Columbia's laws requiring a trigger lock:

> **MR. DELLINGER:** You—you place a trigger lock on and it has—the version I have, a few—you can buy them at 17th Street Hardware—has a code, like a three-digit code. You turn to the code and you pull it apart. That's all it takes. Even—it took me 3 seconds.
>
> **JUSTICE SCALIA:** You turn on, you turn on the lamp next to your bed so you can—you can turn the knob at 3-22-95, and so somebody—
>
> **MR. DELLINGER:** Well—
>
> **CHIEF JUSTICE ROBERTS:** Is it like that? Is it a numerical code?
>
> **MR. DELLINGER:** Yes, you can have one with a numerical code.
>
> **CHIEF JUSTICE ROBERTS:** So then you turn on the lamp, you pick up your reading glasses—
>
> (Laughter.)[130]

The multiplication of concrete objects (the trigger lock, the lamp, the bed, the reading glasses), the specification of an imaginary numerical code (3-22-95), the introduction of a place of purchase (17th Street Hardware), the specification of temporal duration (three seconds) all display the inevitable thrust of the Second Amendment toward the concrete even when speaking hypothetically.

More important, the formal written arguments of the *Heller* court, both the majority and the minority, are, as noted earlier, drenched in historical details (making it in Cass Sunstein's judgment the paradigm of an originalist case). Justice Breyer in his dissent provides an eloquent description of the necessity for the concrete, arguing that the right of self-defense cannot be thought through by means of abstractions:

> This historical evidence demonstrates that a self-defense assumption is the *beginning*, rather than the *end*, of any constitutional inquiry. That the District law impacts self-defense merely raises *questions* about the law's constitutionality. But to answer the questions that are raised (that is, to see whether the statute is unconstitutional) requires us to focus on practicalities, the statute's rationale, the problems that called it into being, its relation to those objectives—in a word, the details. There are no purely logical or conceptual answers to such questions.[131]

Conclusions can be reached not through principles and logic but only through "practicalities . . . —in a word, the details."

Although the principle of materiality sometimes surfaces in mystifying attention to the tattered covers of an infantry manual or the length of a barrel of a gun or the sudden introduction of reading glasses, in fact what is being registered is the transformation of military structures into civil structures, the basic miracle of the social contract.

The principle of solidity and weight is itself audible in the doctrinal formulation, "the right to bear arms." To bear arms is to authorize the bearing of arms, to bear them in the sense of carrying them; to bear them in the sense of standing up under them; to bear them also in the sense of risking the hazard to which having them obligates us. The word *bear*—with its complicated undertow of physical weight and the physical actions of sustaining, pressing, or (as in giving birth) bringing forth that weight—has throughout its history licensed the conflation of things within the body (to bear a baby, Shakespeare's to bear eyes, Scott's to bear a brain, Byron's to bear a heart) with things on or close to the body (the bearing of clothes and of weapons).[132]

The crucial work of material uniformity is to make irrelevant material characteristics of personhood: age, geography, class, and property.[133] Because evenness in a rule permits everything else to be uneven, "collective" or "uniform" rights simultaneously allow high degrees of individuality and hence come to be misidentified as themselves "individual." The insistence that solid infantry books be dispersed evenly across the entire geography (or age or class range) relieves the population from being required to occupy a specific geography or be a certain age or belong to a particular social class to become eligible for full political empowerment. Uniformity of the right, and of the arms themselves, encourages diversity of personal attributes because the right is utterly independent of any given attribute; it is equally available to the bearers of all attributes.

The stress on material solidity is deepened and clarified by the second attribute which emerges beneath the surface of the call for uniformity: sentience, the capacity for representative feeling, or, as it was repeatedly called during the ratification debates, fellow-feeling. The etymology of consent is from "con-sentir," meaning "to feel with," and designating a continuity of feeling across persons.[134] The overt descriptions of the militia turn on such terms. Not everyone must serve, but delegates from all geographical areas, class, age, and property levels must be present to have "fellow-felling" and judge the aversiveness or the worth of the actions undertaken. The issue is ethical; it is conceived as a matter of fairness, an attempt to establish what in twentieth- and twenty-first-century discussions of distributive justice is called a "symmetry of everyone's relations to each other."[135] Thus at the Virginia Assembly, Mr. Mason had formulated the uniformity argument on the militia using these terms. A standing army, a militia chosen from the central government, or a militia drawn unevenly across geography, age, and class, is nonsentient, without a knowledge of the population's feelings and interests: "The representation being so small and inadequate, they will have no fellow-feeling for the people."[136] The phrase "fellow-feeling" recurs, almost as an incremental refrain, in Patrick Henry's brilliant analysis of contract before the same Virginia Assembly.[137]

The center of the collective case against the standing army is precisely its being nonsentient, severed from the knowledge of the sentience of the population. "A standing army is still a standing army by whatever name it is called; they are a body of men distinct from the body of the people."[138] The idea of the standing army as cut off from the feelings of the citizenry—separated from any base in sentience—recurs constantly.[139] It eventually gives rise to the most frequently invoked trope associated with the standing army: the image of the nonsentient "engine," a word that passes up and down the Atlantic coast during the ratification period in the letters of Luther Martin, the letters of Centinel, the *Essays by a Farmer*, and the writings of Brutus.[140] The mute nonsentient missiles of the twentieth century, almost wholly independent of the human population they are empowered to destroy, are a vast magnification of this most dreaded attribute of the standing army.

Through the idea of "sentience," "con-sentir," or "fellow-feeling" opens out into the notion of political representation, it preserves at its most *minimal* the guarantee of "self-representation"—the certainty that participants *at least* have "fellow-feelings" for their own embodied personhood. For both the eighteenth and nineteenth centuries, that capacity for "self-interest" was the greatest safeguard on military power, the final defense of the contract, the "palladium" of all republican liberties. Sumner's *Inquiry into the Importance of the Militia to a Free Commonwealth* unfolded the principle of self-interest as the center from which the capacity for con-sentir and, in turn, the possibility of civil structures emerge: "The history of all ages proves that large armies are dangerous to civil liberty. Militia, however large, never can be; for it is composed of citizens only, armed for the preservation of their own privileges."[141]

The social contract acquires from its members the solidity needed for validation and resistance, consent and dissent. The solidity of the contract is based not on inert matter (as a fortress wall might provide) but on living persons—sentient, capable of self-regard and regard of others. The aspiration toward this sentient materialization of the social contract requires a rigorous stress on numbers. Simultaneously, it holds within it an idea about political self-authorization. I want to end by elaborating each of the two ideas because together they enable us to picture the consensual act in the material plane where the founders pictured it. A social contract is almost a living thing because it has no existence, no reality, other than in the living bodies of its participants.

NUMBERS COUNT

Numbers count. High numbers potentially perform a braking function on the rush to go to war. The framers worked to make the initiation of war difficult and its cessation easy. During the convention, Oliver Ellsworth's judgment that it "should be more easy to get out of war, than into it"[142] was shared by most other delegates. George Mason said, "He was for *clogging* rather than facilitating war; but for facilitating peace."[143] The notion of "clogging" played a critical role throughout the convention, the ratification debates,[144] and later legal commentary. Joseph Story saluted the principle of clogging when he wrote: "It should therefore be difficult in a republic to declare war; but not to make peace.[145] William Rawle similarly saluted this principle when he observed: "[C]ongress alone can subject us to the dubious results of formal war, a smaller portion of the government can restore us to peace."[146]

Those forming the Constitution, whether at the Federal assembly, in the ratification conventions, or in the newspaper debates, always aspired to small armies when they spoke in terms of the nation's injuring power.[147] But they always pictured large numbers when speaking in terms of the base of authorization.[148] They aspired toward a situation that is the opposite of the one we have today, in which the injuring capacity has been pushed to extremely large levels, but the base of authorization has been reduced to the smallest possible number of people.

President Nixon's announcement about his ability to kill 70 million people in 25 minutes[149] had the important effect of calling attention within the government to the presidential first-use arrangement which had previously gone largely undiscussed. It led—in Senate Hearings and elsewhere—to a genre of discussion that centered on the question of how many people a presidential order to launch, or alternatively a submarine captain's order to launch, must pass through before the signal reaches the Minuteman[150] or Polaris[151] missiles. During the Senate Hearings on Presidential First-Use, George H. Questor conceptualized the issue in a way that ties it back to the "clogging" formulations of the Federalists. Questor asked: *"[H]ow many intervening layers of possibly resistant humanity does he have to pass through?"*[152] Questor, as though reassured, at one point remarks:

> The published accounts suggest that the positive decisions of as many as three or four [submarine naval] officers altogether are required, to decide whether a duly authorized signal to launch their missiles had indeed been received, and that the physical act of firing them involves the turning of keys at locations physically remote from each other.[153]

The order must pass through the authorization of four or five before the weapons pass through the bodies of many millions. Repeatedly, in discussions of nuclear arms, fears about authorization by only one are calmed by reassurances that it is actually two, as fears about two are calmed by reassurances that it is actually twenty, and fears about twenty by reassurances that it is actually twenty-five. But in terms of the structure of the Constitution, talk of 2 or 25 or 225 is simply a species of category error.

It is worth remembering how many "intervening layers of possibly resistant humanity" the Constitution envisioned us as having to pass through before war could be fought. In arriving at these numbers, a general principle was continually enacted: it was always the largest possible base over which the founders had control. When the Constitutional Convention determined in Article I, Section 8, that the full

Congress should have the power to declare war, they were choosing the highest numerical body within the government. So, too, when the Constitution then went to the states, the Ratification Assemblies urged that the second consensual locus become the entire population.

These decisions were made despite the pressures toward "emergency" and "speed" that have always been urged in association with war.[154] Justice Story wrote an eloquent passage about the logic of including both houses in Article I, Section 8, and it is not hard to see how the argument would be extended as well to the necessity of enlisting the consent of the full population. He began by acknowledging that "[l]arge bodies necessarily move slowly" and that this cumbersomeness might seem at odds with the "dispatch, secrecy, and vigor ... often indispensable" in declaring war. He then said that this recognition, though important, was greatly outweighed by the arguments on the other side, arguments that follow from the fact that "the power of declaring war is not only the highest sovereign prerogative, but that it is, in its own nature and effects, so critical and calamitous, that it requires the utmost deliberation, and the successive review of all the councils of the nation." He then arrived at the heart of his argument:

> War, in its best estate, never fails to impose upon the people the most burdensome taxes, and personal sufferings. It is always injurious, and sometimes subversive of the great commercial, manufacturing, and agricultural interests. Nay, it always involves the prosperity, and not unfrequently the existence, of a nation. It is sometimes fatal to public liberty itself, by introducing a spirit of military glory.... It should therefore be difficult in a republic to declare war; but not to make peace.[155]

Far from concluding that the pathway into war should be simplified or abbreviated, Story ended by proposing that if anything, the path to war should be made more difficult by requiring a two-thirds vote (rather than a simple majority) in both houses.

One of the great peculiarities of the numbers question is the belief that the president is more than one person. The fact that presidential election[156] involves the whole population is wrongly taken as putting greater numerical weight behind the president's solitary action than behind congressional action, even though Congress entails a much larger body of persons and is collectively elected by the entire national population. The numerical juxtaposition of the presidential electorate with the electorate of an isolated congressional district is a mental act that would be relevant only if one were choosing whether a president or a solitary member of Congress or a solitary citizen had more authority to kill 70 million persons. That numerical comparison is instead inappropriately used to invalidate the entire congressional authorization of this most fundamental of contractual events. The proposal to go to war has to stand up under the scrutiny of 535 members of Congress who are in turn (because the proceedings are public) witnessed by millions of people. That declaration of war then (in a nation commited to conventional weapons) has to be ratified by the nation's citizens.

Locke, urging that military powers be held within the social contract, warned that anyone is "in a much worse condition, who is exposed to the arbitrary power of one man, who has the command of 100,000, than he that is exposed to the arbitrary power of 100,000 single men."[157] A population that believes it is more safe to be subject to a solitary executive empowered to kill millions than to confront conventional troops has become blind to the ground of its own authority within the social contract.

What would be the numbers—*how many intervening layers of possibly resistant humanity*—would make nuclear technology consonant with the Constitution? What numbers are needed to turn a thermonuclear monarchy into the democracy we have always expected our contributions to safeguard? It would begin, but only begin, with the 535 of Congress. The term "people" in early constitutional writings is used, according to legal opinion in one court case, "to express the entire numerical aggregate of the community, whether state or national, in contradistinction to the *government* or *legislature*."[158] Today that would be approximately 314 million. If one takes instead the 14 percent who participated in World War I, the number would be 44 million. If one takes the 3 percent estimated to have fought in the seventeenth- and eighteenth-century wars, today it would be over 9 million.[159] If one takes a two-thirds figure at one point introduced as the number needed from the states to authorize the raising of an army (a proposal Madison thought went too far) the number today would be over 209 million. Numbers are dangerous, but the widely straddling figures from 3 percent to 66 percent—from 9 million to 209 million persons—are invoked here simply to indicate that they are not in the neighborhood of the one or two or twenty persons that enter into nuclear discussions and that have been for the last six decades presented to this population in a deeply insulting and gravely unconstitutional mimesis of collective decision-making. Because democratic weapons have always allowed some rough equivalence between the ratio of those injured and those authorizing the injury,[160] perhaps the number required for launch authorization ought to be set by those figures—Nixon's 70 million, for example.

POLITICAL SELF-AUTHORIZATION: CIVIL RIGHTS AND RIGHTS TO ARMS

Another great peculiarity in the language of nuclear argument is the concern that only the president, rather than a military officer, should control the firing of nuclear weapons because the Constitution tried to guarantee "civilian control." In fact, discussions of the militia and of the right to bear arms did stress the category of civilian, but "civilian" expressed distance from, not proximity to, executive control. Adam Smith wrote: "In a militia, the character of the labourer, artificer, or tradesman, predominates over that of the soldier: in a standing army, that of the soldier predominates over every other character; and in this distinction seems to consist the essential difference between those two different species of military force."[161] Nothing in the early writings lends support to the notion that the insistence on civilian, rather than military, control could ever have been addressed by imagining a *single* civilian in control (or even worse, and as is today the case, a single civilian containing the military might of the whole nation in automated systems that he hoards). As New Jersey Senator Case argued in the 1976 congressional hearings on the United States' nuclear policy of presidential first use:

> It was pointed out by Abraham Lincoln in a letter to his great friend, William Herndon, that it was this power of the kings to involve their countries in war that our Constitution understood to be the most oppressive of all kingly oppressions. The Founding Fathers resolved to frame the Constitution so that no man could keep that power for himself.[162]

Today, one man does keep that power for himself.

Executive control of the army was, from the infancy of the republic onward, consistently seen as the subversion rather than the fulfillment of the contractual requirement for civilian authority. Among the "[f]acts... submitted to a candid world" in the Declaration of Independence were two yoked clauses: "He has kept among us, in times of peace, Standing Armies without the Consent of our legislature. He has affected to render the Military independent of and superior to the Civil Power."[163] Nuclear weapons constitute the ultimate standing army.

The yoking of these two—the prohibition of an executive armed force and the assertion of the supremacy of civil over military institutions—recurs in many of the state bills of rights: Virginia (1776), Massachusetts (1780), and New Hampshire (1783).[164] The phrasing of the Massachusetts Declaration of Rights—"and the military power shall always be held in exact subordination to the civil authority and be governed by it"[165]—clarifies the way the issue was pictured.

Whenever early tracts on the military introduce an "aesthetic" idiom, whenever they begin to speak of the "beauty" of the militia, what has instigated the language of beauty is not the luxuriance of the uniforms or the display of military might, but the reverse. What is beautiful is the miracle of watching the principle of force brought into and held within the contractual frame. In his 1786 report to Congress on his plan for the militia, Secretary of War General Knox periodically uses an aesthetic vocabulary of light—"luster," "splendor," "glorious"— in close proximity to statements stressing the principle of equality on which the militia must be based.[166] It is this that the parade of the militia displays. The bright uniforms signal uniformity: the decentering, diffusion, distribution, and hence fundamental alteration of the principle of force now relocated from its original position outside to its new position inside the "national pact."[167]

The loss of the distributive is the loss of civil beauty, as is audible in the way Cassius phrases his lament about titles: "They have laid in ruins that fine, plain, level state of civil equality, over which the sight of the beholder passed with pleasure."[168] In his extraordinary treatise, William Sumner invokes John Adams as the "civil" father and describes the militia as a "civil" institution that is the palladium of "civil" rights because of its distributive character.[169]

Both Knox in 1786 and Sumner in 1826 perceive the continuous uniformity of the civil militia as a cloth or fabric spanning—sheltering, like a bright canopy—the whole country. Knox writes:

> [F]or a sum less than four hundred thousand dollars annually, which, apportioned on *three millions of people*, would be little more than one-eighth of a dollar each, an energetic republican militia may be durably established, the invaluable principles of liberty secured and perpetuated, *and a dignified national fabric erected on the solid foundation of public virtue.*[170]

Sumner, while stressing the importance of nationally determined uniformity, simultaneously credits the states' decentering of power through the militia "as the grand physical characteristic of state sovereignty.

Without it, *the pillars of the Union would be too slender to support the national fabric.*"[171]

In the atomic age, this once-beautiful protective fabric has come to be repictured as a canopy held aloft *not* by millions of the country's citizens but by a single presidential shaft: the "nuclear umbrella." First publicly visible during the Nixon-Kissinger era, the nuclear umbrella continues in the country's 2010 Nuclear Posture Review; over the decades it has indicated to other countries (accurately or inaccurately) that U.S. nuclear weapons will be fired on their behalf, pledges made by heads of state over the heads of their unconsulted populations.[172]

Thus at the very moment technology seduced the United States into a decisive break from its revolutionary and constitutional foundations, the government took special care to falsely assert a continuity with those origins. A major instance is the Minuteman missile: the official publications of the Air Force often showed, superimposed over the missile, a man with a musket in a tricornered hat; as Gretchen Heefner observes, "North American Aviation, the primary contractor for the Minuteman's guidance system, didn't even bother showing the missile . . . instead using a familiar Revolutionary minuteman statue with rifle in hand, vigilantly watching the horizon."[173] Despite its 1.2 megaton warhead, the missile was sometimes designated a "rifle."[174] This imagery was chosen, she argues, to foster the deeply misleading idea that the new weapons embodied the "ideal of an antimilitaristic, antiaggressive people, responding only when provoked by tyranny."[175]

The profound inappropriateness of ever applying the phrase "civilian control" to a president's solitary control of nuclear weapons is evident in the insistently decentered meaning of "civilian," an emphasis visible in the conflation of the right to bear arms with the right to vote, a final, and critically important, distributive attribute of the amendment. The very small number of Supreme Court cases on the Second Amendment have affirmed its connection to citizenship in the Fourteenth Amendment,[176] to voting,[177] and to the right of assembly.[178]

Even more serious evidence of the interweaving of voting and arms occurs in the history of the extension of the franchise itself. Both the House and Senate judiciary hearings on the Twenty-Sixth Amendment repeatedly cite the participation of those fighting in Vietnam and of those exercising power to consent by refusing to be drafted as having earned for that generation and all that followed the right to vote at a younger age.[179] In fact, in the Senate Judiciary Committee report, the original age of twenty-one is itself located in military service:

> The 21 year age of maturity is derived only from historical accident. In the eleventh century 21 was the age at which most males were physically capable of carrying armor. But the physical ability to carry armor in the eleventh century clearly has no relation to the intellectual and emotional qualifications to vote in twentieth century America.[180]

The report actually proceeds to argue that the new generation can physically carry its armor at eighteen, again signalling the curious persistence with which the issue of arms is anchored in the notion of material weight.[181]

So, too, and far more profoundly, the Fifteenth Amendment, which extended the vote to blacks during the Reconstruction period, was inseparable from the military record: 180,000 blacks had fought in the Union Army, and this fact was used in arguments supporting the new amendment in Republican newspapers like the *Chicago Tribune* and *New York Tribune*,[182] in the 1868 presidential campaign,[183] and on the floor of Congress.[184] Lincoln's "Emancipation Proclamation" had itself been a brilliant merging of two separate verbal acts—a proclamation of emancipation and a call to arms:

> I do order and declare, that all persons held as slaves... are and hereafter shall be free... and I further declare and make known, that such persons of suitable condition will be received into the armed service of the United States, to garrison forts, positions,

stations, and other places, and to man vessels of all sorts in said service.[185]

The Fifteenth Amendment reenacted in reverse the merged logic of self-authorization: as liberty in 1863 made inevitable the eligibility to bear arms, so eligibility to bear arms in 1869 made inevitable the liberty to vote.[186]

The association of the right to bear arms and the right to vote has sometimes worked to contract, rather than continually to extend, the franchise for blacks[187] and for women. Section 2 of the Fourteenth Amendment, for example, bypassed the possibility of women's suffrage by expressing its protection of the voting population in an idiom invented to express the requirements for the militia: "male inhabitants of such State, being twenty-one years of age, and citizens of the United States."[188]

But women's suffrage was eventually achieved, both in the United States and in other countries, in part by linking the capacity to vote with the capacity to serve in war. Suffrage pageants in the United States linked the two imagistically by the inclusion of songs such as "Onward Glorious Soldiers," whose chorus moves back and forth between the literal act of "marching *on to* war" and the metaphorical act of "marching *as to* war"[189] Women's capacity for military service, boxing, and the handling of guns continually reappeared in suffrage plays such as *Back of the Ballot, Unauthorised Interviews, The New Woman*, and *A Suffrage Rummage Sale*.[190] In the United States and in other countries, news articles coupled the contribution of women in World War I with the coming vote.[191] In more recent decades, those urging the inclusion of women in military service (whether a voluntary or a drafted army) argued that the burden of defending the country must be distributed across genders so that the civil rights attached to those military obligations are also fairly distributed across genders.[192]

The same arguments were made in securing military rights for gays.[193] The logic of that coupling is clear: from the earliest moments of the Republic to the most recent, the concept of the civil franchise has been inseparable from the record of military participation. The historical record also makes clear the implications of the present nuclear situation: a form of weaponry that eliminates the population of men and women from the sphere of military authorization eventually divests them of their civil authority as well.

In both the negative and, more often, positive instances, the structural equivalences between voting and bearing arms underscore the shared access they provide to the governing of the country, in peace and in war. Elections, reapportionment cases, and constitutional care about numerical translations from the population base to representation all exemplify what the Supreme Court in *Baker v. Carr* called the "distribution of political strength for legislative purposes."[194] So, too, the right to bear arms holds within it the assertion of a just distribution of military power for war-making purposes.

THE REQUIREMENT FOR DOUBLE AUTHORIZATION IN BOTH WAR MAKING AND CONSTITUTION MAKING

Throughout this and the previous chapter, war making and law making have been steadily implicated in one another, as those acts are performed by the population and by Congress. The distribution of arms, I have argued, mimics the goals of fair *reapportionment* and distributed taxation. The bearing of arms is inseparable from the history of voting. The draft, said Alexander Bickel, entails a series of informal *referenda*. Jacob Javits, as he ushered the War Powers Resolution through the Senate, described "the exclusive authority of Congress to 'declare war'" not as one of Congress's powers but as that power "which the framers of the Constitution regarded as the keystone of the whole Article of Congressional power." Justice Story identified the moment of shifting the nation from a state of peace to a state of war as "the highest act of legislation." Rather than allowing the coupling of law making and war making to remain a loose analogy, I want to end by stressing that the equation is quite literal.[195]

Congressional legislation obviously lacks the weight of constitutional law. The greater authority of the latter derives not from its age—the Constitution will always be under continuous revision—but from the fact that it has two consensual locations. Like statutory law, it originates in verbal actions (declarations, proposals, resolutions) confirmed by the full bicameral congressional assembly. But unlike statutory law, it then migrates out to the population where it must be ratified. The very congressional vote that within the statutory framework transforms a verbal proposal into a "law," within the constitutional framework merely transforms a proposal into a more formal proposal. It retains its character as a verbal construct. A two-thirds vote in the House and a two-thirds vote in the Senate—the size of the vote that with ordinary legislation passes a law even over a presidential veto—makes it only a "proposed" constitutional amendment that then goes before the state assemblies for ratification.[196] The requirement of authorization both from the Congress and from the people tests the nature of representation. The population votes for representatives who vote for a proposed law, which is then sent back to the population for their approval. The process constitutes a literal referendum: an act of referring back and a return to the original ground of political empowerment and linguistic delegation.

The Constitution reserves this requirement for a double location of authorization almost exclusively for constitution making. A jealous guardian of its own exalted status, the Constitution places encumbrances on its own genesis that ensure its separation from all other legislative products. The single other phenomenon to which the Constitution accords this double authorizing ground, and hence the single other phenomenon that acquires a gravity equal to its own, is that of war making. The two doctrinal sites on war—Article I, Section 8, and the Second Amendment—literally reenact this double location of certification. War originates in Article I, Section 8, as a proposition, a verbal performative, a "declaration" in Congress. The proposal must then be substantiated by the call to arms, in which the proposal either is ratified or refused, depending on what portion of the population approves of the country's military participation. This is the Second Amendment. At the original Constitutional Convention, the last-minute shift in the phrasing of Article I, Section 8—replacing "to make war" with "to declare war"[197]—registered the fact that the act of "making" war is reserved for the people. Though the declaration, once affirmed by Congress, has tremendous weight and authority, it has not yet left the realm of verbal performance.

The declaration of war is extraordinary because, in front of the eyes of the world, the representative assembly puts at risk the very population it exists to represent. It puts at risk the ground of its own authorization. The acceptance or rejection of the risk by the population—the referenda, the ratification—is therefore crucial. As only the population can "make" the constitutional changes that Congress "proposes," so only the population can "make" the war that Congress declares.

The fact that Article I, Section 8, was written by the Federal Assembly, and that the Second Amendment emerged out of the ratification debates, reconfirms the double consensual location. The argument is often made that the emergency context of international security in a nuclear age necessarily entails some abbreviation or relaxation of the consent procedures followed during peacetime. But together Article I, Section 8, and the Second Amendment make it clear that the Constitution guarantees just the reverse: consent processes will be more rigorous, not less rigorous, in wartime. It guarantees that the act of consenting will be more express, not less express, for it requires a literal "declaration." It guarantees that the distributive mechanisms will be heightened and amplified through the full vote of both houses and the popular referenda, not relaxed and contracted down to a central authority. Accidental convergences of language are not actually accidental. The language of consent became explicit during ratification (we the people of Virginia, of South Carolina, of New York do assent to and ratify . . .), just as the word *consent* became explicit in, indeed almost inseparable from, the colonial, prerevolutionary, and postrevolutionary dialogue on the standing army. The persistent reappearance of this word—consent, consent, consent, consent—makes visible the insistence on distribution in both constitution making and constitutionally sanctioned war making.

In both constitution making and war making, this heightened process of consent takes a visible, material form. The materiality is signaled in the fleeting iteration of the awkward but strangely positive little word *clog*. We saw that George Mason described the participation of both houses and the slowing down of war that results as "clogging," and Madison, complaining of the delay in the New York State ratification convention that would lead to the Bill of Rights, described it as a "clog" that would lead to some "condition." Both the making of constitutions and the making of war must be thickened with matter—clogged with "intervening layers of possibly resistant humanity"—to give them a gravity and weight consonant with the gravity of the risks brought about. Precisely because human sentience is at stake in the outcome of constitutional revisions and wars, human sentience must also be acutely and elaborately present when both are authorized. The importance of sentience and embodiment to the social contract—which in these first two chapters we have only begun to glimpse—is steadily clarified in the chapters ahead.

An obstructionist materiality or (in its positive expression) a substantiating materiality resides at the center of both constitution making and constitutionally sanctioned war making. This materiality lies beneath the insistent bodily idiom that occurs in both spheres. In the sphere of war making, the idiom has surfaced throughout this chapter in an unexpected array of locations: the stress on "firmness" in Gandhi's conception of nonviolent resistance, the idiom of "ruggedness" and "boasted weight and strength" in the advocacy of a distributed American militia, the odd invocation of the physical properties of a shotgun in *Miller v. United States*, or the multiplication of gun locks into lamps and reading glasses in *District of Columbia v. Heller*, the collaborative "road-clogging" performed by combatants and hungry horses in World War I France. The same physical idiom of weight, firmness, and embodiedness has from the earliest moments of the nation been used to describe acts of legislative ratification. Among the "Facts [to] be submitted to a candid world" by the Declaration of Independence was the charge that the king "has dissolved Representative Houses repeatedly, for opposing with manly *firmness* his invasions on the rights of the people."[198] So echoic of *military resistance* is this description of the population's *legislative resistance* that it might with ease be mistaken for its kindred form of obstruction.

During the later period of actual constitutional ratification, the participants repeatedly described the process as one of materialization. While Madison's attribution of the word *clog* to the New York ratification was uttered derisively, those resisting passage of an unamended Constitution—the Constitution that did not yet include the Bill of Rights—announced their clogging materiality with pride. The most articulate exegeses came from Patrick Henry:

> I declare, that if *twelve states and a half* had adopted [the unamended Constitution], I would, with manly *firmness*, and in spite of an erring world, reject it.[199]

> Gentlemen strongly urge, its adoption will be a mighty benefit to us; but, sir, *I am made of so incredulous materials*, that assertions and declarations do not satisfy me.[200]

Henry's language was echoed by similar declaration in the other states' debates, where ratification was repeatedly envisaged either as a bodily internalization of the document or instead as a fusion of body and document.[201] The proposed document was perceived as an insubstantial piece of paper: "[T]he paper on the table," said Madison;[202] "[T]hat on your table," said Patrick Henry;[203] "[T]he paper before you," said Governor Randolph;[204] "[T]hat paper on your table," said Mr. Nicholas.[205] These phrases suggest how fragile, how provisional the document was prior to its confirmation, seemingly deriving its sturdiness from the table alone. For the participants during the debates, the document did not yet have any substantial weight, and it could only acquire weight by annexing the participants' own materiality: "You have not solid reality—the hearts and hands of the men who are to be governed"[206] "Will gentlemen, then, lay their hands on their hearts, and say that they can adopt it in this shape?"[207] The Constitution would only become law, they repeatedly said, if they put a hand to it, if they put their hearts to it, if they stood behind it.[208] The ratification assemblies—whose whole purpose is to substantiate or decline to substantiate the document under review—somewhat remarkably, made vocal and explicit the nature of the materialization process.

The very requirement of materiality impedes the alteration of the Constitution and protects it against unexamined legal flights of fancy. Over 5000 amendments have in two centuries been proposed. Of these 5000, 33 have left the Congress with a two-third vote in both House and Senate; of these 33, 27 have then received the ratifying vote of the states.[209] Thus 4973 have been prevented from acquiring constitutional reality by the encumbering process, the same encumbering process that has given the surviving 27 their weight and solidity.[210] We lack the means to calculate how many thousands of wars have passed through the minds of solitary individuals, how many fewer of these wars would have seemed plausible once reviewed by a council, and how many still fewer of these would have received the population's enactment. Perhaps, like the ratio of amendments, we collectively fight 27 of every 5000 wars that are individually imagined. Though numerically incalculable, the clogging process at least can be glimpsed in the story of the wild La Courtine horses blocking the road in World War I France, as well as the many other occasions in which the encumbering actions of strike, demonstration, or rebellion, at the threshold or the center, have impeded the waging of war, bringing it (at least for a time) to a stop.[211]

This requirement for materiality—the assent of person after person after person iterated thousands of times—makes it hard to make constitutions and hard to make war with speed and efficiency. But it is also precisely this encumbering materiality that gives both constitution making and constitutionally sanctioned war making their capacity to secure our liberty. William Sumner articulated the relation between armed resistance and legislative resistance. Describing the way the distribution of military authority to a wide population endows the country with a thick materiality or a highly textured surface, he wrote, "The general unevenness of our country; the numerous *obstructions* to the progress of an enemy, which its woods, rocks, ravines, rivers, meadows, mountains, mills, stone walls, and villages present, are peculiarly favourable to militia operations."[212] Sumner then describes at length the way this impedes an enemy's entry into the country far more effectively than does a centralized army, which may disappear after a single battle. In discussing the constitutional guarantees provided by the doctrinal formulation of the right to bear arms, Sumner returned to the word "obstruction" as the mysterious center of political liberty: "Obsta principiis."[213]

The Constitution, through a provision such as the Second Amendment, works by obstruction; it anticipates and eliminates the possibility of executive tyranny. It thereby eliminates the need for the population even to have to speculate about so ungracious a possibility. Only if the population is itself eliminated—as is the case with current out-of-ratio weapons—does the possibility of executive tyranny return. Both our Constitution and our constitutionally mandated requirements for a distributed defense system seek to protect our political liberty through the benign material principles of obstruction and substantiatiation.

I have been arguing that nuclear weapons themselves constitute a large tear in the social contract. When one contemplates the physical attributes of nuclear war—the scale of the hurt involved in images we all know—it may seem beside the point to add that there is a tear in the social contract. But those physical attributes—the irrecoverable injury to people, to all they have made, and to the earth—that *is* the tear in the contract. For that reason, it seems important to bring our own contract to bear on the problem. The right to bear arms has been said, not uncontroversially, to contain within it the right of revolution.[214] Either we ourselves can bear arms and change the situation by revolution or, as seems more plausible and desirable, we can bring into view the prerevolutionary situation and call for judicial recognition of the distributive intent of the right to bear arms.

PART TWO

THE SOCIAL CONTRACT
OUTLAWS NUCLEAR WEAPONS

A Prelude and Summary

On the first day, parts of the Northern Hemisphere are pitch black. As the smoke rises and spreads globally, vast regions darken, eventually receiving just 1 percent of the sunlight formerly received. Photosynthesis stops. The forests die. Oxygen levels plunge. If it is July, the temperature is –10°F. If it is January, the temperature is –50°F. There is no fresh water. No food. Violent storms rage along the coasts. Those animals, plants, and people who at first survived now die of cold, starvation, thirst, and disease. Civilization in the Northern Hemisphere has disappeared, and civilization in the Southern Hemisphere might also disappear. Gone for certain are the tropical forests, and with them most of the species on earth. This is the description of nuclear winter given by seventy scientists working independently in many different countries in the l980s: their research helped convince world leaders to reduce nuclear arsenals so that they are today one-third their former size.

But current research—published in the leading science journals between 2007 and 2012—shows that today's much smaller nuclear arsenal, if used in a major exchange, will still produce nuclear winter, causing a drop in the average temperature across earth larger than what occurred in the Ice Age 18,000 years ago, and reducing rainfall by 45 percent. Temperature drops will be especially severe over large landmasses such as Eurasia and North America, bringing agriculture to a halt and leading to the starvation of human beings and many other species. This new research also models what will happen if a tiny fraction (not even 1 percent but 0.015 percent) of today's total arsenal is used in a regional exchange of fifty Hiroshima-size weapons: 44 million people will die at once; 1 billion will die from starvation.[1]

This is what the tearing up of the social contract looks like. This is why Judge Weeramantry at the International Court of Justice said that even the threatened use of nuclear weapons carries us back to a world antecedent to the social contract. We saw in Part One that nuclear weapons are deeply incompatible with one particular social contract, the U.S. Constitution. The existence of either is premised on the disappearance of the other: either the Constitution, as now seems to be the case, will disappear and our arsenal will thrive; or alternatively, our Constitution will be reaffirmed, causing our nuclear arsenal to disappear.

But Judge Weeramantry was talking not just about one specific social contract, that of the United States. He was talking about the essential phenomenon of social contract that underlies any concrete instance: "a world order dependent upon terror would take us back to the state of nature described by Hobbes in *The Leviathan*."[2] The two antiwar or war-impeding provisions in the U.S. Constitution are together not just an accidental or secondary feature—a lucky feature— of what it is. (Of course, even if it *were* just a lucky feature, we should reach for it as a blessing and proceed from there).[3]

Although Part One focused on one constitution in particular— that of the United States—other countries have constitutional provisions that may (along with international law) eventually enable their populations to eliminate their nuclear arsenals. For example, Article 35 of the French Constitution stipulates that "[a] declaration of war must be authorized by Parliament." Article 34, Clause 3, confers on parliament the obligation to "determine the basic principles of the general organization of national defence." The present arrangements in France—a presidential first-use policy, the inclusion of fewer than twenty people in the formation of nuclear policy,[4] and the issuing of executive edicts that sweep aside legislative authority[5]—all violate the constitution and would themselves, in turn, be eliminated if the constitution were applied.

In India, Article 246, Clause 1, of the constitution stipulates the "Subject Matter" for which Parliament is responsible: "Defense of India and every part thereof including preparation for defence and all such acts as may be conducive in time of war to its prosecution and after its termination to effective demobilization." Subsequent items for which the legislature is responsible include all forms of military force.[6]

The 1993 Constitution of the Russian Federation is widely perceived as conferring vast power on the country's president, but some of its structural features resemble those found in the United States. If Russia is attacked—if its borders are violated by armed aggression—the president may begin to act at once to defend the country (Article 87) and then notify the legislature. But while the president may take unilateral action to defend the interior of the country, Article 102 stipulates that the use of military force *outside the borders* requires the authorization of the Federal Council (the analog of the U.S. Senate); and Article 106 assigns to the Federal Council the responsibility for protecting the borders and overseeing war and peace. Legislative debate, deliberation, and testing of the proposition that a foreign population deserves to be injured therefore appear to be key parts of the structure of governance. Russia also has a constitutional provision that resembles the Second Amendment of the U.S. Constitution: Article 59 distributes to the entire population shared responsibility for defending the country. The only way to make nuclear weapons compatible with these three constitutional requirements is to eliminate those weapons altogether.[7]

Part Two shows that far from being an accidental feature of particular constitutions, the war-impeding feature is essential to the social contract, part of its deep structure—so much so that without it the contract is profoundly incoherent and simply ceases to exist. The nuclear-weapons states, then, cannot hope to keep their weapons by rewriting their social contracts.

Once the elementary form of the social contract is made visible, we see that its fundamental design entails three essential steps: the social contract is a brake on injuring; the brake works by providing an actual material obstruction to the act of injuring; the material of that obstruction is the human body. While the major work of Part Two is to show that it is not just one particular constitution but the social contract itself that prohibits nuclear weapons, a second major undertaking is to comprehend this role of the material impediment—the aliveness of all persons—in the contract.

This reliance on the human body has already become visible throughout the earlier chapters. "How many intervening layers of possibly resistant humanity" stand between a leader's decision to injure a foreign population and the enactment of that decision? In stark contrast with nuclear strategy, the United States Constitution requires 535 intervening layers at the congressional gate, and many millions of intervening layers at the popular gate. The double gating is itself a manifestation of the impediment strategy: outside of war making, it is found in no other constitutionally stipulated national action except the making of the Constitution itself. Live human bodies of citizens are called upon to defend the home country against injury that originates from outside its borders: the dead and wounded in any war make the importance of the body tragically unmistakable. But so, too, resistance to injuring originating at home entails the resistance of the human body, as the clogging of roadways with horses and bodies made clear in the La Courtine resistance in World War I France, as was again clear in the soldiers' strikes throughout England and Canada at the end of World War I, and as was visible once more in the assemblies of protestors during the Vietnam War. Peaceful resistance to wrongful authority requires bodily stiffening—as Gandhi's Satyagraha, "firmness in the truth," confirms. One may become an "intervening layer of possibly resistant humanity" as part of a large group, or instead as a solo performance, as when Rosa Parks refused to get up out of her seat on a bus in Montgomery, Alabama, an act that became the flash point of the civil rights movement: "When that white driver stepped back toward us, when he waved his hand and ordered us up and out of our seats, I felt a determination cover my body like a quilt on a winter night."[8]

The nuclear technology enables a leader to make foreign policy decisions without enlisting the consent of the home population. It makes him independent of the will of the people. Since no human beings are needed to carry the weapons onto the battlefield, there is no need to persuade that population of the wrongdoing of the foreign country, no need to persuade them that all avenues of diplomacy are useless, no need to persuade them that stopping this foreign wrong is even more important than their own lives (a proposition for which a very high standard of proof is needed). Thus the ordinary features of civic life—speech, contestation, debate, persuasion—disappear and are replaced with secret meetings in the leader's private chambers.

As we see over the course of the three chapters that follow, once a population loses the right of bodily self-defense, it loses the right of dissent and consent. Dissent and consent originate in the capacity for self-defense. When nuclear weapons first came into existence, people throughout the world thought about them day and night. Because we have now lived with them for many decades, we rarely think of them at all (unless they are aimed at us). It may at first seem perplexing to be told that so profound a phenomenon has taken place as the loss of the right of bodily self-defense and, with it, the capacity for consent and dissent. When we check our own pulses and ask ourselves whether we consent to or dissent from these new arrangements, it is hard to get any traction on the feeling at all. One's own arms are empty of feeling. But that is exactly what it feels like to lose the capacity for consent or dissent: because the weapons are utterly independent of our consent, our consent is irrelevant; and because it is irrelevant, it is unexercised; and because it is unexercised, it atrophies. Once we internalize our own irrelevance, the idea of nuclear weapons incites neither applause nor indignation; we can set aside the thought of savage world-ruining weapons with a shrug or brief lament, then turn to other thoughts.[9]

While the truth of our disenfranchisement is argued slowly in the chapters to come, it may be helpful, here at the threshold, to contemplate—as a kind of shorthand—an area of life where every individual's capacity for consent remains vibrantly intact, and then contemplate a hypothetical technology that would permit the practice of this form of consent to be lifted away from the population and put in the pocket of a solitary leader alongside the card containing the nuclear codes (which President Clinton attached to his credit cards with a rubber band,[10] and which, when lost, remained missing for several months before the Pentagon was informed that it was astray in the world.)[11]

People reproduce themselves by having children. A couple's decision about having children is a profound way in which consent and the human body are elaborately intertwined (as will be elaborated in Chapter 5). Although childbearing is a phenomenon brought about by individual decisions, a population as a whole may seem to act in concert to change its rate of reproduction, even though the members of that population have not deliberated in an assembly or even openly consulted each other about their own individual decisions. The birthrate in Eastern Germany after the opening of the Berlin Wall provides a striking example. Compared to the 1989 birthrate, the 1991 births fell by 45 percent, the 1992 births fell by 55 percent, and the 1993 births fell by 60 percent.[12] Closely related to a decision about childbearing is the decision to marry. The number of new marriages in Eastern Germany declined sharply during this same three-year period. In the months considered high-wedding months—May, June, July, August, and September—the 1989 figure was 17,000 weddings per month; the 1990 figure was 10,000 per month; the 1991 figure, 6000 per month.[13] As historians have observed, the birthrate figures "exceed fertility changes in Germany brought about by war, hunger, or the introduction of liberal abortion and birth control policies."[14]

Although the birthrate of a geographical region is the collective outcome of tens of thousands of highly individual decisions, such a phenomenon can affect the well-being of a country, and it is therefore not surprising that government leaders sometimes take note of such events. French President Giscard d'Estaing in an April 1979 television appearance announced the declining population of France; he ranked it, along with France's future economic strength, military security, and influence in the world, as one of four "real problems facing France."[15] While the number of families having one child or two children was the same as in earlier years, what alarmed President d'Estaing was the drop in the number of families who had three children. The country therefore initiated a program of monetary subsidy to families raising three or more children. In April 1984 the European Parliament, noting a "marked trend towards population decline," passed a "Resolution on the Need for [European Economic] Community Measures to Promote Population Growth in Europe."[16] Sometimes government measures are more coercive than the monetary incentive in France: in 1967–68 the Romanian government increased fertility by blocking "access to legal abortion," which temporarily raised the number of persons giving birth from 14 per 1000 in 1966 to 27 per 1000 in 1967–68. A government may, of course, take measures not to accelerate but instead to slow down the birthrate, as in the one-child policy introduced into many parts of China in 1978 and continuing today.

Government measures to accelerate or slow down the birthrate may impinge on an individual's consent (just as in the realm of national defense in the era of conventional weapons, a person's individual consent about going to war might be greatly affected—but by no means entirely lost—by government actions, such as monetary incentive to enlist or punitive measures for those who do not enlist). But questions about the person with whom one will create a child or the timing of the childbearing or the number of children ordinarily remain within a highly personal sphere. It is precisely because we retain this authority over our own bodies that government tampering is noticed and assessed and, if aversive, quarreled with.

But now imagine for a moment a situation that has no equivalent in present-day reality, a situation in which the generation of children from harvested cells has now become technologically feasible. It has even become—through huge scientific research and government expense—technologically perfected. A leader finding that his population is failing to reproduce itself (as the residents of Berlin did when their birthrate fell by 52 percent between 1942 and 1946) can now simply reproduce that population. At first the government supplements the population of new children that are still being brought into being by individual pairs of parents. But before long the renewal of the population is considered the exclusive province of the country's executive office—so much so that its procedures, practices, and protocols are pretty much top secret and considered none of the population's business. Occasionally an annoying citizen or citizen's group files a Freedom of Information inquiry into some aspect of the program, but such actions have no power to alter the arrangements. The government's ability to renew the population is now almost wholly independent of the existing adult population. In fact, the government, which formerly had to ensure just economic arrangements and transportation systems to keep its population minimally happy and therefore reproducing itself, can now ignore such problems.

Is it conceivable that a population would accept this profoundly altered situation without an outcry? Surely not in the first decade. Probably not in the second or perhaps even the third. But by the sixth decade, the population might now have forgotten that in the past decisions about population renewal and growth were made by millions of people making individual decisions that had collective outcomes. Although the government might justify the new arrangements on the grounds of national defense—rival countries are producing huge populations that will outnumber and crush us if we do not keep pace—people will remind each other that the new system also has some very legitimate personal advantages. For example, the many months of pregnancy was extraordinarily hard on women in the past, even leading to the deaths of some women; the fact that women bravely endured these hardships in the era when it was the only form of self-replication available should not prevent us from celebrating their new freedom. So, too, the old form of population self-renewal created an unjust bias toward heterosexual relations; now lovers can make their choices about partners without considering the question of childbearing.

It might well be that here in the sixth decade the subject of population renewal still comes up. For example, one country's leader might renew the population wholly from his own cells or from the cells of his ethnic group, while another country's leader might harvest random cells from the staircases in subway stations and public avenues to ensure a wider distribution of the renewal privilege. These different practices might lead to many public discussions about why one's own country is morally right to own this technology while other nations are morally wrong. All states would agree that it would be disastrous for a nonstate actor ever to get his hands on this technology. In fact, not only the leaders but also the populations would live in dread of a nonstate actor (or terrorist) obtaining the technology, even though the nonstate actor can do no more harm with the technology than can the official leaders.

Such meandering public discussions (in this hypothetical world we are imagining) cannot disguise the fact that the astonishingly important and fundamental right of a population to choose to regenerate and perpetuate itself or to refrain from doing so—a collective decision arrived at by hundreds of thousands of individual decisions—would now be gone. Gone as well would be the need to keep the population's economic and moral confidence high through just arrangements in many other spheres of life. Government leaders, even if still elected, would on the day they take office, find themselves in the startling position of being almost wholly independent of the very population that a day ago elected them.

Is this imaginary shift laughable? Yes. Likely to happen? Highly unlikely. But it is crucial to see that precisely the situation that is inconceivable and laughable in the context of a population's right of self-regeneration is factually the case in the context of the right of self-defense. The profound consent and dissent exercised by individual persons but having an indisputable collective outcome in military assemblies fighting for their country, or declining to fight, has been set aside by the fact that government leaders have a technology that permits them single-handedly to carry out offense or defense wherever and whenever they choose.

Do we need some law that anticipates, and makes impossible, the science-fictional situation of population replication? We might say such a law is unnecessary: the very nature of bodily reproduction means it will always be ours to protect and, should some aberrant technology be invented, there would be such a hue and cry from the population that no such anticipatory law would be needed. That is, as we saw in Chapter 2, exactly the argument that Hamilton and Madison made against the fear that military might could ever be concentrated in the hands of a leader. The need to include an explicit right-to-bear-arms provision in the Constitution seemed unnecessary since concentrations of military power in a central location could never take place unopposed: "Can it be supposed that there would not be found one man discerning enough to detect so atrocious a conspiracy, or bold or honest enough" to oppose it? asked Hamilton incredulously in *The Federalist No. 26.* Can we imagine that the "people of the [United] States should silently and patiently behold the gathering storm and continue to supply the materials until it should be prepared to burst on their own heads?" asked Madison in *The Federalist No. 46.* Yet the people of the United States have watched the gathering storm and continued to supply the materials until it is prepared to burst over their own heads and the heads of all people on earth.

Fortunately, the safeguards against such a catastrophe do not depend on improvised opposition but reside, as we earlier saw, in two major provisions of the U.S. Constitution that enable us to dismantle the nuclear arsenal. And as we see in the chapters that follow, centuries of thinking about social contract seek to safeguard the consent of the individual over his or her live body. None of the nuclear states can hope that by amending their constitutions they can retain their weapons. Maintaining nuclear weapons places a country wholly outside the social contract; there is no minor or even major reconfiguring of a country's contract that can accommodate these weapons. Submerging ourselves in the writings of Thomas Hobbes and John Locke, no matter which way we turn, brings us face to face with the very conclusion recently announced by former Secretary of Defense Robert McNamara writing in the pages of *Foreign Policy*: "U.S. nuclear weapons policy [is] immoral, illegal, militarily unnecessary and dreadfully dangerous."[17] McNamara's essay, "Apocalypse Soon," is an urgent plea to his countrymen to wake up to the ghastly reality we minute-by-minute inhabit.

We begin in Chapter 3 with the basic recognition that the social contract is a contract for peace. This simple principle needs to be put securely into view so that we can comprehend how concrete, how insistent, Hobbes is on this fundamental vision. *Peace* is not a word that can be skated over anymore than one could walk across the surface of the earth without coming to the oceans and mountain ranges: for Hobbes, peace structures and contours everything else across the surface of his philosophy. It is therefore Hobbes, as others have urged us to see, who is the philosopher who might best have helped us as we stood on the threshold of the nuclear age, and it is Hobbes who even at this late hour may help us now. Along the way, we will try to come to terms with the way the nuclear age deformed the principles of Hobbes to turn him into an apologist for the very condition he identified as the worst possible outcome of total nongovernance: the massacre of a population.

But how can a social contract enact this commitment to peace? Is it merely an aspirational goal? On the contrary: we will see that it is palpable, graphic, and material. In Chapter 4 we enter the brilliant interior design of the Hobbesian social contract, the internal architecture that enables a government to prohibit its population from injuring and that, in turn, enables the population to prohibit its government from injuring unless it provides an explicit release from the overarching "never injure" rule.

It has been observed that Hobbes's great invention is peace and Locke's great invention is liberty. While Chapters 3 and 4 bring us into the presence of the peace contract, Chapters 5 and 6 let us turn to everyday liberties and the way the relations of consent and the body continue in these spheres. Across the four chapters it will become clear that the social contract is a brake on injuring: that is its fundamental— almost its only—purpose. But it does not act as a brake on living or on lovemaking or on debating or on skiing: that is why it is the guarantor of liberty. Stop (stop injuries) and go (stay alive, write books, get married, laugh): these are the two motions the great invention was designed to bring about; but it cannot do the second if it has forgotten how to do the first.

CHAPTER 3
THE SOCIAL CONTRACT IS
A COVENANT FOR PEACE

Constitutions are encumbrances on the urge to injure other people. Accordingly they are often disparaged as slowing down a war-making process that requires decisiveness and speed. But that work of "encumbrance" is essential to the design of the social contract—that is the very thing it was called into being to accomplish. The social contract is, first and foremost, a brake on going to war.

Social contract theory does not originate in the seventeenth-century writings of Thomas Hobbes and John Locke; it has many antecedents in the medieval period, and much further back in Roman, Greek, and Hebrew writings.[1] But it is Hobbes and Locke on whom the next two chapters focus since they lift the logic of its inner structure into much greater visibility than had existed before. The scaffolding of that inner structure has three key elements: the social contract is an obstruction to injury; the obstruction is material; the material is the human body. We look at each of the three in turn.

THE SOCIAL CONTRACT IS AN OBSTRUCTION TO INJURY

The covenant among people exists to eliminate the action of injuring. Injury and the covenant are fundamentally at odds. Hobbes states in

Leviathan that injury is to the social contract as logical absurdity is to discourse: *"Injury,* or *Injustice,* in the controversies of the world, is somewhat like to that, which in the disputations of Scholers is called *Absurdity."*[2] His earlier work, *On the Citizen,* anticipates the idea that injury and absurdity are analogous: "And there is an analogy between what in ordinary life is called [injuria] and what in the schools is usually called *absurdity."*[3] In a third work, *De Corpore,* Hobbes again puts the analogy in front of his readers:

> The breach or violation of covenant, is that which men call *injury,* consisting in some action or omission, which is therefore called *unjust.* . . . There is a great similitude between that we call *injury,* or *injustice* in the actions and conversations of men in the world, and that which is called *absurd* in the arguments and disputations of the Schools. . . . And so *injury* is an *absurdity* of conversation, as absurdity is a kind of injustice in disputation.[4]

Hobbes is not simply denouncing injury by calling it "absurd." He is making a much more extreme statement: as absurdity is starkly incompatible with and represents the dissolution of intelligent argument, so injury is incompatible and enacts the dissolution of social contract. The dissolution of the contract, in turn, is a reversion to the condition of injury.

Like Hobbes, Locke throughout the *Second Treatise of Government* centrally identifies injury as the action the social contract exists to prohibit. Though the "injury" is not specified as, or limited to, "bodily injury," it takes its force from that original context. Locke, for example, uses the verb "injures" both where the object is the material reality of the body and where the object is freedom,[5] just as he speaks of "invading" another's body, invading another's property (the "annexed body"), or instead invading another's rights.[6] When Locke uses the idiom of "invasion" for a nonphysical object, he often immediately follows it by the word "rapine," to anchor the word in the physical world. Persons enter the social contract for mutual security: the contract comes into being to "secure them from injury and violence," which is a "trespass against the whole species."[7] Is that last phrase an exaggeration: does the will to harm other human beings really embed within it the aspiration to "trespass against the whole species"? The history of weaponry that has culminated in nuclear arms surely validates and literalizes Locke's claim.

The social contract prohibits us from trespassing across the boundaries of another person's body. Locke's concreteness, his sense of persons as embodied, reflects the fact that he was a physician; one of his biographers writes that until at least 1683 Locke "regarded himself as before everything else a doctor."[8] He collaborated extensively with Thomas Sydenham, then a controversial physician, now widely regarded as "the father of English medicine."[9] Locke accompanied Sydenham on visits to patients; he wrote a prefatory poem to Sydenham's treatise on epidemics and planned a preface for a second volume never completed; each sent his medical notes and manuscripts to the other for annotation.[10] The two also planned to coauthor a book reviewing "the whole state of clinical medicine."[11] Their correspondence reveals two key facts: Locke was extremely sensitive to his own pain;[12] more important, he was extremely sensitive to other people's pain and was able to describe it with unusual vividness and precision.[13] Locke's concern for the bodily integrity of others expressed itself not only in terms of individual patients but also in terms of the health of the public: he worked to create mortality tables in Ireland at a time when the concepts of state medicine and public health were just emerging.[14]

Like Locke, Hobbes was thinking about injury that was (however intensely individual) community-wide: he was thinking about war. His statement about injury cited earlier might accurately be rewritten as a statement about war: "War is to the social contract as logical absurdity is to discourse." The stark antagonism between war and social contract is one he repeats frequently thoughout *Leviathan*:

The finall Cause, End, or Designe of men . . . is . . . getting themselves out from that miserable condition of Warre.[15]

They accomplish that end, as the full passage shows, by creating the social contract:

> The finall Cause, End, or Designe of men, ... in the introduction of that restraint upon themselves, (in which wee see them live in Common-wealths,) is the foresight of their own preservation, and of a more contented life thereby; that is to say, of getting themselves out from that miserable condition of Warre.

So stark is the opposition between the social contract and the state of war that Hobbes often refers to the social contract as "Articles of Peace":

> The Passions that encline men to Peace, are Feare of Death; Desire of such things as are necessary to commodious living; and a Hope by their Industry to obtain them. And Reason suggesteth convenient Articles of Peace, upon which men may be drawn to agreement.[16]

He also specifies that these Articles of Peace can be called the Law of Nature (a potentially confusing term, but one which in *De Cive* he carefully distinguishes from "state of nature," a synonym for "state of war").[17] So different are the two—the one meaning "peace" and the other "war"—that Hobbes writes, "The laws of Nature are silent in the state of nature."[18] Using the phrase "Law of Nature" he repeatedly designates "peace" as the raison d'être of the social contract, and war as the contract's very opposite:

> [T]he first, and Fundamentall Law of Nature ... is, *to seek Peace, and follow it.*[19]

> [To] remain still in the condition of *War* ... is contrary to the first and Fundamentall Law of Nature, which commandeth men to *Seek Peace.*[20]

He that…is guilty of the warre…doth that, which is contrary
to the fundamentall Law of Nature, which commandeth *to seek
Peace*.[21]

The prohibition on war, the aspiration to peace, then, is not simply a
feature of the social contract but what he repeatedly designates "the
first, and Fundamentall Law."

The idea that the social contract simply *is* a contract for peace is so
fundamental to the writings of Hobbes that it should be unnecessary
to belabor it. But it is necessary to do so for three reasons. The first is
the world in which we now live. As Bernard Gert writes in his preface
to *De Cive*, "In this day of nuclear weapons, when whole nations can be
destroyed almost as easily as a single man in Hobbes's day, we would do
well to pay increased attention to the one philosopher to whom the attain-
ing of peace was the primary goal of moral and political philosophy."[22]
The second is that peace has been underemphasized in writings about
Hobbes: in an article entitled "Thomas Hobbes's 'Highway to Peace'"
(a phrase from Hobbes's "Preface to the Readers" in *De Cive*), Donald
Hanson laments the discrepancy between the major position Hobbes
accords peace and the marginal position it is accorded in Hobbes scholarship.[23] The third is the erroneous—it would not be inaccurate to say,
preposterous—idea that because Hobbes sanctioned a strong sovereign
he would sanction a sovereign armed with genocidal weapons. Nothing
could be further from the truth. The absolute power Hobbes conferred on
the sovereign was the power to do one thing: stop injury. How so erroneous a view could come about (and how linked the general distortions of
Hobbes's philosophy are to the onset of the atomic age) will be addressed
at a later point; for now we return to the underappreciated centrality of
Hobbes's dedication to "getting us out of the miserable condition of war."

Because the aspiration to peace is "the first, and Fundamentall
Law," many other principles and rules follow from it. Most important
among these other principles is the equality of all people in the formation of the social contract. A contract for peace can only be achieved if,

as Hobbes writes in *Leviathan*, all participants are equal, or are treated as equal to one another:

> If Nature therefore have made men equall, that equalitie is to be acknowledged: or if Nature have made men unequall; yet because men that think themselves equall, will not enter into conditions of Peace, but upon Equall terms, such equalitie must be admitted.[24]

Like other principles that Hobbes considered crucial, this one is announced earlier in *On the Citizen* where he writes: "If then men are equal by nature, we must recognize their equality; if they are unequal, since they will struggle for power, *the pursuit of peace* requires *that they be regarded as equal.* And therefore . . . *everyone should be considered equal to everyone.*"[25] Each person must be equal in the eyes of the law, otherwise "the Controversies of men cannot be determined but by Warre"; and there also follows from this "the equall distribution to each man, of that which in reason belongeth to him," which Hobbes calls "Equity" and "distributive Justice."[26]

Among the 20,000 letters that Gottfried Leibniz wrote to fellow mathematicians and philosophers in Europe and England was a set of letters to Thomas Hobbes. Leibniz had read and greatly admired the brilliance of *De Cive.* "[I]n your little book *De Cive* you seem to have surpassed yourself in the strength of your reasoning and the weight of your opinions, so that one might think you were giving the pronouncements of an oracle rather than handing down the theories of a teacher. . . . I examined the inner fibers of your doctrines down to their very roots." He singles out, as one key fiber, Hobbes's insistence on equality; and the truth of the observation that all people are equal because the strongest can be killed by the weakest.[27] Hobbes had earlier been challenged on this point by a letter writer who asserted that "invalids, madmen, fools, pigmies, and poltroons . . . prevent one from being able truthfully to assert that all men are equal."[28] But Hobbes had remained committed to the doctrine, reiterating it in *Leviathan*.

Although this is not Hobbes's only[29] and certainly not his most optimistic ground of recognizing the equality of all people, it is, as Leibniz saw, directly relevant to his conception of peace; and it is a surprisingly relevant corrective to the arms race in the twentieth and twenty-first centuries. As international relations theorist Hedley Bull saw four decades ago, an individual group of people might hope to achieve "inequality" by acquiring a "superior" power to injure.[30] But before long a second group of people will inevitably acquire the same weapon (as Russia acquired the atomic bomb soon after the United States did). Then six more will acquire the weapons (as Britain, France, China, India, Pakistan, and Israel have now done).

Soon the original country lives in dread that even a lone nonstate actor may get hold of the weapon. This fear is realistic: a recent report assesses the multiple paths by which a nonstate group can either initiate an actual launch by hacking into the apparatus of a nuclear state or can instead generate a false image of a missile, causing a nuclear state to fire a weapon.[31] We have not been informed of any nonstate actor[32] attempts to hack nuclear weapons systems, but in 1998 international hackers successfully inserted an image of a mushroom cloud onto the website of the Bhabha Atomic Research Center in India,[33] in 2000 a thirteen-year-old boy in Connecticut hacked into the U.S. Air Force plane tracking system,[34] and in 2009 Iraqi rebels hacked into the video system of U.S. drones.[35] The fact that a country with 10,000 nuclear weapons (5000 active; 5000 inactive but not yet dismantled) recognizes that it could suffer a nuclear strike or be made to respond to a false missile image introduced by a nonstate actor is a reminder that all people are equal, even independent of their group numbers.[36] Finally, as scientists who work on nuclear winter have stressed, the effects of nuclear weapons spread globally; any country that uses a nuclear weapon will therefore be carrying out an act of "suicide" on its own population; no adversary is required.[37] Hobbes's formulation of equality in terms of equal power to injure and be injured, regardless of apparent strength, is a reminder of how nuclear weapons violate the basis of social contract that obliges us to give to all others any right we would wish to retain for ourselves.[38]

An equality based on equal susceptibility to injury and to death is simultaneously an "equality of aliveness." People do not need to calculate their merits and faults but only the self-evident fact of their shared aliveness to recognize their equality. Many other rules are derived from Hobbes's fundamental opposition between social contract and war, such as laws of safe conduct for intermediaries and laws of gratitude in areas of nonreciprocity.[39] But equality of aliveness, equality in the eyes of the law, and distributive justice are the most important corollaries to the grounding of the social contract in peace and its stark prohibition of war.

As it was crucial to recognize the literal basis of the word "injury" in John Locke's medical practice, so it is crucial to hold on to the fact that when Hobbes says the word "warre" he first and foremost means the literal fact of war, the willful infliction of physical injuries on persons designated enemies, or a contest of reciprocal injuring to determine which side can outinjure the other. If his meaning sometimes extends to figurative and miniaturized uses such as verbal disputations, insults, and acts of petty greed, it begins and ends here in intentional acts of killing, maiming, and physical disablement. Hobbes championed a powerful sovereign, stipulating many times throughout *Leviathan* that by "sovereign" he meant either the legislature or the executive, whichever the population had authorized: "their Sovereign, be it an Assembly, or a Monarch."[40] In *De Cive* the assertion of the alternatives—"the *Man* or *Assembly*," "one man or one assembly," "the assembly or the man," "one man or council [curia]"—occurs on almost every other page.[41] This same insistence on the two alternatives continues in his final book on the social contract, *A Dialogue between a Philosopher and a Student of the Common Laws of England*.[42] But the whole reason for championing a powerful sovereign legislature or a sovereign executive is to eliminate dissension and ensure peace and safety—the peace and safety of the people, *salus populi*. It is inconceivable that he would have accepted a monarch armed with the power to annihilate the species. The vast map of annihilation contemplated every day by nuclear states in the late twentieth and twenty-first centuries enacts everything Hobbes had dreaded and devoted his life to opposing.

Jean Hampton's book—*Hobbes and the Social Contract Tradition*— opens by acquainting us with the literal basis of Hobbes's use of the word *war*:

> He was born in 1588, just before Philip II of Spain sent the Armada to attack England during Spain's war with The Netherlands. During his childhood, a civil war raged within France between the Protestant Huguenots and the Catholic crown. The Thirty Years' War ravaged Europe during all of his early adult years, from 1618 to 1648. And England itself was plunged into civil war and disorder from 1642 to 1649. Cromwell waged war against Ireland, Scotland, and Holland during his protectorship, and two other wars between England and The Netherlands erupted in 1665 and 1672. During the 1670s, Holland was also engaged in a war against France, along with Austria, Spain, and the German principalities. And in 1679, the year of Hobbes's death, political turmoil in England was increasing as, once again, opponents of a Stuart king prepared to overthrow him.[43]

In effect, Hampton requires us to cross over the literal fact of wars in Hobbes's lifetime before we ever read in her book a single other fact about him or about his conception of the social contract.

Precisely this same requirement is placed on us when we turn to Hobbes's own autobiography in verse, which he published first in Latin (1679) and then in English (1680). Once we have entered the interior of the poem, we encounter many pieces of information about his aspirations, his fears, his teaching, books, and exile. But to get there, we must—like the newborn infant Hobbes—cross over the doorsill of war:

> *In Fifteen hundred eighty eight, Old Style,*
> *When that Armada did invade our Isle,*

Call'd the Invincible; *whose Freight was then,*
Nothing but Murd'ring Steel, and Murd'ring Men;
Most of which Navy was disperst, or lost,
And had the Fate to Perish on our Coast:
April *the fifth (though now with Age outworn)*
I'th' early Spring, I, a poor worm, was born.[44]

Murdering men and murdering steel—yet these people are quickly revealed to be as susceptible to death as those they attack, many perishing on the coast of England before they have landed. The poem will now stop to describe the town into which Hobbes was born, the borough of Malmesbury, and then returns to the birth of the "poor worm," explaining how he was pushed into the world prematurely because of his mother's dread of the approaching Spanish Armada:

For Fame had rumour'd, that a Fleet at Sea,
Wou'd cause our Nations Catastrophe;
And hereupon it was my Mother Dear
Did bring forth Twins at once, both Me, and Fear.[45]

This threshold act is a fascinating feature of the poem, because Hobbes here requires us to enact precisely the act that we perform mentally in entering the social contract. We should understand that we have, always at our backs, the state of mayhem and war; we step over the line into the alternative world of the covenant for peace. That contractual space inside the poem is the small town of Malmesbury.

MALMESBURY: THE SIMULTANEOUS CREATION OF A TOWN, A COUNTRY, A KING, AND A PARLIAMENT

Though it is our goal here to understand Hobbes's relation to national and international ground, it is useful, for a moment, to contract our attention to the local ground of Malmesbury, the place to which Hobbes affixed his name on every title page he published. Of the 136 portraits in *Aubrey's Brief Lives*, the account of Thomas Hobbes is singular for the emphasis John Aubrey places on Hobbes's stature as an international intellectual. Three-quarters of the way into the portrait, Aubrey simply suspends his narrative and breaks into a list of those who loved, or befriended, or admired him: Galileo Galilei, Robert Hooke, William Harvey, John Dryden, Descartes...[46] Having lived in France for eleven years and traveled abroad during others, Hobbes might have on his title page specified his country as the whole world. His unswerving affiliation with one small town cannot be attributed to the temporal depth of his residence there: by the age of fourteen, he had already left Malmesbury for Oxford, and we know from Aubrey that the last of his infrequent visits was a weeklong stay in August 1634.[47]

For Hobbes, the town into which he was born and baptized was a dramatic exemplar of the social contract. Malmesbury had come into being through, and was among the first towns in England to receive, a contract. Regarded by many historians as the oldest town in England, some date its origins from the 880 CE charter issued by King Alfred.[48] Others, including Hobbes, date it from the charter King Æthelstan granted sometime between 924 and 939 CE in language that stresses the townsmen's freedom and freedom from injury:

[I], Æthelstan, king of the English, grant, for me and my successors, to my burgesses and all their successors of the borough of Malmesbury, that they may have and hold all the taxes and their free customs... without diminution and honourably. *And I direct all under my power that they should not do them injury....* And I give and grant to them that royal heath of five hides of land... on account of their assistance in my fight against the Danes.[49]

Hobbes was well aware of this history: his poem directly specifies the benefits Æthelstan gave to the town in return for the townsmen's assistance in defeating the Danes; as his poem further specifies, the bones of Æthelstan—the first leader to consolidate the British territories and thus widely regarded as England's first king—are buried in Malmesbury. Hobbes's awareness of the contractual nature of the town might have been still further heightened by the fact that, shortly after his last visit home, Malmesbury renewed its town charter in 1635 when Hobbes was forty-seven and on the eve of writing *De Cive*. The contract reaffirmed the population's liberties and franchises, added a new market area and three new fair days, created the position of a legal advisor or steward to the town, specified a court session every third week, and (from our point of view, perhaps most important) added a preamble emphasizing the need to find better ways of securing the peace.[50]

Philosophers often remind us that the social contract is a thought experiment, a mental performance, and that its historical reality or unreality is not important. That is perhaps a good thing since the Æthelstan contract is believed by charter scholars to have been written in the late thirteenth rather than the tenth century. S. E. Kelly not only designates the borough charter "a forgery" but, citing Tait's *Medieval English Boroughs,* confers on it the distinction of being "the most obvious of post-Conquest forgeries." The charter was submitted to Richard II for official confirmation, which it received in 1381, with later confirmations following in 1411, 1462, and many later dates.[51] The town's famous abbey—Malmesbury Abbey—itself holds a vast assortment of charters (granting it certain lands and privileges), a significant number of which are believed to be of later manufacture than the period specified inside the charter itself.[52] In some cases, a given charter is thought to be a copy of the earlier original; in other cases, a writing out of an orally transmitted history; in still others, a naked fabrication.

What we need to appreciate is the fact that Malmesbury, long before Hobbes lived there, was charter obsessed and contract rich. It had almost as keen an appreciation of the importance of "foundational legends" as its native son had. The factual details interior to the Æthelstan charter are real and uncontested: Æthelstan really did favor the town, chose to be buried there, and conferred the greatest treasures he had on the abbey.[53] Reciprocally, the town's assistance in the defeat of the Danes is real. What is in doubt is whether the contract is accurately signed and dated by this particular king and these particular witnesses, or instead retroactively manufactured several centuries later. Malmesbury was in the Middle Ages one of the country's mints; one might say that, in addition to minting money, it seems to have undertaken the manufacture of contracts.

In Hobbes's autobiographical poem, the lines devoted to Malmesbury stress, in addition to its long-standing position as a center of learning, its early charter from Æthelstan and its history of parliamentary representation, which had begun in AD 1275 and continued with greater frequency than all but a handful of English towns:[54]

Many things worth relating had this Town;
And first, a Monastery of Renown,
And Castle, or two rather it may seem,
On a Hill seated, with a double Stream
Almost environ'd, from whence still are sent
Two Burgesses to sit in Parliament.
Here lie the Bones of Noble Athelstane,
Whose Stone-Effigies does there remain;
Who for reward gave them the Neighbouring Plains,
Which he had moistned with the Blood of Danes.[55]

Given its early charter and its long history of self-governance, it is no wonder that Hobbes chose to yoke his own name to the town, not only in the title of this autobiographical poem—*The Life of Mr. Thomas Hobbes of Malmesbury*—but on the titles pages of all his books: *De Cive* by Thomas Hobbes of Malmesbury, *Leviathan* ... by Thomas Hobbes of Malmesbury, *De Corpore* by Thomas Hobbes of Malmesbury.[56] That this international intellectual, who left home at fourteen and visited the town for one week in the summer of 1634, should so insistently and proudly yoke his name to the place justifies our staying inside Malmesbury a bit longer.

The frontispiece of *Leviathan* depicts a town that summons to mind an aerial view of Malmesbury. We see there an abbey and a row of abbey houses extending out to the city's perimeter wall, which is two-tiered.[57] The town in the engraving may fairly be described as a generic British or continental town. The beautiful aerial maps of English towns—such as Bath, Bedford, Carlile, Kendal, Norwich, Rochester—published by John Speed in his 1611 *Theatre of the Empire* often have one or several features in common with the frontispiece; but none of them specify a two-tiered wall or abbey houses directly adjoining the city wall.[58] Other key features of the frontispiece match the town where Hobbes was born. Malmesbury's most prominent geographical features are its hilltop location and the convergence of two tributaries of the Avon River that almost meet at the northwestern edge of the town—where they are separated by only 200 meters—and do meet at the southwestern corner.[59] The city is, as Hobbes writes in his poem, "On a Hill seated, with a double Stream / Almost environ'd."

A recently discovered 1648 painting of Malmesbury suggests what the city looked like in the mid-seventeenth century (figure 1);[60] and

Figure 1. Annotated painting: Aerial view of Malmesbury as it was in October 1646 during civil war (1648). Artist unknown. Shared features of figures 1 and 2 can more easily be seen at www.pbase.com/hobbes where figures 1–5 are reproduced in color.
REPRODUCED BY PERMISSION OF THE WARDEN AND FREEMEN OF MALMESBURY.

Figure 2. Engraved title-page of Hobbes's *Leviathan* (1651) by Abraham Bosse. Shading added by author to indicate features shared with 1648 painting (figure 1).

in turn, helps to suggest how close the town on the *Leviathan* frontispiece is to Malmesbury (figure 2). Both are aerial views, the painting from just outside, the frontispiece from just inside, the town periphery. Both depict a swath of the town's northeast corner where its famous abbey and abbey houses reaching a perimeter wall reside. The orientation of the painting is from the west (or southwest) looking east (or northeast).[61] Hobbes's provides a different line of vision, which is perhaps from the northeast looking to the southwest.[62] If this reading of the frontispiece direction is correct, it means that the onlooker of the painting is standing on the same ground as the Leviathan stands in the frontispiece; thus, in the painting, we would be looking back at the town from his perspective; he would see on the skyline not a giant like himself but centuries of readers looking across the landscape at him.[63]

Though Malmesbury's resides on a high ridge that falls down to the river below, the wider landscape beyond the riverbed eventually climbs upward again: both painting and lithograph show rolling hill-tops beyond the low plain that surrounds the hilltop city. The stream encircling the town is visible in the 1648 painting and in the frontis-piece is easily recognizable (here made more visible by the addition of shading) and the two-part geometric walls, so prominent in the paint-ing, are again easy to pick out in the frontispiece.

In the painting, the town's hilltop location is indicated by the fact that the houses outside the city walls are much smaller than those inside, suggesting they are farther below us vertically even though they are in the foreground. The writing on the upper-left-hand portion of the painting specifies that the town is "Renowned for its natural streinth Seated on a step hill, unclimable by reason of the manie Rockes." In the drawing for the frontispiece (figure 3) that may have either pre-ceded or followed the engraved version and that was given by Hobbes to Charles II, the town's location on a high ridge is implied by the fact that it is much darker, hence nearer to us, than the surrounding plains which, by being much lighter in tone, seem much farther away—as though they have dropped to a lower elevation. Even without the clar-ity provided by the drawing, that hilltop perch is recognizable in the engraving, as several scholars have observed: "Nearer to the spectator [of the frontispiece], on a central bluff with plateau top, lies a consider-able city."[64] Not all features of the drawing and frontispiece conform to Malmesbury: the double tower on the church is a more familiar sight in northern Europe than in England, where churches had single spires or a rectangular steeple with four spires; scholars of the frontispiece point out that the double tower may be there to remind readers of the pluralities of religions—both Roman and reformed—and to prevent the church from having the unitary quality that the social contract has.[65]

Comparing the beautiful drawing with the engraved frontispiece, Keith Brown stipulates what he and no doubt most observers regard as by far the most important difference: the drawing's outward-looking faces more successfully convey Hobbes's central thesis that "what Leviathan wills is what we will."[66] Collectively, we constitute

Figure 3. Drawing of frontispiece of Hobbes's *Leviathan* (1651) by either Wenceslaus Hollar or Abraham Bosse.

BRITISH LIBRARY, EGERTON 1910 F1. COURTESY OF THE BRITISH LIBRARY BOARD.

the Leviathan. His body—the guarantor of our peace—is constituted by our own bodies, which even in aggregate remain highly individualized (as we can see in figure 4). In fact, is that the face of Hobbes in Leviathan's right thumb, given pride of place but looking somewhat startled to find the shadow of the hilt crossing his forehead?

Of course it is misleading to suggest that by "social contract" Hobbes in *Leviathan* means only the city-state or, as he often calls it, *civitas*, for he also means the nation-state. It is therefore useful to return to a detail quickly passed over above: the bestower of the town charter, Æthelstan, was simultaneously the first king of England, credited with unifying the island, defending it against external aggressors, and then presiding over it peacefully.[67] He issued law codes that required the distribution of food, and prohibited distribution through theft.[68] He asserted the new political unit of "England" through the form of crown

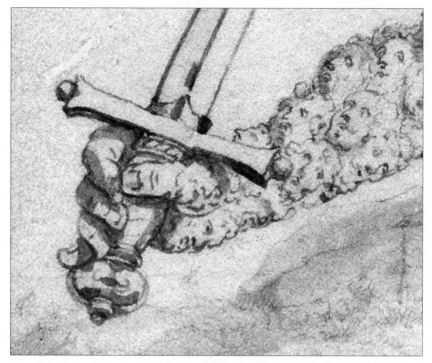

Figure 4. Leviathan's right arm. Detail from drawing of *Leviathan* frontispiece (figure 3).

he wore, replacing the long-standing headgear associated with war—the helmet—with one associated with peace; and through the form of the coins he issued, with *rex totius Britanniae* on one side and his crowned face on the other.[69] He is credited with inventing the majestic language of the charters—beginning with the designation, "Æthelstan, king of the English"—which in their sweeping sentences initiated what afterward became the standard for charter language.[70] In effect, the town of Malmesbury and the state of England came into being at the same time and by the same hand.

Remarkably (for the hero of our verse autobiography), so too did Parliament. In *The Origins of the English Parliament, 924–1327,* J. R. Maddicott writes that Æthelstan created the first "truly national assemblies," which were both the cause and the consequence "of a newly unified English state."[71] Unlike the ad hoc councils that had attended the regional kings and had held only sporadic meetings, Æthelstan's assemblies were "large," "socially diverse," and "frequent and regular in occurrence."[72] The central activity of the assembly was the generation of laws and charters, which were consented to and witnessed by a large number of men, who were also responsible for transmitting news of any legislative act to the large territory of the country and therefore also for enforcing it. Three of Æthelstan's charters, for example, had, respectively, 101 signed witnesses, 92 witnesses, and 59 witnesses.[73] The number of witnesses was constrained by the size of the parchment, one of which ends by indicating that many others were present ("et plures alii milites"), leading Maddicott to surmise the assemblies were much larger than even the witness list suggests: "the witness list is a minimum statement of those attending the assembly."[74] The assembly members were not just witnesses but "active consenters" to the charters and codes: the wording of these documents shows that they "derive[d] their authority" from the joint action of king and councilors.[75] "[A]ssemblies," Maddicott concludes, "thus helped to stabilize and harmonize the relationship between the king and his great men on which the peace ultimately depended."[76]

Hobbes's own account of the historical roots of the English Parliament resembles (though in briefer form) what has just been described above. He in fact dedicates the final pages of his final work of political philosophy to this very subject. *A Dialogue between a Philosopher and a Student of the Common Laws of England*—a work that, unlike his earlier writings, stresses that any act by the monarch must have Parliament's authorization—closes with the lawyer and the philosopher describing the assemblies called by early Saxon kings, the gathering of these territories into the unified country of England with a single king and a single Parliament, the privilege that walled (or fortified) towns had of sending burgesses to Parliament, and the similarity between the earliest Parliament and that in Hobbes's own day.[77] Hobbes does not tell us the name of the king. Nor does he tell us the name of the town where that king lies buried, a walled town that long held the privilege of sending burgesses to Parliament. But since these are the final paragraphs of the book, one sees upon closing it the name of that town printed on the front next to the author's name.

This, then, is the alternative to war: a social contract—a city, a country, a set of laws, a flowered crown (instead of a helmet),[78] a Parliament where charters and codes are generated, witnessed, communicated to the country's people, and enforced. To see a city or a country savaged by war is to see the contract torn. England suffered a civil war from 1642 to 1651, a period during which Hobbes (who specified the war dates as 1640–60) fled to France and lived abroad. But what did this sentence mean for any one town like Malmesbury? Historians show that it was under constant siege, taken now by Parliamentarians, now by Royalists, changing hands either five or seven times:

> At the outbreak of war in 1642 Malmesbury apparently held to the parliamentary side and the committee for Wiltshire met there. The town submitted to the royalists on 3 February 1643, the day following Prince Rupert's capture of Cirencester, but on 23 March it was taken by Sir William Waller for parliament. Sir Edward Hungerford was appointed governor but changed his allegiance and surrendered the town to the royalists on 5 April. Malmesbury may have changed hands twice more before 24 May 1644 when Col. Edward Massey recaptured it for parliament.[79]

A garrison of 1000 men was housed in the city, a number that is almost certainly larger than the town's adult population.[80] The residents filed a petition protesting both the cost of the garrison and its failure to protect them from raids of the other side.[81] Some of Malmesbury's houses were burned to the ground. It is not hard to understand how one (even one who had gone into exile in Paris and was therefore himself not among those injured) could come to believe that such disputes entailed a lethal magnification of inconsequential differences and that choosing either one—the legislature or the king—would be far better than suffering the torment of unending dispute.

It is often observed that civil war was the form of war Hobbes most dreaded. In the preface to *De Cive*, Hobbes explains to his reader why— having originally planned a book that would start with "the body," then proceed to "the man," and then end with "the citizen"—he has instead jumped ahead to publish his work on the citizen:

> While I was filling [the section on the citizen] out, and putting it in order, writing slowly and painfully (for I was thinking it through not composing a rhetorical exercise), it happened that my country, some years before the civil war broke out, was already seething with questions of the right of the Government and of the due obedience of citizen, forerunners of the approaching war. That was the reason why I put the rest aside and hurried on the completion of this third part.[82]

The word *seething* in the passage above is tonally consistent with the "miseries, and horrible calamities," the reduction to "the first Chaos of Violence" that Hobbes, throughout *Leviathan* associates with "Civil Warre," which he defines as "that dissolute condition of masterlesse men, without subjection to Lawes and coërcive Power to tye their hands from rapine, and revenge."[83]

But Hobbes's scathing descriptions of war often do not stipulate "civil" war and clearly extend as well to wars between nations. In 1629 and 1630, Hobbes and his tutee, Gervase Clifton, traveled on the Continent and were for some months confined to Geneva. Nearly every letter home to Clifton's father (also named Gervase) confirms how conscious Hobbes was of the ongoing state of war. In March he writes of their plan to travel to Venice, "but by what way I knowe not, because the ordinary high way through the territory of Milan is encumbered with the warre betweene the French and the Spaniards."[84] In April, he speculates that if they remain in Geneva until the fall, they may still have the chance to go to Italy: "But I have no hope of it, the warres have made all the wayes so dangerous, and difficult, that not a man here, or any where by the way to whom we discovered our purpose but dissuades us from it."[85] In May, he again describes the intrusion of war into their plans: "There is no possibility for the present nor hope for the future of going into Italy, in respect of the warres, and going up and downe of troupes in all partes betweene us and it."[86] In fact, a map of the Thirty Years' War (figure 5) shows that in the 1630–32 period, Switzerland is a partial island of peace surrounded on all sides by conflict; to the north, south, east, and west of Geneva armed struggle is never far away. The arrows indicate the southward movement of the Swedish campaigns. The boxed area at the bottom center indicates the 1628–31 conflict between the French and the Spanish in northern Italy, the part of the Thirty Years' War called the War of Mantuan Succession.[87] It was this latter branch of

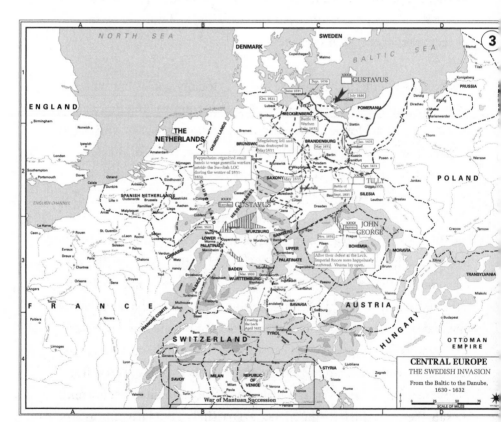

Figure 5. Historical map of the Thirty Years' War: Swedish invasion. War of Mantuan Succession added by author.

COURTESY OF DEPARTMENT OF HISTORY, WEST POINT MILITARY ACADEMY.

the war—the French coming into the Spanish-ruled Milan to support the attempts of a French aristocrat to fill the vacancy in Mantua—that made unthinkable Hobbes's proposed trip to Venice.

THE CONTRACT FOR PEACE IN THEORY AND PRACTICE

The stark opposition that Hobbes and Locke make between war and contract, or between injury and contract will be restated with more precision in Chapter 4 to follow. But for the time being it is useful to appreciate the fact that the opposition is recorded not just in theoretical writings like theirs but in actual historical contracts, specifically, the city contracts that long predate Hobbes and Locke and, equally, the national constitutions that follow in their wake, shaped by their writings.

Legal scholars describe how, in the eleventh and twelfth centuries, many of the 500 major European cities came into existence as mutual aid societies to protect the inhabitants against external sources of human aggression. The cities did not accidentally emerge. They came about through explicit acts of oathtaking and contract making. "A solemn collective oath, or series of oaths," writes Harold Berman, "[was] made by the entire citizenry to adhere to a charter that had been publicly read aloud to them."[88]

Often called "communes for peace," "sworn communes," or "conjurations," their very names memorialized the remarkable verbal process by which they had come into being. The purpose of that verbal act was to forge a strong link between self-governance and the diminution of injury. The founding charter of Freiberg, for example, emphasized the guarantee of "peace and protection."[89] The Flemish charter of Aire opened by identifying the assembled persons about to take the oath, "All those who belong in friendship to the town," and then promised, "Let each help the other like a brother."[90] The articles of the charter for Beauvais in Picardy began: "All men within the walls of the city and in the suburb shall swear the commune; Each shall aid the other in the manner he thinks to be right."[91]

The fundamental goal of "peace"—present in the framing statements of the city communes—was additionally audible in many of the
administrative details. The criminal law of the city—the law against
injuring fellow residents—was sometimes called "the peace" or "peace
of the city" (*pax villae*). So, too, municipal magistrates were called
"warders of the peace" or "jurors of the peace" in cities such as Ver-
dun, Cambrai, and Valenciennes.[92] William Blackstone—compiling
his *Commentaries on the Laws of England* in the eighteenth century—
observes that an offense against a country, palantine, corporation, or
town is always designated an offense "against the peace" of that particular jurisdiction: "contra pacem domini regis," "contra pacem domini,"
"contra pacem ballivorum," "contra pacem vice-comitis."[93]

Like the city contracts of the eleventh and twelfth centuries, the
national constitutions that come into being in the eighteenth through
twentieth centuries announce the framing opposition between contract
and injury. The social contract is essentially a covenant for peace, as we
can see in the fact that so many national constitutions explicitly designate *international* peace a central aspiration, either in the preamble (for
example, the constitutions of Andorra, Azerbaijan, Bahrain, Benin, Bra-
zil, Bulgaria, Burkina Faso, Cameroon, Central African Republic, Chad,
China, Croatia, Egypt, Germany, Indonesia, Japan, Oman, Pakistan,
Senegal, and Turkey) or in an early article (for example, the constitutions
of Albania, Angola, Cape Verde, Ecuador, Finland, Italy, and Laos). It
is also the case that many countries identify *domestic* peace as a central
aspiration in either their preamble (for example, the constitutions of
Cambodia, Ecuador, Guatemala, Honduras, Laos, Macedonia, Turkey,
and Uganda) or an early article (for example, the constitutions of Cambodia, Cameroon, Croatia, Djibouti, Equatorial Guinea, and Ireland).[94]

At issue here is not the extent to which each of these countries
lives up to this aspiration but simply the stark fact that peace is the
goal aspired to. The inclusion of the word *peace* is not an accident or
an ornament, but an essential statement of what the constitution is—a
covenant for peace.

*   *   *

When one hears the name Hobbes, the first word that should come to mind after the words *social contract* is the word *peace*. The deep philosophic momentum of Hobbes toward international peace was recognized by Immanual Kant. As Richard Tuck has compellingly shown, Kant in *Perpetual Peace* as well as in many other writings seized upon and made luminously available the implications of Hobbes's stress on peace that had eluded even Rousseau.[95] Kant argued against the legitimacy of preemptive strikes, and the unending preparation for harm: "We have to admit that the greatest evils which oppress civilized nations are the result of *war*—not so much of actual wars in the past or present as of the unremitting, indeed ever-increasing *preparation* for war in the future."[96]

More important, even, than such philosophic elaboration has been the concrete instantiation of the peace Hobbes envisioned. The social contract tradition inaugurated by Hobbes and continued by Locke, Rousseau, and Kant helped to bring about the array of democracies whose aversion to war has been celebrated by Bruce Russett and countless other observers. (This phenomenon of democratic pacifism—and its sabotaging by nuclear weapons—will be scrutinized in Chapter 4.) Hobbes's contributions to nonviolence have also been recognized by thinkers in disciplines distinct from political philosophy. In *The Better Angels of Our Nature*, for example, cognitive scientist Steven Pinker documents the diminution of many forms of violence over fifty centuries. When at the end of the book he comes to the difficult task of designating the cause of this decrease in injury, he puts in front of us one leading candidate: the Leviathan—both Hobbes's book and what followed the book, the creation of Leviathans, states whose citizens were prohibited from injuring.[97]

Given that Hobbes has over four centuries been successful in both the theory and practice of reducing injury, why should it matter to us that his obsessive aspiration to peace has come in recent decades to be decoupled from his name. The answer is this: at the onset of the nuclear age, at the very moment that democracy was being dismantled by weapons that made democracy impossible (a moment when Hobbes could have brought us to our senses), a view of Hobbes became dominant that not only severed him from the aspiration for peace, but made him an apologist for authoritarian nuclear regimes and for international anarchy.

The originator of the social contract was now invoked to authenticate what amounted to the tearing up of the social contract. Scanning the "standard image" of Hobbes in the classroom at the end of the 1980s, D.J.C. Carmichael found that in the preceding decades the "standard picture of Hobbes" had three features: his "political theory [was] rigidly authoritarian, anchored in a repellent view of human nature and argued with more precision than anyone can bear."[98] Carmichael shows that standard picture is currently undergoing a glacial revision, with the work of Richard Tuck at its center and many scholars contributing. But the distorted image of Hobbes is still available to those who champion thermonuclear monarchy and our permanent state of nuclear readiness. How, given the fact that Hobbes issues statements about peace on every third or fourth page, is it possible that his center of gravity could be ignored—omitted as is usually the case or, alternatively, mentioned but mentioned as though it were itself an inert idea with no implications? Here is one example of the latter. In the nuclear age, Hobbes's name has often been coupled with that of Carl Schmitt, the German philosopher who argued that in a state of emergency the führer may suspend the constitution. (Though this view of emergency was written during the German Third Reich, it would also license the arrangements nuclear states have for presidential first use.) As Tom Sorell shows, Schmitt, in endorsing the führer's *personal* action in dissolving the constitution, thought Hobbes also endorsed the *personal*. But this, as Sorell argues, is utterly wrong: in Hobbes's commonwealth, everyone transfers their decision-making power to the sovereign precisely because the sovereign transcends the personal and acts on the citizenry's behalf.[99] Yet Schmitt is not someone who failed to notice the word *peace*; in one of his writings on Hobbes—*The Leviathan in the*

State Theory of Thomas Hobbes—many passages acknowledge peace as Hobbes's central passion.[100] For Schmitt, the idea of peace apparently implied no obligatory real-world pressure toward preventing injury.

But it is not our purpose to dwell on the modern dismantling of Hobbes; rather, to recover the extraordinary architecture of his vision, to which we here and in the chapter immediately following return.

The social contract, we have begun to see in this chapter, has this profound and brilliant feature: it is perfectly designed for a species whose members—though themselves terribly vulnerable to physical injury— have a hard time comprehending the aversiveness of future injuries, whether their own or other people's. Left to their natural inclinations, they will recklessly commit injuries on the smallest provocation. The social contract closes down the possibility that any injuries ever take place; it simply categorically prohibits them. It does not matter whether the person one contemplates injuring is a neighbor, a business partner, a lover, a stranger on the road, or a foreigner: the injury is not allowed. It does not matter whether one's desire to injure has been long contemplated or surfaces on the spur of the moment: the injury is not allowed. It does not matter whether one has at hand a gun or arrow or knife or poison: the injury is not allowed. Thus our inability as a species to assess the aversiveness of future injuries is not fatal to us because the option of injuring has been largely eliminated from our thoughts and, more decisively, from our actions.

But what if someone in our midst *does* break the no-injury prohibition? Or what if an entire group of foreigners from outside our midst breaks the no-injury prohibition and threatens to invade our shores? Are the remaining members of the social contract helpless in this situation: do they continue to be bound by the never-injure rule? Does not the right of self-preservation—the one right Hobbes says we cannot give up—require their action? These are precisely the two situations in which the members of the social contract—using an intentionally encumbering procedure described in detail in Chapter 4—may be released from the no-injury rule: injury is permitted in the case of punishing a criminal (someone who himself has broken the no-injury rule) or stopping a foreign aggressor by declaring war and fighting those who have sought to dissolve the contract.

Let us restate the no-injury prohibition so that its absolute form (the form we were looking at above) and its form-with-two-exceptions (the form we will be looking at now) are clear. The social contract exists to prohibit injury. In its purest form—were a pure form possible—no injury would ever be legal. The social contract that in its ideal state has as its first and fundamental law a never-injure rule even in reality, as we will eventually see, seeks to stay as close as possible to the never-injure rule. But there are—as both Thomas Hobbes and John Locke make explicit—two *and only two situations* in which the absolute prohibition on injuring can be lifted: the punishment of criminals and going to war.

Another way of saying this—the way Hobbes says it in Chapter 28 of *Leviathan*—is that there are three categories of injury, two legal and the third made up of all those injuries that do not meet the test of the first two and are therefore atavistic acts of destroying the social contract. One legal category of injury is against "a *declared* enemy. . . . [In] *declared* Hostility, all infliction of evill is lawful."[101] The twice-repeated stipulation "declared" emphasizes an impediment to the seemingly straightforward permission slip, as does his foregrounding of the formal act of judgement: "But against Enemies, whom the Common-wealth judgeth capable to do them hurt, it is lawfull by the originall Right of Nature [the right of self-preservation] to make warre."[102] Without these acts of judgement and declaration, any injury is only a hostile act of the kind the social contract was designed to eliminate.

The second permissible release from the never-injure rule is criminal punishment. Hobbes begins his chapter on punishment by noting what an exceptional phenomenon it is:

> Before I inferred any thing from this definition, there is a question to be answered, of much importance; which is, by what door the Right, or Authority of Punishing in any case, came in.[103]

As with legally declared war, only an infliction of injury that has passed through an encumbering deliberative gate is permissible, otherwise it will be the debased form of injury the social contract exists to make impossible:

> The evill inflicted by publique Authority, without precedent publique condemnation, is not to be stiled by the name of Punishment; but of an hostile act; because the fact for which a man is Punished, ought first to be Judged by publique Authority, to be a transgression of the Law.[104]

As Hobbes's own margin glosses announce: "Private injuries, and revenges [are] no Punishments"; "Nor pain inflicted without publique hearing"; "Nor pain inflicted by Usurped power." And to these stipulations he adds, "Nor pain inflicted without respect to the future good." The only goal of punishment is deterrence: "it is of the nature of Punishment, to have for end, the disposing of men to obey the law."[105] This last point is crucial, for it underscores the fact that the purpose of the injury in punishment can only be to restore the commonweath to the state of noninjury by dissuading would-be criminals from carrying out any such future act. According to Mario Cattaneo, Hobbes's emphasis on deterrence makes his conception of punishment far more liberal than Rousseau's, Montesquieu's or Kant's.[106] Cattaneo bases his assessment of the liberalness of Hobbes on four grounds: Hobbes's understanding of the rule of law (stipulating that no law can be passed and then applied to an act after the act has been committed);[107] his conviction that torture produces only false evidence; his insistence that punishment can be undertaken only for deterrence; and his belief that the right of self-preservation gives any person the right to resist the death penalty.[108]

That injury which (with encumbering deliberation) is done to a subject who has himself broken the never-injure rule is called punishment; that injury (with encumbering deliberation) that is done to a foreign people that has broken, or threatened to break, the never-injure rule is called the right of war; all other harms are forbidden.

John Locke makes the same two exceptions to the never-injure rule. The opening chapter of the *Second Treatise of Government* concludes, "*Political power*, then, I take to be a *right* of making laws with penalties of death . . . and in the defence of the commonwealth from foreign injury."[109] Later in section 88, Locke returns to the commonwealth's power to punish transgressions of the law, as well as "to punish any injury done unto any of is members, by any one that is not of it, (which is the *power of war and peace*;)."[110] In section 131, Locke once again stipulates that under the rule of law, force can be used "*only in the execution of such laws*, or abroad to prevent or redress foreign injuries, and secure the community from inroads and invasion."[111] Each of these three passages ends by insisting that the twin release clauses—on behalf of punishment and war—can only be activated if in the service of the public good: "[A]nd all this only for the public good," he writes at the end of his opening chapter; "And all this to be directed to no other *end*, but the *peace, safety*, and *public good* of the people," he writes in section 131.[112]

If such acts are not carried out for the public safety and health, those acts themselves are illegal injuries and, in turn, release us from the never-injure rule, licensing for Locke the right of revolution, a right anticipated in Lutheran and Calvanist theories of resistance and writings on resistance by George Buchanan, Fernando Vazquez de Menchaca, Huge Grotius, and John Milton.[113] For Hobbes, such resistance was seditious. But its being seditious and itself deserving of death did not mean it should not be done: "There are commands that I would rather be killed than perform."[114] While he prohibited tyrannicide, he did not prohibit "hosticide": "If [a sovereign rules] without right, he is a public enemy [*hostis*] and is rightly killed, though this should not be called *Tyrannicide* but *hosticide*."[115]

Now it may seem that a large contradiction has emerged. On the one hand the social contract and war are stark opposites; so, too, social contract and physical injury are stark opposites. But then we find that exceptions will be allowed and the exceptions turn out to be the very phenomena the social contract seemed designed to eliminate, war and personal injury. How can this be?

We will eventually see that what at first looks like a paradox or contradiction is instead a brilliant double-breaking system in the elementary design of the social contract. At level one, the social contract provides an absolute never-injure rule. The never-injure rule works because those who wish to violate the rule see that they will be impeded either by punishment or by having war declared against them. The impediments to injuring—which we name by the abstract words "punishment" or "war"—are actually very material brakes made up of all the human beings in the social contract who have agreed there will be no injury and have further agreed that they themselves (and at their own risk) will stand in the path of any who ignore the rule.

Now we come to level two: just as at level one, the clogging mechanism of fellow human beings stands in the way of injuring, so in turn this structure of inhibition and deterrence (punishment, war) itself has folded into it further inhibiting mechanisms (numerous persons and cumbersome deliberative requirements) designed to make it very hard to happen—able to happen only with tiring amounts of evidence, stamina, and time. (If one is motivated by anything other than the imperative to uphold the never-injure rule, one might give up in exhaustion.) We might call level one the never-injure rule, and level two the seldom-punish/seldom-make-war rule (or punishment-made-difficult/war-made-difficult rule). One can punish only after being explicitly and laboriously released from the never-injure rule; one can make war only after being explicitly and laboriously released from the never-injure rule. We will get a clearer picture of how this works if we return to the claim that at each level the brake is material and the material is the human body.

Is it *literally* the case that the human body is the brake on injuring? Yes, it is *literally* the case.

But before doing so we should acknowledge a problem that we can already see on the horizon. If punishing and warring are costly, people might decline to punish and decline to go to war out of laziness, and gradually develop a disregard for upholding the never-injure rule. That would be fatal to the social contract. Equally fatal would be to find short-cuts to punishing and shortcuts to carrying out war—ways of carrying out those acts without much effort. Each of the two would dissolve the social contract. The first would replace the never-injure rule with an injure-if-you-wish rule; the second would make punishment and war themselves the biggest violators of the never-injure rule.

CHAPTER 4

THE SOCIAL CONTRACT AND THE DOUBLE BRAKES ON INJURY

I have claimed that the social contract has a two-story architecture. Level one is the never-injure rule that, with the exception of self-defense, prohibits the population from *any* act of injuring. Level two is a release from the never-injure rule: it gives to the government the power to injure in the case where a person or persons have broken the never-injure rule thereby necessitating punishment and war making. Because this is explicitly a power of the government and not of individual persons (who cannot initiate punishment or war on their own), this second level is often referred to as "the state monopoly on violence" or "the state monopoly on force." Once we look closely at the second level—the intentionally encumbering double braking system that must be gone through before the government secures the right to injure—we will see that here the case is reversed: it is the population that serves as a constraint on the government. At level one, then, the government acts as a brake on the population, using the threat of punishment to enforce laws that deprive the population of the power to injure. At level two, the population acts as a brake on the government, making it difficult for the government itself to be released from the overarching never-injure rule. With respect to injuring, the population's hands are tied;[1] but the government's hands are also tied until and unless the people untie them.

The population can never injure; the government can sometimes injure, and it is the population's work to determine when that time will be. In the pages that follow we enter the interior architecture of this braking system, both the braking system in the case of punishment (which we look at briefly) and in the case of war (which we look at in more length). Even though the subject of this book is war, the architecture of punishment helps us see the architecture of war with fresh eyes. Whereas we earlier saw that punishment and war are part of an *external*, overarching design to uphold the never-injure rule, now we will see that *interior* to each of the two we again find a double brake at work.

THE BRAKES ARE MATERIAL; THE MATERIAL IS THE HUMAN BODY

Early in the English system there emerged what Leonard Levy identifies as a "double trial": the grand jury reviewed the charges made against a person and determined whether it was appropriate to authorize an indictment and announce it in written form; only then did a second jury, the petit jury, determine guilt or innocence.[2] By 1376, this double jury was well established. Before the accused could be formally indicted, the accusation was tested by twenty-three persons. If the indictment survived this first test, the charge of guilt would be more elaborately tested by another twelve persons. A guilty verdict required, then as now, unanimous assent from the trial jury; a single dissenter invalidated the charge.[3] These thirty-five jurors—twenty-three from the grand jury and twelve from the petit jury—each had strong reasons to resist careless indictment and conviction: first was the juror's *regard for the defendant*; second (and probably often more pressing) was the juror's *self-regard*—a moral terror of a wrongful conviction that would make him guilty of murder and lead to his own damnation. James Whitman documents this moral terror at length, arguing that the "beyond a reasonable doubt" standard that eventually emerged in the late eighteenth century was as much a way of showing jurors how to navigate the waters of moral jeopardy as it was a protection of the defendant.[4] Whitman also shows two other motives the jurors had for resisting indictment and conviction: acts of retaliatory vengeance by the defendant's family members and actual punishment by the law courts if a juror error were discovered; both practices had subsided by the 1660s or 1670s.[5] But while these other sources of fear fell away, spiritual terror remained high through all these centuries—even, according to Whitman, intensifying in the seventeenth and eighteenth centuries[6]—and provided the major motive for careful deliberation and a predilection to err on the side of innocence.

This double jury, needless to say, did not prevent unjust convictions and punishments. Nor does the Anglo-American system today prevent unjust outcomes, even though it has many more layers of impediments than did the seventeenth century: the beyond-a-reasonable-doubt standard (which emerged in the late eighteenth century), the presence of a defense counsel (which developed between 1690 and 1780),[7] far more rigorous rules of evidence (such as the exclusion of hearsay), and safeguards on defendant rights (such as the rule against self-incrimination which Hobbes advocated in the seventeenth century,[8] which was more widely advocated in the eighteenth, and which became operative in the nineteenth and twentieth centuries[9]). But compared to a government's ability to suspect, convict, and punish without any intervening layer of testing (as might happen if a president or governor were able, upon suspicion that someone were a wrongdoer, simply to fire a drone that sought out and killed the suspected wrongdoer), the safeguards provided by a double jury system are high. Its intentionally cumbersome structure is meant to ensure that the error, if it is to occur, falls on the side of noninjury: thus the king can pardon a defendant who is convicted but cannot convict a defendant who is acquitted.[10]

Hobbes was attentive to the double jury system: he refers to the grand and petit juries in his examination of criminal law in *A Dialogue between a Philosopher and a Student of the Common Laws of England.*[11] He unequivocally respects the twelve-person jury, and the population from which it springs—a population to whom, he says, statute books ought to be as readily distributed as Bibles so they do not feel intimidated by lawyers and legal commentators (such as Edward Coke, the commentator against whom the work is addressed).[12] Even without these books, jurors regularly decide not just questions of fact but questions of law, determining whether a given act is robbery or instead theft, whether another act is murder, manslaughter, or accident.[13] Out of their own reasoning powers, jurors determine questions of equity and use it to fill in where statutory law is piecemeal.[14] The jury system, in Hobbes's view, validates his conception of equality and consent: the fact that cases are tried in the neighborhood where the alleged crime occurred and that the parties can reject any jurors they wish increases the willingness of the participants to consent to the proceeding and to accept the verdict.[15]

Hobbes credits the way the trial acts as an "impediment" to the punishment, as when he observes how difficult it is for a jury to convict a person of treason: "But the Question is not here of the Treason (which is either Fact, or design) but of the Proof, which, when it is doubtful, is to be Judged by a Jury of 12 Lawful Men." He thinks his way into the difficulty of ever proving treasonous intent from the (mere) purchase of armour or gun-powder. "But how a Jury from providing, or buying of Armour, or buying of Gun-Powder, or from any other overt Act, not Treason in it self, can infer a Design of Murdering the King, unless there appear some words also, signifying to what end he made such Provision, I cannot easily conceive."[16] Impediments to the state's power to punish reside not only in this resistance of the jury and inherent difficulty of proof but also in the requirement for a precedent law[17] and in the inviolability of the jurors' eventual verdict. (Hobbes was two decades in advance of the legal ruling on this crucial matter.)[18]

Is this idea of "intervening layers of possibly resistant humanity" in the jury system just a theoretical idea? Let us look at figures that are close to the time of Hobbes and Locke, taking first the grand jury screening of prosecution, and then actual criminal proceedings of the jury trial. Legal historian John Langbein, drawing on John Beattie's *Crime and the Courts in England 1660–1800*, describes the way the grand jury regularly acted as a "filtering mechanism" for "groundless or insubstantial" prosecutions:

> For the years 1660–1800 Beattie found that the Surrey grand juries dismissed 11.5 percent of the bills of indictments for property offenses punishable by death and 17.3 percent of those brought for noncapital property offenses, 14.9 percent for murder, 27.4 percent for infanticide, 25.8 percent for wounding, 44.4 percent for rape.[19]

As striking as the figures for the grand juries are those for the actual jury trials in the same period in Surrey where a third of all defendants charged with a felony were acquitted.[20] Taking the grand and petit juries together we see that for the crime of murder, for example, roughly 44 percent of those originally accused are exonerated, and for infanticide 52 percent.

Although the figures for Wiltshire—the county in which Hobbes's Malmesbury resides—are less complete, they appear to be consistent with the Surrey figures. Of those accused of larceny or compound larceny in the three years for which reliable figures exist (1616, 1619, and 1623) 44 percent were released: either they were not indicted at the first stage; or, if indicted, they were acquitted.[21] In the second half of the eighteenth century, the acquittal figures in Wiltshire appear to be even higher. Of those accused of infanticide, for example, 86 percent were acquitted; of those accused of homicide, 56 percent were acquitted.[22]

We can see, then, very directly the way the double jury is designed to act as a constraint on the government's right to punish. While it is the government's power to punish that prevents the population from injuring their neighbors, lovers, coworkers, and strangers, it is, in turn, the population (in the person of the thirty-five grand and petit jurors) that prevents the government from carrying out that power to punish too easily.[23]

In the pages of this chapter that follow, we will see the double braking system at work in the case of war—the constraints imposed first by the assembly and then by the population at large—that is the equivalent of the grand and petit juries in the case of punishment. But it is here, with the relatively simple example of punishment freshly in view, that we can perhaps appreciate the enormity of the error of our arrangements for twentieth and twenty-first century war making premised on weapons of mass destruction. Imagine—in the realm of criminal punishment—that there were no double jury, no requirement for a formal indictment, no requirement for unanimous jury, no appeal—nor any of the scores of encumbrances we know as the Miranda rule and rules of evidence. Imagine that a charge could be leveled and punishment accomplished without going through such gates. Imagine that a president or a governor, who conceived the suspicion that someone was guilty, could send out an automated drone to track down and kill that person with no such intervening encumbrances, just efficient nonstop progress from the governor's mental suspicion to the wrongdoer's physical punishment. If this were to happen at all, it would be accompanied by a hue and cry.

But now look at the war situation. Every official or unofficial description we have tells us that our nuclear weapons are ready to fire within fifteen minutes of a president's giving the order. No impediments. No intervening layers of possibly resistant humanity. To do... what? Execute a solitary criminal with a drone strike who may or may not have done anything? No: to execute millions of human beings who could not possibly have done something to deserve mass execution (however guilty of error their individual leaders may be). But we are getting ahead of ourselves and have simply presumed that war making, like punishment, has a double brake. Let us scutinize that double brake in some detail.

We saw this double brake on war in the United States Constitution in the requirement for an assembly (Chapter 1) and in the distribution over the country's injurying resources in the Second Amendment (Chapter 2)—and we saw equivalents, or partial equivalents, in the constitutions of other states such as France, India, and Russia. We now need to reposition those two back in terms of social contract. It is Locke who emphasized the assembly provision: for him, the legislature was "the soul" of the state. And it is Hobbes who contributes to our understanding of the popular ratification—or refusal—when soldiers are asked to carry out the war. Each of these—the assembly and the soldier's power of affirmation or dissent—will be looked at below. We will focus on Hobbes because it is his work which ought to have been of greatest help to us at the dawn of the nuclear age and it was instead his work which suffered the greatest distortion during that era, temporarily short circuiting his brilliant designs for diminishing injury.

THE FIRST BRAKE ON WAR: THE ASSEMBLY

By sovereign, as we have seen, Hobbes repeatedly insists that he means either an assembly or a person, whichever the population has chosen. Even in a state that has chosen to become a monarchy, that monarchy has legitimacy only because it has been constituted by an actually assembled people, a people residing in a physically coherent location and actively consenting. This is why Richard Tuck identifies Hobbes as a "radical democrat" who originated a "new constitutional theory of monarchy" and "an equally plausible new theory of democracy."[24] Far from being "a theorist of despotism," Hobbes took the notion of "extreme democracy" that Aristotle had attacked in Book IV of the *Politics* and shows "it was in fact the only legitimate form of political association."[25] In *De Cive*, the work of Hobbes that had by far the greatest influence on the next two centuries, Hobbes shows that democracy is "the paradigm" from which all specific forms of government derive.[26]

His other writings restate this central argument. So in *De Corpore Politico, or The Elements of the Law*, Hobbes writes that while a government may take the form of democracy, aristocracy, or monarchy, each of them is premised on and is derived from an antecedent democracy:

> [A]nd it must be so of necessity, because an aristocracy and a monarchy, require nomination of persons agreed upon, which agreement in a great multitude of men, must consist in the consent of the major part; and where the votes of the major part involves the votes of the rest, there is actually a democracy.[27]

This insistence on the population as the source of all governing authority led some of Hobbes's contemporaries to identify him as a radical threat to existing hierarchies of power. Robert Filmer opens his treatise against Hobbes with precisely this point: Hobbes erects "a building" around the rights of sovereignty, says Filmer, and that is fine; but then Hobbes makes the imperiling error of erecting this "building" on "the foundation" of the people's consent (rather than on inherited royal right): "In his pleading the cause of the people he arms them with . . . a right for all the people to govern."[28] Filmer also identifies the principle of equality—a principle on which Hobbes insists—as the key element in "the whole fabric of this vast engine of popular sedition."[29]

Hobbes did not invent monarchy, that was long in existence. What he invented was the stipulation that a monarch's legitimacy (like the legitimacy of any other form of state) depended on the authorization of the people. So essential is a unified and assembled population to Hobbes that when in *De Cive* he wants to explain why an international religious leader can never be a transnational sovereign, the impossibility is assigned to the absence of an actually assembled transnational population.[30]

Assemblies and meetings were, then, crucial to Hobbes. For example, he argued that a democracy exists only while it is meeting or when it has an upcoming meeting scheduled; so, too, an aristocracy's existence depends on its schedule of meetings; since a monarch is always with himself (except while sleeping) this form of government has the advantage that it is always in existence.[31] But Hobbes's view of parliaments or legislatures in particular was very rocky, damning in those books written during the civil war, much more positive and balanced in his later writings.

Hobbes thought Parliament was largely to blame for the English Civil War and (as his major books are written during this period) he generalized this culpability in his writings so that in *De Cive*, for example, he talks about the way discussions in Parliament lead to disagreements, disagreements to factions, and factions to civil strife. Even in this period, however, he never assumes the dissolution of Parliament. He is in the position of people in the United States today who rail against the incoherence and incompetence of Congress, and yet are far from advocating the dissolution of the legislative branch.

Parliament takes center stage in Hobbes's final book, *Dialogue between a Philosopher and a Student of the Laws of England*. In fact, he begins and ends the work with it. Here Hobbes dramatically reverses what had often in the past been a negative and complaint-filled view of Parliament. More striking, he treats this positive view as self-evident: the philosopher and lawyer agree that any valid state action must have Parliament's approval: when the lawyer later restates this requirement for validity, the philosopher reminds him that they are already in agreement on this matter. Finally, and most important for the problems we are addressing here, the key question about parliamentary validation is whether it is needed when the country goes to war. It is here that the discussion of Parliament—and the book as a whole—opens.

Not only will the Philosopher agree with the Law Student that Parliament is necessary; he will assure us that "of course" Parliament is necessary; and further, that there never has been or could be a king who could think that it was possible to act without the authorization of Parliament. In distinguishing between the king's private or natural person and the king's political being, he says any act that has not yet been validated by Parliament is only a personal act; once it has been acted on by Parliament, it is now the king as a political being that is present:

> But as to the Acts and Commands, they may be well distinguished in this manner. Whatsoever a Monarch does Command, or do by consent of the People of his Kingdom, may properly be said to be done in his politick Capacity; and whatsoever he Commands by word of Mouth only, or by Letters Signed with his hand, or Sealed with any of his private Seals is done in his natural Capacity: Nevertheless, his publick Commands, though they be made in his politick Capacity, have their original from his natural Capacity. For in the making of Laws (which necessarily requires his assent) his assent is natural: Also those Acts which are done by the King previously to the passing of them under the Great Seal of *England*, either by word of Mouth, or warrant under his Signet, or privy Seal, are done in his natural Capacity; but when they have past the Seal of *England*, they are to be taken as done in his politick Capacity.[32]

Even a king's act that sets in motion a parliamentary act is, until that parliamentary act itself is completed, only a private or natural act of an individual man. Once the assembly has acted, the king's private act is itself transformed, alchemized, into a national act.

The profound reversal in Hobbes's attitude toward Parliament has been eloquently described by both Joseph Cropsey and Susan Okin. But perhaps left out of their accounts, or understated, is the fact that what is centrally at issue during the discussion is the country's procedure for going to war. This military focus does not mean that parliamentary assent is needed *only* in the case of war; we are certainly meant to understand that a general principle of governance (applicable to many different national acts) is being set forth; but the question of parliamentary authorization of war must be understood as at the very heart of the general principle. Just as juries are an impediment to government infliction of injury, so Hobbes explicitly frames the requirement for parliamentary assent to war as an impediment. The Philosopher says, "Those Statutes [requiring parliamentary assent] are in themselves very good for the King and People, as creating some kind of Difficulty, [f]or such Kings as for the Glory of Conquest might spend one part of their Subjects Lives and Estates, in Molesting other Nations, and leave the rest to Destroy themselves at Home by Factions."[33] The impediment is not, then, an accidental entailment or a regrettable side feature. The brake on war remains fixed until the right of release is achieved. The release mechanism, by design, requires difficult labor to set it in motion.

The phenomenon of an assembly as a brake on war is one that Hobbes encountered in elaborate detail when he many years earlier translated Thucydides' *The Peloponnesian War*, the first of his many books. Thucydides' pages again and again record the speeches given in the Greek assemblies on the eve of war, speeches that—like the American congressional deliberations we saw in Chapter 1—stop to test the accuracy of the word *enemy*, even in one instance permitting representatives of the enemy city of Athens to address the Lacedaemon assembly explaining their position.[34] Tested in the Athenian assembly is the proposition that the entire male population of Mytilene should be executed for the city's betrayal of Athens. A political or military leader who has decided to carry out a massacre does not ordinarily return to the assembly and lay out the case; here, the assembly listens to arguments for and against; votes yes; then, with ships already sailing to carry out the execution, redebates the question and votes no. The massacre does not take place.[35] The assembly's key feature of slowing down the action of injuring is rigorously critiqued and just as rigorously championed.[36] Also prominent is its feature of a conspicuously staged vote, as when Sthenelaidas, unable to decipher the voice vote in the first Lacedaemon assembly, proposes that all who think Athens has violated the peace walk to one side of the room, all who do not, the other side.[37] Far from repudiating the assembly, Hobbes sees himself writing for an audience that—as a result of his translation—will read and think as though participating in an assembly; for in his opening address "To the Readers," Hobbes tells us that Thucydides "setteth his reader in the assemblies of the people and in the senate at their debating; in the streets, at their seditions; and in the field, at their battles."[38]

The philosopher and the lawyer in Hobbes's *A Dialogue* agree that without "force" there is no way for a sovereign to uphold laws or to protect the population from external threat, that he therefore has the right to raise an army: "the King cannot make his Laws effectual, nor defend his People against their Enemies, without a Power to Leavy Souldiers, and consequently, . . . he may Lawfully, as oft as he shall really think it necessary to raise an Army (which in some occasions may be very great)."[39] But this act must be done with Parliament: the Philosopher says, "therefore unless you say otherwise, I say, that the Kings Reason, when it is publickly upon Advice, and Deliberation declar'd, is that *Anima Legis*, and that *Summa Ratio*, and that Equity which all agree to be the Law of Reason, is all that is, or ever was Law in *England*, since it became Christian, besides the Bible."[40] The Lawyer then asks: "In the said Statutes that restrain the Levying of Money without consent of Parliament, Is there any thing you can take exception to?"[41] To which the Philosopher responds, "I am satisfied that the Kings that grant such Liberties are bound to make them good, so far as it may be done without sin." Then he and the lawyer agree that it is a sin to obstruct defense if needed as it is also a sin to go to war if unneeded. When the Lawyer later says the King sins against god "if he will not Consult with the Lords of Parliament and hear the Complaints, and Informations of the Commons, that are best acquainted with their own wants," the Philosopher says, "We are Agreed upon that already."[42]

The philosopher and the lawyer proceed through this matter as though one were the king and the other were Parliament. The Lawyer voices the laws and since the laws are the voice of the king, he ventriloquizes the king's position. Since the Philosopher is often called upon to assent to, or dissent from, the laws, his position is itself closer to that of Parliament, though he tells us at one point that he represents not

Parliament (the representatives of the population) but the population itself: "I am one of the Common People, and one of that almost infinite number of Men, for whose welfare Kings, and other Soveraigns were by God Ordain'd: For God made Kings for the People, and not People for Kings."[43] In the dialogue's constant pressure to reach agreement, the book essentially enacts the way individual citizens both study and, through their consent to the law, make the law.

Embedded in this discussion is a distinction between what the king may do on his own (as a "natural person" in Hobbes's terms)[44] and what requires the validation by Parliament. If the country is invaded he may begin at once to bring the army out to defend the population. If, in contrast, he wants to take soldiers outside the country's own borders, then an act of Parliament is required. We hear of a law (13 Car.2.c.6) that asserts "disposing of the Militia of England ... to be, and always to have been the Antient right of the Kings of *England*." The passage then stipulates: "But there is also in the same Act a Proviso, that this shall not be Construed for a Declaration, that the King may Transport his Subjects, or compel them to march out of the Kingdom, nor is it, on the contrary declared to be unlawful."[45] The philosopher worries about how the money can be raised in an emergency; perhaps there should be money or arms in reserve, prior to the emergency. But we then learn of two separate laws—both from the reign of King Edward I and "Confirmed by divers other Kings, and lastly by the King that now Reigneth"[46]—stipulating that such money cannot be raised without the assembly's consent: "*We have granted ... that for no Business from henceforth, we shall take such Aids, Taxes, or Prizes, but by the common Consent of the Realm*"; and again, "*No Taxes, or Aid shall be taken or Levyed by us, or our Heirs in our Realm, without the good will, and assent of the Arch-Bishops, Bishops, Earls, Barons, Knights, Burgesses, and other Freemen of the Land.*"[47]

Hobbes here makes—or comes close to making—the distinction that, as observed in the Introduction, is crucial in twenty-first-century Scandinavian countries, where a king may act up to but not over the border; one step beyond the border requires parliament's authorization.

So, too, the president in the United States becomes commander-in-chief under two circumstances: either the country is invaded and he (as well as the population) may therefore begin at once to act within the borders; or he has a congressional declaration of war and can therefore carry military force outside the borders. On December 7, 1941, an enemy trespassed onto the home ground of the United States, thereby licensing President Roosevelt, even as he called Congress into joint session, to authorize defensive actions; what he was not yet licensed to do was attack Japan.[48] On September 11, 2001, the people on the hijacked Pennsylvania plane were legally right to begin at once their act of defending the country; what was not permissible on that day or the days following was the president's or the population's invading Iraq or Afghanistan without a formal congressional declaration of war.

Hobbes's philosopher and lawyer agree that an invasion licenses the calling forth of the militia within the country's borders, and agree, as well, that Parliament is needed to go outside. But now the philosopher introduces what he thinks of as a hybrid example. What if it is not one's own country but an immediately adjacent country that is invaded. Can one not begin to act immediately, since the enemy may, after conquering that adjacent country, then invade you? The lawyer holds to the parliamentary requirement, arguing that if that is so, Parliament will see the wisdom of it and make a declaration.[49] The philosopher then protests that there may not be time: the assembly may not be in session and it might require six weeks to gather them. The problem raised— whether an adjacent country's border should be treated as one's own or as foreign—is not decisively answered.

Hobbes's whole treatment of law in this book, then, begins and ends with Parliament; furthermore, at issue is not Parliament decontextualized from any specific circumstance but Parliament in the case of war. This yoking of Parliament and war suggests that Parliament primarily exists to address questions of war. Historians who study Parliament have shown decisively that the English and European assemblies come into being for no other purpose than precisely to get the people's consent for going to war. Whereas today we treat war as a crisis in which Congress should be shoved to the side and ignored, historically the first and fundamental reason assemblies were invented was to act as a braking power on the executive desire to go to war or, where the assemblies endorsed the proposal, as an enabling power.

In the tenth century, the association between war and the origins of the assembly can only be inferred from circumstantial evidence. Huge springtime assemblies—called Easter assemblies—met during years when military events soon followed: so, for example, Æthelstan's 928 Easter Assembly at Exeter precedes his campaign into west-country Britain, just as Edgar's 959 Easter Assembly precedes his huge "naval expeditions around the coasts of Britain."[50] J. R. Maddicott stresses that the assemblies and the armies blend into one another, as the space of the open-air forum blends into the space of the army camp ground. Later in the tenth and early eleventh centuries, the association between parliamentary authorization and the military becomes explicit in laws and codes, as in Æthelred's law of 1008 stipulating that as a defense against possible Viking attack, Navy ships be made ready shortly after Easter, providing that the Easter Assembly so decrees.[51]

This yoking of military authorization and Parliament continues throughout the eleventh and twelfth centuries. The distinction visible in Hobbes between the level of consent needed to act inside the country's borders and the higher standard of consent needed if the king aspires to act outside the borders is one that the research of Thomas N. Bisson confirms. Drawing on events such as the 1089 Winchester assembly, he describes the principle according to which "defensive wars and field strategy required no more than a prudent consultation or notification of the vassal-warriors, [whereas] the undertaking of foreign expeditions and offensive wars necessitated obtaining their consent."[52] Maddicott also observes the centrality of "foreign affairs" in parliamentary business.[53] While parliaments deliberated about many nonmilitary matters, Bisson stresses how indebted even the seemingly nonmilitary dimensions of the assemblies were to a military template: the form of the parliamentary summons, for example, is modeled on its precursor, the military summons.[54]

In the thirteenth century, the link between war making and the growth of representative assemblies in England and Europe becomes increasingly visible. Historian Gaines Post shows that it was precisely occasions of military "emergency" or "necessity" that required the king, in the midst of raising taxes and armies, to get the consent not just of the landed barons but of the "lesser freemen in the communities of shires and towns." Although the lesser freemen were not strictly part of the feudal system, they "were now directly touched by the national emergency."[55] Of major influence was the legal and ethical principle: "that which touches all must be approved by all," *Quod omnes tangit ab omnibus approbetur.*[56] This principle—so crucial to the next six centuries—has been wholly erased in the nuclear age, now dominated by the idea that that which touches all requires the approval of only one or two powerful men.

Gaines Post shows the way feudal law and Roman law converged in the attempt to guarantee the inclusion of all who were touched by the threat of war. Articles XII and XIV of the 1215 Magna Carta stipulated that the levying of military taxes ("scutage or aid") required—in the document's own language—the "general counsel of the realm." Feudal law thus required the king to "obtain the consent of all whose rights and liberties were affected."[57] While the Magna Carta and the accompanying Charter of the Forest were at first intended to secure the rights of wealthy earls and barons, the liberties and privileges enumerated in these documents were by the mid-thirteenth century extended to those with much less economic power, such as knights, precisely because the king required the assistance of those knights in the crusades.[58] Later in the same century under the influence of Roman law, both secular and religious authorities began to stress that any emergency touching the rights and well-being of the population required the consent of that same population.[59]

Whereas in the twentieth and twenty-first century, the claim of "emergency" has been repeatedly invoked by state leaders to silence their populations and explain why all consent procedures must be abridged, in the thirteenth century it was precisely such an emergency, by virtue of its potentially touching all, that required everyone's consent and led to the ever-more inclusive reach of Parliament. The king or his delegate had to come before the assembly and give a persuasive speech justifying the new subsidy, new law, or the raising of an army:[60] "[t]he case of necessity was, as it were, tried in the assembly, and the representatives were, in a sense, attorneys protecting the rights and interests of the communities against the royal claim of public utility and binding the communities by their consent to the decision."[61] Like the aristocrats, the delegates from the boroughs and shires had the right to hear the case and even to negotiate the sum.[62]

While freemen and townsmen came to be included in the assemblies, it is of course the case that only a fraction of the full numerical population was present. Kings had a great stake in finding a way to secure the consent of that missing population, in making sure that whatever actions the parliamentary delegates took would be binding on the population they represented. Thus the doctrine of *plena potestas* (full power of representation) developed, with representatives often having to show through signed petitions that they were authorized by their population to act for them. J. G. Edwards writes that "[f]or a considerable time after 1294 the borough representatives commonly appeared in Parliament bringing with them a formal document, sealed with the borough seal, stating that the mayor and the whole community of the borough concerned had given them full power to act."[63] What the borough citizens agreed to bind themselves to was not the action of the king or the decision of the barons but the deliberations of the general assembly—"to do what shall be ordained by common counsel."[64] The principle of "Quod omnes tangit" lasted for six centuries and provided the foundation for parliamentary sovereignty.[65]

While securing the consent of the wider population had large benefits for that population, so too it had a large benefit for the king who might otherwise be stopped or hindered in many ways. A community could delay parliamentary proceedings by delaying the arrival of their representatives; or following the meeting, it could demand a referendum on a line of action Parliament had endorsed.[66] Developing the notion of fully empowered representatives was intended to cut down on the number of such referenda, occasions when the issue went directly back to the boroughs. So in France in 1302, King Philip IV demanded "delegates with full powers of 'consenting... without excuse of making reference back."[67]

But however successful such efforts were to diminish the number of referenda, the moment when soldiers were called forth to participate in a war was always, in effect, a referendum. This is, as we will see, the second major brake on war, the individual soldier's consent or dissent—and like the first, it is one about whose existence Hobbes was acutely aware. Every parliamentary act licensing war had a referendum if the population was called upon to serve in the defense or the expedition.

We will turn to this second brake in a moment. But we can already appreciate that like the grand and petit juries that act as a filter on the government's ability to punish, so the assembly acts as a brake on the government's arguments for going to war. When a king proposed war and the assembly agreed, war followed and history records the battles. When, in contrast, a king proposed war and the assembly dissented, no martial events followed and the royal attempt was likely to remain unelaborated in the historical record. Hence we are much less likely to know about Parliament's braking action than its enabling action.[68]

But some instances are known in England, Spain, and France. In England in the middle of the thirteenth century, Henry III attempted to raise men and money to defend his duchy of Gascony against an imminent invasion from Castile. Parliament on January 27, 1253, rapidly responded to the king's request and, by February, already had arrangements in place both for troops and money; in March the king sent still more urgent messages home from the Continent, even writing a letter to the whole political community and promising to ensure that rights granted in Magna Carta would be enforced in the local counties. But the momentum toward war was suddenly halted when in the April 1253 Parliament, as Madicott describes it, "Simon de Montfort ... appeared, hotfoot from Gascony, and 'announced the truth', meaning presumably the absence of any danger from Castile and the falsity of the king's assertions. The assembly then broke up in indignation."[69] Similar resistance is documented in Spain of the thirteenth and fourteenth centuries, where the king faced powerful town representatives and nobles in the assembly and sometimes had to withdraw his demand for money and troops. Gaines Post writes of the assembly: "the Cortes ... through its *Disputacion* 'watched over the observance of the laws,' limited the king's right to interpret necessity and public utility, and audited the royal accounts in order to be sure that a subsidy granted was actually spent for the public good."[70] Even when successful, a king's proposal to prepare for war could be an elaborate, many-stage process: in the fourteenth century, Philip V of France, fearing a war with Flanders, held a sequence of assemblies beginning in April 1318 and continuing until the winter of 1319. The assemblies were both central and regional, one in July consisting of representatives from forty-six towns in northern France. The king would use one assembly to urge delegates to return to the towns and help to shape public opinion for the next assembly. Some of the assemblies were held to elicit consent to the general principle of a subsidy; other meetings then followed to adjudicate the specific amount and to smooth out local pockets of resistance.[71] The very elaborateness of the consultation process ordinarily worked to discourage kings from even contemplating frivolous campaigns.

THE SECOND BRAKE ON WAR: THE SOLDIERS' REFERENDUM

Even more resistant than this parliamentary brake on war is the second brake, the population. If the first brake is a trial by discussion,[72] the second is a trial by participation. It acts as a referendum on any decision made by king and council. Hobbes in all his writing acknowledges the key part played by the soldier's consent. In *Behemoth*, he writes, "[I]f men know not their duty, what is there that can force them to obey the laws? An army, you will say. But what shall force the army?"[73]—a set of three sentences I had occasion to quote at the opening of Chapter 2. It might be imagined that this is a free-floating triad that surfaces in some odd corner of the work. Nothing could be further from the truth, for so much does every page illustrate the principle announced there that it would be fair to identify the sentence as the key sentence in the book. Throughout *Behemoth, The History of the Causes of the Civil Wars of England*, we see whoever controls the militia has sovereign power;[74] we see each side courting the army's support but unable to ensure that outcome; we see the army electing its own leaders or adjutators and forming its own parliament;[75] we see the army levying taxes for its own support; we see it voting on whether to carry out a requested massacre; we see it directly defy orders and refuse to go to Ireland; we see it issuing proclamations and petitions.[76] "What made [Cromwell] refuse the title of King?" asks Speaker B in the dialogue. Speaker A answers, "Because he durst not take it at that time; the army ... would have mutinied against him."[77]

Political philosopher Stephen Holmes, who provides an introduction to the Chicago University edition of *Behemoth*, identifies a different sentence as the most electric and edifying: "the power of the mighty hath no foundation but in the opinion and belief of the people."[78] Now it is my argument here that the two statements—"An army, you will say. But what shall force the army?" and "Power ... hath no foundation but in the opinion and belief of the people"—are, in important respects, identical sentences.

In recognizing the population's power to enable or disable war, Hobbes fulfills the description of him as (in Richard Tuck's language) "a radical democrat." Earlier we saw that Hobbes trusted jurors—trusted them not simply to answer questions of fact but to understand the law as well as a highly educated jurist like Edward Coke. The pool of jurors was relatively inclusive: it has been estimated that jurors were drawn from 25 percent of the population (the ineligibility of women cut the number by 50 percent and it is thought that poverty and other factors probably eliminated another 25 percent).[79] But soldiers were drawn from a wider spectrum. Today we take it as self-evident that soldiers have a high status because they risk their lives and because they determine whether a given war is even fought. But was that high moral stature self-evident to anyone other than Hobbes at the moment he was articulating that view?

Historian Stephen Stearns describes the way soldiers were levied in the late sixteenth and seventeenth centuries, concentrating on the years 1624 to 1627 when 50,000 men or 1 percent of the population were indentured. (Hobbes at this time was in his midthirties.) While gentry and yeoman were trained to defend the country and would be called upon if the country were invaded, they were exempt from the levy, which instead fell heavily on the rural landless and small property holders. In the county of Wiltshire, for example, where Malmesbury resides, two-fifths were husbandmen.[80] The contempt in which the indentured were held, visible in the arbitrary process by which they were rounded up and the privative conditions in which they served, is also audible in many contemporary descriptions of them as "jail sweepings" and "drunkards."[81] Once a recruited band of men was delivered to an officer, he was allowed to "refuse substandard men": one officer returned "120 of 200 men sent to him from Hampshire because they were [in his words] 'such creatures he was ashamed to describe them.'" Another officer complained that his troops included "four 'purblind' men, a minister, a 'frantic,' a simpleton, a case of severe palsy, two men with lame or imperfect arms and four foreigners"—in short, "the pitiable wreckage of humanity."[82] (Of those who did serve—neither rejected by their officers nor deserted—the description given remains constant: vagabonds, etc.)

Enter Thomas Hobbes: "[I]f men know not their duty, what is there that can force them to obey the laws? An army, you will say. But what shall force the army?" The vision of soldiers as "the pitiable wreckage of humanity" has here evaporated and in its place is a vision of men voting, raising taxes, forming a parliament, determining not just whether a battle will be won but whether it will even be initiated, and determining whether a country's leader will take a title (just as in the American Civil War, as we saw in Chapter 2, soldiers, using a boot as a ballot box, not only voted in the field, but took and publicized a preelection straw vote to educate the civilian public about their support for the re-election of Lincoln). Throughout *Behemoth*, Hobbes's esteem for the soldier is as high as his regard for the civil war is low. In his other writings, he makes little distinction between the population as a whole—the very population who authorize the form of government that has sovereignty—and the army; for it is, quite simply, the population who must collectively secure the safety of the country from any foreign enemy or assailant originating from within.

Modern legal historians observe that in tenth-century England a "tithing"—composed of ten households—was the same civic unit as the "town" and was invented as a way of securing the peace.[83] Ten tithings, in turn, were grouped into a unit of 100 households to act as a peace guild. In *A Dialogue between a Philosopher and a Student of the Common Laws of England*, Hobbes gives precisely this historical account, though he refers to the "tithings" or "towns" as "decennaries." Almost no one, man or woman, adult or child, is ineligible for the work of defense: close to 100 percent of the population must stand "ready to resist an invading army":

> You know also, that the whole Land was divided into Hundreds, and those again into Decennaries; in which Decennaries all Men even to Children of 12 years of age, were bound to take the Oath of Allegiance: And you are to believe, that those Men that hold their Land by the service of Husbandry, were all bound with their Bodies, and Fortunes to defend the Kingdom against invaders by the Law of nature: And so also such as they called Villains [peasants or serfs], and held their Land by baser drudgery, were obliged to

defend the Kingdom to the utmost of their power. Nay, Women, and Children in such a necessity are bound to do such service as they can, that is to say, to bring Weapons and Victuals to them that fight, and to Dig.[84]

When defense is needed, it is quite literally the population—"bound with their Bodies" and having promised to "perform with the hazard of my Life, Limbs and all my Fortune"[85]—who act as a material impediment to the aggressor.

The strength of a defended town against a foreign aggressor can be inferred from what was required to take the town, as battles were gradually replaced by siege warfare. According to strategists of the 1690s, a siege of a fortified town required a force ten times the size of the garrison defending it and took between twenty-six and sixty days depending on the town's size and morale. A forty-day siege, according to Surirey de St. Rémy's *Mémoires d'artillerie*, required 60,000 men, 18,000 horses, "3,300,000 food rations and 730,000 issues of forage . . . 40,000 rounds of 24-pounder shot . . . 30,000 rounds of musket ammunition . . . 550,000 cubic feet of timber for gun platforms and trench-shoring . . . 18,000 picks and mattocks, 4,000 baskets" and more.[86]

Hobbes's identification of the whole citizenry with the capacity for collective self-defense was perceived by his great opponent, Robert Filmer. Filmer's complaint that Hobbes had erected the "building" of sovereignty on the seditious "foundation" of the population straightforwardly recognizes this identification. Earlier his complaint against Hobbes was given in elliptical form, but here is what his full statement says. "In [Hobbes's] pleading the cause of the people he arms them with a very large commission of array, which is a right in nature for every man to war against every man when he please, and also a right for all the people to govern."[87] As the editor of Filmer's tract explains, a commission of array was "a commission issued by the king to mobilize the militia."[88] But now, according to Filmer's rendering of Hobbes, it is the population that issues its own commission of array; it has become self-mobilizing, and it is this power that confers "a right for all the people to govern."

We have seen that the population—in their own embodied persons—act as a bulwark, a profound material impediment, against invasion. But this same capacity to act as a material impediment can forestall the actions of a sovereign or a commander as well, as Hobbes's many empirical observations about soldiers in *Behemoth* attest. This is why readers of Hobbes—whether in the seventeenth century or the twentieth and twenty-first—have repeatedly noted the way the Hobbesian right of self-preservation or right of self-defense directly contradicts what otherwise seems the unqualified authority of the Hobbesian sovereign.

In his own time, the license to disobedience or noncompliance conferred by the right of self-preservation was observed by friend and foe alike. Thus Leibniz writes to Hobbes:

> [E]ven though you seemed to assert that every right was transferred from the subjects to the state, you correctly observe elsewhere that even in the state one retains the right to look after one's own interests, when one is threatened by the fear of destruction, either in the state, or by the state itself.[89]

In elaborating this right, Leibniz begins with what is explicitly stated in Hobbes—the right of a person being led to death to rebel—and goes on to what he believes must follow:

> So that if someone's execution is ordered by those who exercise sovereign power, he still has the right to turn the world upside-down for the sake of his preservation; whereas the other subjects owe their rulers obedience by the force of their original agreement. But will you not agree, most distinguished Sir, that a strong suspicion of great danger will justify taking preventative action against harm.... I think you will not deny that even on your philosophical principles, people who see danger approaching will have the right

to join together in alliances. . . . For I think that all the conclusions which you correctly draw about sovereignty can be summed up as follows: in the state, the covenant between the people must not be broken lightly or on any slight suspicions, since a great degree of safety is guaranteed by it.[90]

What the admiring Leibniz had inferred was inferred as well by Hobbes's most passionate opponents.

It was precisely Hobbes's stress on the right of self-preservation (which included not only the defense of one's body but one's reputation) that, as Jean Hampton has persuasively shown, led Bishop John Bramhall to confer on *Leviathan* a new title, *A Rebel's Catechism*, and incited equal alarm in Robert Filmer and in Edward Hyde Clarendon.[91]

Filmer was especially troubled by the seditious license embedded in Hobbes's assertion that "'No man is bound by the words' of his submission 'to kill himself or any other man.'" The only time we have no freedom to disobey, according to Hobbes, is when doing so would frustrate the end for which sovereignty was invented, *salus populi*. But that— Filmer argues with complete accuracy—has two outcomes. First, "[i]f no man be bound by the words of his subjection to kill any other man, then a sovereign may be denied the benefit of war." Second and just as appalling, if "refusal to obey" now "depend[s] upon the judging of what frustrates the end of sovereignty, and what not" we are faced with the conclusion that the authority to judge resides with the population—"of which [Hobbes] cannot mean any other judge but the people."[92]

We find in the writings of Hobbes, then, a powerful validation of the double braking system in war: the trial by discussion and the trial by participation, the test points of the assembly and the population. Just as in the jury system that monitors the sovereign's license to punish, the actual petit jury is an even more rigorous and publicly scrutinized process than the grand jury, so in wartime the population's braking action is more elaborate and prolonged, even, than the assembly, though the assembly is the all-important first line of defense against a potentially lethal inundation. This second brake, as we have seen, is vividly present both in Hobbes's empirical writing (his recitation of the actions of soldiers throughout *Behemoth*) and in his theoretical writings (his account of the right of self-preservation in *Leviathan*, which undercuts the duty to obey the sovereign).

This second brake on war, the potential disobedience of the individual soldier—and once this individual dissent is multiplied, the capacity of the population to enable or disable the war plans of the country's leader (a brake completely absent in weapons of mass destruction)—has one additional manifestation in Hobbes's writings, his translation of the *Iliad*. Every concrete situation of consent (as we will see in Chapter 5) has some theorists who say we exercise consent only at the threshold (once we say yes we relinquish our ability later to say no) and other theorists who say we have both threshold and ongoing consent (we say yes or no at the start of something; but even after we say yes, we retain the power to say no at later stages). Hobbes has often been seen as a threshold-only theorist: we consent to the social contract at the front gate, after which we no longer retain the power to consent or dissent since our only option is to obey. But as we have seen, his writings about defense—both defense of the country and of one's own individual person—show a different picture. Without ongoing consent, the soldier would simply be an empty vessel enacting and transmitting the commander's or sovereign's orders. We have seen how implausible the empty vessel account is, and we will see so once more in the *Iliad*.

Not every reader of this chapter may wish to read the following account of the decisions Hobbes made about word choice in translating the *Iliad* and may prefer instead to move forward to the chapter's conclusion. But the choices visible there are fascinating in and of themselves and essentially reinforce and clarify what appears in *Behemoth* and *A Dialogue*, as they also reinforce the set of essays Hobbes wrote late in life on heresy, the right to express views that depart from what authorities promulgate as the correct view.[93] Just as we, living in the fourth century after Hobbes, are the beneficiaries of his legacies, so he recognized his own world as inheriting legacies from the medieval English and European past out of which so much thinking about towns and nations emerged, as well as from the yet more distant Greek and Roman past. His social contract writings carry us back not just across seven centuries but across twenty-five centuries; just as it is to be hoped that his own writings carry us forward not only into our own constitutional history, but, if we survive our present misdeeds, forward by twenty-five centuries more.

Three key points about Hobbes's *Iliad* may help to keep the larger portrait of social contract in view. First, the *Iliad* is centrally about the soldier's capacity for dissent. Because disobedience, then as now, has a very high cost, it is ordinarily far easier to obey than to disobey. Nonetheless, when soldiers obey they have chosen to do so; when they disobey, they have chosen to do so. One might object—as one watches these conclusions unfold—that such a vision, while surely Homer's, is not necessarily Hobbes's; for it is not Hobbes who first sang the story we are hearing. Yet Hobbes chose to translate this work—chose to translate all 16,000 lines of ancient Greek. He had many fields other than translation that interested him (math, physics, optics, legal theory, history, political philosophy) and even within the single choice of translation, he had scores of other poems, plays, histories, and political treatises from which to choose.

Second and of greatest concern in what follows, Hobbes's word choices in translation make emphatic the dissent of Achilles and the failure of the sovereign, Agamemnon, to dedicate himself to the common good. Hobbes's translation also foregrounds the social contract frame that is embedded in the poem.

Third, Hobbes recognized how portentous were the potential effects of such a poem. In *Leviathan* and *Behemoth* Hobbes states that "one of the most frequent causes" of "Rebellion . . . against Monarchy . . . is the Reading of the books of Policy, and Histories of the Antient Greeks, and Romans. . . . From the reading . . . of such books, men have undertaken to kill their Kings, because the Greek and Latine writers . . . make it lawfull, and laudable, for any man so to do; provided before he do it, he call him Tyrant."[94] In summary, he continues, the classics teach us "*Tyrannophobia*."[95]

What are we to make of a political philosopher who repeatedly observes that the ancients teach tyrannophobia, and even tyrannicide, but who *starts* his career by translating Thucydides' *History of the Peloponnesian War*, and *ends* it by translating Homer's *Iliad*? According to Hobbes's first biographer and constant associate, by the age of fourteen he had already translated Euripides' *Medea* (the work he will later cite in the climactic sentences of his chapter about insurrection in *On the Citizen*),[96] and throughout his life, he kept the ancient texts constantly by his side. Aubrey writes, "He had very few Bookes. I never sawe . . . above halfe a dozen about him in his chamber. Homer and Virgil were commonly on his Table; sometimes Xenophon, or some probable historie, and Greek Testament, or so."[97]

That these sourcebooks on tyrannophobia and tyrannicide were his constant reading is crucial, but even more crucial is the fact that he carried out the gigantic labor of translation, thereby making the writings available to many other people. Far from cautioning his reader to be wary in the presence of such works, he states in his introduction to Thucydides that "Homer in poesy, Aristotle in philosophy, Demosthenes in eloquence," and Thucydides in history are among the Greek writers who have never been "exceeded, some not approached, by any in these later ages."[98]

Disobediance, dissent, rebellion, and tyrannicide (or, as Hobbes would correct us, hosticide) are not, as Leibniz saw, acts to be carried out lightly or, in all likelihood, ever; they are emphatically and repeatedly discouraged in Hobbes's writings; but they are not prohibited. Our always insightful Filmer saw that the right of self-preservation in *Leviathan* already contained regicide as a corollary: "Hereby any rogue or villain may murder his sovereign."[99] In *On the Citizen*, Hobbes was explicit. He several times complains that people too often use the word "Tyrant" simply to mean "I do not like the king," rather than reserving it for one who has betrayed the obligations to secure the population's safety, where "hosticide" may become legitimate. "If [a leader] rules without right, he is a public enemy [*hostis*] and is rightly killed, though this should not be called *Tyrannicide* but *hosticide.*"[100] This does not mean that thirty decades of commentaries saying Hobbes encourages obedience are wrong: his writings urge obedience as the default state.

As in his other writings, what we see in the *Iliad* is a preoccupation not with rebellion but with the overarching architecture of the social contract. The first brake on war, the assembly, had been the central subject matter of the very first work Hobbes ever wrote, his translation of Thucydides. The second brake on war, the soldier, is the central subject of almost the last work Hobbes wrote, his translation of the *Iliad*.

THE SOLDIER'S DISSENT IN THE HOMER OF HOBBES

On the threshold of entering war, soldiers exercise the power of consent to, or dissent from, the act of going to war. As we saw in Chapter 2, once soldiers have agreed to enter the war, their power of consent does not end: it continues far beyond this initial gateway into the third day, the 300th day, the 3000th day of the fighting. Here in the *Iliad*, the act of dissent occurs in the ninth year of war; the event the poem records is the dissent of Achilles and the vast consequences of that dissent. The wrath of Achilles is my theme, Sing Goddess, the rage of Achilles at King Agamemnon. That Achilles' act *is* an act of dissent, a solo rebellion against his king and field marshal, might get lost to view in the brilliant poetry and complex transactions of Book I. But it cannot get lost in Hobbes's translation; for his margin gloss, printed on the top of every page of the opening book, reads, "The discontent and secession of Achilles... The discontent and secession of Achilles... This discontent and secession of Achilles."

Agamemnon (perhaps like many civilians today) thinks that the dissent of a solitary soldier does not matter: "*Desert*, by all means—if the spirit drives you home! / I will never beg you to stay, not on *my* account. / ... What if you are a great soldier? That's just a gift of god. /

Go home with your ships and comrades, lord it over your Myrmidons! / You *are* nothing to me—you and your overweening anger!"[101] The poem is about the vast consequences of the individual soldier's dissent.

The lines just invoked are from Robert Fagles's powerful translation, a translation usually cited here prior to giving Hobbes's translation of the same Greek passage for three reasons: first, Fagles's late twentieth-century diction is much closer to our own than Hobbes's seventeenth-century diction and hence makes the story more easily audible; second, the poetry of Fagles's English is magnificent and we should hear the poem in a magnificent version; third, a juxtaposition of what Fagles says and what Hobbes says—while showing the inferior poetic abilities of Hobbes—nevertheless makes dramatically visible Hobbes's refusal to minimize the hero's act of dissent.[102]

What are the grounds of Achilles' dispute with Agamemnon? Like the soldiers in the American Civil War who formulated high-minded debates in their tents along the Potomac, Achilles addresses from the outset questions of ethical symmetry and justice. The argument is about the problem of unequal distribution. The unequal distribution takes four forms. First, there is an unequal distribution of motive: the leaders have a motive for going to war; the soldiers have none. (I have no quarrel with Troy, says Achilles; it was not my wife that Paris abducted; nor did the Trojans raid any of his homeland's agrarian treasures.) Second, there is an unequal distribution of risk: the soldiers fight out in front; Agamemnon skulks behind the lines. Now these two problems were ones known to Achilles almost from the outset of the war (the first nine years that are antecedent to the poem and that we do not directly see).

The next two complaints are far more crucial to the emerging catastrophe of the *Iliad*; and they concern the just distribution of the spoils of war. Either the spoils of war should be uniformly distributed across all the soldiers, says Achilles, or if they are to be unevenly distributed, that unevenness should correspond to an unevenness in risk taking, unevenness in accomplishment during battle.[103] Neither of these distributional models is followed since King Agamemnon takes none of the risks and almost all the prizes of war; he has already offended the gods and caused his soldiers to die of plague because he repeatedly violated Chryseis, the daughter of the priest; and in the course of Book I, will soon deprive Achilles of his beloved Briseis, his captive, his prize, and the woman whom Achilles will describe in Book IX as "the wife I love."[104] Crucially, Achilles' parsing of the unjust forms of distribution begins *before* Agamemnon announces that he will take Briseis.[105] He protests unjust distribution on behalf of all the soldiers even before he is himself the specific victim of it. He sees from the grief of the priest and the soldiers dying of the plague that it has imperiled the very people the leader should be doing everything to safeguard.

Achilles' dissent is an act of astonishing verbal defiance. Here is a small piece in Robert Fagles's translation:

> "*Shameless—*
> *armoured in shamelessness—always shrewd with greed!*
> *How could any Argive soldier obey your orders,*
> *freely and gladly do your sailing for you*
> *or fight your enemies, full force? Not I, no.*"
>
> (Fagles, bk. I, ll. 174–78)

Hobbes is not as vivid a translator as is Fagles. But what is crucial to recognize is that Hobbes—the theorist who is described in countless books and articles as prohibiting *all acts of disobedience* and as recommending an unchallenged sovereign (thus making irrelevant the ongoing consent or dissent of the population)—does *nothing* to temper or modify the verbal transgression of Achilles. Here are the same lines:

> *O impudence! Achilles then replied,*
> *What other of th' Achaeans willingly,*
> *Will, when you only for yourself provide,*
> *Go where you bid, or fight with th' enemy?*
>
> (Hobbes, bk. I, ll. 145–48)[106]

Achilles' cry, "O impudence!" is a close synonym for "shamelessness": it is from the root *in* meaning "not" and *pudere* meaning "to cause shame." But Fagles's word "shamelessness" designates a state of moral deficit that could occur at any level of the political hierarchy, from its lowest rung to, as here, its highest. "Impudence," in contrast is an allegation that is normally reserved for a subordinate, for one with less majesty and status than the person making the accusation. But that is exactly the allegation that Achilles makes to the monarch in Hobbes's translation.

Hobbes uses the word *impudence* only once in *Leviathan*. In Chapter 6 on the passions, he provides a crisp single-sentence definition: "The *Contempt* of good Reputation is called IMPUDENCE."[107] "CONTEMPT," in turn, is "nothing else but an immobility, or contumacy of the Heart."[108] Immobility of the heart is an accurate description of Agamemnon, but the other word Hobbes adds is important as well. The entailment of "contumacy"—usually defined as "resistance to authority"—reinforces our sense that Hobbes, in choosing to use the word *impudence* to describe King Agamemnon, has conspired with Achilles to reverse the normal understanding of power lines. The sovereign is not (as the Hobbesian sovereign is always said to be) unchallengeable. The king in Hobbes's translation is addressed by Achilles as someone below the authority of others and ignorant of their claim on his respect. Hobbes's use of the word *impudence* in *The Whole Art of Rhetoric* and again in *Behemoth* bears out these devastating connotations.[109]

After the charge of impudence comes the next wave of Achilles' insults, first as it is phrased by Fagles:

No, you colossal, shameless—we all followed you,
to please you, to fight for you, to win your honor
back from the Trojans—Menelaus and you, you dog-face!
What do you care? Nothing.

(Fagles I. 186–89)

Here now is Hobbies: his poetry does not have the adrenalized push of Fagles's; but the insult is keyed to a high, possibly higher, level:

Against the Trojans I no quarrel have. . . .
Only for yours and Menelaus' sake,
To honour gain for you we came to Troy,
Whereof no notice, dogs-head, now you take,
But threaten me my prize to take away.

(Hobbes I. 149, 153–56)

Robert Fagles's phrase "You—you dog-face!" is a powerful act of name calling, but at least it includes the vocative "you," a repeated "you," and the explosive "dog-face!" is a collapsed predicate nominative or predicate adjective. It does not completely totalize (and exhaust) Agamemnon's identity the way Hobbes's unadorned, undiluted vocative, "dog's head" does: "Whereof no notice, dog's head, now you take."

It is at this point that Agamemnon announces he will seize Briseis. Though Achilles, at Athena's insistence, stops short of killing Agamemnon, his verbal defiance mounts:

But Achilles rounded on Agamemnon once again,
lashing out at him, not relaxing his anger for a moment:
"Staggering drunk, with your dog's eyes, your fawn's heart!
Never once did you arm with the troops and go to battle. . .
Safer by far, you find, to foray all through the camp,
commandeering the prize of any man who speaks against you.
King who devours his people!"

(Fagles I. 262–65, 268–70)

It is here that Achilles swears his great oath of dissent, that he will not fight the Trojans, that without him the Greeks will lose, and that when Agamemnon comes to him begging for his return, he will *not* do so.

As it is relevant to take note of the way Hobbes translates Achilles' acts of dissent, so it is key to note that in describing the harm done to Achilles, Hobbes repeatedly uses the physically stark word *injury* that—as was visible in the previous chapter—is the fulcrum word in social contract writings: "Injury is to social contract as logical absurdity is to discourse." Injury is not an insult to or diminution of the social contract but a nullification of it (in the same way that logical absurdity is a nullification of discourse). The only two legal forms of injury are punishment and war,[110] and each of these two is permissible only after passing through the double brakes of the grand and petit juries in the case of punishment, and the assembly and the population in the case of war.

How Hobbes thought about the taking of Briseis can be gleaned from a passage in the *Leviathan* where he writes:

> Justice...consist[s] in taking from no man what is his...not to deprive their Neighbors, by violence, or fraud, of anything which ...is theirs. Of things held in propriety, those that are dearest to a man are his own life, & limbs; and in the next degree, (in most men,) those that concern conjugall affection; and after them riches and means of living."[111]

In the world we live in today, the act of interfering with other people's conjugal affections is sometimes depicted as an interesting or semi-harmless pastime. That is not Hobbes's view. Interfering with conjugal affection is only one degree less bad than taking a person's life or severing one of his limbs. The *Leviathan* passage stipulates that this definition of justice as prohibiting the violation of life, limb, or love *is to be taught to the population by the sovereign*. Far from teaching justice, Agamemnon by taking Briseis enacts its dismantling in front of the full assembly of soldiers.

Thus Hobbes repeatedly uses the word *injury* (where Fagles, for example, uses *outrage* or *grief*) as when Achilles says to Athena (who has come down to the shore to stop him from killing Agamemnon):

Come you, said he, to see the injuries
That are by Agamemnon done to me?

(Hobbes I. 195–96)

Or a short time later in praying to his mother as Briseis is led away, he says he could have endured the short life assigned to him if not "forced to bear such open injury."[112] Later books continue to refer to Agamemnon's act as an injury to Achilles. It is of course the case that Agamemnon's taking of Briseis from Achilles reenacts *inside* the Greek lines the very injury that when carried out by a foreign people is cause enough to go to war. That is, the taking of Briseis by Agamemnon reenacts the taking away of Helen from Menelaus by Paris. Does Achilles—whom both Fagles and Hobbes describe as heartbroken—*over*react by refusing to fight with the Greeks and thereby put them at tremendous risk? But he is no more overreacting than Agamemnon and Menelaus are in going to war over Helen. There is only an open question in the first case if there is an open question in the second case.

Herodatus in his *Histories* tells us the Greeks *were* overreacting. In his account of Helen he observes that the theft of a woman by a foreign people happened repeatedly in the ancient world; and he faults the Greeks for making such a fuss about it. But though we now rightly fault the epic for trafficking in women, at the same time the willingness of the Greeks to see the taking of a woman as a profound violation of the polis and the rule of law is something we must appreciate, especially when we hear the contrary view of Herodotus.

Herodotus gets to Paris by the second page of *The Histories*, after first giving a sequence of parallel acts in which one group of people carries off the king's wife or daughter. Then he writes:

> Thus far there had been nothing worse than woman-stealing on both sides; but for what happened next the Greeks, they say, were seriously to blame; for it was the Greeks who were, in a military sense, the aggressors. Abducting young women, in their opinion,

is not, indeed, a lawful act; but it is stupid after the event to make a fuss about avenging it. The only sensible thing is to take no notice; for it is obvious that no young woman allows herself to be abducted if she does not wish to be. The Asiatics, according to the Persians, took the seizure of the women lightly enough, but not so the Greeks: the Greeks, merely on account of a girl from Sparta, raised a big army, invaded Asia and destroyed the empire of Priam.[113]

Again, the Greeks in going to war over Helen are including in their self-definition the membership of women in their marriages and in their cities that other peoples—Herodotus assures us—regarded as too minor to make a fuss about.

Achilles makes the direct connection between the stealing of Helen and the stealing of Briseis. He reminds the ambassadors who try to assuage his grief that the Greeks only came to Troy because the wife of Menelaus was abducted, and continues in Hobbes's translation: "What then must no man love his wife but they? / Yes, all men of their own wives much should make, / If they have either wit or honesty. / And I love mine as well as he loves his, / Although she be my captive."[114]

We will come back to Book I after looking at two key scenes of dissent in Book II of the *Iliad*. It is precisely the fact that Homer gives us three major scenes of dissent in an unbroken series (one in the first book, two still to come in the second) that shows how unnegotiable this subject is. The relentless emphasis on dissent—which today often seems to be missing in everyday conversations about the poem—is clearly present in writings dedicated to twentieth- and twenty-first-century soldiers. Jonathon Shay in *Achilles in Vietnam* looks at the analogy between war trauma suffered by Achilles and by American soldiers in Vietnam; in both cases the trauma was deepened by the soldiers' sense of the unjust acts carried out by leaders.[115] Elizabeth Samet in *Soldier's Heart* describes how her students at West Point, when studying the *Iliad*, focus on the way Achilles contests what the leaders say.[116] Book II, like Book I, makes the subject of consent and dissent impossible to ignore, for anyone who believes in citizen-soldiers.

Homer opens Book II with two scenes—Agamemnon's test of his army and the dissent of Thersites. Here Homer makes even more emphatic than in Book I the soldier's freedom to disobey. Indeed, the poem makes it clear that under some circumstances it is the soldier's obligation to disobey. What soldiers do is *not* a matter of rote unreflecting obedience, but the result of deliberative decisions. As this second book opens, Zeus sends Agamemnon a dream (a false dream but one which Agamemnon believes is true) that they will today take the city of Troy, and that he should therefore assemble the troops (all the troops except Achilles) and command them into battle. Agamemnon is elated, thrilled by the anticipation of victory. But he decides that before entering battle, he will "test" the loyalty of his armies by coming before them, announcing his despair at ever defeating Troy, and urging them (in the language of Fagles) to "cut and run." Here are the last nine lines of Agamemnon's speech, from Fagles:

> *"And now nine years of almighty Zeus have marched by,*
> *our ship timbers rot and the cables snap and fray*
> *and across the sea our wives and helpless children*
> *wait in the halls, wait for our return... And we?*
> *Our work drags on, unfinished as always, hopeless—*
> *the labor of war that brought us here to Troy.*
> *So come, follow my orders. All obey me now.*
> *Cut and run! Sail home to the fatherland we love!*
> *We'll never take the broad streets of Troy."*
>
> (Fagles II. 157–165)

"So come, follow my orders. All obey me now. / Cut and run! Sail home to the fatherland we love!" This speech is an extraordinary structure for exposing the meaning of loyalty. The soldiers, commanded to flee, are expected to stay: they will show their obedience by refusing to carry out the command they have been given, by instead contradicting it, and Agamemnon has met with his "ranking chiefs in council" immediately before meeting with the full assembly of soldiers to instruct them (his closest councilors) to move among the armies persuading them *to disobey* their king and great field marshal, Agamemnon.

An easy understanding of obedience is one in which a subordinate, in this case a soldier, carries out a physical action to match the verbal instruction of a superior. Homer directly dismisses—just pushes off the table—this facile notion of obedience. In fact, this scene in Book II serves as a template for the opening in Book IX where Agamemnon will again order his troops to "cut and run": whereas in Book II, the monarch is not uttering a sincere speech act, is instead testing his men, in Book IX he *is* uttering a sincere speech act. Because Achilles is absent from the lines, the Achaeans are being relentlessly slaughtered and Agamemnon orders them back to the ships to "sail to the fatherland we love." Agamemnon's orders will again be disobeyed. Here are the lines in Fagles:

> *Finally Diomedes lord of the war cry broke forth:*
> *"Atrides—I will be first to oppose you in your folly,*
> *here in assembly, King, where it's the custom."*
> (Fagles IX. 35–37)

The assembly is the space where "it is the custom" to oppose the king. Diomedes continues:

> *Desperate man! . . .*
> *Desert—if your spirit drives you to sail home,*
> *then sail away, my King! The sea-lanes are clear,*
> *there are your ships of war, crowded down the surf, . . .*
> *But the rest of the long-haired Achaeans will hold out,*
> *right here, until we've plundered Troy. . . .*
> *And all the Achaeans shouted their assent.*
> (Fagles IX. 46, 48–50, 52–53, 58)

It would almost be impossible to locate ourselves ethically in this desperate moment in Book IX if we had not had a very explicit rehearsal for it at the opening of Book II in Agamemnon's test. Further, it is crucial to see that back here in Book II, the test of the soldiers that valorizes their disobedience is set within a wider framework of disobedience. Zeus has commanded Agamemnon to lead the Achaeans into battle. The dream figure says to the king, in Fagles's translation:

Zeus commands you to arm your long-haired Achaeans,
to attack at once, full force—

(Fagles II. 32–33)

an instruction that Agamemnon in turn recites to his council of ranking chiefs:

Zeus commands you to arm your long-haired Achaeans,
to attack at once, full force—

(Fagles II. 77–79)

a command which Agamemnon *disobeys* by then proceeding to issue the instruction to his men to disarm and cut and run. So, just as it is *not true* that a soldier will make his action conform to a commander's verbal instruction, so it is apparently *not the case* that a great field commander will make his actions conform to a sentence uttered by the gods.

Finally, of course, Zeus is lying. He expects the Greeks to be slaughtered by the Trojans this day; he has sent the king this false and "murderous dream"[117] precisely to bring about that result. Why? To accommodate the beloved Achilles—or more precisely, to accommodate the beloved mother of Achilles, Thetis, who has petitioned Zeus on her son's behalf.

The mental somersaults Homer expects of us in Book II are quite overwhelming. Through successive levels of dissent—Agamemnon disobeying the instruction of Zeus; the Achaeans disobeying the instruction of Agamemnon in order to bring about a catastrophe; the resumption of battle that will lead to the slaughter of the Greeks—we witness the validation of the dissent of Achilles in Book I, his oath that he will no longer fight on the behalf of the Greeks and that without him they will lose. Agamemnon, we remember, thinks the individual soldier is expendable. He says to Achilles in Book I, "What if you are a great soldier? That's just a gift of god. / Go home with your ships and comrades, lord it over your Myrmidons! / You *are* nothing to me—you and your overweening anger!"[118] Again, while Achilles fights in the lines, the Trojans will only fight defensively; but as soon as they recognize he is not there, they fight offensively.[119] Just as Sophocles' play, *Philoctetes*, interrupts the Trojan War in the tenth year of fighting in order to meditate on the nature of a soldier's physical injury, so Homer's *Iliad* interrupts the Trojan War at the end of its ninth year in order to stop and contemplate the nature of the soldier's consent. That is not just a feature of the epic. That *is* the epic.

How does Hobbes translate these amazing circumstances—these nested acts of disobedience that will serve to validate Achilles' act of dissent? Three acts of translation seem especially notable. First, whether it is a god or a human leader who is speaking, there is never the assumption that soldiers necessarily do what a leader wants them to do. Hobbes repeatedly underlines that uncertainty. When Agamemnon tells the council that after testing the assembly he will take the troops into battle, he uses the provisional language of trying:

> *This said, the dream went off again, and I*
> *How to th'assault the army may be brought*
> *As far as we can safely fain would try.*
>
> (Hobbes II. 62–64)

When Nestor hears Agamemnon's recitation of the dream, he suspects it must be a false dream and yet says that because it is the king's dream, they must follow through on it and get soldiers to battle. Here is Hobbes's phrasing of Nestor's speech:

> *But since the king is th'author (if we can)*
> *Let us persuade the people to take arms.*
>
> (Hobbes II. 72, 73, emphasis added)

Again, when the soldiers are in the midst of running to the ships in *nominal obedience* to Agamemnon's command to cut and run, Hera[120] tells Pallas Athena to go down to earth and dissuade them from fleeing:

> *Go quickly then, try if you can prevail,*
> *With hopeful words to stay them yet ashore,*
> *And take away their sudden list to sail,*
> *And let the ships lie as they did before.*
>
> (Hobbes II. 145–48, emphasis added)

Athena "leaps to the ground," stands "on the sand" of the shoreline and says to Odysseus almost these same words:

> *[Odysseus],[121] said she, do you mean to fly,*
> *And here leave Helen after so much cost*
> *Of time and blood, and show your vanity;*
> *And leave the Trojans of their rape to boast?*
> *Speak to each one, try if you can prevail*
> *With hopeful words to stay them on the shore,*
> *And take away this sudden list to sail,*
> *And let the ships lie where thy lay before.*
>
> (Hobbes II. 153–60, emphasis added)

These two speeches—by Hera speaking to Athena[122] and by Athena speaking to Odysseus—make more visible the uncertain outcome of the acts of persuasion than, for example, in Fagles whose Hera says to

Athena, and Athena in turn to Odysseus, "With your winning words hold back each man you find—/ don't let them haul their rolling ships to sea!"[123]

In Hobbes we hear: If we can...if we can...try if you can prevail...try if you can prevail. This is not to say that in other translations the uncertainty by any means disappears: in Fagles, for example, both Agamemnon and Nestor acknowledge the provisional nature of their commands: "Come—see if we can arm the Achaeans for assault."[124] But of the four descriptions, two of Hobbes's are as equivocal of outcome as Fagles's while two are more emphatic in their equivocation.[125] Here we should stop to stress again that there is nothing exceptional in the Greek acknowledgment of the leader's dependence on the agreement of his soldiers: there is no military general one can read or read about—whether Napoleon or Grant or Lee or Rommel or Montgomery—who does not similarly acknowledge that he can only *try* to get soldiers into battle, and that the decision is in the end the soldiers' own.

A second striking feature of Hobbes's translation is that moment where the voice of the poem—let us call it Homer's voice or the narrator's voice, the voice that describes events in the poem and stands outside any one of the combatants—describes King Agamemnon's foolishness in believing the dream. Here is Fagles right after the dream departs:

> *He thought he would take the city of Priam then,*
> *that very day, the fool. How could he know*
> *what work the Father had in mind? The Father,*
> *still bent on plaguing the Argives and Trojans both*
> *with wounds and groans in the bloody press of battle.*
>
> (Fagles II. 43–47)

Here is Hobbes's translation of those lines:

> *the Dream departed. And the king*
> *Believ'd it as an oracle, and thought*

To take Troy now as sure as anything;
Vain man, presuming from a dream [Zeus's] will,
Who meant to th'Greeks and Trojans yet much woe,
And with their carcasses the field to fill
Before the Greeks should back to Argos go.

(Hobbes II. 30–36)

Though Hobbes is a far less radiant writer than Fagles, his conception of a field filled with carcasses is arguably more devastating. Hobbes's vocative address, "Vain man," is less derisive than Fagles's description, "the fool," in part because the contemptuous word is in Hobbes only an adjective while in Fagles a noun, thereby exhausting the king's identity; and in part because vanity is, in the council of war, probably less damning than being a fool. But Hobbes's, by coming close to a direct address, places the narrative voice in insolent or defiant relation to the king, rather than standing outside the frame of events. A few lines later, Hobbes's Nestor uses the word *foolish* to describe the dream—"This dream, had it been told b'another man, / Feigned and foolish would have seem'd to me"[126]—an attribution Fagles does not at this point use. Hobbes has, then, captured both the monarch's vanity and his foolishness.

A third and final attribute of Hobbes's translation is his use of the idiom of social contract, such as the word *assembly* and *consent*. It is not that Hobbes is importing these words into the poem. The poem *is* centrally about consent and dissent; it has no other subject that competes with it as the key matter. The nature of "assembling" (which is integrally connected to the commander's reliance on the soldiers' consent) is therefore key to the poem. Cedric Whitman's classic study, *Homer and the Heroic Tradition*, identifies scenes of assembly as a fundamental principle of structure in the *Iliad*, assemblies among the gods, among the councils of advisors, and among the full array of soldiers. This crucial matter is of necessity present in any translation, as when Fagles writes, "The troops assembled. The meeting grounds shook."[127]

The meeting grounds are the space of deliberation and debate. But Hobbes uses the words *assembly* and *consent* in his translation in a way not found in other translations, and that foregrounds its connections with his own work on social contract. In the opening 200 lines of Book II, the explicit words "assembly" or "consent" occur six times in Hobbes and three times in Fagles. At the opening of Fagles's Book II, Zeus in devising the false dream says the gods on Olympus, who had earlier been divided in their preferences for Greece or instead Troy, now "clash no more … and all agree: / griefs are about to crush the men of Troy."[128] Here is Hobbes's alternative:

> *The Gods no more thereon deliberate,*
> *But all consented have....* [129]
> *No longer to delay the Trojan fate.*
>
> (Hobbes II. 10–12)

So, too, it is revealing to compare the way the troops, instructed to cut and run, obey in Fagles and in Hobbes. Fagles's poem is a work of genius, probably not a description that even the most ardent reader would give of Hobbes's poem; but Hobbes's epic is aligned with the vocabulary of social contract, a constant reminder that both the solitary soldier and the assembly of soldiers may affect the fate of their country. Here is Fagles:

> *And the whole assembly surged like big waves at sea,*
> *the Icarian Sea when East and South Winds drive it on,*
> *blasting down in force from the clouds of Father Zeus,*
> *or when the West Wind shakes the deep standing grain*
> *with hurricane gusts that flatten down the stalks—*
> *so the massed assembly of troops was shaken now.*
> *They cried in alarm and charged toward the ships*
> *and the dust went whirling up from under rushing feet*
> *as the men jostled back and forth, shouting orders—*

"Grapple the ships! Drag them down to the bright sea!
Clean out the launching-channels!" Shrill shouts
Hitting the heavens, fighters racing for home,
knocking the blocks out underneath the hulls.

(Fagles II. 168–80, emphasis added)

Here is Hobbes, beginning a few lines earlier with the end of King Agamemnon's address to his armies:

Come, then, and all agree on what I say,
Let's put to sea, and back t' Achaea fly.
We shall not win the town although we stay.
This said, the army with applauses high
Consented all *(save those that had been by*
In council of the princes of Achaea)
And moved were like to the billows high
That rolled are by some great wind at sea.
Or as, when in a field of well-grown wheat
The ears incline by a sharp wind opprest;
So bow'd the heads in this assembly great
When their consent *they to the king exprest.*
Then going to the ships cry'd Ha la la! . . .
and to the sky
Went up the noise.

(Hobbes II. 121–33, 137–38, emphasis added)

The consent of the soldiers is twice foregrounded in Hobbes's translation.

Hobbes is not importing the conception of social contract into the poem. The conception of the social contract is already amply there. J. V. Luce, in an article on "The Polis in Homer and Hesiod," shows how richly present the polis is in the *Iliad*. "It is," Luce writes, "for Homer, the outstanding feature of human society." The word *polis* occurs 109 times in the *Iliad* and 89 times in the *Odyssey*; the closely related word *astu* occurs 88 times in the *Iliad*, 49 times in the *Odyssey*; the two "often interchangeable" words occur 335 times in the two poems.[130] The climactic portrait occurs in the tour de force account of the shield of Achilles in Book XVIII: the polis, depicted on the shield both at war and at peace, "dominates the whole composition" with the depiction of peace centering on the act of marriage and on the law courts.[131]

Book XVIII contains the most concentrated account: the fact that the entire polis has been collapsed down to a size that can fit on the surface of the shield means that it can, for the duration of that book, be contained within the boundaries of the human mind. But the concern with the polis radiates throughout the entire poem and is used for both sides in the conflict. The word *acropolis*, which contains the word *polis*, occurs only once (in a description of the "citadel of Troy" in the eighth book of the *Odyssey*), but the "periphrastic" equivalent of acropolis—"the high polis" or "the highest polis"—is common, as are such phrases as "the well-walled *polis* of Troy," "the *polis* of Priam," the "broad-roaded *polis* of the Trojans."[132] For Homer, the nonpolis is depicted in the *Odyssey* Book IX, in the account of the Cyclops: "They have no assemblies where policies are proposed and no customary ordinances (*themistes*). / They dwell on the mountain in hollow caves. / Each lays down the law for his own wives and children, and they pay no heed to one another."[133] This is a passage Plato cites in the *Laws* as an example of patriarchal systems preceding the polis.[134] All this, to return to our starting point, is to say that Hobbes is *not* reenvisioning the coast of Troy using *extrinsic* notions of contract; yet by so overtly and repeatedly using the explicit vocabulary of consent, dissent, assembly, he is making inescapable the structures that we might otherwise need J. V. Luce's assistance to decipher.

Before proceeding to the crucial later parts of Books II, we should take note of the striking difference in the straightforward language of Achilles and the false language of Agamemnon and of Zeus, the first of whom uses a series of insincere imperatives to test his men and the second of whom directly lies to the king. Achilles' speech and the speech of Agamemnon are directly contrasted because each speaks an oath holding up a scepter. Each performs a key speech act of the kind we examined in Chapter 1. Achilles' oath that he will stay separate from the fighting is taken on a scepter whose physical attributes he describes in detail, a scepter that the heralds pass to anyone in the assembly wishing to speak and that according to Bernard Knox "stands for the rule of law and due process in the community."[135] Agamemnon's very different scepter is the royal scepter that originates with the gods and has passed down to him through a lineage of named gods and kings. Homer lists the royal lineage—name by name—immediately before telling us that Agamemnon, leaning his weight on this scepter, issues his false command.

A spectacular and convincing portrait of Achilles' language in the original Greek text (audible in all translations, though to varying degrees) is given in an article cowritten by Paul Friedrich and James Redfield in 1978. In it the two scholars try to account for the sense that people have had for two millennia that Achilles' speech is different from all the other participants', an intuition people articulate by saying "'He's more forceful', 'harder to scan', 'uses odd words', and 'just feels different.'"[136] Much about Achilles' speech is continuous with the other characters: everyone in the *Iliad* speaks in complete hexameter lines.[137] To get at the answer, Friedrich and Redfield take the ten scenes in which Achilles appears and through which he inexplicably dominates the poem, and compare the 897 lines of poetry he speaks with the 890 lines that he either listens to (because they are directly addressed to him) or overhears (because they are addressed to someone else).[138]

Their astonishing analysis of Achilles' language—his "richness of detail," his use of "hypothetical imaginings" and "similes," his "poetic directness" and "tone of detachment," his refusal ever to "concede a point to an adversary," his use of vocatives, titles, and forms of affectionate address (as when Achilles calls Patroclus "delight of my heart"), his use of imperatives in which the clauses are unlinked (and are therefore said by linguists and rhetoricians to be "in asyndeton"), his use of the phrase *nûn de* ("actually") to pivot between his commitments to "imagination and realism"[139]—all contribute to our sense that Achilles occupies an exceptional linguistic zone. Redfield and Friedrich conclude that Achilles "is the only hero in the *Iliad* who is himself a bard":

> In one passage, we actually see him outside his tent in the evening, playing the lyre and singing "the deeds of men" (IX.186–9)— including, we assume, his own; Homer intends him to be taken not only as a poet, but as a poet of his own acts. The poetry which makes his rhetoric so powerfully expressive does not, however, enable him to manipulate men effectively; and so the others are not persuaded to join him against Agamemnon. But its power does enable him to touch a second audience, namely the reader, and so to create an ironic complicity.[140]

By the beginning of Book II, following the compromised dream speech of Zeus and false command of Agamemnon, we already have a strong auditory sense of the distinct language of Achilles that Redfield and Friedrich find in the epic as a whole.

By the end of Book II, the Achaeans—with the exception of Achilles and his comrades—will be moving forward into battle and we will be given the magnificent catalogue of ships and the review of the coalition of the armies fighting for Troy. As the poet Allen Grossman has observed, the ship's catalogue at the end of Book II was to the ancient world what the table of chemical weights was to the modern world. Cedric Whitman also celebrates the beauty and power of the incantatory recitation of names and numbers of the troops on both sides. By the opening of Book III, we will be standing on the walls of Troy with Helen and the city elders, watching the Greeks moving across the plain and listening to Helen as she (once herself an intimate Argive insider) describes to the Trojan elders the attributes of the magnificent individual soldiers who are approaching.

But in order for this to happen—before the ship's catalogue and the review of the heroes on two sides—one additional scene of dissent has to occur: the verbal eruption of Thersites and his decisive silencing as Odysseus beats him black-and-blue; and the witnessing soldiers laugh and jeer at his physical deformities, his cowardice, and his impudent dissent. *His* act of verbal dissent is permitted none of the nobility accorded to Achilles; it is described as though it were as misshapen as his body, as degraded as his alleged cowardice in fighting (although we also have to read this backward: his act of dissent causes him to be perceived as cowardly and physically misshapen).[141] It would be impossible—given the thoughtful crediting that Homer has earlier given to disobedience—for us now to move into the resumption of battle, so dissent must be discredited: Thersites must be permitted to make his rude entry and just as rudely be made to exit.

Here is Hobbes's rendering of the excruciating scene. Odysseus has just moved through "the assembly," persuading people to return to battle, urging—in a line that is deeply compatible with *Leviathan*— "Let one be king (we cannot all be kings)." The assembly falls quiet, and now comes the scene:

> *Thersites only standeth up and speaks.*
> *One that to little purpose could say much,*
> *And what he thought would make men laugh would say.*
> *And for an ugly fellow none was such*
> *'Mongst all the Argives that besieged Troy.*
> *Lame of one leg he was; and look'd asquint;*
> *His shoulders at his breast together came;*
> *His head went tapering up into a point,*
> *With straggling and short hair upon the same.*
>
> (Hobbes II. 188–96)

This cruel description of Thersites' body is unnegotiably present in the Greek and shared by all translations. In fact, in most translations,

Thersites' voice is made equally unpleasant, as when Fagles writes (in contrast to the opening lines above), "But one man, Thersites, still railed on, nonstop. / His head was full of obscenities, teeming with rant, / all for no good reason, insubordinate, baiting the kings— / anything to provoke some laughter from the troops."[142] Through his omissions, Hobbes here and in the passage to come (where Fagles has Odysseus describe Thersites' speech as "babbling," "mouthing," "flinging indecencies" "blithering on in this way") actually confers a measure of dignity on Thersites' speech:

> And Agamemnon now aloud he rated,
> And thereby anger'd all the Greeks beside.
> What is't, Atrides, said he, stays you here?
> Your tent is full of brass; women you have
> The best of all that by us taken were,
> For always unto you the choice we gave.
> Or look you for more gold that yet may come
> For ransom of some prisoner whom I
> Or other Greeks shall take at Ilium,
> Or for some young maid to keep privately?
> But kings ought not their private ease to buy
> With public danger and a common woe.
> Come, women of Achaia, let us fly,[143]
> And let him spend his gettings on the foe.
> For then how much we help him he will know,
> That has a better than himself disgrac'd.
> But that Achilles is to anger slow,
> That injury of his had been his last.
> This said, [Odysseus] straightway to him went,
> And with sour look, and bitter language said,
> Prater, that to thyself seems eloquent,
> How darest thou alone the king t'upbraid?
> A greater coward than thou art there's none

'Mongst all the Greeks that came with us to Troy.
Else 'gainst the king thy tongue would not so run.

(Hobbes II. 199–223)

Hobbes's act of permitting Thersites to maintain power and dignity is especially evident toward the end of the passage. Odysseus's charge of cowardice almost seems a non sequitur, since the only basis he gives seems suggestive not of cowardice but of courage: "How darest thou alone the king t'abraid? . . . 'Mongst all the Greeks that came with us to Troy." Only then does Hobbes have Odysseus surmise that Thersites "seeks an excuse to run away." In Fagles, in contrast, the charge of cowardice saturates the lines, and thus the defiance of Thersites is deflated. Here it is not, as in Hobbes, Thersites' solo act of speaking out against Agamemnon that makes him singular but the extremity of his inadequacy as a soldier: "Who are *you* to wrangle with kings, you alone? / No one, I say—no one alive less soldierly than you, / none in the ranks that came to Troy . . . So stop your babbling, . . . your eyes / peeled for a chance to cut and run for home."[144] In both translations, Thersites is presented as one-of-a-kind, but it is based on his defiance in one case and in the other, his sordid and slippery fear.

The point of these comparisons is not to marvel at the accuracy or inaccuracy of Hobbes's translation and omissions. It is to take note of the fact that this philosopher—whose name in the commentaries is wrongly yoked to an automaton level of obedience—has not only chosen to translate a poem whose major subject is dissent but who has made many small decisions along the way that reveal his willingness to credit dissent. The capacity of soldiers to dissent is crucial to the overall work of the social contract because if soldiers are incapable of dissent, it means there is no second brake on the sovereign's decisions to go to war. Nothing, therefore, could be more important.

Odysseus threatens that if in the future Thersites ever speaks so again he will beat him, but then proceeds to beat him in the present, an act treated as a cause of cruel merriment among the troops:

This said, he basted him both back and hips.
Thersites shrugg'd, and wept, sat down, and had
His shoulders black and blue, dy'd by the staff;
Looked scurvily. The people that were sad
But just before, now could not choose but laugh.

(Hobbes II. 236–40)

The scene, like the scenes that precede it, shows that the act of challenging a sovereign's will is not one topic among many in this poem; it is the poem's center. The dissent of Thersites is a comic grotesque mirror of Achilles' own dissent. Achilles' arguments about just distribution—that the spoils of war must be equal across persons, or if unequal, must follow in their inequalities the unequal contributions of those who fought—are repeated by Thersites, repeated in conflated and condensed form but a form clearly recognizable as echoic of Achilles. The two scenes together provide a stark example of the principle that what occurs the first time as tragedy, occurs the second time as farce (or, to take the model of Greek drama, the tragedy is followed by a condensed satyr play). Homer has to have us repicture dissent as a negative event, after having allowed it to acquire great depth and power, else we would not be able to return to the Trojan War, to the courage and vulnerability of soldiers on both sides, and to the eventual portrait of the cost to the Greeks of losing the consent of a solitary soldier, Achilles.

On the surface, a negative portrait of dissent should be one Hobbes very much appreciates since he is so often seen as someone unequivocally opposed to disobedience. It will therefore be useful to contemplate what he thought of Thersites' dissent in more detail. What he thought of this scene can be gleaned by looking at the commentary written by an earlier translator, John Ogilby, commentary that Hobbes not only read but greatly praised in his own preface to the poem. In fact, Hobbes's praise for Ogilby forms the closing sentences of the preface: "But why [am I publishing the poem] without annotations? Because I had no hope to do it better than it is already done by Mr. Ogilby."[145] Not only has Hobbes given him the final sentence in the preface, but he is the only contemporary even named in the preface, whose pages otherwise invoke only Homer, Virgil, Lucan, Cicero, and Eustathius.[146]

When John Ogilby dedicated his own 1660 translation of the *Iliad* to Charles II, he stated that he dedicated it to the newly coronated king because the poem is "the noblest Oblation of the Muses" and because the poem is "a most constant Assertor of the Divine right of Princes and Monarchical Government." He then—still addressing Charles in the dedication—offers as proof of the poem's faultless proauthority, promonarchy stance, the portrait of Thersites in Book II: "all Anti-monarchical Persons [Homer] describes in the Character of Thersites":

> *Who fondly vented incoherent Things*
> *'Gainst Soveraign Power and Majesty of KINGS:*
> *The most deformed Piece of All who came*
> *To th' Ilian siege; squint-ey'd crook-back'd & lame;*
> *His breast bunch'd out; round was his head; a thin*
> *And callow downe vested his meager Chin.*[147]

This translation of Homer's description of Thersites, like Hobbes's translation of the same passage cited earlier, is devastating. If Charles II were to read no further in the poem than its dedicatory page, he could indeed conclude that Homer savages anyone holding antimonar-chic views. But what if Charles II were to read Book I or the full scene in Book II from which the cited passage comes? We know that after Hobbes gave his own handwritten copy of *Leviathan* to Charles II, his formerly cordial relations with the king abruptly ended.[148]

In one of his annotations, Ogilby notes disapprovingly that Thersites addresses Agamemnon as "Atrides" rather than as *King* Atrides; and Ogilby's own dedication to Charles II is lavishly addressed "To the most High and Mighty MONARCH CHARLES the Second of England, Scotland, France and Ireland KING Defender of the Faith Ec." Ogilby was, almost without question, a Royalist: it was John Ogilby who was selected to choreograph the elaborate coronation pageant for Charles II, the restoration of monarchy in England (though the pageant included striking details that call his royalist sympathies into question, such as the fact that in one sequence he made the figure of Rebellion far more vivid than the figure of the Monarch).[149] But does John Ogilby really believe this poem is pro-Royalist, so pro-Royalist that it can accurately be said that "all Anti-monarchical Persons he describes in the Character of Thersites"? Ogilby explicitly registers his answer to that question—an emphatic No—in his annotations to the poem, annotations that Hobbes read and knew in detail.

John Ogilby is certainly aware of the parallel between Thersites and Achilles: in one of his footnotes, he faults Thersites for merely duplicating the arguments Achilles has already made in the first assembly, rather than, as the poem itself claims, "stir[ring] up fresh Debate."[150] Thersites himself invokes the injustice done to Achilles and observes that the injustice might have justified regicide: only because Achilles is slow to anger, says Thersites, is Agamemnon not dead.

John Ogilby in his marginalia to Book I—that is, long before we get to Thersites—makes this same point. He cites the sixteenth-century European classical scholar Julius Scaliger as "find[ing] fault with Homer for making Achilles put up [with] so high an indignity and affront as he did, so tamely; taking no revenge upon Agamemnon than by words onely."[151] Ogilby then defends Homer by saying, what is in fact true, that Achilles in these lines *does* contemplate killing Agamemnon and only abstains because he must obey Athena: our nominal pro-Royalist writes, "the greatnesse of his Spirit in attempting to kill the Generall," is matched and subdued by his "piety" and obedience to Athena.[152]

That the defiance of Achilles and of Thersites both introduce the hypothetical of regicide is crucial when we recall the oddity of the fact cited early: the very political philosopher who repeatedly stated that ancient Greek writers teach the public "tyrannophobia" is the same political philosopher who begins his career with a translation of Thucydides (a translation from the Greek that was not available to the

English public until Hobbes gave them one[153]) and ends his career with a translation of Homer.[154]

A third feature of Ogilby's marginalia (marginalia Hobbes judged difficult to surpass) again demonstrates his recognition that the anti-monarchical act belongs to Achilles, the poem's hero, and not merely to a minor figure who makes a short and painful appearance in Book II, as the dedication to Charles II misleadingly announces. John Ogilby's multiple glosses on Agamemnon are almost more devastating than what Achilles himself says.

No soldier in Book I steps forward to defend Achilles by taking up his arguments against Agamemnon and extending them.[155] But so consistently does Ogilby do so that he almost acts as that missing comrade. For example, after Achilles, under Athena's tutelage, refrains from killing Agamemnon and restores his sword to its sheath, he redoubles his verbal insult, "Thou Dog-Eyd Drunkard, hearted like a Deer!"[156]—an insult we have heard earlier from Fagles and Hobbes but that we are now hearing in Ogilby's translation. This is the powerfully offensive line that Hume later objected to at the end of his essay "Of the Standard of Taste."[157] As though this line were not already powerful enough on its own, foot soldier John Ogilby steps forward with the following margin gloss: "Drunkenness, Impudence, and Cowardice, the greatest Vices and defects in a Souldier and Commander. The Athenian Law instituted by Solon . . . punished the Archon, or chief Magistrate taken drunke with death."[158] That is not a piece of marginalia designed to make the reader (and Hobbes was a reader) dismiss the charges against Agamemnon lightly. He is in effect saying: These are not merely unattractive characterological faults; they are the kind of faults for which in a later age kings deserve to be, and are, executed. Hobbes would not have been startled by this note. In *On the Citizen* he says that "drunkenness is an offense against the natural law." Just as it is wrong to forego reason or one's duty, so it is wrong to do anything that will predictably impair one's ability to reason or to do one's duty. The forms of behavior called for in peacetime differ from the forms of behavior called for in war, but two prohibitions are common to both peace and war: the prohibition on drunkenness and the prohibition on cruelty.[159] Though Hobbes does not go nearly as far as Ogilby in condemning drunkenness (since Ogilby awards it the death penalty), he clearly judged it a serious misdeed.

Even more devastating a gloss on Agamemnon occurs very early in Book I. Before Agamemnon takes Briseis he has taken Chryseis, the daughter of the priest. The Greek encampments have been scourged by plague, and when Achilles calls a council to decipher the cause of the plague, the seer Calchas reveals that the cause is Agamemnon's unlawful act and that he must restore the dark-eyed virgin to her father. Agamemnon at first refuses, saying he cannot bear to part with her. Achilles tries to reason with the king, arguing that though there is not at present a substitute, they will certainly find one after they defeat Troy. But Ogilby—the self-appointed aide-de-camp of Achilles—steps up to the plate with the following crushing observation: Here we see that Agamemnon could part with his daughter Iphigenia "to serve his Ambition" but because of his lust "would not part" with Chryseis even "though the welfare of his Army . . . depended upon it." The reminder at this moment that the man who refuses "the disappointing of his Lust" is the same man who "to serve his ambition, sacrificed his own Child," pushes him much closer to an object of pure disgust than anything that has yet been said inside the poem.[160] Ogilby's act of bringing these two phases of Agamemnon's life into direct juxtaposition is shocking and revelatory. Even if one knows well both the Iphigenia story and the Chryseis story, they normally inhabit different mental landscapes and so remain stranded from one another. Ogilby's powerful act of placing them side by side almost delivers a physical blow to the reader.

The dispute about which the muses sing in the *Iliad* is not a private dispute between two men. Achilles' dissent is based on the allegation that Agamemnon has violated the public trust, as in the lines just cited where he is reluctant to give up his mate even though the "welfare" of his plague-stricken soldiers requires it. He believes he is entitled, as

Achilles will later say, to "rob the Souldier of the publick Gifts... Thou the devourer of thy People art."[161] To this line Ogilby appends a note saying kings enrich their subjects, a "tyrant" impoverishes them.[162]

Certainly in his translation of the *Iliad*, Hobbes captures the public violation that would convert a legitimate sovereign into an illegitimate tyrant—or, in the term Hobbes preferred, *hostis*, enemy.[163] A striking instance occurs in the Thersites passage invoked earlier:

> *But kings ought not their private ease to buy*
> *With public danger and a common woe.*
>
> (Hobbes II. 209, 210)

In one crisp line—"With public danger and a common woe"—Hobbes has Thersites deliver what from the point of view of the social contract is a damning accusation. A polis intact is a "Common Wealth"—that is a term that looms large in *Leviathan*, beginning with its appearance in the book's subtitle.[164] But to satisfy his private hungers, Agamemnon has converted the common wealth into the common woe—"the common woe" in the form of the man-killing plague that results from his trespass against the priest of Apollo's daughter, "the common woe" that the Greeks will suffer at the hands of the Trojans now that Achilles "ha[s] the war declined."[165]

As "common woe" is a stark inversion of "Common Wealth," so "public danger" is a stark inversion of "Publick Safety." Throughout *Leviathan*, Hobbes repeatedly states that "the Sovereign" may be either a monarch or an assembly. Two features (and two features only) are required for the sovereign to remain the sovereign: first, that it get its authority from the consent of the people (the "seditious" foundational feature of Hobbes's social contract according to his foes); second, that it be dedicated to *salus populi*, the well-being of the people.[166] *Salus populi* has for its opposite the "Public Danger" Hobbes has so adroitly coupled with the common woe.

The song the muses are called upon to sing in the *Iliad* is not a private dispute but a public matter. Homer and Hobbes are deeply compatible because each is so centered in the question of dissent. Someone wishing to challenge the gravity of Hobbes's commitment to the *Iliad* might remind us now of what he states in his own preface to his *Iliad*—"Why then did I write it? Because I had nothing else to do." Is it really the case that this political philosopher, this practicing mathematician, this sometimes physicist, this correspondent of Leibniz's, this man who at the end of his life wrote a series of essays arguing that heresy was legal (and in *Behemoth* he says "heresy" and "rebellion" are the same thing)[167]—that this person had nothing better to do? Rather than a way of minimizing what he has done, the formulation that "he had nothing better to do" should be taken literally. For a political philosopher who believes that the sovereign derives its authority from the consent of the people, and that the sovereign has no other purpose but the safety of the people, translating the *Iliad* was the very best thing he could do.

The capacity to consent or to dissent is not just one human capacity among hundreds. Hobbes says in *On the Citizen* that it is the soul of an individual person. This same capacity for giving or withholding consent is the soul of the commonwealth:

> Because man has a soul, he has a will [*voluntas*], that is, he can assent [*velle*] and refuse [*nolle*]; similarly a commonwealth has a will, and can assent and refuse through the holder of *sovereign power*, and only so.[168]

In order to show why a solitary soldier's dissent matters, Homer makes Achilles a glistening hero: because he is "the best of the Achaeans," a brilliant runner and fighter, the Greeks learn that their cause is lost without him and the elated Trojans become more confident and daring. For those inside the story—comrades, countrymen, opponents, enemies—his dissent matters because he is the best of the Achaeans; but for those standing outside the epic listening to it—whether in ancient

Greece or seventeenth-century England or in the twenty-first century—the opposite is the case: his being the best of the Achaeans helps make legible the astonishing fact that an individual soldier's consent matters.[169] Solitary military dissidents today—such as Joseph Darby who turned in to the Army the Abu Ghraib torture photographs—exemplify the way an isolated act of dissent by a single soldier (even one whose mother is not a goddess and who is not himself the fastest runner) can have worldwide consequences: "a firestorm of global outrage"[170] and the eventual end of U.S. acts of torture. Where it is not a single soldier but many—as in the numerous historical instances invoked in Chapter 2—the consequences may alter their country temporarily or even permanently.

When Hobbes asserted (and he asserted many times) that the sovereign was identical with the people whose consent brought the social contract and its sovereign into being, he was basing this identification on two key facts. First, that the sovereign and the people share the same advantages and disadvantages: "[t]he first and greatest advantage is Peace and defence, and it is the same for both. For both the ruler and the ruled employ the united forces of all their fellow citizens for the defence of their own lives."[171] Hobbes gives a second reason (though it sounds close to the first). Their shared dependence on one another's safety means that if the sovereign does anything to diminish the well-being of the people, the sovereign's own well-being will be jeopardized: "if the holder of sovereign power exacts so much money from the citizens that they cannot feed themselves and their families and maintain their physical strength, it is as big a disadvantage for the ruler as for themselves, since however rich he may be, he cannot protect his own wealth and Power without the physical aid of the citizens."[172]

If by some unimaginable seventeenth-century magic, the sovereign were to obtain a weapon that made that sovereign wholly independent of the citizenry, then the identification and mutual dependence of the two would dissolve. Noted a moment ago was Hobbes's belief that the sovereign and the citizens share identical advantages and disadvantages.

But only their shared advantage—peace and defense—has so far been registered here. What did he regard as "the greatest disadvantage that can occur in a commonwealth"? His answer: "massive slaughter of the citizens."[173]

This is the fate nuclear weapons hold out as a daily, hourly, minute-by-minute possibility. As many scientists have warned, any country that uses nuclear weapons against another country is also committing an act of national suicide since its own citizenry will in the weeks following the event become casualties. Even if only a single country in the world were to have nuclear weapons, its accidental or intentional firing of the weapon would be lethal to its own population. When Hobbes names this "massive slaughter of the citizens" as the greatest disadvantage he can imagine, he says that it cannot arise in any of the three forms of government he describes (monarchy, aristocracy, democracy) but only from anarchy, which is the dissolution of all three forms:[174]

> [W]ho does not see that *Anarchy* is equally opposed to all the kinds in the list? For the word means that there is no government at all, i.e. there is no commonwealth at all. And how can it be that a *non-commonwealth* is a kind of *commonwealth*?[175]

The phrase "thermonuclear monarchy" seems the most accurate description of the form of government in today's eight (or more) nuclear states, since the standing arrangements for nuclear weapons depend on the will of a few men within each of those eight states. Hobbes would be revolted by the arrangements we have invented, but would almost certainly reject the phrase "thermonuclear monarchy" to describe it, replacing it with "thermonuclear anarchy." He would not be able to locate his own conception of a sovereign—whose entire raison d'etre is to secure peace—with the target-ready arrangements for nuclear weapons coupled with nonstop conventional violence: in over sixty years since the invention of atomic weapons, there have been only three and a half years when the United States has not been simultaneously involved in conventional combat.[176] That nonstop record of conventional combat— always without a constitutionally mandated congressional declaration and, after Vietnam, without a distributed army required by the Second Amendment—is an important demonstration of the falsity of the claim that nuclear weapons prevent conventional war.

This chapter has shown that the social contract is nothing else than an architecture for the prevention of injury and war. It has a two-tiered structure. At level one, there is an absolute never-injure rule. This rule is enforced by level two, where arrangements are in place to punish or go to war against any person or persons who break the never-injure rule. But punishing and going to war (both of which entail injury) are not easy: within both the act of punishment and the act of going to war, a double brake is in place that must be released before the enforcing act can be carried out: two juries in the case of punishment; an assembly and multitudes of citizen-soldiers in the case of war. As at level one the government constrains the population, at level two the population constrains the government. The double brakes are designed to place "many intervening layers of possibly resistant humanity" between the government suspicion that persons or foreign peoples have broken the never-injure rule and the conviction that that is the case.

Only part of this work can be attributed to Thomas Hobbes; his writings are a window back into many earlier centuries of philosophic meditation and real-world institution building, just as his writings are a window into the future works of Locke, Rousseau, Kant, and the institution building of the American Federalists and constitution writers in many countries. But it is important to see how foundational is Hobbes's passionate and indefatigable call for a covenant of peace: the word that occurs more than eighty times in *Leviathan*, and seventy-three times in *De Cive*, often preceded by some designations such as "the first law," "the fundamental law."

It is also crucial to recognize how distorted the view of Thomas

Hobbes became in the period immediately following the invention of nuclear weapons. Just as nuclear weapons could only come into being by silently bypassing constitutional requirements for war making, so their existence changed the way people regarded the Constitution: suddenly long-revered protocols seemed like archaic and embarrassingly feminine constraints on our gigantic masculine war machine. Swaggering and unstoppable, surpassing in blast and burn power every weapon the world had ever seen, nuclear weapons could not be stopped by armies of opposition, let alone by a few words of script on a piece of paper. Their existence also changed the way those thinking about international relations would think—or rather, stop thinking—about the ethical norms embedded in centuries of moral and political philosophy. This ethics-free arena required a deformation in the way Hobbes was viewed.

Political theorist Brian C. Schmidt has tracked the "divorce between political theory and international relations" that occurred in the 1950s, 1960s, and 1970s. While political theory continued to address "normative issues, such as the nature of justice, freedom, [and] equality," international relations underwent a "bizarre detour" in which it prided itself on a "value-free" school of "realism," marginalizing all "old-fashioned" values in the name of "a theory of survival."[177] Insofar as it wanted to dignify this ethical vacuum with a philosophic name, a name was chosen: Thomas Hobbes. Historian David Armitage has shown in detail that it was not the philosophy of Hobbes that led to the twentieth-century theory of international anarchy; just the reverse; only after a position of international anarchy was invented was Hobbes dragged (kicking and screaming) into this arena:

> Hobbes was only identified as a theorist of international anarchy once a consensus had emerged that the international realm was indeed anarchic.... Hobbes did not directly inspire the conception of the relations between states as fundamentally anarchic. It was instead the proponents of a "discourse of anarchy" in international relations who co-opted Hobbes.[178]

Noel Malcolm has also provided a tour de force account of the puzzling "asymmetry" between Hobbes scholars who barely mention international relations (because Hobbes so seldom addresses it) and international relations scholars who present Hobbes as the champion of ethics-free realism, power politics, and imperialism.[179]

None of the three (Schmidt, Armitage, Malcolm) explicitly attributes these detours into philosophic lawlessness to the invention of nuclear weapons, but the timing of the many writings they review coincides with the period of intense nuclear standoff, a period that both Schmidt and Armitage see ending with the twenty-first-century return of moral and political philosophy to the international arena.[180] The Cold War period pushed to the background Hobbes's identification of the laws of nations with the laws of nature which require us to seek peace, and foregrounded instead Hobbes's account of "the state of nature" as a war of all against each, as though this were the state Hobbes advocated, rather than the state he dedicated his life to eliminating. Every schoolchild during the nuclear age would come to know Hobbes's statement that life is "nasty, brutish, and short" without learning that Hobbes says this is only what life is like when we choose war over social contract. The passage from which the three famous words come warns that without the social contract, there can be no "Industry ...no Culture of the Earth; no Navigation...no commodious Building;...no Instruments of moving...no Knowledge of the face of the Earth; no account of Time; no Arts; no Letters; no Society."[181] This is not the condition Hobbes recommends. Nor is it the condition Hobbes says we are fated to endure. It is the condition he warns we will suffer if we tear up the social contract and disregard the laws of nature which require us to seek peace.

Constitutional democracy (as described in Part One) conforms to the architecture of the social contract with its two-tiered, injury-reducing structure (our subject in Part Two). Does it only aspire to peace or does its braking system ensure peace? Many observers agree with Bruce Russett's conclusion that democracies are peace loving:

democracies do not go to war with democracies.[182] Russett not only amasses empirical evidence but also enumerates features that he and others put forward to help to explain why this outcome should be the case. But how different each feature looks depending on whether the nation-state's military is conventional or instead nuclear. Each feature, true in the first case, becomes false in the second.

Here is Russett's list of peace-creating features (followed, in each case, by the deformation that occurs with nuclear weapons). First, democracies, unlike autocracies, are inherently transnational: "Democracies foster, and are fostered by, the pluralism arising from many independent centers of power and influence" and therefore encourage "transnational linkages."[183] *A nuclear monarchy has no interest in sharing nuclear weapons with other countries, though it may ask other countries to station its own weapons and communications systems on their grounds.* Second, democracies are "dovish" because "democratic processes produce restraint by the general populace which will have to pay the price of war in blood and money."[184] *The population in nuclear states has almost no knowledge about, and certainly no say over, the country's nuclear weapons; it has no power to exercise any restraint over their use.* Three, "the complexity of the mobilization process"—the gigantic labor of amassing and moving tens of thousands of fighters and pieces of equipment—"means that leaders will not readily embark" on war.[185] *Nuclear weapons eliminate mobilization: the total injuring power is already amassed, the weapons themselves are in the location from which they will be fired, already programmed into the weapons are the longitude and latitude of both probable and possible targets.* Four, in a democracy "[d]issent within broad limits by a loyal opposition is expected and even needed for enlightened policy-making, and the opposition's basic loyalty to the system is to be assumed in the absence of evidence to the contrary."[186] *No "loyal opposition" to nuclear weapons exists on the floor of Congress, inside the White House, or at any other level of governance such as the state legislatures. Only once people retire from their government positions and are therefore out of power do they sometimes express opposition.* Five, in a democracy "the process [of war preparation] is immensely more public than in an authoritarian state."[187] *Little to no information is publicly available about nuclear weapons, their location, their targets on any given day (even the commander of a submarine is not told what "destination" is indicated by alphanumeric codes he is instructed to program into the missiles on his ship); executive discussions about their contemplated use are released decades after the president is out of office.* It is not possible for an authoritarian country to be less public or less subject to restraint by the public than is currently true in the nominally democratic nuclear states.

If the war-impeding features on Bruce Russett's list disappear in the presence of nuclear weapons, that is because democracy itself disappears in the presence of nuclear weapons. Is it only the war-impeding features of democracy that disappear? As social contract theory reminds us, a constitutional state exists to impede injury and war. If it has lost its braking powers on war, it stands to lose everything on Hobbes's list: industry, agriculture, commodious buildings, navigation, transportation, knowledge of the face of the earth, arts, letters, society. What features of democracy do we imagine can continue if there is earthwide slaughter? Shall we write songs of regret and sorrow after the weapons are fired, or work to make their firing impossible by dismantling them today?

PART THREE

EVERYDAY CONSENT AND EMERGENCY DELIBERATION

A Prelude and Summary

Nuclear weapons cannot be reconciled with governance. Since their invention, their ungovernability has been registered in many direct and indirect ways. During the 1970s and 1980s, the obsessive writings on "command and control" made audible the recognition that they were always, at best, just barely "under control." Today, in the second decade of the twenty-first century (after twenty additional years of proliferation), the "controllability" of nuclear weapons has come to seem hopeless: worldwide, most people agree that it is just a matter of time before they slip out of official hands into the hands of terrorists or, alternatively, slip out of human hands altogether and explode by accident or inadvertence.

Perhaps two nuclear-missile submarines will collide (as happened in February 2009, when England's HMS *Vanguard* and France's *Le Triomphant* collided in the Atlantic).[1] Perhaps a nuclear weapon carried on a plane will—as a result of that plane's exploding, crashing, or sliding off a ship—fall into the ocean or onto land (as happened in 1956, 1957, 1959, 1961, 1965, 1966, and 1968[2]). Perhaps a reliable submarine commander will suddenly lose his reliability (in December 2008, the commander of the Ohio-class submarine USS *West Virginia* was relieved of his command;[3] athough his ship carried twenty-four Trident II nuclear

258 THERMONUCLEAR MONARCHY

missiles with up to 408 warheads, no public account of his dismissal
could be given because such a report, according to the Navy, would
violate his "personal privacy"[4]). Perhaps, the early warning system of a
nuclear state will misconstrue a benign atmospheric event (the rising
moon in 1960, a flock of geese in the 1950s, a Norweigan rocket fired to
explore the aurora borealis in 1995) as an enemy missile and prepare to
fire a lethal missile in response (NORAD went on high alert in response
to the moon and the geese; and in 1995 Boris Yeltsin came within five
minutes of firing a missile at the United States in response to the Norwegian exploration of the northern lights[5]). Perhaps a terrorist will
obtain the capacity to use a nuclear weapon by buying enriched uranium that has slipped out of a Russian factory into the black market.[6] Or
perhaps the parts he needs will simply arrive unexpectedly in the mail
(in August 2006, the Taiwan military, expecting to receive helicopter
batteries from the U.S. Air Force, instead received "four fuses designed
to trigger Minuteman III intercontinental ballistic missiles"[7]). With luck,
the watchful terrorist may discover an already fully assembled set of
missiles sitting unattended on the tarmac of a U.S. military base, ready
to be flown to a chosen destination: in August 2007 six nuclear missiles
sat attached to a B-52 bomber on an open airfield for thirty-six hours,
first at Minot Air Force Base in North Dakota and then at Barksdale
Air Force Base in Louisiana. In introducing the Senate Hearings on the
incident, Senator Carl Levin noted that the six bombs were each ten
times the strength of the Hiroshima bomb, and continued:

> The issue this morning is very, very serious. Over a 2-day period last
> August, the Air Force lost control and knowledge of six nuclear war-
> heads.... Through an extraordinary series of consecutive failures of
> process, procedure, training, and discipline, the nuclear warheads
> flew [1,400 miles] on the wings of a B-52 bomber from Minot to
> Barksdale inside of cruise missiles. No one knew where they were
> or even missed them for over 36 hours.... Luckily, these weapons
> weren't stolen or permanently lost, or accidentally dropped from

the wings...or jettisoned because of bad weather or mechanical problems, with the pilots not even aware that they were jettisoning nuclear weapons containing deadly plutonium....The three investigations...have found that the underlying root cause is the steadily eroding attention to nuclear discipline in the Air Force and, indeed, the whole DOD [Department of Defense].[8]

With alternative forms of skill and luck, a terrorist might be able to bypass even the fully assembled bomb sitting unattended on an airfield and instead introduce a command directly into a missile system by hacking into that system (in April 2009, foreign hackers made their way into America's Joint Strike Fighter—the F-35, a 90 percent digitized plane designed to carry B61 free-fall nuclear bombs and upgraded in 2012 to carry precision-guided nuclear bombs; the 2008 breach was one of 18,050 hacking incidents suffered by the U.S. federal government in that year).[9] Another strategy would be to reside in the neighborhood of the president of a nuclear state who, at least in the case of the United States, has the nuclear codes on him round-the-clock and will surely, sooner or later, let them slip out of his hands whether for a single day (as when President Carter sent to the cleaners a suit jacket with the card containing the nuclear codes in its pocket),[10] or for several months (as when President Clinton mislaid the card and declined to notify the Pentagon until directly confronted).

When we openly acknowledge, as most inhabitants of earth do, that a nuclear weapon could strike as the result of an accident or accidental availability to a terrorist, it is an admission that nuclear weapons are ungovernable; they cannot be kept securely within a legitimate command structure. So, too, when people conclude that—unlike thousands of other humanly made artifacts—nuclear weapons, once made, cannot be unmade, they are voicing the judgment that missiles are wholly outside human control (an object that can be controlled can be unmade). Bill Joy's controversial 2000 article in *Wired* magazine argued that robots may eventually have so much intelligence and power built into them that they will be able to disable their human makers before those human makers can disable them: he cited nuclear weapons—the objects we appear incapable of eliminating and that stand on the verge of eliminating us—as the first prototype.[11]

But these three species of radical ungovernability—their susceptibility to accidental detonation, their susceptibility to procurement by a terrorist, their greater ability to eliminate us than we have to eliminate them—provide a very incomplete and therefore misleading portrait of their profound injury to governance. Parts One and Two of this book have shown that even in the hands of legitimately elected leaders, nuclear weapons are ungovernable: they and their would-be users are outside the frame of law, they are outside the most elementary frame of government. "Even" in the hands of national leaders? It is more accurate to say "especially" in the hands of national leaders for the size of the arsenal such leaders can trigger is vastly larger than what a terrorist or accidental plane crash can instigate, and the preparations in place for their use are orders of magnitude greater than what could occur in the other two scenarios. The capacity to destroy entire nations and the whole earth is in the hands of national leaders. The possession of these weapons by "legitimate leaders" is also what makes them an object of aspiration and emulation by nonnuclear states and stateless terrorists alike, and ensures that they will keep spreading.

Crucially, the other three genres of ungovernability achieve their immunity to control from design features intentionally built into them in this fourth, putatively legitimate arena: genocidal power in a small number of human hands or in a hands-free computerized system.[12]

Some may protest that a vast distance separates terrorist use of a nuclear weapon from state use of a nuclear weapon; but what exactly are the differences? Each works without benefit of sunlight, each works without "intervening layers of possibly resistant humanity," each aims to bring about a catalogue of harms that not even Dante's nine rings of hell can outpace. How far any terrorist has gone in actually aspiring to such an outcome is unknown to us; what we do know is that nations have worked to hone every step of the many-thousand-step procedure required. If a terrorist is able to use this weaponry, it is only because the nation-states have readied it for use.

Despite the widespread dread of accidental detonation or terrorist appropriation of nuclear weapons, there is insufficient momentum toward their elimination. Part of what impedes our ability to get rid of them is the deeply erroneous view that—in contradistinction to the accidental and terrorist uses—there exists some benign or legitimate or lawful use of these weapons. If they could just be kept in Fort Knox (side by side with our gold!) so that we alone could use them . . . ; if they could just be confined to the nuclear club and monitored with greater care . . . But this is a starkly mistaken description. No legal or democratic or contractual option exists.

Thermonuclear weapons are at least as savage and prelegal in the hands of a tiny group of national officials as in the hands of a tiny group of self-described terrorists. Compare the ideologies of five terrorist groups: variations appear among them in coherence, in moral argument, and in degree of dedication to a given people. Now compare those ideologies with the ideologies of any five of the nuclear states: again variations in coherence, in moral argument, and in dedication to a given people appear among them. But do any of these variations (within the terrorists, within the nationals, or across the full array of terrorists or nationals) make the massacre of the residents of New York or New Delhi or Tehran or Beijing by any one group less savage or atavistic or unforgiveable? Nuclear weapons—whether used by national leaders, by terrorists, or by the robotic instruction embedded inside them to accomplish the work for which they were designed—have only a single objective, massacre of all living creatures, of all they have built, and (as seems especially possible when used on the scale available to national leaders) of the earth itself.

Given these four genres of radical ungovernability, why do the populations of nuclear states stand by in silence?

The answer is contained in the question: to say nuclear weapons are "ungovernable" is to say that they are unreachable by the human will, the populations of earth can have no access to them. As though residing in another dimension, they exist in tubes of sealed space that run parallel to our own world but that we cannot enter. The membrane that separates us from their lethal corridors is one-directional: the weapons may suddenly unzip the barrier, erupt into our world, eliminate us; but we cannot, standing on the other side, unzip the barrier, step into their world, and eliminate them.[13]

But this arrangement need not be enduring. We have seen that nuclear weapons *most certainly can* be subjected to governance, using—what?—governance itself: constitutions backed by centuries of social contract theory and practice. The constitutional provisions described in Part One give us a way to reach these unreachable objects and, more, give us a lever to act as a direct brake on their use and, more, give us a tool to dismantle them. Their appearance of unreachability comes about in part because the weapons reside in a physically separate zone (corridors deep in the sea or high in the sky). But our sense that we cannot get traction on them also comes from decades of secrets, lies, and smug officialdom that—like layers of oil, slime, and sludge—obscure the tactile surfaces of the weapons and make our fingers unable to recognize the off-switch even as our hands pass over it. While there have been tens of thousands of specific untruths, the three thickest layers of distortion will be removed even as the weapons are dismantled: the first is the demeaning of constitutions in the nuclear age; the second is the demeaning of political philosophy, severing it from the international arena or worse, distorting it into an apparatus to license mass carnage; the third is the demeaning of the population—the creation of an ontology of inequality whereby populations are deemed unqualified to speak about their own self-preservation, unless (and often not even then) they have personally manned a minuteman silo, participated in the creation of an atomic bomb, or served as secretary of defense.

The need to repair the first of these was addressed in Part One, the second in Part Two, and we turn to the third here in Part Three.

What we call "a constitutional principle of authorization" when embedded in a legal document, and "social contract" when embedded in a philosophic document, we call "consent" when embodied in a living human being. It is to the problem of consent that we now turn. Because the populations of nuclear states have been severed from military responsibilities by long-standing nuclear arrangements, one's day-to-day awareness of one's responsibility for self-preservation, for the defense of one's country, for the protection of other peoples, and the protection of the earth may have grown less acute, even though we may know—and not just from Hobbes—that our soul resides precisely in those avenues of self-preservation and defense.[14]

Although our agile practice of consent and dissent has been blunted in the military realm, we have retained its acuity in the day-by-day actions of peacetime. Attributes of consent that when described in earlier chapters might have sounded remote to the reader, or as merely wishful thinking—the relation of consent to one's own body, the difference between threshold and ongoing consent—will be immediately recognizable as self-evidently life-shaping when now re-encountered in the nonmilitary contexts in Chapter 5. Everyday consent will be contemplated in three spheres: in medical practice, in ordinary experience of political citizenship, and in marriage or intimate relations. We will see here (as we had occasion to see earlier) that consent (like contract) exists to diminish injury. We will see that the body—the thing that must remain intact and alive on behalf of all that is either bodily or nonbodily—is not only the thing protected, but also the ground across which all other rights are generated and without which we can have no rights.

It might be argued—presidents and the executive officers of nations have argued this many times—that the democratic operations of consent that we see in Chapter 5 are all well and good for peacetime, but have to be suspended in wartime and other emergencies. But we see in Chapter 6 that this claim is preposterous. Constitutions, social contract, and consent exist in order to safeguard against injury: to say that in a situation of potential injury they must be put aside is a logical absurdity. The equivalent would be to train someone in CPR and then tell the person that in the event that someone's heart stops pumping, one should set aside CPR since this is now an emergency. Consent comes into being where there is a possibility of injury and where self-preservation is at issue. It is therefore extremely odd to be told that in cases of extreme danger, our consent is suddenly without merit, interest, or availability. The structures of power in the nuclear age have corralled populations into a philosophically untenable proposition according to which we are in charge of our own self-preservation except where our actual preservation is at stake.

We saw in Part One that two constitutional provisions—the requirement for a declaration of war and the requirement for a population-wide distribution of authorization for any war—together provide a concrete tool for dismantling nuclear weapons. As we moved from Part One to Part Two, we saw that this tool can act to undo those weapons not with the light hammer tap of a 300-year-old constitutional implement but with the weighted blow of an implement that emerged into view with Homer in the eighth century BCE; that over the next 2400 years was relentlessly deliberated, practiced, and passed from one generation to the next by townsmen, freemen, kings, and councillors all over Europe; that was then focalized and sharpened by a set of seventeenth-and eighteenth-century philosophers beginning with Thomas Hobbes and continuing through John Locke and Jean-Jacques Rousseau; and that then arrived at full legibility as a pair of written constitutions in two countries, America and France, lands from where its lightsome agility coupled with its vast weight and gravity enabled it to spread to scores of other countries. But neither that light constitutional American implement nor the massively weighted twenty-eight-century-old contract concealed in its interior (like the scepter around which civilizations have assembled and vowed to stand by one another) can deliver that blow to nuclear weapons unless living human beings lift them up off the ground where they lie waiting, available for use.

Part Three is about the act of lifting them up.

CHAPTER 5
CONSENT AND THE BODY

The phenomenon of consent, as a verbal act, is extremely protean: it continually slides in and out of varying conceptual locations such as contract, signature, partnership, promise, waiver, voting lever, warning, and warranty. So, too, its tonal range extends from the negative extreme of "acquiescence" and "privation" (as when one consents to a dire medical operation) to the positive extreme of an affirmation so generative it may bring into being a new child (as when two people consent to an act of lovemaking) or a new nation (as when an assembly votes for constitutional ratification). Overburdened with meaning, the richness of its sites and citations may seem to suggest an instability or incoherence in the concept.

But as one scans across these various locations, it turns out that far from being incoherent, a small and stable set of structural attributes resides at the center of its many invocations. This chapter introduces three portraits of consent from three separate peacetime spheres—medicine, political philosophy, and marriage law—to identify a recurring set of structural elements: their shared emphasis on the human body, their purposeful mystification of active and passive, and their displacement of the contingent by the artifactual. Of these three, it is the first—the material anchoring of consent in the body—that is most crucial.

PORTRAIT 1: MEDICINE

This physical emphasis is most immediately visible in the context of medicine and medical experimentation. In case law surrounding the problem of consent in surgical operations, the single sentence which emerges again and again is that of Judge Benjamin Cardozo in the 1914 case, *Schloendorff v. Society of New York Hospital*: "Every human being of adult years and sound mind has a right to determine what shall be done with his own body."[1] More compelling than that now canonical sentence is the verbal context in which it arises: "In the case at hand the wrong complained of is not merely negligence. It is trespass. Every human being of adult years and sound mind has a right to determine what shall be done with his own body; and a surgeon who performs an operation without his patient's consent commits an assault, for which he is liable in damages." The body, in this language, is conceived of as a palpable ground: the body has edges; it has specifiable boundaries; to cross over those boundaries without the authorization of the person is an act of trespass.

Judge Cardozo sets this in a political and philosophic framework by citing the 1905 Illinois Court of Appeals case, *Pratt v. Davis*, in which Justice Brown had asserted "Under a free government at least, the free citizen's first and greatest right, which underlies all others—the right to the inviolability of his person, in other words, his right to himself—is the subject of universal acquiescence."[2] Here as legal commentators have noticed, the private relation (or what might have been conceived of as merely "the private" relation) between physician and patient is placed within the frame of the "civil rights of citizenship."[3] But it is crucially important to notice that it is not simply designated "a right" but "the first and greatest right," the right "which underlies all others," an "underlying of all others" that is asserted to be the "subject of universal acquiescence." The body is here conceived of not simply as something to be brought in under the protection of civil rights, but as itself the primary ground of all subsequent rights. The substratum of all other political and civil rights is the relation of the person to her or his own embodied personhood.

Four features of the portrait of consent that U.S. medicine provides are key.

The portrait is canonical. The sentence cited ("Every human being of adult years and a sound mind has a right to determine what shall be done to his own body") is not some fragile utterance, spoken once, recorded once, and found in some obscure research into the transcripts of consent cases. It is a sentence spoken once, and then respoken countless times, as it comes to be invoked in case after case following *Schloendorff v. Society of New York Hospital*. It is, along with its political framing, the canonical statement that gets incorporated into everyday courtroom practice. Further, it is incorporated not only into courtroom practice but also into classroom practice, since the interpretive stress on a civil, rather than an exclusively personal, physician-patient relation is part of the casebook, *Law, Science, and Medicine*, and the case routinely enters other classroom texts such as *Law, Medicine, and Forensic Science*.[4] Just as Judge Cardozo underscores the political implications by citing earlier case law, so those designing classroom texts further underscore Cardozo's own act of underscoring, and this becomes part of the education of each generation of law students as they read that text.

This process of underscoring is worth stressing because both literary and legal deliberations every day entail a confrontation with two forms of language, a "language of erasure" and a "language of heightening": in the first, language can come to seem self-canceling because a sentence will be given, then retracted, given, then qualified or complicated beyond recognition; in the second, the meaning is continually lifted out and made more visible through a continuous sequence of clarifications. It is therefore no wonder that in articles on medical consent in the law journals and ethics journals, one reencounters (if often only latently) precisely the same two-part structure of perception—the recognition of the body as the ground of consent, and this in turn as the ground of subsequent civil rights, with a recurring salute to John Stuart Mill's statement in *On Liberty*, "Over himself, over his own body and mind, the individual is sovereign"[5] and to John Locke's statement from section 27 of the *Second Treatise of Government*: "Though the earth, and all inferior creatures, be common to all men, yet every man has a *property* in his own *person*: this no body has any right to but himself."[6]

The continuity between medical consent law and political philosophy is unsurprising, especially when we recall the fact—encountered in Chapter 3—that Locke was himself a physician, and that he collaborated extensively with Thomas Sydenham, both in his treatment of patients and in his theoretical writings on medicine.[7] If medicine is open to prior political philosophy, it is in part because that prior political philosophy has itself been partially shaped by medicine. Whether or not their writings explicitly name the phenomenon of "consent" in patient care, the two physicians regularly credited the patient's sovereignty over his or her own body by using the optative idiom of "letting" the person follow a therapy. The instructions, rather than issuing imperatives or commands, express the hope or wish that they be followed.

In, for example, the manuscript on "A Dysentry" sent to Locke in 1670, Sydenham writes:

> Take 4 gallons of whey, *let* the patient drinke thereof... and *let* him doe the same successive ... and *let* the rest be put up by way of clyster.... *let* him goe to bed and in a little time he will of his owne accord fall into a gentle breathing.[8]

Again, in a 1679 letter responding to Locke's request for advice on the treatment of a particular patient, Sydenham writes:

> I would advise that you give him a dram thereof, finely powedered and made up with syrup of oranges into a bole every eighthe hour untill he hath taken an ounce drincking a draught of any wine *that best likes him* after it; and *that he be allowed* to eat and drinck *what*

best pleases his appetite, excepting onely fruit and all cold liquors. But when he shall have mist two or three fitts and hath strength *I wish* he were in London under my eye for a few days, provided it consists not with your occasions to be with him, in regard that somewhat is to be don that is a litle nice in order to the preventing accidents that usually follow these things.[9]

How these physicians spoke directly to patients may perhaps be generalized from Sydenham's own letters to Locke when sick. In one, Sydenham explains how the sequence of recommended steps has been adapted to accommodate the peculiarities of Locke's own body: "As to injections, in your case these things dissuade the use of them." The language invites, rather than requires: "'twill be highly necessary that you cherish yourself as much as possibly you can by going to bed very early at night even at 8 o'clock, which next to keeping bed, that is unpracticable, will contribute more to your reliefe than can be imagined."[10]

How dire a physician's uninvited trespass across the boundaries of the body is can be appreciated by recalling that diseases themselves trespass across the boundaries of the body. A physician who carries out such an act is thereby mimicking the very phenomena his profession exists to oppose. A disease does not ask the person whose body it inhabits for permission to dwell there: thus from the earliest study of medicine, the onset of disease has been described in the language of criminal assault, as when Hippocrates throughout the *Epidemics* opens many of his case histories with the "seizing" of the patient: "Erasinus lived by the gully of Boötes. Was seized with fever after supper; a troubled night."[11] The idiom of "seizing," "attacking," or "taking hold" has been used by physicians as different as the eighth-century Persian Rhazes in his treatise on smallpox ("they are seized with the Small-pox"),[12] the sixteenth-century French surgeon Ambroise Paré in his treatise on the plague ("This pestiferous poison principally assail's the vital spirit.... the hostile assault.... everie-where seiz' upon the common sort.... it seized upon manie more than it killed"),[13] the seventeenth-century British Nathaniel

Hodges in his writings on the plague ("the Persons first seized with it"),[14] and Sydenham in his writings on scarlet fever and measles ("This attacks infants most"; "The measles generally attack children.... The spots take hold of the face first").[15] When Daniel Defoe in his *A Journal of the Plague Year* says of that 1665 epidemic—"how they were surprized, when it came upon them as it did; for indeed, it came upon them like an armed Man, when it did come"[16]—he is only being slightly more explicit and elaborate than the physicians whose descriptive verbs uniformly register the coercive quality of illness, its bypassing of consent, its insult to, and attempt to defeat, the patient's will.

Of course, not every assailant is openly aggressive; some enter the premises by indirection and stealth; so Locke in his essay on disease entitled "Morbus" repeatedly describes the way the seeds of a disease "insinuate them selves into the body," their "slow & secreat begining" as they first "lie dormant & insensible," the "cruel" work of eventually destroying tissue and bone "with soe much speed & vigor."[17] Since physicians over many centuries have labored to understand which diseases arrive from an external source and which originate inside the body, it might seem that the language of assault and insinuation takes a position on one side of that question; but the language is in fact ordinarily independent of that debate.[18] The idiom of assault and assailants and border-crossings is used to describe not only the onset of disease but also its later phases and symptoms when it has already been residing within the boundaries of the patient's body for some days or weeks, as when Hippocrates notes that on the eightieth day of his illness Clean-actides was "attacked by acute fever"[19] or when Paré describes a plague patient, already laden with symptoms, as now "*molested* with a desire to vomit... green and black matter."[20] The language is appropriate even if the disease has been in residence since birth. What we today identify as genetic diseases "molest" the will as aggressively as those arising from external epidemics and, like them, are paradigmatically nonconsensual. Given the molesting action of disease, medical practice must seek to place itself as far from molestation as possible. It is perhaps for this reason that of the ten sentences that comprise the Hippocratic Oath, six prohibit injuring a patient, sexually trespassing the patient's body, or betraying to anyone outside the perimeter of the patient's household the intimate facts known to the physician.[21] Centuries later, the aspiration not to trespass over the borders of the body can be heard in the gentleness with which Locke conceives of the physician's touch. The Bodleian Library at Oxford houses Locke's cutout paper design for a truss (probably for allaying the discomfort of a hernia) onto which he has inscribed instructions for its fashioning from leather, for moistening specified sections of the leather to stiffen it, and for fastening it, all of which stipulate the way the truss must accommodate the shape of the patient's body, as in the instance of the opening (probably designed to accommodate the male patient's genitals): "The middle part to be bent gently the other way that it may stand with a hollow suited to the convexity of the body in that part."[22] Touch the patient's body with extreme respect, the instructions seem to say, instructions that—by having been inscribed directly onto the truss cutout—seem to hover a millimeter or so over the surface of the body itself.

Equally striking is Locke's transmission of the recipe for making and applying an ointment for burns (originally invented by Prince Rupert to treat burned soldiers and used by Locke for treating a woman burned by an iron and a man scalded by boiling water):

> Lay it on the part [that has been burned] with a feather and then cover the part with a thin linin rag, which need not, nay should not, be taken off at all till the patient be quite well but be anoynted twice a day with a feather to keep it moist with the oyntment.[23]

Locke in a later note to himself repeats the instruction "to anoint the part burnt with a feather dipd in the dissolved oyntment," to use "very thin fine linin such as fine worne cambrick to keep the air from it," and when the first layer of ointment is dry, to "lay it on with a feather upon the thin linnin cloth that lies immediately on the part and then bind it up with an other linnin cloth." Locke ends this second note by reporting that the patient healed "cito tuto jucunde [swiftly, safely, and pleasantly]."[24]

The emphasis here on the canonical quality of Judge Cardozo's words—both in its continuity with earlier political and medical thinking and in the steady invocations of *Schloendorff v. Society of New York Hospital* in the decades following the case—is in part inspired by legal theorist Daniel Farber's engaging essay in *The New Republic* entitled "The Case Against Brilliance." Farber argues, there and in a series of later legal writings, that the problem with brilliance is precisely that it is nonconsensual: "brilliance is not merely *evidence* that a theory is invalid, but a likely *cause* of its invalidity" and inappropriate to legal and economic theory, since "if only a brilliant person can think of [it]," it is not likely to stand as a valid description of what most people do or think: "'brilliance'—new ideas that turn conventional thinking on its head—should count heavily against an economic or legal theory."[25] The canonical, in contrast, *is* the conventional, is the consensual even if one day in 1914 it originated in a particular brilliance or elegance of mind. Thus it is a consensual theory of consent.

So, the first point is, whatever is being said, what is being said has become canonical. Farber's ingenious claim is itself a version of an argument canonical in U.S. political theory from Tocqueville onward, that genius violates and disregards the ethic of camaraderie and equality and that, conversely consensus or equality inhibits genius.[26] The second, third, and fourth features of the medical portrait of consent go back to the content, the what, of what is being said. The most important of these is the emphasis on the body.

The body is the core of consent. The fact that the medical issue of consent takes place on behalf of the body is (as we have seen both in the phrasing of the *Schloendorf* case itself and in prior centuries of language used by physicians in their treatment of patients) so self-evident that it would be hard to unfold or elaborate the point were it not that someone else has already found a way to do so "brilliantly." Marjorie Shultz's legal analysis of medical consent in *The Yale Law Journal* draws on a thick history of twentieth-century case law to demonstrate the intricacy and inextricability of this identification. Shultz provides glacial evidence that whether a medical case involving consent is tried under battery rules or instead under negligence rules, the cases are body dependent or "touch" dependent. Thus in battery cases, an unconsented act of touch is itself an injury: the "right to be secure against unconsented touching is close to absolute."[27] Surgery often provides the model of "an invasive touching."[28] Touch is the "trigger" for such cases: if there has been no touch, there has been no battery. In negligence cases, where one might anticipate a shift in standard, physical contact is again used "to determine when to impose a duty to disclose for purposes of securing informed consent."[29] In both legal forms of redress, physical contact is the "trigger mechanism" for requiring consent and for bringing a complaint for failure to obtain consent.

Shultz's framing argument differs from the central argument here. Shultz believes that the phenomenon of "autonomy" has become confused or conflated with the "physical." She aspires to decouple the two so that battery and negligence rules can be extended to those who have not technically been touched (patients, for example, for whom the physician has prescribed a particular medication).[30] The argument here, in contrast, holds that the insistent coupling of "consent" and the "body"—far from being a confusion or a mistake—reveals the deep structure of consent. This does not mean the cases cannot be extended to other medical problems. Even if the merging of consent and the body is, as I argue, essential to the structure of consent, Shultz's admirable goal of extending the rules to cases without touch should be attainable. Product liability law in the United States, for example, began with objects that either entered or touched the surface of the body but was soon extended to objects very distant from the body.[31]

This conclusion—that the body is inseparable from the deep structure of consent—will gradually become increasingly compelling once we watch precisely the same coupling of consent and the body reappear in the arenas of political philosophy and marriage law. For the time being, whether one calls their inextricable yoking a "confusion" or instead an "essential grounding," whether one sees it as unnecessary or instead necessary, it is in any event that inextricability in medical contexts that becomes luminously clear in Shultz's expert account.

The body is, then, the thing protected. But the body is also the lever across which sovereignty is gained, authorization achieved. This carries us to the third feature of this portrait, the emphasis on citizenship.

Consent credits the citizenship of strangers. Judge Cardozo's original statement contains a haunting phrase: "Relativ[e] to this transaction, the plaintiff was a stranger," a use of this word that recalls Michael Ignatieff's historical and philosophic study, *The Needs of Strangers*, in which he suggests that the nature of any polis is best measured by the provisions it makes for strangers, or for the habits of contact it encourages or discourages between strangers: criminal assault is one pattern; a very different pattern is the way in a welfare state strangers make assessments about one another's intimate needs. Ignatieff writes: "It is this solidarity among strangers, this transformation through the division of labour of needs into right and rights into care that gives us whatever fragile basis we have for saying that we live in a moral community."[32] "Stranger" in this context does not mean foreigner, but one who is among us, yet simultaneously unknown to us, and whose claims on us depend in no way on any specificity of knowledge. The hospital becomes in this regard a miniature nation-state. Judge Cardozo's statement about the hospital reads almost like a poem by Emma Lazarus (the stone edifice of the hospital becoming like the ingathering skirts of Lady Liberty): "A hospital opens its doors without discrimination to all who seek its aid. It gathers in its wards a company of skilled physicians and trained nurses, and places their services at the call of the afflicted, without scrutiny of the character or the worth of those who appeal to it, looking at nothing and caring for nothing beyond the fact of their affliction."[33]

The central place of "strangers" in medical practice is visible not only in Judge Cardozo's use of the legal meaning of the word in *Schloendorff v. Society of New York Hospital* but also in Charles Rosenberg's monumental study of the hospital, *The Care of Strangers: The Rise of America's Hospital System*, in Robert A. Burt's *Taking Care of Strangers: The Rule of Law in Doctor-Patient Relations,* and in Morris Vogel's *The Invention of the Modern Hospital: Boston, 1870–1930.* Diverse forms of hospitals emerged in the nineteenth century (charity, government, private, ethnic), but all of them drew on a single shared ethic: "widespread acceptance of the propriety of going, when ill, among strangers for treatment."[34] These histories of the hospital sometimes use the word "stranger" for its psychological rather than political content: the word registers the psychological complications posed by the impersonal structures of modern medical systems rather than the notions of citizenship, membership, contract, or obligation.[35] Yet the hospital is "impersonal" in part for a deeply benign reason: its availability to the sick must be independent of any "personal" relation that the patient does or does not have with its physicians, nurses, and administrators.

Rosenberg repeatedly attends to the way the American hospital mirrors in its own structures the large structures of the polis. Originating in the country's port cities, the hospital's own institutional history is intimately bound up with the story of immigration.[36] Morris Vogel provides a concrete instance in his study of the Boston hospitals. The economic aristocracy of nineteenth-century Boston opposed the influx of Irish immigrants into "their" city but welcomed those Irish suffering illness or injury into Massachusetts General and Children's Hospital, at that time both charity hospitals. The hospital thus acted as a transformative portal, contributing to the changing perception of Irish-American citizenship.[37] In the 1870s, "immigrants were substantially overrepresented among city hospital patients"; but eventually middle class and wealthy patients began to enter the hospitals for treatment, so that by 1920, the sociological distribution within the hospital was almost identical to the statistical breakdown of classes in the city as a whole.[38] The gradual mixing within one building of all classes eventually ensured a better distribution of medical care to even its poorest inhabitants.[39]

It is true that more than one institution has been invoked in political theory as a microcosm of the polis: Michael Walzer, for example, has elaborated the difference between the liberal state and the communitarian state through the oppositional models of the Hilton Hotel (receptive to all but sterile, empty) and Home (restricted in its reception but warm, full).[40] But the hospital, as Cardozo's suggestive language encourages us to see, has a special claim on our attention as a model of the polis—particularly as a model of the aspirations and defects of the liberal, contractual state. Because the polis, according to contract theorists, comes into being to eliminate injury (as we saw throughout Chapters 3 and 4), an institution that exists solely to address the problems of the injured is likely to make graphically visible the virtues and defects of the larger political system. Not surprisingly, the best and worst features of rival political systems in the late-twentieth and twenty-first centuries have sometimes seemed best summarized in their rival medical systems.

To pretend that the concept "citizen" is wholly good would be to sentimentalize it. Many arguments can be imagined that would discourage such a vocabulary, whether occurring in a medical or any other context. Alexander Bickel, for example, criticizing the emphasis on citizenship in liberal political theorists of the past or present, calls attention to the fact (indeed he applauds the fact) that the United States Constitution and law endow the concept of "citizenship" with the most minimal content possible: he sees the elaboration of citizenship vocabulary as dangerous, because he can imagine circumstances in which a group of people—a jury, a group of lawmakers, a neighborhood—might be willing to deprive someone of status if they believed that what they were taking away was that person's "citizenship" whereas if they realized that what they were about to take away was the individual's "personhood," they would be much more reluctant to do so.[41] But the opposite tradition, from Aristotle to Locke to Michael Walzer has seen it as the safeguard of personhood (as Bickel himself notes since it is precisely this tradition against which he is writing). The concept of consent in medicine, as ethicist William May observes, "encourages full respect for the dignity of the patient who has not, through illness, forfeited his sovereignty as a human being."[42] Here "citizenship," far from acting as a dangerous decoy away from the concept of personhood, instead exists to protect it: the word "sovereignty" is lifted up out of the sentence as a shield over "human being."

This centering of the body in citizenship provides a doorway for the continual entry of political philosophy into medicine. The importation into medical thinking about consent of Mill's or Locke's statements on the body is indicative of a wide and constant reflex. Thus the President's Commission for the Study of Ethical Problems in Medicine and Biomedical and Behavioral Research attempted to find an appropriate theoretical basis for compensating research injuries (compensation not derivable from consent since the participants have consented): the proposed solution entailed using H.L.A. Hart's and John Rawls's concept of "justice as fair play," a concept primarily invented to justify "arrangements such as taxation and national defense."[43] Again, Charles Fried addresses the problem of consent in random clinical trials, a problem because the person does not know what position she or he will occupy within the experiment and thus cannot give consent; or alternatively, the person receives a medical therapy without knowing it has been arrived at by a random procedure. Fried both proposes and criticizes a solution that uses the notion of "distributive justice": the burden of sacrifice must be fairly distributed across the participants in the experiment.[44] The structural affinity between the two spheres emerges more fully by turning to the portrait of consent provided by political philosophy; but before leaving the medical portrait, its fourth and final feature should be briefly introduced, its apparent mystification of active and passive.

Consent erases the division between active and passive. Situations of sickness, injury, or operation often entail heightened forms of the passive and the active. The patient is in a situation of extreme passivity; the physician or surgeon, extreme activeness. In fact, if one imagines the normal distribution of activity and passivity in the ordinary act of touch and being touched, it becomes clear that both are, in medicine, magnified. Normally, the magnification takes place in the direction of healing, but if the patient's consent has been abridged, then it is magnified in the opposite direction. Now the active physical act of touching is raised to the more overtly or aggressively active act of injuring (even if no wound exists separate from the place the body was touched without consent). So, too, the passive recipient of the touch has now entered the more extreme receptivity of being injured.

This magnification of active and passive occurs even if the patient is awake, and may be still further magnified if, as is often the case, the patient is asleep or unconscious or under anesthesia, as is true in most operations. The patient may even be dead, since many consent issues occur in conjunction with the problem of autopsy as well as organ donation or (as it is actually called) "anatomical gifts." Yet it is precisely here—in the injured, sleepy, anesthetized, dying body—that we have the sudden grounding of rights, sovereignty, dignity.

The stately cadence of the language used to confer this dignity occurs in both legal and ethical writings: it is audible in Marjorie Shultz's account of the patient's peculiar status "as the bearer of consequences"[45] or in William May's account of consent "encourag[ing] full respect for the dignity of the patient who has not, through illness, forfeited his [or her] sovereignty as a human being." Has not forfeited it through illness and, we can add, or through anesthesia, or unconsciousness, or even death. The whole issue of consent, by holding within it the notions of sovereignty and authorization, bears within it extremely *active* powers. Yet it often arises precisely at the point where by any conventional description there seems an extreme of passivity.

What may at first strike an observer as a mystification of active and passive eventually emerges into view as a willful redistribution of active and passive. This redistribution recurs in the other sites of consent, and so is a point to which the chapter will return. Ultimately we will see that consent seeks to guarantee the integrity of the individual will at precisely those moments where the will is nominally suspended.

PORTRAIT 2: DEPARTURE (BODILY MOTION)

The emphasis on the body found in medical attention to consent is equally visible in political philosophy. The social contract, we learn in Hobbes's *Leviathan* and *De Cive*, is a compact for peace. Human beings enter the social contract for mutual security: the contract comes into being to "secure them from injury and violence" which, says Locke, is "a trespass against the whole species."[46] As we saw throughout Chapters 3 and 4, the social contract is a double-tiered structure by which the government prohibits the population from injuring (by reserving to itself the threat of punishment and war) and, in turn, the population prohibits the government from injuring by an architecture that subjects that government to the same no-injury rule unless and until the population explicitly releases it from that prohibition.

Therefore, in showing the material grounding of consent, one could—in moving from the medical picture to the picture provided by political philosophy—stay with this first, most essential feature of the body, its susceptibility to injury. But within political philosophy there emerges a second key feature of the body, its capacity for motion: almost as graphically physical as the prohibition on injury is the mapping of consent onto the actions of physical departure, movement, or return to the polis. The generation of the nation-state and one's political obligation arise from one's sheer bodily presence within the boundaries of a nation-state, one's decision not to travel out of that country that has come to be known by the label "tacit consent through residence," a phrase Locke uses in section 119 of the *Second Treatise of Government* and an idea that recurs in "A Review and Conclusion" of Hobbes's *Leviathan*, and Book IV, Chapter 2 of Rousseau's *Social Contract*.[47]

When our attention shifts from the "prevention of injury" to "physical motion," we have not strayed from the individual's right of self-defense, or from her responsibility for keeping herself alive; we have instead shifted from desired outcome (peace, absence of injury) to the active means of achieving that outcome (liberty). It has been observed that in social contract theory, the legacy of Hobbes is "Peace" and the legacy of Locke is "Liberty." As Robert Faulkner writes, "Locke ... combines Hobbes's universally effective protector of peace with the requirement of a universal political liberty. *Pax ac Libertas*, Locke once wrote as a motto in his *Two Treatises*."[48] Another way to understand this shift from injury to motion is as a transition from what is absent to what is present, from the prohibitive and privative (what we cannot do: injure others) to the enlarged sphere of action this newly acquired immunity from injury confers on us. As we saw many times throughout Chapters 3 and 4, the social contract is a brake on injuring; it is *not* a brake on making love (unless injury is entailed), reading books (unless injury is entailed), making money (unless injury is entailed), or making a journey (unless injury is entailed). It is designed to minimize the fragility and simultaneously to magnify the powers of human sentience.

The phenomenon of consent through residence (like consent in the earlier medical context) makes it clear that what is at stake is not an unanchored notion of autonomy but autonomy as grounded in the human body. In medical contexts the body was *first*, the thing protected by powers of consent; *second*, the lever across which the ground of self-authorization is brought into being. These two are certainly present in the arena of political philosophy, but now a *third* dimension of the body is present as well; it becomes the locus of the act of consent itself. That is, it becomes the site of the performative act. We acquire a clear view of this feature by first looking at the inseparability of physical motion and volition (quite independent of a person's relation to the nation), and then by focusing more narrowly on physical motion and consent (the specific volitional act of choosing to reside within a specific community).

Even in contexts where social contracts and political obligations are not immediately at issue, the attempt to discuss "liberty" or "will" or "volition" seems always to require the image of unimpeded or impeded physical movement. Complaining (unfairly) that "no writer has explained what *liberty* and *servitude* are," Hobbes in *On the Citizen* proceeds at once to do so:

> LIBERTY (to define it) is simply the *absence of obstacles to motion*; as water contained in a vessel is not *free*, because the vessel is an obstacle to its flowing away, and it is *freed* by breaking the vessel. Every man has more or less *liberty* as he has more or less space in which to move; so that a man kept in a large jail has more *liberty* than a man kept in a small jail.[49]

In his famous arguments with Bishop Bramhall, Hobbes again insists that liberty is freedom to perform physical motions and that constraints on liberty are impediments imposed from without ("the water is said to descend freely, or to have liberty to descend by the Chanell of the River, because there is no impediment that way, but not across, because the banks are impediments").[50] We say that something or someone is deprived of liberty if the constraints are imposed from the outside (as when the river is deprived of lateral motion by the riverbanks) but not, says Hobbes, if the constraint arises from within (as when the water cannot ascend a hill or when a person who is sick cannot walk). Other philosophers include both external and internal impediments to motion as constraints on liberty; but the key point here is how inseparable liberty and motion are, despite otherwise important variations in definition. For Hobbes, "Life it selfe is but Motion."[51]

Locke shares this identification of freedom with physical motion.

In his account of volition and the will in *An Essay Concerning Understanding*, he writes:

> If Freedom can with any propriety of Speech be applied to Power, it may be attributed to the Power, that is in a Man, to produce, or forbear producing Motion in parts of his Body, by choice or preference; which is that which denominates him free, and is Freedom it self.[52]

So yoked together are motion and liberty that when Locke wishes to describe the absence of liberty, he must do so using instances of motion in which freedom plays no part: a tennis ball struck by a racket, a man falling when a bridge collapses beneath him, a person whose arm convulsively strikes a friend, a man carried while asleep into a room where he is locked with a friend he is glad to see.[53]

It might be argued that Hobbes and Locke are, whenever speaking about volition, just a hair's breadth away from speaking about consent; and so before turning explicitly to consent and its definition within political philosophy, we should briefly contemplate the description of volition decoupled from that context. The connection between volition and physical motion has been affirmed by philosophers from the first to the twenty-first century. John Searle's essay on "The Freedom of the Will" is an instance. Searle throughout contemplates freedom in terms of mental and psychological attributes, "choices, decisions, reasonings, and cogitations" as they impinge on "our actual behavior."[54] Yet the examples he invokes to illustrate how we distinguish human wills from determined phenomena are always framed in terms of physical movement. He writes, "If somebody predicts that I am going to do something, I might just damn well do something else. Now, that sort of option is simply not open to glaciers moving down mountainsides or balls rolling down inclined planes or the planets moving in their elliptical orbits."[55] The essay then proceeds through images of motion and arrested motion, molecules swerving from their paths, persons moving at gunpoint across the floor.[56]

This is not to say that in the history of writing about the will—from the Greeks down through Augustine, Schopenhauer, Nietzsche, to Arendt—the will has never been spoken about outside the idiom of physical motion. But it is almost to say that. Discussions of freedom are almost invariably couched in terms of physical movement, and this linguistic couching seems to reflect the phenomenon it seeks to describe: the will itself is couched in embodiment. Movement locates, rather than merely illustrates, the will. Thus Gilbert Ryle, impatient with what he calls "the tangle of largely spurious problems, known as the problem of the Freedom of the Will," argues that the "prime function of volitions, the task for the performance of which they were postulated, is to originate bodily movements."[57] Volitions, he says, are talked about as special acts in the mind "by means of which a mind gets its ideas translated into facts."[58] William James's whole chapter on the will in *The Principles of Psychology* proceeds through an analysis of physical movement: "The only ends which follow *immediately* upon our willing seem to be movement of our own bodies."[59] For Augustine, in the *City of God*, the will is present not only in acts of walking or lifting one's arms, but in the exercise of mouth, face, ears, breath, voice;[60] and moving still further back in time, Epictetus accounts for his Freedom with the simple declaration, "I go where I please, I come whence I please."[61]

That passage from Epictetus was quoted by Maurice Cranston—biographer of Locke, translator of Rousseau—in his address to an international convention on the right of exit that gathered in Sweden in the early 1970s and that compiled a map of the actual passport and exit laws along the borders of twenty-five countries: what it was like to be a woman attempting to pass out of Switzerland without her husband's permission,[62] or to be a person with an alcohol problem trying to leave Denmark. Cranston, after invoking Epictetus, says that the Greek word, "eleutheria, in its etymology meant 'to go where one wills'"[63] and he goes on to claim, somewhat more controversially, that the Roman word for freedom, "libertas," also originates in freedom of movement.[64]

Cranston invokes these etymologies to put forward the claim that "there are grounds for considering the right to freedom of movement as the first and most fundamental of man's liberties."[65] In other words, he comes close to the language used by U.S. medical case law in identifying the right that underlies all other rights. It may seem as though this clause—the right that underlies all other rights—is coming to have a promiscuous sound, and indeed there is a temptation, whenever one is examining any one right, to see all others following from it. But while the two contexts seem very different—one entailing movement in and out of one's country, the other immobilization under anesthesia—in fact what is being honored in both instances is one's capacity to dispose of one's body as one wishes, turning it over into the hands of a physician, carrying it outside the state, holding it within the state, and so forth.

When one shifts from the broad notion of liberty and freedom to the narrower notion of consent, then, the grounding in movement—specifically movement inside or outside one's own country—becomes even more palpably physical. This is strikingly the case in the classic articulation of "tacit consent through residence," Socrates's statements on political obligation in Plato's *Crito*, a text that bears the same relation to consent within political philosophy that *Schloendorff v. Society of New York Hospital* bears to consent within medicine. At the dawn of the day before Socrates' execution, offered by comrades the chance of escape from Athens, in (in other words) a situation of high emergency, Socrates outlines the reasons why he cannot leave, why he is obligated to obey Athenian law even when mistakenly applied: he is obligated because he has in a daily and ongoing way consented to the construction of the state.

Socrates gives multiple grounds for consent, multiple paths by which he has consented. He does so not in his own person but by an act of *ventriloquism* in which the Athenian laws and Athenian Constitution, as though animated objects, begin to speak, explaining, talking, pressuring, saying: Socrates, you of all men have consented to this state, you of all men have, in receiving its benefits (of life, parenting, and education), understood the reciprocity of loyalty entailed, you of all men have considered and, despite complaints, credited its justness, and you of all men cannot duck *out* from under its laws even if falsely judged in a trial.[66] Plato's animation of the inanimate reappears in many of his dialogues, but this is a particularly beautiful instance because it makes it clear that through one's consent, one generates a political obligation, and through that obligation the state and its laws come into being. Consent *is* an act of ventriloquism, an apparently mute disposition of the body that becomes a throwing of the voice into the political realm.[67]

The refusal physically to exit from the country over a seventy-year lifetime is the major ground of consent. Thus Socrates tells Crito (still speaking through the laws): you know, Crito, with the exception of military service, I've never left this city, never crossed the borders for "a festival or for any other purpose," never "traveled abroad as other people do," "never felt the impulse to acquaint [myself] with another country or constitution"—despite the fact that Sparta and Crete were "favorite models of good government."[68] This is a breathtaking moment because suddenly the image of Socrates walking by the stream in *Phaedrus* and through the other dialogues, rushes in and one understands that what he was doing, meandering, walking, *patrolling the borders*, was nothing less than *generating a state*. His presence within the borders has been uniform and total: You could not, the laws tell him, have absented yourself less had you been "lame or blind or decrepit in some other way."[69] Though only one of several grounds of manifest consent, his act of residing is without question the most vivid, not only because it is what he has done over the last seventy years, but because, now in his final hours, the decision to stay or to leave once again confronts him for the duration of the dialogue. The escape Crito has devised *is* itself the act of exiting from the city, and as through residence one makes the state, so through departure one withdraws consent and unmakes the state. The constitution and laws speak:

Now, Socrates, what are you proposing to do? Can you deny that by this act which you are contemplating you intend, so far as you have the power, to destroy us, the laws, and the whole state as well? Do you imagine that a city can continue to exist and not be turned upside down, if the legal judgments which are pronounced in it have no force but are nullified and destroyed by private persons?[70]

Thus the past performative act is placed before him one more time: the subject of this dialogue *is* physical exit; the drama of the dialogue *is* the act of residing.

Plato's *Crito* tends to be invoked in discussions of tacit consent through residence, in part because the form of the argument, dramatic dialogue, makes more palpable the fact of embodiment. The urgency is heightened by the approach of the state galley on its return from its mission to Delos, a mission that has delayed Socrates' execution. The fact that the execution cannot take place during the absence of the mission displays the immobilization of the state that occurs when its citizens are outside the borders. It loses its own executive powers. Only with the ingathering of its citizens (the return of the mission) can it reconstitute itself and regain its powers to act.

But while most concrete in Plato, certainly the physical location of that generative act is recognizable even in the more abstract argumentation of Hobbes, Locke, or Rousseau. If "tacit consent through residence" has a single doctrinal location, it is a solitary sentence by Locke in section 119 of the *Second Treatise of Government*. Here Locke uses a triptych of verbs followed by a fourth which asserts the fact of residing. One's possession of the state takes various forms, "whether this his possession be of land, to him and his heirs for ever, or a lodging only for a week; or whether it be barely traveling freely on the highway; and in effect, it reaches as far as the very being of any one within the territories of that government."[71] In other words, he moves in this series from owning, to renting, to traveling on the highway, in order to get to the universal state of residing. As Locke moves across the three, the depth of the citizen's investment in, or literal connectedness to, the ground of the polis is growing progressively more shallow: as owner, the citizen is anchored to the earth; as lodger, he merely occupies that ground for a week (and thus though temporarily fixed is also detachable); and by the third term, the citizen (no longer rooted in or even temporarily attached to the earth) is now so free of the ground that he has become mobile and moves down the highway. But this steady diminution of rootedness, this more and more minimal investment, at the same time entails a steady increase in activeness and hence in the overtly displayed agency of the will. This leads to Locke's climactic landing on the fourth, and wholly passive, term of residence.

Rousseau, too, locates the performative act of consent in the physically manifest actions of moving or refraining from moving. Although his commitment to tacit consent through residence is most explicit in the fourth book of the *Social Contract*—"After the state is instituted, residence implies consent: to inhabit the territory is to submit to the sovereign"[72]—it shapes earlier books as well. Book 3, for example, ends climactically with his invocation of Grotius, and the right of every citizen (whether alone or collectively) to withdraw from the state and "renounce" membership.[73] That same book opens with a passage grounding consent in physical movement: "Every free action has two causes which concur to produce it, one moral—the will which determines the act, the other physical—the strength which executes it. When I walk towards an object, it is necessary first that I should resolve to go that way and secondly that my feet should carry me. When a paralytic resolves to run and when a fit man resolves not to move, both stay where they are."[74] As though envisioning the continual drift of populations across countries or national boundaries, Rousseau measures the scale of populations against the physical expanse of the territories they inhabit.[75] This habit of picturing person against physical ground is perhaps most eloquently summarized in his original title page: "*The Social*

Contract or Principles of Political Right by J.-J. Rousseau, Citizen of Geneva.—foederis aequas / Dicamus leges (Aeneid, XI)."[76] Significantly, Rousseau at the age of fifteen had inscribed his name in the same way— "Jean-Jacques Rousseau, citoyen de Genève, 1727"—in a country gate,[77] thus directly locating it not only in the physical terrain but in a portal of entry and exit.

Plato, as we saw, not only made the capacity for choosing between residence or departure the central subject matter of the *Crito* but built it into the formal structure of the dialogue since the central drama is Socrates' decision about whether to escape the city-state or remain in Athens awaiting execution. Though Hobbes, Locke, and Rousseau are less concrete and pictorial, they each aspire to make the right of exit a formal feature of their account. Hobbes ends Chapter 7 of *On the Citizen* with a discussion of the ways we may be released from the sovereign power of the commonwealth, one of which is by exercising the right of exit to go live abroad:

> This can happen in two ways: either by permission, as when one gets leave and voluntarily departs to live elsewhere, or by command, as an *Exile*. In both cases he will be free of the laws of his former commonwealth, because he is now bound by the laws of his new country.[78]

Crucially, this comes as the final sentence, right when we are exiting the chapter entitled "Three Kinds of Commonwealth." By presenting alternative kinds of commonwealth, the chapter reminds us that we have exercised consent over the commonwealth we have chosen; and Hobbes invites us, at the very moment we are exiting that chapter, to imagine exiting from a given state. Form reenacts content, as we saw it do in Rousseau, where the reader exits Book 3 with Grotius's climactic announcement on right of exit.

But the philosopher who comes close to Plato in building right of exit into the formal features of his treatise is John Locke. Indeed, it could be argued that the inexplicably large impact of the

Second Treatise of Government—its influence not just as an idea but as an inspiration for designing an actual social contract, the American Constitution—should be attributed in part to the brilliance of its form. In the very first sentence of the *Second Treatise* Locke makes what appears to be a self-disparaging joke:

> Reader, thou hast here the beginning and end of a discourse concerning government; what fate has otherwise disposed of the papers that should have filled up the middle, and were more than all the rest, it is not worth while to tell thee.[79]

Reader, Locke seems to say, I am giving you the door of entry and the door of exit, there is no middle ground. In fact, when we look at the form of the *Second Treatise* it gradually becomes clear that this portal of entry and exit is the essence of the social contract: Reader, I am giving you the door of entry and the door of exit because that is what a social contract is.

This principle, announced in the opening sentence of the preface, everywhere shapes the form of the *Second Treatise*. Even before we get to the preface, the page facing the title page tells us the treatise is "AN ESSAY CONCERNING THE TRUE ORIGINAL EXTENT AND END OF CIVIL GOVERNMENT." Apparently, origins and ends will be our only concerns. By such terms, Locke of course refers to the teleological meaning of origin and end, and he tells us many times throughout the *Treatise* that the two are identical. The beginning is peace; the end is peace. Political societies are brought into being by a voluntary act of the original compact[80] for "peaceable living,"[81] they are "peaceful beginnings,"[82] they are "begun in peace."[83] So, too, are the ends of society. "The great end of men's entering into society ... peace and safety,"[84] he writes; and elsewhere, "the end of government being the good of the community,"[85] "safety, ease, and plenty,"[86] "The end of government is the good of mankind."[87] While, then, origin and end mean peace, they also mean portal, entry and exit. Locke's final chapter is appropriately entitled "Of the Dissolution of Government"; but even more telling is the fact that at almost the midpoint of the work—what should be the middle pages—he positions side by side two chapters, "Of the Beginning of Political Societies" (Chapter 8) and "Of the Ends of Political Society and Government" (Chapter 9), once again affirming that consent simply IS the capacity to enter and to exit: the middle ground has disappeared. We can say Locke simply ignores—or according to his own description, has lost—the middle ground. Or we can say more accurately, logically speaking, a contractual state has no middle ground. The social contract is like a doorway on rails that slides into reach no matter where one is in the book or where one stands in one's own country, because (as we know from section 119) one is always traveling freely on a highway.

Locke likes minimums. Whenever he reminds us that the social contract comes into being by the voluntary act of "agreeing to unite," we encounter reminders such as "This is all that it is," "This is nothing but," "That only could give beginning." In a single paragraph of Chapter 8, he repeats the "This and this only" structure three times:

> And this is done by barely agreeing to *unite into one political soci-*
> *ety*, which is *all the compact* that is, or needs be. . . . And thus that,
> which begins and actually *constitutes any political society*, is noth-
> ing but the consent of any number of freemen capable of a major-
> ity to unite and incorporate into such a society. And this is that,
> and that only, which did, or could give beginning to any *lawful*
> *government* in the world.[88]

But what about the rest of the *Second Treatise*? Is Locke exaggerating when he says there are no middle pages?

In fact, the mental act of exiting from and reentering the social contract is required of us on almost every page of the *Second Treatise*. We can comprehend the form of the work if we picture the social contract as the ground inside a circle:

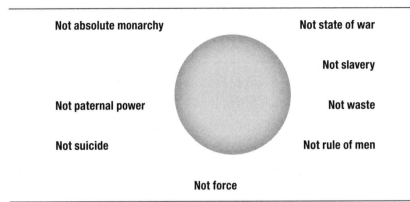

Not absolute monarchy   Not state of war

Not slavery

Not paternal power   Not waste

Not suicide   Not rule of men

Not force

Outside the social contract lie all the things that the social contract IS NOT, and from which it must distinguish itself. Thoughout the treatise, we contininually progress through a series of these NOT-constructions. The social contract is *not* patriarchy. It is *not* a rule of men. It is *not* absolute monarchy. It is *not* force. It is *not* slavery. It is *not* waste. It is *not* suicide. These are not epigrammatic statements; in most case an entire chapter is devoted to the "not"[89] and sometimes much more, as in the instance of paternal power whose ejection from the inner circle occurs at many places in the treatise.[90] Each time we encounter Locke's argument about one of these not-constructions, we mentally exit from, and then reenter the contractual circle. Mentally, we must keep crossing and recrossing the threshold until it becomes a membrane as flexuous as our own breath. The work—rather than simply abstractly instructing the reader—actually instills in us the mental habit of consent by making us deeply conversant with the practice of exit and entry. In effect, the *Second Treatise of Government* is all membrane.

Again, the relation between consent in medical contexts and consent in political philosophy makes visible their common ground: the human body. Injury, overtly the issue in medicine, is also overtly at issue in the social contract, all the contractarians conceiving of the state as brought into being to prohibit or diminish injury. So, too, the "trigger" notion of *touch* in medicine reappears in political philosophy. In early European courts and parliaments, as we saw in Chapter 4, the

Roman principle *quod omnes tangit*—"that which touches all must be approved by all"—determined the structure of the summons that in turn determined who was required to be present, in residence, during the court or counsel proceeding. From its original appearance as a Justinian maxim, *quod omnes tangit* developed in the West into a major constitutional principle of representation, consent, and due process.[91] Just as the phenomena of physical injury and touch, immediately visible in medicine, are equally recognizable in political philosophy, so conversely the phenomenon of residence, articulated in vivid intricacy only in political philosophy, can be observed with ease in medicine. It is visible, for example, in the right of exit in the Nuremberg principles guaranteeing that anyone participating in a medical experiment may choose to leave the experiment at any time. It appears again in procedures for establishing residency among new physicians,[92] and again in the use of "community standards" and "locality rules" in litigation about medicine.[93]

The two phenomena—the susceptibility to injury, the capacity for willed movement—are two among hundreds of facts about the body. But it seems true to say that these are not simply any two, but a complementary framing pair, and in this sense fundamental. What is at stake in the medical operation or injury is the issue of touch but also the entry into the inside of the body, whereas the issue of political departure turns this inside out: it is the ability to place the body itself inside a particular world or to carry it outward. In each instance there is a pronounced physical boundary that in the first case cannot be crossed without consent and in the second case the crossing of which constitutes consent. Thus there is an extreme heightening of the categories of inside and outside as they occur in sentience. Though in each instance one is only disposing of a relatively tiny piece of matter—one's own body—in fact by having absolute authority over what can touch, or pass across, the boundaries of one's own person, and, conversely, to be able to exercise authority over the world space in which one places or displaces oneself, one has just gained absolute authority vis-à-vis the rest of the world.

Locke and Rousseau would surely recognize the kinship between the boundaries of nation-state and body in the consentual relation of medicine or (anticipating the subject toward which we soon turn) marriage. We already saw in the medical section of this chapter Locke's extreme respect for the boundaries of a patient's body in his touchgently design for a truss and again in the extreme delicacy of his instructions for dressing burns. It is also not accidental that, as Lawrence Stone observes, "John Locke seems to have been the first to protest vigorously against the encasing of young bodies in tight corsets reinforced with metal and whalebone," a practice that Rousseau in *Emile* protests on both "aesthetic" and "biological" grounds;[94] similarly, both Locke and Rousseau opposed the "swaddling" of infants that originated in Roman times;[95] and one of Locke's most insistent metaphors in the *Second Treatise*, that of the fence, is used as a marker of both bodily and nation-state boundaries.[96]

But the discrepancy between the scale of the boundaries of the body and the boundaries of the nation-state—in other words the discrepancy between the very modesty of one's powers of authorization and the largesse of the asserted outcome—is related to a second general attribute connecting the two portraits of consent in medicine and political philosophy, the mystification of the active and passive. The surgeon's obligation to secure our consent in an operation leads us down a path where resonant concepts like sovereignty, citizenship, and rights emerge forth, an affirmation of the sanctity of personhood, of the *robustness* of the sanctity of personhood; yet, as we saw earlier, this is occurring at a time when the ground of personhood is most in jeopardy, most *fragile*, most passive—so passive that the person may be ill (with the cognitive and perceptual disturbances often entailed in illness), or asleep, or anesthetized, or even dead.

This disruption of the ordinary categories of active and passive is almost equally descriptive of the social contract: it involves those who are governed and those who govern. As Rousseau himself notes, the social contract (between "the people and the magistrates it sets over itself") seems, according to some theorists, to be "a contract which stipulates between the two parties the conditions under which the one undertakes to command and the other to obey. It will be admitted, I am sure, that this is a strange way of contracting."[97] In general, the whole notion of consent stands the distinction between passive and active on its head, since consent theory claims that it is by the will of the apparently passive that the active is brought into being.

If the distance between governors and governed itself entails extremes of the passive and active, the locating of the universal ground of consent in "tacit consent through residence" circles us back and plunges us into a deeper extreme of passivity. We are initially presented with a problem: here are the governed, subjected to laws; by what route have they been subjugated? We are then presented with a solution: they are not subjugated to the laws; they have willed those laws; they have brought that state into being; they have generated it. This quiets our alarm about subordination, but a moment later inspires a second occasion of bafflement: And now *how* exactly did they do that? To which we are given the answer: By staying still. In other words, we (by means of the construct of consent) mentally loop our way out of the passive only to find ourselves, seconds later, more deeply entrenched in what at least *appears* to be the wholly inert state of not moving. Even the etymology of *residence* underscores this: *re-sedere*; that which sits or stays, that which is left behind, that which resides, a residue.

Despite the palpability of physical movement in Plato, Locke, and Rousseau, one never feels completely confident that residing, refraining from movement, *is* a performative act. Rousseau worries that unanimity in a population can indicate either an extreme of will or, alternatively, an utter collapse of the will, a "lapse into servitude"[98] and the same can be said of residence: it may represent a majestic display of free will or a complete immobilization and the anesthetization that implies. When the laws speak to Socrates, they tell him that if he had been "lame, blind, or decrepit in some other way" he could not have been "less absent" from the city-state—a statement meant as a great tribute, for it is at this point that they tell him he "stands out above" all other Athenians in his "affection for this city and us its laws"; yet simultaneously in its compounding of negatives ("could not have been less absent") it seems a precarious acknowledgment of the inextricability of disability and ability in political matters. These same ambiguities are audible in Rousseau's conflation of what would usually be understood as disability and ability: "When a paralytic resolves to run and when a fit man resolves not to move, both stay where they are."[99]

A puzzling dimension of consent, then, is the peculiar place of the active and the passive. Three explanations of that mystification seem plausible.

One way of interpreting the paradox is to worry that there is something fraudulent about the whole notion of consent.[100] If it seems to assert and celebrate sovereignty of personhood, and the continuation of the will, at the very moment of that will's being anesthetized and subject to the talents of another's hand, then one might think this consent is fictitious, unreal, even though we might allow it to be generously motivated. Though we are subjugated to governors, though we are anesthetized and subject to someone else's hand, we tell one another narratives about our sovereignty, how it is the will of the anesthetized patient that guides the hand of the surgeon, how it is the residence of the citizen within the state that brings that state into being. We recite these narratives, as though they were the placating poems of Plato, and Locke, and Rousseau.

A second way of interpreting the paradox is close to the first except that instead of understanding fiction to mean unreal or fraudulent or a lie, fiction is taken in its familiar and positive sense: consent becomes, by this path of comprehension, an exercise of the artifactual response at a moment when the will is in danger of being impaired. That is, an actual re-creation of one's own relation to one's external circumstances comes about. The artifactual holds within it the voluntaristic, and thus the generation of the artifact by those in a position of passivity at a moment of great polarization from the active (the surgeon; the governors) equalizes the relation. This interpretation is the one I believe to be most accurate: it entails understanding consent as a redistributive site where inequalities are transformed into equalities, and vice versa.

The evidence for this second interpretation is provided by many of the writers just encountered. Augustine's description of the bond between the will and bodily motion, for example, leads him to celebrate our inherent artistry: observing the ease with which we move our hands and feet at will, he in the next breath describes the seemingly supernatural feat visible in the hands of craftsmen in whom "natural powers which lack strength and speed are developed by active training."[101] He marvels at the way we effortlessly introduce motion into our vocal chords and lungs, and says we make of our bodies a musical instrument: as "bellows serve the purpose of smiths and of organists, the lungs are obedient to the will of a man when he breathes out or breathes in, or speaks or shouts or sings."[102] Delighting in the volitional gift that enables some individuals to wiggle their ears ("either one at a time or both together"), or move the scalp down to the forehead and back again, or perfectly imitate a bird's call, Augustine presents the human being as a magician of disappearing and reappearing toys: "Some can swallow an incredible number of various articles and then with a slight contraction of the diaphragm, can produce, as if out of a bag, any article they please, in perfect condition."[103] The theologian Nicolas of Cusa, the poet John Donne, and the painter Leonardo da Vinci, each picture the brilliant "toys" of civilization (a pair of drawing compasses, a book, a bell) inside the body, a mental reflex that expresses the idea that the human will can revise—or re-create—even the inside of the body (an achievement we today take for granted).[104]

When we move from volition to consent—from the will in general to the specific will to belong to a human community of one's own choosing—the intuitions about the alliance of consent with creation become more emphatic. We saw, in the description of Plato's *Crito*, that Socrates' act of physical residence is presented as an act of ventriloquism, a transformation of bodily motion into the city's laws, a throwing of one's voice into the public sphere. Socrates explicitly reminds us that the laws are the result of human artistry, for he ends by saying, "That, my dear friend Crito, I do assure you, is what I seem to hear them [the laws] saying, just as a mystic seems to hear the strains of music and the sound of their arguments rings so loudly in my head that I cannot hear the other side." [105]

The social contract theorists of the seventeenth and eighteenth centuries may not explicitly liken consent to the composition of music. But they certainly conceive of the social contract as an invention whose sole purpose is to reinvent us. Hobbes (as we saw in Chapter 4) starkly contrasts life outside the social contract ("solitary, poore, nasty, brutish, and short") with life inside the social contract, graced with geography, navigation, transportation, "commodious [b]uilding," arts, letters, society. [106] Rousseau, too, conceives of the social contract as a created object designed to re-create us: "it produces a remarkable change in man." Across the artifactual lever of the social contract, a being whose conduct is guided by "instinct" is transformed into a being whose conduct is guided by "justice." "Physical impulse" is transformed into "duty," "desire" is transformed into "right," and "inclination" into "reason." "[A] narrow, stupid animal" becomes "a creature of intelligence" whose mind is "enlarged," whose sentiments are "ennobled," and whose spirit is "elevated." Possession by force is now constrained by the legal right of property. Formerly subject to the "slavery" of his appetites, each person now acquires "moral freedom." [107]

Rousseau has dedicated the eighth chapter of the first book exclusively to this enumeration of the ways persons are re-created, holding back the single most important transformation for the end of Chapter 9 and the close of the first book:

I shall end this chapter—and Book I—with an observation which might serve as a basis for the whole social system: namely, that the social pact, far from destroying natural equality, substitutes, on the contrary, a moral and lawful equality for whatever physical inequality that nature may have imposed on mankind; so that however unequal in strength and intelligence, men become equal by covenant and by right.[108]

This is close to, but not identical with, Hobbes's account of equality: either we all are originally equal (and I for one, says Hobbes, believe this is the case) or we must at every moment act "as though" we were, for the first premise of the social contract is our shared equality and without this principle, the social contract cannot survive for more than a few minutes. Here we see the benign shift from the first interpretation (social contract as untruth) to the second (social contract as artifact that redesigns us): whether or not equality exists in the state of nature, we shall will it into actuality when we create the social contract. Hobbes has simply carried the artifactual act further than Rousseau, retroactively locating it—with only the smallest waver of equivocation—in our original state.

These first two readings assume that human action can be understood as occurring along a spectrum that goes from passive to active. Each of the two explains consent as that crossover point from the passive to the active (the precise moment where the less and less passive suddenly becomes the active). The first reading simply says that what catapults you from the passive to the active is a lie: the civilization invents a construct of consent and asserts that, all appearances to the contrary, you are authorizing every incision the surgeon makes, or all appearances to the contrary, you are bringing the state into being just by being there. The second says an actual artifact is invented, given a shape and material form that enables you to get from one to the other: the consent form can be understood as an actual direction to the surgeon for his or her acts, just as going to the physician originates the instruction to "heal me"; and by the alternatives of consent and revolution, we do not just pretend to make governments; we make and unmake them.

But a third reading would say that active and passive are so mystified in consent that the phenomenon of consent actually calls into question the reality or usefulness of the categories of passive and active.[109]
Each time "consent" emerges, it is an alarm bell saying something is
wrong with these categories; they do not refer to anything that actually exists. Or alternatively, it may be that consent itself acts to explode,
or at least disturb, those categories; and this disturbance of categories
might be seen as one of its negative or instead one of its most attractive features. If feminist discourse often critiques consent, feminist
discourse as a whole can itself be understood as deeply centered in the
phenomenon of consent.[110] One of the features of consent that makes
it so potentially resonant for feminist theory is this disruption of the
categories of passive and active. The mystification of active and passive in consent may originate from the mystification of the active and
passive in the body. If it is the case that consent is a redistributive site,
then it is also appropriate that consent entails an immersion in the
body where active and passive are already profoundly confounded.[111]
One is forced to discard old patterns of active and passive and emerge
with a new set in hand.

As is audible in this sequence, though the three represent alternative explanations for the phenomenon of consent, it may be that each is
an extension of the others: the covering narrative (interpretation one)
is the prelude for an actual instantiation of that narrative in the world
(interpretation two), and this in part comes about not merely by shifting what was in the sphere of the passive into the sphere of the active
but by disrupting the categories themselves (interpretation three). This
disruption and redistribution turn on the assertion of bodily continuity between the active and the passive persons, now made partners in
a shared work.

This claim about the interior continuity of bodies emerges more
fully in the third portrait—marriage. It is in the sphere of marriage that
we are most likely to be struck by the etymology of con-sentir, and the
continuity of "sentience-across-persons" the word implies. It is also in

the sphere of marriage that we can most quickly recognize the intimacy between "consent" and "creation."

PORTRAIT 3: DESIRE

Marriage is a reciprocal act[112] of consent, a contract, but a contract that has very little specified content. It lacks the particularized elaboration of intricate agreements that many other forms of contract have.[113] This lack of specific content makes it difficult to determine when its terms have been violated and the contract is dissolved; it is for this reason that the dissolution of marriage requires the special procedures of divorce or annulment.[114] In its minimalness, the marriage contract recalls the political contract: we saw in the previous section Locke's repeated reliance on a "this and this only" structure—"and this is done by agreeing to *unite into the political society,* which is *all the compact that is.*"[115] While marriage has minimal content, that minimal content, by its very minimalness, underscores the material grounding of the volitional act.

Consent is not simply an aspect of marriage or a requirement of marriage. It *is* the marriage. The shared exchange of vows is a ritualized performance of reciprocal consent. As in the earlier medical and political contexts, consent is here inseparable from the physical body; but now it is the act of lovemaking or procreation, the body in its generative capacity, that is its special province rather than the body in its susceptibility to injury or in its willed options of departure and residence. The canon law description of the matrimonial consent has two sections. First: "Marriage is constituted by the duly manifested consent of persons juridically able to marry; which consent can not be supplied by any human power." And second, "The marriage consent is an act of the will by which each party gives and accepts a perpetual and exclusive right over the body for the exercise of acts suitable of themselves for the procreation of children.[116] As the meaning of these two gets unfolded in the commentary, the sovereignty over that small piece of terrain that was visible in the political and medical becomes once more visible. The clause stating that the consent cannot be supplied by any other human power was elaborated by Pius VI, in 1789: "It can not be supplied by paternal authority or by the supreme authority of the Church or of the State; for it belongs exclusively to the bride and bridegroom to transfer to each other ownership of their bodies";[117] and quoting further, "The marriage consent is an act of the [free] will with a definite, specific object" and that object is the body; or, as another commentator writes: "The essential object of the consent is a right over each other's body with a view to certain specific acts."[118] Marriage *is* the reciprocal transfer of rights of the body to the other person. That is what one stands witness to at the wedding.

The transfer of rights over the body, audible in the language of the legal rule, has during many periods been explicit in the language of the marriage vow itself as it often continues to be today: ["A]nd so I join thee in faith to my body, that I may bring thee faithfully and loyally to my body," say the words of the French vow from the city of Barbeau in the 1100s,[119] in the marriage vow of Combrai from the 1300s,[120] the man and the woman each say, "[W]ith my body I thee honor . . . in faithful fellowship and companionship"; and in Avignon in 1300 the man says, "I give to thee my body as spouse and husband" and the woman says, "I give to thee my body as wife."[121] The transfer of bodily rights to the beloved in the Protestant religions is, though less explicit, still audible, as in the primacy of the word "desire" in the highly simplified Lutheran vow originating in 1542,[122] and in the phrase from the 1549 Anglican vow that carries forward the resonant Medieval and Renaissance Catholic wording into many later Protestant denominations: the words "have her and hold her" consented to by the man, and the words "have him and hold him" consented to by the woman become the simplified single phrase spoken identically by man and woman, "to have and to hold."[123]

As the early pronouns make clear, the word *hold* in the phrase *to have and to hold* means to physically embrace and "to have" means "to have sexually." Joel Foote Bingham's commentary on the phrase at first makes it sound as though it is a general legal phrase for validating a claim, but he then, in citing *Corinthians* 7:4 makes clear the physical referent: "*To have and to hold.* This is the so-called phrase of Habendum et Tenendum, which . . . is the firmest and most solemn formula known to our language for delivering and assuming possession of one's claims. By this solemn formula, the Man and Woman put themselves into the power and possession of each other. So that, henceforth, in the words of the Apostle, 'the wife hath not power of her own body, but the husband, likewise the husband hath not power of his own body, but the wife'"[124] The two people promise a lifetime of faithful partnership that goes beyond decisions about lovemaking, for the vows promise "to love and to cherish" (in the Anglican phrasing) and are made "in tenderness" (as the Presbyterian vow registers) and in "friendship" (as the majestically simple Quaker vow states).[125] But bodily care and protection are primary, as the widespread inclusion of the phrase "in sickness and in health" indicates; and some versions of the marriage vow state openly that henceforth the only sexual intimacies that will take place are those consented to by one's mate.[126] In fact, so entwined are the consent and the body that, as Bernard Andrew Siegle writes, the energy of formal church argument was expended trying to answer the question of whether the couple are married immediately after the moment of speaking the vows or instead immediately after the bodily consummation:

> Historically a great debate existed in the Church on what was the essential factor constituting a marriage. The Canon Law School in Bologna [under Gratian] maintained that *consummation* was this factor; this made the marriage. While the School of Paris at the time [under Peter Lombard], maintained it was *consent* which made the marriage valid. Eventually this debate was settled when Pope Alexander III in the twelfth century], using tradition as his basis, stated that *consent was* the essential factor that made the marriage valid.[127]

This phrasing of the solution makes it appear that one can arrive at an either-or decision, thus suggesting the separability of the two, yet subsequent Church commentaries reimport qualifications that at once reestablish the difficulty of decoupling them: "Thus mutual consent is sufficient to constitute marriage in its essence; consummation adds an accidental perfection and more absolute indissolubility."[128]

Although sexual consummation (or contact with the interior of the body) does not usually take place inside the liturgical rite of marriage itself, it often occurs in close proximity to the marriage vows, perhaps most strikingly in the Jewish "Yichud," the brief period between the wedding and the wedding feast when the pair are secluded from the guests for the explicit purpose of actual or nominal consummation.[129] In medieval Christian weddings, the decorating and blessing of the marital bed was part of the celebration, and a special church service welcomed the married couple back into the assembly after consummation.[130] Perhaps more relevant is the fact that while sexual lovemaking does not take place at the same moment as the speaking of vows, bodily intimacy does. The right hands of the couple are joined in the 1542 Lutheran liturgy.[131] In the Anglican ceremony of 1549 (as well as in the many Protestant variants descended from it) the woman's hand is enclosed inside the man's hand while he speaks his vow; for the space of a breath their hands separate; the woman then encloses the man's hand in hers as she speaks her vow.[132] A Quaker marriage comes about during a weekday meeting when a pair stand up, take one another's hand, and promise to be faithful.[133]

The "solemnization" of body for body that in the church ceremony is carried out by the enclosing of hands is accomplished in the civil ceremony by the kiss.[134] The kiss of the couple toward the end of the religious ceremony celebrates their marriage state but does not itself bring that state into being. In the secular rite, in contrast, it is the kiss in combination with the spoken consent that creates the marriage.[135]

As the kiss of the civil ceremony reminds us, the framing description of marriage as consisting essentially of an act of consent by which there occurs the transfer of rights of the body to the other person is not confined to the religious imagination but surfaces in more secular contexts. Thus Locke in the *Second Treatise*, says, "*Conjugal society is made by a voluntary compact between man and woman, [which] consist[s] chiefly in such a communion and right in one another's bodies as is necessary to its chief end, procreation.*"[136] Kant in the *Metaphysics of Morals*, while decoupling the contract from procreation or childbearing, writes that marriage is "the union of two persons of different sexes for lifelong possession of each other's sexual attributes." In fact, unmindful of the Church's twelfth-century decision, Kant states that "a marriage contract is *consummated* [fulfilled, vollzogen] only by the *conjugal sexual intercourse*."[137] Blackstone's *Commentaries on the Laws of England* describe civil marriage as valid if three conditions are met: the persons are "*willing* to contract," "*able* to contract," and "*did* contract."[138] Willingness to contract, he goes on to write, consists in consent. He later cites the statue of Henry VIII, that "all marriages contracted by lawful persons in the face of the church, and consummated with bodily knowledge, and fruit of children, shall be indissoluble."[139]

Wedding vows spoken by same-gender couples in the late twentieth and early twentieth-first centuries are often identical with, or similar to, vows that in the past were spoken only by different-gender couples and continue to entail the reciprocal transfer of rights over the body, sexual intimacy, and shared decisions about whether and when to have children. The list of countries[140] and states[141] that recognize same-sex marriage grows every day, as does the list of churches throughout the world that confer blessings on the civil marriages of same-sex couples and in some instances welcome the couple's marriage inside the church where their vows are spoken.[142]

In, finally, contemporary U.S. civil law, an unconsummated marriage is still today more easily annulled than a consummated one, though this is less often true now than in the past.[143] But the detail is the reminder that the near inextricability of consent and the body (the authorization of the physical ground of personhood) is not confined to the descriptions of one church or to canon law or to rites that belong to the past. In fact, consummation is often referred to as *"the ratification"* of the marriage contract[144] or the *"validation"* of the marriage in U.S. family law.[145] The verb "to ratify" in these texts means "to make love."

Again, when cases of fraud or misrepresentation in the contract are brought, the misrepresentation must go "to the essence" of marriage, and "going to the essence of marriage" tends to mean "going to the body." While a misrepresentation about money does not invalidate the contract, a misrepresentation about the desire to have children does;[146] ability to consummate and willingness to consummate are also often considered to "go to the essence of marriage."[147]

We saw at the opening of this chapter that "consent" may fall along a tonal spectrum that runs from the extremes of aversion (the reluctant yes a person gives when she consents to a dangerous medical operation) to that of jubilance (the eager yes of those consenting to marriage or to making love, as in Molly Bloom's words that end James Joyce's *Ulysses*: "all perfume yes and his heart was going like mad and yes I said yes I will Yes").[148] In many cultures, the wedding celebration is as elaborate as the marriage rite itself is minimal, often entailing the gathering of people from great distances, lavish forms of dress, many hours, even days, of festivities: the sequence of seven blessings in the Jewish wedding ends, "let there be heard in the cities . . . and in the streets . . . the voice of mirth and the voice of gladness, the voice of the bridegroom and the voice of the bride, the voice of the merriment of the bridegrooms at their nuptial feasts, and of youths from their musical entertainments"[149]—a description compatible with the tone of many secular and religious ceremonies and for which one theologian uses the word "hilarity,"[150] laughter-filled exhilaration.

The earlier chapters have all stressed that the work of consent—the thing for which it is designed—is the diminution of injury: the higher the possibility of injury, the more explicit and highly staged the consent must be. This being so, it is clear why one needs highly visible consent procedures before going to war or before punishing or before a medical surgery or before choosing a homeland. But why do such explicit consent practices arise in the context of jubilation and mirth?

It is precisely because bodily boundaries are about to be crossed that the consent to a love partner must be highly self-conscious and explicit.[151] Sustained bodily proximity brings with it the possibility of injury: during all hours of day and night, during all seasons of the year, during all stages of alertness from full wakefulness, to inattentive relaxation, to deepest sleep, the two persons will be in each other's company, bringing with it (were the relation entered into without deliberation) the potential for harm not present when one is standing in the midst of a thousand anonymous people in a public city square (and where elaborate consent procedures are therefore unneeded). Not only the marriage vow itself, but the many religious and secular addenda to the starkly simple marriage vow—rituals of engagement, public announcement, the gathering of an assembly, the paced and musically scored motion of walking—are meant to increase the chance that the acts of intimate union that might be accomplished on the wings of rapture or intoxication alone are attended by scrutiny, deliberation, and testing. Even here, then, we may say consent serves as a brake that must be released before the action goes forward.

The portrait of marriage places before us the possibility of consent free of the mystified categories of active and passive, especially when, as here, we focus on two-person marriage (rather than polygamy) and on secular and religious forms that require the consent of both parties and the speaking of identical vows.[152] But were we to linger over the marriage portrait, it would soon turn out that we have not entirely escaped that mystification. It has been long and widely noticed that the promised reciprocal transfer of rights over the body has historically tended to be one-directional, favoring the man: the contractual provision for equality has been, as John Stuart Mill observed, subverted either by laws "annexed" to the contract or by background social practices. And so we have circled back to the optimistic assertion of equality in a two-party relation—patient and physician, governed and governors, wife and husband—only to see it slipping asymmetrically in one direction once more.

Even the most intense exclusivity of passion (the realm of shared desire, *con-sentir*, consenting adults) does not ensure a reciprocity of volition or eliminate the categories of domination and subordination. Sartre, for example, in *Being and Nothingness*, says that the lover, by wanting steadily amplified desire on the part of the beloved, actually wants that person's "unfreedom," wants him or her to be entranced, enchained.[153] And other sites that appear to present a reciprocal model of consent—such as contract law—may also in the end carry us quickly back to the realm of inequality.[154]

But it may also be the case that over the long run sexual desire equalizes, that the hard-won equality of women with men could not easily have come into being without it. During the long centuries when the two genders were unequal, desire perhaps served as a daily reminder of how counterfactual that asserted inequality was. We can catch glimpses of this pressure toward equalization in the more extreme history of inequality between different religious, racial, or economic groups. Historically, groups that have been separated by social rules holding them to be ontologically distinct and by laws prohibiting their members from intimate union have been challenged and eventually defeated by physical desire which brings persons face to face with their equality, even if in the short run (as elaborate documentation has shown) such union has entailed exploitation and abuse by the partner having the higher cultural status (man over woman, white person over black, rich over poor, favored religious group over disfavored one). But over time, erotic desire may serve as a wake-up call to the fact that the persons in the two racial, gender, religious, or economic groups are actually equal, and that the laws and cultural norms asserting otherwise are manifestly false.

Consent between two persons from separate groups (two genders, two races, two religions, two economic spheres) may invite from onlookers the same skepticism about the reality of consent that we saw in the medical and political portraits: is consent—whether given in marriage or in a single act of lovemaking—only a fiction? If so, is it a fiction in the sense of fraud? Or is it instead a fiction in the sense of actual re-creation, a site across which standing power arrangements are called into question and redistributed in a new form? When Sally Hemings was in France, she was eligible to become a free woman; she was therefore reluctant to travel back to the United States with the widowed Thomas Jefferson; after much pleading from him, she eventually agreed to do so on condition that their children, once reaching maturity, would be freed.[155] Is her consent here "fraudulent" because race, wealth, and gender favored Jefferson, or were those sites of inequality called into question and redesigned through their reciprocating acts of consent? If a black woman in the same year were to stand on United States soil (without the bargaining power given by French soil) and consent to an ongoing intimate relation with a white owner,[156] would her consent be unreal? The argument here is that her desirability to him, and his to her, might themselves create a French soil before there were any such national ground on which to stand.

The mysterious nature of active and passive recurs across the medical, political, and marital portraits, and the three have other shared features. In each sphere, for example, a distinction can be made between the threshold consent and the perpetual consent we found earlier in the structure of war. Within marriage law, whether a given civil or religious institution prohibits or instead sanctions separation and divorce turns on whether the consent of the two people is seen as an exclusively threshold act (that once given, cannot then be retracted) or instead as perpetual (consent is each day renewed; it may therefore also be retracted). Within U.S. medicine, ethical norms in therapeutic practice and in experimental research are distinguishable by the much greater emphasis in the second on consent as ongoing. The 1947 Nuremberg Code, the 1975 Declaration of Helsinki, as well as state codes (such as the California Act on the Protection of Human Subjects in Medical Experiments), all overtly state as a central thesis the ongoing and revisionary nature of consent: "He or she should be informed that he or she is at liberty to abstain from participation in the study and that he or she is free to withdraw his or her consent to participate at any time."[157] In a hospital stay, in contrast, patients are ordinarily not told that their consent is ongoing, that the food and the medicines they are handed are (like the operations they undergo) subject to their consent, and that they may change their minds about a plan of treatment to which they have previously agreed. Within social contract theory, whether a particular theorist endorses or instead disdains revolution often turns on whether the person believes consent is a perpetual act or instead a solitary act performed (and afterward relinquished) at the threshold. Sometimes political philosophers acknowledge the existence of both forms and give them separate names.[158]

A third common feature across the medical, political, and marital spheres is what can be called the ideological neutrality of consent: in medicine, political philosophy, and law, the concept has been useful to both conservative and liberal voices. It has been invoked to advocate revolution; but with equal urgency, it has been called upon to explain why the citizenry has an obligation not to enter revolution. Again, within medicine, it has been identified as the safeguard of patient rights; it has alternatively been seen as protecting the surgeon against patient rights. Marriage, too, has been seen as conserving existing power lines or instead as liberalizing them. The term "ideological neutrality" is used not because consent is empty of ideological content but because it is richly present across a wide spectrum of cultural meaning, and therefore belongs to no one camp.

The three shared features we have just looked at—the mystification of active and passive, the competition between threshold and perpetual forms of consent, and the ideological richness of the phenomenon— should not deflect attention from the most important and emphatic common ground shared by medicine, political treatises, and marriage law: their insistent locating of consent in the body. They share this feature with the portrait of consent in wartime that turns on the population's right of self-defense. We have turned to these three spheres of consent in peacetime because they are electric in their familiarity; consent in wartime, in contrast, has faded with disuse, and so seems obscure, lost to view, as though it were an antique, or even a foreign, idea.

Without consent, medical surgery is either a crime or a tort; without consent over one's own bodily location in a given country, one ceases to be a citizen and becomes instead a political prisoner; without consent, sexual intimacy is rape. When we stop to contemplate how crucial the capacities for consent and dissent are in medicine, in civil society, or in marriage, we regain our sense of how momentous they may be in war and how momentous is their loss. Of course, the three peacetime manifestations of consent can themselves be lost. The statewide violation of medical consent was most egregiously carried out in the medical experiments of Nazi Germany when thousands of people were coerced into obscene pseudo-scientific studies and hundreds of thousands were sterilized. The right of free movement in and out of the polis was most completely abridged in Communist countries such as East Germany, where a double wall around Berlin and similar walls around the country's border closed down the free movement of the populations for several decades and so worked to silence them. Smaller-scale tyrannies—Reverend Moon, Jim Jones—have abridged marital consent among their followers by pairing people who themselves exercised no choice over their sexual partnerships. We have not yet had a state that arrogates to itself the reproduction of children, but the vision of what that would look like—and its analogy to the state's arrogation to itself of the right of self-defense—were set forth in the Prelude to Part Two.

The grounding of consent in the body is not just one of its structural features; it is the most fundamental. The matter of consent is in each case primarily living matter. Problems in consent always have to do with the body—a sodomy law in Georgia, the testing of blood for AIDS in a Texas hospital, the testing for drugs on an Amtrak train, a defense against rape in a British court, a labor contract regulating hours of employment. And finally the problem to which this book is dedicated, the way in which a shift in military technology has altered the social contract, fundamental because it is *quod omnes tangit*, that which touches all.

The attributes of the material grounding that emerge in the three portraits from medicine, political philosophy, and marriage make clear the attributes of the body and hence what is jeopardized. The body is: first, the thing protected; second, the lever across which rights are generated and political self-authorization is achieved; third, the agent and expression of consent, the site of the performative; and, fourth and finally, a ratifying power. These, then, are what are jeopardized when consent is lost. Together they underscore the scale of political alteration should we fail to call back—through demonstration or negotiation or argument or court action—the powers of consent that have so disastrously slipped away with the advent of nuclear arms.

CHAPTER 6
THINKING IN AN EMERGENCY

This chapter is a reminder of what in the nuclear age we sometimes seem to have forgotten: that we have both the responsibility *and the ability* to protect one another, both within the boundaries of our own nations and across national boundaries. Once we hold in front of our eyes the landscape of actual emergencies—as the central sections of this chapter ask us to do—we can recognize the deep principles of mutual protection that consistently appear, whether in the act of a midwife in Zambia trying to save a newborn with CPR, a commune in Saskatchewan building a raft to rescue stranded villagers, or an entire national population in Switzerland working in concert to uphold their commitment to "equality of survival." We can and ordinarily do retain our ability both to think and to act in emergencies, and should not be misled by governments into believing that the speed of modern life requires that populations step aside and stop thinking while larger and larger arsenals are accumulated whose only purpose is to injure.

THE SEDUCTION TO STOP THINKING

In his mid-twentieth-century book on *Constitutional Dictatorship*, Clinton Rossiter predicted that the atomic age would soon be governed by emergency rule and a solitary executive figure.[1] He was right. A recent report by the Geneva Center for the Democratic Control of Armed Forces reviews the governance structures of the earth's eight nuclear states: the United States, the United Kingdom, France, the Russian Federation, China, Israel, India, and Pakistan. All eight have ceded control of nuclear weapons to their presidents or prime ministers: all eight have permitted their legislative assemblies and their citizenry to disappear.[2]

There are, of course, distinctions among the eight nuclear weapons states. Of 22,600 weapons held worldwide, the United States and Russia hold 21,600 of them.[3] The countries vary in their readiness to fire: both China and India keep their warheads "unmated" to the delivery vehicles;[4] the United States and Russia together keep 2000 ready for launch, day and night. Strategic policies vary: India is committed to a "second-use only" policy,[5] whereas the United States and Britain have a first-use policy. The number of people who will initiate any launch also varies from country to country: in the United States, the president alone issues the order to launch;[6] in Pakistan, three people—the prime minister, the president, and a third unidentified person—must act in concert to launch a weapon, as is also true in Russia, where the president, the defense minister, and the chief of the general staff share control over the release codes.[7]

While these and other differences are important, what unites the eight countries should be kept steadily in view. Each has the capacity to kill millions of people; each has placed that capacity in a small number of hands; each has bypassed the distributional structures that characterize democratic governance; and each has a population that could bring its own national laws (as well as international laws) to bear on ridding itself of both the nuclear weapons and the legal deformations those weapons cause.

Legal scholars have shown that by the end of the twentieth century many countries had come to live in the state of "chronic emergency" that Clinton Rossiter predicted, with more and more powers ceded to the country's president or prime minister. Hans Born, the author of the Geneva study, judges that among the eight nuclear states, the United States has a strong chance of reestablishing democracy both because of various constitutional provisions and because of a robust civil society. Given this democratic potential, it is revelatory to see how saturated with emergency rule this particular nation has become. Supreme Court attorney and constitutional scholar Jules Lobel calls attention to a Senate report acknowledging that by the 1970s "470 statutes existed delegat[ing] power to the executive over virtually every aspect of American life," presidential power that since then has increased, appearing in presidential control of drug wars, civilian transportation, and civilian nuclear plants.[8] Astonishingly, even the constitutionally specified arrangement for presidential succession has itself been replaced by two separate lines of presidential succession, determined not by constitutionally legal procedures but by private councils within the executive.[9] Counterparts of many of these legal deformations can be found in the other nuclear states. For example, both Russia and France have set up lines of succession that diverge from the constitutionally mandated sequence;[10] in Britain, two deputies are appointed, one of whom can launch the weapons if the prime minister is not available to do so.[11]

In the United States, the dissolution of law in the second half of the twentieth century accelerated in the twenty-first. In the first eight years of the new century, the claim of emergency and the momentum toward unconstrained executive power became increasingly legible, with a presidential office that sanctioned the practice of torture, detention without charge, widespread surveillance of its citizens, and a private mercenary army answerable only to the president.[12] The first in this list—the practice of torture—carried the United States into the deepest region of war crime. The international and national prohibition on torture is not just one law among many but a foundational prohibition underlying the larger framework of laws. Torture ceased in 2009 when a new president entered the White House, but the practice of extrajudicial executions, already in place, greatly increased: by 2012, U.S. drones had killed more than 3000 people in Pakistan, Yemen, and Somalia. These nonbattlefield targeted killings were carried out without any trial to determine the guilt of the targeted persons, and without any authorization by the legislature or the citizenry.[13]

As these many acts indicate, the overall shift in government across the last sixty years has entailed setting aside distributional mechanisms in favor of centralized ones, setting aside democratic arrangements in favor of monarchic ones, setting aside constitutional provisions for nonconstitutional ones.

Among these monarchic and nonconstitutional arrangements, the arrangements for nuclear weapons are the most grave.[14] In the United States, as we saw in Part One, nuclear weapons and the strategic doctrines for their use have bypassed two major provisions of the Constitution: the prohibition on initiating war without a formal declaration of war by the full legislative assembly (Article I, Section 8, Clause 11), and the prohibition on an executive military force that acts independently of the population's authorization and consent (the Second Amendment). Together, these two provisions place a large brake on the attempt to go to war; they stipulate that the United States cannot begin to injure a foreign population unless reasons can be given that are so persuasive that they survive scrutiny and testing by both the national assembly and the population at large. These provisions were meant to ensure that military authority would be distributed to the whole population. In turn, that distribution was meant to guarantee that the country would remain a democracy, not a tyranny. By setting aside these constitutional provisions, the country gives up the form of government it should rightfully treasure and protect. We give it up whether or not the weapons are ever actually fired. And if they are fired? We then exterminate another population, as well as millions of other living creatures.

The legal principle *Quod omnes tangit*, "that which touches all," as we saw in Chapter 4, is only the first half of a sentence. The entire sentence reads: *Quod omnes tangit, ab omnibus decidetur*, "That which touches all requires everyone's agreement."

This chapter looks at the way a spurious invocation of emergency in the nuclear age has acted on the people of the world to make us surrender our powers of resistance and our elementary forms of political responsibility. The chapter also shows that, correctly understood, we collectively and thoughtfully address many forms of emergency conditions, and do so by honoring—not abandoning—procedures that are legal, open, widely understood, and carefully prepared in advance of the crisis to make possible a democratic, not a dictatorial, response.

We need to reacquire our responsibility for our own governance. If it is perilous to cede our collective political responsibilities to any single authority under normal peacetime conditions, it is far more perilous to do so when vast injuries to the earth's people, and to the earth itself, are at stake.

THE CLAIM OF EMERGENCY

The implicit claim of emergency is that all procedures and all thinking must cease because the emergency requires that (1) an action must be taken, and (2) the action must be taken relatively quickly. It is odd to set the first of these, the requirement that an action be taken, in opposition to deliberative thinking. The unspoken presumption is that either one can think or one can act, and given that it is absolutely mandatory that an action be performed, thinking must fall away. But at least one whole genre of thinking—what Aristotle called "deliberation"—has no other function than precisely to enable the taking of actions. In *De Anima*, he differentiates thinking that is directed toward an apprehension of "what is," which he calls "perception" and elsewhere "contemplation," from a form of thinking directed toward decisions about "whether to do one thing or another,"[15] which he designates "deliberation."

Even if we now move back from the specific genre of deliberation to the more encompassing act of thinking, it is clear that the claim is an odd one: the call to suspend thinking is precisely a call to suspend governance, whether self-governance or the governance of the polis. How integrally governing and thinking are coupled is most rapidly displayed by recalling that our major political treatises tend to be written by people who have also written treatises about how we think. *The Republic* and *The Laws*, themselves saturated with observations about cognition, were written by that same Plato who wrote about the mind in the *Timaeus*, *Theatetus*, and *Phaedrus*. Aristotle's *Politics* exists side by side with writings such as *Prior Analytics* and *Posterior Analytics*, as well as writings on cognition: *De Anima, Sense and Sensibilia, On Memory, On Dreams*. Hobbes's *Leviathan* opens with chapters interrogating the nature of the mind—"Of Sense," "Of Imagination," "Of Reason, and Science"—an interrogation also present in *De Corpore*, an early exemplar of the computational theory of mind. And Locke wrote not only *The Second Treatise of Government* but the *Essay on Human Understanding* and *Conduct of the Understanding*. John Stuart Mill wrote *On Liberty* and *Considerations on Representative Government*; he also wrote *A System of Logic* and an essay "On Genius." This insistent coupling reflects the intimate association between understanding governance and understanding understanding. As we shall see, the two are nearly a single merged subject.

The first of the two seductions to giving up thinking in an emergency—the argument that emergency requires an action—is not, then, a very creditable one. The second seduction—the argument that the action must be done soon—is more problematic because more plausible. Aesop tells a tale about a young boy who is drowning.[16] He calls to a nearby huntsman for help. The huntsman, disapproving of the boy's rashness, begins to lecture him. The boy calls out: "No. Save me now. Lecture me later." At the end of Aesop's tale, which lasts only as long as the sentences just recited, the moral seems to be that in an emergency there is no time for thinking or deliberating, certainly not for lecturing.

Now, this would be an odd piece of advice for Aesop to give, since the fables collectively constitute a small treatise on emergency thinking—a set of lectures to those who are drowning, or were, or might someday in the future be, drowning. And in fact, true to his own emergency primer, the explicit moral we now come to in the postscript to the story of the drowning boy repudiates the huntsman's posture of reprimand (while simultaneously reenacting it), for it counsels that one ought not to get into a situation that licenses anyone else to reprimand you. The fable, then, provides two rules about emergency. The first rule of emergency thinking is that one ought not to get into one; the huntsman delivers this rule. Aesop backs it up one more step: one ought not to get into a situation that makes it appropriate for someone to remind you that the first rule of emergency is not to get into one. There is surely a third rule at work here: whatever happens, keep talking.

The second great seduction to giving up thinking in an emergency, then, the argument that the speed of emergency requires action without thought (the drowning boy's position), is displaced in Aesop by the advocacy of cognitive acts that have the power to anticipate and eliminate the conditions of emergency. Aesop calls for thinking that preempts the emergency. Rather than emergency bringing about the end of thinking, thinking should bring about the end of emergency.

But how is this to be done? The basic assumption during peacetime is that the world stays the same and persons change. The stability of the world acts as the background for the display of our changes, our circuitous thoughts, our contemplative digressions. In an emergency this is inverted: the world is changing more quickly than we can change. Baudelaire's poem about a swan misplaced in Paris suffering the conditions of exile, "trailing his white plumes on the raw ground,"[17] provides an image for those displaced by emergency: Andromache bewildered by the loss of Hector and the Trojan War, an African immigrant searching the Parisian sky for the palm tree of her home. In an emergency, the mind is in exile like Baudelaire's swan, "with his frenzied gestures,

ridiculous and sublime." The thinking mind is this big beautiful creature, helpless in exile from the conditions of its own thought.

THE MIND IN EXILE IN EMERGENCY

Aesop's recommendation to remain coherent in an emergency is difficult to carry out. Thucydides gives the classic account of the dissolution of conventions during the plague of Athens. No medical therapy
helped, he writes. "Nor was any other human art or science of any
help at all. Equally useless were prayers."[18] Soon no one even attempts
remedy. Thucydides designates this immobilization the most "terrible
thing of all"; when people realize they have the plague, "they would
immediately adopt an attitude of utter hopelessness, and, by giving in in
this way, would lose their powers of resistance."[19] People become indifferent to "every rule of religion or of law," disregarding even funeral
ceremonies, adopting "most shameless methods" of disposing of the
bodies. Thucydides calls this a "state of unprecedented lawlessness."[20]
The dissolution of laws, customs, and religious ceremonies entails at its
heart a dissolution of language: "words indeed fail," says Thucydides.
Aesop's dictum to "keep talking" is lost among all the other lost rules.

The portrait of cognition Thucydides gives is consistent with the
more familiar experience of emergency in everyday life. Language disappears. Words are replaced by loud noises, crude sirens, harsh horns—
one-syllable sounds that act as placeholders for language until it can
return. The few words that remain tend to be the minimalist vocabulary
of counting, as in the rules for cardiopulmonary resuscitation ("ONE
one thousand, TWO one thousand, THREE one thousand") with its
15:2 ratio for a rescuer acting alone, its 5:1 ratio for two rescuers acting as partners. So fragile is our hold on emergency language that—as
in Aesop's well-known tale about the boy who cried wolf—there must
exist special rules for keeping it intact, special constraints on invoking
the vocabulary of alarm lest we exhaust its too easily exhausted powers

before the actual problem arrives. This fragility is also registered in the special legal categories that have been designed to protect and regulate emergency language: fighting words, dying words, crying fire in a theater.[21]

One might conclude from historical portraits of actual catastrophes (whether in ancient Athens or today) that human beings lose their social and political structures in an emergency not simply because they have suddenly been subjected to an asocial and anarchic framework but because they are, in their own deepest impulses, asocial and anarchic. Certainly Thucydides is often understood to be illustrating this account of humanity.

But it is not at all clear that this conclusion is warranted. A Canadian quarterly publication called the *Emergency Preparedness Digest* reviews a constant stream of actual and hypothetical emergencies (grain elevator fires, laboratory disease outbreaks, tornadoes, chemical spills, ice breaks in spring, tsunamis in all seasons); and it analyzes existing civil defense procedures, hypothetical rescue strategies, communications problems whose solutions range from meteor-burst warning systems (radio signals relayed across the continuous sequence of meteors available in the heavens) to the establishment of community agreement about the meanings of a siren "yelp" as distinguished from a siren "wail." The portrait repeatedly presented here is that people in emergencies—or at least Canadians in emergencies—are neither asocial nor anarchic. We would be social if we knew what gestures or actions to perform, and even without that knowledge, we are often diffusely social. So, too, we would be responsive to leadership if a clear site of authority were visible. The absence of direction may come from the fact that there is no one present, or instead from the fact that there are too many people present; Quebec Civil Defense finds in some emergencies between "200 and 300 persons on the scene from various organizations responsible for emergency measures,"[22] itself providing the grounds for the type of crowd panic described by Elias Canetti in his classic book *Crowds and Power.*

It is in spite of our socialness and lawfulness that the framework of norms and laws dissolves, not because of an inherent wish to be free of such constraints. In the absence of any mental stays, one may become vulnerable to the most rigorous stays, orders issuing from outside. The psychology of this susceptibility is unapologetically elaborated in Antonin Artaud's writings on the immobilization of the theatrical audience in his Theatre of Cruelty, where the play assumes a potentially dictatorial power over the audience, stunning them into full attention that has no object other than the spectacle. Artaud, who claims the plague as an analogue for the theater, is clearly fascinated by Thucydides.[23] The single most influential sentence in Thucydides's account is the surrender to hopelessness that deprives the population of resistance. The goal of the emergency spectacle, says Artaud, is to bring about "a genuine enslavement of the attention."[24] "I propose then a theatre," he writes, "in which violent physical images crush and hypnotize the sensibility of the spectator seized by the theatre as by a whirlwind of higher forces."[25] If Artaud's audience were equipped with the procedures from Canada's *Emergency Preparedness Digest* (and somewhere in its pages there must exist an article on what to do if one finds oneself at a play by Artaud), or if they had the 901,000 days a year of active practice that the Swiss population collectively has for its fallout shelter system, or even if they had practiced the "scrum" gesture that (for many decades) every scout who received a Fireman's Badge had to be able to perform, they would have the capacity for resistance.

Artaud is important because he unashamedly displays the theater director's own monarchic motives for emergency decrees. A political leader who brings about chronic emergencies may have these same motives: to stun the mind, to immobilize, to bring about a genuine enslavement of attention. But he is unlikely to author a political treatise on this subject, for it would arm the reader with the very skepticism that enables resistance.

As one scans across the plagues of Thucydides and Artaud, across the tidal waves and grain elevator fires in Canada, and the Swiss vision of unspecified war, three alternative political descriptions of the population recur: the first is immobilization; the second is incoherent action; the third is coherent action. The first alternative is one in which a population is incapable of initiating its own actions and highly susceptible to following orders imposed by someone else, as illustrated in Artaud's account of audience passivity in France, or in Hannah Arendt's account of the obedience of Eichmann in Germany, or in the notorious Milgram experiments in the United States, where subjects willingly inflicted electric shock on other people if instructed by a scientist to do so. The other two alternatives entail the performance of an action in which some level of self-authorizing agency remains. The rest of this chapter focuses on the extraordinary role played by habit in shaping these two alternative forms of self-authorization. In an emergency, the habits of ordinary life may fall away, but other habits come into play and determine whether the action performed is fatal or benign.

The seduction against thinking in an emergency comes, as we have seen, from two sources: first, from a false opposition between thinking and acting; second, from a plausible (but in the end, false) opposition between thinking and *rapid* action. Now a third, equally potent, form of seduction becomes visible: the acts of thinking that go on in emergencies are not recognized by us as acts of thinking. We misrecognize them. More precisely, we correctly recognize the presence of habit in these mental acts but incorrectly conclude that habit is incompatible with, or empty of, thought. We are therefore willing to set these mental acts aside. Our derisive attitude toward habit prevents us from seeing the form of thinking embedded in these cognitive acts and hence makes us willing to give up, or set aside, the most powerful mental tools that stand ready to assist us.

The first two seductions entail an overt repudiation of the act of thinking. This third one is, on the surface, just the opposite. Out of a deep regard for thinking, in the name of thinking, we set aside practices that—because they correctly appear as habit—are *incorrectly* taken to be removed from the realm of thought. We need to see that not only mental habits but also their codified counterparts, procedural pathways and legal rules, are deeply compatible with the most rigorous forms of thinking. Far from being set aside, they need to be respected, revered, and practiced.

THE ROLE OF HABIT IN EMERGENCY

The habits of everyday life, as Thucydides makes clear, often fail to serve in an emergency.[26] But in the absence of our ordinary habits, a special repertoire of alternative habits may suddenly come forward. It is not the case that ordinary life is habitual and emergency life is nonhabitual. Both coherent and incoherent emergency actions appear to have their source in habit.

The habits that suddenly surface may have been culturally received without our self-consciously aspiring to acquire them. A friend in Philadelphia was alarmed when she opened the oven door and saw a mouse. More accurately, she was stunned not to see the mouse but to hear the sentence that came out of her mouth: "Eek. A mouse." There are many serious illustrations of this same phenomenon. In a book called *Running Hot*, an ambulance emergency worker describes the difficulty of obtaining and transmitting to the hospital accurate medical information, because by the time the ambulance crew arrives at the home, fifteen people may be moving anxiously about the room. So, too, at the hospital: the information the ambulance team gives to the physician or nurse receiving the patient at the door may not reach the physician who then treats the patient in an interior room. As both the portrait of ambulance work and many other forms of emergency work make vivid, coherent deliberative acts are made extremely difficult by seriatim thinking—by a sequence of temporally or spatially distinct locations for the various stages of examination, inquiry, and decision making. The alternative to seriatim structure is an assembly structure where all contributors to the emergency decision are co-present in a single space and a single time. Governmental structures designed to guarantee the most careful and thought-laden decision making have this assembly form; thus, in the United States the constitutional requirement for a congressional declaration of war (Article I, Section 8, Clause 11) and for jury deliberation (Fourth Amendment) seek to insure that information, rather than being passed from person to person, is examined under the pressure of consistent attention across participants.

A seriatim structure is, of course, a necessity in the case of a patient whose injury or illness originates in a location distinct from the hospital or treatment center. The condition of the patient being transported by the ambulance is likely itself to be in a state of rapid change. Often, once the ambulance begins its run, a person who seemed to have been unconscious in the home may turn out not really to be unconscious. "Patients have no basis for judging what is appropriate," writes Donald Metz.[27] They have been known to pretend they were unconscious until loaded into the ambulance, because they did not know what was expected of them and so adopted a stereotyped role of the 'ambulance patient.'" Contained in this account is *no* implication that the patient has been faking, or melodramatizing the situation, or inappropriately seeking sympathy; indeed, the person is often gravely injured or ill and, in addition, deeply mystified about what to do. Because the cultural image of an ambulance patient is one of unconsciousness, the person may simply absorb that cultural habit and mime unconsciousness.

Many stories about emergency are precisely about the appropriateness or the inappropriateness of the habits that surface during them. Aesop tells the story of a little donkey who carries a heavy burden of salt one day and finds that when he wades through the river, the salt dissolves and his burden disappears. So the next day he again carries his heavy load into the river. But this time he is carrying sponges (which absorb the water) and he drowns. Aesop has many other tales about applying the wrong habit or instead, by foresight and preparation, applying the right one. It is because a set of given actions will either accelerate the emergency or instead bring it to a halt that carefully chosen emergency preparations must be put in place. Far from being structureless, a crisis is an event in which structures inevitably take over. The only question is whether the structures will be negative or positive.

Because this chapter will go on to speak about philosophic assessments of habit, it will be useful to set before the reader four concrete instances of emergency preparation that depend, for their essential design, on the willful instilling of deeply formed habits in advance of the catastrophe. The fact that the four models come from widely different contexts suggests that a key feature cuts across and unites many genres of emergency preparation.

FOUR MODELS OF EMERGENCY THINKING

MODEL 1: CPR

Classic CPR procedures consist of a rigid set of rules about counting. Almost all actions are accompanied by a number, and the counted actions are paced by the inclusion of filler words: "ONE one thousand, TWO one thousand, THREE one thousand." The distribution of the rescuer's efforts between two locations, the chest and the mouth, is also numerically specified: thirty compressions at the chest for every two breaths at the person's mouth. If the rescuer has a partner, fifteen acts are carried out at the chest for every two that the other rescuer performs at the mouth. The few pieces of language that are not numerical are as terse as numbers and, again, rigidly specified. Because, for example, CPR is physically demanding and might have to go on for a long period (ten minutes, twenty minutes, forty minutes), the two rescuers may need to change positions; this change is signaled by the person at the chest substituting the word "change" at the place where one would normally say "four": "ONE one thousand, TWO one thousand, THREE one thousand, CHANGE one thousand, FIVE one thousand." A breath is now given by the rescuer at the mouth and the two rescuers change locations.

The procedures for CPR confirm a feature that is often cited in critiques of habit, its rigidity, while at the same time vividly illustrating the mistake those critiques make when they attribute to rigidity a robotic (or automaton-like) lack of thought. Built into those 30:2 and 15:2 ratios is a deep knowledge about the number of times a minute the heart must pump to support the body and the minimum amount of oxygen that must be in that pumping blood to keep the tissue—and in particular, the brain—unharmed; built into those ratios also is a deep knowledge about the difficulty of thinking clearly if a child's or a friend's or a stranger's heart suddenly stops beating. The acts, far from being thoughtless, are thought laden; they are designed to carry out the actions of breathing, circulating, and thinking during the period while those three internal actions are in a state of suspension. Further, the very fact that the rescuers know precisely what to do increases the chance that they will retain their ability to think clearly. The procedures are so efficiently internalized that mental space is left over for addressing additional complicating problems.

CPR conflates the extraordinary with the ordinary. It enables someone who has died—or who will within a very few minutes be dead—to turn around and step back onto the path of life. Given its connection to reanimation, it is appropriate that historians have glimpsed the earliest traces of the aspiration for CPR in ancient Egypt and ancient Hebrew, both civilizations receptive to the miracle of reanimation. The discovery of an ancient Egyptian mouth-opening instrument, believed to be connected to the cult of the dead, has prompted the thesis that the practice of artificial respiration may have begun five millennia ago.[28] The Hebrew scriptures also provide possible precedents, such as the description in 2 Kings of Elisha the Prophet bringing a child back to life: "He placed himself over the child. He put his mouth on his mouth, his eyes on his eyes, and his hands on his hands, as he bent over him. And the body of the child became warm... Thereupon, the boy sneezed seven times, and the boy opened his eyes."[29] Despite these and other fascinating precedents, false starts, and successful first-second-and-third steps across many centuries and geographical regions, the actual invention of CPR is usually assigned to the year 1959, when five scientists—Peter Safar, James Elam, James Jude, Guy Knickerbocker, and William Kouwenhoven—brought together their two independent lines of research on breathing and circulation.[30]

Are its miraculous powers of reversal certain, or even likely? CPR only sometimes brings the person back to life, and only some of those who recover go on to live a long time. But that sentence is equally accurate with the twice-repeated "only" removed: CPR sometimes brings the person back to life; some of those who recover go on to live a long time. One study of a rural hospital in Kenya looked at 114 children who were given CPR in a two-year period from 2002 to 2004: 82 had stopped breathing (and were therefore a short time away from their hearts stopping as well); 32 had suffered arrest of both lungs and heart.[31] All were severely ill from one of three causes: malaria, extreme malnutrition, or septicemia. Most were younger than six years old.[32] Of the eighty-two children who had stopped breathing, twenty-five began to breathe again after being given CPR; of those twenty-five, eighteen lived long enough to be discharged from the hospital. Of the thirty-two children whose heart and lungs had both stopped, five regained breathing and heartbeats after CPR. Although none of these five lived long enough to be discharged from the hospital, the temporary return of breath and circulation would have given them a chance for longer life had it been possible to reverse the dire sickness each had—as may, someday in the future, be possible. Of the 114 children, then, 30 regained life: 12 very briefly, 18 long enough to become healthy and leave the hospital.

The survival rate following CPR is tracked at the Kilifi District Hospital in Kenya and at hospitals in many other countries in the world precisely because the expectation is that it should be, and will with study become, higher. Indeed, the survival rate for the Kenyan children who had suffered respiratory arrest represented a significant increase over the survival rate a few years earlier.[33] Similarly, a 2003 study of Nigeria's Lagos University Teaching Hospital found that during 2147 operations in a one-year period, thirteen patients suffered cardiac arrest. The average age of the patients was thirty.[34] All thirteen were given CPR but only five survived. The authors of the study report these figures to urge the repair of the two major causes for the unacceptable level of survival: extreme loss of blood (a problem that can be solved through a better hospital blood bank) and inadequate conformity to the international guidelines on administering CPR, issued in 2000, again in 2005, and most recently in 2010.[35]

The potential miracle of CPR grows out of the nonmiraculous fact of repetition—repetition carried out on three levels. First, as noticed earlier, the act itself is comprised of a set of repeated actions. In the case of Lagos University Teaching Hospital, the mean duration before the person regained spontaneous circulation was twenty-five minutes; the person or persons compressing the heart repeated that action more than 2500 times (100 beats per minute for twenty-five minutes). In the case of the children in Kenya, no child given more than fifteen minutes of CPR survived. Even this much briefer duration would require 1500 compressions of the child's chest and 100 breaths.[36] Infants are given cheek-puffs of breath, rather than the deep, forceful, double breath given to adults; the presses on the center of the sternum are done with two fingers backed by the strength of the arm, rather than, as with adults, two overlapping hands and the weight of rescuer's full upper body.

Second, both the initial acquisition of the skill and the maintenance of the skill entail repetition and practice. The goal of the initial training is to impress a small set of facts into the learner's mind so vividly that they might, at that moment, seem indelible. The brilliantly designed 1959 handbook on artificial respiration—*Resuscitation of the Unconscious Victim: A Manual for Rescue Breathing*, coauthored by Peter Safar and Martin McMahon—provides an example. The tiny, bright-yellow book, eighty pages long and as big as one's hand, ends by singling out in its penultimate paragraph one fact in particular without which all other facts will fail: "We believe that the teaching of the 'head tilt, chin up' position will save more lives than the teaching of any method of artificial respiration." Almost fifty years later, the 2005 international guidelines still specify the importance of the "head tilt, chin up" position as the best way of assuring a clear airway.

A person who is unconscious often has his head falling forward with his chin "sagging" toward his chest. In this position (and even in the normal position with the chin perpendicular to the chest), the back of the tongue completely blocks the passage from the throat to the airway leading to the lungs. Only when the head is arched back and the chin is pulled up so that the throatline is taut does the airway fully open so the rescuer's breaths can reach the lungs. This fact is artfully enfolded into the 1959 manual's verbal analysis *thirty-one* times (in one two-page section it recurs seven times).[37] In addition, it is visually represented with twelve illustrations of the correct position of the victim's head, throat, and neck: ten are full-page, two are half-page. The ostensible purpose of many of these drawings is some additional instruction, but the "head tilt, chin up" position continues to be vividly rendered. The use of stark line drawings is crucial, for bodily learning—the ability of viewers to reproduce in their own bodies what is depicted in the visual field—happens much more rapidly with sketches and cartoons than with photographs or paintings.[38]

Six of the twelve illustrations incorporate another key instruction— "watch the chest"—either by stamping those three words onto the visual diagram or by a dotted line going from the rescuer's eyes to the person's chest. Once the chest rises, one takes one's mouth away from the person's mouth, so that air is expelled before the next breath is given—a principle restated thirteen times in the verbal text. Can one, after reading the handbook, ever forget these two rules: "head tilt, chin up" and "watch the chest"? Safar and McMahon assume the answer is yes. The handbook advises practicing every six months, the same interval that today, fifty years later, is still advocated.[39]

One 2009 study of neonatal resuscitation in delivery clinics in Lusaka and Ndola, Zambia, found that the performance capacity of college-trained nurse midwives (who already had an average of sixteen years of experience) more than doubled after being given explicit training in CPR. Before training the midwives carried out many acts correctly, such as warming the infant sufficiently, but did not know aspects of resuscitation such as the depth of the chest compression that would give the infant the best chance of survival. Despite a great improvement after training, the study also found that the abilities of the midwives fell off markedly after six months; in fact, their skills were only slightly better than they had been prior to training.[40] Worldwide, 4 million newborns die each year, 1 million of them from the arrest of heart and lungs; and since neonatal resuscitation is "simple, inexpensive," and "readily available," the study urges retraining in CPR every six months (and introduces the possibility that it should be done as often as every three months). The Nigerian study cited earlier similarly urged that all anesthetists in the Lagos University Teaching Hospital participate in "organized simulations" and "continuing training," and pointed out that the International Guildelines explicitly counsel periodic retraining. The Kilifi, Kenya, study also specifies that the learning achieved in any pediatric advanced life-support course is "*short-term* knowledge" only and that "recertification is important if the concepts... are to be retained."[41]

The consequence of failing to refresh knowledge every six months has been observed in countries all over the world. An unannounced 2010 test of CPR in the Hospital of Brigham and Women's in Boston, Massachusetts, revealed that only the physicians and nurses whose specialty was emergency medicine showed complete conversancy with CPR; even those physicians and nurses working in the cardiology sections of the hospital performed substantially below the recommended standard.[42] The *learning* and *relearning* of CPR, like the *act* of CPR, is built on repetition.

The existence of international guidelines, protocols, and handbooks carries us to the third level of repetition. Knowledge of CPR must be distributed across millions of people in every country to be effective. It must become not only an individual habit but an earthwide habit.

Concrete instances of the practice of CPR in hospitals have been given above because accurate statistics can be more easily gathered in the controlled situation of a hospital than on the street or in widely dispersed homes or workplaces. But most instances of cardiac arrest do not occur in the hospital; three-quarters of them happen in the home or at work or on the street.[43] Even the time it takes for an ambulance to arrive may be too much time. Sixty seconds after a person stops breathing, his oxygen level begins to drop; it continues falling rapidly. While many organs can survive a brief interruption of oxygen, the brain begins to suffer damage three to five minutes after it stops receiving oxygen.[44] Both the chance of survival and the chance of surviving without brain damage therefore depend on rapid response. The Lagos Teaching Hospital study found that the chance of survival tripled if CPR was begun in the first minute of cardiopulmonary arrest. If everyone in the hospital knows CPR, no time is lost running through the ward to find the one person who does know it. Studies of the street similarly emphasize the advantage of a small time window. One study of bystander CPR found that the survival rate was greater than 18 percent if the CPR was started in under two minutes and 12 percent if over two minutes.[45]

Only if knowledge of the practice is widely disseminated can the practice itself be practiced. Distribution is therefore not just a tertiary attribute of CPR; it is the heart of what it is. Physician Mickey Eisenberg's historical study of CPR, *Life in the Balance: Emergency Medicine and the Quest to Reverse Sudden Death*, is of necessity as much about the strategies of distribution as it is about medical research. That is in part because the founders of CPR themselves saw distribution as the key to its lifesaving powers. James Elam's medical research, for example, provided crucial evidence about the life-giving quality of expired air; though the oxygen level of breath is lower during exhalation (16 percent) than inhalation (21 percent), it provides enough oxygen to allow the blood of the subject to reach (and hold) a 100 percent saturation level.[46] He also demonstrated that the then-current forms of manual respiration delivered *zero* oxygen. But while continuing his research, he also met on Saturday mornings with Buffalo fire and ambulance squads and gave them theatrical demonstrations of the oxygen levels in the competing forms of assisted respiration, all registered on a giant dial visible to everyone in the room. When he moved to Baltimore, he (along with Peter Safar) constantly lobbied the Army, the Red Cross, and the National Research Council to endorse and thereby assist the distribution of the new procedure. He also made a film, *Rescue Breathing*.[47]

Like Elam, Peter Safar from the outset coupled medical research with distribution. His 1959 manual described above, *Resuscitation of the Unconscious Victim*, was simultaneously published in the United States, Canada, and the Commonwealth Nations of Great Britain.[48] Safar's coauthor, Martin McMahon, was the captain of the Baltimore fire and ambulance service, a partnership that began when Safar gave regular classes to firemen who in turn trained others.[49] Crucially, it was this attempt to carry the results outside the exclusive domain of physicians and onto the streets that in turn suddenly accelerated the medical research itself, for it was Fireman McMahon who was responsible for bringing together the two independent avenues of research, one on assisted respiration (Safar and Elam), the other on assisted circulation (Knickerbocker, Kouwenhoven, and Jude) that otherwise might have remained stranded from one another, as they had been throughout earlier decades and centuries.[50]

Blood needs to be laden with oxygen, but blood also needs to be (in Eisenberg's well-chosen word) "propelled" throughout the body. Conclusive evidence that circulation could be accomplished by massaging the chest—massaging it without cutting open the chest and acting on the heart directly, as originally attempted—was the work of James Jude, Guy Knickerbocker, and William Kouwenhoven at Johns Hopkins University Hospital, who also determined the best location, direction, and speed of the compressions. Crucial to the dissemination of their findings were two 1960 journal articles, the first of which, in the *Journal of the American Medical Association (JAMA)*, carried it to the international medical community, and the second of which, in *Reader's*

Digest, carried it to the public at large. *JAMA* reported that of twenty patients who suffered cardiac arrest in the hospital, fourteen had survived with the assistance of heart compressions lasting as little as one minute or as long as sixty-five minutes. The youngest person was two months; the oldest, eighty. But while the *JAMA* article focused on the work of the top research scientists, it simultaneously made clear that the procedure belonged not to physicians and nurses but to the people everywhere: "Anyone, anywhere, can now initiate cardiac resuscitative procedures. All that is needed is two hands."[51] *Reader's Digest*—which in 1960 had an international circulation of 23 million[52]—carried the news much farther. It chose to describe not in-hospital cases but an out-of-hospital case, narrating the story of the first person (as the magazine framed it) to be "snatched from death by a layman using the closed-chest method."[53]

Bystanders who give CPR greatly increase the chance that the person suffering cardiac arrest will survive. A 1994 study of New York City, for example, found that bystanders who gave CPR on average initiated it within one and a half minutes of the heart attack and that the people they helped had a three times higher chance of survival than those not receiving help.[54] A 2005 study of Los Angeles similarly found that bystanders doubled the chance of a person's surviving, and tripled the chance if the bystander was present at the moment the person first collapsed.[55] A 1998 study of large areas of urban and rural Sweden again found that bystanders doubled the chance of survival.[56]

Yet what is being doubled and tripled in all these geographies is a very low survival rate to begin with. Without bystander help, fewer than 1 in 100 (0.8 percent) survive in New York; almost 3 in 100 (2.8 percent) survive with bystander help; thus the overall New York average is 1 person in 100.[57] Los Angeles and Chicago[58] similarly have a 1-in-100 survival rate, as does Johannesburg, South Africa.[59] Sweden's overall rate is 5 people in 100, due to the much shorter time it takes for the ambulance to arrive and for defibrillation to begin. Shortening the time to defibrillation and the arrival of professional paramedics is key to increasing the numbers: traffic congestion is credited with causing the slow arrival time of New York ambulances (11.4 minutes); ambulances in need of repair and sections of the city lacking street names and numbers are credited with the fact that so few patients in Johannesburg live long enough to be eligible for defibrillation.[60] Key, too, to higher survival is raising the number of bystanders who feel competent to assist. The number is already high,[61] but increasing it still further will contribute to better survival rates, as citizen education in other regions of the United States and other countries of the world has shown.[62]

A country in which one has a greater chance of surviving an out-of-hospital cardiac arrest is Japan, where 1.4 million people are trained in CPR every year. One study tracked bystander intervention in Osaka during an eight-year period (1998–2006) when residents were learning CPR and ambulance personnel were for the first time permitted to use a defibrillator without a physician present. As a result of citizen training, the cases of cardiac arrest in which bystanders delivered CPR rose from 19 percent to 36 percent. The time that elapsed before CPR was initiated shortened, as did the time it took to contact the emergency service. The overall survival rate in Osaka rose to 12 percent.[63] The 12 percent survival figure can be contrasted with the 1 percent survival figure in New York, Chicago, and Los Angeles, and the 5 percent survival rate in the Swedish cities of Stockholm, Gothenburg, and Malmö and surrounding rural regions. Most studies give—in addition to overall survival rate—the much higher survival rate for a subset of cardiac arrest that begins with ventricular fibrillation: in this category the overall survival rate in the three American cities was 5 percent, in Sweden 9.5 percent, and in Osaka 16 percent.

Equally striking evidence of the importance of population-wide training is the help bystanders in Kyoto gave to the 5170 children who suffered out-of-hospital cardiac arrest during a two-year period between 2005 and 2007.[64] The children's heart attacks were brought on by internal causes such as heart problems, respiratory diseases, and tumors, or by external causes such as hanging, drug overdose, and drowning.[65] Bystanders gave CPR to 2432 of the children, almost half of the total number (47 percent).[66] The study differentiates between those bystanders who used classic CPR—both chest compression and breathing—and those who used compression alone, and found that the first had greater life-sustaining powers and better neurological outcomes.[67] But it also stresses that *any* version of CPR more than doubled the child's chance of not only surviving but doing so with a minimum of neurological damage.

While, then, CPR is a habit structure built on repetition—repetition within the act, repetition in the initial acquisition and subsequent maintenance of the practice, repetition of the practice across millions of people in every country of the world—it has high levels of thinking and research built into it. Indeed, Columbia University president Jonathan Cole's recent book about brilliant discoveries carried out by American research universities cites the 1959 invention of CPR as an instance of why the United States—and by implication, every other country—should continue to support universities.[68] True of the original discovery of CPR, so too the ongoing refinement of our understanding of the conditions under which it best works requires huge investments of intellectual labor, whether—as the studies cited above illustrate— at the University of Johannesburg, the Lagos Teaching Hospital, or the thirteen hospitals and medical centers in Kyoto, Osaka, Senri, and Seattle that contributed to the eight-year Osaka study.

This constant research also means that the practice is continually reviewed and refined when evidence indicates the procedures should change. Classic CPR is still the recommended procedure for professional caretakers, for bystanders giving CPR to children and infants, and for confident, well-trained bystanders giving CPR to adults. But the international guidelines now suggest that if one is an untrained or an unconfident bystander, or a bystander hesitant to place one's mouth in contact with an adult's mouth, one can deliver only the chest compressions.[69] Much more research is needed to confirm the benefits of this shift in recommended procedure.

Some recent studies of bystander assistance during adult cardiac arrest show that (as with the Kyoto children) classic CPR is more beneficial than compression-only. But other studies suggest compression alone may be equally effective. Several explanations have been given for this puzzling fact. First, compression-only is much easier for an untrained bystander; the instructions for compression-only can be given by a telephone dispatcher to a bystander more easily than can the steps of classic CPR. Carrying out one part of CPR correctly may be as, or more, effective than doing both parts haphazardly. It is also the case that the chest compressions must be given rapidly and forcefully at 100 beats per minute; interrupting that action for too long an interval to give breaths can jeopardize the momentum of the compressions. Finally, a reluctance to place one's mouth on a stranger's mouth may make the bystander carry out both actions with less commitment and passion than are needed; it may even make bystanders hesitant to begin. The 2005 guidelines called for much more research on this question, whose results affected the next set of guidelines issued in November 2010. An interim 2008 advisory from the American Heart Association recommended "hands only" (compression-only) CPR. Its title, "A Call to Action for Bystander Response," indicates the hope that this recommendation will recruit more people into the practice of CPR.[70]

This first emergency procedure looked at here—CPR—is one that focuses on individuals. The arrest of heart and lungs (whether in a newborn or in an adult) happens one person at a time; so, too, the acquisition of the knowledge and skill embedded in CPR happens one person at a time. The next section turns away from the individual to emergency procedures that are collective in nature and that enlist the efforts of small assemblies of people. We will see the part played by habit in emergency procedures that together constitute civil society.

But before turning away from CPR, it is useful to take note (even in the midst of this highly individualized act) of the part played by civil society—municipal fire departments, schools, churches, the

International Red Cross, the American Heart Association, the National Research Council, Boy Scouts, Girl Scouts—in encouraging the distribution of the rescue practice across the world's population. Eisenberg's history of CPR provides striking evidence of the part played by civil society at every stage of the long endeavor to discover the best set of steps for restoring breath and heartbeat. The Amsterdam Rescue Society was formed in 1767 to recommend procedures for resuscitating those who had drowned; in response to Amsterdam's act, the cities of Venice and Milan began similar societies in 1768; in 1769 the city of Hamburg required a reading in all churches of the best steps to follow to assist "the drowned, strangled, frozen, and those overcome by noxious gases"; Paris started its rescue society in 1771; St. Petersburg, in 1774; London, in 1774. What is today known as the Royal Humane Society in England began as the Society for the Recovery of Persons Apparently Drowned when physicians in London read the reports of successful resuscitations in Amsterdam.[71]

Recommending an anthology of procedures (some of which would still today be credited, and many others wholly discredited), these eighteenth-century societies not only saved lives but helped create the wide aspiration to find the way to, in effect, restore the heart and lungs to their habitual actions. Here is the fourth level of habit embedded in CPR: the human heart beats 31 million times a year.[72] How could it suddenly "forget" how to do this? CPR is a procedure in which a conscious understanding of the pumping motion of the heart is directly relayed to the heart by the rescuer's hands. After what may be as little as one minute or as long as sixty-five minutes, the heart remembers and reacquires its habitual motion.

MODEL 2: MUTUAL AID CONTRACTS

The arrangements for mutual aid in the dispersed communities on the plains of Canada's Saskatchewan province illustrate a second model of emergency action. There, small constellations of towns and farms sign an explicit social contract promising mutual aid. In the language of the contract of the Quill Plains Mutual Aid Area: "each party to the agreement will assist any other party to the agreement in the event of a disaster."[73] This language, or a close equivalent, is repeated in many of the other social contracts from the Saskatchewan province, such as that of the Battlefords Mutual Aid Area. The contracts vary in size. The Quills Plain contract binds together three towns and four rural districts, each in itself sparsely populated (approximately 700 people) but together becoming 5000. The Battlesford contract brings together 23,000 residents.[74] The signing of these local contracts predates their formal authorization by the Legislative Assembly of Saskatchewan which in 1989–90 passed "An Act Respecting Emergency" whose Article Eleven stipulates that local communities "may enter into agreements" with other communities for "mutual aid" and the "pool[ing] of resources."[75] The provincial government by this act endorses and facilitates what the local communities have in many cases already brought into being.

The power to declare the emergency is also local: Article Twenty of the Emergency Planning Act specifically gives to the "local authority" the right to make the declaration and stipulates that if, because of the crisis, the members who together constitute the local authority are dispersed, some one member can make the declaration on behalf of the local authority as a whole, thereby setting into motion a series of legal powers and paths of financial support.

On July 3, 2000, for example, the eighty-house village of Vanguard suffered a torrential downpour of rain. In this part of the Saskatchewan prairie, the annual rainfall is eleven inches. But on this single evening—between 4 p.m. and midnight—over thirteen inches of water fell; its impact on Vanguard was amplified by the fact that the tiny village is situated at the bottom of a valley and thus received additional water flowing in from surrounding hills.[76] Streamflow records for nearby Notuku Creek had been kept for over sixty years by a hydrometric station. Streamflow is measured in cubic decameters (dam^3): a decameter is ten meters, a cubic decameter is 1000 cubic meters. The *annual* discharge of Notuku Creek averaged 28,500 dam^3 with a monthly figure of zero in the dry periods of each year. During this one storm, the discharge was 73,000 dam³, by far the highest level it had ever reached.[77] A few minutes after midnight, the deputy mayor and another council member met by candlelight to put the formal declaration of emergency into effect.[78] Next morning at daybreak the full council met at the mayor's house.

The Vanguard storm was an intensified version of a storm that was hitting a 1700-square-kilometer region. With 353 million cubic meters of water reaching the ground, it was "the largest eight-hour storm ever documented on the Canadian prairies."[79] The rain was accompanied by other sources of terror: between 6 p.m. and 7 p.m., 1051 strokes of lightning were recorded (and in the storm as a whole, four times that number), and immediately southwest of Vanguard a band of hail fell that produced "100% crop damage." But by far the greatest problem was the water. The lower bands of the storm over Vanguard consisted of air that three days earlier had been "on the ground" in a corridor of farm states from Texas up to North Dakota absorbing moisture from "rapidly growing agricultural crops"; the upper bands of air had three days earlier been "near ground-level" in the fertile central valley of California, again absorbing moisture from the fast-growing crops. Once the storm reached Vanguard, it became "anchored" to that spot by a strong wind blowing from the north that prevented the storm itself from continuing its northward-moving direction.[80] The Saskatchewan plains often receive severe weather but usually that weather sweeps rapidly by; on this night, it stayed fixed in place for many hours.

Vanguard was now an island surrounded by water. How then could people from the outside who wanted to help get in? A small Hutterite community ten kilometers to the south, Cypress Hutterite Colony Farm, immediately built a barge and carried in fifty volunteers that first day and on the days following.[81] A farmer with a small plane landed on a patch of available ground to lift out those who were stranded and needed to leave. The residents (all of whose homes had two to eight feet of sewage in the basements) were offered accommodations in a small, nearby college that was empty for the summer; but the residents declined to abandon their homes.[82]

For three months (July, August, September) Vanguard residents had no water. Individual wells and the village reservoir were contaminated with *E. coli* bacteria and with the herbicides that had been put on the fields in the preceding four weeks. Though no pesticides had been recently used in the fields around Vanguard, waters rushing in from other regions brought this third form of contaminant as well.[83] A bottled-water company in the town of Swift Current brought in the first truckload of water, which ten bottling companies around the province continued to deliver without interruption, and without cost, during the three months.[84]

Supplying Vanguard and the immigrant volunteers with food was a complex, but apparently (for the people of Saskatchewan) not a difficult, problem to solve. Communities such as Swift Current and Regina—separated from Vanguard by 72 kilometers and 260 kilometers, respectively—were among the many that provided the residents with food day after day.[85] The backbreaking work of clearing and bleaching the basements, and digging a deep pit to bury and treat the contents of the storm-ruined abattoir, was carried out by residents and neighboring communities. Communication was carried out during this period by a series of letters hand-delivered to each house—for example, urging the residents not to drink the water even if it appeared clear, and later providing instructions on the procedure for clearing and testing the wells. The letters were delivered by high school graduates who a day before the storm had returned to their single-building K–12 school for a July 1 Canada Day town reunion.[86] This house-by-house form of communication (rather than anonymous media announcements) was singled out as key in all the after-action reports: "Concise information is needed quickly and people may not absorb this in the normal manner. Hand delivery is the recommended option."[87]

The Saskatchewan mutual aid contracts specify procedures for determining lines of authority and communication. Equally important, the contracts may explicitly require that lists be made of materials (such as welding equipment or maps or trucks) that individual owners have agreed to contribute during any crisis.[88] The compilation of such a list itself acts as a rehearsal; it requires the community to think through a starkly specific set of questions about the tools required in a flood, in a mudslide, in a fire, in a chemical spill, in a plow wind, in a tornado, and to designate the actual location where each tool exists and the person who will bear the responsibility for bringing it to the site.

Early in the morning of April 18, 1990, a grain elevator caught fire in Naicam, a town of 900 residents and a member of the Quill Plains Mutual Aid area. A grain elevator (which typically holds 168,000 bushels of grain) is itself a cooperative structure in which many farmers pool their produce.[89] Historians have attributed Saskatchewan's inclination toward progressive politics (the province originated Canada's Progressive Party and was the first region in North America to have a health care system) to its early habits of cooperative ownership of grain elevators.[90] In the late nineteenth century, these structures were privately owned, but by 1911 they had become associations; by 1975, almost all of them (79 percent) were farmer-owned rather than privately owned.[91] The Naicam grain elevator is shared by 300 farms in the region. On this day in 1990, the burning elevator itself became the beneficiary of another voluntary association, the Quill Plains Mutual Aid contract.

Within five minutes of the fire report, the Naicam all-volunteer fire truck arrived; a truck from Spalding (eleven kilometers away) arrived in fifteen minutes; a truck from Melfort (fifty-four kilometers away) arrived in fifty-five minutes with an aerial ladder that would prove decisive during the course of the day.[92] Forty minutes later, as the winds changed and the fire became more threatening, a request for the Watson fire truck (thirty-three kilometers away) was issued. Three fans of branching telephone calls brought waves of food and volunteers with shovels during the nine-hour fire fight.[93]

As was true at Vanguard, any major problem in these prairie towns usually, at some point, involves a question of water. With four fire trucks together pumping 10,000 liters a minute, the problems of exhausting the water supply began to loom, even with the water shut off in parts of the town. Thus, two hours into the fight a convoy of twenty farm trucks with large and small water tanks—the large-capacity trucks already designated for this job in the Quills Plain Mutual Aid contract, the small trucks spontaneously volunteering—began a steady tour to and from Round Lake, five kilometers from the town.[94] Because the mayor had declared an emergency at the time the request to the trucks was made (9:15 a.m.), crews were legally able to barricade the entire roadway so that the trucks could proceed without interruption or danger.[95] By 11:15, the town well still had 391,500 liters remaining, but at 10,000 liters a minute that would have permitted only thirty-nine minutes of water had there been no farm trucks assisting.[96]

Equally concrete as the plan for confronting fires is the elaborate Saskatchewan design for evacuation and billeting. Communities that agree to be "receiving communities" keep their houses stocked with materials to accommodate those evacuated; the registry of houses is reviewed twice a year; one receiving community practiced once a month, and at the end of two years had a major simulation in which people were housed and fed for two weeks.[97] The Saskatchewan town of Kindersley devised a billeting plan that would accommodate 1500 persons. Rather than testing it with an evacuation exercise, they arranged for a week of indigenous games in December 1994 and used the billeting arrangements to house 1500 athletes. The arrangements for housing and food were so well distributed that only a few additional people were needed to register the guests and keep them informed.[98]

Such exercises, not only in Saskatchewan but in other Canadian provinces, are forward-looking rather than backward-looking; they are designed not only "to test" the procedures that are already in place, but "to design" systems that will be increasingly supple in their response. One exercise in Nova Scotia, for example, confronted that province with a daylong hypothetical emergency that consisted of 415 separate incidents spiraling out of hurricane-force winds, freezing rain, and fire.

The test, involving both civilians and military, drew on the resources of seventeen municipalities, six companies, and twelve federal departments. The exercise revealed military reliance on acronyms that civilians could not decipher; it also made visible the need to design smaller mutual aid areas, to decentralize lines of authority, and to enhance the powers of local municipalities.[99]

These varying levels of mental rehearsal enable participants to become competent and confident. Equally important, if there are politically problematic procedures, those come to the attention of the community long before they are put into actual practice.[100] For example, the Saskatchewan Emergency Planning Act has a number of provisions that permit the suspension of ordinary democratic procedures once a formal declaration of emergency has been made by either the national or the local government. It allows immediate conscription; it allows entering a house without a warrant; and it includes provisions for both prohibiting and requiring movement, thereby restricting the ordinary right of entry and exit (as was true when the road between Round Lake and Naicam was sealed off to all vehicles other than farm trucks carrying water). But because the procedures have been subjected to public scrutiny, additional clauses have been added that place restrictions on the emergency powers, both by limiting the number of days an emergency declaration can last and by requiring compensation for damage done during the emergency.

However problem-laden such provisions are, they should be contrasted with the situation of a country where no civil defense procedures have been specified, or where procedures have been specified by one branch of the government but are not known to the population at large because (as in the United States)[101] no public discussions and practice of civil defense ever take place.

The Saskatchewan social contracts are sometimes highly specific in their content, detailing the piece of equipment that any one person will be relied on to bring. The necessity of this kind of specification is amplified by the distances separating members of the mutual aid contract; one might otherwise drive fifteen kilometers to the site of a problem only to find that the tool one has brought has already been carried there by several other rescuers and that some other highly needed tool can only be supplied by circling back home in a thirty-kilometer round trip during which the calamity will continue to unfold. While this specificity may prove crucial, even more crucial is the fact of regularly working and planning together, whatever the content of that work or planning session.

This principle, vividly at work in Saskatchewan, was dramatically demonstrated in the immediate aftermath of the Kobai earthquake that in 1995 killed 6000 residents of Japan and left 350,000 people homeless. The government—as media from Japan and from around the world soon noticed—was immobilized by "ineptitude" and "jurisdictional disputes," whereas 1.2 million volunteers moved in with speed and precision, donating not only their labor but $1.6 billion to the devastated districts.[102] According to Robert Pekkanen, the surge of spontaneous assistance is correctly attributed to the remarkable fact that Japan has 300,000 small neighborhood groups (or, to be precise, 298,488). As one study of Yokohama makes clear, the association—though on average comprising between 100 and 300 households—may be as small as 7 homes or as large as 3000.[103] These neighborhood associations do not mentally rehearse how to clear rubble after earthquakes; but they do habitually clean parks, maintain roads, clear streams, and repair street lamps. They do not practice attending to the injured and homeless, but they do regularly support children's groups, youth groups, and the elderly. They do not organize disaster relief, but they do routinely organize neighborhood celebrations of festival days.[104]

One might call these practices "habits of mutual aid," or one might instead use the designation Alexis de Tocqueville long ago assigned to them: "habits of the heart."[105] In his travels through America in the nineteenth century, Tocqueville was astonished by the practice of voluntary association that he saw in people "of all ages, all conditions, and all disposition" organized around every conceivable subject, "religious, moral, serious, futile, general or restricted, enormous or diminutive," collectively attempting to carry "to the highest perfection the art of pursuing in common the object of their common desires."[106] Although not so extravagantly diverse, the voluntary associations in Japan certainly take varied forms: urban, suburban, rural, neighborhood associations (*chounaikai*), local retailers' associations (*shotenkai*), "self-government associations" in high-rise apartment complexes and labor unions (*jichikai*).[107] The response of the Japanese neighborhoods to the Kobai calamity is consistent with Tocqueville's description of the effect of voluntary associations: "Feelings and opinions are recruited, the heart is enlarged, and the human mind is developed only by the reciprocal influence of men upon one another."[108]

As observed earlier, the question is not *whether* habit will surface in an emergency (it surely will) but instead *which* habit will emerge, and whether it will be serviceable or unserviceable. Japan's governmental bureaucracy certainly had its own well-practiced, deeply entrenched habits, but these turned out to be incapacitating while the "habits of the heart" practiced by the neighborhood associations turned out to be enabling. As it happens, these groups are almost entirely independent of the government, so much so that Japan has often been described as a country that suppresses civil society.[109] Unlike many democracies, Japan does not grant to voluntary associations a tax-exempt status, or give them the virtually free mailing privileges that equivalent groups elsewhere receive, or grant them legal recognition as incorporated "persons" that would let them receive donations or gifts. The spectacle of 1.2 million volunteers putting themselves at risk (despite the fact that none of them were covered by insurance) led to a countrywide demand for a major modification in Japan's relation to its own civil society. A 1998 Non-Profit Activities Law now allows such voluntary groups much greater freedom from bureaucratic oversight than they had earlier, and confers legal recognition on them.[110]

While, then, habit is often seen as a phenomenon unresponsive to "change," habits inevitably come into play when people face world-changing events such as torrential storms, fires, and earthquakes. In turn, habits that prove beneficial in an emergency may also bring about—as in the case of Japan's Non-Profit Activities Law—significant changes in formerly unyielding governmental structures.

The compatibility between mutual aid compacts and the necessity of confronting change has been documented in many other countries. In Africa, voluntary associations—what one scholar calls "economies of affection"[111]—existed long before colonial rule and the emergence of states. These "long-standing informal solidarities" sometimes retained the same form when the population confronted rapid urbanization, and elsewhere gave rise to new forms.[112] During the third, fourth, and fifth decades of the twentieth century, for example, thousands of rural residents in West Africa migrated to Lagos, Nigeria, and Accra, Ghana—cities that had no provisions for assisting them if they were sick, injured, unemployed, orphaned, or distressed by the dislocation of their sudden move. The practice of voluntary association, which many of the migrants carried with them from their hamlets or villages, provided for pooling of resources that covered the cost of illness, disability, funerals, court appearances, newly arriving babies, the formation of schools, and scholarships for promising children.[113] By 1956, for example, almost 17,000 people in Accra belonged to at least one voluntary association, most of them comprised of 30 to 100 people but sometimes much smaller or much larger. The society membership was sometimes based on the village from which the migrants came (*association d'originaire*) but other times based on common interest or form of work.[114]

Regularly addressing individual emergencies, these societies "were also in the habit of providing a lump sum to each member in rotation"[115] by establishing a carefully designed system to facilitate savings. For example, market women in the Ghanaian association called Nanemei Akpee (Society of Friends) provided working capital for one another through their weekly meetings; each week, each member made a carefully recorded contribution to a collective sum which was given to one member, until all members had taken a turn, after which the rotation would begin anew. Named "rotating credit associations" by Clifford Geertz,[116] this form of mutual aid society exists not only throughout West Africa but also throughout the world, in places such as China, Vietnam, India, and England.[117]

In Africa—as in Saskatchewan and Kobai—nature continues in the late twentieth and early twenty-first centuries to provide countless hazards that must be protected against. A form of association still visible in the twenty-first century is the assistance farmers give one another in places such as the Oromo region of eastern Ethiopia. Here "seed insecurity" is a large problem. Most farmers grow a form of sorghum that requires eight or nine months to mature; if too much or too little rain falls during this time, they need to reseed, using the slow-growing cultivars if the season is still early and the more rapidly growing, but less nutritious, forms if the season has progressed. Each farmer saves seed—storing it "above the cooking fire" or "in an underground pit"—but often there is not enough for multiple sowings; then farmers rely on the seed stores of neighbors (as well as the marketplace if they have money). The voluntary associations are not family-based: during 1998, for example, no farmer reported receiving seed from kin; neither did any farmer receive seed from an NGO source.[118] Because "mutual aid associations are common among the Oromo, and norms stress generosity with seed," large volumes of seed move from farm to farm, leading to great diversity in the plants.

This long-standing cooperation among eastern Ethiopian farmers has many analogues, such as the practices of mutual aid among farmers in Zimbabwe that, even during the severe famine of 1982–84, helped peasant farmers survive. During the drought, women often had to walk fifteen kilometers each way to obtain water; teachers in the Matabeleland and Masvingo provinces reported children fainting in the classrooms; the Ministry of Health reported that 70 percent of the children in these provinces were undernourished; more than a third of the cattle died. Here, as in the case of eastern Ethiopia in the early 2000s, it was voluntary association rather than biological association that was relied upon. As the "drought deepened" over the course of one year, the number of households that could no longer feed themselves rose from 16 percent to 56 percent; but people did not go to family members for help. Assistance given by relatives (who often live at a distance) was never higher than 9 percent and fell to lower levels as the drought grew more severe.[119] The voluntary associations, in contrast, grew stronger as the famine grew more severe despite the fact that the sharing of oxen, a central practice of the associations, was diminished by the death of so many of the animals.[120] Mutual aid not only enabled the people to survive but, as Michael Bratton writes, led to the "amazing" fact that "peasant families grew and sold more maize in the first five years of independence [1980–85] than during the previous years."[121]

What in Africa or Japan or Canada is the effect of the mutual aid contracts and voluntary associations on the larger population, the population outside the boundary of the association itself? Do these "habits of the heart," "economies of affection," and "norms of generosity" spill outside the associations, affecting other people and even the state as a whole? The examples above all suggest the way the "norms of generosity" overflow from the interior to the exterior. In Saskatchewan, the Hutterite village that made the barge for rescuers trying to reach Vanguard, and the town of Regina that contributed to the food, are not formal members of the town's voluntary association. In Japan, the neighborhood groups who assisted the earthquake victims of Kobai became their neighbors at the moment the earthquake struck. In the mutual aid communities of eastern Ethiopia, 50 percent of the farms that provided seed to their fellow association members also gave seed to farms outside the association.[122]

This same principle of transfer appears to describe the relation of civil society to the state as a whole.[123] Voluntary associations help to protect the entire population of a state because, as Tocqueville long ago stressed, they act as a safeguard, diminishing the impact the executive power of a state can have on the people.[124] A second effect (or perhaps instead, a second way of saying the same thing) is that such voluntary

associations increase "the accountability" of a government to its population.[125] A third effect (or alternatively, a third restatement of the first
two) is that such voluntary associations appear to address the governments of the countries in which they reside not for personal favors but
for actions in the public interest.

In his widely known study *Making Democracy Work: Civic Traditions in Modern Italy,* Robert Putnam compared towns with weak and
robust habits of voluntary association (such as sports clubs, community
organizations, and youth groups). Citizens of towns with extensive
practice of voluntary association contacted their governmental officials
much less often; and when they did, the issue raised was almost always
some problem of public interest. The citizens in towns with low levels
of voluntary association contacted their government officers frequently,
but did so to ask for jobs or personal favors (the "average councilor" in
such districts receives eight to ten inquiries about personal favors every
day)—almost never to call attention to an issue affecting the public
good.[126]

The first two examples of emergency preparation—CPR and mutual
aid contracts—address hazards that usually come from nature: earthquakes, torrential rain, severe drought, fire, disease, and the fallibil-
ity of the human body that can suffer a heart attack even when the
sun is shining and the ground is still. The third and fourth genres of
emergency preparation—which will be looked at in the sections that
follow—come not from nature but from the other profound source of
hazard, the phenomenon of war. In moving to these next two forms of
emergency preparation, the subject shifts from injuries decoupled from
human intention to injuries that are the direct outcome of such intention. The focus also shifts from small collaborative groups (collectively
called by the name "civil society") to the much larger and more unitary
collective that is the nation-state.

Before moving away from voluntary associations, however, it is
important to notice a feature that has so far been ignored. While our

attention has here centered on voluntary associations as remedies against natural disasters, it is also the case that they have often been instigated as a response to—a way of heading off—the possibility of war. As we saw in Chapter 3, hundreds of European cities came into being as "sworn communes for peace" and for mutual protection, as one clause in the Beauvais charter announces: "If any man who has sworn the commune suffers a violation of rights, . . . [the peers] shall do justice against . . . the offender."[127] It is logical for clauses of the charter promising mutual defense to be followed by clauses arranging for jury trial because such compacts seek to diminish injury issuing from outside the city (war or armed attack) and from inside the city (crime). One oath for mutual assistance from the Bologna region makes the coupling explicit: the members "should maintain and defend each other against all men, within the commune and outside it."[128] The "communes for peace" seek to secure their members from both sources of injury.[129]

The town's commitment to protecting its members from outside aggression by no means implied that outsiders were themselves subjected to aggressive treatment. On the contrary: Harold Berman writes that "immigrants were to be granted the same rights as citizens [the right to vote, the right to bear arms, the right to a jury trial] after residence for a year and a day."[130] Before gaining those rights, the immigrant was seen as someone deserving of special care. A 1303 guild statute from Verona, one of the oldest in existence, specifies the categories of people who should be the recipients of special aid: one had the obligation to give "fraternal assistance in necessity of whatever kind," to give "hospitality toward strangers, when passing through the town," and to offer "comfort in the case of debility."[131] The mutual aid contracts and communes for peace out of which Europe's cities grew came into being to protect insiders and outsiders from injury—injury that could arise either from crime or from war.

It is a remarkable fact, as we saw throughout Chapters 3 and 4, that the nation-state in social contract theory of the seventeenth and eighteenth centuries has almost precisely the same point of origin. The contract comes into being, as Hobbes repeatedly urged, "to get us out of the miserable condition of war"; and both Hobbes and Locke repeatedly stressed that protecting oneself against crime and war was at the heart of consent theory. While, then, the interaction between civil society and the state can take many different forms, it is the urge to protect against wrongfully inflicted injury that brings both into being.

MODEL 3: SWISS SHELTER SYSTEM

A third extraordinary model of the place of habit in emergency preparation is the Swiss shelter system, which is shaped by three underlying assumptions. The first assumption (as the Swiss Office of Civil Defence observes in one of its widely distributed pamphlets) is that the locus of injury in any future war will be civilians. The ratio of civilian to soldier deaths jumped sharply from World War I to World War II, and then jumped again in the Korean War, and then jumped once more in the Vietnam War. In a nuclear war, the casualties will be close to 100 percent civilians.[132]

The second assumption is that a sturdy shelter system will almost certainly save the country. If an area is directly hit by a nuclear weapon, the people will die; but if, according to Swiss medical research, a weapon explodes even two kilometers away, a fallout shelter will give 500 times the protection available outside the shelter.[133] The fallout shelter is treated in the widely distributed pamphlets as a living, breathing entity that must be continually checked and kept in sturdy working order. Over the past four decades, the shelter has been continually subjected to new forms of testing, such as the 2000–2001 tests on the shelter's immunity to electromagnetic pulse issuing from a nuclear explosion or from electromagnetic weapons.[134]

The third assumption is that a democracy must guarantee "equality of survival." Any solution to the threat of nuclear disaster must therefore be distributed across the entire population.[135] This requirement for universal access to the means of survival, repeatedly stressed in the country's 2001 *Civil Protection Concept*, is anchored in Article 2 of the federal constitution of Switzerland, which includes the guarantee of "equal opportunity" among the rights and liberties the constitution exists to safeguard, as well as Article 61, which assigns to the federal government responsibility for protecting the population against armed conflict.[136] "Equality of survival" was, from the outset, restated many times in the early decades of the shelter system: *The 1971 Conception of Swiss Civil Defence* lists first, among its principles, "A place in a shelter for *every inhabitant* of Switzerland," and later reaffirms, "Equal chances of survival for all," insisting that "the same chance of survival during wartime must be offered to *all inhabitants* of our country."[137] As the word *inhabitant* indicates, the shelter system aims to ensure equality of survival to foreign residents as well as citizens.

"Equality of survival" may be a principle that is always embedded in preparations for emergency. CPR is knowable; one can learn it if one chooses. But one cannot know who will one day be the recipient of that embodied knowledge; it is there *for anyone.* Even if one has been motivated to learn CPR because one has a child who is a swimmer or a brother who has a weak heart, the knowledge is not specific to that child or brother; it is available to every person whose path crosses one's own. Of the thousands of people giving bystander CPR in the studies cited earlier, many did not know the person they were helping. The booklet on artificial respiration that so successfully teaches the "head tilt, chin up" and "watch the chest" instructions was published in a year—1956— when racial relations in the United States were still deeply strained, yet it assumes that the person learning the steps is equally likely to be giving artificial respiration to a person who is black or white. The booklet specifies the places on the surface of a white person's body and a black person's body where oxygen deprivation (signaled by the color blue) will be most visible. The same commitment to "equality of survival" is true of mutual aid compacts; all participants agree that they will take on (and distribute, or equalize, among themselves) the adversity that may fall on any one member of their association. But the Swiss shelter system makes this principle of "equality of survival" astonishingly explicit and astonishingly concrete. To have carried out this principle across an entire population is a feat of civic and moral engineering.

Swiss law requires that every house have, and maintain in good condition, a fallout shelter. The "obligation to build," for many decades a Swiss requirement, is currently encoded in Article 46 of the Federal Law on Civil Protection System and Protection & Support Service, a law passed by the federal parliament on October 4, 2002, and ratified by the population on May 18, 2003, with 80.6 percent voting in favor. A federal requirement, the obligation to build is currently enforced by the cantons (the country's twenty-six states). People who do not build a shelter must pay compensation to help pay for public shelters.[138] The shelter system underwent review and revision in the 1990s and again in the early years of the twenty-first century. Almost all aspects of the original system have been reaffirmed, even though it is now hoped that the country will have a two-year lead time before armed conflict—much less time than the time required to build the shelters but enough time to restock them.[139] In addition to the use of shelters in wartime, their use for natural disasters and epidemics—phenomena with less lead time—has been stressed since the 1990s and continues today.

Swiss law makes provisions that go beyond the shelter requirements. It assigns specific obligations to its male citizens beginning at the age of twenty and continuing until the age of forty, an upper age that can be increased to fifty or reduced to thirty-five depending on the parliament's assessment of the likelihood of armed conflict.[140] Participation by female citizens and foreign residents is voluntary.[141] The law requires conscripts and volunteers to practice approximately four days a year.[142] Article 36 of the Federal Law on Civil Protection specifies a yearly refresher course of two to seven days, in addition to the two to three weeks of original training (Article 33) and two weeks of advanced training every fourth year (Article 35). In 1988, for example, the Swiss citizenry collectively devoted 901,000 days to rehearsing their individual assignments; in 1998 (when world tensions were lower), 600,000 days.[143]

Any Swiss man can, when asked, specify a highly precise task. One friend in Zürich, for example, is on the Committee for Special Objects. He is required during practice days to go into a particular church in Zürich, gather the altarpieces and all the statues of the saints, including the statue of Saint Roch with the accompanying statue of Saint Roch's dog who in turn holds in his mouth a ceramic Eucharist wafer.[144] Saint Roch protects against plague because in his own life he moved among plague-stricken people distributing medicine and food. The dog first began to accompany the saint when the saint himself had the plague; the dog brought him bread each day. In caring for the Zürich statue, the man or woman assigned this task enacts the very principle of protection the statue celebrates. Further, in saving any one precious object, what is preserved is not only that object but the population's link, through that object, to many kindred objects outside of Switzerland, which may or may not survive a nuclear war. Transnational as well as national culture is at risk. Artifacts depicting Saint Roch reside in Zürich, but they also reside in Venice (the paintings by Jacopo Tintoretto and Bernardo Strozzi in the Scuola of San Rocco), and in museums in Marseille, Budapest, Toronto, Philadelphia, and Sarasota, as well as in hundreds of towns and villages throughout the world that contain carved and painted depictions of the saint by unknown hands.

The civil defense conscript assigned to this Zürich church carefully wraps each artifact (including the ceramic wafer) and carries it to a specified shelter. At the end of several days, he carries each object from its shelter back to the church, unwraps it, dusts it off, and restores it to its original position. The Swiss believe that preserving a population means not just keeping individual residents free from physical injury but keeping intact networks of families and friends, and the cultural artifacts that are precious to that population.

In addition to shelters for every person within its borders, Switzerland has built 290 shelters providing 7,416,000 cubic feet of storage for cultural objects.[145] Elaborate inventories, diagrams, and tracings have been, and continue to be, made of both movable and immovable artifacts. Preparation for protecting treasured objects includes not only securing an appropriate shelter, but also making certain that the roads, paths, and staircases to the shelters are specified. If the object is too wide to be carried up a given staircase, a new route or a new destination must be found. The Swiss laws on cultural property follow from the 1954 Hague Convention on the Protection of Cultural Property and the 1999 Second Protocol, which increased the level of protection beyond that originally provided.[146]

Switzerland has been accurately described as a "reverse Potemkin village."[147] A Potemkin village has visible facades with no actual construction behind them. Switzerland is the opposite: its shelter system has few visible structures, but inside many mountains are hidden hospitals and beneath nearly every house is a fully stocked and working fallout shelter. Dispersed throughout the countryside are shelters for the artworks and artifacts held in common by the population that connect them to one another and to a transnational culture.

The shelter system gives Switzerland political autonomy. The Bern pamphlets many times repeat that one purpose of the shelter is to make Switzerland less vulnerable to "blackmail" or "extortion."[148] During the second half of the twentieth century and the beginning of the twenty-first, the country has had little power to persuade the superpowers to dismantle their nuclear arsenals; nor would it have been endurable to be in a permanent posture of petition, continually requesting the United States and Russia to stop speaking about sending missiles on trajectories crossing above Swiss land. The shelter system restores to the Swiss their power to affect their own destiny. It provides a form of "vertical evacuation."[149]

During these same decades in the United States, the population—without actual debate or deliberation or medical research—somehow came to the conclusion that shelters were useless and only increased the chance of going to war. No referendum (such as that in which 80.6% of the Swiss population validated the "obligation to build") was held; the decision to ignore shelters was a presidential decision. What made this outcome especially startling was that the government leaders of the United States, the very individuals who had the nuclear arsenal at their disposal, continued to spend billions of dollars on an extensive shelter system for themselves in Mount Weather in the Blue Ridge Mountains of Virginia, a man-made cavern large enough to contain three-story buildings and a lake—"a lake," as one journalist observed, "large enough for water-skiing."[150] The Federal Emergency Management Agency (FEMA) later spent $2.9 billion on a mobile shelter to supplement the fixed shelter for the president.[151]

It could be argued that the White House is a certain target, whereas the risk to the homes of the citizens is distributed over a wide area and therefore only a small risk is suffered by any one citizen. But a nuclear weapon does not "take out" a single house, whether the White House or any other house; if the White House is a likely target, all houses in Washington, DC, and the mid-Atlantic region should have shelters. A fully democratic arrangement might be one in which every twenty-four hours the president (on the basis of a daily lottery) were assigned a random household to go to in the event of nuclear war; the way to protect him would be—following the Swiss example—to make certain all homes were equally protected, so that wherever the lottery took him, he would have a chance of surviving.

This arrangement might even give the president a greater chance of surviving since wherever he or she was, a shelter would be nearby. Exercises designed to test White House evacuation to Mount Weather have called into question whether members of the executive branch will be able to reach the Blue Ridge Mountains, since their path to the shelter is likely to be blocked by roadways clogged with people trying to flee the East Coast. Those eligible to enter the shelter all carry a special pass that, when shown to the population, is supposed to license them to move to the front of all lines. But since most of the population has not been consulted about this arrangement, it is not self-evident that such a pass will have the hoped-for effect: during one exercise, a bus driver refused to let the cardholder jump to the front of the queue, and in another instance a presidential cavalcade was brought to a standstill by a farmer's truck loaded with pigs coming toward them on a narrow road.[152] The exercise of consent surfaces in unexpected ways: firing nuclear weapons does not require the population's consent; building fallout shelters for the upper echelon of government does not require the population's consent; but the president's ability to get through a clogged road *will* require the population's assistance and consent. Were there to be frequent exercises for the use of the governmental shelter, the unjustness of the arrangement would become so vivid that it would no doubt increase the pressure to eliminate the country's vast nuclear arsenal altogether, giving the United States (for the first time) a reasonable position from which to ask the rest of the world to abstain from obtaining such weapons.

Ted Gup, who has written an extensive series of investigative articles on the presidential shelters,[153] has also provided a lengthy inquiry into the secret underground shelter built for Congress at Greenbrier Hotel in White Sulphur Springs, West Virginia. One of the twelve-by-fifteen-foot doors is nineteen inches thick and weighs twenty-eight tons; the two hinges of another door weigh 1.5 tons. Since almost no congressmen knew about the shelter, they cannot be held accountable for the painful discrepancy between what the government leaders spent on their own protection and what they spent on that of the country's population.[154] Once Congress learned of Greenbrier, it renounced its access to the shelter.

In contrast to the presidential and congressional shelters, in the ten-year period between 1978 and 1988, Switzerland built 3 million new home fallout shelters (roughly 300,000 per year). In addition, they built 127 emergency operating rooms, 311 first aid stations, 892 first aid posts, and 96,000 hospital bunks.[155] Switzerland now has enough shelter space (including home dwellings, institutions, hospitals, and public shelters) for 114 percent of its population. Sweden and Finland currently have shelters for 81 percent and 70 percent of their populations, respectively; Austria has 30 percent; Germany, 3 percent.[156]

It is crucial to understand that what differentiates Switzerland and the United States is not that one country believes shelters are potentially effective and the other country believes they are ineffective. Both countries have devoted vast resources to the belief that they are effective. What differentiates Switzerland and the United States is the beneficiaries of the shelters: the population in the case of Switzerland, the government leaders in the case of the United States. Switzerland's goal is to make certain it can enact "legal equality" by making certain "every inhabitant of our country has the same chance of survival."[157] In contrast, not only was the money spent on the U.S. presidential fallout shelter vastly in excess of the amount spent on fallout shelters for the population (billions of dollars to protect the president, zero dollars to protect the population), it was vastly in excess of *all* civil defense allocated for the population, for floods, fire, hurricanes, and other catastrophes.[158] This is not gallant. Neither is it coherent.

One of two things is true. Either fallout shelters are useless, in which case neither the population nor the government should have them. Or they are useful, in which case both the population and its leaders should have them. Only a monarchic political structure could excuse an arrangement that has for its citizens no civil defense—either shelters or established practices—while lavishing elaborate structures over their own heads. The adjective "monarchic" or "tyrannic" is invoked here not merely as an expression of disapproval but as a literal designation of the form of government that results when constitutional arrangements (the just distribution of authority and risk) are dismantled. Such constitutional arrangements themselves, when adhered to, constitute the fourth example of the way custom—here, legal customs—can be formed to preempt emergencies, and will be turned to shortly.

Before turning to that fourth model of emergency preparation, it is useful to pause and contemplate the place of democracy in emergency preparation. The contrast between the all-population Swiss shelter system and the president-only shelter system in the United States uncovers a stark discrepancy between the democratic commitment of the first country and its absence in the second. This difference in the two shelter systems is indicative of a much larger difference: Switzerland's commitment to equality of survival, shown in its shelters for all its own residents, is even more evident in the fact that the country has no nuclear weapons that put the residents of other countries at risk; the United States' lack of commitment to equality of survival, shown in its spending all emergency money on the executive alone, is much more evident in the fact that it is by far the largest nuclear-weapons holder in the world. By this arsenal, it retracts from *all people of the world* the right of self-defense and the capacity to ensure their own survival. Needless to say, it is not just "democracy" and "democracies" that stand to be annihilated by nuclear weapons; it is all civilization, as well as the natural world that has long been the companion of that civilization. As it is civilization, not democracy alone, that is in the direct line of fire, so, too, it is civilization, not democracy alone, that seeks to act as the guarantor of survival. This recognition is not to put democracy aside but only to step away from it briefly, so that when we return to it—in the fourth model of emergency procedure below—we better comprehend what it is we are seeing.

Habits of emergency preparedness are much wider than, and anterior to, democracy. It is hard, for example, to contemplate the Saskatchewan grain elevators or the strategies for seed security in Ethiopia or the Swiss shelters without recalling China's tradition of "ever normal granaries," which were flourishing by the time of the Han dynasty (206 BCE to 220 CE). The grain shelters—some round, others rectangular or square, usually on stilts high off the ground—were intended to store grain as insurance against famine, as well as to house it when it was plentiful and prices were low so it could be distributed when prices were high, thus providing a system of government price control. Like the Swiss shelters, the structures were built according to specifications: thus we find descriptions of them in the *Book of Odes*, beautiful drawings in ancient scrolls, and stone engravings, all intended to distribute ideas about the best design.[159] As Joseph Needham writes, the structure "looks impregnable" with its frame of "heavy timber, the roof of closely laid tiles, and the solid door—often there are two—has double leaves and is fastened with a heavy timber beam."[160] Beginning during the Han dynasty and continuing, unevenly, across two millennia come manuals of instructions that, like the counting rules of CPR, give exact specifications of the best way to build granaries. Treatises such as *Nung Cheng Chhüan Shu* and *Shou Shih Thung Khao* specify even the "bricks and tile to be used and the characters with which they were to be stamped"; internal bays, each with its own door, measure 4.25 meters high by 3.5 meters wide by 5 meters deep; one bay is left empty so that the grain in each bay can be rotated to the next bay every six months, ensuring the grain will be "cooled and aired."[161] Needham's only sorrow is that none of the surviving manuals specify the exact design for the lanterns in the roof that ensure ventilation. Intended to equalize the availability of food across irregularities in the population and irregularities in the harvest, the "ever normal granary" (or "constantly normal granary" as it is first called in 54 BCE)[162] is accompanied by systems to ensure "equable transport" in 115 BCE and "equalization and standardization" of measure in 110 BCE.[163]

Elaborate records from the Qing period show that the aspiration to ensure food for the population was carried out. In earlier dynasties, the principle is stated and there are references to the use of the granaries during famine, but the records are too fragmentary to be certain.[164] But by the Qing period (and especially 1644–1790, the very period during which Hobbes, Locke, and Rousseau were formulating the social contract theory that would underlie Western democracy) there is elaborate archival evidence. In the early eighteenth century, at least twelve Chinese provinces each stored at least "one million bushels of grain." By the second half of the eighteenth century, year-by-year records exist for twenty provinces, showing stores in three types of granaries: the ever-normal (state-run) granary, the community granaries, and the charity granaries.[165] As Pierre-Etienne Will and R. Bin Wong conclude, "The mid-Qing grain storage system was much more ambitious than any comparative storage program in Chinese history, not to mention that of other pre-modern civilizations."[166]

The country had three motives for guaranteeing the availability of food: Confucian morality required nourishing the population for its own sake and taught that a population could only aspire to virtue if survival were ensured; the governors needed the support of the population for their expansionist plans; regular distribution of 30 percent of the grain prevented spoilage and freshened the supplies.[167] These three motives could be fulfilled only if the shelters themselves were made impregnable by design and maintenance. As the Swiss shelters need to keep out radiation, so the Chinese shelters had to keep out rain, fermentation, and infestations by fungi, birds, insects, or rodents.[168] As the Swiss system involves elaborate work beyond the physical constructions, so too the Qing attempt to ensure survival involved elaborate record-keeping, documenting yearly rainfall, harvest conditions, forms of ventilation, and storage amounts. Distribution itself was recognized as "an art," and alternative forms of distribution were developed for lean, fertile, and normal production harvest.[169]

The millennium-long aspiration for equality of survival makes all the more startling the spectacle of nuclear countries that spend money on weapons and on shelters for those executive branch officers issuing the orders to fire the weapons, but not on shelters for the population at large. As the United States abandoned the project of shelters for its citizenry, so too did the United Kingdom. Multiple documents show that prime ministers from Clement Attlee to Harold Wilson—the period from 1945 to 1970—concluded that it was impossible to protect the population "at an affordable cost"; the damage, Attlee observes in one document, would be of "a scale . . . against which any civil defence preparations that were possible at the present time would be ineffective."[170] If leaders perceive that a given form of weaponry is so devastating that "no known protection" can be effective, should not those leaders begin to work frantically and relentlessly to eliminate such weapons from their own country and worldwide?

Instead, various British leaders procured the weapons, as well as an already existing shelter for themselves inside Box Hill in Wiltshire.[171] The recently declassified documents studied by historian Peter Hennessy reveal a 1963 War Cabinet compiling a list of who would be included in the 210-person Cotswold bunker, a list that omitted the Queen— the nuclear architects reasoned that she would be safer on the royal yacht, *Britannia*.[172] (Is a surface ship really a prudent place to be during a nuclear war?) A planning document entitled "Government War Book" was discreetly circulated in ninety-six copies during this same year, but not until two years later—two years after the Cuban Missile Crisis—did anyone notice that no copy had been sent to Buckingham Palace.[173] The Cotswold bunker was conceived of as a place, as the former head of the Ministry of Defence described it, "from which you could hope to restore some kind of government and make all kinds of arrangements from medical to food."[174] The documents Hennessy surveys, however, do not themselves show any preparatory thinking about "arrangements from medical to food"; and it is hard to picture how such arrangements could be initiated, let alone carried out, once an exchange of missiles had taken place. Did the War Cabinet imagine that though no shelters could protect against the bomb, somehow a surviving legion of nurses and cafeteria workers would be reachable by phone and able to start administering aid?

Far from working to ensure an equality of survival, the British executive officers at moments appear to have regarded the population's desire to survive as a detriment to the war effort. A report commissioned to describe the potential breakdown of government during nuclear war hypothesizes that "breakdown" occurs when

> the government of a country is no longer able to ensure that its orders are carried out. This state of affairs could come about through ... the mass of people becoming preoccupied with their own survival rather than the country's war effort.[175]

Like the United States' repudiation of its citizenry, the disregard for the population of the United Kingdom helps us to contemplate the scale of achievement in the Swiss arrangements for a countrywide "vertical evacuation."

Vertical evacuation attempts to reestablish the right of exit, a right that has, for more than 2000 years, been recognized as essential to liberty. Some philosophers go further, asserting that it *is* liberty, as we saw in Chapter 5, not only among social contract theorists but thinkers from Plato and Epictetus forward. Although the inhabitants of countries practice their consent through many acts (such as forming constitutions, voting to ratify or reject a constitutional amendment, voting for an officeholder, voting for a new law, running for office, acquiring citizenship), Locke argued that their willingness to reside inside a specific society which they were free to leave was the manifestation of their agreement to it, even if they had been born into a set of legal arrangements and had never voted for them.

Among other unspeakable harms, the weapons held by the eight nuclear states have eliminated the right of exit. With the exception of the Swiss underground, there is no space on earth that cannot be reached by the weapons. Many nations have worked to create nuclear-weapons-free zones that will increase the chance of survival and also create a sphere in which the right of exit is restored.[176] Those treaties— the 1996 Treaty of Pelindaba (Africa), the 1995 Treaty of Bangkok (Southeast Asia), the 1968 Treaty of Tlatelolco (Mexico, Central, and South America), the 1985 Treaty of Rarotonga (South Pacific), the 1972 Seabed and Ocean Floor Treaty, the 1959 Antarctic Treaty—together cover a vast geographical spread. Crucially, they eliminate the possibility of possessing nuclear weapons from their own member states; the Treaty of Pelindaba, for example, which encompasses every country on the African continent as well as Madagascar, persuaded two countries with nuclear ambitions, South Africa and Algeria, to renounce those weapons.[177] In addition, such treaties encourage "habits of dialogue" among countries in any given region.[178] Each treaty serves as a model or precedent for the next (the language in Rarotonga is explicitly used in Pelindaba) and together they work to "delegitimize" nuclear weapons.[179] They may, in combination with many other avenues, eventually rid the earth of them.

But what the nuclear-weapons-free zones do not do, at present, is provide a shelter over the heads of the inhabitants or create a place of exit. Long-range U.S. weapons can easily reach these populations. Nuclear weapons ships are not banned from entering nearby waters. In 2002, U.S. President George Bush declined to sign the Bangkok Protocol, complaining that its provisions for protecting territorial waters limited U.S. "freedom of navigation."[180] The only other nuclear-free-zone treaty that extends its protection to ocean waters is the Latin American Treaty of Tlatelolco; while it contains no blanket prohibition on the transit of ships carrying nuclear weapons, it gives member states individual discretion over whether such ships are permitted to pass through their waters. The United States signed but stated that it rejected any aspect of the treaty compromising its "freedom at sea."[181] Thus the United States—while eliminating the right of free movement from almost all human beings on earth—has invoked principles of free movement to legitimate its right to station its nuclear weapons in any coastal ocean of the world. Over the last fifty years, "freedom of the seas" has repeatedly been invoked when any international constraint on the movement of submarines was proposed. When, as part of the 1971 Seabed Treaty, Yugoslavia stipulated that the United States contact a country whose coastal waters were about to be entered by a submarine, the United States strenuously objected.[182] When in 1985 New Zealand insisted that ships carrying nuclear weapons stay out of their coastal waters and ports, the United States retaliated by disrupting the trilateral security treaty joining the United States, Australia, and New Zealand.[183] The control these treaties give their populations is limited. The Rarotonga Treaty, for example, permits the United States to test its delivery systems (though not the weapons themselves) in the regional waters of the South Pacific, and permits the United States to station nuclear command and control instruments on Australian ground.[184] In fact, none of the treaties prohibits support facilities for some other country's nuclear weapons on the soil of their member states.[185]

While, then, these treaties have accomplished critically important work, they do not make the populations living in the zones immune to nuclear weapons. The Swiss shelter system aspires to do exactly that. It is one of the few pieces of evidence we have that the right of exit (as well as the right to *exist*) is still imaginable in the nuclear age.

MODEL 4: THE CONSTITUTIONAL BRAKE ON WAR

The best exit, the only exit, from the obscene damage that nuclear weapons are designed to bring about is the elimination of the weapons themselves. That outcome is precisely what the fourth model of emergency preparation would have brought about had its procedures been practiced over the last sixty years. That outcome can still be brought about—methodically and decisively—if the United States population begins to follow those procedures now. The two provisions in the U.S. Constitution that stipulate what must take place before we ever begin to injure a foreign population are on every plane (logical, strategic, technical) profoundly incompatible with any form of weaponry that permits a president to authorize and enact the killings of tens of millions of people within several hours.

The fourth model of emergency thinking is therefore one the reader is already well aware of since it has been the central subject of this book. Nonetheless, it will be useful to review it briefly here in the company of the other three models.

The question in an emergency, as we have seen, is not *whether* habit structures come into play but *which* habit structures come into play. Our nuclear weapons, and the presidential first-use arrangements for their firing, are deep, elaborately practiced habits. Our fourteen Ohio-class submarines—each carrying the equivalent of 4000 Hiroshima bombs—are moving across the ocean floor without cessation, day in and day out. The submarines come into their home ports in Kings Bay, Georgia, and Bangor, Washington, only long enough to shift crews; each submarine has two crews (one designated Gold, the other Blue), and each crew stays under the ocean for three months. During those ninety days—as Gerrit Oakes, an electronics technician on the USS *Maine*, reports—the crew keeps "busy doing drills, training." Only on a single day out of the ninety days—"halfway through the patrol"—is there a special day and night "where we don't do any training."[186] As the Secretary of the Navy, Donald Winter, recently stated: "Although our nation has never fired a submarine-launched ballistic missile in anger, our Trident fleet [has the ability] to do so 24 hours a day, 7 days a week, 365 days a year."[187] Secretary Winter said this at a ceremony "commemorating the completion of 1,000 Trident strategic deterrent patrols"—that is, 3000 months (or 250 years) of Ohio-class submarine patrols during which the fleet has maintained its instant nuclear-weapons-launch abilities. Like the submarines, the U.S. land-based and air-based missiles stay in a constant state of practiced readiness.

The executive branch, too, stays in a state of readiness, with the briefcase containing the nuclear codes never more than one room away from the president. Hugh Shelton, Chairman of the Joint Chiefs of Staff under Bill Clinton, describes the "Night Blue" telephone exercises the Pentagon and President (or "a role player assuming the part of the President") constantly practice—often in the middle of the night—so that a presidential order to launch can be carried out at once:

> It was just past 2:00 A.M. when the computer-synthesized voice crackled to life and repeated, *"Missiles inbound, missiles inbound."* ... I spun around and grabbed the red notebook labeled TOP SECRET, then sailed through my checklist almost by rote. ... My "office" was an impenetrable vault deep inside the Pentagon's National Military Command Center (NMCC), with secure 24/7 links to the President, direct contact with U.S. missile-tracking stations worldwide, a safe containing nuclear codes behind my desk,

and the key to initiate nuclear launch at my fingertips.... While my Assistant DDO was patching in commanders of NORAD..., STRATCOM.... and the Secretary of Defense, I was being connected to the President's military aide, one of five whose primary responsibility was to shadow the President at all times with the "football," a forty-pound black-leather-covered titanium briefcase that contains the nuclear-retaliatory options and a small laminated card of presidential authorization codes. Within seconds I would be speaking with the President.[188]

Like the crew on the submarine, such exercises are constant: "Our guiding philosophy was—and still is—practice, then practice again."[189]

War plans are not remote and dust-accruing hypotheticals but active instructions. As the Natural Resources Defense Council points out: "The [strategic] war plans are not an outline of possibilities for the future *but a directive of what weapons must be put in place*: for key targets identified in the plan, *a warhead must be available and assigned to hit it at all times*."[190] The Natural Resources Defense Council also reports that during the George W. Bush administration, much work was undertaken to make the "preplanned strike options" more "adaptable" and "rapid," with an increased reliance on computerized computation.[191]

Standing against this lethal, genocide-ready arsenal are two provisions of the Constitution. As Locke notes, a population can "take sanctuary under the established laws of government."[192] While the United States does not at present have a civil defense shelter system that protects its population, it does have a Constitution that was designed to protect that population—and through that population, the people of other countries. The Constitution does not eliminate the possibility of war. But it does seek to ensure that war cannot be (1) entered into, and (2) sustained over a prolonged period, without reasons convincing enough to persuade large assemblies of people, both within the national legislature and within the population at large, of the need to injure foreign peoples.

Two crucial provisions—Article I, Section 8, Clause 11, and the Second Amendment—each ensure a distribution of military authority. One, as we have seen, specifies that the power to declare war will be given to Congress, the full representative assembly. The option of giving this power to a smaller group—either the president acting alone or the Senate acting alone—was explicitly discussed and explicitly rejected at the Constitutional Convention. The power to declare war was given to the full assembly for three reasons: to ensure deliberation, to distribute authority, and to act as an emergency brake on the urge to go to war. The congressional obligation to oversee the nation's entry into war has been called by eighteenth- and nineteenth-century jurists "the highest act of legislation."

While the constitutional provision for a congressional declaration of war is a "law" consisting of a small number of words—"The Congress shall have power to declare war"—an elaborate protocol of steps is embedded in that clause, a protocol that includes the presentation in written form of what precisely is being declared; the guarantee of an equal voice to all members, majority or minority, that in turn ensures that if there is a counterargument to be made (most centrally, about whether a particular country does in fact deserve to be regarded as an "enemy"), it will be made; the explicit person-by-person polling and written recording of a vote by all 535 members; and the presentation to the U.S. population—either during the event or in the hours immediately after—of a complete transcript of both the debate and the vote. Each of these, in turn, consists of a sequence of specified steps: the written form of the declaration must be read aloud three times so that all assembled understand what is at issue, and the speakers must proceed according to rules (such as the requirement that each speaker refer to other speakers by their office rather than their name) set out in advance in Thomas Jefferson's *A Manual of Parliamentary Practice* and by *Robert's Rules of Order*.

Congress was designated—along with the population as a whole— as the body responsible for overseeing our entry into war in part because

Congress (in eras when it is functioning) practices the art of debating day in and day out. Imagine an assembly that only waited until it was on the threshold of war to decide what rules of speaking it would follow, what forms of verbal opposition it would hold to be fair and unfair, how the array of speakers would be sequenced, what rules of evidence it would accept. It could be said that all congressional deliberation during peacetime, no matter how trivial or grand the subject, is a rehearsal, a constant act of practicing, for the moment when it will be called upon to debate the gravest matter of all, the matter of going to war.

The same logic underwrites the Second Amendment. A population that bears the responsibility for questions about going to war becomes a population capable of high level of debate; conversely, a population that forfeits that responsibility allows its powers of deliberation to deteriorate. Just as Article I, Section 8, Clause 11, distributes the declaratory power to the full assembly, so the Second Amendment distributes authority to the whole enfranchised population. It rejects the notion of "a standing army," a fixed form of military force subject to executive control and cut off from civilian life (as exists in magnified form today in nuclear weapons which are available to the executive and wholly cut off from civilian life). It insists instead on a "militia" or "citizen's army," an army drawn from the full population uniformly across geography and wealth. According to the record of the ratification debates at the time the Constitution was circulating to the states, without a proper distribution of arms, an executive army presents as much threat to the social contract as does a foreign army, since in both cases the population is "invaded," "disarmed," and infantilized back into a state of precontractual coercion.

The Second Amendment, as we saw in Chapter 2, does not stipulate how much injuring power the country will have; it may have very little or a great deal. The amendment stipulates, instead, that however much the country has, the authority for its use must be equally distributed across the population. This principle of equal distribution has also been saluted in other countries by militarists and pacifists alike. In the first General Assembly in France in 1789 Mirabeau said that the aristocracy had been created merely by endowing one group of citizens with arms and depriving the other group of arms. Similarly, Gandhi said that of the eleven evil acts committed by the British against India, the worst was the disarming of the population ("Give us back our arms," he said, "and then we'll tell you whether or not we're going to use them").[193]

Congress and the population in concert act as a double brake on the executive urge to identify another population as an enemy. We saw this double brake in the U.S. Constitution in Chapters 1 and 2; and we saw the double brake in the overarching architecture of social contract theory in Chapter 4 (as we also saw potentially relevant constitutional provisions in other nuclear states such as France, India, and Russia).[194] Legal rules are meant to be internalized into a set of practices that automatically go into effect: when a crisis arises, Congress begins to deliberate and the population begins to debate. But since the invention of nuclear weapons, there has been no congressional declaration even for the conventional wars in Korea, Vietnam, the Gulf, the former Yugoslavia, Iraq, or the invasions of Panama and Haiti.[195] Following Vietnam, the disappearance of the draft eliminated the distribution of military responsibility across the population, eliminating as well the exercise of popular debate and dissent. Because in the present era these constitutional provisions have lapsed, when a crisis arises Congress and the population wait passively for an announcement from the president and the joint chiefs of staff about what "the country" will do.

Complaints are often made that involving Congress and the population in war decisions will slow down the act of going to war because so much energy is needed to persuade them. That is precisely what the Constitution intended. Here we encounter a key attribute differentiating our first three models of emergency preparation—CPR, voluntary associations, and the Swiss shelter system—and the constitutional provisions for overseeing our entry into war.

Rather than specifying the taking of an action, the Constitution instead requires that we stop and deliberate about whether to take an action. This difference arises because of a starker difference. In those emergencies where the diminution of injury is at stake, all deliberative habits are directed toward determining *how* to minimize the injury, not to the question of *whether* we ought to minimize the injury. If a fire has broken out in a grain elevator, we do not wonder whether to put it out but how to put it out in the most efficient and damage-minimizing way. If a swimmer has stopped breathing, no one deliberates whether we ought to help him start breathing, but only the sequence of acts that will bring his breath back.

There exist highly anomalous situations where we do debate whether to continue administering aid, such as extended care for tiny premature infants or for injured persons on full life support. But these perplexing problems warrant a great deal of our attention precisely because they are so at odds with the ordinary imperative to give aid. Furthermore, the very reason they occasion deliberation is because a grave question has arisen about whether the aid that is being administered diminishes the injury or instead perpetuates or even amplifies it. Far from contradicting the norm, then, these apparently anomalous cases instead confirm it: deliberation is directed to how, not whether, to diminish the injury.[196]

Precisely the opposite is the case where the action to be performed is not the diminution of injury, but its infliction. Now rather than clearing all paths to ensure speed, gates must be closed until the claim that "inflicting injury is necessary" has been subjected to rigorous testing and until those carrying out the test themselves step forward and take responsibility for opening the gate by voting and openly attaching their name to the vote. As we saw in Chapters 3 and 4, the social contract in its ideal form prohibits injury altogether. Even in the real world it allows two *and only two* situations in which the absolute prohibition on injuring can be lifted: the punishment of criminals and going to war. Both of these situations are ones in which the wrongdoers—the criminals, the enemy population—have acquired the status of wrongdoer precisely by having broken the never-injure rule and so must themselves be stopped, even if stopping them requires injuring them. But because by inflicting injury on the criminal or on the enemy, members of the social contract perform an action that is deeply at odds with the first rule of that contract, their act of injuring can be done only after going through exhausting procedural gates (for example, a two-tiered jury trial, a two-tiered war authorization involving both the congressional declaration of war and the deliberation by the population) designed to test whether it is really the case that the alleged wrongdoers have in fact broken the never-injure rule. Only if the allegation of wrongdoing withstands the sustained scrutiny of both the grand and petit juries in the case of criminal wrongdoing and 535 people in the case of the congressional declaration, will the never-injure prohibition be lifted and the criminal punished or the enemy attacked.[197] Only if hundreds of thousands of citizens ratify that congressional decision by agreeing that the country designated "enemy" needs to be stopped will the war (declared by Congress) ever become materialized reality.[198]

The two part rule of emergency—act quickly if the goal is to prevent injury; act slowly if the goal is to inflict injury—has been turned upside down by Congress in the twenty-first century: Congress has thrown aside its major legislative task of acting as an obstructive testing ground for war and simultaneously made itself an obstacle to health care, to student education, to bridge and highway repair, to financial bailouts, and other forms of rescue. In other words, it has acted to impede CPR and mutual aid while keeping open the highway to war. It has acted like Aesop's donkey bringing the right habit (obstruction) to the wrong situation (the saving of lives).

The overarching framework of emergency depicted in this chapter has three alternative outcomes: immobilization (Artaud's theatergoer; Arendt's Eichmann; the unconscious ambulance patient) or incoherent action (Aesop's donkey failing to distinguish salt and sponges) or coherent action (CPR, the Canadian mutual aid contracts, the Swiss shelter system, the U.S. constitutional provisions overseeing war). Those are the three alternatives. Clearly immobilization and incoherent action are not outcomes to emulate. What needs to be undertaken, then, is an assessment of a coherent action, and almost all instances of coherent emergency action entail high degrees of habit. In all four models, planning, practicing, and virtuoso performance occur in advance of the actual emergency.

The question is not, Do emergency and habit go together? They do go together. If we can act, we do so out of the habitual. Habit yokes thought and action together. If no serviceable habit is available, we use an unserviceable one and become either immobilized or incoherent. Instead the question is, To what extent are the habitual and the deliberative compatible? Behind the question of the habitual is the question of laws, since habit is an internalizing regulating mechanism that has its external equivalent in law; the bond is manifest in the nearby term "custom," used in everyday speech as a synonym both for habit and for law. Insofar as this chapter provides an argument about finding and following good habits, it also provides an argument about finding and following, binding ourselves to, good constitutional procedures. Conversely, it also reveals that our contempt for our laws, the suspension of constitutional requirements overseeing our entry into war, is in part based on our contempt for the habitual that is undeserved.

The Constitution assigns to both the legislature and the population the obligation to deliberate on the eve of war and in days following. Such acts of deliberation require the kind of year-in, year-out practice visible in other realms of emergency action. Far from being at odds with habit, these acts of deliberation are constituted by it. In the remaining pages we will try to recover how compatible deliberation and habit are.

THE PLACE OF HABIT IN ACTS OF THINKING

The rejection of procedures and constitutional guarantees, this chapter has so far suggested, comes from three sources: first, the belief that action requires putting aside thinking; second, the belief that action does in fact normally require thinking but that *rapid* action requires putting aside thinking; and third, the belief that thinking requires setting aside habit. In the first two, thinking is rejected in the name of action. In the third, habit is set aside in the name of thinking. This third error is as grave as the first two. We have seen that habit is everywhere visible in effective emergency preparation. In turn, thinking is profoundly visible in the lineaments of habit.

It is not hard to see why the kind of deliberative act connected to an emergency has some features that make it hard to recognize as an act of deliberation. Deliberation normally inhabits a temporal space close to the action which is its outcome. If one deliberates about the best book to read, that is usually followed by reaching for the book. If one chooses the best horse to ride, that is usually followed by mounting the horse. The same is true of group decisions; a faculty that debates a rule change usually takes a vote and institutes the decision soon after the deliberations. But in the case of emergency procedures, there is apt to be a long temporal break between the deliberation and the actual enactment, which must wait for the emergency. There is a long pause between figuring out CPR procedures and the moment one is called upon to use that knowledge. There is a long pause between designing and building the shelter system of Switzerland and the moment of its use. There is a long pause between the debates on the best constitutional procedures to protect a country on the threshold of war and the moment 40, or 100, or 200 years later when the crucial test of the braking power of these procedures comes.

The mystification that is caused by the distance between the deliberation and the action is compounded by a second problem. Not only must the procedure be made habitual, but it must be inscribed as habit in the most highly self-conscious way. In ordinary life, the more useful a habit is the stronger it grows, simply because each day provides the occasion to practice it. There is no need to set aside a few days a year to practice reading or driving a car; life keeps putting in front of us daily problems that occasion the practice of those actions. But emergencies do not occur often, and therefore there is no naturally arising occasion on which the appropriate procedure can be practiced. The habit must instead be acquired by a highly willed act of internalization and may seem to be an artificial exercise without an object. Emergency procedures may come to seem the empty offspring of the space of waiting and the place of drill.

Our everyday estimate of habit unreflectingly places it outside thought, outside human will, outside ethics. But a rich philosophic tradition—classical Greek and Christian writers,[199] Anglo-American thinkers,[200] and continental theorists[201]—has seen habit as a powerful tool of cognition. It is the relation between habit and one specific form of thinking, deliberation, that most directly illuminates the way we think in an emergency, since deliberation is thinking directed toward the taking of an action. But the place of habit in deliberation will itself be clearer if it is preceded by a consideration of two other mental events, sensory perception and creation—mental events that are themselves elaborately in play in an emergency.

HABIT AND SENSATION

Habit is never seen as something that makes a slight adjustment in the character of sensory perception, dulling perception (if one judges habit to be a negative) or enhancing it (if one judges it as positive). It is instead understood to cut to the heart of sensation, closing it down entirely or building up perception at its own interior and even bringing it into being. If these two views are taken together, they do not balance one another or cancel one another out. Remarkably, they together work to validate the positive view. They together show that habit is an immensely powerful agent for regulating, even creating, the acuity of sentience. Just as one may regulate the amount of light by opening and closing one's eyelids or by turning and tilting one's head through hundreds of angles and planes, so habit acts to set in place countless gateways that either open and allow the world to rush toward one or instead close it to keep it wholly at bay. The way the negative and positive account together validate the positive account becomes clearer if we for a moment contemplate the two views in isolation from one another.

The negative account sees habit as incompatible with sensory acuity and, ultimately, with sensation itself. Habit makes us—in some almost literal way—insensate, insensible. Montaigne articulates this view. He takes smell as his model instance. How quickly we grow used to the presence of an odor, and when we grow used to it, it at once diappears: "Habit stupefies our senses.... My perfumed doublet is pleasant to my nose, but after I have worn it three days in a row it is pleasant only to the noses of others."[202] Any sensation that is enduring, repetitive, or perpetual may similarly become lost to us. The extraordinary adaptability of the sense of smell, rather than being taken as "exceptional," becomes for Montaigne paradigmatic of all the senses. What is true of smell is true of hearing, as he illustrates with a story about his gradually acquired ability to sleep through troublesome church bells. But we sleep not only through church bells; we even sleep through the music of the spheres, the "marvelous harmony" produced by the solid bodies of the spheres "coming to touch and rub on one another as they roll." Thick and leaden with habituation, we become insensible to the perpetual sound of the cosmos, a deprivation that in turn works to deepen our leadenness. Church bells and the music of the spheres are not randomly chosen: the habitual (Montaigne argues) closes us out from things of great beauty and spirit.

When Montaigne complains that habit makes us insensible, he is not simply using a loosely pejorative word; he means very literally that sensory perception is incapacitated, "stupefied," "put to sleep." This conception of habit is today presented as a general complaint about the way it disposes us to be "insensitive," "robotic," "automatic," or "inanimate." Samuel Beckett called habit "a great deadener" (despite the fact that throughout his plays, lifesaving rules of survival always entail elaborate repertoires of habit).[203] The very vividness of these words, and the unmarked modulation from "insensitive" to "insensate" to "inanimate," might make us lose sight of the literalness of the claim that lies behind each.

Aliveness is perceived to be at issue, not only by the great detractors of habit but by its champions. Philosophers as separated in time as Aristotle, William James, and John Dewey have seen habit not as diminishing but as magnifying sensitivity, sensation, and sensory aliveness. Far from cutting us off from the music of the spheres, it is exactly the work of habit, says Aristotle, to bring the highest things within our reach, even if they appear to arrive by some path beyond our own agency. In the *Nicomachean Ethics*, he questions whether the greatest excellences, and the happiness that attends them, come from the gods or instead from "learning or by habituation or... training." He concludes that though "godlike," they are often not "god-sent" but acquired by "some process of learning or training."[204]

Any theorist who holds that sensory acuity is achieved by habit will also be a theorist committed to education. So William James writes, "Could the young but realize how soon they will become mere walking bundles of habits, they would give more heed to their conduct while in the plastic state. We are spinning our own fates.... Every smallest stroke of virtue or of vice leaves its never so little scar."[205] Aristotle's formulation is even stronger: "It makes no small difference then, whether we form habits of one kind or another from our youth; it makes a very great difference, or rather all the difference."[206]

Precisely this constellation of claims about habit—its connection to sensation, to the highest spiritual accomplishments, and to education—is central to John Dewey, whose positive account of sensory perception is as concrete as Montaigne's negative account. Even to be able to pick out of the world a specifiable odor such as the perfume of Montaigne's doublet, or to sort out the sound of the church bell from a welter of other sensory sensations (such as the feel of the bed on which Montaigne is tossing and turning) is a labor; in the time prior to actually hearing the church bell, we have, according to Dewey, constructed our own ability to do so. Dewey's example is not sound or odor, but color:

[D]istinct and independent sensory qualities, far from being original elements, are the products of a highly skilled analysis which disposes of immense technical scientific resources. To be able to single out a definitive sensory element in any field is evidence of a high degree of previous training, that is, of well-formed habits. A moderate amount of observation of a child will suffice to reveal that even such gross discriminations as black, white, red, green, are the result of some years of active dealings with things in the course of which habits have been set up. It is not such a simple matter to have a clear-cut sensation. The latter is a sign of training, skill, habit.[207]

If, as Dewey argues, it takes "some years of active dealing with things" to reliably discriminate green, blue, or red, how many years of practice are required to reach the adult state in which the average human being is capable of distinguishing 26,000 colors, or over 2.3 million if "gray value" (or lightness) is included?[208] In turn, what ardor and practice are required to move beyond these "average" capacities to become an exquisite colorist like the Venetians (with their habits of optical mixing), or like Matisse (whose paintings induce retinal arabesques), or like the virtuoso landscape gardeners Gertrude Jekyll or Claude Monet?

In addition to habits of sensation, Dewey frequently speaks of habits of acute observation and inference,[209] habits of thought and active inquiry.[210] But the acuity of sensory perception remains key. It allows us "to respond freshly and generously to each incident in life."[211]

The negative and the positive accounts, so strikingly at odds, eventually reinforce one another. For Montaigne, we start with a sensation and habit acts to dampen it down, threatening to subtract it all together from the perceivable surface of the world. For Dewey, there is no sensation to begin with, only a welter of confused and scrambled signals; eventually the active and labor-intensive effort of attention enables us to distinguish a discrete sensory event. For Montaigne, habit puts aliveness in peril by making sensory perception closer to sleep than to waking. For Dewey, habit heightens the felt experience of aliveness and by steadily heightening our perceptual acuity greatly contributes to our ability to keep ourselves alive. The two views not only coexist, but coexist within any one writer. (Thus Montaigne, as we will see in a moment, sometimes greatly celebrates the power of habit, as Dewey periodically interrupts his celebratory account to voice complaints about the negative outcomes of habit.)[212]

The fact that habit is held responsible for both insensitivity and supersensitivity works to credit the positive place of habit in sensory cognition. (It means that through habit we can affect our perceptual acuity, dampening down aversive or distracting sensations while magnifying the acuity of desirable sensations. The neurological basis of this two-directional plasticity has been worked out with extraordinary clarity in one particular realm of sensory perception, not color or odor or sound or taste but that of touch, specifically physical pain. The revolutionary but widely accepted "gate control theory of pain"—developed by neuroscientist Ronald Melzack and biologist Patrick Wall—rejects the Cartesian picture of an external pain stimulus acting on the surface of the body and ringing a bell cord that proceeds in a linear fashion to the brain. It posits instead a gate on the spinal cord where—even before we begin to feel the pain or identify the part of the body where it is taking place—cultural habits, familial habits, and individual habits are brought to bear on the apprehension of the pain, either closing down the gate so that we do not feel the sensation as acutely as the stimulus itself would warrant or opening the gate more widely so that its aversive affects are felt in full force.[213] The complex neurobiology at work in the brain's gate control structure may one day help us come to understand the neural structures that clarify the way habit and learning work in wholly pain-free forms of sensory perception, whether seeing color or hearing a bird's song. It will help to explain why learning, and self-directed habits of attention, can vastly magnify our sensory powers.

HABIT AND CREATION

As in the realm of sensation, so in the realm of creation we find both a damning and a celebratory account of habit. Familiar to most people is the view that artistic improvisation and engineering inventiveness exist at one end of a spectrum that has at its opposite pole the phenomenon of habit. The poet, the dancer, the composer, the painter, the inventor seem at some far remove from the realm of habit. Yet equally familiar to most people is the key part played by habit in achieving and maintaining creative virtuosity: the labor-intensive daily drill ballet dancers undergo, the five-hours-a-day-every-day practice of violinists. Gershwin first learned his instrument as a child when he went to play at the home of a friend whose family had an automatic player piano (an instrument he first saw in the penny arcade at the age of six); he placed his hands on the moving keys and eventually found that when he carried his hands to a piano that was not automated, he could reproduce the same virtuosity.[214]

The richness and depth of the two opposing views can be efficiently apprehended by concentrating on one person of great inventive genius, Benjamin Franklin, and the ways in which he is described by two people, both themselves hugely influential artists, one of whom is dazzled by Franklin and the other of whom scorns him. The positive account is provided by the American architect and architectural theorist Robert Venturi, who has reconstructed Franklin's house in Philadelphia and attached to it a celebratory museum. The negative account is provided by the British poet and novelist D. H. Lawrence.

Benjamin Franklin provides a good case for three reasons. First, he is a great inventor: bifocals, grocer's stick, swimming fins, a university, reading clubs, street lights, and international treaties are among the things he invented or helped to create. Second, his inventions were often occasioned by what he saw as a latent emergency; throughout Franklin's autobiography and letters, his recognition of a problem—such as a dark street—occasions an adrenaline rush of invention. Third, his idea of invention is directly yoked to habit. Franklin believes that to make a creditable invention one must first make the object, and then make certain that the instructions for making it are legible enough so that everyone else can make it too. A pair of bifocals or a glass harmonica only becomes a successful creation once it is distributable, habitual.

This principle applies to what Franklin regarded as one of his greatest inventions: himself. His autobiography is a set of instructions on how to make a Benjamin Franklin—how, in effect, to make a great inventor, or whatever that person is who throughout the book stands in front of us. This desire to make the conditions of his own construction legible in turn occasions his inclusion of the charts of vices and virtues that enabled him deliberately to shape needed habits. Inventors who lived after Franklin have sometimes taken his instructions to heart. Tolstoy's early diaries have lists to regulate what he will do at the gaming table, lists for what he will say in the drawing room, lists for how he will inscribe a new prose style into himself, and these lists are punctuated with open acknowledgments that his teacher is Benjamin Franklin.[215] But Tolstoy's admiration—and his great crediting of the link between habit and creation—are encoded in his own imitation of Franklin rather than in an extended set of descriptions, and so for the positive and negative views it is illuminating to turn to Venturi and Lawrence.

Venturi's architectural portrait of Benjamin Franklin—his reconstruction of Franklin's house and the museum (or hall of fun) that adjoins it—dedicates itself to the attributes of capaciousness and vivacity. One section of the museum contains a closet whose silver interior is covered with mirrors on all four walls; on the mirrors in flashing neon script are the words "Inventor," "Statesman," "Printer," "Revolutionary," "Treaty Maker," all pulsing in bright colors. As one stands inside the closet, the endlessly reflected waves of script seem to be moving toward and away from one in all directions, so that one experiences what it must have been like to be inside the pulsing consciousness of Benjamin Franklin, his hot pink inventorliness passing through his bright green statesmanship and nearly colliding with the blue of his revolutionary dimension which in turn has braided to his treaty making. One senses his largeness and largesse.

Lawrence's portrait is precisely the opposite. Not capaciousness but a closing down is what he stresses. Though Franklin receives many adjectives from Lawrence, the main ones are littleness and the absence of color. "He was a little model, was Benjamin. Doctor Franklin. Snuff-coloured little man!" And again, "Middle-sized, sturdy, snuff-coloured Doctor Franklin, one of the soundest citizens." And again, "I'm not going to be turned into a virtuous little automaton as Benjamin would have me." On the final page, Franklin is still in Philadelphia "setting up this unlovely, snuff-coloured little ideal, or automaton, of a pattern American."[216]

Venturi pictures the interior of Franklin in throbbing Technicolor; Lawrence pictures him as snuff-colored and miniaturized. Oddly, it is not that Lawrence fails to see how many actions Franklin performed: he includes a Franklinesque list—that he "lighted the streets of young Philadelphia...invented electrical appliances...was a member of all the important councils of Philadelphia...won the cause of American Independence at the French Court, and was the economic father of the United States." Lawrence even pictures Franklin as single-handedly overthrowing Europe: "He wanted the whole European applecart upset"; he made "a small but very dangerous hole in the side of England, through which hole Europe has by now almost bled to death."[217] Yet precisely the teeming layering of persons in Venturi's mirrors are what Lawrence claims are shut down by Franklin—he asserts that he, Lawrence, is many men and Franklin wants him to choose and be only one. Lawrence, however large, seems homogeneous when standing by the side of the heterogeneous Benjamin Franklin, who seems to be carrying a small crowd of persons around inside of him.

The other image Lawrence uses as persistently as small and snuff-colored is the barbed-wire fence: "This is Benjamin's barbed wire fence. He made himself a list of virtues, which he trotted inside like a grey nag in a paddock"; "Here am I now...sitting in the middle of Benjamin's America looking at the barbed wire...the American corral"; "Benjamin tries to shove me into a barbed wire paddock"; "America ...Absolutely got down by her own barbed wire of shalt-nots."[218]

The view is once again in precise opposition to Venturi's. Reconstructing Benjamin Franklin's house, Venturi leaves the walls entirely un–filled in; he gives us only the outline of the house, etched in steel, like an elegant architectural pencil sketch. Far from being constricting, the house is airy, open to the sky and the sounds of the street. The domestic habits of self-construction, despised by Lawrence, are venerated by Venturi: he inscribes into the floor passages from Benjamin's letters from France to his wife, listing the blue material for house curtains, consulting with her whether the material is appropriate for the hangings. The phantom blue curtains are as airy as the sky. The fleeting sound of a voice making its way across the Atlantic is Venturi's salute to Franklin's charts, lists, and daily letters of domestic self-invention.

The division between the constricting and the expansive stands for a large split, for the two reactions are applicable to many contexts where invention and procedure are coupled. Is "equality of survival"—at work in all four of the emergency models we looked at—a profound and colossal ethical invention or is it something that can be swept away with scorn? Is the Swiss shelter system Venturi's image of throbbing Technicolor ingenuity? To me it is: I believe the Swiss and their procedures for protecting their population and their special objects will survive anything. Or is it instead the case, as many people believe, that Switzerland is correctly described as snuff-colored, small, full of barbed-wire regulations? Should we give a standing ovation to the residents of the Saskatchewan plains for their lists specifying what equipment each person must bring to a fire, or should those lists be dismissed as "virtue in columns"? Is learning CPR a boring act of self-miniaturization or is it closer to a glass harmonica in its otherworldly virtuosity?[219]

Above all, are the laws specifying the gates the people of the United States are obligated to pass through before they injure a foreign population—Article I, Section 8, Clause 11, and the Second Amendment—snuff-colored procedural regulations that we can shrug off with impunity as we have tried to do for the last six decades, or are they vibrant inventive genius writ large, the palladial alphabet of a country that aspires to be a great and a good democracy? When the citizens of Athens were scheduled to meet in assembly, a flag was raised above the city at daybreak so that the city's 30,000 citizens would remember to come. Those who arrived late were marked with paint and fined for their tardiness.[220] In the United States, neither the congressional assembly nor the citizens convene as the issue of going to war is debated in private conversations behind closed doors at the White House.

Before he was a presidential candidate, Senator Barack Obama spoke at the John F. Kennedy Library about the painful discrepancy between the Illinois state legislature, where attendance by all members is required during deliberations, and the U.S. Congress, where during most debates the hall is empty, with a few staffers milling in and out.[221] As President George W. Bush prepared to invade Iraq in February 2003, Senator Robert C. Byrd stood on the floor of the Senate and denounced its muteness:

> [T]his nation stands at the brink of battle...yet this Chamber is for the most part ominously, dreadfully silent.... There is no debate. There is no discussion. There is no attempt to lay out for the Nation the pros and cons of this particular war. There is nothing.

Silent, despite the fact that—as Byrd went on to say—the United States was about to launch "a massive unprovoked military attack on a nation which is over 50% children." Silent, despite the fact that the executive branch was about to introduce a dangerous new doctrine of preemption, attacking not a country that was a present threat but a country that might someday in the future become one. Silent, despite the fact that the executive "recently refused to take nuclear weapons off the table when discussing a possible attack against Iraq."[222]

If the U.S. Constitution is a great invention, its system of checks and balances, its distribution of power across three branches of government, is the heart of that invention. Yet the elimination of the congressional declaration of war, and the consequent devolution of all military power to the executive, has eliminated that principle of equal branches.

We saw at the opening of this book Richard Nixon's assertion that the legislature and judiciary are not equal to the executive because only the executive has an army. That same view has recently been voiced by Dick Cheney, the once-powerful vice president under George W. Bush. Explaining, as Nixon had before him, why the executive branch cannot be checked by the legislature or the judiciary, he gave a four-word summation: "We've got the helicopters."[223]

It is not, of course, an army or helicopters but nuclear weapons that have produced the specter of executive omnipotence. Nixon recognized that merely by lifting his hand to his face he could bring about 70 million deaths in twenty-five minutes. Cheney holds the same picture in front of his mind's eye. In the aftermath of the Bush administration, while the country was still reeling from the White House authorization of torture and other abuses, Cheney was confronted on a television news show about the illegal actions of the president. Rather than assuring the questioner that the presidential power was more constrained than it appeared, he asserted the opposite. Public complaints about Bush's abuse of power come from an insufficient appreciation of the true scale of the president's power. Accompanied round the clock by a military aid carrying the nuclear football,

> [The President] could launch the kind of devastating attack the world has never seen. He doesn't have to check with anybody. He doesn't have to call the Congress; he doesn't have to check with the courts. He has the authority because of the nature of the world we live in. It's unfortunate, but I think we're perfectly appropriate to take the steps we have.[224]

Locke's description of the legislature as the soul of a contractual state[225] has a counterpart: a state without a living legislature has lost its soul. It as, as Simon Schaffer has written, "the death of the social body."[226] Does the country not yet look dead? Any among us who briefly survive the opening moments of thermonuclear war should remember this sentence as we survey the darkened sky and scorched earth: this is what a country that has lost its soul looks like.

If we should someday have a president who recognizes that he or she cannot legally go to war without first going to Congress and asking for a declaration, would Congress even remember how to carry out such deliberations? Equally important, would the population of the United States recognize the necessity of restoring this constitutional provision? Four days before he was elected president, Bill Clinton said in an interview that he would never take this country to war without a congressional declaration,[227] a statement that might have prompted people to dance in the streets. But there was no confetti; the streets remained quiet, and even the interviewer appeared not to have noticed what the candidate had just said and simply changed the subject. Once he was elected, President Clinton invaded Haiti and the former Yugoslavia on his own authority, oiling the machinery of illegal executive habits that would make it easier for the next president to roll into Iraq, killing more than 100,000 civilians—and reinforcing the long-standing nuclear arrangement for presidential first use.

HABIT AND DELIBERATION

Are there—as there were in the spheres of sensory perception and creation—both negative and positive accounts of the place of habit in mental deliberation? Certainly both accounts are audible in the concrete instance of the deliberation required for a congressional declaration of war. On the one hand, it is perceived as the greatest and gravest safeguard of the social contract because it specifies that we can only be released from the never-injure rule by going through a deliberately encumbering set of steps before lifting the prohibition. When Justice Story called Article I, Section 8, Clause 11, the "highest act of legislation," he argued that far from being too encumbering, it would be reasonable to add "greater restrictions" to it.[228] On the other hand, the requirement for a congressional declaration has been (and continues to be) denigrated by many people in the twentieth and twenty-first centuries as a set of baffling and unnecessary impediments to the taking of an urgent national action.

Detractors of habit, believing that it shuts down sensation and that it exists at an opposite pole from creation, are not likely even to get to the question of its relation to deliberation. But what is striking is the fact that deliberation and habit share key attributes, and their relation can be approached by looking at the overlapping accounts of these attributes. Crucially, the role of material obstruction (which we regularly associate with habit) turns out to be assigned a key role in the philosophic accounts of deliberation: the focus on impedimenta in debates about the congressional declaration of war, for example, is consistent with a broader perception of the place of impedimenta in deliberation of any kind. Conversely, governance (which we regularly associate with deliberation) turns out to be assigned a key role in the philosophic accounts of habit. We begin with the second, before turning back to the first.

Habit, like deliberation, governs. Deliberation and governance are so inextricably linked that—as we saw at the opening of this chapter—political philosophers who have written treatises on the one tend also to have written treatises on the other: Plato, Aristotle, Locke, Hobbes, Hume, and Mill convince us that the two subjects occupy shared ground.

Ideas govern the state because, as Locke writes in *Conduct of the Understanding*, they govern our individual actions: "in truth the ideas and images in men's minds are the invisible powers that constantly govern them, and to these they all universally pay a ready submission."[229] It is precisely because the understanding exercises this governing power that the "conduct of the understanding" is so important. As good ideas make possible good governance, so bad ideas that take over the mind are described by Locke in images of illegal governance: "matters" can "take possession of our minds with a kind of authority and will not be kept out or dislodged, but, as if the passion that rules were for the time the sheriff of the place and came with all the posse, the understanding is seized and taken with the object it introduces, as if it had a legal right to be alone considered there."[230]

Almost as strong as the link between deliberation and governance is the link between habit and governance. The two are yoked together both by those who denigrate habit and by those who celebrate it, the first seeing habit as resulting in tyrannical governance, the second seeing habit as responsible for governance in its benignly effective workings. The opening sentence of Montaigne's essay on custom tells the story— one that later reappears in Locke[231]—about the village woman who lifted a calf each day from its infancy onward and found that eventually she could still lift the animal even after it had grown to be an ox. On the face of it, this seems to be a story about the extraordinary enabling power of daily habit. Surprisingly, in a not uncharacteristic non sequitur, Montaigne writes in the very next sentence: "For in truth habit is a violent and treacherous schoolmistress . . . furious and tyrannical."[232] Later in the same essay he writes, "But the principal effect of the power of custom is to seize and ensnare us in such a way that it is hardly within our power . . . to reflect and reason about its ordinances."[233]

It is because habit exerts such "force" that it is credited as governing, whether by celebrators or detractors: "The nature of habit," writes John Dewey, "is to be assertive, insistent, self-perpetuating."[234] Habits are "demands for certain kinds of activities . . . they will . . . they form . . . they furnish . . . they rule."[235] Montaigne himself in the course of his essay shifts from perceiving custom as tyrannizing to custom as governing: "Pindar calls her, so I have been told, the queen and empress of the world."[236] He continues a short time later, "Let us return to the sovereignty of custom." Montaigne's essay ends with his famous warning not against disobeying the law (that would be unthinkable) but even against merely making a suggestion that the law be amended![237] Montaigne throughout this essay is using the word "custom" both for everyday behaviors and for law. While law is a form of habit (regularizing and making customary certain procedures and rules), laws also act to inscribe habits in us, as has been recognized from Aristotle forward: "Legislators make the citizens good by forming habits in them, and this is the wish of every legislator; and those who do not effect it miss their mark, and it is in this that a good constitution differs from a bad one."[238]

Deliberation, like habit, entails material impediments. Habit is closely associated with materialization. The emergency procedures looked at throughout this chapter often take an externalized or materialized form: a written and memorized rule about counting, an emergency kit, a fallout shelter with thick walls and a ventilation system, a written contract with the specification of a twenty-foot ladder to be brought to the disaster site and the name of the person who will carry it there. Quite apart from the presence of any literal form of materialization, the sheer "force" of habit, described by Montaigne and Dewey, gives it its quality of "substantiveness" as though it were a *physical* presence. That substantiveness certainly constrains our freedom; if a friend's heart stops, the person who has learned CPR does not do any one of the hundred inventive things he might otherwise have done (flail his arms about, run for help, cry, shake the afflicted person, cover him with kisses) but begins to move through a very confined set of actions. The same is true in every other case. Having internalized the habit, as Montaigne complains, we lose our freedom and "no longer have the liberty of even raising our eyes."

Deliberation, too, entails just such a loss of liberty, as the word itself—de-liberation—announces. Thomas Hobbes makes the point unmistakable: "And it is called Deliberation, because it is a putting an end to the Liberty we had of doing, or omitting, according to our Appetite, or Aversion.[239] Brilliant and deeply crediting accounts of the material encumbrance of deliberation are provided by John Locke, on the one hand, and by John Dewey and Charles Peirce on the other.

Throughout *Conduct of the Understanding*, Locke criticizes rapid and unrestrained thinking, complaining that speech usually out-paces thinking, and thinking outpaces evidence.[240] The mind has a fast-forward momentum that makes it skip from one part of knowledge to another without "due examination of particulars."[241] This forward momentum is a species of "laziness" which allows the mind to take the first object that comes along. Locke calls this rapidity a state of "prostituting the mind" because the mind gives itself to the firstcomer.[242] It then wanders off to another subject, and then another, and then another.[243]

When Locke speaks of "well-grounded arguments" he has physical ground in mind. In his argument against haste he speaks of one who rides through a country:

> [one acquires a] loose description of here a mountain and there a plain, here a morass and there a river.... Such superficial ideas and observations as these he may collect in galloping over it. But the more useful observations of the soil, plants, animals and inhabitants, with their several sorts and properties, must necessarily escape him; and it is seldom men ever discover the rich mines without some digging. Nature commonly lodges her treasure and jewels in rocky ground. If the matter be knotty and the sense lies deep, *the mind must stop and buckle to it, and stick upon it* with labour, and thought, and close contemplation.[244]

Objects of thought have weight, and are elsewhere, as here, described in terms of physical ground. Locke even develops a term for thinking that arrives at evidentiary and weighted objects; he calls it "bottoming." In a section devoted to reading, Locke says one must go through the encumbering process of locating where the argument "bottoms," a process so thick that it is at first experienced as a "clog" in one's studies, a word he repeats admiringly several times.[245] The instruction to see where "the argument bottoms" may seem offhand in the section on reading, but late in the book "bottoming" becomes a formal term to which a special section is devoted: "Section 44: Bottoming." He illustrates the aspiration to find where any issue or question bottoms with the idea of the equality of all men, a certainty that can be carried reliably through all debates and questions.[246]

This same vision of material encumbrance is central to the accounts of deliberation given by Dewey and, earlier, by Pierce. In *How We Think*, Dewey outlines the sequence of steps entailed in deliberation. It begins with the "felt-experience" of a difficulty, a state of "undefined uneasiness" or "perplexity." This perception of unease leads to an interruption in one's normal action, whether physical or mental. Deliberation is an interruption and a search for an object to restore the forward momentum.[247] This state of suspended motion is uncomfortable, even painful, and is therefore one that must be "endured"; one must resist easy or arbitrary suggestions that would let one return prematurely to the "inertia" of forward "gliding" motion.[248] One mentally tries out various possibilities, conducting a series of mental experiments; because the solutions are carried out in the imagination only, the consequences are "not final or fatal" as they would be if actually enacted.[249] Eventually this mental testing enables one to find an object that releases one from the uncomfortable state of deliberation.

Charles Peirce provides a strikingly similar account of deliberation, describing the act of thinking as motivated "by the irritation of doubt," an uncomfortable state that is only "appeased" once the act of thinking finds an appropriate object of belief, which in turn leads to "the establishment in our nature of a rule of action, or, say for short, a *habit*."[250] Both Peirce and Dewey mean their accounts to apply across a wide range of instances that includes everyday acts such as deciding which path to take when the road forks or whether to pay one's transportation fare with the five coppers or the nickel one has just pulled from one's pocket.[251]

But the opposite end of the spectrum, where emergency and survival are at stake, is clearly crucial. "Now, the identity of a habit," Peirce writes, "depends on how it might lead us to act, not merely under such circumstances as are likely to arise but under such as might possibly occur, no matter how improbable they may be."[252] For improbable events where deliberation is especially crucial, we develop forms of what Peirce calls "self-notification"[253] and what the later theorist Jon Elster calls "self-binding."[254] Dewey writes:

> By thought man also develops and arranges artificial signs to remind him in advance of consequences, and of ways of securing and avoiding them.... [C]ivilized man deliberately *makes* such signs; he sets up in advance of wreckage warning buoys, and builds lighthouses where he sees signs that such events may occur. ... The very essence of civilized culture is that we deliberately erect monuments and memorials, lest we forget; and deliberately institute, in advance of the happening of various contingencies and emergencies of life, devices for detecting their approach and registering their nature, for warding off what is unfavorable, or at least for protecting ourselves from its full impact.[255]

Dewey's buoys, lighthouses, monuments, and memorials of deliberation are what Elster means by forms of self-binding or precommitment in which "we temporarily deposit our will in some external structure" until "after some time [it] returns to its source and modifies our behavior"; capable of both rationality and irrationality, we invent forms of self-binding to "protect [ourselves] against the irrationality."[256] Dewey's general account of deliberation serves well as an account of the transnational rules for CPR, the Saskatchewan mutual aid contracts, the Swiss shelter system, and—of greatest importance here—the constitutional requirements overseeing the United States' entry into war, the channel markers and lighthouses that mark out a highly specific and constrained path into war. To sail outside those channel markers may feel like freedom, but we are careening into an abyss that places the entire earth in peril.

Emergency procedures are laden with deliberation. There may well be, as we have seen, a long temporal hiatus between the deliberation and the actual enactment of the procedure: the Swiss debate about whether to have a shelter system and the population's actual act of inhabiting the shelters when a nuclear weapon is fired. The fact that there is a temporal interruption between the deliberation and the performance of the action does not mean that the final action—the inhabiting of the shelters—was nondeliberative, nonvolitional, outside the population's will or choice. Aristotle says choice is "what has been decided [by] previous deliberation"; a choice is "that which is chosen before other things."[257] Of course, deliberation may be strikingly visible both in the creation and in the enactment stages; deliberation may be not only the path by which the emergency procedure was arrived at but also the specified content of that procedure. That is precisely the case in the United States' requirement for a congressional declaration of war, a provision debated and determined at the country's Constitutional Convention and one whose very content stipulates the action of debate and voting by a large assembly of people. Of the four models of emergency procedure, the deliberative act remains most visible in the provision for a declaration of war; but the capacity for ongoing deliberation is part of what is being protected in all four. The key point here is that each of the four—CPR, the Canadian or Ethiopian or Japanese mutual aid contracts for shared rescue, the Swiss shelter system, and the constitutional provision for a congressional declaration—is the outcome of a deliberative process, and all are objects of choice.

Aristotle lists the things that *cannot* be objects of deliberation: (1) the elementary, (2) heavenly movements such as the solstice, (3) arbitrary things that could just as easily be something else, (4) objects of deliberation for other populations—that is, things indeed arrived at by deliberation but not by one's own deliberation, and (5) impossibilities. What makes the Swiss shelter system an instance of Venturiesque throbbing Technicolor ingenuity is that, though Switzerland conceives of itself as having almost no influence on the superpowers, and though it acknowledges that geographically speaking it could well be in the direct or indirect line of fire, it conceives of the survival of its population as an object of deliberation, not as an impossibility. And what is disheartening about the disavowal of our own emergency preparation in the Constitution is that it takes our fate out of the sphere of deliberation and designates it either an impossibility, a phenomenon akin to the solstice, an arbitrary thing, or an outcome to be determined by another population.

This chapter holds that the two constitutional provisions overseeing our entry into war provide the best possible protection for our democracy, protection—first and foremost—against monarchic weapons, whether the nuclear form of monarchic weaponry invented in the 1940s or some future form of monarchic weaponry invented in the 2040s. Some people may wish to argue that these two constitutional provisions (and their equivalents in other countries) have flaws and that we need to amend the Constitution to provide some other, better form of protection. If so, the conclusions we can reach about thinking in an emergency need to be kept in mind. First, because technology makes what was once the mere ritual ceremony of monarchy a concrete reality backed by genocidal killing power (the capacity to annihilate at will all the peoples on earth), civil society is in a new situation and has to secure appropriate laws and procedures that make the return of monarchy impossible. Second, these procedures must be as explicit as the CPR protocol or the Swiss shelter system with its extraordinary specification for Saint Roch, his dog, and the heart-shaped ceramic Eucharist wafer the dog holds in its mouth. Third, this kind of specificity is the only resource that has been shown to work in medicine, in floods, in search-and-rescue missions, or in any context of injury from the present back through history to the tales of Thucydides and Aesop and Aristotle. Inventing these and making sure they are widely understood—understood by the entire population—is one of the philosophic and civic responsibilities of our age.

CONCLUSION

AGAINST US ALL

When the commander of the United States Strategic Command (STRATCOM), was asked in January 2008 to compare "the nuclear mission" with "other missions," he gave a simple answer:

> We have a lot of balls we juggle every day in this command. All but one of them are rubber. One is crystal. Most of them that we drop, they're going to bounce. We can pick them back up, throw them back into the stream and juggle them. But the nuclear mission is a crystal ball. We cannot afford to drop that. This is a mission area where we as human beings are challenged to be perfect. We are not perfect.[1]

In a sequence of short sentences, General Chilton makes visible the enormity of the nuclear problem: it is a crystal ball being kept in the air by the hands of human beings who are, as a species, imperfect jugglers. Once dropped, it will permit no reversal, no repair, no recovery—no starting over.

But is the description completely accurate? Is it the "nuclear mission" that is shatterable, or is it instead the case that nuclear weapons have converted the earth's surface into something shatterable. This resilient spinning planet, revolving in its path over millions of years, tracing circles in the air while all the time weathering heat and ice to produce the most unthinkable array of beautiful creatures—dazzling in their numbers, colors and forms—has by the solitary invention of nuclear weapons been converted into a surface where all that swims or swoops or skips or sways—arabesques of aliveness so hilariously inventive they are like laughter itself—can, within a few hours be burned, sickened, and slain.

If constitutions seem too slender a tool to save human beings, their scale may seem even more inadequate to the task of saving the other inhabitants of earth. "Sequoia," once the name of one of the most enduringly alive organisms on earth, is now the name of the fastest supercomputer on earth, dedicated to simulating nuclear weapons testing so that the nuclear capabilities of the United States will not be thwarted by restrictions on actual testing.[2] How did this achievement, the culmination of work done over six decades by thousands of inventive human beings, come to be dedicated to nuclear weapons rather than, say, solving the problem of famine, or deciphering illness, or decoding the migratory intelligence of arctic terns that fly from pole to pole twice a year?

The tool we have for restoring the planet to a stable spin is the U.S. Constitution. A delicate tool, perhaps, when looked at in its American incarnation, the monolithic blow it can deliver to illegal governance is legible in the pushback coming from century upon century upon century of antecedent theory and practice. Tools for protecting the earth's human population and tools for protecting nonhuman life-forms have long gone hand in hand. The constitutional rule of law, we know, has a great debt to the thirteenth-century British document, the Magna Carta. Historian Peter Linebaugh has made us aware that the Magna Carta originally contained another charter, which then grew up side by side with it. It was called the Charter of the Forest. It sought to guarantee that the bounty of earth was available to all people, not just to kings, as had been true earlier.[3] So, too, the obligation to protect the earth belonged to all people, not just to kings. It is cited in our own country in law cases involving the public's access to natural resources: "Since Magna Carta and the Charter of the Forest, the ownership of birds, fish and game...has been uniformly regarded...as a trust for the benefit of all the people in common."[4]

Among other things, the Charter of the Forest sought to protect the right of self-defense—the right that by the agency of nuclear weapons, has now been retracted from all the populations of earth. The forest's "greenhue" or "vert," as Edward Coke explained in his seventeenth-century margin glosses to the 1224 document, was "whatsoever beareth green Leaf." It was available to the population for diverse uses such as shelter ("Haw-Thorn, Black-Thorn") and food ("as Pear-Trees, Chestnut-Trees, Apple Trees"). Included among these primary uses—explicitly and repeatedly—was self-defense: Oakes, Beeches, Ashes, Poplers, Maples, Alder, and Elder.[5] The charter addressed not just the need to distribute the resources of earth away from kings and toward the people but also the need to distribute them across generations. A 1608 supplement to the charter is entitled *A Proclamation for Preservation of Woods.* The king urges his "loving subjects" not to lop off the tops of trees, not to "bark or girt" them, not to cut down young saplings that will over time become "Oake, Elme, Ashe, Beech." Though the forest is theirs, they should take only what is "meete and necessary" to their needs. Generations of the future should find not just that the forest still stands, but that it stands yet more ample and full, its luxuriance certifying the earlier generation's capacity to be mindful of people still to come: the goal is "to worke the meanes not only of better preservation of our said woods in times to come, but also of a present multiplication and increase of Timber and Wood to all future ages. And to the end that our care may appear to extend to the preservation and increase of Timber, as well in general to others, as to our selves."[6] Could the author of this tract, James I, have imagined all the woodlands of England burned and blasted beyond regeneration? No longer available for food, self-defense, and shelter?

It is often said that our military prowess today is so great that earlier peoples simply could not have imagined such destructive powers (and that therefore their musings are irrelevant to our problem). Nothing could be further from the truth. These legal instruments—and with them all the other things Hobbes lists on the side of civilization and opposed to the life without a social contract (arts, science, society, geography, navigation, industry, commodious building, transportation, instruments for measuring time)—came into being precisely because earlier people not only *could*, but *did*, imagine the human capacity for destructive rage.

This recognition is addressed in our earliest writings. The *Iliad*, as the poet Allen Grossman shows, is about the human impulse toward "obliterative rage," the attempt to erase and deface the human form that comes when Achilles drags Hector's body around the leveled city attempting to scrub away layer after layer, until his body disappears. The gods will not allow it and place a protective golden envelope around the warrior's body. "What ... is the purpose of the *Iliad*? It is this: *the establishment of a limit to violence at the point of the defacement of the human image*."[7] The oldest epic we have, *Gilgamesh* (more than three thousand years old) tells the story of this same "obliterative rage" exercised at the outset not against human beings but against the forest, the grove of giant Blue Cedars. Does Gilgamesh seek to obliterate the spirit of the Blue Cedars only because the Sumerians have deforested the plains of Mesopotamia and now need to plunder more wood? No, answer Robert Harrison, there is a "deeper" reason: Gilgamesh is enraged that the giant trees surpass him in stature, cover the earth with a reach his name can never match, and most important, will like the earth itself, long outlive him and each successive king in turn.[8]

Like the legal instruments at the center of this book, these poems exist because earlier people—far from being incapable of imagining the scale of destruction on which we boast and congratulate ourselves—precisely did see it and tried to put protocols and poems in our path, warning buoys in our coastal waters and beacons in the forest canopy. The Charter of the Forest has been seen by legal scholars as an important constituent in the modern Public Trust Doctrine that in turn has been called upon to protect forests and thereby help prevent global warming.[9] If that doctrine can be enlisted to protect against global warming, it may also one day become eligible to assist the struggle against the far more condensed catastrophe of nuclear war. In the meantime and for the time being, the beauty of earth and the Charter of the Forest are invoked here as reminders of our obligation to use whatever tools are available today, and to put our hands to the work. It has often been the beauty of earth that has inspired constitutions,[10] as well as legislation[11] designed to protect both people and their environments.[12]

If the authors of the social contract writings of the seventeenth and eighteenth centuries—the precursors of national and state constitutions—focused centrally on human beings and not on other living creatures or on the earth itself, they were certainly highly alert to these others. Thomas Hobbes's first published writing is a long poem in Latin about a series of geographical wonders in Derbyshire: peaks; caverns; medicinal springs; the origin of rivers; an abyss so deep that he stands terrified at its edge, listening to eleven widely spaced rebounds of a dropped rock—the next-to-last a whisper, the last only the mental image of that whisper. Hobbes makes himself intimate with the earth's surface—he walks, climbs, crawls on all fours, stands erect again, moves like a crab, bathes naked in crystal waters—and often the earth's features mimic his body, its steep ravine "sucking with dark lungs the pliant air," its "veins" carrying healing waters, the buttocks and female genitals of its giant rock formations embarrassing and delighting him with their magnification of human surfaces.[13]

At the poem's opening, his thoughts are with aristocrats and the artfulness of piped water in a country estate; but soon, in a wilder geography, he lets himself come face to face with miners forced by hunger to work in subterranean spaces ("A people expert in experienc'd wo"), two of whose dead bodies are visible there and whose kinship with his own body he stops to salute.[14] The poem memorializes, too, a peasant once suspended on a rope 300 feet into a bottomless cave; instructed by an earl to carry out depth soundings with a basket of stones, he emerged so terrified he died.[15] As with the miners, Hobbes stresses his own bodily continuity with the peasant, for that man's acoustical experiment comes after Hobbes has twice, from a far safer location, carried out the same fear-inducing experiment. Hobbes's thoughts are also about his living girl guide with "accent clear"; her knowledge of the geography, "steady foot" and emboldening cheerfulness link her with the poetic muses whom he coaxes unsuccessfully to describe the female rock formations: "Tell me, tell't me alone, tell't in my ear. / Whisper't, that none but thou and I may hear; / She's dumb, as conscious of the form obscene."[16] Hobbes may be traveling with aristocrats; his companions are unnamed and undescribed.[17] It is instead two miners, a peasant, and a clear-speaking girl (decisive in her speech as in her silence) who are intimate with the hidden wonders of the earth's undersurface. They will later be among all those who have, according to Hobbes, uncontested equality in the social contract.[18]

Stones, water, and sunlight preoccupy Hobbes on the Derbyshire peaks; and perhaps for that reason, or perhaps because it is early autumn, we do not hear of wildflowers and grasses. But then we come to John Locke, who collected wildflowers—not "now and then" but on eighty-eight different days in 1664 and ninety-four days in 1665,[19] resulting in what is credited with being among "the oldest surviving collection of English wildflowers,"[20] numbering 3000 by some accounts, just shy of 1000 by others.[21] Peter Anstey and Stephen Harris describe the care entailed in mounting, dating, and labeling the flowers (not a daffodil but a "Double white Daffodill," not a violet but a "Single white Dames Violet") in both English and Latin, after drying each flower for a week, with a change of paper every day, the source of paper being that "previously used for exercises by Locke's pupils at Christ Church."[22] His 970 wildflowers required 6790 rotations of drying paper.

Anstey and Harris carefully document the many reasons for recognizing Locke not as an amateur plant gatherer (as some early historians have supposed) but as a member of a network of "botanically aware virtuosi." The fifteen botanical books in his library, the seventy plant references in *An Essay on Understanding*, and even the magnificent hand-pressed book of 970 wildflowers are only the beginning.[23] Equally telling are Locke's sophisticated and highly knowledgeable gathering of seeds in England, France, and Netherlands, his correspondence with leading plant men of the day, and the fact—as Anstey and Harris scrupulously show—that the seeds he gathered parented major streams of plants in two important herbaria in Oxford and one in London: "Of the 200 seeds on the lists which Locke sent Jacob Bobart the Younger, twenty-four, or 12%, ended up in the Hortus siccus; forty-two, or 21%, ended up in the Morisonian Herbarium.... Furthermore, an initial foray into Hans Sloane's massive archive has revealed that progeny from at least four of Locke's seeds ended up in the Sloane Herbarium."[24]

Amateur or virtuoso, Locke was consumed with these fragile eruptions on earth's surface in the spring, summer, and fall of each year. We lose a large part of his mental world if his love of wildflowers is overlooked. Less in danger of being forgotten—because published and read widely—are Rousseau's *Botanical Writings* where he lingers over, and meticulously describes, the anatomical structure of buttercups, daisies, hyacinths, and lilies; marguerites, sunflowers, and china asters.[25] Here he asserts that "beautiful knowledge" of plants is a prerequisite for becoming a philosopher.[26]

Civilization's tools for placing brakes on war protect the earth and other species, not just humans. Any tool that by eliminating nuclear weapons can secure the life of a girl on the Derbyshire peaks or her sister on a mountainside in Iran or China will simultaneously secure the migrating snowy owls and double white daffodils. And conversely any tool that by eliminating nuclear weapons can reattach the name "Sequoia" to its high home in an ancient tree will also secure the surface and undersurface of the earth and the human beings who crawl or walk over its surface and bathe in its crystal waters. There is no separation among earth, its human inhabitants, and its other species because nuclear weapons are *Quod omnes tangit*, that which touches all.

At the close of the *Second Treatise of Government* (in the chapter examining the legitimate grounds for rebellion), Locke quotes a memorable observation about one of history's tyrants: "And of Caligula ... he wisht that the people had but one neck, that he might dispatch them all at a blow."[27] Nuclear weapons and the highly practiced arrangements for their use have made Caligula's wish come true: the people of earth now have but one neck and can be dispatched all at a blow. It does not matter that the thermonuclear monarchs who preside over us today are ordinarily much nicer people than Caligula, for it is the nuclear architecture itself that literalizes and monumentalizes Caligula; the individual personalities of our monarchs, and the always amusing differences among them, are at best a temporary check on a vast structure of cruelty that stands ready to be used. It is national monarchs, not terrorists, who have put this in place and readied it for use, whether by themselves or by stateless actors. And it is these colossal structures of illegitimate nongovernance that must be dismantled.

Some will say that the two constitutional provisions presented here—Article I, Section 8, clause 11, and the Second Amendment—are not the best tools for dismantling thermonuclear monarchy. To this I say: if these tools look inadequate, that is only because they are at present lying unused on the ground. They will become very great tools once human hands pick them up and use them. We should use whatever tool can best accomplish the dismantling. If there is a better tool, please tell us what it is, and help us to see how to use it.

NOTES

INTRODUCTION: THE FLOOR OF THE WORLD

1 Each Ohio-class submarine has 24 missiles; each missile has 8 warheads; hence each ship has a total of 192 warheads. The Trident II warhead (Mark 5 W87) can be either 300 or 475 kilotons. Three hundred kilotons times 192 warheads equals 57,600 kilotons or 57.6 megatons. The weapon used in Hiroshima was between 12 and 15 kilotons; therefore, a middle figure of 13.5 kilotons can be used. More arithmetic: 57,600 kilotons divided by 13.5 kilotons is 4266; therefore, each Ohio-class submarine carries the injuring power of 4266 Hiroshimas. If the submarine instead uses a 475-kiloton Trident II warhead, the submarine carries the injuring power of 6755 Hiroshima explosions (for the Trident II warhead figures, see William Arkin, Thomas Cochran, and Milton Hoenig, *U.S. Nuclear Forces and Capabilities, Nuclear Weapons Databook*, vol. 1 [Pensacola, FL: Ballinger, 1984], p. 15).

The numbers just given here are conservative. Often officials give much higher numbers. A Department of Energy newsletter quotes Congresswoman Patricia Schroeder as reporting that the SSBN *West Virginia* carries the equivalent of 7680 Hiroshima blasts ("Tuck Tells House Panel Rocky Flats Start Up Off until Third Quarter," *Inside Energy/with Federal Lands*, March 26, 1990). Schroeder's figure is based on the calculation that the submarine has 192 warheads each with forty times the power of that used against Hiroshima. The number of missiles on each Ohio-class submarine is consistently reported as 24; the number of warheads on each missile is usually designated as 8, but is sometimes as high as 17.

2 Sixty-one countries participated in World War II. The number given here—each submarine as eight times the World War II figure—is again conservative. The total blast power of World War II has been calculated as three megatons by the International Commission on Nuclear Non-Proliferation and Disarmament.

Using that figure, a single Ohio-class submarine is *nineteen* times the total blast power expended in World War II. For the three-megaton figure, see the International Commission's report co-chaired by Gareth Evans and Yoriko Kawaguchi, *Eliminating Nuclear Threats: A Practical Agenda for Global Policymakers*, Part II, sec. 1.2.

3 "Written Statement of the Government of Qatar: Legality of the Threat or Use of Nuclear Weapons (Request for Advisory Opinion)," (Dr. Najeeb Al-Nauimi, Minister Legal Advisor), June 20, 1955, p. 2.

4 "Letter dated 18 May 1995 from the Permanent Representative of the Democratic People's Republic of Korea to the United Nations" (Pak Gil Yon, Ambassador), p. 1; and "Letter dated 20 June 1995 from the Ambassador of India, together with Written Statement of the Government of India: Status of Nuclear Weapons in International Law (Request for Advisory Opinion of the International Court of Justice)," pp. 2, 5, 7. India argued that both the use (whether first use or second use) and the making of nuclear weapons are illegal.

5 "Note Verbale dated 20 June 1995 from the Embassy of Sweden, together with Written Statement [10 June 1994] of the Government of Sweden," pp. 3, 5 (referring generally to "international law," to Hague, and to Geneva 1925); "Note Verbale dated 19 June 1995 from the Embassy of the Islamic Republic of Iran, together with Written Statement of the Government of the Islamic Republic of Iran," p. 2; "Communication dated 20 June 1995 from the Embassy of Egypt, together with Written Statement of the Government of Egypt," pp. 8, 11, 13, 14, 15. Egypt, noting that the survival of her population depends centrally on river water, ocean water, and agricultural land, identified herself as "a leading country in the efforts for... [worldwide] nuclear disarmament" and in the efforts to make the Middle East a nuclear weapons–free zone (p. 2).

6 "Letter dated 22 June 1995 from the Permanent Representative of the Marshall Islands to the United Nations, together with Written Statement of the Government of the Marshall Islands," pp. 1, 3–4.

7 "Written Statement of the Government of India," pp. 1, 2, 5.

8 "Letter dated 14 June 1995 from Minister at the Embassy of Japan, together with Written Statement of the Government of Japan," p. 1.

9 The United States' arguments against the applicability of these protocols sometimes center on original intent. For example, the St. Petersburg Declaration forbidding weapons "that render death inevitable" was written with antipersonnel weapons in mind, not with weapons that merely have "a high probability of killing persons in its immediate vicinity" (p. 33). Sometimes, as in the instance of the Rio Declaration, the protocol is set aside on the grounds that it is a "political," rather than a legally binding, document (p.40). In general, the United States dismisses international rules on one of two bases: (1) nuclear weapons are not included in the text (either because the text predates the invention of nuclear weapons or postdates the invention of nuclear weapons but fails to include a specific clause), or (2) if

nuclear weapons are explicitly mentioned, that explicit mention constitutes not a prohibition but an "aspirational goal" (p. 46).

While an array of arguments are put forward to explain why international protocols and covenants are inapplicable to a determination of the legal status of nuclear weapons, the United States provides a single, overarching argument that recurs throughout the document: the use of nuclear weapons belongs to the future and therefore a formal ruling would constitute "judicial speculation about hypothetical future circumstances" (p. 2); "the Court should not, on a matter of such fundamental importance, engage in speculation about unknown future situations" (p. 4); a judgment cannot "be made in advance or in the abstract" (p. 30); to rule that nuclear weapons would bring "severe damage" to neutral countries (and therefore violate neutrality rules) would be "in any event highly speculative" (p. 32). The Court is repeatedly chided for agreeing to give an Advisory Opinion on a subject that is "vague" (p. 5), "hypothetical," "abstract" (p. 30).

10 "Written Statement of the Government of the United States," p. 33 (the final phrase quoted is a citation from Article II of the U.N. Convention).

11 On May 14, 1993, the World Health Organization asked the International Court of Justice for an Advisory Opinion on the legality of nuclear weapons. On December 15, 1994, the U.N. General Assembly requested (in Resolution A49/75K) that the International Court of Justice provide an Advisory Opinion on the subject: "Is the threat or use of nuclear weapons in any circumstance permitted under international law?" On February 8, 1995, the International Court of Justice wrote to governments inviting them to contribute their view by June 20, 1995. On October 5, 1995, hearings began. The International Court issued its Advisory Opinion on July 8, 1996.

12 The Navy has not disclosed what antenna or alternative technology has replaced the no-longer-used antenna in Michigan and Wisconsin. In response to the author's Freedom of Information inquiries, the Navy implied that no new systems or aerials are in use. But over the many years when the Michigan-Wisconsin ELF antenna was in use, the Navy insisted that it was desperately needed, that its work could not be duplicated by any other already existing communication system, and that without it there was no way to communicate from land to a deeply submerged submarine.

If the Navy has not expressed alarm about the communication problem following the elimination of the ELF system, the defense industry has. According to Raytheon senior manager William Matzelevich, "One of the missing capabilities, when you look out there today at submarines, is how do you build a simple messaging system that allows someone to pick up the phone and talk to a submarine … Submarine communications today either have to be scheduled broadcasts that could take from eight to 12 hours from delivery to confirmation of the message or using floating wire antennas" (Geoff Fein, "Raytheon Developing Technology for Submarine Communications," *Defense Daily*, vol. 234, no. 7, April 11, 2007).

Raytheon is developing a new communications technology called "Deep Siren Tactical Paging System" that will be based on buoys ejected from the submarine to the surface.

The problem is not that the "valuable" ELF system has not yet been replaced, but that the ELF system itself enhanced communication "only marginally at best," as Wisconsin Senator Russ Feingold (acting on behalf of the residents of his state—most of whom deplored the antenna) three times argued before Congress in his efforts to have the system terminated: "ELF is a one-way, primitive messenger system designed to signal to—not communicate with—deeply submerged Trident submarines.... If it is a first-strike weapon, then it is destabilizing and threatening" ("Department of Defense Appropriation Act, 1996," Amendment 2413 [limiting the cost of terminating ELF to $12 million], Congressional Record, Senate, August 10, 1995, pp. 23026, 23027).

If the colossal antenna had a benefit, it was that for several decades it made Wisconsin residents acutely aware of the country's SSBN fleet. Those residents, in turn, made some of the rest of the U.S. population aware of the otherwise invisible fleet.

13 A third communication system pursued during the 1980s and 90s involved a blue-green laser; it was unable to penetrate to the depth of ELF waves, and though much faster than ELF in its transmission of data, it lost time scanning the ocean trying to locate the submarine.

14 In its coupling of giant force with giant ignorance, thermonuclear monarchy is a vast magnification of an attribute of monarchy noticed long ago. Thomas Paine, in *Common Sense*, describes the monarch as one whose isolation cuts him off from information: "There is something exceedingly ridiculous in the composition of monarchy; it first excludes a man from the means of information, yet empowers him to act in cases where the highest judgment is required. The state of the king shuts him from the world; yet the business of a king requires him to know it thoroughly; wherefore the different parts, by unnaturally opposing and destroying each other, prove the whole character to be absurd and useless" (Thomas Paine, *Common Sense* in *Political Writings*, ed. Bruce Kuklick [Cambridge: Cambridge University Press, 1989], p.6).

15 This goal of minimal injury was explicit at the time of the writing of the U.S. Constitution (see Chapter 2) and is still today a stated goal of the U.S. military. For example, the three overarching rules of war in the Navy are symmetry, chivalry, and necessity. Necessity, far from serving to excuse brutality, is understood as a brake on injuring: it requires there be used, in any conflict, only the smallest amount of force needed for accomplishing the goal. Necessity, symmetry, and chivalry are each starkly out of line with nuclear weapons; and some of the most articulate objections to U.S. nuclear weapons have come from members of the Navy. Objections to nuclear weapons may also contribute to the low retention rate of nuclear submarine officers, as reported to Congress by Vice Admiral F. L. Bowman, U.S. Navy, Chief of Navy Personnel (National Security Subcommittee

of the House Appropriations Committee on Military Personnel Programs, April 16, 1996).

16 Cited in *First Use of Nuclear Weapons: Preserving Responsible Control: Hearings before the Subcommittee on International Security and Scientific Affairs of the Committee on International Relations of the House of Representatives*, 94th Cong., 2d Sess. (1976), 218.

17 The nuclear briefcase came into being after the Cuban Missile Crisis. Even before the crisis, Kennedy worried about the speed and clarity of the procedures for a presidential launch. Here is a portion of a memo he sent on January 17, 1962 (designated "Top Secret" for over twenty-five years):

Question Number 1:

Assuming that information from a closely guarded source causes me to conclude that the U.S. should launch an immediate nuclear strike against the Communist Bloc, does the JCS Emergency Actions File permit me to initiate such an attack without first consulting with the Secretary of Defense and/or the Joint Chiefs of Staff?

Question Number 2:

I know that the red button on my desk phone will connect me with the White House Army Signal Agency (WHASA) switchboard and that the WHASA switchboard can connect me immediately to the Joint War Room. If I called the Joint War Room without giving them advance notice, to whom would I be speaking?

Question Number 3:

What would I say to the Joint War Room to launch an immediate nuclear strike? (From memo entitled, "ALERT PROCEDURES and JCS EMERGENCY ACTIONS FILE," JCS 1/62-12/62, Box 281, John Fitzgerald Kennedy Library, Boston, MA).

18 Fred Barbash, "Carters Find Peace, Quiet in Idaho Wilderness," *Washington Post*, August 24, 1978, p. A2; "Nuclear Code Briefcase Remained Near Reagan," *New York Times*, March 31, 1981, p. A5.

19 The 1952–54 National Security Council Memoranda and 1959 Presidential Memoranda in which Eisenhower contemplates using atomic weapons in Taiwan straits and again in Berlin are cited at length in Chapter 1, which analyzes the differences between presidential and congressional forms of deliberation. Another instance of a long time lapse between presidential action and public notification concerns predelegation. In 1959, Eisenhower pre-delegated to a small set of military commanders authority (in case he was unreachable) to launch nuclear weapons in response to either a conventional weapons attack or a nuclear attack. These instructions were declassified forty-two years later, in May 2001, following repeated requests from the National Security Archive at George Washington University, requests originally declined on the grounds that the top-secret material was relevant to war plans currently in effect. ("First Declassification of Eisenhower's Instructions to

Commanders Predelegating Nuclear Weapons Use, 1959–60," ed. William Burr, National Security Archive Electronic Briefing Book No. 45, May 18, 2001). On pre-delegation of authority to launch nuclear weapons, see also William Burr, "U.S. Had Plans for 'Full Nuclear Response' [against Russia and China] in Event President Killed or Disappeared during an Attack on the United States," National Security Archive Electronic Briefing Book No. 406, December 12, 2012.

20 Extended interview with McNamara in *The Fog of War* (director and interviewer, Errol Morris, 1994). On the release of documents showing Johnson's consideration of a pre-emptive strike in China, see Jim Mann, "U.S. Considered '64 Bombing to Keep China Nuclear-Free," *Los Angeles Times*, September 27, 1998. On the forty-two-year lapse between the time Nixon contemplated using tactical nuclear weapons in response to North Korea's shooting down of a reconnaissance plane and the notification of the public, see Chapter 1, note 137 and accompanying text. On Nixon's October 1969 act of flying eighteen B-52 bombers loaded with nuclear weapons toward Moscow during the Vietnam War, and the declassification of this event thirty-five years later, see Jeremi Suri, "The Nukes of October: Richard Nixon's Secret Plan to Bring Peace to Vietnam," *Wired Magazine*, February 28, 2008. Attached to Suri's article are three documents: "Memorandum for the President from Henry A. Kissinger. Subject: Military Alerts," October 9, 1969; "Memorandum for Colonel Haig. Subject: Significant Military Actions," October 8, 1969; and a January 1970 after-action report, "SAC History Study #136: Notes on Increased Readiness Posture of October 1969." On Nixon's 1972 proposal to use nuclear weapons in North Vietnam, see Deb Riechmann, "Nixon Discussed Nuclear Strike in Vietnam," *Boston Globe*, March 3, 2002.

21 Natural Resources Defense Council, "Faking Nuclear Restraint: The Bush Administration's Secret Plan for Strengthening U.S. Nuclear Forces" (February 13, 2002, describing Nuclear Posture Review). According to defense analyst Norman Polmar twelve new SSBN(X) ships are scheduled, the first due to arrive in 2019, the second in 2022, and one each year from 2024 to 2033 (U.S. Naval Institute, *Proceedings Magazine* [July 2011]: 86, 87).

A March 3, 2013, Congressional Research Service Report indicates that in the Navy's FY2013 budget request, it has now proposed moving the date for the building of the first ship from 2019 to 2021 and the twelfth ship from 2033 to 2035, thereby spreading the preliminary research and development costs over more years and enabling them to lower the current year's request from last year's figure of $1067 million to $564.9 million (Ronald O'Rourke, "Navy Ohio Replacement [SSBN(X)] Ballistic Missile Submarine Program: Background and Issues for Congress," Congressional Research Service Report, March 3, 2012, pp. 1, 16). The fact that Congress approved the budget request on March 21, 2013, suggests that it has accepted the Navy's proposed two-year delay (Telephone Conversation with Ronald O'Rourke, Specialist in Naval Affairs, Congressional Research Service Office, March 22, 2013). A 2012 Government Accounting Office Report estimates the overall cost of the twelve new Ohio-class submarines as $90 billion: $11 billion in research, $79 billion to build ("Defense Acquisitions: Assessments of Selected Weapons Programs," GAO-12-400SP, March 2012, p.152).

22 President Barack Obama's 2009 speech in Prague made many people throughout the world hopeful that he would work to eliminate nuclear weapons: "[W]e must stand together for the right of people everywhere to live free from fear [of nuclear weapons] in the 21st century. . . . [A]s a nuclear power, as the only nuclear power to have used a nuclear weapon, the United States has a moral responsibility to act. We cannot succeed in this endeavor alone, but we can lead it, we can start it. So today, I state clearly and with conviction America's commitment to seek the peace and security of a world without nuclear weapons" ("Remarks by President Barack Obama," Hradcany Square, Prague, Czech Republic, April 5, 2009).

But, as the forward momentum of the new land-based, sea-based, and air-based delivery systems indicates, the nuclear arsenal of the United States in unlikely to disappear unless the population itself acts to bring this about. Inside the U.S. government, the Prague sentences just cited tend to be given less weight than the two that immediately followed: President Obama continued, "I'm not naive. This goal will not be reached quickly—perhaps not in my lifetime" (quoted by Amy F. Woolf, "U.S. Strategic Nuclear Forces: Background, Developments, and Issues," Congressional Research Service Report, January 14, 2013, p. 2).

23 Another period that illustrates our collective willingness to suppress questions about our own nuclear weapons is the day of September 11, 2001, and its immediate aftermath. On 9/11, President Bush—who was in Texas when the World Trade Towers were hit—immediately boarded Air Force One but delayed returning to Washington because he was advised that the White House might be a terrorist target. Of the many Air Force bases in the United States where he might have landed that day, the president chose to land at Offutt Air Force Base, Nebraska.

Prior to 9/11, Offutt Air Force Base, was publicly described as the "nerve center of America's nuclear strike force" not only against the Soviet Union but "against terrorist states or rogue leaders who threaten to use their own nuclear, chemical or biological weapons" ("Head of Nuclear Forces Plans for a New World," *New York Times*, February 25, 1993, p. B7; this article is specifically about the shift in U.S. nuclear targeting to include terrorist leaders or terrorist-harboring states). Offutt is the location of the strategic command that "consolidates control of all long-range nuclear bombers, . . . missile-firing submarines and EC-135 command planes." Did President Bush stop at Offutt Air Force Base because nuclear retaliation was among the options on the table that day and in the days following? Neither Congress nor the media nor the public nor even the 9/11 investigative commission appears ever to have mentioned the *nuclear* status of Offutt or asked a single question about it. The official *9/11 Commission Report* states, "Offutt Air Force Base in Nebraska was chosen because of its elaborate command and control facilities, and because it could accommodate overnight lodgings for 50 persons.

The Secret Service wanted a place where the President could spend several days, if necessary." In context, "command and control facilities" seems only to refer to the "video teleconferencing" apparatus that allowed Bush to speak with Condoleezza Rice and George Tenet as soon as he landed, and the emphasis is on Offutt's commodious sleeping accommodations (*The 9/11 Commission Report: Final Report of the National Commission on Terrorist Attacks upon the United States* [New York: Norton, 2004], pp. 325, 326).

24 Natural Resources Defense Council, "Table of U.S. Strategic Nuclear Forces, 2002."

25 Jonathan Elliot, ed., *The Debates in the Several State Conventions, on the Adoption of the Federal Constitution, as Recommended by the General Convention at Philadelphia in 1787, Together with the Journal of the Federal Convention, Luther Martin's Letter, Yates's Minutes, Congressional Opinions, Virginia and Kentucky Resolutions of '98–'99, and Other Illustrations of the Constitution*, vol. 3, "Convention of Virginia" (Philadelphia: Lippincott, 1861), p. 590 (hereinafter Elliot, *Ratification Debates*).

26 The 1991 Gulf War had a "conditional" declaration of war (it specified certain events that if occurring on a future date would then automatically place the country at war). As discussed in Chapter 1, in all five of the country's legally declared wars (preceding the War of 1812, the Mexican-American War of 1846, the Spanish-American War of 1898, World War I, and World War II) the "conditional" was explicitly rejected as a legal form of "declaration" on the grounds that such phrasing would allow Congress to initiate the spilling of blood and the spending of national treasure without facing their own full responsibility for that horror. Article I, Clause 8, requires Congress to declare war (not to specify conditions which if not met will carry the country into war "automatically" and "calendrically" and "by some hand other than Congress's own") precisely so that by facing their full responsibility for the horror, they will adequately test whether that horror is truly in the nation's interest.

27 Shortly before his 1992 election, Bill Clinton stated that as a youth he had declined to served in Vietnam because there had been no Congressional Declaration of War (Interview with David Frost, October 31, 1992). In that same interview, he promised that if elected, he would never take the country to war without a congressional declaration. As president, however, he invaded Haiti without a congressional declaration (stating in an August 3, 1994, news conference, "Like my predecessors of both parties, I have not agreed that I was constitutionally mandated to get [Congressional support])"; and later, he took the country into an undeclared war in former Yugoslavia.

28 *Washington Post*, June 21, 1992, p. A18.

29 Nixon's position during the impeachment proceeding was summarized by Sam Dash, Chief Counsel to the Senate Select Committee: "He was taking the position [that he was above the law] since he was commander-in-chief of the army, and had all the power, and the court has no army and the Congress has no army" (interview

in Foster Wiley, director, *Watergate Plus 30: Shadow of History*, PBS documentary, 2003).

30 Nixon's lawyer quoted by Sam Dash, Chief Counsel of Senate Select Committee (interview in Foster Wiley, *Watergate Plus 30*).

31 Paul Fussell, *Uniforms: Why We Are What We Wear* (Boston: Houghton Mifflin, 2002), p. 98.

32 "If I ask a man in America if he wants a king, he retorts, and asks me if I take him for an idiot" (Thomas Paine, *The Rights of Man*, Part I in *Political Writings*, p. 126).

33 Fussell surmises that they were donated to a high school marching band—a plausible destination since the spectacle of royal uniforms can be tolerated, even enjoyed, when wholly decoupled from any aspiration to physical force.

34 The term was invented by Walsh McDermott, a physician in the Department of Public Health at Cornell Medical Hospital. The problem of statistical compassion is looked at in detail in my essay "The Difficulty of Imagining Other People," which can be found in *Handbook of Interethnic Coexistence*, ed. Eugene Weiner (Abraham Foundation, 1998); and also in *Human Rights and Political Transition*, ed. Carla Hesse and Robert Post (Berkeley: University of California Press, 1999). A brief version occurs in *For Love of Country*, ed. Martha Nussbaum and Joshua Cohen (Boston: Beacon, 1996). The German version, "Das Schwierige Bild der Anderen," appears in *Schwierige Fremdheit: Über Integration und Ausgrenzung in Einwanderungsländern*, ed. R. Habermas, P. Nanz, and F. Balke (Frankfurt: Fischer Verlag, 1993), pp. 229–64.

35 This discrepancy also characterizes the difference between the president and the home population as centers of suffering, as is elaborated in the account of fallout shelters in Chapter 6, "Thinking in an Emergency."

36 Theodore C. Sorensen, *Decision-Making in the White House: The Olive Branch or the Arrows*, Foreword by John F. Kennedy (New York: Columbia University Press, 1963), pp. 11, 12; italics added.

37 Theodore C. Sorensen, appended note to the conclusion of Robert F. Kennedy, *Thirteen Days: A Memoir of the Cuban Missile Crisis*, introd. Robert S. McNamara and Harold Macmillan (New York: Norton, 1969).

38 "Sixth Debate: Lincoln's Rejoinder [to Judge Douglas]," October 13, 1858, in *Abraham Lincoln: Speeches and Writings 1832–1858*, ed. Don E. Fehrenbacher (New York: Library of America, 1989), vol. 1, p. 769. "Has [popular sovereignty] not got down as thin as the homoeopathic soup that was made by boiling the shadow of a pigeon that had starved to death?" Lincoln repeats the image four sentences later, receiving (according to the historical record) "Roars of laughter and cheering" after each iteration.

39 Constitution of Norway, Article 25. My thanks to Dagfinn Føllesdal for first directing my attention to the Norwegian Constitution (Conversation, Wissenschaftskolleg zu Berlin, 1990).

40 Constitution of Norway, Article 30, para. 3.

41 Declaration of Rights (1688), *Journals of the House of Commons*, 1688–89, p. 115, quoted in J. A. Downie, "Politics and the English Press," in *The Age of William III and Mary II: Power, Politics, and Patronage 1688–1702: A Reference Encyclopedia and Exhibition Catalogue*, ed. Robert P. Maccubbin and Martha Hamilton-Phillips (Williamsburg: College of William and Mary, 1989), p. 340. Justice Joseph Story also cites the 1688 Declaration of the Peers and Commons (quoting from Blackstone's *Commentaries*, ed. George Tucker [1803], pp. 211, 222, 232) in *Commentaries on the Constitution of the United States with a Preliminary Review of the Constitutional History of the Colonies and States Before the Adoption of the Constitution*, 2 vol. 4th ed. With notes and additions by Thomas M. Cooley (Boston: Little Brown, 1873), vol. 1, p. 238.

42 William A. Speck, "Religion, Politics, and Society in England," in Maccubbin and Hamilton-Phillips, eds., *Age of William III and Mary II*, pp. 49, 58. This paragraph also draws on essays in the Maccubbin volume by John W. Yolton ("John Locke," pp. 153–55) and by Frank H. Ellis ("The Glorious Revolution as Farce," p. 333).

43 Charles H. Taylor, "Assemblies of Towns and War Subsidy, 1318–1319," *Studies in Early French Taxation*, ed. Joseph R. Strayer and Charles H. Taylor (Cambridge, MA: Harvard University Press, 1939), pp. 109ff., esp. 143, 167–72; and Charles H. Taylor, "An Assembly of French Towns in March 1318," *Speculum* 13:3 (July 1938): 295ff., esp. 297, 298. For the connection between war making and the assembly during the reign of Philip the Fair in the 1301–03 period, see C. H. McIlwain, "Medieval Estates," in *The Cambridge Medieval History*, ed. J. R. Tanner, C. W. Previté-Orton, and Z. N. Brooke (Cambridge: Cambridge University Press, 1932), vol. 7, ch. 23, p. 644ff. esp. 682–85.

44 "Dissenting Opinion of Judge Weeramantry," International Court of Justice, July 8, 1996, p. 83. The International Court had specified many circumstances in which nuclear weapons are illegal, and designated both their use and threatened use contrary to international law; but—unlike Judge Weeramantry—it did not hold "directly and categorically that the use or threat of use of the weapon is unlawful *in all circumstances without exception*" (p. 4).

A PRELUDE AND SUMMARY FOR PART ONE

1 Kenneth A. Shepsle provides a digest: "Low in the public's esteem, the American legislature has suffered through aged and out-of-touch committee chairs, gridlock-inducing filibusters, financial corruption, lobbying and sexual scandals, partisan strife and an accompanying decline in comity and civility, incumbent protection, earmarking and pork barreling, continuing resolutions and omnibus appropriations reflecting an inability to finish tasks on time, and a general sense that the 'people's business' is not being done (well)" ("Dysfunctional Congress?" in *Symposium: The Most Disparaged Branch: The Role of Congress in the Twenty-First Century, Boston University Law Review* 89, no. 2 [April 2009]: 371). See this issue for many other essays criticizing or defending Congress: See also Lawrence

Lessig, *Republic, Lost: How Money Corrupts Congress—and a Plan to Stop It* (New York: Twelve, 2011).

2 Program on International Policy Attitudes, 2004 poll, cited by Lawrence S. Wittner, "Protest Against Reliable Replacement Warhead," *Bulletin of Atomic Scientists*, October 16, 2007. In the interest of increased transparency, the Obama administration in 2010 disclosed the size of the U. S. nuclear stockpile as 5113 warheads—a considerable reduction. The term "stockpile," however, is not the same as "overall inventory of assembled weapons." The Federation of American Scientists—which accurately calculates and publicizes the number of nuclear weapons during eras when the government withholds that information—puts the number in that latter category as 9600 (Hans M. Kristensen, "United States Discloses Size of Nuclear Weapons Stockpile," Federation of American Scientists Strategic Security Blog, May 3, 2010). Until a weapon is dismantled, it can be taken out of storage and redeployed. The number 10,000 (or 9600) must be used in describing U.S. weapons until the assembled weapons that are nominally scheduled for disassembly are actually disassembled.

3 A poll conducted by the Center for International and Security Studies at University of Maryland provides the 73 percent figure for Americans and a 63 percent figure for Russians (Lawrence Wittner, "Portents of an Anti-Nuclear Upsurge," *Bulletin of the Atomic Scientists* December 7, 2007). In Canada, 73 percent "strongly support" complete elimination of nuclear weapons and 15 percent moderately support complete elimination (Simons Foundation of Canada, "The Canada's World Poll," January 2008, p. 41).

4 United Press International, "Domestic News," October 14, 1989.

5 More hopeful is the British response to Tony Blair's 2006 announcement of a next-generation Trident submarine which led to a year-long protest at Faslane Naval Base and thousands of protestors in London (see, for example, Severin Carrell, "Renewing Trident: The Protestors: 'They Keep Arresting us for Breach of Peace. Trident Is the Breach of Peace,'" *Guardian*, December 5, 2006, p. 7; "16 Arrested as Greenpeace Tries to Blockade Trident Submarine Base," *The Times* [London], February 24, 2007, p. 33).

6 Originally designed to carry between one and three warheads, the ICBMs are each restricted to a single warhead by the New START Treaty. However, as Amy F. Woolf points out in her January 14, 2013, Congressional Research Service Report, unlike START I, New START does not require that the front end of the missile be redesigned to accommodate only a single missile: "As a result, the United States could restore warheads to its ICBM force if the international security environment changed." Woolf also puzzles over an October 2003 *Air Force Magazine* article quoting General Robert Smolen describing the missiles as collectively having "up to 800 warheads" (Amy F. Woolf, "U.S. Strategic Nuclear Forces," p. 11).

7 Gretchen Heefner, *The Missile Next Door: The Minuteman in the American Heartland* (Cambridge: Harvard University Press, 2012), ch. 3, p. 60. The doctrine of

"eminent domain" enabled the Air Force and the Army Corps of Engineers to bury the missiles wherever they wished deep in the fields of Wyoming, Colorado, Nebraska, and South Dakota, even moving farm houses if they were too close to the chosen field. According to Heefner, urban Bostonians—and specifically the antinuclear group SANE, which refused to respect the Air Force protocol of invisibility—may be responsible for the government's cancellation of the 150 ICBMs originally destined for the meadows of Massachusetts, New Hampshire, and Maine (pp. 71, 72).

8 Thomas Paine, *Rights of Man, Common Sense, and Other Writings*, ed. and introd. Mark Philp (Oxford: Oxford University Press, 1995), p. 147.

CHAPTER 1: THE CONSTITUTION REQUIRES A CONGRESSIONAL DECLARATION OF WAR

1 Andrei Sakharov, "Sakharov on Gorbachev and Bush," *Washington Post*, December 3, 1989; "Presidents' Answers Don't Always Answer," *International Herald Tribune*, December 4, 1989.

2 See, for example, Jeremy J. Stone, "Presidential First Use Is Unlawful," *Foreign Policy* 56 (1984): 94–112; Francis Wormuth, Edwin Brown Firmage, and F. Butler, *To Chain the Dog of War: The War Power of Congress in History and Law* (Champaign, IL: University of Illinois Press, 1986), pp. 267–77; H. Bartholomew Cox, "Raison d' Etat and World Survival: Who Constitutionally Makes Nuclear War?", *George Washington Law Review* 57 (1989): 1614; Ray Forrester, "Presidential Wars in the Nuclear Age: An Unresolved Problem," *George Washington Law Review* 57 (1989): 1636; Yonkel Goldstein, "The Failure of Constitutional Controls Over War Powers in the Nuclear Age: The Argument for a Constitutional Amendment," *Stanford Law Review* 40 (1988): 1543; Paul A. Hemesath, "Who's Got the Button? Nuclear War Powers Uncertainty in the Post-Cold War Era," *Georgetown Law Journal* 88, (2000): 2473.

3 Judge John P. Vukasin, Jr., "Transcript of Proceedings," Dellums v. Reagan, No. c-87-2587-JPV (N.D.Cal. Nov. 19, 1987), p. 8. The defendant in a legal case about nuclear weapons may be the president alone or may instead be the president and others in a first-use position, such as those in the line of presidential succession as specified in the 1976 congressional hearings on first use: *First Use of Nuclear Weapons: Preserving Responsible Control: Hearings before the Subcommittee on International Security and Scientific Affairs of the Committee on International Relations of the House of Representatives*, 94th Cong., 2d Sess. (1976) at 39, 79, 94, 128, 213, 215 (describing situations in which persons other than the president might be in first-use positions). Testimony during those hearings suggested that, during that era, the captains of the U.S. strategic submarines were also in first-use positions (Hearings: *First Use of Nuclear Weapons*, pp. 76, 77, 215). The gravity of this constitutional anomaly surrounding thirty-five unelected strategic submarine commanders was not attended to by the press and public in the decade following the 1976 hearings, but eventually

was addressed in the late 1980s and corrected in 1990s by the addition of "permissive action links" (or PALs) to submarines necessitating presidential authorization to unlock the missiles (Miller, "Who Needs PALs?", in *Proceedings: U.S. Naval Institute*, July 1988, pp. 50–56; Norman Moss, "Water Bombs," *The New Republic*, October 3, 1988, p. 20; Stuart Hampshire, "Engaged Philosopher," *New York Review of Books*, February 2, 1989, p. 7; Elaine Scarry, "A Nuclear Sub Accident Waiting to Happen," *Philadelphia Inquirer*, November 6, 1988, p. 9E, col. 1. Attention to the issue was in part prompted by a 1987 study by Peter Stein and Peter Feaver documenting the absence of locks on submarine-carried nuclear weapons in *Assuring Control of Nuclear Weapons: The Evolution of Permissive Action Links* [Lanham, MD: University Press of America, 1987], pp. 72–89, 99–103).

In addition to cases about presidential first use, Article I, Section 8, has been the constitutional basis of law cases about nuclear weapons unconnected to presidential action, such as the sequence of lawsuits about accidental computer launch brought by Clifford Johnson. See Johnson v. Weinberger, 851 F.2d 233 (9th Cir. 1988); Johnson v. Chain, No. 89-20265-sw (N.D.Cal. 1990); Johnson v. Weinberger, No. c-86-3334-sw (N.D.Cal. 1986). Also, either Article I, Section 8, or the 1974 War Powers Resolution (a weakened form of the constitutional requirement) has been at the center of congressional lawsuits against presidents acting with conventional troops, in Iraq, see Dellums v. Bush, No. 90-2866 (D.D.C. Dec. 13, 1990); in the Persian Gulf, see Lowry v. Reagan, 676 F.Supp. 333 (D.D.C. 1987); in Grenada, see Conyers v. Reagan, 578 F.Supp. 324 (D.D.C. 1984); in Nicaragua, see Sanchez-Espinoza v. Reagan, 568 F.Supp. 596 (D.D.C. 1983); and in El Salvador, see Crockett v. Reagan, 558 F.Supp. 893 (D.D.C. 1982).

4 U.S. Department of State, "Memorandum of Discussion at the 214th Meeting of the National Security Council, Denver, September 12, 1954," *Foreign Relations of the United States 1952–54*, vol.14, p. 618 hereinafter cited as *FRUS*). The participants at this meeting also discussed whether United Nations authorization would make it easier to obtain, or even bypass altogether, congressional authorization (pp. 620, 621). I am grateful to Marc Trachtenberg for his generous advice in locating and deciphering various materials in the declassified Eisenhower papers that are periodically referred to in this chapter.

In addition to repeated explicit mentions of atomic weapons in the September 1954 and January 1955 presidential meetings about Quemoy and Matsu, the participants sometimes refer to Document 291: "Memorandum by the Chairman of the Joint Chiefs of Staff (Radford) to Secretary of Defense (Wilson), September 11, 1954." Here Chairman of the Joint Chiefs Radford, Navy Chief Carney, Air Force Chief Twining, and Marine Commandant Shepherd (as well as Army Chief of Staff for the Far East Hull) provide assessments of what will be gained and lost by going to war. The document three times insists that if the United States embarks on military action in China, atomic weapons must be included from the outset as an option (See Enclosure A 3c; Enclosure B 6c, Appendix to Enclosure B, no. 9, in FRUS 1952–54, vol. 2, pp. 598, 604, 608, 610).

5 U.S. Department of State, "Memorandum of Discussion at the 233d Meeting of the National Security Council, Washington, January 21, 1955, 9 A.M.," *FRUS* 1955–57, vol. 2, p. 94. Similar language is used in the September 12 meeting, without any explicit reference to impeachment or the bypassing of congressional authorization: "The President suggested...that everyone could be sure of one thing, and that is that the vital interests of the U.S. in that area will be protected, and if we think that those interests are in danger we will take appropriate action to help our friends out there" (*FRUS* 1952–54, vol. 14, p. 623).

6 See *FRUS* 1955–57, vol. 2, pp. 92–93.

7 On the question of whether the country had a constitutional declaration against Iraq in the Gulf War, see Michael J. Glennon, "The Gulf War and the Constitution," *Foreign Affairs* 70 (Spring 1991): 84–101.

8 Although political obligation is traditionally understood as an "obligation" to one's own country, Joseph Nye extends the concept to include our "obligation to foreigners" in *Nuclear Ethics* (New York: Free Press-Macmillan, 1986), pp. 27–41.

9 "Deliberations for the Declaration of the War of 1812, *Annals of Congress*, 12th Cong., 1st sess. (1812), 298, 2322 (hereinafter "Deliberations for the 1812 Declaration").

10 Embedded in discussions of both linguistic and political representation is the issue of the safety of persons and populations; it is, therefore, not surprising that a nuclear arms policy that imperils achieves that imperilment by abridging constitutional as well as linguistic paths of representations.

11 J. L. Austin, *How to Do Things with Words*, 2d ed., ed. J. O. Urmson and Marina Sbisà (Cambridge, MA): Harvard University Press, 1962), p. 16.

12 Howard Warrender, *The Political Philosophy of Hobbes: His Theory of Obligation* (Oxford: Clarendon Press, 1957), pp. 14–17. Austin's conception of the speaker tends to be exclusive (no one can successfully utter the speech act except the designated speaker) while Warrender's conception tends to be inclusive (everyone can successfully utter the speech act except people explicitly disqualified by, for example, "immaturity" or by "insanity").

13 Austin says of the marriage, it "does not come off, is not achieved" (*How to Do Things with Words*, p. 16).

14 Austin, *How to Do Things with Words*, pp. 23, 59. 43.

15 Jürgen Habermas, *The Theory of Communicative Action, vol. 1, Reason and the Rationalization of Society*, trans. Thomas McCarthy (Boston: Beacon Press, 1984), p. 321. See also John Searle's analysis of the "differences between those acts that require extralinguistic institutions for their performance and those that do not" (*Expression and Meaning: Studies in the Theory of Speech Acts* [Cambridge: Cambridge University Press, 1979], p. 7). Searle observes that Austin "sometimes talks as if he thought all illocutionary acts" required extralinguistic institutions, but of course many of the acts Austin is talking about do have that requirement. This is the genre of speech acts that particularly interests Austin.

16 Tim Reiterman, *Raven: The Untold Story of the Rev. Jim Jones and His People* (New York: Penguin, 2008), pp. 173–74, 254, 332, 393, 586.

17 Hugo Grotius, *The Rights of War and Peace including the Law of Nature and of Nations*, trans. A. C. Campbell, introd. David Hill (Washington: Dunne, 1901), pp. 317, 321.

18 Austin explicitly uses the word *transmissible* in comparing the special way the phrases "I know" and "I promise" allow others to act and to rely on those spoken words (J. L. Austin, "Symposium: Other Minds II," in *Logic and Reality: The Symposia Read at the Joint Session of The Aristotelian Society and the Mind Association at Manchester*, July 5–7, 1946, supplementary vol. 20 [New York: Johnson, 1946], pp. 171, 172). But the analysis and taxonomy of speech acts can be understood as centrally addressing the issue of "transmissibility" even if the term is not explicitly used. It is present, for example, in John Searle's attention to "the way the speaker gets the job done" (*Speech Acts: An Essay in the Philosophy of Language* [Cambridge: Cambridge University Press, 1969], p. 61), to the level of "illocutionary force" that differentiates various sentences (Searle, *Expression and Meaning*, p. 2), and to the distinction between speech acts that "commit the speaker . . . to some future course of action" and those that enlist the hearer into a future action (Searle, *Expression and Meaning*, pp. 13, 14; also see Habermas, *Communicative Action*, pp. 319, 320).

19 While it is accurate and useful to think of all three forms of address taking place simultaneously, historical evidence suggests that the primary recipient of the declaration has varied from one period to another. In his 1848 treatise on the law of nations, Archer Polson identifies 1763 as a dividing line between second-person and first-person forms of address. "The custom," Polson writes, "of making a declaration of war to the enemy, previous to the commencement of hostilities, is of great antiquity, and was practiced even by the Romans. . . . [E]arlier jurists . . . generally consider a war, undertaken without this previous declaration, to be contrary to the law of nations. . . . Since, however, the peace of Versailles, in 1763, such declarations have been discontinued, and the present usage is for the State with whom the war commences to publish a manifesto within its own territories, communicating the existence of hostilities, and the reasons for their commencement. The publication of this manifesto was looked on as so essential, that nations have demanded a restitution of everything taken before such a publication" (*Principles of the Law of Nations, with Practical Notes and Supplementary Essays on the Law of Blockade and on Contraband of War* [London: Griffin and Co., 1848], §6, pt. 3, p. 38).

20 In *The Second Treatise of Government*, Locke insists on the nondelegability of legislative acts: "The *legislative cannot transfer the power of making laws* to any other hands; for it being but a delegated power from the people, they who have it cannot pass it over to others" (§141; see also §§212–19 on the dissolution of the government that occurs "when the legislative is altered" by either the appropriation or delegation of its legislative powers; *Second Treatise of Government*, ed. and introd. C. B. Macpherson [Indianapolis: Hackett, 1980], pp. 75, 107ff.).

The current congressional habit of delegation has been severely criticized by people on both the Left and the Right. Both John Ely and Justice Rehnquist, for example, have urged the revival of the nondelegation doctrine. Ely argues that it helps "ensure that decisions are being made democratically" and also "reduce[s] the likelihood that a different set of rules is effectively being applied to the comparatively powerless" (*Democracy and Distrust: A Theory of Judicial Review* [Cambridge, MA: Harvard University Press, 1980], pp. 131–34, 177). In the 1980 benzene case, Justice Rehnquist rejects "uncanalized delegations of legislative power," and with these words echoes Justice Cardozo's analysis of delegated powers "not canalized within banks" in the landmark 1935 *Schechter* case (Industrial Union Department, AFL-CIO v. American Petroleum Institute, 448 U.S. 607 [1980], reprinted in Stephen G. Breyer and Richard Stewart, *Administrative Law and Regulatory Policy: Problems, Texts, Cases*, 2d ed. [Boston: Little, Brown, 1985], p. 93). Rehnquist invokes a long tradition of arguments against delegation, citing John Locke as well as the 1892 case, *Field v. Clark*: "That Congress cannot delegate legislative power to the President is a principle universally recognized as vital to the integrity and maintenance of the system of government ordained by the Constitution" (Industrial Union in *Administrative Law*, p. 92). For a rigorous analysis of the arguments against congressional delegation to the executive, see Paul Gewirtz, "The Courts, Congress, and Executive Policy-Making," *Law and Contemporary Problems* 40 (1976): 46–85; as well as David Schoenbrod, "The Delegation Doctrine: Could the Court Give It Substance?" *Michigan Law Review* 83 (1985): 1224–90.

21 The gravity of the exact wording of a speech act is illustrated by President Barack Obama's thoughtful decision to retake his 2009 oath of office after the initial attempt misfired: Justice John Roberts, on the first attempt, accidentally recited the incorrect words of the oath, making Obama uncertain whether he would successfully carry out the speech act by now himself uttering the correct words of the oath, or instead by echoing the incorrect words Roberts had just offered him.

22 For accounts of the shooting, Haig's announcement, and the constitutional and "crisis management" lines of succession, see the *New York Times*, March 31, 1981, and April 1, 1981. For nonconstitutional lines of succession authorizing the firing of nuclear weapons, see House of Representatives, Subcommittee on International Security and Scientific Affairs of the Committee on International Relations, *Hearings: First Use of Nuclear Weapons*, pp. 39, 42, 76, 79, 128, 213, 215.

23 Vacancies in the House of Representatives remain empty until filled by election. Even in the Senate, where the number of members is comparatively small, the Seventeenth Amendment to the Constitution arranges for the election, rather than the predetermined succession, of a new senator: it stipulates that the governor (or other "executive authority") of the given state "shall issue writs of election to fill such vacancies." In some states (e.g., Kansas, Kentucky, Maine, Massachusetts, Minnesota, Nebraska), the governor arranges for the election to occur during the November period when general elections are normally held. In other states (e.g.,

Arkansas, Louisiana, Mississippi, Oklahoma), the governor arranges for elections in a month closer to the announcement of the vacancy: for example, South Dakota law requires that if the vacancy occurs more than six months before a regularly scheduled election, a special election shall occur between eighty and ninety days after the seat became vacant; and Vermont has a similar law.

The Constitution therefore anticipates that the House and Senate will continue to function during the interim period prior to the election while the seat remains vacant. In the case of the Senate, the Seventeenth Amendment permits, *but does not require*, the state legislature "to empower" the governor "to make temporary appointments" until the vacancy can be filled by election. While many states (e.g., North Carolina, Ohio) have laws stipulating that the governor "shall" make such a temporary appointment, other states (e.g., New Jersey, North Dakota, South Dakota, Virginia) merely provide that the governor "may" make such an appointment; and still others (e.g., Arizona, Oklahoma, Oregon) omit the possibility of temporary appointment altogether (Committee on Rules and Administration of U.S. Senate, *Senate Election Law Guidebook 1990: A Compilation, of Senate Campaign Information, Including Federal and State Laws Governing Election to the United States Senate* [Washington DC: GPO, 1990], pp. 174, 200, 202, 204, 210, 215, 227, 236, 238, 239, 240, 248, 257).

24 "Memorandum Prepared by the Secretary of State, Washington, September 12, 1954," *FRUS* 1952–54, vol. 14, p. 611. Here Dulles's notes on the need for congressional authorization are framed within explicit acknowledgments that "holding" or "defending" Quemoy would probably entail "general war with Red China" and "would probably lead to our initiating the use of atomic weapons." See also *FRUS* 1952–54, vol. 14, pp. 615, 620, 621. Dulles argues that the president needs either congressional authorization or a United Nations authorization. A U.N. authorization may eliminate the need for a congressional act or may instead make obtaining such an act easier. Another document records Dulles's complaint that "some of the Chiefs [Joint Chiefs of Staff] did not seem to be at all familiar with the constitutional requirements relating to the employment of U.S. Armed forces in hostilities." The document differentiates the military's ability (if empowered by a congressional authorization) to act on "the massive retaliation theory" from its ability (if waiting for congressional authorization) merely "to defend Formosa from invasion" (Douglas MacArthur II, "Memorandum of Conversation," October 30, 1954, John Foster Dulles Papers, White House Memoranda Series, Box I, File "Meetings with the President 1954" [1], 4).

25 *FRUS* 1955–57, vol. 2, pp. 92–93.

26 *FRUS* 1955–57, vol. 2, p. 92. "In some anxiety, the Attorney General inquired whether the President intended to change his plan to seek additional authority from the Congress. The Attorney General thought it still highly desirable to seek this authority. The President assured the Attorney General that he had not changed his ideas on this subject."

27 Dulles periodically summarizes the British reluctance: "The British fear atomic war and would not consider the reasons for our action to be justified" (*FRUS* 1952–54, vol. 14, p. 619). Again, in the January 21 meeting, Dulles attributes the British Cabinet's unease with U.S. action on the offshore islands to the "British feeling that in order to make this commitment stick, we might be obliged to use atomic weapons. … The British were always very sensitive about this subject" (*FRUS* 1955–57, vol. 2, p. 90). See also Eden to Dulles, April 28, 1954, John Foster Dulles Papers, Subject Series, Box 3, File "Atomic Weapons and Proposal 1953–54, 55" [2].

28 *FRUS* 1955–57, vol. 2, p. 91.

29 House Joint Resolution 159, 84th Cong., 1st sess.

30 "Deliberations on Formosa Resolution," *Congressional Record*, 84th Cong., 1st sess., January 28, 1959, p. 942.

31 "Deliberations on Formosa Resolution," pp. 841, 842.

32 "Deliberations on Formosa Resolution," p. 949; in the House, see Brooks at p. 664, Kilday at p. 672, Holifield at p. 674, and Rivers at p. 675.

33 S. Con. Res. 21, *Congressional Record*, 84th Cong., 1st sess., April 1, 1955, p. 4218.

34 "Deliberations for the Declaration: Spanish-American War," *Congressional Record*, 55th Cong., 2d sess. (1898) 3777 (hereinafter, "Deliberations for the Spanish-American Declaration"). The purpose of the conditional was to give President McKinley more time for negotiation; but this apparently pacific motive did not keep it from being, in its construction, slippery and dangerously open-ended.

35 "Deliberations for the Declaration of War for World War I," *Congressional Record*, 65th Cong., 1st sess. (1917), 210, 214, 256 (hereinafter, "Deliberations for the World War I Declaration"). The phrasing gave Germany notice that a "willful violation of the rights of American ships and American citizens…is an act of war…and thereupon, *without further declaration or notice*, the President be, and he is hereby, authorized and directed to employ the entire naval and military forces of the United States and the resources of the Government to carry on war against the offending country; and to bring the conflict to a successful termination all of the resources of the country are hereby pledged by the Congress of the United States" (italics added). Again, the motivation for the conditional was benign, giving Germany one more chance, but the outcome is no less dangerous.

36 The authorization of force was conditional on whether Iraq complied with U.N. resolutions by January 15, 1991 (for the full text of the resolution, see S. J. Res. 2, Authorization for Use of Military Force Against Iraq, *Congressional Record*, 102d Cong., 1st sess., Daily ed. 5403–4; also printed in the *New York Times*, January 14, 1991). According to Jonathan Winer, a legislative assistant for Senator Kerry, certain Democrats discussed in committee the plausibility of changing the wording from a "conditional" authorization to a straightforward declaration. However, the change was judged implausible because the Democrats would clearly be seeking to introduce a wording that they themselves would then vote against, and that was designed to increase the number of negative votes (telephone conversation with

Jonathan Winer, February 1991). The fact that the predictable outcome of such a shift of wording would be to increase the negative vote underscores the way an overt declaration inhibits a positive vote by requiring those voting for it to acknowledge responsibility. The final vote on the conditional declaration (42 percent "no" in the House, 47 percent "no" in the Senate) was already so negative that the resolution would almost certainly not have passed if that phrasing were eliminated.

37 Locke's prohibition of delegation turns on this distinction: "The power of the *legislative*, being derived from the people by a positive voluntary grant and institution, can be no other than what that positive grant conveyed, which being only to make *laws*, and not to make *legislators*" (*Second Treatise of Government*, p. 75).

38 There are, of course, many other subordinate linguistic features not attended to in this account. Though the major speech act is the declaration, the deliberations are studded with many assisting forms of speech act: the morning prayer, formal messages from the other house, roll call votes on subordinate issues, and so forth. So, too, there are informal linguistic features that vary from one congressional war deliberation to the next. For example, World War II has highly charged language, not found in the other deliberations, that was almost certainly prompted (not excused) by the fact that the country had just been attacked at Pearl Harbor. This charged language takes two forms. First, an astonishingly unrestrained racist idiom used for the Japanese; the European enemies, in contrast, are described in a language consonant with the idiom used in the four earlier declarations ("Deliberations for the Declaration of War for World War II," *Congressional Record*, 77th Cong., 1st sess. (1941), 9523, 9530, 9531, 9532; see page 9530 for an exceptional moment when the language describing Hitler approximates that used for the Japanese [hereinafter "Deliberations for World War II Declaration"]). Second, a falsely poetic, or mock poetic, form of speech: the day of the Pearl Harbor attack is repeatedly referred to as "yesterday morn" rather than "morning"; "yon" recurs rather than "yonder" or "that" or "over there"; and there is repeated talk of the fact that soldiers will have to "don" their uniforms (pp. 9521, 9528, 9530, 9535).

39 These three structural attributes will be contrasted with linguistic features of presidential deliberation. The population's legal power to stop presidential first use comes from the fact that it is constitutionally prohibited rather than from a reasoned argument about the unique deliberative powers of the congressional assembly. Whether a call in a game can be determined by the referee or by the spectator in the stand does not turn on the phenomenological attributes of the two calls: if one could show that the spectator's seat permitted a more reliable angle of vision, that would be an argument that the referee's seat should be changed, not an argument that the accidental occupant of the seat should be given the obligation. So, too, if a spectator has a particular optical genius, that is an argument for why he or she should seek to become a referee, not an argument for why the spectator should be permitted to make calls. Similarly, a president's great knowledge of foreign affairs or superb ability to assess material dangers is not an argument for why he should

be permitted to wage war single-handedly, but an argument for why he should address the Senate and House on the floor of Congress where he can openly make an argument to his congressional colleagues and persuade them to wage war.

40 As noted earlier, the wording for the 1812 Declaration ("Deliberations for the 1812 Declaration," p. 298, Appendix, p. 2322) has close equivalents in the other wars; the variations are described in "The False Form of Materiality" in this chapter.

41 Only with a majority assenting will it become a declaration. The vote for the War of 1812 was 79 to 49 in the House, 19 to 13 in the Senate; for the Mexican War, the vote was 174 to 14 in the House, 40 to 2 in the Senate; for the Spanish-American War, 310 to 6 in the House, 42 to 35 in the Senate; for World War I, 373 to 50 in the House, 82 to 6 in the Senate; for World War II against Japan, it was 388 to 1 in the House, 82 to 0 in the Senate; against Germany, 393 to 0 in the House, 88 to 0 in the Senate; against Italy, 399 to 0 in the House, 90 to 0 in the Senate. The 1991 conditional authorization of force in Iraq was 250 to 183 in the House (42 percent negative vote) and 52 to 47 in the Senate (47 percent negative vote; data from "The Vote to Authorize War with Iraq: Never Before Has Congress Been So Divided," Council for a Livable World, Washington, DC).

42 A senator watching the 1812 Declaration gradually gain credibility and the assent of more and more people said, "I understand that ever since the prospect of war began to thicken" ("Deliberations for the 1812 Declaration," p. 273). The sense that verbal acts performed in Congress have, or eventually acquire, a material form is openly registered in various ways. Sometimes the acts of the voice (speaking, listening, or reading) are referred to their material counterparts, as when one speaker on the eve of World War I says, "We have submitted to the dictates of every first-class power on earth during the past four years. Do some of you new Members of Congress realize that you or I could not ship this reading stand to Norway, a neutral country, until we had received a permit from the British Embassy in this city to do so? . . . Do you realize that you could not send a pen or pencil to Switzerland, another neutral country, without first getting the consent of Great Britain in London?" ("Deliberations for the World War I Declaration," p. 318). Speech takes place in, and is subject to the physical obstructions of, the material world; just as in turn those physical obstructions may themselves have been created by verbal acts of treaty making or legislation.

Similarly, the attributes of the physical world may be annexed to the verbal sentences describing and evaluating that physical world. During the deliberations for the Mexican War, for example, the question of Mexico's invasion of the United States became a key issue. The reality of that physical act became conflated with the verbal acts of assessing the invasion. The issue of invasion actually entailed two questions: (1) has "it" been invaded; and (2) if so, is the "it" that has been invaded "ours." These questions, in turn, led various senators to use the language of "debatable ground" and "undebatable ground," though at all times what was being talked about was the concrete earth: "I was under the impression that it was on the east side of the river, that it was to be limited to undebatable ground," said Senator Davis, and he continued, "But if it turns out that this territory is debatable ground, a serious responsibility rests somewhere, and presents the questions of war in a very different aspect from what it would have possessed had the invasion been made within the acknowledged limits of this country" ("Deliberations for the Declaration of War against Mexico," *Congressional Globe*, 29th Cong., 1st sess. [1846] 786 [hereinafter "Deliberations for the Mexican War Declaration"]). Representative Abraham Lincoln's "Spot Resolutions" questioned whether the ground on which blood had been spilled belonged to the United States (U. S. House of Representatives, RG 233, HR 30).

43 The Mexican War deliberations contain debates about the exact wording of the declaration that are commented upon even during the roll call vote; see footnote 67 below.

44 The term "exact repeatability" was invented by William Ivins, *Prints and Visual Communication* (Cambridge, MA: MIT Press), p. 162; and is cited and elaborated by Allen Grossman in his treatise on poetry, *Summa Lyrica*, in *Western Humanities Review* 44 (Spring 1990):15.

45 "Deliberations for World War II Declaration," p. 9537.

46 Douglas MacArthur II, Memorandum of Conversation, October 30, 1954, John Foster Dulles Papers, White House Memoranda Series, Box I, File "Meetings with the President 1954" (1), p. 4.

47 "Memorandum of Conference with the President, March 6, 1959, 10:30 A.M.," Declassified Documents Collection 1981/597B. *FRUS*, 1958–60, vol. 8, p. 434.

48 Bertrand Russell, *Unpopular Essays* (New York: Simon and Schuster, 1950), p. 31.

49 The conclusions that follow about presidential deliberation are based primarily on documents concerning the Taiwan Straits Crisis (1954) and the Berlin Crisis (1959), during both of which the Eisenhower administration contemplated the use of atomic weapons as well as the possibility of general war (with China and Russia in 1954, and with the German Democratic Republic and Russia in 1959). The repeated references to atomic weapons are unambiguous in the documents. Hence, the emerging scholarly literature is consistent on this point. The declassified papers about the Taiwan straits, for example, have also been analyzed in Gordon H. Chang, "To the Nuclear Brink: Eisenhower, Dulles, and the Quemoy-Matsu Crisis," *International Security* 12 (1988): 96–123; H. W. Brands, Jr., "Testing Massive Retaliation: Credibility and Crisis Management in the Taiwan Straits," *International Security* 12 (1988): 124–52. For an analysis of the Berlin Crisis that takes into account the available archives, see Marc Trachtenberg, *History and Strategy* (Princeton: Princeton University Press, 1991), esp. pp. 209–15; and *A Constructed Peace: The Making of the European Settlement 1945–1963* (Princeton: Princeton University Press, 1999), chapter 7.

It might be argued that the conclusions about presidential deliberation arrived at in the present study must be understood as tentative until a larger array of presidential administrations can be surveyed. Such a survey is, of course, seriously impeded by the unavailability of much of the evidence. The set of formerly classified presidential papers that have now been partly declassified only goes up to the early 1960s, except for patches such as the papers about Vietnam. While the conclusions reached here will be strengthened by subsequent studies of presidential deliberation, two factors strengthen the reliability of those conclusions in their present, incomplete form. First, the unavailability or (where papers exist only in a small number of libraries) the impeded availability of presidential papers itself confirms the portrait of deliberation reflected in those papers that are available.

Second, if study of further presidential papers should reveal occasional instances of the two linguistic features described here as missing, that would not change the overall argument. If, for example, Eisenhower or Kennedy or Reagan at a certain moment asked those around the table to vote yes or no on a certain question, that would certainly be an instance of designating a concrete set of sentences in which the counselors now inlaid their voices, thus constituting an explicit moment of consent and "exact repeatability." But such an instance would not then show that "exact repeatability" is a structural feature of presidential deliberation. The feature would instead be only discretionary, depending on the choice and disposition toward voting of a particular president. Hence, we merely return to the photograph in President Bush's pocket, and to national arrangements that depend on the psychological accident of presidential dispositions. We submit to "a rule of men" rather than to "the rule of law."

50 *FRUS* 1955–57, vol. 2, p. 94.

51 Robert Kennedy, *Thirteen Days: A Memoir of the Cuban Missile Crisis*, introd. Robert S. McNamara and Harold Macmillan (New York: Norton, 1969), p. 112.

52 Kennedy, *Thirteen Days*, p. 117.

53 Theodore Sorensen, *Decision-Making in the White House: The Olive Branch or the Arrows*, introd. John F. Kennedy (New York: Columbia University Press, 1963), p. 60. The transcripts of the Cuban Missile Crisis confirm the possibility of a counselor persuasively contradicting a president ("October 27, 1962: Transcripts of the Meetings of the ExComm," transcriber, McGeorge Bundy, ed. James G. Blight, *International Security* 12, no. 3 [1987–88]: 48, 57, 61). However, a president's toleration, or even welcoming, of disagreement does not permit us to conclude that "disagreement" is a structural feature of presidential deliberation: these instances, like those described in note 49 must be understood as discretionary and individually laudable rather than as (as in Congress) structurally necessary.

It might well be that individuals with objections make arrangements to speak with the president privately, because it is "unseemly" to challenge the president openly in the meeting. But this confirms the crucial role of congressional deliberation, where the nonhierarchical nature of the participants ensures the possibility of an attack by one speaker against any other speaker. Objections are not silenced by unseemliness. This means, crucially, that both the arguments on behalf of the recommended action and the opposition arguments are not merely voiced but heard and scrutinized by a large number of people listening.

Finally, the counselors are, with the exception of the vice president, themselves unelected officials, as Paul Gewirtz reminds us ("The Courts, Congress, and Executive Policy-Making," p. 47, n. 2).

54 *FRUS* 1952–54, vol. 14, p. 616.

55 *FRUS* 1952–54, vol. 14, p. 621.

56 *FRUS* 1952–54, vol. 14, p. 622.

57 "Memorandum of Conference with the President, March 6, 1959, 5:00," Declassified Documents Collection 1981/597B. Perhaps because of the volatile and explicit nature of Senator Fulbright's question, the formerly "Top Secret" Memorandum for this 5 p.m. meeting is not reprinted in *FRUS*. Instead, the meeting and the list of its participants are briefly mentioned in a *FRUS* footnote to a meeting between the President and several members of Congress that had taken place at 10:30 a.m. on the same day, a calm meeting that Vice President Nixon designated of "great significance" and that President Eisenhower, agreeing, then had photographed, as though to provide a record of the participation of this four-person miniature Congress (see *FRUS*, 1958–60, vol. 8, pp. 428, 435). Senator Fulbright appears to have been a thorn in the side of executive war plans. In a telephone conversation that took place shortly after the 10:30 a.m. meeting, Acting Secretary of State Herter reports to absent Secretary of State Dulles about what has just transpired ("we've convince them we can't do it by ground"), and also mentions the upcoming 5 p.m. meeting with Senator Fulbright. Dulles is surprised that Fulbright has been invited to the White House. Herter explains the invitation has been necessitated by Fulbright's announcement in the morning newspapers that he plans to call Acting Secretary Herter in to testify before the Senate Foreign Relations Committee ("[Herter] thought this was extremely bad") (*FRUS*, 1958–60, vol. 8, p. 438).

58 As observed in notes 49 and 53, even if a thorough examination of the historical record were to show that presidents do sometimes overtly poll their counselors, this act is still contingent on the individual's discretion and cannot be understood as a structurally necessary part of presidential deliberations.

59 "Letter from the President to the Supreme Allied Commander, Europe (Gruenther), [Washington] February 1, 1955," *FRUS* 1955–57, vol. 2, p. 192.

60 Sorensen, *Decision-Making in the White House*, pp. 9, 10.

61 Bob Woodward, *Bush at War* (New York: Simon & Schuster, 2002), pp. 145–46.

62 "Deliberations for the 1812 Declaration," pp. 266, 298, and Appendix, p. 2322.

63 S. J. Res. 1, "Deliberations for the World War I Declaration," p. 305; second italics added.

64 S. J. Res. 116, "Deliberations for World War II Declaration," pp. 9505, 9537 (Declaration against Japan); second italics added.

65 In the debates on the declarations, a perceptual rather than a verbal idiom is sometimes used: Roosevelt requests from Congress its declaration against Germany and
Italy by asking Congress "to recognize" a state of war between the United States
and those countries ("Deliberations for World War II Declaration," p. 9652; see
also "Deliberations for the Mexican War Declaration," pp. 793, 796). Precisely the
same ambiguity is involved as in the verbal idiom. Ultimately, the "recognition" is
a formal performative act: the recognition of another country or of the existence
of war helps bring it into being while seeming to be an act made possible by a pre-
existing fact. For a philosophic study of recognition, see Axel Honneth, *Kampf
um Anerkennung* (Frankfort am Main: Suhrkamp, 1992).

66 "Deliberations for the Mexican War Declarations," pp. 795, 804. The declarations
for both World War I and World War II had preambles asserting that the other
country had committed repeated "acts of war" or "unprovoked acts of war," but
not asserting the war to be already in existence (S. J. Res. 1, "Deliberations for the
World War I Declaration," p. 305; S. J. Res. 116, "Deliberations for World War II
Declaration," p. 9505).

67 The title of the bill reflects the same division: "An act providing for the prosecution
of the existing war between the United States and the Republic of Mexico," where
the gerund makes the war's existence prior to its prosecution. The entire debate
during the deliberations for the Mexican War (far more than for the other four
wars) became a sustained analysis of whether a declaration of war is a descriptive
sentence or a performative sentence. The debate was necessitated by the preamble
and gerund forms.

The final vote in the Senate was preceded by a vote on whether to eliminate
the preamble: eighteen voted yes; twenty-eight, no. The final vote had forty yes
votes and seven votes expressing various forms of resistance to the preamble,
two persons saying "aye except preamble," two voting no, and three remaining
silent at roll call on the express ground that the preamble made the act of voting
impossible ("Deliberations for the Mexican War Declaration," p. 804). The preamble, therefore, determined the shape of the vote. It also shaped the discussion
by causing extensive debate about which of two committees would consider it,
Military Affairs (if the declaration merely says the United States will repel invasion and prosecute hostilities) or instead the Committee on Foreign Relations (if
it is a declaration of war; p. 784).

68 A small number of other performative speech acts also appear to introduce the possibility of backdating. For example, should marriage vows that confer legitimacy
on an already conceived baby be understood as an act of backdating the marriage?
Legally, at least in the United States, no backdating has occurred because the term
legitimate refers to the marital status of the parents at the moment of birth rather
than at conception. So, too, in states where it is possible through marriage to legitimate a child after birth, the child is a "nonmarital legitimate" offspring; hence,
again, there is no backdating (see Harry D. Krause, *Child Support in America:*

The Legal Perspective [Charlottesville: Michie Law Publishers, 1981], pp. 105, 112). Annulment would appear to be a stark performative act of backdating, but there are some signs that the annulment cannot be understood as retroactively happening in the same temporal space as the enunciation of the marriage vows, such as the fact that, in many states, a child conceived between the marriage and the annulment is legitimate (Krause, *Child Support*, p. 111). A judge's or jury's verdict is another area where a question about backdating can be raised: does a guilty verdict mean "guilty starting at the moment the word is formally pronounced in court" or instead "guilty starting at the moment of performing the action for which the person is being tried"?

69 H. Res. 10086, "Deliberations for the Spanish-American Declaration," pp. 4244, 4254.

70 H. Res. 246 and S. Res. 158, April 25, 1898, "Deliberations for the Spanish-American Declaration," p. 4231.

71 "Deliberations for World War II Declaration," p. 9505.

72 It may be that the action of *postdating* is the structural counterpart of delegation, since delegation can be understood as an act of *predating*. During the passage of the Formosa Resolution, for example, Senator Morse repeatedly referred to the bill as an act of predating, since it gave the president authority to use the military in advance of any facts that warrant that use ("Deliberations on Formosa," pp. 841, 955). Delegation can, in general, be understood as authorizing outcomes prior to the existence of the very facts required to motivate those outcomes. This emphasis on the temporal complication of delegation makes its kinship to "conditional declaration" clearer (see "Authority in a Declaration of War ..." in this chapter).

73 "Deliberations for the World War I Declaration," p. 249.

74 "Deliberations for the Spanish-American Declaration," p. 3783.

75 "Deliberations for the Mexican War Declaration," p. 800.

76 "Deliberations for the 1812 Declaration," p. 1630.

77 "Deliberations for World War II Declaration," p. 9505 (against Japan).

78 "Deliberations for World War II Declaration," pp. 9523, 9525, 9526, 9532, 9524.

79 "Deliberations for World War II Declaration," pp. 9532, 9528.

80 "Deliberations for World War II Declaration," Representative Scott on p. 9529; and Representative Angel on p. 9525.

81 For the most eloquent articulations of this point, see Calhoun's speeches in "Deliberations for the Mexican War Declaration," pp. 784, 785, 796, 798; also see Moorhead and Archer, p. 784; Allen, p. 785; Lucid, p. 793.

82 "Deliberations for the World War I Declaration," p. 121; see similar appropriations, p. 131.

83 "Deliberations for the World War I Declaration," pp. 159, 161, 165; of the $62 million budget, $38 million is in war debt.

84 "Deliberations for the World War I Declaration," pp. 138, 209, 223, 357, 402.

85 "Deliberations for the World War I Declaration," p. 272.

86 "Deliberations for the World War I Declaration," p. 278.

87 "Deliberations for the World War I Declaration," p. 284.

88 "Deliberations for the World War I Declaration," pp. 285–92.

89 "Deliberations for the World War I Declaration," p. 158.

90 The coupling of "persons and things" implies that things are extensions of persons (as is perhaps most straightforwardly the case in the detail of the artificial limbs). On this continuity, in both war and peace, see Elaine Scarry, *The Body in Pain* (New York: Oxford, 1985), pp. 108–13, 117–23, 281–307.

91 "Deliberations for the Spanish-American Declaration," pp. 3792, 3341, 4229. (The declaration of war is both introduced and passed on April 25, but earlier weeks have a series of interventions declared and it is here, starting on April 13, that the House passes these bills.)

92 "Deliberations for the 1812 Declaration," p. 321.

93 "Deliberations for the 1812 Declaration," p. 1490.

94 "Deliberations for the 1812 Declaration," p. 1577.

95 Because any performative sentence introduces a new set of circumstances into the world, it has what Hegel and others observed as the annihilative power of a creative act, its inevitable destruction or disturbance of what is already given. In the performative of war, of course, this annihilation becomes not just a secondary or tertiary attribute of the act but its central content and direction. The congressional deliberations habitually entail a verbal recognition of what stands to be annihilated, in contrast to the arrangements for nuclear first use, which permit enactment with no sustained registration of the people and worlds to be destroyed.

96 "Deliberations for the Mexican War Declaration," p. 783; Deliberations for the World War I Declaration," p. 158. Curiously, the 20,000 figure occurs in both Congresses.

97 "Deliberations for the 1812 Declaration," p. 291; see also Senator German, p. 277: the different geographies, climates, and customs of the civilians will slow down the transformation into a soldiery.

98 "Deliberations for the 1812 Declaration," p. 291; see Senator German, pp. 272–74, who slowly rotates his attention across the geography of New Orleans, New York (Bedlows and Ellis Island), Rhode Island (from "three to five thousand men can defend that island"), Boston ("perhaps, the only secure place of considerable consequence on the seaboard"), and so on to Maine, Detroit, and Albany, imagining the aggregate required for defense.

99 "Deliberations for the World War I Declaration," p. 284.

100 "Deliberations for the World War I Declaration," p. 207.

101 "Deliberations for the 1812 Declaration," p. 1490.

102 "Deliberations for the 1812 Declaration," pp. 1515, 1570.

103 "Deliberations for the Spanish-American Declaration," p. 3451.

104 The phrase "blood and oil" used by American protestors during both the 1991 and 2003 wars against Iraq is a transformation of "blood and treasure," or a

deformation since it expresses the idea of exchanging blood for unneeded treasure, rather than a population giving both blood and treasure in exchange for some third thing warranting so profound a commitment. The phrase is often, of course, invoked in these earlier contexts precisely to question whether that third thing does warrant the spending of the people's blood and treasure.

105 For example, the phrase occurs in *The Danger of the Protestant Religion*, *The Two Great Questions Consider'd*, *Reasons Against a War with France*, *The Succession of Spain Consider'd*, *The Felonious Treaty*, and *Imperial Gratitude*, in *The Political and Economic Writings of Daniel Defoe*, ed. P. N. Furbank (London: Pickering and Chatto, 2000), vol. 5, pp. 35, 62, 88, 110, 115, 123, 159, 162, 181.

106 Bernadette A. Meyler, "Daniel Defoe and the Written Constitution," *Cornell Law Review* 94, no. 73 (November 2008).

107 For the association in Europe between a new interest in counting signatures and an emerging idea of democracy, I am grateful to Peter Burke, Institute for Advanced Study, Berlin, March 1990.

108 *The Federalist No. 6*, in *The Federalist Papers*, ed. Clinton Rossiter (New York: Mentor, 1961), p. 55.

109 "Deliberations for the 1812 Declaration," pp. 1554, 279, 281, 283, 292, 1638, 1655. For a sustained use of the term, see Mr. Taggart's speech in the House reprinted in the *Virginia Gazette*; while the phrase seems casually introduced, it provides the underlying structure of the long speech, three pages of which are about blood and three about treasure (pp. 1657–63).

110 "Deliberations for the World War I Declaration," p. 209, italics added (quoting Senator Vardamen); see also p. 212. For its occurrence in a later war, see for example, "Deliberations for World War II Declaration," p. 9668. During the Civil War, Jefferson Davis used the phrase in his November 1864 address to the Confederate Congress at Richmond (cited in *The Civil War: An Illustrated History*, narrative by Geoffrey C. Ward, based on documentary filmscript by Geoffrey C. Ward, Ric Burns, and Ken Burns [New York: Knopf, 1990], p. 334).

111 The others took place behind closed doors.

112 "Deliberations for the World War I Declaration," pp. 156, 208, 216, 262–63, 265, 283. The galleries had been full since the opening of the deliberations; their applause, according to the House record, occurs even during President Wilson's speech.

113 For example, "Deliberations for the World War I Declaration," pp. 307, 317, 349.

114 In the deliberations for both the Spanish-American War and World War I, the applause occurs at moments when speakers have urged a declaration of war ("Deliberations for the Spanish-American Declaration," pp. 3780, 3781, 3784; "Deliberations for the World War I Declaration," pp. 119), even though petitions and polls in various regions suggested the population opposed the war by 10 to 1. An exchange between Mr. Britten and Mr. Glass provides one emphatic instance (House, April 5, 1917):

MR. BRITTEN: The truth of the matter is that 90 per cent of your people and mine do not want this declaration of war, and are distinctly opposed to our going into that bloody mire on the other side. There is something in the air, gentlemen, and I do not know what it is, whether it be the hand of destiny, or some superhuman movement, something stronger than you and I can realize or resist, that seems to be picking us up bodily and literally forcing us to vote for this declaration of war when away down deep in our hearts we are just as opposed to it as are our people back home.

MR. GLASS: How do you know our people do not want it? [Applause on the floor and in the galleries.] (p. 317)

Two explanations seem plausible. It may be that the deliberations on the declaration would attract prowar people, or that the deliberations create their own urgent momentum toward that declaration. A declaration of war is what they have come to see; a nondeclaration is a nonevent.

A second explanation is that the pressure to express consent comes precisely at those moments when the thing described is so costly that it requires consent, that it provides every reason for presuming hesitation, and that, therefore, nonhesitation (if it exists) must be overtly and vigorously expressed. So during Wilson's address to the Congress on the eve of World War I, "It will involve... It will involve... It will involve the immediate full equipment of the navy... It will involve the immediate addition to the armed forces... It will involve... taxation" (p. 119). Each time Wilson recites an entailment, applause follows. This is crucial because it is of course here that consent is required. Precisely where the government cannot go on without the population, the population expresses its willingness to come along.

115 "Deliberations for the World War I Declaration," pp. 132, 133, 261.

116 "Deliberations for the World War I Declaration," p. 136.

117 "Deliberations for the World War I Declaration," p. 258.

118 "Deliberations for the World War I Declaration," p. 256.

119 "Deliberations for the World War I Declaration," p. 141.

120 "Deliberations for the World War I Declaration," p. 259. The second and third genres of representational slippage bear a resemblance to what are normally considered legitimate forms of representational magnification, as when a member of Congress claims to speak for a district of 7 million, only 3 million of whom voted and 1.8 million voted for him.

121 Two congressmen even formally poll their constituencies and report the vote ("Deliberations for the World War I Declaration," pp. 362, 366). The many other acts of voting—in churches, clubs, and town halls—are, as noted earlier, initiated by the citizens themselves (see, for example, pp. 129, 130–36, 140–55, 186–88, 225, 242, 254–61, 305, 365).

122 "Deliberations for World War II Declaration," p. 9505 (Vandenberg).

123 "Deliberations for World War II Declaration," p. 9523.

124 "Deliberations for World War II Declaration," p. 9525. This shift may be completely fair: it is in part why the Constitution has different procedures in the case of attack. Prescience, guessing the will of the people, is permissible in the extraordinary circumstance of direct attack. The very permission in the Constitution for the president to act without Congress when the country is invaded is precisely that kind of presumption of knowledge about the population's will.

125 "Deliberations for World War II Declaration," p. 9534 (Jennings).

126 "Deliberations for World War II Declaration," p. 9521 (House, Mrs. Byron); see also p. 9531.

127 "Deliberations for World War II Declaration," p. 9532. Representative Scanlon, who himself served in World War I, describes his "only son" as "ready to serve his country in whatever military or naval capacity he is needed" and then attributes this same readiness to the larger population: friends and constituents "have called me seeking advice whether to enlist or await the call under the draft machinery ...set up by Congress. These people are typical of every citizen in the Thirtieth Congressional District of Pennsylvania. I know that *every person in that district*, I might even say that *everyone in the great Commonwealth of Pennsylvania*, will back up the votes that my colleagues and I make" (italics added).

128 "Deliberations for World War II Declaration," p. 9528.

129 "Deliberations for World War II Declaration," p. 9525.

130 "Deliberations for World War II Declaration," p. 9525.

131 "Deliberations for the World War I Declaration," p. 219. Deliberations for the other declarations also include expressions of the weight of both the individual's and the assembly's vote (see, for example, "Deliberations for the 1812 Declaration," pp. 287, 291, 1638, 1678).

132 "Deliberations for the World War I Declaration," p. 208.

133 "Deliberations for World War II Declaration," p. 9531.

134 "Deliberations for World War II Declaration," p. 9537.

135 "Deliberations for the World War I Declaration," p. 322.

136 The World War II deliberations have two genres of exclusion—hence two lapses from the inclusive and impersonal—not characteristic of the other deliberations. The first is the extreme racist idiom noted earlier. The second is a self-interested iteration of obvious arguments: because the assembly is close to unanimous, the speeches seem (unlike those in the other deliberations) less arguments intended to enlighten or persuade than recitations of the self-evident intended to put the speaker on record as having correct sentiments. Such passages have the tone of personal anecdotal narratives, though they are very different in content. The recitation of the obvious, however, while not admirable, is not wholly without merit, since it ensures that the common understanding is, indeed, the common understanding. Certainly, the assembly's overall act of putting itself on record is crucial, even if the individual ambition to "be on record" is personally driven.

137 "Memorandum: Secretary of Defense Laird to NSA Kissinger, June 25, 1969. Subject: Review of US Contingency Plans for Washington Special Action Group," Tab L, declassified October 2006 (Document 12, "How Do You Solve a Problem Like Korea," Electronic Briefing Book 322, National Security Archive, George Washington University). See also Chris McGreal, "Papers Reveal Nixon Plan for North Korea Nuclear Strike," *Guardian*, July 7, 2010.

138 It may at first seem that conversely, a performative sentence tolerates, even requires, substitutable content while a descriptive sentence insists on (or aspires to) the nonsubstitutability of its content; but, as the foregoing argument has shown, the performative sentence achieves high constraints on its content through the constraints on the speaker and the testing of all his or her descriptive statements leading up to the final speech act.

CHAPTER 2: NUCLEAR WEAPONS VIOLATE THE SECOND AMENDMENT REQUIREMENT FOR AUTHORIZATION BY THE CITIZENRY

1 I. Kant, "On the Proverb: That May Be True in Theory, But Is of No Practical Use," in *Perpetual Peace and Other Essays on Politics, History, and Morals*, trans. Ted Humphrey (Indianapolis: Hackett, 1983), p. 88.

2 Kant, "On the Proverb: That May Be True in Theory," p. 88.

3 Thomas Hobbes, *Behemoth: Or, the Long Parliament*, ed. Ferdinand Tönnies (London: Simpkin, Marshall, and Co., 1889), p. 59.

4 The most comprehensive attempt to track the paper record through which U.S. presidents have assumed control over nuclear weapons is Frank Graham Klotz's unpublished Oxford University PhD dissertation: "The U.S. President and the Control of Strategic Nuclear Weapons" (1980). In the thirty years following his dissertation research, Lt. General Klotz went on to become the commander of Air Force Global Strike Command (in charge of all Air Force nuclear weapons) at Barksdale, Louisiana; he retired in March 2011.

No published account of the sequence of presidential directives formalizing this strategic policy is available to the population. No president has addressed the population (in his State of the Union speech or on any other occasion) about this national policy. The silence on this subject means that most Americans are not aware of the first-use policy which continues under President Barack Obama today.

Even in decades when the nation's first-use policy was more publicly discussed than is true today, the U.S. population remained largely unaware of it. A 1984 Public Agenda Foundation poll found that 81 percent of the U.S. population believed that the country had nuclear weapons for defensive purposes only (see Daniel Yankelovich and John Doble, "The Public Mood: Nuclear Weapons and the U.S.S.R.," *Foreign Affairs* 63 [1984]: 45, citing study by Public Agenda Foundation & Center for Foreign Policy Development, "Voter Options on Nuclear Arms Policy: Briefing Book for the 1984 Elections"). The poll followed an eight-year period during which the issue had been openly, but only occasionally, addressed by political and religious leaders. See, for example, *First Use of Nuclear Weapons: Preserving Responsible Control: Hearings before the Subcommittee on International Security and Scientific Affairs of the Committee on International Relations of the House of Representatives*, 94th Cong., 2d Sess. (1976) [hereinafter *Hearings: First Use of Nuclear Weapons*]; McGeorge Bundy, George Kennan, Robert McNamara and Gerard Smith, "Nuclear Weapons and the Atlantic Alliance" (originally an influential 1982 *Foreign Affairs* article) reprinted in *No-First-Use*, eds. Frank Blackaby, Jozef Goldblat, and Sverre Lodgaard (New York: Taylor and Francis, 1984); National Conference of Catholic Bishops, *The Challenge of Peace, God's Promise and Our Response* (Washington, DC: United States Catholic Conference, 1983), p. vii (urging NATO to adopt a no first-use policy).

Political, legal, and religious concern tends not to be widely reported in the press: when 1988 presidential candidate Jesse Jackson pledged no first use, the *L.A. Times* devoted its headline to the announcement. See "Jackson Sees First Use as Irrational," *L.A. Times*, May 27, 1988, pt. I, at p. 1, col. 1. Their act was unusual, though, and the issue did not become part of the election contest. On January 3, 1989, Representative Weiss of New York introduced a joint resolution on first use, which was referred to the Committee on Foreign Affairs and the Committee on Armed Services (March 1, 1989), but did not receive public attention. See House of Representatives Joint Resolution 46, 101st Cong., 1st Sess. (1989). Nor was press attention given to the 1987 lawsuit against presidential first use brought by California Representatives Ron Dellums and Don Edwards (see Chapter 1).

The American public's attention to the subject is often prompted by international, rather than national, sources, such as China's April 2012 urging that the United States and other first-use states renounce the policy (Fredrik Dahl, "China Wants 'Drastic' U.S., Russia Nuclear Arms Cuts," Reuters, April 30, 2012) or the Soviet Union's 1990 reiteration in Vienna of its own 1982 pledge against first use; or Andrei Sakharov's editorial shortly before his death urging the United States to abdicate first use (described in Chapter 1); and the November 1990 Stockholm Declaration made by the Swedish Initiative for the Prevention of Accidental Nuclear War (a coalition of all six political parties of the Swedish Parliament and nine professional organizations against nuclear arms) which called for the nonproliferation of nuclear weapons to countries where they do not yet exist and the international delegitimization of nuclear weapons in countries where they already exist. The Swedish Initiative stipulated that first use should be eliminated, even before international delegitimization of all nuclear weapons can be fully achieved:

> Delegitimize the use of nuclear weapons. . . . [O]ne realistic step towards the complete elimination of all nuclear weapons, should be to negotiate an international convention banning the use, of threat of use, of nuclear weapons. Consequently, all nuclear weapons countries should declare a policy of no-first-use and adapt their military structures to this policy.

(*Action Program for the Prevention of Accidental Nuclear War*, ed. Sven Hellman

[Stockholm: Swedish Initiative for the Prevention of Accidental Nuclear War, 1990]; see pp. 9, 14, 19.)

5 Alexander Bickel, *The Morality of Consent* (New Haven: Yale University Press, 1975), pp. 102–3.

6 Bickel, *The Morality of Consent*, p. 102.

7 Bickel, *The Morality of Consent*, p. 102.

8 See James McCague, *The Second Rebellion: The Story of the New York City Draft Riots of 1863* (New York: Dial Press, 1968), p. 143. Many of the incidents, as well as the names of participants and those killed are reconstructed in Adrian Cook, *The Armies of the Streets: The New York City Draft Riots of 1863* (Lexington: University of Kentucky Press, 1974). Resistance may also, as Joseph Story's editor observed, be initiated by national or state authorities: "When the late civil war broke out, and the President issued his call for 75,000 militia, apportioned among the several States which had not declared their secession, the governors of several of the border States responded with either a peremptory or a qualified refusal. The governors of Virginia, North Carolina, Kentucky, Tennessee, Missouri, and Arkansas refused in the most positive, and some of them in insulting terms . . . [and they contested its constitutionality]" (Joseph Story, *Commentaries on the Constitution of the United States: With A Preliminary Review of the Constitutional History of the Colonies and States Before the Adoption of the Constitution*, 4th ed., Notes and additions by T. Cooley [Boston: Little, Brown, and Co. 1873], vol. 2, p. 117, n. 5).

9 See Theodore Dwight, "History of the Hartford Convention (1833)," pp. 358–62, cited in Story, *Commentaries on the Constitution*, p. 99, n. 1.

10 Vietnam desertion rate given by Paul von Zielbauer, "U.S. Army Revises Upward the Number of [Iraq War] Desertions," *New York Times*, March 23, 2007.

11 Neil Sheehan, *A Bright Shining Lie: John Paul Vann and America in Vietnam* (New York: Random House, 1988), p. 364.

12 Sheehan, *A Bright Shining Lie*, pp. 316, 342.

13 Sheehan, *A Bright Shining Lie*, pp. 351, 355, 357, 371.

14 Sheehan, *A Bright Shining Lie*, p. 374; see also 3, 13–14, 503–8.

15 James C. Scott, *Weapons of the Weak: Everyday Forms of Peasant Resistance* (New Haven: Yale University Press, 1985), p. 30.

16 Ella Lonn, *Desertion During the Civil War* (1929), introd. William Blair (Lincoln: University of Nebraska Press, 1998), p. 23.

17 Lonn, *Desertion During the Civil War*, p. 28. During four months from October through February, a report lists the desertions of 72,000 Confederate soldiers east of the Mississippi (p. 27).

18 Lonn, *Desertion During the Civil War*, pp. 8, 15, 32.

19 Lonn, *Desertion During the Civil War*, pp. 46, 59–60.

20 James M. McPherson, *For Cause and Comrades: Why Men Fought in the Civil War* (New York: Oxford University Press, 1997), pp. 93–94. Here are descriptions

given by one soldier: "November 30. Took part on the affirmative of Resolved that the Constitutional relations of the rebel states should be fixed by Congress only. ... Witnessed some rare outburst of untutored eloquence. December 14. Had an interesting debate at the Lyceum on the subject of executing the leaders of the rebellion. Made my speech on the negative. The affirmative carried by just one vote in a full house.... December 31. Sergeants Rollins & Need discussed ably the rights of the South. Sergt. Miller expanded on the revolution of ideas."

21 Joseph Allan Frank (with Barbara Duteau), "Measuring the Political Articulateness of United States Civil War Soldiers: The Wisconsin Militia," *Journal of Military History* 64 (January 2000): 73–74.

22 Richard M. Watt, *Dare Call It Treason*, introd. Colonel John Elting (New York: Simon and Schuster, 1963), p. 275. The French source on which Watt bases his narration of the mutiny—P. Poitevin, *La Mutinerie de la Courtine: Les Régiments Russes Révoltés en 1917 au Centre de la France* (1938), p. 149—goes on to describe the events of September 17–19, 1917, in the same images of road clogging, though soon it is between 6000 and 7500 men rather than horses:

> This release of horses was only the beginning and at two o'clock the rebels having gathered in the barracks of Laval emerged with their belongings, without arms, and formed groups of four waving little white flags. The movement of surrender had begun. The vast majority of the troupe, despite the dictates of the ultimatum, headed for La Courtine, by a small road that led to the church, next to which was the command post of the French general staff.... The total number of submissions reached almost 7500 men. Some came on foot, others in vans, in wagons, carts, on horseback, etc., all without arms.... Despite the congestion produced at the same place by the traffic of thousands of soldiers.

(Id. at 149–51 [translated from the French]). My thanks to D. A. Miller for providing an English translation of this passage, as well as those cited in the notes below.

23 Watt, *Dare Call It Treason*, p. 275.

24 Raymond Poincaré, *Au Service De La France: Neuf Années De Souvenirs* (Paris: Plon, 1932), vol. 9, p. 153. The original French reads: "Des hommes ont refusé d'aller aux tranchées. L'ordre est menacé partout. La fièvre s'étend." Continuing the metaphor of bodily disablement, Poincaré asks, "Will we need to wait for a new Marne victory to be cured?" (cited by Watt, *Dare Call It Treason*, p. 275 [translated from the French by D. A. Miller]).

25 B. H. Liddell Hart, *History of the First World War* (London: Pan Books, 1972), p. 302.

26 See Dirk Dähnhardt, *Revolution in Kiel: Der Übergang Vom Kaiserreich zur Weimarer Republik* (Neumünster: Karl Wachholtz Verlag, 1978), pp. 48, 50–54.

27 Liddell Hart, *History of the First World War*, p. 379.

28 See Andrew Rothstein, *The Soldiers' Strikes of 1919* (London: Macmillan, 1980), pp. 37–85, esp. 37–38.

29 Rothstein, *The Soldiers' Strikes of 1919*, p. 39.

30 The emphasis military leaders put on morale is looked at in more detail in Elaine Scarry, *The Body in Pain: The Making and Unmaking of the World* (New York: Oxford University Press, 1985), pp. 104–7, 153–57, 345–46.

31 Martin Gilbert, *Winston S. Churchill* (London: Heinemann, 1975), vol. 4: 1917–1922, p. 235, cited in Rothstein, *The Soldiers' Strikes of 1919*, p. 95. For a discussion of the British soldiers' awareness of the plan, see p. 100.

32 Gen. Bernard M. Serrigny, *Trente Ans avec Pétain* (Paris: Plon, 1959), p. 146, cited in Watt, *Dare Call It Treason*, p. 215.

33 David Lloyd George, *War Memoirs* (1934), vol. 4, p. 335, cited in Watt, *Dare Call It Treason*, p. 218.

34 Jean Gueyras, "La colère des pasdarans," *Le Monde*, August 21–22, 1988, at p. 1, col. 1, and p. 5, col. 1 (translated from the French by D. A. Miller).

35 See "E. Germans Deserting," *Newsday*, March 1, 1990, p. 12; *International Herald Tribune*, March 1, 1990, p. 1, col. 2; Trumbull, "News Currents," *Christian Science Monitor*, March 1, 1990, p. 2, col. 1.

36 See Anatol Lieven and Mary Dejevsky, "Vilnius Anger over Seizure of Deserters," *The Times* [London], March 28, 1990, p. 1, col. 1.

37 Ian Urbina, "Even in Families Sworn to Duty, Misgivings Arise as War Goes On," *Sunday New York Times*, July 15, 2007, pp. 1, 14.

38 William H. McMichael, "Desertions Highest Since 2001," *Army Times*, November 15, 2007. McMichael gives a higher number than does Urbina for 2006, but since it is the exact figure he also gives for 2007, it seems a misprint. Though the Army has the highest presence in Iraq, other branches of the military who serve there also experience desertions: from September 2005 to September 2006, the number of desertions was 1036 among Marines, 1129 among Navy, and 16 among Air Force. Five percent of the 2006 Iraq deserters were court-martialed; most were discharged "in non-criminal proceedings on less-than-honorable terms," and some were "allowed to return to their units" (Estes Thompson, "Military Makes Little Effort to Track Deserters," *Army Times*, June 28, 2007).

39 Simon Tisdall, "Will the US Really Withdraw from Iraq and Afghanistan?" *Guardian*, June 8, 2011.

40 Report by the Department of Army's Center of Military History, "Historic Review on the 65th Infantry Regiment Court-Martial," pp. 11, 17, 18, 28 (available online under its title).

41 "The War over Pity: Why the Deserters Have Been Forgiven," *The Economist*, August 17, 2006.

42 Alexander Hamilton, *The Federalist No. 26*, in *The Federalist Papers: Hamilton, Madison, Jay*, ed. Clinton Rossiter (New York: New American Library, 1961), p. 172.

43 Hamilton, *The Federalist No. 26*, p. 172.

44 Hamilton, *The Federalist No. 26*, p. 173.

45 James Madison, *The Federalist No. 46*, in *The Federalist Papers*, pp. 298–99.

46 In the 2008 Supreme Court case about the right to bear arms, *District of Columbia v. Heller* (554 U.S.), Justice Scalia writing for the majority urged that while the Second Amendment gives individuals the right to carry a gun for self-defense, this obviously does not mean that felons or mentally ill people may carry guns. But both Justice Stevens in his dissent and Justice Breyer in his dissent point out that Scalia provides no argument or evidence for why these persons should be disallowed while the instances addressed in *Heller* should be allowed. See Syllabus, p. 2; Majority opinion, pp. 54, 57 ("nothing in our opinion should be taken to cast doubt on longstanding prohibitions on the possession of firearms by felons and the mentally ill"); Stevens's dissent, p. 3, n.3, and p. 9 ("for even felons... may invoke the protection of those constitutional provisions. The Court offers no way to harmonize its conflicting pronouncements"); Breyer's dissent, p. 43 (referring to prohibitions on felons and the mentally ill: "Why these? Is it that similar restrictions existed in the late 18th century? The majority fails to cite any colonial analogues").

47 The Second Amendment cannot be categorically separated from the pleasures of hunting since the European and American history of that pleasure is itself entwined with issues of distributive justice. The conflation was visible, for example, during the French Revolution. In August of 1789, the majority in the General Assembly voted for a decree abolishing "the exclusive right of dovecotes and pigeon houses.... Pigeons will be encaged at times determined by the communities, and during this time, they will be regarded as game. Everyone will have the right to kill them" (Michel Winock, "Chronique de 1789: L'année sans pareille," *Le Monde*, August 16, 1988, at p. 2, col. 1; translated from the French). The decree, according to Mirabeau, asserted the principle of equality: "Every man has the right to hunt on his land, none has the right to hunt on someone else's land: this principle is as sacred for the monarch as for anybody else" (trans. D. A. Miller).

The conflation of the personal right to hunt with the political right of arms also occurred in the United States. A proposed constitutional amendment emerging from the Pennsylvania ratification assembly included a provision asserting the people's "right to bear arms for the defence of themselves and their own State or the United States, or for the purpose of killing game" (Bernard Schwartz, *The Bill of Rights: A Documentary History* [New York: Chelsea House, 1971], vol. .2, p. 665). The perception of intimacy continued into the nineteenth century in military tracts. William Sumner, for example, speaks of shooting game as a way the population remains limber in the use of its arms; see "An Inquiry into the Importance of the Militia to a Free Commonwealth, in a Letter from William H. Sumner, Adjutant General of the Commonwealth of Massachusetts, to John Adams, Late President of the United States; with His Answer," in *Anglo-American Antimilitary Tracts 1697–1830*, ed. Richard H. Kohn (New York: Arno Press, 1979), pp. 39–40 (hereinafter "An Inquiry into the Importance of the Militia").

Legal theorists in both the United States and Britain recognized the implications of hunting laws. "Blackstone," wrote William Rawle, saw "that the prevention of popular insurrections and resistance to government by disarming the people, is oftener meant than avowed, by the makers of forest and game laws" (William Rawle, *A View of the Constitution of the United States of America* [Philadelphia: H. C. Carey & I. Lea, 1825], pp. 122–23 [citing Blackstone, *Commentaries*, vol. 2, p. 412]).

48 Meeting, August 18, 1789, *Archives Parlementaires*, vol. 8, p. 455, cited in Dieter Contrad, *Gandhi und der Begriff des Politischen: Staat, Religion und Gewalt* (München: Wilhelm Fink Verlag, 2006), p. 194.

49 Gandhi, cited in Conrad, *Gandhi und der Begriff des Politischen*, p. 193.

50 Mahatma Gandhi, *An Autobiography or the Story of My Experiments with Truth*, trans. Mahadev H. Desai (Ahmedabad: Navajivan, 1927), p. 666.

51 Marion Georges, "Les autorités judiciaires doivent convaincre l'opinion de leur détermination," *Le Monde*, December 14, 1989, at p. 5, col. .3.

52 See District of Columbia et. al. v. Heller, 554 U.S. (June 26, 2008); United States v. Miller, 307 U.S. 174 (1939); Miller v. Texas, 153 U.S. 535 (1894); Presser v. Illinois, 116 U.S. 252 (1886); United States v. Cruikshank, 92 U.S. 542 (1876).

Prior to *Heller*, the call for a Supreme Court reinterpretation was implicit in many law review articles observing the small number of cases, and was sometimes explicit, as when David Hardy wrote: "The formation of jurisprudence of the Second Amendment is nearly two centuries overdue" ("Armed Citizens, Citizen Armies: Toward a Jurisprudence of the Second Amendment," *Harvard Journal of Law & Public Policy* 9 (1986): 559, 638. Sanford Levinson is also among those who had urged a new interpretation, writing in 1989 that "The Supreme Court has almost shamelessly refused to discuss the issue." He also argued that both liberals and the legal academy continue to ignore the amendment at their peril, and he urged that "serious, engaged discussion" begin (Levinson, "The Embarrassing Second Amendment," *Yale Law Journal* 99 [1989]: 637, 654, 656–59). Whether the Heller decision fulfills the need Hardy and Levinson point to is a matter of ongoing debate.

53 For an analysis of the consistent emphasis in the country's first four Supreme Court cases on the Second Amendment as a collective, rather than an individual, right, see Roy Weatherup, "Standing Armies and Armed Citizens: An Historical Analysis of the Second Amendment," *Hastings Constitutional Law Quarterly* 2 (1975): 995–1000, reprinted in Senate Committee on the Judiciary, 97th Congr., 2nd Sess., *Report on the Right to Keep and Bear Arms* (1982), pp. 130, 164, 166 (hereinafter *Senate Report on Second Amendment*). Don B. Kates, Jr., adds to the nineteenth-century list two cases in which the amendment figures more tangentially than in those cited above: Robertson v. Baldwin, 165 U.S. 275 (1897), and Scott v. Sanford, 60 U.S. 393 (1856). See Kates, "Handgun Prohibition and the Original Meaning of the Second Amendment," *Michigan Law Review* 82 (1983): 204, 246–50. Kates

provides strong arguments for the individual interpretation; but, more crucially, he points out the "false dichotomy between the exclusively state's right and the unrestricted individual right interpretations" that have inappropriately absorbed legal commentary (p. 273). "In fact," he adds, "the arms of the state's militias were and are the personally owned arms of the general citizenry, so that the amendment's dual intention to protect both was achieved by guaranteeing to the citizenry a right to possess arms individually" (p. 273). The confusion of individual and collective rights is addressed later in this chapter.

54 Writing for the majority, Justice Scalia said *Heller* was the Supreme Court's "first in-depth examination" of the Second Amendment, and therefore could only accomplish a limited amount (*District of Columbia v. Heller*, p. 63).

55 *District of Columbia v. Heller*. As Justice Breyer points out in his dissent, "The majority spends the first 54 pages of its opinion attempting to rebut JUSTICE STEVENS' evidence [in his dissent] that the Amendment was enacted with a purely militia-related purpose" (Breyer, "Dissent," p. 41). This does not mean the majority rejects the prominence of the militia-related purpose. Justice Scalia writes, "It was understood across the political spectrum that the right helped to secure the ideal of a citizen militia"; "[T]he threat that the new Federal Government would destroy the citizens' militia by taking away their arms was the reason that right—unlike some other English rights—was codified in a written Constitution" (Scalia, "Majority Opinion," p. 26; Breyer, "Dissent," citing Scalia, p. 36). Justice Scalia argues that in addition to the collective right, the individual right of self-defense in the home is included and is of major importance, possibly even more important than the military right (Scalia, "Majority Opinion," p. 26). Justice Stevens's dissent argues for the amendment being limited to the defense of the country. Justice Breyer joins Justice Stevens but also writes a second dissent arguing that even if the individual right of self-defense in the home is protected by the amendment, it is a subsidiary right and a right that can be regulated by DC or state laws, as evidenced by early colonial regulations.

56 Cass R. Sunstein, "Second Amendment Minimalism: *Heller* as *Griswold*," *Harvard Law Review* 122, no. 1 (November 2008): 248–49, 272.

57 Sunstein, "Second Amendment Minimalism," pp. 252–53, 270. In addition to opinion polls, Sunstein observes the bipartisan support: "majorities of both houses of Congress supported a robust individual right in an amicus brief and . . . both nominees for the presidency—John McCain and Barack Obama—greeted *Heller* with general enthusiasm."

58 Sunstein, "Second Amendment Minimalism," p. 249. Not only is the number of Second Amendment cases prior to *Heller* extremely small, but those cases themselves are history-light. Justice Scalia in *Heller* complains about the absence of historical detail in *United States v. Miller*: "The Government's Miller brief thus provided scant discussion of the history of the Second Amendment—and the Court was presented with no counterdiscussion. As for the text of the Court's opinion itself, that discusses *none* of the history of the Second Amendment. It assumes

from the prologue that the Amendment was designed to preserve the militia,... (which we do not dispute), and then reviews some historical materials dealing with the nature of the militia, and in particular with the nature of the arms their members were expected to possess,... Not a word (not a word) about the history of the Second Amendment. This is the mighty rock upon which the dissent rests its case" ("Majority Opinion," *District of Columbia v. Heller*, pp. 51–52). As Sunstein's observation about originalism makes clear, the *Heller* court (in both the majority and minority opinions) more than makes up for the earlier inattention to history.

59 The Virginia Ratification assembly, for example, both opened and closed by stressing the fact that the Constitution was (until voted upon) only a piece of paper. "Suppose," said Mr. Pendleton during the opening of the debate, "the paper on your table dropped from one of the planets; the people found it, and sent us here to consider whether it was proper for their adoption." Toward the close of the debate, Madison referred to those who wrote the Constitution at the Federal Assembly as "those who prepared the paper on the table"; and Mr. Harrison led into his summary of his vote by asking: "How comes that paper on your table to be now here discussed?" (*The Debates in the Several State Conventions, on the Adoption of the Federal Constitution, as Recommended by the General Convention at Philadelphia in 1787, Together with the Journal of the Federal Convention, Luther Martin's Letter, Yates' Minutes, Congressional Opinions, Virginia and Kentucky Resolutions of '98– '99, and Other Illustrations of the Constitution*, ed. Jonathan Elliot [Philadelphia: Lippincott, 1861], vol. 3, pp. 38, 618, 628 [hereinafter Elliot, *Ratification Debates*]). Additional instances of the Constitution as "that paper" come later in this chapter.

60 The use of these words is explicit and self-conscious, as when Patrick Henry asks, "Have they said, We, the states? Have they made a proposal of a compact between states?... Is this a monarchy, like England—a compact between prince and people?" Henry also asks what it would mean to be ruled, regulated, or taxed "not by your own consent, but by people who have no connection with you." Whether or not Patrick Henry at any given moment overtly uses the word "compact" or "contract," his arguments and comments at the Virginia Ratification Debate collectively constitute a brilliant treatise on social contract or, more precisely, on the phenomenology of the action of contracting (Elliot, *Ratification Debates*, vol. 3, pp. 44, 56).

The explicit language of contract is also used by many others, as when Mr. Grayson, stressing the assembly's freedom to reject the proposed contract, observes: "In all parts of the world there is a reciprocity in contracts and compacts. If one man makes a proposition to another, is he bound to accept it?" Mr. Nicholas concludes his comments on the nature of amendment by saying: "If thirteen individuals are about to make a contract, and one agrees to it, but at the same time declares that he understands its meaning... (what the words of the contract plainly and obviously denote)...." Almost all the participants speak about the action of making a country, as when Mr. Zachariah Johnson describes the "happy operation [of government] when [it is] judiciously constructed"; when Mr. Tyler observes that "[w]e are not passing laws now, but laying the foundation on which laws are to be made"; and when Mr. Nicholas discusses how varying forms of ratification affect the "binding" character of the compact (Elliot, *Ratification Debates*, vol. 3, pp. 614, 626, 644, 641, 626).

61 Elliot, *Ratification Debates*, vol. 3, p. 656.

62 Elliot, *Ratification Debates*, vol. 4, p. 338.

63 Elliot, *Ratification Debates*, vol. 4, p. 342, citing David Ramsay, *The History of South-Carolina: From Its First Settlement in 1670, to the Year 1808* (Charleston: David Longworth, 1809), vol. 2, p. 432.

64 Robert Allen Rutland, *The Birth of the Bill of Rights 1776–1791* (Chapel Hill: University of North Carolina Press, 1955), p. 175, citing "Letter from John Jay to Mrs. Jay (July 5, 1788)," reprinted in *The Correspondence and Public Papers of John Jay 1782–1793*, ed. Henry Phelps Johnston (New York: G. P. Putnam, 1970), vol. 3, pp. 347–48.

65 *Senate Report on Second Amendment*, p. 163. For Governor Clinton's letter, see Elliot, *Ratification Debates*, vol. 2, pp. 413–14; on the New York circular letter, see also Merrill Jensen, *The Making of the American Constitution* (Princeton: D. Van Nostrand Co., 1964), pp. 138–50.

66 In his dissent in *Heller*, Justice Stevens reviews the proposed right to bear arms amendments forwarded by Virginia, New York, North Carolina, and New Hampshire. North Carolina withheld its ratification until the Constitution was supplemented with the Bill of Rights. Other states during the ratification debates— Massachusetts, Maryland, and Pennsylvania—discussed the need for protecting the right but the proposed amendment did not receive the majority vote in those states and was not forwarded to Congress. Jusice Stevens, dissenting (joined by Justices Souter, Ginsburg, Breyer), 554 *U.S. District of Columbia v. Heller* (2008), pp. 20–23.

67 Arthur Taylor Prescott, *Drafting the Federal Constitution: A Rearrangement of Madison's Notes Giving Consecutive Developments of Provisions in the Constitution of the United States, Supplemented by Documents Pertaining to the Philadelphia Convention and to Ratification Processes, and Including Insertions by the Compiler* (Baton Rouge: Louisiana State University Press, 1941), p. 515; see also pages 519 and 736 for Gerry's opposition to the centralization of the military (hereinafter *Madison Rearranged*).

68 Prescott, *Madison Rearranged*, p. 515.

69 "Letter from James Madison to Edmund Randolph (July 16, 1788)," reprinted in Elliot, *Ratification Debates*, vol. 5, p. 573.

70 See Elliot, *Ratification Debates*, vol. 2, p. 412.

71 Akhil Amar, "Our Forgotten Constitution: A Bicentennial Comment," *Yale Law Journal* 97 (1987): 286, invoking the description of ratification in Hamilton's *The Federalist No. 22*, p. 152, and Madison's *The Federalist No. 40*, p. 253. See also

Akhil Amar, "Philadelphia Revisited: Amending the Constitution Outside Article V," *University of Chicago Law Review* 55 (1988): 1094 (hereinafter "Philadelphia Revisited"). Here Amar argues that the ratification conventions have a greater claim to being "the people" than has the Congressional Assembly because of the smaller influence of agency costs in the ratification conventions and because the delegate selection process of the conventions focused only on ratification and not on a "bundle" of oddly assorted issues.

72 Perhaps the most adventuresome or unrestrained articulation of this idea is made by William E. Nelson who, in a standard reference work, states that a single sentence within the Fourteenth Amendment—"No state shall make..."—has become the text upon which most twentieth-century constitutional law is a gloss (William E. Nelson, "Fourteenth Amendment [Framing]," in *Encyclopedia of the American Constitution*, vol. 2, ed. Leonard Levy, Kenneth Karst, and Dennis Mahoney [New York: Macmillan, 1986], p. 757).

Other writers, even if more cautious, are also tempted into comprehensive statements. Coupling the Fourteenth Amendment's "equal protection" with the First Amendment's "freedom of expression," Michael J. Perry asserts that the "two categories are, by consensus, among the most important in the whole corpus of constitutional law. The third category ['substantive due process'] is, again by consensus, the most controversial" (Michael J. Perry, *The Constitution, the Courts, and Human Rights: An Inquiry into the Legitimacy of Constitutional Policy-Making by the Judiciary* [New York: Oxford University Press, 1982], p. 5). Ward E. Y. Elliott also observes the reach of the Fourteenth Amendment: "[W]hile nobody actually said that they understood the Fourteenth Amendment to be a blank check to posterity, the framers and the members of the state legislatures who ratified the amendment might not have been shocked to find language like 'equal protection,' 'due process,' and 'privileges and immunities' extended to deal with problems like wiretapping, which they were in no position to anticipate" (Ward Elliott, *The Rise of Guardian Democracy: The Supreme Court's Role in Voting Rights Disputes, 1845–1969* [Cambridge: Harvard University Press, 1974], p. 60).

73 Within social contract theory, whether a particular theorist endorses or instead disdains revolution often turns on whether the person believes consent is a perpetual act or instead a solitary act performed (and afterward relinquished) at the threshold. Sometimes political philosophers acknowledge the existence of both forms and give them separate names. For example, Patrick S. Atiyah identifies the "promise" as a subspecies of consent, in which, at a single decisive moment, there is a willed abdication of the power of successive revision normally operating in consent. See Patrick Atiyah, *Promises, Morals, and Law* (Oxford: Oxford University Press, 1981), p. 177. John Locke differentiates "express consent" from "tacit consent" on this basis. The first occurs in a decisive moment and is not revocable; here, the obligation incurred, rather than the action performed, becomes "perpetual." The second is open, iterative,

revocable; it can be withdrawn at any time. See John Locke, *Second Treatise of Government*, ed. C. B. Macpherson (Indianapolis: Hackett, 1980), p. 65.

On threshold and perpetual consent in marriage and in medicine, see Chapter 5, the section entitled "Portrait 3: Desire."

74 In general, the decentering of power at the ratification conventions, rather than opposing the centralizing tendency of the Constitutional Convention, can be seen as extending the distribution of power occurring there through the "separation of powers" doctrine. The idiom of "checks and balances" expresses distribution in a defensive or negative language, the withholding of all power from any one location. But this can alternatively be phrased as a positive dispersal of power across all locations.

The language of "distribution" is used by Hamilton, who speaks of checks and balances as "[t]he regular distribution of power into distinct departments" (*The Federalist No. 9*, p. 72). So, too, it is a natural mental habit for Madison to go from "separation of powers" to the image of people as a whole. In his February 6, 1792, article in the *National Gazette,* he writes, "In bestowing the eulogies due to the particular and internal checks of power, it ought not the less to be remembered, that they are neither the sole nor the chief palladium of constitutional liberty. The people who are authors of this blessing, must also be its guardians" (James Madison, "Government of the United States," reprinted in *The Writings of James Madison Comprising His Public Papers and His Private Correspondence, Including Numerous Letters and Documents Now for the First Time Printed*, ed. Gaillard Hunt [New York: Putnam, 1906], vol. 6, p. 93).

On the "separation of powers" doctrine as a distributive mechanism, see Akhil Amar, "Of Sovereignty and Federalism," *Yale Law Journal* 96 (1987): 1425. Amar has analyzed the "majoritarian," "structural," and "educational" characteristics of the Bill of Rights that have been obscured by what he describes as a "clause-bound approach" to "constitutional discourse" (Akhil Amar, "The Bill of Rights as a Constitution," *Yale Law Journal* 100 [1991]: 1201–10).

75 It is appropriate that the Second Amendment was, as David Hardy observes, "one of the least controversial" and, thus, one of the most consensual of the ten amendments. See Hardy, "Armed Citizens, Citizen Armies," p. 606.

76 Story, *Commentaries on the Constitution*, vol. 2, p. 87.

77 This constitutional requirement of declaration by the full bicameral assembly strongly indicates that the policy of presidential first use cannot be remedied by giving the decision to a congressional committee, or to "sample" members of each house, or to a council of state chosen by Congress, as several authors have recommended. See articles cited in Chapter 1, note 2: Cox, "Raison d'Etat and World Survival," p. 1633: Forrester, "Presidential Wars in the Nuclear Age," p. 1641; Goldstein, "The Failure of Constitutional Controls Over War Powers in the Nuclear Age," p. 1587; Stone, "Presidential First Use is Unlawful," p. 107. For

a more elaborate analysis, see William C. Banks, "First Use of Nuclear Weapons: The Constitutional Role of a Congressional Leadership Committee," *Journal of Legislation* 13 (1986): 1. The requirement for numerical participation is looked at later in this chapter.

78 See Locke, *Second Treatise of Government*, pp. 8, 46, 47, 66–68, 101–24. See also John Dunn, "Consent in the Political Theory of John Locke," in *Life, Liberty, and Property: Essays on Locke's Political Idea*, ed. Gordon J. Schochet (Belmont, CA: Wadsworth Publishing Co., 1971), p. 154. The opposition between contract and force is central to the writings of Thomas Hobbes, as we see in detail in Chapter 3. The self-consciousness with which the American founders, as well as earlier contractual societies, positioned contract against force is elaborated later in this chapter.

79 These seven states are Virginia, Pennsylvania, Maryland, North Carolina, New York, Massachusetts, and New Hampshire. See *The Complete Anti-Federalist*, ed. Herbert J. Storing (Chicago: University of Chicago Press, 1981), vol. 2, p. 447, n. 26. For a contemporary argument that the state-controlled militia is a distributive mechanism designed to act as a "check on the abuse of military power by the federal government," see Perpich v. United States Department of Defense, 666 F. Supp. 1319 (D. Minn. 1987), affirmed, 880 F.2d 11(8th Cir, 1989), affirmed, 110 5. Ct. 2418 (1990).

80 Prescott, *Madison Rearranged*, p. 524.

81 Resolutions of the Massachusetts House of Representatives, June 29, 1769, quoted in John Phillip Reid, *In Defiance of the Law: The Standing-Army Controversy, the Two Constitutions, and the Coming of the American Revolution* (Chapel Hill: University of North Carolina Press, 1981), p. 166; italics added. On John Locke's use of the idiom of invasion, see Chapter 3 in this book.

82 "Letter from Benjamin Franklin to Samuel Cooper (June 8, 1770)," cited in Reid, *In Defiance of the Law*, p. 171.

83 See Cassius, *Considerations on the Society or Order of Cincinnati, Lately Instituted by the Major-Generals, Brigadiers, and Other Officers of the American Army, Proving That It Creates, a Race of Hereditary Patricians, or Nobility, and Interspersed with Remarks on its Consequences to the Freedom and Happiness of the Republick*, in Kohn, ed., *Anglo-American Antimilitary Tracts* (hereinafter *Order of Cincinnati*).

84 *Order of Cincinnati*, p. 10. The importance of prohibiting titles in a distributive society is saluted by Madison:
> Could any further proof be required of the republican complexion of this system, the most decisive one might be found in its absolute prohibition of titles of nobility, both under the federal and the State governments; and in its express guaranty of the republican form to each of the latter.
> (*The Federalist No. 39*, p. 242.)

85 James Winthrop, "Letters of Agrippa," *Massachusetts Gazette*, no. 406 (February 5, 1788), reprinted as "Agrippa XVIII" in Paul Leicester Ford, *Essays on the*

Constitution of the United States Published during Its Discussion by the People 1787–88 (Brooklyn: Historical Printing Club, 1892), pp. 11–19; italics added.

86 "Letters of Luther Martin," *Maryland Journal*, no. 1021 (March 18, 1788), reprinted as "Luther Martin, III" in Ford, *Essays on the Constitution*, pp. 358–59.

87 See U.S. Constitution, Amendments II, III, and IV.

88 The word "disarm" has the peculiarity of being, on the one hand, a neutral descriptive term registering the state of being deprived of one's weapons and, on the other hand, a concussive term within strategic writings, now most familiar to us in Clausewitz's formulations, registering total defeat by the opponent. See Carl von Clausewitz, *On War*, ed. and trans. Michael Howard and Peter Paret (Princeton: Princeton University Press, 1976). As the quoted passages suggest, the first meaning (the deprivation of arms) is often referred to as though it were the second (total subjugation), precisely because the first is perceived as inevitably entailing the second. Or, phrased in the other direction, "disarm" in strategic writings can have the resonance of total subjugation precisely because the apparently neutral deprivation of arms always involves an open or obscure state of coercion.

89 Weatherup, "Standing Armies and Armed Citizens," p. 973 (quoting the Bill of Rights, 1 W. & M., sess. 2, c. 2 [1689]). See also Hardy, "Armed Citizens, Citizen Armies," pp. 1–87 (detailing the development of the political right to bear arms in seventeenth-century Britain).

90 Weatherup, "Standing Armies and Armed Citizens," p. 973.

91 Max Farrand, ed., *The Records of the Federal Convention of 1787*, vol. 2 (New Haven: Yale University Press, 1966), p. 385.

92 Luther Martin, "Mr. Martin's Information to the General Assembly of the State of Maryland," reprinted in Storing, *The Complete Anti-Federalist*, vol. 2, pp. 59–60.

93 "The Address and Reasons of Dissent of the Minority of the Convention of the State of Pennsylvania to Their Constituents, 1787," reprinted in Schwartz, *The Bill of Rights*, vol. 2, p. 665.

94 Centinel, "To the People of Pennsylvania (Jan. 5, 1788)," reprinted in Storing, *The Complete Anti-Federalist*, vol. 2, p. 182.

95 Aristocrotis, "The Government of Nature Delineated or An Exact Picture of the New Federal Constitution" (1788), reprinted in Storing, *The Complete Anti-Federalist*, vol. 3, p. 210. This idiom of "disarming"—as well as the less serious "disabling" or "depriving"—continued into the nineteenth century. For examples, see Presser v. Illinois, 116 U.S. 252, 265 (1886); Rawle, *A View of the Constitution*, pp. 122–23.

96 Rawle, *A View of the Constitution*, p. 121. On the use of the word "palladium" for defense achieved through distribution, see Elliot, *Ratification Debates*, vol. 4, p. 338.

97 Sumner, *An Inquiry into the Importance of the Militia*, p. 68.

98 Story, *Commentaries on the Constitution*, vol. 2, p. 620. For an overview of the association of arms distribution with democracy in the wider philosophic framework of Aristotle, Cicero, Machiavelli, Locke, Sidney, Rousseau, and others, see

Stephen P. Halbrook, "The Second Amendment as a Phenomenon of Classical Political Philosophy," in *Firearms and Violence: Issues of Public Policy*, ed. Don Kates, Jr. (Pensacola: Ballinger, 1984), pp. 363–83.

99 Story, *Commentaries on the Constitution*, vol. 2, p. 620.

100 See Madison, *The Federalist No. 46*, p. 300.

101 Elliot, *Ratification Debates*, vol. 2, p. 176; italics added. Justice Story noticed this language and commented on its peculiarity. See Story, *Commentaries on the Constitution*, vol. 1, p. 248.

102 Madison, *The Federalist No. 39*, p. 244.

103 Elliot, *Ratification Debates*, vol. 3, pp. 616–17.

104 Hamilton, *The Federalist No. 1*, p. 33.

105 Hamilton, *The Federalist No. 85*, p. 527.

106 Rawle, *A View of the Constitution*, p. 13.

107 Elliot, *Ratification Debates*, vol. 3, p. 418.

108 Elliot, *Ratification Debates*, vol. 3, p. 426.

109 Richard Henry Lee, "Observations of the System of Government Proposed by the Late Convention. By a Federal Farmer" (hereinafter *Letters from the Federal Farmer*), in *Pamphlets on the Constitution of the United States*, ed. Paul Leicester Ford (Brooklyn: 1888), p. 277. On the contested authorship of these letters, see Storing, *The Complete Anti-Federalist*, vol. 2, pp. 214–17; Gordon S. Wood, "The Authorship of the Letters from the Federal Farmer," *William & Mary Quarterly* 31, no. 2 (April 1974): 299–308.

110 Lee, *Letters from the Federal Farmer*, p. 305; italics added.

111 Lee, *Letters from the Federal Farmer*, p. 306. Inequities in distribution across age continued to be a concern in the nineteenth century. In *An Inquiry into the Importance of the Militia*, Sumner charted the gradual contraction in the age of those serving in the militia: at first those exempted from service (aged forty to forty-five) participated by contributing money, but when a still younger rung of men (aged thirty-five to forty) was later excluded, those originally exiled were relieved of even the obligation to contribute financially. See *An Inquiry into the Importance of the Militia*, pp. 49–51.

112 Here, Gandhi's autobiography is again illuminating. In a chapter called "Miniature Satyagraha," he describes the acts of noncompliance taken by himself and other Indians in a voluntary corps in the army. Their actions protested not the existence of the military (they themselves had volunteered) but inequities in authority between the English students appointed as their corporals and themselves. They insisted that the position of corporal either be eliminated altogether or that it come about by the vote of the corps rather than by the appointment of the commanding officer. In effect, they established as the only permissible alternatives either complete equality or a nonequality brought about by the explicit vote of the participants, as Gandhi himself was the "chairman" and "unofficial" representative of

the corps. See Gandhi's *Autobiography or the Story of My Experiments with Truth*, vol. 2, pp. 525–29.

113 See Aristocrotis, in Storing, *The Complete Anti-Federalist*, vol. 3, p. 202.

114 Aristocrotis, in Storing, *The Complete Anti-Federalist*, vol. 3, pp. 202–3.

115 Lee, *Letters from the Federal Farmer*, p. 305.

116 Lee, *Letters from the Federal Farmer*, p. 305.

117 Cassius, *Order of Cincinnati*, p. 13.

118 DeWitt, "To the Free Citizens of the Commonwealth of Massachusetts," *American Herald*, October/December 1787, reprinted in Storing, *The Complete Anti-Federalist*, vol. 4, p. 36.

119 Sumner, for example, calls people at the time of the revolution "that rugged people" and speaks of the "masculine virtues of constancy, fidelity, and firmness, which governed her conduct." See *An Inquiry into the Importance of the Militia*, p. 60. Though Sumner here calls the virtues "masculine," it would in the long run be an error to read the idiom as narrowly gendered. See notes 120 and 121, below.

120 The same constellation of words, for example, recurs in Gandhi's conception of resistance. Judging the English phrase "passive resistance" inadequate to express the actions in which he was engaged, Gandhi designed a public contest to elicit an alternative phrase. Out of the contest emerged the then newly invented, but now familiar, word *Satyagraha*, chosen because it means "firmness" in the "truth" ("Sat = truth, Agraha = firmness"). See Gandhi, *Autobiography or the Story of My Experiments with Truth*, vol. 2, p. 474.

Female pacifism reveals the same stress on bodily materiality. It is evident, for example, in the protest strategies of women at Greenham Common Women's Peace Camp who conceived of their bodies as a "constant source of freshly invented obstructions" (Ann Snitow, "Holding the Line at Greenham," *Mother Jones* [February/March 1985]: 30, 42).

121 An emphasis on "firmness" and "materiality" occurs in conjunction with women soldiers, military leaders, and heads of state. Antonia Fraser devotes a chapter of *The Warrior Queens* to "Iron Ladies." Though the designation of Golda Meir's "iron hand" originates with a later president of Israel, and the designation of Margaret Thatcher as the "Iron Lady" originates with the Soviet Union's *Red Star*, the attributions were accepted by the women themselves. See Antonia Fraser, *The Warrior Queens: The Legends and the Lives of the Women Who Have Led Their Nations in War* (New York: Alfred A. Knopf, 1989), pp. 312, 315.

In her poem on Boadicea, Judy Grahn salutes the same resistant materiality: "I am the wall at the lip of the water / I am the rock that refused to be battered" (Fraser, *The Warrior Queens*, p. 304). When woman soldiers themselves speak, the stress on a resistant materiality becomes evident less in the materials of metal, iron, or stone than in the fact of the resistant body. In a missive to the English military leadership, Joan of Arc writes:

King of England, and you Duke of Bedford, calling yourself Regent of France
...do right.... Surrender to the Maid sent hither..., the keys of all the good
towns you have taken and laid waste in France.... And you, archers, comrades
in arms, gentles and others, who are before the town of Orleans, retire in God's
name to your own country. If you do not, expect to hear tidings from the Maid
who will shortly come upon you to your very great hurt.... I am sent here in
God's name, the King of Heaven, to drive you body for body out of all France.
(Marina Warner, *Joan of Arc: the Image of Female Heroism* [Berkeley: University
of California Press, 1981], p. 68).

A Palestinian woman, Nuha Nafal, expressing her readiness to fight whenever
called, describes her political resistance in terms of the body:

Often there are applications and documents to fill out and always there is the
question of where one is born.... [W]hen the application is returned, Palestine
is always crossed out and Israel written in, instead.... [N]ow, I write what they
wish and I say nothing. But I am Palestinian. My hair is Palestinian, my body is
Palestinian, and the words I speak are Palestinian. My death will be Palestinian!
(Nuha Nafal, in Sally Hayton-Keeva, ed., *Valiant Women in War and Exile: Thirty-
Eight True Stories* [San Francisco: City Light Books, 1987], p. 58).

The emphasis on bodily materiality found among female soldiers, whether in the
medieval or modern period, should be distinguished from the external concentration on one narrow attribute of the body: the sexual. Antonia Fraser has observed
the tendency of women soldiers to be described obsessively by men as alternately
chaste and insatiable (Fraser, *The Warrior Queens*, p. 11).

122 Farrand, *Records of the Federal Convention of 1787*, vol. 2, p. 386.

123 Prescott, *Madison Rearranged*, pp. 520–21.

124 Sumner, *An Inquiry into the Importance of the Militia*, p. 65.

125 Sumner, *An Inquiry into the Importance of the Militia*, pp. 65–66.

126 307 U.S. 174 (1939).

127 307 U.S. p. 178. On the judicial attention to the physical properties of weapons,
see Halbrook, "What the Framers Intended: A Linguistic Analysis of the Right to
'Bear Arms,'" *Law and Contemporary Problems* 49 (1986): 158–59; Kates, "Handgun Prohibition and the Original Meaning of the Second Amendment," pp. 248,
249, 259–60; Weatherup, "Standing Armies and Armed Citizens," p. 168.

128 Justice Scalia in his majority opinion in *Heller* refers to the emphasis on physical
attributes in the earlier case: "JUSTICE STEVENS can say again and again that
Miller did 'not turn on the difference between muskets and sawed-off shotguns' but
the words of the opinion prove otherwise" (*District of Columbia v. Heller*, p. 50).

129 307 U.S. p. 181.

130 Oral Argument, *District of Columbia et al., Petitioners v. Dick Anthony Heller*, no.
07-290, Washington, March 18, 2008, beginning 10:06 a.m., pp. 83, 84.

131 Justice Breyer, dissenting (joined by Justices Stevens, Ginsburg, and Souter) *District of Columbia v. Heller* (June 26, 2008), pp. 7, 8.

132 These references for "bear" are drawn from the four-page entry for the word in *The Oxford English Dictionary* (Oxford: Clarendon, 1933), pp. 731–34.

133 Similarly, race is later made irrelevant and, still later, gender. See the section of this chapter entitled "Political Self-Authorization: Civil Rights and the Rights of Arms."

134 While many etymologies are controversial, the derivation of "consent" in "con" and "sentire" is consistent across numerous authorities. See Ernest Klein, *A Comprehensive Etymological Dictionary of the English Language* (Amsterdam: Elsevier, 1971); C. T. Onions, ed., *The Oxford Dictionary of English Etymology* (Oxford: Clarendon Press, 1995); Eric Partridge, *A Short Etymological Dictionary of Modern English* (New York: Macmillan, 1966), s.v. consent. The sense of the word as "a feeling with or across persons" is apprehensible in the closely related word "consentient."

135 John Rawls, *A Theory of Justice* (Cambridge: Harvard University Press, 1971), p. 12.

136 Elliot, *Ratification Debates*, vol. 3, p. 426.

137 Schwartz, *The Bill of Rights*, vol. 2, pp. 766, 770, 809, 817. Common to Patrick Henry's position during the Revolution and during the ratification were both his framing of all political issues in contractual language and his insistence on the distribution of military authority. His most widely known revolutionary speech (which climaxes "Give me liberty or give me death") was spoken to support a sequence of three resolutions before the Virginia assembly on the eve of the revolution, the first asserting the importance of a militia to a free government, the second calling out the militia, the third arming that militia. See Robert Meade, *Patrick Henry: Practical Revolutionary* (Philadelphia: J.B. Lippincott, 1969), pp. 28–29, 35.

138 *Essays of Brutus* (quoting a speaker before the British House of Commons) in Storing, *The Complete Anti-Federalist*, vol. 2, p. 407.

139 See, for example, *Essays by a Farmer*, describing how troops in countries that have lost political and civil liberties "must not feel like" the population and must have "separate interests" from them. In Storing, *The Complete Anti-Federalist*, vol. 5, p. 22.

140 See Mr. Martin's *Information to the General Assembly of the State of Maryland* and *Letters of Centinel to the Freemen of Pennsylvania, Essays by a Farmer*, and Brutus, *To the People of the State of New York*, in Storing, *The Complete Anti-Federalist*, vol. 2, pp. 27, 140, 418; vol. 5, p. 33.

141 Sumner, *An Inquiry into the Importance of the Militia*, pp. 7–8.

142 Prescott, *Madison Rearranged*, p. 514.

143 Prescott, *Madison Rearranged*, p. 514. In Madison's notes, the record of Mason's argument leads directly to the record of the shift from the word "make" war to "declare" war in Article I, Section 8. The passage was also cited by Richard B. Morris in his statement before the Foreign Relations Committee (March 9, 1971, p. 80) during the hearings on congressional war powers, and is requoted in 93 *Congressional Record* 1408 (January 18, 1973).

144 For example, Brutus, one of the most important of the anti-Federalists, sometimes was absorbed with counting the numbers involved in military decisions. See Storing, *The Complete Anti-Federalist*, vol. 2, p. 413.

145 Story, *Commentaries on the Constitution*, vol. 2, p. 87.

146 Rawle, *A View of the Constitution*, p. 106.

147 At no point in these writings does the call for universal military service express an aspiration for a massive offensive military power. In the Federal convention, suggestions are made that only one-fourth or one-tenth of the militia be in training at any one time and that the entire militia be kept fit by a gradual "rotation" across the fractions. See Prescott, *Madison Rearranged*, p. 518.

148 This insistence on a wide base of authorization is visible in writings about inclusiveness across differences in age, class, and geography. It is also visible in the recurring preoccupation with the discrepancy between the small size of an army and the large size of a militia, a disproportion ensuring the population's capacity for self-defense and resistance. For example, Madison writes:

> The highest number to which, according to the best computation, a standing army can be carried in any country does not exceed one hundredth part of the whole number of souls; or one twenty-fifth part of the number able to bear arms. This proportion would not yield, in the United States, an army of more than twenty-five or thirty thousand men. To these would be opposed a militia amounting to near half a million of citizens with arms in their hands, officered by men chosen from among themselves, fighting for their common liberties and united and conducted by governments possessing their affections and confidence.

(Madison, *The Federalist No. 46*, p. 299). This numerical juxtaposition continually reoccurs. In an 1860 address to Congress on the militia, C. L. Vallandigham contrasts the size of the army and the official returns measuring the size of the militia for the year 1808 when the population was 7 million (3204 and 636,386, respectively). See 36 *Congressional Deliberations* 1130 (1860) (address of Hon. C. L. Vallandigham of Ohio to the House of Representatives). He then contrasts the size of the army and the militia for the year 1858 when the population was about 30 million (17,498 and 2,755,726, respectively; p. 130). The double aspiration—a small numerical base for risk and a large numerical base for authorization—is summarized perhaps most succinctly in an 1836 address to the Congress about the militia: "Let the means of defence be as ample, and the burdens on the people be as light as possible." (*Congressional Globe*, 24th Cong., 1st Sess. 235, 237 [1836] [address of Ransom Gillet to the House of Representative]). Madison describes that same vision of small risk and large authorization in *The Federalist Papers*:

> The Union itself, which it cements and secures, destroys every pretext for a military establishment which could be dangerous. America united, with a handful of troops, or without a single soldier, exhibits a more forbidding posture to

foreign ambition than America disunited, with a hundred thousand veterans ready for combat.

(*The Federalist No.41*, p. 258).

149 Justice Davis once wrote that this nation "has no right to expect that it will always have wise and humane rulers, sincerely attached to the principles of the Constitution." This is why solutions must be structural and independent of psychological accidents. (Ex parte Milligan, 71 U.S. [4 Wall.] 2, 125 [1866], quoted in Story, *Commentaries on the Constitution*, vol. 2, p. 103). Davis's words recall Madison's warning in *The Federalist Papers* that "[e]nlightened statesmen will not always be at the helm" (*The Federalist No. 10*, p. 80).

150 Today's land-based intercontinental ballistic missiles are still called "Minuteman."

151 Today's submarine launched ballistic missiles are Tridents.

152 See *Hearings: First Use of Nuclear Weapons*, p. 18; italics added.

153 *Hearings: First Use of Nuclear Weapons*, p. 215.

154 The strategic report "Discriminate Deterrence," written by the Commission on Integrated Long-Term Strategy (January 1988), provides an example of this pressure. The opening pages make the remarkable suggestion that the country needs more "national consensus" about strategic matters so that it can have "fewer legislative restrictions that inhibit its effectiveness" (p. 2). The complaint about legislative impediments continually reemerges. Restrictions on military persons and restrictions on the training of foreign police forces are called "a self-inflicted strategic wound" (p. 19). The refusal to train armies in countries that do not abide by standards of nuclear control is referred to as a species of "micro-management," and a Congress is imagined that will exercise its powers of partnership with the executive by restraining and effacing itself (p. 47). The legislative prohibitions on testing an antisatellite missile are presented as an impediment, as are Congress's low military appropriations during periods free of crisis and its reluctance to sanction even "modest expenditures in many Third World countries" (pp. 54, 58, 61).

Such impatience with legislative encumbrances is remarkable because the aspiration for an unchecked military-executive implies a tolerance of monarchic or totalitarian forms of government. Far from being embarrassed by this implication, the report unembarrassedly and repeatedly expresses its envy for dictatorships free of legislative restrictions: the "United States has some large competitive disadvantages" in its capacity to move troops "[b]ecause [the Soviet client states] are dictatorships [and] can secretly order aid missions and military units abroad and disguise their missions there" (p. 21). It complains about the crisis-driven "stop-go" military spending of the United States and presents as an object of aspiration the "formidable stability that has long marked Soviet defense investment" (p. 59). Elsewhere it observes that "[a] dictator, or an involuntary coalition dominated by a dictatorship, has less trouble in preparing to launch military operations" (p. 64)

The report is admirable in its emphasis on conventional weapons and in its aversion to nuclear weapons, the use of which can so quickly destroy "a civil society"

(p. 66). But in its contempt for legislative restrictions, in its vision of an unencumbered military-executive partnership, and in its envy of the military advantages of totalitarian states, it seems to have quite lost sight of what a civil society is.

155 Story, *Commentaries on the Constitution*, vol. 2, p. 87.

156 "Election" may actually be less essential to the executive argument than it appears, since versions of the argument occur even where the executive has not been elected. Hanna Pitkin observed that prior to the English Civil War, "the king sought to keep the members of Parliament in their place by arguing that each spoke only for his own separate community; they did not [unlike him] collectively 'represent' the realm" (Hanna Fenichel Pitkin, *The Concept of Representation* [Berkeley: University of California Press, 1967], p. 252).

157 Locke, *Second Treatise of Government*, p. 72.

158 Luther v. Borden, 48 U.S. (1 How.) 2, 21(1849).

159 The 3 percent and 14 percent ratios of participants to total population in earlier wars are given in Quincy Wright, *A Study of War* (Chicago: University of Chicago Press, 1942), pp. 234, 658, 660.

160 For an account of this equivalence, its role in legitimating war, and its disappearance in the shift from conventional to nuclear war, see Scarry, *The Body in Pain*, pp. 151–57.

161 Adam Smith, *An Inquiry into the Nature and Causes of the Wealth of Nations*, ed. Edwin Cannan (New York: Random House, 1994), p. 755.

162 119 *Congr. Rec.* 1395 (1973) (remarks of Sen. Case, N.J.).

163 "The Declaration of Independence," para. 2 (U.S. 1776).

164 The state-by-state Declarations of Rights are reprinted in Schwartz, *The Bill of Rights*, vol. 2, pp. 235, 266, 280, 319, 339, 375.

165 Schwartz, *The Bill of Rights*, vol. 2, pp. 42–43.

166 Shortly after emphasizing that the militia must be organized by the states "under one and the same system, to be established by Congress, including the formation of battalions and uniform equipments," Knox speaks of the importance of instilling "habits which shall give *a lustre* to the American character. The people universally should be furnished with arms, and know how to use them" (Joseph Willard, *Plan for the General Arrangement of the Militia of the United States [Read before the Massachusetts Historical Society]* [Cambridge, MA: J. Wilson & Sons, 1863], p. 8; italics added). For the words "splendor" and "glorious," see id., pp. 33, 38.

167 Brutus, "To the Citizens of the State of New York," in Storing, *The Complete Anti-Federalist*, vol. 2, p. 375.

168 See Cassius, *Order of Cincinnati*, p.10.

169 See Sumner, *An Inquiry into the Importance of the Militia*, pp. 61, 68. In his 1826 paper on the militia, Sumner devotes half of the paper to the issue of uniformity (*A Paper on the Militia Presented to the Hon. James Barbour, Secretary of War in November, 1826* [Washington, DC: B. Homans, 1833], pp. 15–30). The proximity of the words "uniform" or "equal" to the word "beauty" can be sensed in the

frequency with which "*non*uniformity" is explicitly coupled to the words "deformity" or "defect," sometimes even occurring in apposition, as in the phrase "defective, unequal, and oppressive" (p. 18). Observing the variations across states in the numerical composition of companies and regiments, Sumner writes: "All this *deformity* arises from the operation of the existing laws, defeating the *design* of those who granted the power to the National Government, for the sake of ensuring a perfect uniformity of organization" (p. 15, italics added). He then moves immediately from this abstract aesthetic vocabulary to a more concrete aesthetic practice: "[Congress] can provide arms and equipments for both officers and soldiers, and authorize *the delivery of colors and musical instruments* from the national armories" (p. 15, italics added). Similarly, in a speech to the U.S. Congress about arrangements for the militia in the state of New York, Ransom Gillet countless times stresses the "civil" nature of the militia and "citizen soldiers" of all ages and wealth. He speaks of the thrill—"the beating of the high military pulse"—that comes on seeing the militia not in battle but in the "brilliant military array, conducted in an orderly manner" during "training and martial exhibition" (Gillet, *Congressional Globe*, pp. 235, 237). See also Vallandigham, 36 *Congressional Deliberations*, p. 1130, reciting in detail the precise equipment provided for the militia in a 1792 congressional act: "every private among dragoons would be required to find a serviceable horse, of the same height (14½ hands high), with bridal, saddle, mailpillion, valise, holsters, breast-plates, crupper, boots, spurs, pistols, saber, and cartouch-box."

170 Willard, *Plan for the General Arrangement of the Militia*, p. 29; italics added.

171 Sumner, *A Paper on the Militia*, p. 9; italics added.

172 My thanks to Matthew Spellberg for noticing the continuity between the nuclear umbrella and the national canopy of earlier centuries (August 3, 2006). See Department of Defense, "Nuclear Posture Review," April 2010 (Washington, DC), pp. 18, 53, 68. The term has been in use since at least 1965 when R. W. Komer writes a memorandum to McGeorge Bundy recommending that the United States keep offering India "unilaterally a nuclear umbrella" (Secret Memorandum, January 14, 1965, Department of State, Lyndon Baines Johnson Library, National Security File, Committee on Nuclear Proliferation, Box 6, India; available on Digital National Security Archive). My stipulation that the pledges may or may not be sincere is prompted by Francis J. Gavin's account of conversations between Nixon and Kissinger, who felt the nuclear umbrella could only work if the United States' power outmatched its adversaries' by a ratio of 5 to 1: "In an age of parity, the president declared 'the nuclear umbrella in NATO a lot of crap'" ("Nuclear Nixon: Ironies, Puzzles, and the Triumph of Realpolitik," in *Nixon in the World: American Foreign Relations, 1969–77*, ed. Fredrik Logevail and Andrew Preston [Ithaca: Cornell University Press, 2008], p. 134). On the withholding of information about the nuclear umbrella from the American public, see, for example, White House press documents on the question of whether President Reagan offered Pakistan a place

under the American nuclear umbrella (Press Guidance, October 11, 1984, Nuclear Non-Proliferation, NP02152, available on Digital National Security Archive).

173 Gretchen Heefner, *The Missile Next Door: the Minuteman in the American Heartland* (Cambridge: Harvard University Press, 2012), p. 31.

174 Heefner, *The Missile Next Door*, p. 32.

175 Heefner, *The Missile Next Door*, p. 31.

176 See *District of Columbia v. Heller*, 554 U.S 43, 44 (and Stevens's dissent, p. 39); *Presser v. Illinois*, 116 U.S. 252, 257-58 (1886); *United States v. Cruikshank*, 92 U.S. 542, 554-55 (1876).

177 See *Cruikshank*, 92 U.S. at 555-56.

178 See *District of Columbia v. Heller*, 554 U.S 5 (and Stevens's dissent, p. 10); *Presser*, 116 U.S. 264-67; *Cruikshank*, 92 U.S. 551-52. The link between military and civil rights is descriptive of other countries as well. On the connection between the armies of the British citizenry and the emergence of a concept of civil rights in England, see Hardy, "Armed Citizens, Citizen Armies," p. 571.

179 The generational argument—used on behalf of a constitutional change that is transgenerational—occurs throughout the Senate testimony and is prominently displayed in the executive summary report. That report observes that the Cox Commission on student protests at Columbia University had "called the present generation 'the most intelligent,' 'the most idealistic,' the 'most sensitive to public issues,' and with a 'higher level of social conscience than preceding generations'" (Senate Committee on the Judiciary, *Report on Lowering the Voting Age to 18*, 5. Rep. No. 26, 92d Cong., 1st Sess. [1971], p. 3). President Nixon is cited as testifying that the country's youth are "better equipped today than ever in the past.... [They exemplify] the highest qualities of mature citizenship." Senator Goldwater called the country's youth "the finest generation that has ever come along." Anthropologist Margaret Mead observed that it is "not only the best educated generation ..., but ..., more mature than young people in the past" (p. 4).

The double location in which the generation is constantly pictured—the terrain of Vietnam and the terrain of the university—underscores the fact that participation both in war and in war protest provided Congress with its evidence. This double location is also stressed in the executive summary for the House deliberations:

As noted, the 91st Congress by extraordinary majorities in each Chamber approved a Federal statute designed in part to lower the minimum voting age to 18 in Federal, State, and local elections. This action expressed a congressional judgment that the education level reached by 18 year olds, *their civic and military obligations and their readiness and capacity to participate in the political process* rendered unreasonable a minimum voting age classification above eighteen.

(House Committee on the Judiciary, *Report on Lowering the Voting Age to 18*, H.R. Rep. NO. 37, 92d Cong., 1st Sess. 5 [1971] [remarks of Rep. Celler]; italics added [hereafter *House Report on Lowering the Voting Age*]).

The bill for lowering the voting age had first been introduced in 1942, and as the Senate executive report noted, had been reintroduced at least once in every successive year, 150 times in total (*Senate Report on Lowering the Voting Age*, pp. 7–8). The timing of the bill—both its passage in 1971 and its original introduction in 1942—illustrates the principle "[o]ld enough to fight, old enough to vote." See *Lowering the Voting Age to 18: Hearings Before the Subcommittee on Constitutional Amendments of the Senate Committee on the Judiciary*, 91st Cong., 2d Sess. 157 (1970) [hereinafter *Senate Hearings on Lowering the Voting Age*] (statement of Sen. Kennedy).

180 *Senate Report on Lowering the Voting Age*, p. 5.

181 Both anthropologist Dr. Margaret Mead and Vice President Agnew credited the speed of physical maturation and strength which, according to Mead, takes place three years earlier than it did in the eighteenth century, and according to the Vice President happens "sooner" than it did fifty years ago (see *Senate Report on Lowering the Voting Age*, p. 5). In the full text of the hearings, the issue of weight is even more explicit—modern eighteen-year-olds can carry their armor:

> Strange as it may seem, the weight of armor in the 11th century governs the right to vote of Americans in the 20th century. The medieval justification has an especially bitter relevance today, when millions of our 18-year-olds are compelled to bear arms as soldiers, and thousands are dead in Vietnam.

(*Senate Hearings on Lowering the Voting Age*, p. 157 [statement of Sen. Kennedy]). The testimony on behalf of lowering the voting age comes from the full political spectrum. Senator Goldwater, like Senator Kennedy, was a strong exponent of the amendment. See *Senate Hearings on Lowering the Voting Age*, pp. 132–33.

182 Conversation with Kenneth Stampp, October 25, 1987.

183 At their nominating convention in Chicago in May 1868, the Republican Party announced the promise of black suffrage in their presidential platform. The language of the promise directly anchored it in the recent bearing of arms: "The guarantee by Congress of equal suffrage to all loyal men at the South was demanded by every consideration of public safety, of gratitude, and of justice" (*Congressional Globe*, 40th Cong., 3d Sess. 691 [1869]).

184 For example, speeches on behalf of the amendment in the House specifically referred to the war: "If the measure proposed by the joint resolution should be approved . . . , that race which stood firm and battled for the Union in the nation's struggle will have a voice in the selection of our rulers" (*Congressional Globe*, 40th Cong., 3d Sess., app. 92 [1869]). The memory of service in the Civil War continued to be enabling at the polls for many decades. In 1901, for example, the newly formed state constitutions of both Alabama and Virginia listed military participation in the Civil War among the factors that fulfilled the "residency" requirement for voting. See Alabama and Virginia Constitutions reprinted in *Documentary History of Reconstruction: Political, Military, Social, Religious, Educational, and Industrial, 1865 to 1906*, vol. 2, ed. W. Fleming (New York: McGraw-Hill, 1966), pp. 453, 454.

For the coupling of military rights and civil rights in World War II, see Chapter 1, "The Inlaying of the Weight of the World."

185 Abraham Lincoln, The [Emancipation] Proclamation, in *The Liberator*, January 2, 1863, reprinted in *The Antislavery Argument*, ed. William H. Pease and Jane H. Pease (Indianapolis: Bobbs-Merrill, 1965), pp. 481, 482.

186 Lincoln's own correspondence enacted this circular logic of distributive rights. For example, in his 1864 letter to Governor Hahn of Louisiana, he privately urged the inclusion of blacks in the "elective franchise," especially "those who have fought gallantly in our ranks" (Letter from Abraham Lincoln to [Louisiana] Governor Hahn [March 13, 1864]," reprinted in Fleming, *Documentary History of Reconstruction*, vol. 1, p. 112)

187 In 1870, for example, the Senate debated whether black Senator-elect Revels met the constitutional requirement that a Senator must have been a citizen for nine years; those opposing his eligibility cited the exclusions of blacks from the militia in some federal and state statutes between 1792 and 1815. See *Congressional Globe*, 41st Cong., 2d Sess. 125–30 (1870). Courts similarly have limited civil rights by associating them with rights of arms. For example, Chief Justice Taney, in arguing in the *Dred Scott* decision against the plaintiff's status as a free person, pointed out that such status would attribute to the plaintiff the power not only to have standing in court, but also to vote and to bear arms (*Scott v. Sandford*, 60 U.S. [19 How.] 393, 415–18, 420 [1857]; see also Stephen P. Halbrook, *That Every Man be Armed: the Evolution of a Constitutional Right* [Oakland, CA: Independent Institute, 1984], pp. 108–23; Kates, "Handgun Prohibition and the Original Meaning of the Second Amendment," p. 216).

188 U.S. Constitution, Amendment 14, section 2; Conversation with Akhil Amar, October 15, 1987.

189 See Hazel MacKaye, "Susan B. Anthony: A Chronicle Pageant," in *The Suffragist*, December 11, 1915, pp. 7, 8; italics added.

190 See George Middleton, *Back of the Ballot* (1915); Alice Duer Miller, *Unauthorised Interviews* (1917); George Rugg, *The New Woman* (1896); Mary Winsor, *A Suffrage Rummage Sale* (1913), reprinted in *On to Victory: Propaganda Plays of the Woman Suffrage Movement*, ed. Bettina Friedl (Boston: Northeastern University Press, 1987), pp. 325, 363, 130, 243.

191 Both the United States and Denmark are mentioned in "War and Freedom," in *The Suffragist*, December 11, 1915, p. 6. In England, suffragists celebrated soldiers such as Boadicea and Joan of Arc in pageant banners and visual displays. See Sharon MacDonald, "Boadicea: Warrior, Mother and Myth," in *Images of Women in Peace and War: Cross-Cultural and Historical Perspectives*, ed. Shirley Ardener, Pat Holden, and Sharon MacDonald (Madison: University of Wisconsin Press, 1987), pp. 40, 55–56. In Russia, the call for women's suffrage during one period of World War I was closely associated with the creation of a battalion of women volunteers to compensate for the alarming number of male desertions. See Anne Wiltsher,

Most Dangerous Women: Feminist Peace Campaigners of the Great War (London: Pandora Press, 1985), pp. 176–81. Crucial in all these examples is the conflation of a civil right such as voting with possession of authority in military affairs. That voice may be on the side of militarism or instead on the side of pacifism, as in the Puget Sound Project, Greenham Common, and the Seneca Women's Encampment against nuclear weapons.

192 The National Organization of Women, for example, argued this in their report before the 1980 House Hearings on the Draft: "Those who oppose the registration and draft for females say they seek to protect women. But omission from the registration and draft ultimately robs women of the right to first class citizenship. Moreover, because men exclude women here, they justify excluding women from the decision-making of our nation. (*Judiciary Implications of Draft Registration: Hearings before the Subcomm. on Courts, Civil Liberties, and the Administration of Justice of the House Comm. on the Judiciary,* 96th Cong., 2d Sess. 157, 155–68 [1980]).

In his 1869 essay, "The Subjection of Women," John Stuart Mill repeatedly affirmed the ties between civil liberty and military responsibility:

To Englishmen [being governed by a Queen] does not seem in the least degree unnatural, because they are used to it; but they do feel it unnatural that women should be soldiers or members of Parliament. In the feudal ages, on the contrary, war and politics were not thought unnatural to women, because [they were] not unusual.... There can be little doubt that Spartan experience [of bodily exercise and training for women] suggested to Plato... the social and political equality of the two sexes.

("The Subjection of Women," in *Essays on Equality, Law, and Education by John Stuart Mill* ed. J.M.M. Robson [Toronto: University of Toronto Press, 1984], p. 270).

Today, women constitute 19 percent of the Air force, 17 percent of the Navy, 13 percent of the Army, and 7 percent of Marines. No women serve as SEALs or on attack submarines. Until June of 2011, no women were permitted to serve on Ohio-class submarines; eighteen women are now serving there (Lolita Baldor, "SEALs: No Women Need Apply—Yet," *Washington Post,* June 1, 2011, p. B4). As of January 2013, the Pentagon has set out to rescind the 1994 ban on women serving in combat ("Direct Combat Exclusion Rule"), a ban that excludes women from 237,000 Army, Navy, Air Force and Marine positions, all of which are now under review. The year 2016 is the target date for achieving gender equality in the military (Spencer Ackerman, "Here's How the Military Will Finally Accept [Most] Women in Combat," *Wired,* January 24, 2013; and Julian E. Barnes and Dion Nissenbaum, "Combat Ban for Women to End," *Wall Street Journal,* January 24, 2013).

193 Elaine Scarry, "Separate Is Unequal for Gays, Too," *Los Angeles Times,* February 16, 1993. In December 1993 the prohibition on gays serving in the military was repealed but a "Don't Ask Don't Tell" policy was implemented. In December 2010, Congress passed a law repealing "Don't Ask Don't Tell," thereby making it

legal for gays to serve openly. Those pressing for open service for gays and repeal of "Don't Ask Don't Tell" identified military service as a "civil right," even "the last civil rights issue we have" (see speech of Ms. Tausher in *Don't Ask Don't Tell Review: Hearing before the Military Personnel Subcommittee of the Committee on Armed Services*, House of Representatives, 110th Cong., 2d sess., 23 July 2208, p. 30). Comparisons were often made to the achievement of equal rights by African Americans and by women.

Those opposing the open service of gays in the military, however, used "rights" language against gays; for example, freedom of expression (particularly the case of chaplains wishing to express disapproval of homosexuality) surfaced repeatedly to suggest that gay rights and the First Amendment were in opposition (see *The Report of the Department of Defense Working Group that Conducted a Comprehensive Review of the Issues Associated with Repeal of Section 654 of Title 10, USC, Policy Concerning Homosexuality in the Armed Services*, United States Senate, 2d Sess., 2–3 December 2010, pp. 180, 218, 297, 441; and *Repeal of Law and Policies Governing Service by Openly Gay and Lesbian Service Members*, Committee on Armed Services, House of Representatives, 112th Cong., 1st Sess., April 11, 2011, pp. 69, 72, 73). At least one case in the lower courts against Don't Ask Don't Tell—opposing service by gays altogether—was won on First and Fifth Amendment grounds (*Department of Defense Working Group*, pp. 193–94).

194 Baker v. Carr, 369 U.S. 186, 197 (1962), citing Baker v. Carr, 179 F. Supp. 824, 826 (1959).

195 The argument that follows summarizes the relation between war making and constitution making specifically within the U.S. Constitution; but the connections are much broader as we see in Chapters 3 and 4 on Thomas Hobbes and the social contract.

196 See U.S. Constitution, Article V (establishing that proposed amendments may originate either in the Congress or among the population through two-thirds of the state legislatures).

197 Prescott, *Madison Rearranged*, pp. 513–14.

198 The Declaration of Independence para. 2 (U.S. 1776). On the adjective "manly" prefixed to the word "firmness," see notes 119–21, above.

199 Schwartz, *The Bill of Rights*, vol. 2, p. 771; italics added.

200 Schwartz, *The Bill of Rights*, vol. 2, p. 781; italics added.

201 For example, the idiom of internalization is audible in the Massachusetts debate when General Thompson, protesting the absence of a Bill of Rights, speaks of ratification as the "swallowing" and "digesting" of an only partly ingestible document (Schwartz, *The Bill of Rights*, vol. 2, p. 683). The idiom reappears in South Carolina's debate in which Mr. Dollard speaks of the refusal to ratify as provoking the standing army to "ram it down their throats" (Schwartz, *The Bill of Rights*, vol. 2, p. 753).

202 Schwartz, *The Bill of Rights*, vol. 2, p. 823.

203 Schwartz, *The Bill of Rights*, vol. 2, p. 809; see also p. 813.

204 Schwartz, *The Bill of Rights*, vol. 2, p. 821.

205 Schwartz, *The Bill of Rights*, vol. 2, p. 829; see also note 56, above.

206 Schwartz, *The Bill of Rights*, vol. 2, p. 818.

207 Schwartz, *The Bill of Rights*, vol. 2, p. 827. When the amendments were eventually passed, Patrick Henry and Richard Henry Lee believed that the final document still insufficiently protected the population against presidential concentration of power and a standing army. Significantly, both continued to express their reservations in terms of the document's lack of materialization. In a letter, Patrick Henry writes to Lee: "For Rights, without having power & might is but a *shadow*." See *Patrick Henry: Life, Correspondence and Speeches,* ed. William Wirt Henry (New York: Charles Scribner's Sons, 1891), vol. 3, p. 398; italics added. Lee responds: "Your observation is perfectly just.... [T]he English language has been carefully culled to find words *feeble* in their nature...."(p. 402; italics added).

208 Metaphorical use of parts of the body becomes even more literal when describing war. On the use of the body for substantiating issues of war, see Elaine Scarry, *The Body in Pain*, pp. 119–21; 124–39; 143–48; 350, n.138.

209 See Dellinger, "The Legitimacy of Constitutional Change: Rethinking the Amendment Process," *Harvard Law Review* 97 (1983), p. 427. Because amending the Constitution through Article V is so cumbersome, the claim is sometimes made that the Constitution prohibits ongoing consent, subjecting those in the present to the will of the past. But, as argued earlier, by demanding the first ten amendments, the ratifying assemblies transformed threshold consent into perpetual consent (see in this chapter the section entitled "Distribution, Ratification, and the Bill of Rights"). On the reconcilability of democracy and the Constitution, see Stephen Holmes, "Precommitment and the Paradox of Democracy," in *Constitutionalism and Democracy*, ed. Jon Elster and Rune Slagstad (Cambridge: Cambridge University Press, 1988), p. 195, 244. Holmes argues that "imaginative interpretation" by each successive generation is a supplementary way of amending the Constitution. See also Akhil Amar, who describes methods of amending the Constitution outside Article V through the direct actions of the population in "Philadelphia Revisited," pp. 1051–58, 1089–99.

210 Hamilton and Madison both applied the language of "solidity" or "substance" to the population's ratification. See Hamilton, *The Federalist No. 22*, p. 152, and Madison, *The Federalist No. 40*, pp. 252–53.

211 That a population "authorizes" the infliction of injury does not mean necessarily that their actions are "justified." Authorization and justification entail two distinct sets of requirements. Nevertheless, a claim that the waging of a particular war is "justified" must fail in a contractual society if the population has not authorized the war. In this sense, authorization logically precedes justification, even though experientially the chronology may be reversed: to secure the population's authorization, a government may have to begin by identifying the justifying conditions.

The relation of the two terms was clarified for me by a conversation with Stephen Knapp in Berkeley, California, November 19, 1987.

212 Sumner, *An Inquiry into the Importance of the Militia*, p. 21; italics added.

213 Sumner, *An Inquiry into the Importance of the Militia*, p. 37.

214 This is a final instance of the deep structural continuity between constitution making and war making; the right to bear arms contains the right of revolution. Similarly, as Walter Dellinger has argued persuasively, Article V's provision for constitutional amendment represents the right of revolution built into the contract. See Dellinger, "The Legitimacy of Constitutional Change," p. 431.

A PRELUDE AND SUMMARY FOR PART TWO

1 P. Alan Robock, Luke Oman, and Georgiy L. Stenchikov, "Nuclear Winter Revisited with a Modern Climate Model and Current Nuclear Arsenals: Still Catastrophic Consequences," *Journal of Geophysical Research* 112 (July 2007): 3, 5, 6, 9. A drop of temperature worldwide of 12°F to 14°F means that over some large landmasses such as Eurasia and North America the temperatures are freezing in both winter and summer (since the worldwide average includes the temperature over oceans, where the effects are more moderate). The qualities of nuclear winter resulting from the arsenal available in the 1980s are summarized by Carl Sagan, Vladimir Alexandrov, Paul Ehrlich, and Alexander Pavlov, "Nuclear Winter: The World-Wide Consequences of Nuclear War," *UNESCO Courier* 38, no. 5 (May 1985): 26, 28, 29, 30. Recent research on nuclear winter (using more sophisticated modeling) adjusts the original predictions made in the 1980s and shows that those original predictions understate how long the earth will be dark (a period close to ten years) and overstate oxygen loss and temperature drop (which, though still lethal, will be less extreme). This new work shows that even a small regional conflict—the studies posit an exchange between India and Pakistan of fifty weapons 15 kilotons in size—will result at once in 44 million casualties and 1 billion deaths worldwide from starvation in the months following (Owen Toon, Alan Robock, and Richard P. Turco, "Environmental Consequences of Nuclear War," *Physics Today*, December 2008). A 2°F drop in temperature throughout the Northern Hemisphere, in combination with the lack of sunlight and rain, will shorten the growing season by thirty days, preventing crops from reaching maturity (A. Robock, L. Oman, G. L. Stenchikov, O.B. Toon, C. Bardeen, and R. P. Turco, "Climatic Consequences of Regional Nuclear Conflicts," *Atmospheric Chemistry and Physics*, April 19, 2007). This article specifies that one hundred Hiroshima-size bombs are "less than 0.03% of the explosive yield of the current global nuclear arsenal" (hence the exchange of fifty such weapons examined in the *Physics Today* article would be 0.015 percent of our total arsenal). The new work also shows that the scale of the ozone losses will be greater than predicted earlier (Michael J. Mills, Owen B. Toon, et al., "Massive Global Ozone Loss Predicted Following Regional Nuclear Conflict," *Proceedings of the National Academy of Science* 1–5, no. 14 [April 8, 2008]: 5307–12). The scientists carrying out

this work stress the need for abolition of weapons (beginning with those possessed by the United States and Russia) and lament the inattention to nuclear winter by twenty-first-century governments and unclassified research (see Alan Robock and Owen Brian Toon, "Local Nuclear War, Global Suffering," *Scientific American*, January 2010; and Steven Starr, "The Climatic Consequences of Nuclear War," *Bulletin of Atomic Scientists*, March 12, 2010).

2 "Dissenting Opinion of Judge Weeramantry," International Court of Justice, July 8, 1996, p. 83 (cited earlier in Introduction, "The Floor of the World").

3 On the relevance of "luck" to moral life, see philosophers Bernard Williams, "Moral Luck" in *Moral Luck* (Cambridge, U.K.: Cambridge University Press, 1981), pp. 20–39: and Thomas Nagel, "Moral Luck" in *Mortal Questions* (Cambridge, U.K..: Cambridge University Press, 1979), pp. 24–38.

4 Bruno Tertrais, "The Last to Disarm? The Future of France's Nuclear Weapons," *Nonproliferation Review* 14, no. 2 (2007), p. 258.

5 Such as Decree No. 64–46 (January 14, 1964) and Decree No. 96-520 (June 12, 1996) confining authority to engage nuclear forces to the president alone. See Born, "National Governance of Nuclear Weapons," p. 9; Tertrais, "The Last to Disarm?", p. 257; and George Nolte, ed., *European Military Law Systems* (Berlin: De Gruyter Rechtswissenschaften Verlags, 2003), p. 292. Although as in other atomic-age democracies the requirement for a legislative authorization of war has been allowed to deteriorate, Jörg Gerkrath in the Nolte volume calls attention to a 1993 proposal by the Vedel Committee to strengthen Article 35 by amending it to require a parliamentary declaration of war for any military intervention outside French borders (p. 294).

6 The "Subject Matter" of Article 246 is enumerated in a document that accompanies the constitution, the Seventh Schedule, List I, numbers 1, 2, and 2A. India's Constitution also includes environmental clauses on the obligation to protect wild animals, birds, and forests (Article 48A; Schedule 7, clauses 17, 17A, 17B; Schedule 12, clause 8) that may contribute to an elimination of the country's nuclear weapons. Like the Swiss concern for the protection of the country's cultural heritage, the Indian Constitution lists a positive duty "to value and preserve the rich heritage of our composite culture" (Part IV A, Article 51A).

Like many constitutions written after the invention of atomic weapons, the Indian Constitution includes "emergency" provisions (Part XVIII) that potentially subvert other clauses in times of national crisis. In his study of constitutional dictatorship, Clinton Rossiter reminds us that although these emergency clauses have become frequent in the nuclear age, they also antedate the era: Rossiter analyses at length the emergency clause of Germany's Weimar Constitution that made possible Hitler's rise to power and unfettered executive power. For a rich comparative analysis of emergency provisions in a range of constitutions, see Bruce Ackerman's article in which he singles out the Canadian and South African constitutions as having the best safeguards ("The Emergency Constitution," *Yale Law Journal*

113, no. 5 [March 2004]: 1029–91). More convincing, however, is Laurence Tribe and Patrick O. Gudridge's response to Bruce Ackerman arguing that any such emergency article—no matter how loaded with safeguards—carries a high risk of destroying the constitution ("The Anti-Emergency Constitution," *Yale Law Journal* 113, no. 8 [June 2004]).

7 Not all eight of the nuclear states have explicit constitutional provisions that make the legislature or the population a brake on the urge to go to war. But countries that lack such provisions have in recent years sometimes voiced the need to acquire one. In the United Kingdom, for example, proposals to require a parliamentary declaration of war prior to taking British troops into battle have been introduced at regular intervals in the first decade of the twenty-first century (see, e.g., the House of Commons Public Administration Report, HC 422 of 2004, saying Parliament's authorization of war should be required; and Clare Short, "Bill Requiring Parliament's Approval for Declaration of War and Dispatch of Troops," June 22, 2005). In Pakistan, although the constitution has no provision stipulating which branch of the government declares war, the April 2010 passage of the Eighteenth Amendment strengthened the legislative and judicial branches and diminished the power of the presidency (State Department Press Release, "Background Notes: Pakistan," June 11, 2010).

8 Donnie Williams with Wayne Greenhaw, *The Thunder of Angels: The Montgomery Bus Boycott and the People Who Broke the Back of Jim Crow* (Chicago: Lawrence Hill Books, 2006), p. 48.

9 Among the few people who actively dissent to nuclear weapons are retired missile officers, retired generals, retired secretaries of state, and retired secretaries of defense. Because their consent was needed in the chain of command, their power to consent or dissent has not wholly atrophied and they can occasionally appear in public and voice their dissent to a population they helped to disenfranchise, many of whom can now not even recognize what they are talking about. A 2011 example is the quartet called "the Four Horsemen"—Henry Kissinger, George Shultz, William Perry, and Sam Nunn—who have joined the move for "Global Zero" and have attempted to reawaken the public to the severe dangers the world now faces from nuclear weapons. In describing their actions, some newspapers and journals differentiate their "important" dissent from the "unimportant" dissent of ordinary citizens—as when the *Economist* writes, "Suddenly Global Zero was able to recruit people who were a far cry from the old 'ban the bomb' crowd" (*The Economist*, June 18, 2011, p. 69). The deterioration of the national fabric is in nothing so visible as in the belief that dissent only has "authority" if it is voiced by someone who helped to invent nuclear weapons or who was once in a military or governmental position to fire the weapon. The millions of people who stand to be injured have no voice and soon give up speaking, as occurred in the 1995 case at the International Court of Justice, described in "The Floor of the World." As we saw in the legislative

histories of the fifteenth, nineteenth, and twenty-sixth Amendments, civic stature is achieved through military stature; and, conversely, once a population is excluded from military operations and knowledge, they lose their civic voice as well. Needless to say, the disarmament work carried out by people like nuclear scientist Robert Oppenheimer, former Minuteman ICBM launch control officer Bruce Blair, U.S. Pacific Command officer Noel Gayler, or by the Four Horsemen is crucial during the period when the population has been silenced.

10 Robert Patterson, *Dereliction of Duty: Eyewitness Account of How Bill Clinton Compromised America's National Security* (Washington, DC: Regnery Press, 2004), p. 57. This detail at first sounds startling, even obscene; but where exactly should a president carry the card? On a chain around his neck? On the underside of his necktie? The problem resides in the arrangement for presidential use, not in the choice the individual president makes about where on his person he keeps the card, which merely makes the problem graphically visible.

11 General (Ret.) Hugh Shelton, *Without Hesitation: The Odyssey of an American Warrior* (New York: St. Martin's Press, 2010), pp. 174–75.

12 Nicholas Eberstadt, "Demographic Shocks in Eastern Germany, 1989–93," *Europe-Asia Studies* 46, no. 3 (1994): 520.

13 Eberstadt, "Demographic Shocks," p. 527. The total number of marriages in 1989 was 131,000 and in 1992 was 48,000. In 1989, 8 people per 1000 chose to get married and in 1992, 3 people per 1000 (Eberstadt, "Demographic Shocks," p. 526, Table 2).

14 Eberstadt summarized in James C. Witte and Gert G. Wagner, "Declining Fertility in East Germany After Unification: A Demographic Response to Socio-Economic Change," *Population and Development Review* 21, no. 2 (June 1995): 388. Eberstadt says that for industrialized populations, one can only find equally dramatic changes if one goes to the smaller unit of the city. Thus Berlin's "birth rate fell by 52% between 1942 and 1946" (Eberstadt, p. 521).

15 Television interview transcribed in *Le Monde*, April 30, 1979, reprinted in "President Giscard d'Estaing on Fertility Decline in France," *Population and Development Review* 5, no. 3 (September 1979): 571–73.

16 Resolution reprinted in "The European Parliament on the Need for Promoting Population Growth," *Population and Development Review* 10, no. 3 (September 1984). More recently, a 2010 debate about the costs and benefits of eighteen to twenty weeks of maternity leave and two weeks of paternity leave included references to the beneficial effect on fertility rates ("Costs and Benefits of Maternity and Paternity Leave," European Parliament, Press Release, October 11, 2010). The Romanian birth figures come from the document "Romanian Population Policy," *Population and Development Review* 10, no. 3 (September 1984); p. 570.

17 Robert McNamara, "Apocalypse Soon," *Foreign Policy*, May 5, 2005.

CHAPTER 3: THE SOCIAL CONTRACT IS A COVENANT FOR PEACE

1 The Greek, Roman, and medieval backgrounds become visible at various points in this chapter. For the influence of Hebrew writings, see Eric Nelson, *The Hebrew Republic: Jewish Sources and the Transformation of European Political Thought* (Cambridge, MA: Harvard University Press, 2010).

2 Thomas Hobbes, *Leviathan*, ed. and introd. C. B. Macpherson (London: Penguin, 1968, 1985), ch. 14, p. 191.

3 Thomas Hobbes, *On the Citizen*, trans. and ed. Richard Tuck and Michael Silverthorne (Cambridge: Cambridge University Press, 1998), p. 44. Injury and injustice are almost synonyms, as Hobbes's first quotation indicates. Tuck translates the latin "iniuria" in this second passage as "wrong" (or injustice) whereas I retain "injury," as did the 1651 English translation (long thought to be Hobbes's own) and as did Hobbes's nineteenth-century editor, Molesworth.

4 Thomas Hobbes, *De Corpore Politico or The Elements of Law*, in *The English Works of Thomas Hobbes of Malmesbury*, ed. William Molesworth (London: John Bohn, 1811), vol. 4, ch. 3, pp. 95, 96.

5 John Locke, *Second Treatise of Government*, ed. and introd. C. B. Macpherson (Indianapolis, IN: Hackett, 1980), p. 52.

6 Locke, *Second Treatise of Government*, pp. 115, 116.

7 Locke, *Second Treatise of Government*, p. 10; see also pp. 15, 16.

8 Henry Richard Fox Bourne, *The Life of John Locke* (1876; rpt. Darmstadt: Scientia Verlag Aalen, 1969), vol. 1, p. 446. See also Maurice Cranston, "The Physician," in *John Locke: A Biography* (London: Longmans, Green and Co., 1957), pp. 88–105.

9 Ralph H. Major, *Classic Descriptions of Disease: With Biographical Sketches of the Authors*, 3rd ed. (Springfield, II: Charles C. Thomas, 1945), p. 194.

10 Kenneth Dewhurst, "Sydenham on 'A Dysentry,'" in *Bulletin of the History of Medicine* 29 (1955): 393–95.

11 Cranston, *John Locke: A Biography*, p. 117.

12 See Sydenham's 1674 letter to Locke, reprinted in Kenneth Dewhurst, "Sydenham's Letters to John Locke," *The Practitioner* (1955): 315.

13 See Locke's 1675 letter to Sydenham, reprinted in Dewhurst, "Sydenham's Letters to John Locke," p. 316. See Chapter 5, note 10.

14 Kenneth Dewhurst, "The Genesis of State Medicine in Ireland," *Irish Journal of Medical Science* (August 1956): 365–67, 379–81.

15 Hobbes, *Leviathan*, ch. 17, p. 223.

16 Hobbes, *Leviathan*, ch. 13, p. 188.

17 Hobbes, *On the Citizen*, p. 108.

18 Hobbes, *On the Citizen*, p. 69. As astonishing as it may seem, some of the twentieth-century misidentification of Hobbes as an exponent of brutal international realism comes from quoting the term "laws of Nature" as though it meant "state of Nature."

19 Hobbes, *Leviathan*, ch. 14, p. 190.

20 Hobbes, *Leviathan*, ch. 15, p. 209.

21 Hobbes, *Leviathan*, ch. 15, p. 210.

22 Hobbes, *Man and Citizen (De Homine and De Cive)*, ed. and introd. Bernard Gert (Indianapolis: Hackett, 1991), p. 28.

23 Donald W. Hanson, "Thomas Hobbes's 'Highway to Peace,'" *International Organization* 38, no. 2 (Spring 1984): 329–354. The striking description of a social contract as "a highway to peace" is drawn from the English translation of *De Cive* that was long regarded (mistakenly, according to Richard Tuck) as Hobbes's own; this is the translation in the Gert edition cited in the previous note. Tuck's translation of this phrase is "the royal road to peace," which accords with the original Latin, *pacis via regia* (*Elementa Philosophica de Cive* [Amsterodami, Henr. & Viduam Th. Boom, 1642], [pages unnumbered]). *Via Regia* is the title of a book on the art of governance that Charlemagne asked Abbot Smaragdus to prepare in the early ninth century (Olaf Pedersen, *The First Universities: Studium Generale and the Origins of University Education in Europe*, trans. Richard North [Cambridge: Cambridge University Press, 1997, 2007], p. 87). According to Christoph Ernst Luthardt, who says the book is dedicated not to Charlemagne but to Louis the Pious, the book's recommendations to the king about achieving justice include the advice that he "should be anxious for the manusmission of the serfs in his kingdom, as we are all created equal by nature" (*History of Christian Ethics*, trans. W. Hastie [Edinburgh: T. & T. Clark, 1889], p. 302). Via Regia is also the name of a literal highway running between eastern and western Europe: estimates about the century in which it was first built vary greatly (from 1 BCE or earlier to eight or ninth century CE); the first written mention of it is thirteenth century CE. In England, the idea of the via regia has antecedents in Bede, but comes to the fore in the early twelfth-century writings of Henry of Huntingdon, after which it enters many legal treatises (beginning with *Leges Edwardi*) and literary accounts by Geoffrey of Monmouth and Havelok the Dane. The idea of the King's Four Highways, two of which run north-south and two east-west, is elaborately bound up with the guarantee of peace on those roads (see Alan Cooper, "The King's Four Highways," *Journal of Medieval History* 26, no. 4 [2000]: 351–70; and Robert Allen Rouse, *The Idea of Anglo-Saxon England in Middle English Romance* [Cambridge, U.K.: D. S. Brewer, 2005], pp. 100–126).

24 Hobbes, *Leviathan*, ch. 15, p. 211.

25 Hobbes, *On the* Citizen, ed. Tuck, p. 50.

26 Hobbes, *Leviathan*, ch. 15, p. 212.

27 Gottfried Wilhelm Leibniz, "To that distinguished man, Thomas Hobbes," (1674?), Letter 195, in *The Correspondence of Thomas Hobbes*, vol. II: 1600–1679, ed. Noel Malcolm (Oxford: Clarendon, 1994), pp. 731–35.

28 "François Peleau to Hobbes, from Bordeaux," Letter 90 (18/28 August 1656), in *Correspondence of Thomas Hobbes*, vol. I: 1622–1659, p. 300.

29 Hobbes observed, for example, that our equal will to live also gives us an equality of hope.

30 I found, several months after first writing this paragraph, that Hedley Bull had anticipated me by forty years in seeing the association between Hobbes's conception of equality and the ubiquity of nuclear weapons which make equal all the people of the world (*The Anarchical Society*, introd. Stanley Hoffman [New York: Columbia University Press, 1995; 1st ed. 1977], p. 48).

31 Jason Fritz, "Hacking Nuclear Command and Control," 2009 Report for the International Commission on Nuclear Nonproliferation and Disarmament (Barton, Australia and Tokyo, Japan, 2008–2010), p. 18. The central role of hacking in current and future wars is also described by Richard A. Clarke and Robert Knake, *Cyber War: The Next Threat to National Security and What to Do about It* (New York: Harper Collins, 2010).

32 Someone who believes that state superpowers have enduringly superior injuring force might point out that the cyber weapons invented by states—such as the 2009–10 digital worm that subverted the Iranian uranium enrichment plant—greatly surpass in sophistication those invented by solitary hackers. But the malware team that invented the Stuxnet weapon may not involve a higher number of persons than the transnational and state-independent team of five or six people who rapidly deciphered it (Kim Zetter, "How Digital Detectives Deciphered Stuxnet, the Most Menacing Malware in History," *Wired*, July 11, 2011).

33 Cited in Fritz, "Hacking Nuclear Command and Control," p. 18.

34 CNN, "Teen Charged with Hacking into Air Force System," April 24, 2001. The boy "hacked into the secure connection between the Air Mobility Command System at Scott Air Force Base in Belleville, Illinois and US Department of Transportation computer system at the Volpe Center in Cambridge, Massachusetts"; he also "ran a program that destroyed the electronic data files that recorded his presence on the system."

35 BBC, "Iraq Rebels 'Hack' into US Drones," December 17, 2009.

36 In response to the threat that a U.S. nuclear missile might be launched by a hacker, the nation's missiles are now preprogrammed during peacetime to land in the open ocean. The April 2010 *Nuclear Posture Review* refers to this "open ocean targeting" under President Obama as a "continuing" policy that began in 1994 during the Clinton administration (pp. 16, 48, 49). In the past our missiles on alert had the longitude and latitude of particular cities and military sites programmed into them. This shift in targeting (while inspired by hypothetical hackers) is something to celebrate. There is, however, nothing to stop the next presidential administration from reverting to the prior form of targeting. Nor do we have any reason to be confident that under the current policy *every* one of our missiles is at *all* times free of land-based targeting coordinates. A far safer way to address the threat of hacking would be to eliminate the preprogrammed targeting altogether, and decouple the missiles from their delivery vehicles, as is true in some nuclear states.

37 A. Robock et al., "Climatic Consequences of regional nuclear conflicts," *Atmospheric Chemistry and Physics*, April 19, 2007, p. 53.

38 The only inequality he tolerates is to give to oneself *less* than is given to others. Hobbes, *On the Citizen*, ed. Tuck, p. 50.

39 Hobbes, *Leviathan*, p. 213. See also pp. 209–15 passim.

40 Hobbes, *Leviathan*, pp. 237, 245, 297, 376.

41 For example, Hobbes, *On the Citizen*, ed. Tuck, pp. 9, 12, 80 (three times), 82, 84, 86, 88 (twice), etc.

42 Hobbes, *A Dialogue between a Philosopher and a Student of the Common Laws of England*, ed. Joseph Cropsey (Chicago: University of Chicago Press, 1971), pp. 59, 66, 71, 73, 141, 161.

43 Jean Hampton, *Hobbes and the Social Contract Tradition* (Cambridge: Cambridge University Press, 1986), p. 5. Richard Tuck's *Hobbes: A Very Short Introduction* (Oxford: Oxford University Press, 1989, 2002) brought me into contact with Hampton's work as well as that of Mario Cattaneo, cited later.

44 Hobbes, *The Life of Mr. Thomas Hobbes of Malmesbury, Written by Himself in a Latine Poem, and now Translated into English* (London: Andrew Cooke, 1680, reprinted Exeter: The Rota, 1979), pp. 1, ll. 1–8.

45 Hobbes, *The Life of Mr. Thomas Hobbes of Malmesbury*, pp. 2, ll. 25–28.

46 John Aubrey, *Aubrey's Brief Lives*, ed. Oliver Lawson Dick, frwd. Edmund Wilson (Boston: David R. Godine, 1999), pp. 157, 158.

47 Aubrey, *Aubrey's Brief Lives*, pp. 149, 150. This physical absence does not exclude a physical connection to the geography; the first poem Hobbes wrote (not on Wiltshire but on Darbyshire) shows how absorbed he was by geography, both surface and subterranean. (And his friend John Aubrey knew the soil, stones, small shells, ferns, butter flowers, meadow grasses, holly bushes, witch hazel, and oak trees of Malmesbury and surrounding Wiltshire in intricate detail, as his *Natural History of Wiltshire* confirms on every page.) But it seems far more likely, as I argue below, that it is the municipality and contracts and parliamentary and monarchic crossroads that elicited from Hobbes this devoted affiliation.

48 For example, the BBC online history specifies Malmesbury as the oldest town and specifies the King Alfred charter. This charter, however, seems to grant land not to a group of townsmen but to one "faithful *minister*, Dudig by name" (S 356, in S. E. Kelly, *Anglo-Saxon Charters II, Charters of Malmesbury Abbey* [Oxford: Oxford University Press for The British Academy, 2005], pp. 194–95, no. 20. Translation by David A. E. Pelteret at http://www.trin.cam.ac.uk/kemble/pelteret/Malm/Malm 20.htm).

49 S 454 in Kelly, *Charters of Malmesbury Abbey*, p. 291, no. 48; italics added; Trans. Pelteret.

50 D. A. Crowley, ed., A. P. Baggs, Jane Freeman, Janet H. Stevenson, *A History of the County of Wiltshire: Volume 14: Malmesbury Hundred*, 1991 (hereinafter *A History of The County of Wiltshire: Malmesbury*) available at British History Online: http://www.british-history.ac.uk/report.aspx?compid=116149#s12. These details

about the 1635 charter are dispersed throughout the article and can be found at footnotes 546, 559, 581, 587.

51 Kelly, *Charters of Malmesbury Abbey*, p. 292.

52 Kelly counts twenty-one Malmesbury Abbey charters "purporting to come from" the seventh, eighth, and ninth centuries and notes that only one other West Saxon archive (Glastonbury) has this wealth of material (*Charters of Malmesbury Abbey*, p. 1).

53 William of Malmesbury says that Æthelstan had four sisters whose suitors brought him astonishing jewels and artifacts, which he later bestowed on other kings, reserving the most precious gifts for Malmesbury: a piece of "the adorable cross enclosed in crystal; where the eye, piercing though the substance of the stone, might discern the colour and size of the wood; [and] a small portion of the crown of thorns, enclosed in a similar manner" (William of Malmesbury, *Chronicle of the Kings of England from the Earliest Period to the Reign of King Stephen*, ed. J. A. Giles [London: Henry G. Bohn, 1847, Kessinger Legacy Reprints], p. 136).

54 According to *A History of the County of Wiltshire*, Malmesbury's representatives had attended "74 parliaments before 1449," making it the fourth most frequently represented borough in Wiltshire.

55 Hobbes, *The Life of Mr. Thomas Hobbes of Malmesbury*, pp. 1, 2, l. 11–20.

56 The Malmesbury designation occurs on the title pages of the published writings. One unpublished manuscript on optics—"A Minute or First Draught of the OPTIQUES"—announces that the work is "by Thomas Hobbes at Paris 1646" (London, British Library, MS Harley 3360, f.ir.). The preposition "at" in "at Paris" suggest physical location at the time of composition, whereas "of Malmesbury" suggest abiding identification.

57 The tenth-century Wessex document, Burghal Hidage, specifies that Malmesbury had a wall 4950 feet in length (Kelly, *Charters of Malmesbury Abbey*, p. 18). A thirteenth-century document "lists obligations to repair 26 sections of the town's wall, presumably its whole length. Those required to repair the wall . . . were apparently the owners of the plots in the borough adjoining the respective sections" (Crowley et al., *A History of the County of Wiltshire: Malmesbury*, drawing on *Rotuli Chartarum: 1199–1216* [Charter Rolls], ed. Thomas Duffus Hardy [Record Commission, 1837], pp. 213, 222). According to Oliver Creighton, of 719 towns in medieval Britain, 230 of them had either stone walls or at least a circuit of ditch; this is a much lower proportion than towns on the European continent. In comparison to the richly studied European walled cities, British walled cities are greatly understudied. ("'Castles of Communities': Medieval Town Defences in England; Wales and Gascony," [*Château Gaillard: Etudes de castellologie médiévale* 22 (Caen: Publications du Crahm, 2006], pp. 75, 77).

58 John Speed, *The Theatre of the Empire of Great Britaine: Presenting an Exact Geography of the Kingdomes of England, Scotland, Ireland, and the Isles Adioyning: with the Shires, Hundreds, Cities, and Shire-Townes, within ye Kingdome of England,*

Divided and Described by John Speed (London: John Sudbury & George Humble, 1611). Viewable at http://faculty.oxy.edu/horowitz/home/johnspeed/Cities1.htm.

59 Among John Speed's maps, none of the towns are located on a promontory. In two cases—the cities of Kendal and Lancaster—a fortress located *outside the town* resides on a prominent hill. In contrast to the absence of hilltop locations, many of Speed's maps show a river, in one case—Norwich—almost encircling the city, and in two other cases—Chester and York—framing most of the town on three sides.

60 The painting—reproduced here from a high resolution copy sent to me by the Warden and Freemen of Malmesbury—is one I first encountered when reading a report by the North Wiltshire District Council, *Malmesbury Conservation Area Appraisal* (April 2007), p. 10. In tracking down the provenance of the painting, Hobbes's own interest in aerial views of towns should be taken into consideration, as should the fact that Aubrey in the appendix to *The Natural History of Wiltshire* ("Draughts of the Seates and Prospects" [Boston: IndyPublish, n.d.]), lists the paintings or engravings he would like to have made for the book, one of which is the following: "Prospect of Malmesbury Abbey; and also of the Town, and a Mappe of the Town.—Mr. Wharton, &c.-Sir James Long. (Take the true latitude and longitude of Malmesbury.)" Because the provenance of the painting is unknown, it is not impossible that (like some of the Malmesbury social contracts) it will turn out to be of later manufacture than the date specified on its surface.

61 Wiltshire County Archaeology Service, *The Archeology of Wiltshire's Towns: An Extensive Urban Survey: Malmesbury* (Trowbridge, England: August 2004), p. 4, section 3.2.2. This report specifies the orientation of the painting and indicates that it was painted in 1648. The writing on the front of the painting indicates that it depicts the city as it was on October 23, 1646, after the civil war had begun but just before the fortified walls were destroyed.

62 The market cross visible in the painting (a Malmesbury landmark almost as well known as the abbey) would be just below the horizontal line of the Leviathan grid that cuts the title page in two. Much clearer images of Figures 1–5 can be seen at www.pbase.com/hobbes; and I am deeply grateful to Patricia Scarry Jones for her work on the images.

63 The possibility that the painted town and the frontispiece town are views from opposing compass points can be appreciated by holding the frontispiece upside down: many of the architectural features of the painting and frontispiece then reside in the same spatial locations.

If the Leviathan in the frontispiece is indeed standing in the same position as the viewer stands in the 1648 painting—that is, in the southwest—it explains why we see in the distance beneath his left hand the sea and sailing ships. Malmesbury is just twenty-three miles from the port of Bristol which lies to the southwest. That is why Hobbes's mother was so alarmed by reports of the Spanish Armada. Though the eventual path of the Armada did not take it to Bristol, the residents of that city were elaborately engaged in the lead up to that event. Conceivably, the ships behind the Leviathan allude to the Spanish Armada, or instead to the three ships that Bristol contributed to the Royal Navy's defense against the Armada, or even to the many Bristol merchant ships that earlier carried war supplies to Spain and thus inadvertently contributed to the Armada's preparation (see Jean Vanes, *Bristol at the Time of the Spanish Armada, Local History Pamphlets*, no. 69, Bristol Historical Association, pp. 17, 18, 19, 21ff.). Given the Leviathan's peaceful countenance, however, it is more likely that the ships allude to the "Navigation" and "use of the commodities that may be imported by Sea" that, along with the other institutions of civilization, depend for their existence on the social contract (*Leviathan*, ed. Macpherson, p. 186).

64 Margery Corbett and Ronald Lightbown, *The Comely Frontispiece, The Emblematic Title-Page in England 1550–1660* (London: Routledge & Kegan Paul, 1979), p. 220.

65 Keith Brown, "The Artist of the *Leviathan* Title-Page," *British Library Journal* 4, no. 1 (Spring 1978): 31. Brown also surmises that the divisiveness of the double spire may express Hobbes's antiecclesiastical stance.

The walls in the frontispiece zigzag in the leftmost portion, which may just indicate a shift in the geography of the hilltop (note that the walls in the 1648 painting zigzag) or may instead indicate a star fortress, which—like the double spire—would be more typical of a European than an English town. Star fortresses were introduced into England during its civil war, but there is no indication that Malmesbury ever had one. Corbett and Lightbown (*Comely Frontispiece*, pp. 219, 220) identify the structure in the frontispiece as a star fortress, and also observe another star fortress at the fork in the river on the right side of the frontispiece. In general the scholarship on the frontispiece has been very interested in identifying Leviathan's face—Cromwell, Charles I, Charles II, and Hobbes himself are all candidates—but not in identifying the town. John Speed's *Theatre of the Empire* includes at least one town whose fortress has zigzagging walls: Carlile.

66 Brown, "The Artist of the *Leviathan* Title-Page," p. 32. The engraving does, however, accommodate a greater number of people and seems to include women and children.

67 Sarah Foot, *Æthelstan: The First King of England*, The English Monarchs Series (New Haven: Yale University Press, 2011). Foot describes the disunity of the island prior to Æthelstan (pp. 214ff.) and the "perpetual preparedness" for war in regions like Wessex (p. 150). Æthelstan achieved "hegemony over the whole island of Britain" (p. 203) after other kings on the island recognized his power and pleaded for a treaty of peace (p. 152); and after he successfully repelled the Scots and Danes from English ground (pp. 154–56).

68 Æthelstan's "Ordinance on Charities" were his earliest legal injunctions. His law codes placed huge and repeated emphasis on the prohibition of theft: one-third of all Anglo-Saxon legal references to a "thief" are in his ordinances; he saw elimination of theft as way of restoring peace. According to Foot, "Breach of the peace became in his eyes tantamount to treachery, the breaking of a man's oath to the king." Foot quotes William of Malmesbury: "there is a vigorous tradition

in England that [Æthelstan] was the most law-abiding ruler they have ever had." Foot, *Æthelstan*, pp. 128, 130, 131–37, 139.

69 Foot, *Æthelstan*, pp. 207, 208–13.

70 Foot, *Æthelstan*, pp. 139, 204–206. He used the phrase "*rex Anglorum*" in both his codes and his charters. Æthelstan's charismatic use of a crown (probably influenced in its design by Germany) and his highly voiced charter rhetoric are also described by J. R. Maddicott in *The Origins of the English Parliament 924-1327* (Oxford: Oxford University Press, 2010), pp. 19–21.

71 Maddicott, *Origins of the English Parliament*, p. 3.

72 Maddicott, *Origins of the English Parliament*, pp. vii, 4. The frequency of meetings can be inferred by the numerical record of the national assemblies and by the law Æthelstan passed for borough assemblies (*gemot*) specifying that "seven days' notice is to be given before the meeting and that fines are to be imposed on those failing to attend on three occasions" (p. 15). The diversity is inferred by the inclusion on witness lists of names that are Scandinavian, Welsh, and Scottish (pp. 6–8); over the next half century, men from fortified towns are included.

73 Maddicott, *Origins of the English Parliament*, pp. 4, 5, 29. Both Foot in *Æthelstan* and Maddicott in *Origins* stress the importance Æthelstan gave to an itinerate model (not used by later kings) which by traveling from place gave a much wider population an understanding of what the assembly was doing (Foot, pp. 139, 204; Maddicott, pp. 11, 17).

74 Maddicott, *The Origins of the English Parliament*, p. 5. The presence of a royal scribe, Æthelstan A, enabled records to be kept (p. 15). Maddicott contrasts tenth-century England with Carolingian and German parliaments where the "legislative tradition" was disappearing in the tenth century (p. 29).

75 Maddicott, *The Origins of the English Parliament*, pp. 25, 26, 28.

76 Maddicott, *The Origins of the English Parliament*, p. 31.

77 Hobbes, *A Dialogue between a Philosopher and a Student of the Common Laws of England*, pp. 166–67.

78 The open-faced flowers on the crown of Hobbes's frontispiece Leviathan are worth noticing. They read as flowers even more immediately than do the stylized irises of the fleurs-de-lis pattern found on medieval French crowns and on the "St. Edward's Crown" worn for many centuries by English kings and queens.

79 Crowley et al., *A History of the County of Wiltshire: Malmesbury*. For a description of Malmesbury and the surrounding Wiltshire towns during the civil war, see also Samuel Lewis, *A Topographical Dictionary of England Comprising the Several Counties, Cities, Boroughs, Corporate and Market Parishes, Chapelries, and Townships, and the Islands of Guernsey, Jersey, and Man, with Historical and Statistical Descriptions* (London: S. Lewis and Co., 1831), vol. 4, p. 482.

80 I draw this conclusion from the fact that the adult population of the town numbered 860 in 1547 and 1107 by 1801. Crowley et al., *A History of the County of*

Wiltshire: Malmesbury, drawing on *Wiltshire Archeological and Natural History Magazine*, pp. vii, 3.

81 Crowley et al., *A History of the County of Wiltshire: Malmesbury*, drawing on "Accounts of Parliamentary Garrisons" (Wiltshire Record Society, pp. ii, 27–36).

82 Hobbes, *On the Citizen*, ed. Tuck, p. 13.

83 Hobbes, *Leviathan*, pp. 238.

84 "Thomas Hobbes to Sir Gervase Clifton, circ 5/15 March 1629/30," letter reprinted in G. R. de Beer, "Some Letters of Thomas Hobbes," *Notes and Records of the Royal Society of London* 7, no. 2 (April 1950): 200.

85 "Thomas Hobbes to Sir Gervase Clifton, 19/29 April 1630," letter reprinted in Beer, "Some Letters of Thomas Hobbes," pp. 200–201.

86 "Thomas Hobbes to Sir Gervase Clifton, 10 May 1630," letter reprinted in Beer, "Some Letters of Thomas Hobbes," p. 202.

87 To the West Point map of the 1630–32 Swedish arm of the Thirty Year's War I have added the 1630 War of the Mantuan Succession.

88 Harold Berman, *Law and Revolution: The Formation of the Western Legal Tradition* (Cambridge, MA: Harvard University Press, 1983), p. 393. Peter Kropotkin describes how in Iceland and Scandinavian lands the entire body of law would be recited aloud before an assembly, in *Mutual Aid: A Factor of Evolution* (New York: McClure Phillips, 1903), p. 158.

89 Berman, *Law and Revolution*, p. 375.

90 Henri Pirenne, *Medieval Cities: Their Origins and the Revival of Trade*, trans. Frank D. Halsey (Princeton: Princeton University Press, 1925), p. 218. For the full contract, see Kropotkin, *Mutual Aid*, p. 177. Despite their aura of revolution and volatility, the first French communes were brought into being by the desire for self-help: "to protect the town and keep the peace in circumstances where self-help seemed the only hope" (Susan Reynolds, *An Introduction to the History of English Medieval Towns* [Oxford: Clarendon Press, 1977], p. 104). Reynolds's French sources are A. Vermeesch, "Essai sur les origines et la signification de la commune dans le nord de la France" (Huele, 1966); Petit-Dutaillis, *Les Communes françaises* (Paris, 1947); and P. Michaud-Quantin, *Universitas: Expressions du movement communautaire dans le moyen age latin* (Paris, 1970).

91 Berman, *Law and Revolution*, p.366.

92 Pirenne, *Medieval Cities*, pp. 207–9.

93 Sir William Blackstone and Thomas McIntyre Cooley, *Commentaries on the Laws of England: In Four Books* (Chicago: Callaghan and Company, 1872), vol. 1, p. 117. On the debate about whether English town councils were influenced by continental city contracts, see James Tait, *The Medieval English Borough*, pp. 264–65 ff.

94 My thanks to former research assistant Matthew Spellberg for patiently compiling this list of national constitutions.

95 Richard Tuck, *The Rights of War and Peace: Political Thought and the International Order from Grotius to Kant* (Oxford: Oxford University Press, 1999), pp. 209–219, 224–25.

96 Kant, *Conjectures on the Beginning of Human History* and *Perpetual Peace: A Philosophic Sketch*, cited in Tuck, *The Rights of War and Peace*, pp. 217, 219.

97 Steven Pinker, *The Better Angels of Our Nature: Why Violence Has Declined* (New York: Penguin, 2011), pp. 680–82.

98 D.J.C. Carmichael, "Teaching Thomas Hobbes" *Canadian Journal of Political Science* 23, no. 3 (September 1990): 546. Fortunately, Carmichael's article was occasioned by the appearance of eleven new books on Hobbes in the late 1980s and early 1990s that together worked to bring about "a fundamental reorientation" toward Hobbes. As he notes, a distilled version of this profound about-face can be found in Richard Tuck, *Hobbes: A Very Short Introduction*.

99 Tom Sorell, "Schmitt's unHobbesian Politics of Emergency" in *Leviathan Between the Wars: Hobbes' Impact on Early Twentieth Century Political Philosophy*, ed. Luc Foisneau, Jean-Christophe Merle, and Tom Sorell (Frankfurt: Peter Lang, 2005), pp. 130, 138.

100 Carl Schmitt, *The Leviathan in the State Theory of Thomas Hobbes: Meaning and Failure of a Political Symbol* (1938), trans. George Schwab and Erna Hilstein, fwd. Tracy B. Strong (Chicago: University of Chicago Press, 2008), pp. 31, 33, 34, 35, 46. Schmitt reveres Hobbes and makes many accurate statements about the matchless scale of his influence (p. 86 passim.).

101 Hobbes, *Leviathan*, Pt. II, ch. 28, p. 356; italics mine.

102 Hobbes, *Leviathan*, Pt. II, ch. 28, p. 360; italics mine.

103 Hobbes, *Leviathan*, Pt. II, ch. 28, p. 353.

104 Hobbes, *Leviathan*, Pt. II, ch. 28, p. 354.

105 Hobbes, *Leviathan*, Pt. II, ch. 28, p. 355.

106 Mario Cattaneo, "Hobbes's Theory of Punishment," in *Hobbes Studies*, ed. K. C. Brown (Oxford: Basil Blackwell, 1965), pp. 288, 296.

107 Carl Schmitt points out that on the European continent, credit for this idea is given to Anselm Feuerbach ("the father of criminology") when it is actually a principle announced much earlier by Hobbes (Schmitt, *The Leviathan in the State Theory of Thomas Hobbes*, pp. 72, 73.)

108 Cattaneo, "Hobbes's Theory of Punishment," pp. 276–88.

109 Locke, *Second Treatise of Government*, p. 8; italics are Locke's.

110 Locke, *Second Treatise of Government*, p. 47; italics are Locke's.

111 Locke, *Second Treatise of Government*, p. 68; italics are Locke's.

112 So, too, the passage from section 88 ends "and all this for the preservation of the property of all the members of that society, as far as is possible."

113 Martin van Gelderen, "'*So meerly humane*': Theories of Resistance in Early-Modern Europe," in *Rethinking the Foundations of Modern Political Thought*, ed. Annabel

Brett and James Tully with Holly Hamilton-Bleakley (Cambridge: Cambridge University Press, 2006), pp. 149–170.

114 Hobbes, *On the Citizen*, ed. Tuck, p. 82. He also writes that legal action "against the holder of *sovereign power*" can be "undertaken not as a matter of *civil law* but of *natural equity*" (p. 85; italics are Hobbes's).

115 Hobbes, *On the Citizen*, ed. Tuck, p. 133; italics are Hobbes's.

CHAPTER 4: THE SOCIAL CONTRACT AND THE DOUBLE BRAKES ON INJURY

1 The image of tied hands, as we saw earlier, is Hobbes's own: "Lawes and coercive Power to tye their hands from rapine, and revenge."

2 Leonard W. Levy, *The Palladium of Justice: Origins of Trial by Jury* (Chicago: Ivan R. Dee, 1999), pp. 55–68.

3 Levy, *Palladium of Justice*, pp. 22, 46.

4 James Q. Whitman, *The Origins of Reasonable Doubt: Theological Roots of the Criminal Trial* (New Haven: Yale University Press, 2008), pp. 3, 5, and passim. Whitman's richly informative book seeks to over-weight the reasonable doubt standard toward the jury and away from the defendant; he is convincing about the moral comfort it affords the jurors but not about its lack of protection to the accused. On the Continent, a trial system emphasizing the importance of evidence acted as a system of brakes on findings of guilt parallel to the jury system in England. Whitman sees the continental stress on evidence as a way of easing the conscience of the judge rather than as a protection of the accused (p. 17). But here again it is surely, first and foremost, a protection for the accused, as quickly becomes evident if one imagines eliminating entirely the requirement for evidence. Though both the jury system and the evidence system provide great protections for the defendant, it is of course true that these very arrangements can sometimes contribute to an extreme miscarriage of justice, as when the continental emphasis on evidence motivated jurists to use torture (see John H. Langbein, "The Legal History of Torture," in *Torture: A Collection*, ed. Sanford Levinson [New York: Oxford University Press, 2004], pp. 93–104).

5 Whitman, *Origins of Reasonable Doubt*, pp. 10, 11, 161. Whitman provides many signs of jurors' reluctance to convict such as their fourteenth-century preference for giving "special verdicts" (findings of fact) rather than "general verdicts" (pronouncements of guilt): "Parliament petitioned the king in 1348 to allow jurors in all civil cases to enter special verdicts" (p. 154). Whitman also reminds us of the fear of erroneous convictions in Islamic and Buddhist cultures: "medieval Islamic jurists... held that judges who falsely convicted an accused person should suffer exactly the same punishment they had inflicted"; Buddha's sense of justice was shaped by the fact that as an infant he saw his father "sentencing criminals to death" and remembered "that in a past life he too condemned men to death, and that as a result he burned in hell for 80,000 years" (pp. 10–12).

6 Whitman, *Origins of Reasonable Doubt*, p. 129.

7 John H. Langbein, *The Origins of Adversary Criminal Trial* (Oxford: Oxford University Press, 2003), pp. 4, 67–172.

8 Edward G. Andrew, "Hobbes on Conscience Within the Law and Without," in *Canadian Journal of Political Science* 32, no. 2 (June 1999): 210, 217, drawing on Hobbes, *Leviathan*, ch. 14, p. 199, and ch. 46, p. 700.

9 Langbein, *The Origins of Adversary Criminal Trial*, pp. 278–84.

10 Levy, *Palladium of Justice*, p. 46

11 Hobbes, *A Dialogue between a Philosopher and a Student*, pp. 87, 89. Unlike the Court of Common Law, the Court of Admiralty (which mainly tries cases about England's relation with other states) has neither grand nor petit juries but only a judge. Hobbes endorses the multiple-court arrangement.

12 Hobbes, *A Dialogue between a Philosopher and a Student*, pp. 62, 71–72.

13 Hobbes, *A Dialogue between a Philosopher and a Student*, pp. 148–50. Whereas Hobbes in *Leviathan* celebrates the jurors' capacity to make law, in *A Dialogue* he seems (to me) worried about the jurors' going beyond questions of fact to determination of the law; but several scholars write that he approves of this situation and thinks jurors as well qualified as judges to do so. See James R. Stoner, *Common Law and Liberal Theory: Coke, Hobbes, and the Origins of American Constitutionalism* (Lawrence, KS: University of Kansas, 1992), pp. 110–11; and Edward G. Andrew "Hobbes on Conscience," pp. 207, 208, 220. See Andrew, page 222, for the continuity between this idea of juror law-making in Hobbes and the idea in Rousseau and Kant that laws are legitimate because the people make (or pass) the law.

14 Stoner, *Common Law and Liberal Theory*, pp. 110–11.

15 Hobbes, *Leviathan*, pp. 292–93; Andrew, "Hobbes on Conscience," p. 219 (citing, in addition to *Leviathan*, *A Dialogue between a Philosopher and a Student*, p. 80); Stoner, *Common Law and Liberal Theory*, pp. 110–11.

16 Hobbes, *A Dialogue between a Philosopher and a Student*, pp. 108–9. Locke perhaps thought the impediment created by the requirement for "unanimity" was too great, since in his writing of the *Fundamental Constitutions of Carolina*, clause 69, he provided for a verdict based on a majority vote.

17 Hobbes, *A Dialogue between a Philosopher and a Student*, pp. 140, 149; *Leviathan*, ch. 27, p. 339; see also Andrew, "Hobbes on Conscience," p. 217 (drawing on *Leviathan*, ch. 28, p. 355).

18 Andrew, "Hobbes on Conscience," p. 210. The Star Chamber, for example, punished jurors by imprisonment, fine, or requiring them to stand in Westminster Court with papers on their head announcing their wrong verdict, which was most often a verdict of innocent (see Charles Hamilton, "Star Chamber and Juries: Some Observations," *Albion: A Quarterly Journal Concerned with British Studies* 5, no. 3 [Autumn 1973]: 237–42)

19 Langbein, *The Origins of Adversary Criminal Trial*, p. 45. Levy shows that seventeenth-century tract writers—such as John Somers's (1682) *The Security of Englishmen's Lives* and Henry Care's (1698) *English Liberties or Free Born Subject's*

Inheritance—explicitly described this "filtering" action, as when Somers writes "grand juries are our only security," ensuring that people cannot be "drawn into jeopardy by all the malicious crafts of the devil, unless such a number of our honest countrymen shall be satisfied in the truth of the accusation" (Levy, *Palladium of Justice*, p. 64).

20 Langbein, *Origins of Adversary Criminal Trial*, p. 14, citing John M. Beattie, *Crime and the Courts in England 1660–1800* (1986), p. 412. Langbein cites an acquittal rate of 40 percent in the Home Circuits for the earlier period, 1558 to 1625, drawing on J. S. Cockburn, "Introduction," *Calendar of Assize Records: Home Circuit Indictments Elizabeth I and James I* (1985), pp. 113–14.

21 M. J. Ingram, "Communities and Courts: Law and Disorder in Early-Seventeenth-Century Wiltshire," in J. S. Cockburn, ed., *Crime in England: 1550–1800* (Princeton: Princeton University Press, 1977), pp. 132–33. Seventy-nine percent of those accused were indicted; of the 79 percent indicted, 83 percent were convicted.

22 Mark Jackson, *New-born Child Murder: Women, Illegitimacy and the Courts in Eighteenth Century England* (Manchester: Manchester University Press, 1996), p. 155, n. 64. In the case of homicide, 27 percent were convicted of manslaughter and 17 percent convicted of murder.

23 My argument here is that the population acts as a passive constraint on government; only when the population gives the green light can the government go ahead and punish. But in *The Palladium of Justice*, Leonard Levy gives evidence of more-direct ways the population used the jury system to modify government actions. Beginning in 1641, grand jurors in America were empowered "to investigate any abuses of governmental powers and any laxity in town governance" such as not repairing the roads (p. 65); grand juries served as a location of resistance to British government by, for example, "refus[ing] to indict rioters who in 1765 destroyed the tax stamps in Boston" (p. 67); the people of Massachusetts insisted that grand jurors be selected by town meetings, arguing that "the appointment of grand jurors by sheriffs constituted tyranny" (p. 67).

24 Richard Tuck, "Hobbes and Democracy," in *Rethinking the Foundations of Modern Political Thought*, pp. 181, 183, 190.

25 Tuck, "Hobbes and Democracy," pp. 171, 183.

26 Tuck, "Hobbes and Democracy," pp. 172, 184.

27 Thomas Hobbes, *De Corpore Politico, or The Elements of Law*, ch. 2, pp. 138, 139, in *The English Works of Thomas Hobbes of Malmesbury*, vol. 4 (1840), ed. William Molesworth (reprint: Scientia Aalen, 1962).

28 Robert Filmer, *Observations Concerning The Originall of Government, Upon Mr Hobs Leviathan, Mr Milton against Salmasius, H. Grotius De Jure Belli*, p. 186, in *Patriarcha and Other Writings*, ed. Johann P. Sommerville (Cambridge: Cambridge University Press, 1991), pp. 184–85 (herinafter *Observations Concerning the Originall of Government, Upon Mr Hobs Leviathan*).

29 Filmer, *Patriarcha: The* Naturall *Power of Kinges Defended against the Unnatural Liberty of the People. By Arguments Theological, Rational, Historical, Legall,* in *Patriarcha and Other Writings,* p. 3.

30 Hobbes, *On the Citizen,* ed. Tuck, p. 221. "[A] *church* only exists where there is a definite and recognized, i. e. legitimate, authority by which individuals are obliged to attend the meeting either in person or through others. And it becomes *one* and capable of the functions of a *person,* not because it has uniformity of doctrine, but because it has unity of authority to summon Synods and assemblies of CHRISTians; otherwise it is merely a crowd, and several distinct *persons,* however much they agree in belief."

31 Hobbes, *On the Citizen,* ed. Tuck, pp. 91, 94, 96.

32 Hobbes, *A Dialogue between a Philosopher and a Student,* p. 162.

33 Hobbes, *A Dialogue between a Philosopher and a Student,* p. 64.

34 Hobbes, *The Peloponnesian War: Thucydides (The Complete Hobbes Translation),* ed. David Grene (Chicago: University of Chicago Press, 1989), pp. 42–46. Archidamus, King of the Lacedaemons, reminds them in assembly that Athens is a great city (p. 48) as he will again remind his troops, on the eve of invasion, that they are about "to war against a great city" (p. 96).

35 Hobbes, *The Peloponnesian War,* pp. 180ff.

36 Hobbes, *The Peloponnesian War,* pp. 38, 42, 48.

37 Hobbes, *The Peloponnesian War,* p. 50.

38 Hobbes, "To the Readers," *The Peloponnesian War,* p. xxii.

39 Hobbes, *A Dialogue between a Philosopher and a Student,* p. 59.

40 Hobbes, *A Dialogue between a Philosopher and a Student,* p. 62.

41 Hobbes, *A Dialogue between a Philosopher and a Student,* p. 63.

42 Hobbes, *A Dialogue between a Philosopher and a Student,* p. 68.

43 Hobbes, *A Dialogue between a Philosopher and a Student,* p. 61.

44 The king may begin to act, just as any member of the population may begin at once to defend himself and his fellow citizens if the country is invaded.

45 Hobbes, *A Dialogue between a Philosopher and a Student,* p. 60. The law explicitly announces that the king has no right to act over the border but the law does not explicitly state that it is illegal to do so. The lawyer explains that if he begins to act without Parliament, the Parliament will either quickly confirm what he does or, as in the case of a conquest-crazed leader, he will find himself walking on a plank in midair without support at home or abroad.

46 Hobbes, *A Dialogue between a Philosopher and a Student,* p. 61.

47 Hobbes, *A Dialogue between a Philosopher and a Student,* pp. 60–61.

48 In his meeting with cabinet and congressional members on the evening of December 7, Roosevelt avoids answering questions posed to him about initiating retaliatory actions; he says he is calling Congress into joint session for the next day at 12:30 p.m. but when asked, says he does not yet know whether he will be requesting a declaration of war ("Diary Entry of Secretary of Agriculture Claude Wickard,"

December 7, 1941, Claude R. Wickard Papers, Department of Agriculture Files, Cabinet Meetings, 1941–42; Box 13, Franklin D. Roosevelt Presidential Library). The idea of acting up to, but not one step beyond, the borders of the country is literalized in a telephone conversation earlier in the afternoon with Secretary of the Treasury Henry Morgenthau, Jr. "*HM Jr:* We are freezing all Japanese funds. *The President:* Yes. *HM Jr:* We are not going to let any Japanese leave the country or to carry on any communications. *The President:* I see. *HM Jr:* Well, our responsibility is the border. *The President:* Yes, yes. That's right" (Transcript, Telephone Conversation, December 7, 1941, Henry Morgenthau, Jr., Papers; Presidential Diaries, August–December 1941, Box 515, Franklin D. Roosevelt Presidential Library). The conversation then turns to protecting the perimeter of the White House, with Roosevelt accepting only a modest version of what Morgenthau recommends. (Both documents viewable at www.fdrlibrary.marist.edu/archives/pdfs/pearlharbor.pdf.)

49 Hobbes, *A Dialogue between a Philosopher and a Student*, p. 65.

50 Maddicott, *The Origins of the English Parliament 924–1327*, p. 13.

51 Maddicott, *The Origins of the English Parliament 924–1327*, p. 13.

52 Thomas N. Bisson, "The Military Origins of Medieval Representation," *American Historical Review* 71, no. 4 (July 1966): 1209.

53 Maddicott, *The Origins of the English Parliament 924–1327*, p. 273.

54 Bisson, "The Military Origins of Medieval Representation," pp. 1212, 1213. Bisson notes that "in England the earliest extant writ of military summons (about 1072) antedates the first surviving conciliar writ by nearly a century and a half.... [T]he possibility presents itself that Chapter xiv of Magna Carta—providing for a direct summons of greater tenants in chief, and an indirect summons of other king's tenants through the sheriffs, to gatherings of the realm—was modeled on a type of military summons that was already traditional in 1215" (p. 1213).

55 Gaines Post, *Studies in Medieval Legal Thought: Public Law and the State*, 1100–1322 (Princeton: Princeton University Press, 1964), pp. 112–14.

56 Post, *Studies in Medieval Legal Thought*, p. 112. On the principle of *quod omnes tangit*, see Post's Chapter 4, "A Romano-Canonical Maxim, *Quod Omnes Tangit*, in Bracton and in Early Parliaments," pp. 163–238.

57 Post, *Studies in Medieval Legal Thought*, p. 112.

58 Maddicott, *The Origins of the English Parliament 924–1327*, pp. 268–72. While an earl had a salary of £1500, a knight's salary was approximately £20 (p. 220). In England, the lower clergy and knights attended Parliament for the first time in 1254.

59 Post, *Studies in Medieval Legal Thought*, p. 112.

60 Post, *Studies in Medieval Legal Thought*, p. 114–15, nn. 98, 99.

61 Post, *Studies in Medieval Legal Thought*, p.116.

62 Post, *Studies in Medieval Legal Thought*, pp. 114–15, n. 99.

63 J. G. Edwards, "The *Plena Potestas* of English Parliamentary Representatives," in *Oxford Essays in Medieval History, presented to Herbert Edward Salter* (Oxford:

Clarendon Press, 1934), p. 144. Earlier, in the mid-thirteenth century, the idea had emerged that consent to taxes had to be done personally and individually, not through a representative (p. 148).

64 Edwards, "The *Plena Potestas* of English Parliamentary Representatives," p. 151.

65 Edwards, "The *Plena Potestas* of English Parliamentary Representatives," p. 152.

66 Post, *Studies in Medieval Legal Thought,* pp. 127–60.

67 Charles Holt Taylor, "An Assembly of French Towns in March, 1318," *Speculum* 13, no. 3 (July 1938), p. 299.

68 The absence of this historical record perhaps explains why Hobbes's philosopher in the *Dialogue between a Philosopher and a Student of the Laws of England* cannot imagine a king falsely arguing for the necessity of war.

69 Maddicott, *The Origins of the English Parliament 924–1327,* pp. 268–72, 213, 214.

70 Post, *Studies in Medieval Legal Thought,* p. 119.

71 Taylor, "An Assembly of French Towns in March, 1318," pp. 112, 168, 172.

72 The description of an assembly as a "trial by discussion" is given by Bernard Manin in his book on representation in seventeenth- and eighteenth-century England, France, and United States, *The Principles of Representative Government* (Cambridge: Cambridge University Press, 1997), pp. 183, 190, 191, 205, 216. As he stresses, however, it is not the discussion but the moment of consent that is crucial.

73 Hobbes, *Behemoth: The History of the Causes of the Civil Wars of England and of the Counsels and Artifices by which They Were Carried on from the Year 1640 to the Year 1660,* ed. William Molesworth, *The English Works of Thomas Hobbes,* vol. 6, p. 237.

74 Hobbes, *Behemoth,* ed. Molesworth, pp. 264 ("the power of the militia . . . is in effect the whole sovereign power"), 285 ("so stupid they were as not to know, that he that is master of the militia, is master of the kingdom, and consequently is in possession of a most absolute sovereignty"), 344 ("The first article takes from the King the militia, and consequently the whole sovereignty for ever").

75 Hobbes, *Behemoth,* ed. Molesworth, pp. 334–35: "The army being herewith enraged [with Parliament], were taught by Ireton to erect a council amongst themselves of two soldiers out of every troop and every company, to consult for the good of the army, and to assist at the council of war, and to advise for the peace and safety of the kingdom."

76 Hobbes, *Behemoth,* ed. Molesworth, pp. 160, 161, 162.

77 Hobbes, *Behemoth,* ed. Molesworth, p. 400. See also in *Leviathan* Hobbes's disapproving description of the way the "affections of his Army" empowered Julius Caesar (p. 374).

78 Hobbes, *Behemoth, or the Long Parliament,* ed. Stephen Holmes (Chicago: University of Chicago Press, 1990), pp. xi, xxviii, citing Hobbes, p. 16 (p. 184 in Molesworth).

79 Andrew, "Hobbes on Conscience Within the Law and Without," p. 205.

80 Stephen J. Stearns, "Conscription and English Society in the 1620s," *Journal of British Studies* 11, no. 2 (May, 1972): 4–6.

81 Stearns, "Conscription and English Society in the 1620s," pp. 5, 7. Stearns concludes that Shakespeare's depiction of the disreputable Falstaff is vividly accurate, and a rare window into the way the indentured soldier was perceived. Stearns also shows that like the soldiers we encountered in Chapter 2, these soldiers sometimes practiced dissent through desertion: "Sergeant-Major Leigh's returns show 200 runaways out of 2500 men. Another report from the summer of 1625 shows 200 desertions from a levy of 2000 men in the few days time it took to march from where they had been levied to Plymouth. By 1627 the situation was worse, 80 desertions from a press of 400 men" (p. 15).

82 Stearns, "Conscription and English Society in the 1620s," pp. 8, 16. Stearns marvels at the bravery of men who stood their ground in battle—"better men than their selectors had any right to expect" (p. 23).

83 See entries for "Tithing" and for "Town" in Richard Burn and John Burn, *A New Law Dictionary: Intended for General Use, as Well as for Gentlemen of the Profession* (London: T. Cadell, 1792), p. 283. Blackstone, writing in the same century, says the tithing was invented "with a view of obliging each district to answer for the robberies committee in its own division." All acted as "sureties or free pledges . . . for the good behaviour of each other" (*Commentaries on the Laws of England*, §§114, 115). He then makes it clear that the tithing acts as a bulwark against incursions from another country as well (see the description of counties bordering Wales and Scotland in §117). Some historians say the unit of ten households is a distinctly British invention (with credit divided between Alfred and Æthelstan) and attribute to Europe only the 100 household unit; other historians, such as David Pratt, credit Europe with the ten-household unit as well (see *The Political Thought of King Alfred the Great* [Cambridge: Cambridge University Press 2007], p. 235).

84 Hobbes, *Dialogue between a Philosopher and a Student*, p. 164. It is worth pausing over Hobbes's inclusion of women here. Locke in the *Second Treatise* blasts Filmer's advocacy of patriarchy by pointing out that paternal power has no meaning in a state, but only in a family; and even there, says Locke, it should be called "parental power," since it is both mothers and fathers who care for children. Hobbes on this matter goes further than Locke by arguing in *De Cive* that "the mother originally hath the government of her children, and from her the father derives his right, because she brings forth and first nourisheth them." For Filmer's citation of Hobbes and response, see *Observations Concerning the Originall of Government Upon Mr Hobs Leviathan*, p. 192; and see Hobbes, *On the Citizen*, ed. Tuck, ch. 9, pp. 108, 109.

85 The first phrase is spoken by the philosopher and the second by the lawyer who recites the oath of allegiance formalized under Edward II but probably in use earlier (p. 164).

86 St. Rémy summarized by David G. Chandler, "The Art and Science of Fortification and Siegecraft," in *The Age of William III & Mary II: Power, Politics, and Patronage*

1688–1702, ed. Robert P. Maccubbin and Martha Hamilton-Phillips (Williamsburg: College of William and Mary, 1989), pp. 123–25.

87 Filmer, *Observations Concerning the Originall of Government, Upon Mr Hobs* Leviathan, p. 185.

88 Sommerville, ed., *Patriarcha and Other Writings*, p. 185n.

89 Letter 195, Gottfried Wilhelm Leibniz to Hobbes, from Paris (1674?) in Noel Malcolm, ed., *The Correspondence of Thomas Hobbes: Volume II 1660–1679* (Oxford: Oxford University Press, 1994), p. 734.

90 Leibniz, Letter 195, in Malcolm, *The Correspondence of Thomas Hobbes*, pp. 734, 735.

91 Hampton, *Hobbes and the Social Contract*, pp. 197–207. In *The Catching of the Leviathan or the Great Whale* (the appendix to *Castigations of Mr. Hobbes*), Bramhall writes "Rebells Catachism"; some editions of his other writings use the plural possessive, "Rebels' Catachism." Clarendon's work is *A Brief View and Survey of the Dangerous and Pernicious Errors to Church and State, in Mr. Hobbes's Book, entitled* Leviathan. See also William Lucy, *Observations, Censures and Confutations of Notorious Errours in Mr. Hobbes His* Leviathan (1663, reprinted 1996: New York, Routledge), ch. 22, pp. 164–75, where Lucy argues that people do not always consider staying alive to be as important as Hobbes makes out, and that we should act on self-preservation only if that which is requiring us to give up our lives is not the church, the state, or some other "greater good" (p. 174). In support of his assertion that one's own death does not always cause anguish, Lucy tells the story of his own four-year-old daughter "who being sickly, I put out to a neighbours house, in whose care I confided, to attend her; she grew weaker and weaker undo *death*, and almost immediately before her *death* the man of the house coming home from his business, she called the woman, whom she usually called, *old Mother: old Mother*, said she, *goe give the old man his breakfast, he will be angry else; and leave such a boy to rock me in my Cradle*, and so straightway *dyed*" (pp. 171–72). One might have thought even the most unrepentant patriarch would think twice before using this story to discredit the right of self-preservation.

92 Filmer, *Observations Concerning* The Originall of Government, *Upon Mr Hobs* Leviathan, pp. 193, 194. Hampton notes the second of Filmer's two objections in *Hobbes and the Social Contract Tradition*, p. 199.

93 For an analysis of Hobbes's writings on heresy, see Samuel I. Mintz, "Hobbes on the Law of Heresy: A New Manuscript," *Journal of the History of Ideas* 29, no. 3 (July/September 1968): 409–13. Mintz publishes for the first time a manuscript written by Hobbes at the age of eighty-five. Hobbes's three other writings are *De Haeresi* (an appendix to a late edition of *Leviathan* arguing against the punishment of heretics), passages on heresy in *Dialogue between a Philosopher and a Student*, and "Historical Narration Concerning Heresy," an essay in which Hobbes reviews the heresy statutes in England that have been passed and then repealed. Hobbes shows that no laws are in effect in England and that punishing heretics

is therefore illegal, as is any attempt to force them "to abjure" their beliefs. Mintz describes the incident of 1666 (predating most of these writings) when a committee in the House of Commons said *Leviathan* incited profanity and atheism, and when bishops in the House of Lords made a motion that Hobbes be "burn't for a heretique" (p. 409).

While I concentrate on disobedience in wartime, Hobbes's thinking about disobedience in peacetime is also of great interest. In his introduction to *Dialogue between a Philosopher and a Student,* Joseph Cropsey points out that Hobbes himself disobeyed the king by giving his *Behemoth* manuscript to his publisher immediately after the king gave him "a flat prohibition to publish it" (Cropsey, "Introduction," p. 11). A. P. Martinich, Hobbes's biographer, says that Hobbes himself did not initiate the publication of *Behemoth* (even putting himself on record, in at least two letters to friends, as saying it should not be published since royal permission to do so had been "Flatly denied"). But he also gave copies of the manuscript to others, with the instruction to do with it as they wished (*Hobbes: A Biography* [Cambridge: Cambridge University Press, 1999], pp. 214, 219). Somewhere along the way, one of these friends must have wished to see it in print, since publication soon followed.

94 Hobbes, *Leviathan,* ch. 29, p. 369. See also *Behemoth,* ed. Molesworth, p. 193.

95 Hobbes, *Leviathan,* ch. 29, p. 370.

96 Hobbes, *On the Citizen,* ed. Tuck, ch. 12: "On the Internal Causes which Tend to Dissolve the Commonwealth," p. 141. In *Leviathan,* chapter 38, and in *The Elements of the Law,* part II, chapter 8, Hobbes again calls on the dangerous "eloquence" of Medea to illustrate the error of rebellion in the naïve belief that one can reconstitute the state and make it new.

97 John Aubrey, *Aubrey's Brief Lives,* ed. Oliver Lawson Dick, fwd. Edmund Wilson (Boston: David R. Godine Publisher, 1999), pp. 149, 154.

98 Hobbes, "To the Readers," *The Peloponnesian War: Thucydides,* p. xxi.

99 Filmer, *Observations Concerning the Originall of Government Upon Mr Hobs* Leviathan, p. 195.

100 Hobbes, *On the Citizen,* ed. Tuck, p. 133.

101 Homer, *The Iliad,* trans. Robert Fagles, introd. and notes, Bernard Knox (New York: Viking, 1990), bk. I, ll. 204–205, 211–13.

102 Hobbes's foregrounding of dissent would become even more visible if rather than comparing his poem to a single translation (Robert Fagles's) it were possible for us to follow multiple English translations. In *The Iliad—Twenty Centuries of Translation* (Lexington, Kentucky: 2012), Michael Nikoletseas juxtaposes twenty English translations of a few of the poem's passages such as the opening lines; some are translated from the Greek, others from Latin, still others from French. Nikoletseas's own intent is to assess which English translation, in any given line, is most true to the spirit and letter of the original Greek, and he ranks them best to worst.

Although not part of his project, his line-by-line juxtapositions make Hobbes's sensitivity to dissent vividly apparent.

For example, almost all translations open by focusing on Achilles' anger, the destructive passion that will cause so much damage: the word *wrath* is used by George Chapman, Alexander Pope, James Macpherson, William Cowper, William Cullen Bryant, Ernest Myers; the word *rage* is used by John Ogilby, Robert Fagles, Michael Pierce Reck, and Stanley Lombardo; *vengence* is used by the Earl of Derby; *anger* is used by Samuel Butler and Robert Fitzgerald. Hobbes, in stark contrast to all of these, takes as his theme "the discontent" of Achilles; from the outset, Hobbes pivots our attention to Achilles' felt experience of an injustice (the terms of which Homer will shortly describe). One other translator, Francis W. Newman, uses a word that is free of anger: *resentment*. But that, by comparison to *discontent*, conveys a small-minded mental state.

Nikoletseas observes that the original Greek intensifies the anger with an adjective, variously given in the English translations as *destructive wrath, ruinous wrath, deadly wrath, baneful wrath, wrath pernicious, hateful hate, maniac rage, deep and deadly vengeance* (Nikoletseas takes "maniac rage" as the best translation [pp. 90–92]). Hobbes simply omits the adjective altogether (as do two other translations).

Still in the second and third lines, Homer acknowledges the harm that will result from Achilles' mental state. Hobbes registers "what woe [he]...brought to the Greeks," but minimizes the sense of devastating responsibility that other translators foreground and make graphic by including large numbers: "a thousand troubles" [Rouse], "pains thousandfold upon the Achaeans" (Lattimore), "ten thousand woes caused to Achaea's host" (Cowper). Others emphasize the damaging effects by saying they are uncountable: "unnumbered woe" (Rees), "with countless pangs Achaea's army wounded" (Newman), "unnumbered ills" (Earl of Derby), "woes numberless" (Bryant), "countless ills" (Butler), "countless woes" (Murray), "countless losses" (Fagles), "incalculable pain" (Lombardo). Chapman chooses "infinite sorrows" and Ogilby and Macpherson settle for "many" (pp. 94–95).

As I note in introducing my discussion of the *Iliad*, Hobbes foregrounds dissent by placing a margin gloss at the top of every page in Book I that reads, "The discontent and secession of Achilles." Had he translated the opening lines the way others have, a very different gloss would have to appear there: such as "the maniac rage and pains thousandfold of Achilles," or simply, "The wrath and countless ills of Achilles."

103 Fagles, *Iliad*, bk. I, ll. 193–99.

104 Fagles, *Iliad*, bk. IX, p. 262, l. 407. Briseis is "wife," too, in Hobbes's translation (bk. IX, p. 102, ll. 338–42), a passage we look at shortly.

105 The Argive soldiers are dying of the plague; Achilles calls together an assembly to determine the cause of the plague; it is revealed that the cause is Agamemnon's

violation of the daughter of the priest of Apollo; Agamemnon will only give her up if he can have the woman of Ajax, Odysseus, Idomeneus, or Achilles.

106 Thomas Hobbes, *Homer's Iliads, Translated Out of Greek by Thomas Hobbes of Malmesbury*, in *The English Works of Thomas Hobbes of Malmesbury*, vol. 10, collected and edited by Sir William Molesworth (London: John Bohn, 1846; reprint Scientia Verlag Aalen, Germany, 1966). Hobbes's translation has for the most part been unknown and unread. Thus Douglas Bush in a *PMLA* article (vol. 41, no. 2, pp. 335–41) entitled "English Translations of Homer" enumerates translations of the *Iliad*, including even travesties and books of translated excerpts; but Hobbes is not included. John Ogilby's 1656 *Iliad* and 1660 reprint are included. Virginia Woolf's father, Sir Leslie Stephen (*Hobbes*, London, 1904) takes admiring notice of Hobbes's translation: "Nobody has yet, I believe, discovered that the work is a worthy rival of Chapman or Pope; a work which might perhaps have charms for some literary revivalists...a creditable occupation for a man of eighty-six." George Croom Robertson praises its "power and vigor." These last two works are cited in an essay denouncing the translation, G. B. Riddehough, "Thomas Hobbes' Translations of Homer," *Phoenix* 12, no. 2 (Summer 1958), p. 62, n. 8. Attention to Hobbes's final work will be greatly increased by the 2008 Oxford University Press edition of Hobbes's *Iliad* and *Odyssey* edited by Eric Nelson.

107 Hobbes, *Leviathan*, ch. 6, p. 126.

108 Hobbes, *Leviathan*, ch. 6, p. 120.

109 Hobbes's account in *The Whole Art of Rhetoric* (where he says that impudence contains the contrary of every feature of shame) again centers on contempt: "[I]n the presence of such whose judgment most men despise, men are not ashamed. Therefore we are ashamed also in the presence of those whom we reverence" (*The Whole Art of Rhetoric*, in *The Works of Thomas Hobbes of Malmesbury*, vol. 6, ed. William Molesworth [London: John Bohn, 1840], bk. II, ch. 8, p. 460). Agamemnon's lack of regard for other people—so profoundly visible in his indifference to the soldiers suffering from the plague, his disregard for the agony of the priest, and his contemptuous rejection of the advice of his best fighter—is also visible in his naked inability to feel shame. Hobbes also observes how close contempt is to cruelty: "*Contempt*, or little sense of the calamity of others, is that which men call CRUELTY; proceeding from Security of their own fortune" (*Leviathan*, p. 126).

Perhaps not surprisingly, the word *impudence* occurs numerous times in Hobbes's *Behemoth*, his book about the English Civil War, where he couples it with "bestial incivility," "injustice," "hypocrisy," "villainy," "knavery, and folly," adolescent foolishness (the "quibbles" of schoolboys), and international deception (Hobbes, *Behemoth*, ed. Molesworth, pp. 271, 313, 318, 319). As the tonal range of these words suggests, impudence originates in small-mindedness but produces a large moral wrong. In *Behemoth*, it is consistently used to describe the actions of Parliament or "democratic assemblies," pp. 249, 250). In other words, Hobbes attaches it to the side we know he opposed, suggesting that his use of it to describe the monarch in the *Iliad* reveals the side he there holds to be in the wrong. The specific actions that occasion the word in *Behemoth* do genuinely shock the conscience: "when [Parliament] summoned any town, it was always in the name of King and Parliament" (p. 318); Parliament "voted the Queen a traitor, for helping the King with some ammunition and English forces from Holland" (p. 319); Parliament called upon the Scots army to invade England and then called upon the King to pay the £300,000 owed to the Scots soldiers for their work of invasion (p. 272). Whether Hobbes's descriptions of Parliament are wholly accurate is a separate question.

110 Hobbes, *Leviathan*, part II, ch. 28.

111 Hobbes, *Leviathan*, pp. 382–83. In *On the Citizen*, physical intimacy with another person's spouse is again placed side-by-side with murder: ch. 6, §16 begins, *"Theft, Murder, Adultery* and all *wrongs [iniuriae]* are forbidden by the laws of nature" (ed. Tuck, p. 86).

112 Homer, *Iliad*, trans. Hobbes, bk. I, l. 336, p. 7; see also line 220, as well as line 370 describing the "injury" done to Chryses and Achilles' attempt to repair it.

113 Herodotus, *The Histories*, trans. Aubrey de Sélincourt, ed. and introd. John Marincola (New York: Penguin, 2003 rev. ed), p. 4. Several of the acts he describes were committed by the Greeks (carrying off Europa, daughter of King Persius) and abducting Medea (daughter of King of Aea). Herodotus may be reporting a view— "Such then is the Persian story. In their view it was the capture of Troy that first made them enemies of the Greeks" (p. 5)—rather than voicing his own.

114 Homer, *Iliad*, trans. Hobbes, bk IX, ll. 338–42, p. 102.

115 Jonathan Shay, *Achilles in Vietnam: Combat Trauma and the Undoing of Character* (New York: Scribner, 1994), see ch. 1, "The Betrayal of What's Right," esp. pp. 10–14 on "The Fairness Assumption."

116 Elizabeth Samet, *Soldier's Heart: Reading Literature through Peace and War at West Point* (New York: Picador, 2007), see esp. ch. 4, "To Obey or Not Obey."

117 Homer, *Iliad*, trans. Fagles, bk. II, ll. 7–9.

118 Homer, *Iliad*, trans. Fagles, bk. I, ll. 211–13.

119 Homer, *Iliad*, trans. Fagles, bk. IX, ll. 427–28. It is Achilles himself who gives this account. This is how the scheme comes about that Patroclus puts on Achilles' armor, to produce the impression that Achilles is back in the lines, fighting.

120 Juno in Hobbes's text.

121 Ulysses in Hobbes's text.

122 Juno speaking to Athena in Hobbes.

123 Homer, *Iliad*, trans. Fagles, bk. II, ll. 192–93.

124 Homer, *Iliad*, trans. Fagles, bk. II, ll. 85, 99.

125 In trying to persuade his soldiers to turn toward Troy rather than to their ships, Odysseus speaks gently "to prince or peers" but "when a common man he bawling saw, / He bang'd him with his staff, and roughly spake. / Be silent, and hear

what your betters say. ... Let one be king (we cannot all be kings)" (Homer, *Iliad*, trans. Hobbes, bk. II, ll. 165, 176–78, 181). Though the differential treatment of wealthy and poor is not compatible with Hobbes's stress on equality in his political theory, the final line—"Let one be King (we cannot all be Kings)"—is directly in line with *Leviathan's* explanation for why we should all ordinarily obey the sovereign, and also one John Ogilby (whose *Iliad* we will encounter shortly) cites in his dedicatory preface to the monarch as evidence of how pro-Royalist the poem is.

126 Homer, *Iliad*, trans. Hobbes, bk. II, ll. 70–71.

127 Homer, *Iliad*, trans. Fagles, bk. II, l. 111. See Cedric H. Whitman, *Homer and the Heroic Tradition* (Cambridge, MA: Harvard University Press, 1959), especially the chapter on "The Geometric Structure of the *Iliad*." For a sustained analysis of assemblies in the *Iliad*, see David F. Elmer, *The Poetics of Consent: Collective Decision Making and the* Iliad (Baltimore, MD: Johns Hopkins University Press, 2012).

128 Homer, *Iliad*, trans. Fagles, bk. II, ll. 15–17.

129 The line continues "for Juno's sake."

130 J. V. Luce, "The *Polis* in Homer and Hesiod," *Proceedings of the Royal Irish Academy* 78 (1978): p. 5.

131 Luce, "The *Polis* in Homer and Hesiod," p. 1. See also Gregory Nagy, "The Shield of Achilles: Ends of the *Iliad* and Beginning of the Polis," in *New Light on a Dark Age: Exploring the Culture of Geometric Greece*, ed. Susan Langdon (Columbia, MO: University of Missouri Press, 1997).

132 Luce, "The *Polis* in Homer and Hesiod," pp. 5, 7. Luce surmises that "polis" may be from the word essentially meaning acropolis with "astu a lower town" (p. 7). Luce is careful to note that of course the conception of the polis is not that of fifth-century Athens with "coined money, written constitution, ... navies of triremes" (p. 3). (Actually, some of the items Luce lists as not present certainly seem to be present, such as "defensive alliances.") Luce also notes the word *dikaspolos*, meaning "law administering," an epithet "used of ... Telemachus in the *Odyssey*."

133 *Odyssey*, bk. IX, l. 106–13; cited in Luce, "The *Polis* in Homer and Hesiod," p. 9.

134 Luce, "The *Polis* in Homer and Hesiod," p. 9.

135 Bernard Knox, "Notes on the Translation," in Homer, *Iliad*, trans. Fagles, footnote to bk. 1, l. 273, p. 621.

136 Paul Friedrich and James Redfield, "Speech as a Personality Symbol: The Case of Achilles," *Language: Journal of the Linguistic Society of America* 54, no. 2 (June 1978): 265.

137 Friedrich and Redfield note a single exception at bk. 23, l. 855 (p. 265).

138 Friedrich and Redfield, "Speech ... The Case of Achilles," p. 269. "The counter-speakers," they note, "include gods and goddesses, men and women, and one horse. Some are friendly, some angry, some superordinate, some subordinate; the counter-sample, like the basic sample, presents a great range of topics and audiences" (p. 270).

139 Freidrich and Redfield, "Speech...The Case of Achilles," pp. 271, 273, 275, 279, 280, 281, 283.

140 Freidrich and Redfield, "Speech...The Case of Achilles," p. 271. Gregory Nagy describes Achilles in Book IX as both poet and rhapsode (*Plato's Rhapsody and Homer's Music: The Poetics of the Panathenaic Festival in Classical Athens* [Washington, D.C.: Center for Hellenic Studies, 2002], pp. 17, 18).

141 In *Why Societies Need Dissent*, legal scholar Cass Sunstein notes that a dissenter never personally gets the benefits of his or her own dissent; the community reaps the benefit of dissent; the individual dissenter will be repudiated even if his or her views are validated and bring about change (Cambridge, MA: Harvard University Press, 2003). As we will see with the help of John Ogilby's annotations, this crediting reading of Thersites is just below the surface of the poem.

142 Homer, *Iliad*, trans. Fagles, bk. II, ll. 246–49.

143 By "women of Achaia" he means his fellow soldiers who are groveling to Agamemnon's orders and therefore appear unmanly.

144 Homer, *Iliad*, trans. Fagles, bk. II, ll. 287–92.

145 Hobbes, "To the Reader, Concerning the Virtues of an Heroic Poem," p. x. Clearly Hobbes thought he *could* improve on, and even replace, Ogilby's translation. But he did not believe he could improve on the annotations which are often ingenious and brilliantly learned. Ogilby tells his readers, for example, that Thetis strokes the chin of father Zeus in order to elicit the nod of consent; Prometheus captured fire from heaven by trapping lightning in a crystal.

146 In his otherwise fascinating preface to his new edition of Hobbes's *Iliad*, Eric Nelson (mistakenly, in my view) argues that Hobbes is here being sarcastic. I see no evidence that that is the case: it is almost inconceivable that Hobbes would clutter the exalted list of names in the preface with a name derisively invoked. Nelson is here projecting modern biases back onto Hobbes. As biographer Katherine S. Van Eerde points out, Ogilby was highly regarded in his time, even if later generations erased that reputation. He was at various times in his career Master of the King's Revels in Ireland, Royal Cartographer, Royal Cosmographer, and was selected by the city of London to write the coronation ceremony for Charles II, a ceremony that incorporated the talents of the city's many choirs, companies, and bands (for the coronation ceremony of James, Ben Jonson and Thomas Dekker had been selected). See Katherine S. Van Eerde, *John Ogilby and the Taste of His Times* (Folkestone Kent: Wm Dawson & Sons, Ltd, 1976), pp. 47, 48, 71. Hobbes's biographer, A. P. Martinich, shares my view that Hobbes here gives a genuine salute to Ogilby: "Hobbes himself was impressed by the scholarship, and, contrary to his usual practice, mentions Ogilby twice by name" (*Hobbes: A Biography*, p. 340).

147 John Ogilby, "Dedication" to *Homer His Iliads translated, adorned with Sculpture and Illustrated with Annotations* (London: Thomas Roycroft, 1660).

148 Keith Brown writes, "[Hobbes's] full motives for the gift were clearly quite complex, but he knew in advance that the Royalists were unlikely to approve the book,

and simple self-defence must have been one powerful factor. He needed to show that this was not a book that he felt ashamed of in Royalist company: that it was a work of science, presenting permanently valid principles, which only an accident of the times made apt to 'frame the minds of a thousand gentlemen' to conscientious obedience to Cromwell" ("The Artist of the *Leviathan* Title-Page," p. 29). A. P. Martinich thinks "it is plausible that Hobbes [in giving his manuscript to Charles II] hoped that *Leviathan* would enhance his position at the court." But he also quotes a contemporary who describes Londoners' reception of the book as pro-Rebellion rather than pro-Royalist: "'Mr. Hobbes is at London much caressed, as one that has by his writings justified the reasonableness and righteousness of their [the rebels'] arms and actions" (*Hobbes: A Biography*, pp. 214, 219).

149 Ogilby's having designed the coronation pageantry is not altogether decisive in determining whether he was wholly pro-Royalist. Katherine Van Eerde notes that at one point Ogilby's script is very much about the "themes of Rebellion" and about the "Restoration triumphant"; but she also notes that the figure of "Rebellion [makes] a vigorous speech to the King" to which "Monarchy, another lady, but of much less vivid language and personality, made a brief answer" (p. 53). Rebellion claims credit for instigating the civil wars, and then sings these words, "I hope, at last, to march with Flags unfurl'd; and tread down Monarchy through all the World."

150 Ogilby, *Homer His Iliads Translated*, bk. II, p. 39, l. 10; p.40, annotation d.

151 Ogilby, *Homer His Iliads Translated*, bk. I, p.11, annotation z. Ogilby both in his translation and in his notes italicizes all proper names which I am omitting here.

152 Ogilby, *Homer His Iliads Translated*, bk. I, p. 11, annotation z. Ogilby uses the name "Minerva" for "Athena" in this passage. In another of his notes, Ogilby credits the severity of the injury Achilles has suffered by inviting us to picture a scene that, as he observes, Homer has abstained from giving us (because it would distract from the momentum of the book), namely the parting of Briseis from Achilles, "the sad and perplexed condition of a loving Wife, forceably parted from a tender Husband" (p. 18, annotation u).

153 According to A. P. Martinich, the only translation of the *Peloponnesian War* that had been available was an English translation of a French translation of a Latin translation (*A Hobbes Dictionary* [Oxford: Blackwell Publishers, 1995], p. 224, s. v. "Peloponnesian War by Thucydides"). If Hobbes is perceived as advocating a totalitarian sovereign, it is not unreasonable to argue (as some scholars do) that he translated Thucydides because the book has sections celebrating strong antidemocratic claims. But the book also has strong prodemocratic and proassembly sections, and is not, by non-Hobbesian readers, usually taken as a totalitarian meditation. In those repeated passages where Hobbes cautions against ancient texts because they teach tyrannaphobia, he does not say, "except of course Thucydides and Homer." In her book *Thucydides, Hobbes, and the Interpretation of Realism* (DeKalb: Northern Illinois University Press, 1993), Laurie M. Johnson critiques the view that

Thucydides is a neorealist who can be used to ennoble twentieth-and twenty-first-century neorealism in international relations. She quotes Richard K. Ashley's classic 1984 article "The Poverty of Neorealism," which argues that neorealism "subordinates all practice to an interest in control, bows to the ideal of social power beyond responsibility," and produces "a totalitarian project of global proportions" (p. 221). Drawing on the writings of Daniel Garst and others, Johnson argues that the neorealist view of Thucydides systematically ignores the central position he accords to speeches and speech making, as it also ignores the fatal decline that comes about when, in the seventh and eight books of the *History*, speech making deteriorates and is replaced by "dispatches, military harangues, [and] reports of decisions made" (pp. 210–11, 216). While Johnson defends Thucydides, she appears to accept the twentieth-and twenty-first-century appropriation of Hobbes into the neorealist camp, an appropriation my own Chapters 3 and 4 show to be deeply mistaken.

154 Recall, too, that the taking of another person's spouse or partner is listed by Hobbes in the *Leviathan* as only one degree less injurious than taking the person's life or limbs. James Redfield and Paul Friedrich, contrasting the lyric speech of Achilles with the persuasive speech of Odysseus, observe that had Agamemnon taken Odysseus's beloved, Odysseus would have successfully persuaded all the Greeks to dissent and to kill the king. "Odysseus," they write, "responds to the sexually-based insults to the honor of his wife by slaughtering over 100 suitors and hanging dozens of 'disloyal' maidservants. One can speculate that Odysseus, if affronted by Agamemnon as Achilles was, would . . . [eschew] poetic rhetoric, he would use the oratory of the persuader, and his own astuteness, to engineer a successful regicide" p. (285).

155 Nestor, urging Achilles and Agamemnon to stop their struggle (in Fagles, bk. I, ll. 290–333), briefly advises the king that Briseis belongs to Achilles and should stay with him; he then advises Achilles at greater length that he will lose in any contest of strength since, though he is born of a goddess, Agamemnon has more force since he rules many men.

156 Ogilby, *Homer His Iliads Translated*, bk. I, p. 12.

157 David Hume, "Of the Standard of Taste," in *David Hume: Selected Essays*, ed. Stephen Copley and Andrew Edgar (New York: Oxford University Press, 1993, 2008), p. 154.

158 Ogilby, *Homer His Iliads Translated*, bk. I. p. 12, annotation k.

159 Hobbes, *On the Citizen*, ed. Tuck, pp. 53, 54, 58, 64.

160 Ogilby, *Homer His Iliads Translated*, bk. I, p. 8, annotation h.

161 Ogilby, *Homer His Iliads Translated*, bk. I, p. 12, ll. 24, 26. Hobbes's translation of these lines is much less forceful than Ogilby's.

162 Ogilby, *Homer His Iliads Translated*, bk. I, p. 12, annotation l.

163 Hobbes, *On the Citizen*, ed. Tuck, p. 133.

164 *Leviathan, or The Matter, Forme, & Power of a Common-Wealth Ecclesiasticall and Civil* (1651 title page). Hobbes's inclusion of the word "Common-Wealth" in his subtitle was one of the grounds of Robert Filmer's denunciation: "I wish the title of the book had not been of a commonwealth.... Many ignorant men are apt by the name of commonwealth to understand a popular government, wherein wealth and all things shall be common, tending to the leveling community in the state of pure nature" (Filmer, *Observations Concerning the Originall of Government, Upon Mr Hobs* Leviathan, p. 186).

165 Homer, *Iliad,* trans. Hobbes, bk II l. 695.

166 Hobbes describes the solitary goal of "public safety" or "the safety of the people" or *salus populi* in *Leviathan* (pp. 376, 385) and in *Behemoth* (p. 48). That is why the sovereign has the role of "secular salvation" through civil society that a god does on an immortal plane (see Martinich, *A Hobbes Dictionary,* s.v. salvation as peace and defense).

167 Hobbes, *Behemoth,* ed. Molesworth, p. 174. Hobbes says that heresy is in the realm of religion what we call rebellion in the political sphere.

168 Hobbes, *On the Citizen,* ed. Tuck, p. 89.

169 A year later in the Trojan War, all fighting will stop so that Odysseus and the son of Achilles can travel to the island of Lemos where Odysseus had earlier abandoned Philoctetes because the smell of his wound and the sound of his shrieks of pain sickened his shipmates; the Greeks need to retrieve Philoctetes' powerful bow without which they cannot win the war. The war must stop while those hearing the story—told by Sophocles in *Philoctetes*—meditate on why the wounds of the individual soldier matter. It is not that his wounds matter because he is the possessor of the bow (though that is the case for Odysseus and Neoptolemos inside the play); the Greek mind endowed him with the bow so that we would come to understand that the distress of a single wounded soldier matters.

170 2005 Profile in Courage Award description, at John F. Kennedy Presidential Library and Museum, at http://www.jfklibrary.org/Events-and-Awards/Profile-in-Courage-Award/Award-Recipients/Joseph-Darby-2005.aspx?t=1

171 Hobbes, *On the Citizen,* ed. Tuck, p. 116

172 Hobbes, *On the Citizen,* ed. Tuck, p. 117.

173 Hobbes, *On the Citizen,* ed. Tuck, p. 116.

174 Hobbes, *On the Citizen,* ed. Tuck, p. 116, 117.

175 Hobbes, *On the Citizen,* ed. Tuck, p. 92.

176 See, for example, Mary L. Dudziak, *War Time: An Idea, Its History, Its Consequences* (New York: Oxford University Press, 2012), pp. 28–31. Dudziak provides a chart of the almost uninterrupted sequence of years in which the U.S. military has awarded a campaign medal (p. 28). The Disabled American Veterans organization specifies "The only non-war period after World War II, other than a period of seven months in 1990, was from October 15, 1976, to November 4, 1979" (p. 30).

177 Brian C. Schmidt, "Together Again: Reuniting Political Theory and International Relations Theory," in *British Journal of Politics and International Relations* 4, no. 1 (April 2002): 115–140, esp. 121, 122. Schmidt cites the phrase "bizarre detour" from Steve Smith, "'The Forty Years' Detour: The Resurgence of Normative Theory in International Relations," *Millennium: Journal of International Studies* 21:489–506.

178 David Armitage, "Hobbes and the Foundation of Modern International Thought" in *Rethinking the Foundations of Modern Political Thought,* ed. Annabel Brett, James Tully, and Holly Hamilton-Bleakly (Cambridge: Cambridge University Press, 2006), pp. 219–35, esp. 231–32.

179 Noel Malcolm, Chapter 13: "Hobbes's Theory of International Relations," in *Aspects of Hobbes* (Oxford: Oxford University Press, 2002), pp. 432–56.

180 Schmidt describes the many writings that herald the return of ethics and values to the international realm, such as those by philosophers John Rawls and Jürgen Habermas, international scholars Richard Falk and Charles Beitz, feminist theorists Rebecca Grant and J. A. Tichner ("Together Again: Reuniting Political Theory and International Relations Theory," pp. 122, 124–25, 138, 132, 133).

181 Hobbes, *Leviathan,* ed. Macpherson, p. 186.

182 Bruce Russett, *Grasping the Democratic Peace: Principles for a Post-Cold War World* (Princeton: Princeton University Press, 1993). A recent book qualifies this optimistic view of democracy by showing that "states in the early phases of transitions to democracy are more likely than other states to become involved in war" (Edward D. Mansfield and Jack Snyder, *Electing to Fight: Why Emerging Democracies Go to War* [Cambridge, MA: MIT Press, 2005]; citing book summary by MIT Press).

183 Russett, *Grasping the Democratic Peace,* p. 26.

184 Russett, *Grasping the Democratic Peace,* pp. 30, 31 (citing reasons given by other scholars, and showing it is true only when democracies contemplate fighting other democracies).

185 Russett, *Grasping the Democratic Peace,* p. 38. Russett writes, "The greater the scale, cost, and risk of using violence, the more effort must be devoted to preparations in public, and of the public" (p. 39).

186 Russett, *Grasping the Democratic Peace,* p. 31.

187 Russett, *Grasping the Democratic Peace,* p. 38.

A PRELUDE AND SUMMARY FOR PART THREE

1 Rachel Williams and Richard Norton-Taylor, "Nuclear Submarines Collide in Atlantic," *Guardian,* February 16, 2009; and John F. Burns, "French and British Submarines Collide," *New York Times,* February 16, 2009.

2 Lucy Walker, director, *Countdown to Zero* (Magnolia Pictures, 2010). The bombs fell into the Mediterranean in 1956, into the Atlantic off the U.S. East Coast in 1957, onto South Carolina in 1958, into the Puget Sound near Whidbey Island in

1959, onto North Carolina in 1961, into the Pacific near Japan in 1965, onto Spain and into the Mediterranean in 1966, and onto Greenland in 1968. In some cases the bombs were never recovered. In no case did a thermonuclear explosion take place, but in two cases—Spain and Greenland—plutonium was dispersed over a wide geography; a town in South Carolina suffered a huge conventional explosion; one of the bombs that fell on North Carolina had six safety devices, five of which failed, only the sixth preventing a nuclear explosion.

3 "USS *West Virginia* (Gold) Commanding Officer Relieved," US Fed News, December 30, 2008; "U.S. Navy Sub Commander Fired," UPI, January 1, 2009.

4 Letter from D. P. German, Navy Personnel Command, Department of the Navy to Elaine Scarry, Freedom of Information Request 20110347 (July 11, 2011). "Should responsive information exist that reflects detailed rationale for relief/detachment of an officer from command, it would be contained in the Navy Military Personnel Records System Privacy Act System of Records. The acknowledgement that such documentation exists in this record would be damaging to CDR [Commander] Hill's personal privacy. Therefore, I can neither confirm nor deny that such responsive documentation exists."

5 Walker, *Countdown to Zero*,

6 Walker, *Countdown to Zero*.

7 Michael Hoffman, "Details Emerging on How Fuses Got to Taiwan," *Air Force Times*, March 26, 2008; see also Josh White, "Nuclear Parts Sent to Taiwan in Error," *Washington Post*, March 26, 2008. The Taiwan military (a year later at the moment it needed its helicopter batteries) discovered and reported the error. Both the *Air Force Times* and the *Washington Post* stories marvel at the failure of the Defense Department to notice the missing ballistic fuses during periodic inventories in the intervening year, and the *Washington Post* story provides a graphic showing the large discrepancy in size and shape between helicopter battery packages and missile component packages.

8 Committee on Armed Services, U.S. Senate, *Hearing: Air Force Nuclear Security* (Hearing specifically dedicated to the Minot-Barksdale incident; with classified material deleted), 110th Cong. 2d sess. (February 12, 2008), p. 2. The Air Force witnesses testifying at the Hearing several times offered the view that "the American public was never in danger" (Senator John Warner summarizing statement of Lt. Gen. Daniel J. Darnell, p. 72; and see Darnell's written statement, p. 6, and the written joint-statement of Lt. Gen. Darnell, Maj. Gen. Polly Peyer, and Maj. Gen. Douglas Raaberg, "during the incident there was never an unsafe condition," p. 8), a view that Senator Levin and Senator Bill Nelson repeatedly challenged as self-evidently false and misleading (pp. 69, 70, 72, 74). Military witnesses, General Larry Welch and General Darnell, assured the senators that no nuclear explosion could have taken place even if the pilots had jettisoned the bombs not realizing they were nuclear missiles. When then asked whether plutonium could have been spread across the land, they appeared wholly unaware—until informed by the senators—that plutonium

spillages had occurred when U.S. weapons fell on Spain and on Greenland (pp. 73, 78, 79). They later provided written statements to the senators explaining that the conventional explosives (CHE, conventional high explosives) packaged with the nuclear missiles that fell on Spain and on Greenland were far more heat-sensitive than those today (IHE, insensitive high explosives), and that therefore no plutonium could have been dispersed in the 2007 incident (p. 80). At no point did it occur to those testifying that just as many layers of fail-safe procedures had been catastrophically bypassed at Minot and Barksdale (where ninety personnel were initially decertified and twenty-five personnel eventually disciplined)—equivalent forms of errors and shortcutting may also have taken place among those responsible for packaging and fusing the weapons themselves. Although those parts of Air Force practice that were investigated revealed scores of errors, those parts of Air Force practice not investigated were assumed to be error-free.

9 Siobhan Gorman, August Cole, and Yochi Dreazen, "Computer Spies Breach Fighter-Jet Project," *Wall Street Journal,* April 21, 2009. See also David Fulghum, Bill Sweetman, Amy Butler, "Internet Hacking Drives Up Pentagon Costs," *Aviation Week,* February 6, 2012. The degree of reliance on computers (90 percent for the F-35; 70 percent for the F-22) is given by David Fulghum, "Cyperwar Strategy," *Aviation Week,* April 9, 2012. The 2012 shift from free-fall to precision-guided nuclear missiles is described by Richard Norton-Taylor, "Nato Plans to Upgrade Nuclear Weapons 'Expensive and Unnecessary,'" *Guardian,* May 10, 2012. The centrality of tactical nuclear weapons was reaffirmed in the United States' 2010 *Nuclear Posture Review;* formerly carried out by F-16s and by Tomahawk cruise missiles, this task (despite some European requests for removal of munitions from their ground) relies on F-35s supplied with B61 nuclear bombs from European munitions depots completed in 1998 (Rebecca Grant, "Nukes for Nato," *Airforcemagazine.com.* 93, no. 7 [July 2010]).

10 While Clinton's loss of the codes has been confirmed by former Chairman of the Joint Chiefs of Staff Hugh Shelton in his book *Without Hesitation,* Carter's loss is usually referred to as a "rumoured loss" (e.g., David Usborne, "Clinton Mislaid Nuclear Launch Code for Months, General Reveals," *The Independent,* October 22, 2010, p. 2; Alex Spillius, "Lost the Key to Nuclear War?" *Daily Telegraph* [London], October 22, 2010, p. 21; and see Pete Sameson's story in *The Sun* on the same day).

11 Bill Joy, "Why the Future Doesn't Need Us: Our Most Powerful 21st Century Technologies—Robotics, Genetic Engineering, and Nanotech—Are Threatening to Make Humans an Endangered Species," *Wired* 8, no. 4 (April 2000).

12 On the later, see the lawsuits brought by Clifford Johnson, Chapter 1, n. 3.

13 It may seem paradoxical both to say that nuclear materials are within the reach of terrorists and to say they are beyond the reach of the population. But nuclear weapons are (comparatively) easy to turn on and nearly impossible to turn off. Since the nuclear terrorist wants to do the first and the population the second, the weapons are available to one and not to the other.

14 The word "soul" is used here to refer to that part of the human being that wishes to protect himself and others from injury, that entertains the possibility that other populations may not be our enemy and so may deserve to be included in the sphere of protection, and that cares to include in that sphere as well at least some non-human species, wood thrush, beech tree, dolphin, fern. Because our access to this part of ourselves becomes palpable in acts of consent or dissent, the operational vocabulary of "consent" and "dissent" will be used while recognizing that what is at stake in them is not a narrow practice of citizenship but the daily practice of respect for one's own life and the life of fellow creatures.

CHAPTER 5: CONSENT AND THE BODY

1 Schloendorff v. Society of New York Hospital, 211 N.Y. 125, 105 N.E. 92, 93.

2 Pratt v. Davis, 118 III.App.161, 166 (1905), affirmed 224 III, 30, 79 N.E. 562 (1906).

3 Lawrence O. Gostin, Judith Areen, Patricia A. King, Steven Goldberg, and Peter G. Jacobson, *Law, Science, and Medicine*, 3rd ed. (Mineola, New York: Foundation Press, 2005), p. 237.

4 William J. Curran and E. Donald Shapiro, *Law, Medicine, and Forensic Science*, 3rd ed. (Boston: Little, Brown, 1982), pp. 417, 426, 447, 1036. Here the grounding of medical consent in concepts of citizenship is much less visible than in *Law, Science, and Medicine*, which devotes a rich chapter of analysis to "Patients, Subjects, and Citizens" (pp. 234–301).

5 John Stuart Mill, *On Liberty* (Buffalo: Prometheus, 1986), p. 16. Excerpts from Mill's essay are, for example, cited in *Law, Science, and Medicine*, pp. 237–39; and the sentence "Over himself..." recurs in articles such as R. E. Ritts, "A Physician's View of Informed Consent in Human Experimentation," *Fordham Law Review* 36 (1968): 636; and Marjorie Maguire Shultz, "From Informed Consent to Patient Choice: A New Protected Interest," *Yale Law Journal* 95 (1985): p. 220.

6 Locke, *Second Treatise of Government*, §27, p. 19.

7 See Chapter 3, section entitled "The Social Contract Is an Obstruction to Injury." The long debate over whether Sydenham or instead Locke is the major author of the 1668 medical essay "Anatomia" and the 1669 "Ars Medica" appears to have been resolved in Locke's favor by the computational stylistics and content analysis carried out by Peter Anstey and John Burrows. See "John Locke, Thomas Sydenham, and the Authorship of Two Medical Essays," in *Electronic British Library Journal* (2009), available at http://www.bl.uk/eblj/2009articles/pdf/ebljarticle 32009.pdf.

8 Manuscript first published in Dewhurst, "Sydenham on 'A Dysentry,'" p. 396.

9 Letter from Thomas Sydenham to John Locke, August 30, 1679. Printed in Kenneth Dewhurst, "Sydenham's Letters to John Locke," *The Practitioner* 157 (1955): 319; italics added. This letter with some variations in spelling and punctuation can also be found in *The Correspondence of John Locke*, ed. E. S. DeBeer (Oxford: Clarendon, 1976), vol. 2, p. 398.

10 Letter from Sydenham to Locke (1674) printed in Dewhurst, "Sydenham's Letters," p. 315. Locke's attention to the pain of his patients is visible in his 1675 letter to Sydenham requesting advice on how to treat a woman's facial pain. The letter is remarkable in two respects: first, the care Locke takes to register the woman's own precise account of her felt experience; second, Locke's ability to make simultaneously visible to Sydenham what the woman looks like from the outside **during** one of these attacks, and what she is experiencing from the inside. He writes, for example, "When the fit came there was, to use my Lady's own expression, as it were a flash of fire all of a suddaine shot into all these parts, and every one of those twitches which made her shreeke out, her mouth was constantly drawn on the right side towards the right eare by repeated convulsive motions which were constantly accompanied by her cries." Following the attack, she has "only a dull pain ... in her teeth ... and an uneasinesse in that side of her tongue which she phansied to be swollen on that side, which yet when I looked on it, as I often did, had not the least alteration in it in colour, bigness, or any other way, though it were one **of her** great complaints that there was scalding liquor in her fits shot into all that side of her tongue" (Letter, reprinted in Dewhurst, "Sydenham's Letters," p. 316).

11 Hippocrates, *Epidemics I*, in *Hippocrates*, vol. 1, trans. W.H.S. Jones (Cambridge, MA: Harvard University Press, 1984), Case VIII, p. 201; and see Case XI, p. 205, and *Epidemics III*, Case VI, p. 229. Hippocrates uses the language of "seizing" even to mark the onset of a crisis in an already existing sickness; see, for example, the opening of Case XIII, p. 209, or in *Epidemics III*, Case III, p. 223.

12 Abu Becr Mohammed Ibn Zacariya Ar-Razi, *A Treatise on the Small-Pox and Measles* (London: Sydenham Society, 1848), p. 32, reprinted in Ralph H. Major, *Classic Descriptions of Disease with Biographical Sketches of the Authors* (Springfield, IL: Charles C. Thomas, 1932), p. 197.

13 Ambroise Paré, *The Workes of that Famous Chirurgion Ambrose Parey*, trans. Thomas Johnson (London: Cotes, 1644). p. 535, reprinted in Major, *Classic Descriptions of Disease*, p. 88.

14 Nathaniel Hodges, *Loimologia: Or an Historical Account of the Plague in London, in 1665* (London: E. Bell and J. Osborn, 1720), p. 30, reprinted in Major, *Classic Descriptions of Disease*, p. 86.

15 Thomas Sydenham, chapters "On the Scarlet Fever" and "On the Measles," in *The Works of Thomas Sydenham*, trans. R. G. Latham (London: Sydenham Society, 1850), pp. 242, 250, reprinted in Major, *Classic Descriptions of Disease*, pp. 196, 198.

16 Daniel Defoe, *The History of the Great Plague in London in the Year 1665. Containing Observations and Memorials of the Most Remarkable Occurrences, Both Public and Private, That Happened during that Dreadful Period*. By a Citizen, who lived the whole Time in LONDON (London: F. and J. Noble, 1754), p. 139, reprinted in Major, *Classic Descriptions of Disease*, p. 92.

17 Locke, "Morbus" (1666 or 1667), British Library, Add. MS. 32, 554, pp. 232–33, 237, 246, 248–50, transcribed (showing deletions not reproduced here) in Jonathan

Walmsley, "'Morbus': Locke's Early Essay on Disease," *Early Science and Medicine* 5, no. 4 (2000): 391, 392.

18 Although the two concerns are independent, they may of course occur in the same medical essay, as in Locke's "Morbus" just cited, where he is indeed concerned to show that the disease could not originate in the blood since if it were due to the "depravation of [the] bloud, why bloud should at [the] same time corrode one legge soe cruelly and at [the] same time soe courteously nourish ye other" ("Morbus," p. 392) would be difficult to explain. My point is that the same vocabulary of seizure and insinuation occurs even in writings where the disease is understood to originate in the body, or where the question of where the disease originates is not even being asked.

19 Hippocrates, *Epidemics I,* Case VI, p. 199; and see note 11, above.

20 Paré, *The Workes of that Famous Chirurgion,* p. 90.

21 Hippocrates, "The Oath," in *Hippocrates,* pp. 299, 300. I am including in the count of six the two sentences prohibiting abortion and surgery with the assumption that Hippocrates must have assumed these two acts were too close to injury to be part of the physician's work. See Jones's comment on the accepted practice of surgery on pages 293–95, which suggests that Hippocrates considers not the performance of surgery but the performance of surgery by an underqualified person to be the problem. Even excepting the prohibitions on abortion and surgery, four of the ten sentences are dedicated to the problem of physician trespass.

22 MS. Locke C. 29, fol. 121, photograph reproduced and inscription transcribed in Kenneth Dewhurst, "Truss Designed by Locke," *British Medical Journal* 2, vol. 2, no. 4878 (1954): 44.

23 MS. Locke d. 9, p. 17, Bodleian Library, Oxford University, transcribed in Kenneth Dewhurst, "Prince Rupert as a Scientist," *British Journal for the History of Science* 1, no. 4 (December 1963): 372.

24 MS. Locke d. 9, p. 320, transcribed in Dewhurst, "Prince Rupert as a Scientist," p. 373. If the ointment itself contributed to the success of the dressing, it did so because it kept the wound moist and suppressed bacteria. The recipe included oil extracted from cream, "Moonwort, Mousear [chickweed], plantin, Sanicle [plant in carrot family], Adders tongue and the roots of Solomons Seale" (p. 372).

For an extensive review of twenty-first-century burn dressings—from the most widely used "paraffin impregnated gauze" to "films, foams, composites, sprays and gels" to "bioengineered skin substitutes"—see Jason Wasiak, Heather Cleland, and Fiona Campbell, "Dressings for Superficial and Partial Thickness Burns" in *Cochrane Collaboration* (John Wiley & Sons, 2010), available at http://online library.wiley.com/doi/10.1002/14651858.CD002106.pub3/full, an article that draws on a vast data set provided by studies carried out in the second half of the twentieth century and opening of the twenty-first. The ideal dressing acts as substitute skin, allowing drainage of the wound, keeping the wound moist, permitting liquid and gas transfer while keeping bacteria out. The article compares the rival dressings on the basis of pain, time to healing, and rate of infection.

The problem of delicate touch that Locke tried to solve with a feather is today addressed by foams and sprays, and by leaving (as Locke did) the dressing in place because "frequent change" of dressing "traumatizes newly epithelialized surfaces and delays healing." The dressing in some of the studies drawn on in Wasiak et al. is left in place for five or six days before change, with a second dressing (as in Locke's recommendation) placed over the first when needed (see, e.g., the section on "Silicon coated nylon dressing"). The article has a section directly assessing the "Level of pain associated with the application and removal, or both, of the wound dressing," and explicitly compares rival dressings on the basis of how many times each must be changed and how many minutes it takes.

25 Daniel A. Farber, "Too Clever by Half: The Case Against Brilliance," *The New Republic*, September 1, 1986, pp. 11, 12. Farber puts forward "the case against brilliance" more elaborately in two *Minnesota Law Review* articles from 1986 and 1987, and later in his book coauthored with Suzanna Sherry, *Desperately Seeking Certainty: The Misguided Quest for Constitutional Foundations* (Chicago: University of Chicago Press, 2002), where he critiques six leading constitutional theorists—Robert Bork, Antonin Scalia, Akhil Amar, Richard Epstein, Bruce Ackerman, and Ronald Dworkin—as "thinkers" whose "work" is "characterized more by brilliance than by soundness" (p. 57); see also pp. 1, 6, 133, 151. As is evident in my citations to some of these theorists in earlier chapters, I myself believe their brilliance (and brilliance in general) is often compatible with accuracy and with the soundness of thinking that eventually comes to be regarded as canonical.

26 Alexis de Tocqueville, *Democracy in America*, trans. Henry Reeve, rev. Francis Bowen, rev. and ed. Phillips Bradley (New York: Vintage-Random, 1945), vol. 2, p. 273f.

27 Shultz, "From Informed Consent to Patient Choice," p. 224.

28 Shultz, "From Informed Consent to Patient Choice," p. 228.

29 Shultz, "From Informed Consent to Patient Choice," p. 233.

30 Shultz's emphasis on "touch dependency" sensitizes us to the fact that some areas of the law address one sense modality but not another. In her analysis of "The First Amendment Right against Compelled Listening," Caroline Mala Corbin notes that the First Amendment is much more likely to be used to protect against coerced listening than against coerced viewing: judges have consistently ruled that viewers have the option of closing their eyes or looking away, even when their mobility is restricted (*Boston University Law Review* 89 [June 2009]: 939, text accompanying n. 22–26).

31 American Law Institute, *Second Restatement of the Law of Torts* (St. Paul, MN: American Law Institute Publishers, 1966), vol. 2, sec. 402A (Reporter: William L. Prosser), 349ff. and appendix, vol. 3, 1ff. See also the multivolume *Restatement of Torts, Third: Product Liability* (1998), *Restatement of Torts, Third: Apportionment*

of Liability (2000), and *Restatement of Torts, Third: Liability for Emotional and Physical Harm* (vol. 1: 2010) all of which were occasioned by, and greatly extend the discussion of, section 402A in the original *Second Restatement* (as explained by Lance Liebman, director of the American Law Institute, in the foreword to *A Concise Restatement of Torts*, 2nd ed. [2010], pp. ix, x). In these later volumes, laws that originally addressed exclusively physical events (whether touching the body or at greater remove) are extended to the nonphysical: as the reporters for the volume on *Liability for Emotional and Physical Harm* explain, "Begun in the mid-1990s, the *Restatement Third of Torts: Liability for Physical and Emotional Harm* addresses the core principles of liability for physical harm. It provides rules for liability for intentional, negligence, and strict-liability torts that result in physical injury. Later, it was expanded to include liability for emotional harm, and it now encompasses claims for stand-alone emotional harm" (Michael D. Green and William C. Powers, *A Concise Restatement of Torts*, 2nd ed., p. xi).

32 Michael Ignatieff, *The Needs of Strangers* (New York: Penguin-Sifton, 1984), p. 10.

33 *Schloendorff v. Society of New York Hospital*, at p. 95.

34 Morris Vogel, *The Invention of the Modern Hospital: Boston, 1870–1930* (Chicago: University of Chicago Press, 1980), p. 4.

35 Robert Burt, in particular, analyzes and attempts to redress negative consequences of impersonality for both physicians and patients in *Taking Care of Strangers: The Rule of Law in Doctor-Patient Relations* (New York: Free Press, 1979).

36 Charles Rosenberg, *The Care of Strangers: The Rise of America's Hospital System* (New York: Basic Books, 1987), pp. 337, 349.

37 Vogel, *The Invention of the Modern Hospital*, p. 15.

38 Vogel, *The Invention of the Modern Hospital*, pp. 118, 119.

39 Rosenberg, *The Care of Strangers*, p. 260.

40 Michael Walzer, Lecture, Mellon Seminar on Human Nature, University of Pennsylvania, Spring 1987. For the Hilton Hotel analogy, see also Walzer's *Interpretation and Social Criticism: The Tanner Lectures on Human Values* (Cambridge, MA: Harvard University Press, 1987), p. 15. In *Thick and Thin*, he again uses the example of the hotel to exemplify a "minimalist universalism" (*Thick and Thin: Moral Argument at Home and Abroad* [Notre Dame, IN: University of Notre Dame Press, 1994], p. 52). Morris Vogel's study of the nineteenth-century Boston hospitals explicitly focuses on "the hotel" dimension of the hospital: wealthy and middle-class patients were seen and treated in their own homes; the giving of hospital lodgings—effectively, as Vogel notes, hotel rooms—to the poor was part of how that institution served them, and eventually the more wealthy as well (Vogel, *The Invention of the Hospital*, pp. 100, 104, 115, 119).

41 Alexander Bickel, "Chapter 2: Citizen or Person? What Is Not Granted Cannot Be Taken Away," in *The Morality of Consent* (New Haven: Yale University Press, 1975), pp. 33–54. See especially pp. 36–38, 53.

42 William F. May, "Code, Covenant, Contract, or Philanthropy," *Hastings Center Report 5* (December 1975), p. 33.

43 Bernard R. Boxill, "Appendix C: Consent and Compensation" in President's Commission for the Study of Ethical Problems in Medicine and Biomedical and Behavioral Research, *Compensating for Research Injuries: The Ethical and Legal Implications of Programs to Redress Injuries Caused by Biomedical and Behavioral Research* (Washington, DC: GPO, 1982), vol. 2, pp. 42, 50.

44 Charles Fried, *Medical Experimentation: Personal Integrity and Social Policy* (New York: Elsevier, 1974), pp. 59–66. For philosophic discussion of informed consent that enlists John Rawls's *Theory of Justice*, see, for example, James Wilson's summary and critique of O'Nora O'Neill's recent writings on autonomy and consent in "Is Respect for Autonomy Defensible?" *Journal of Medical Ethics* 33, no. 6 (June 2007): 353–56, esp. 355–56.

45 Shultz, "From Informed Consent to Patient Choice," p. 220, n. 3.

46 Locke, *Second Treatise of Government*, p. 10, see also pp. 15, 16.

47 Just as within medicine the act of consent floats among different locations—the selection of a doctor; the taking of a prescription; the actual signing of a consent form—so too the act of consent forming the social contract has many locations. An elegant graphing of these locations—voting, running for office, receipt of benefits, fair play, as well as the classical and contemporary exponents of each—appears in A. John Simmons's book, *Moral Principles and Political Obligations* (Princeton: Princeton University Press, 1979). Despite the multiplicity of sites, the "real battleground" for consent theorists, according to Simmons, is "tacit consent" (p. 79); of the varying forms of tacit consent, the most absorbing because most universalizing is "tacit consent through residence."

48 Robert Faulkner, "The First Liberal Democrat: Locke's Popular Government," *Review of Politics* 63, no. 1 (Winter 2001): 15.

49 Hobbes, *On the Citizen*, ed. and trans. Tuck and Silverthorne, p. 111. In this passage, Hobbes soon changes from liberty per se to civil liberty; and to the fact that children, slaves, and free adults all maintain the right of self-preservation under any threat.

50 Hobbes, *A Treatise of Liberty and Necessity*, transcribed, translated, and printed from oral debate in France by John Davys, quoted by John Bramhall, *A Defence of True Liberty from Antecedent and Extrinsecall Necessity*, introd. G. A. J. Rogers (London: Routledge, 1996; reprint of 1655 edition), no. 29, p. 210.

51 Hobbes, *Leviathan*, ch. 6, p. 130. Throughout Part I, chapter 6, Hobbes describes the "Interior Beginnings of Voluntary Motions; commonly called the PASSIONS" (p. 118) in terms of motion: sensations, for examples, are "onely Motion, caused by the action of externall objects" (p. 121); and the effect of such sensation "is nothing but Motion, or Endeavour; which consisteth in Appetite, or Aversion, to, or from the object moving," the former appearing as "DELIGHT" and the latter,

"TROUBLE OF MIND" (p. 121). Hobbes at every point stresses that even these interior motions (perception, desire, aversion) are literal, physical, bodily motions; and he disparages those who think the vocabulary is being used metaphorically: "For the Schooles find in meere Appetite to go, or move, no actuall Motion at all; but because some Motion they must acknowledge, they call it Metaphoricall Motion: which is but an absurd speech: for though Words may be called metaphoricall; Bodies, and Motions cannot" (p. 119).

52 Locke, *An Essay Concerning Human Understanding*, ed. Peter H. Nidditch (Oxford: Oxford Clarendon Press, 1979), bk. II, ch. 21, §16, p. 241.

53 Locke, *An Essay Concerning Human Understanding*, bk. II, ch. 21, §9, pp. 238–39. Locke, like Hobbes, says thinking entails motion (though it is not clear whether he would describe that motion as literal or metaphorical). In a 1702 letter, Locke addresses the question of whether the understanding is free by saying in one sense it is, in another sense it is not. We have freedom of understanding insofar as we can move from one mental object to another: "I can think about Adam's sin, or remove my cogitation thence to the city of Rome or to the art of war in the present age. In all these actions and in countless others of the kind I am free because I am able at my pleasure to think or not to think about this or that." But he goes on to differentiate this meaning of understanding (the freedom to move toward or away from a mental object) from "an act of understanding" meaning "that action by which I perceive that something is true." Here one does not have freedom; for example, one has not the freedom to *not* understand that the three angles of a triangle are the equivalent of two right angles, once that truth has been demonstrated (Letter #3192, John Locke to Philippus Van Limborch, September 28, 1702, translated from the Latin, online at *Past Master*, reprinted from *The Correspondence of John Locke*, ed. E. S. De Beer, vol. 7, p. 680). On "Thinking and Motion" as two parallel but not identical events, see *An Essay Concerning Human Understanding*, bk. II, ch. 21, §§4–8, pp. 235–37.

54 John Searle, *Minds, Brains, and Science* (Cambridge: Harvard University Press, 1984), p. 87.

55 Searle, *Minds, Brains, and Science*, p. 88.

56 Searle, *Minds, Brains, and Science*, pp. 92, 96. Our movement across a room is not the only physical action Searle pictures: "Raise your arm or walk across the room or take a drink of water" he coaxes, framing the walk across the room with two other embodied actions. But it remains the major one. At two crucial points, Searle uses an extended example of the movement of a person across the floor under coercion. As is suggested below, once the context changes from "volition" to "consent" (that is, once the philosophic context is explicitly political) the examples change from the domestic and psychological movement across a floor to persons moving across the national terrain.

57 Gilbert Ryle, *The Concept of Mind* (London: Hutchinson, 1949), pp. 71, 67.

58 Ryle, *The Concept of Mind*, p. 63.

59 William James, *The Principles of Psychology,* 1890 ed. (New York: Dover, 1950), vol. 2, p. 486. James's descriptions of physical movement are stunning; see, for example, his account of the difficult and precise movements requiring a "premonitory weighing [that] feels so much like a succession of tentative sallyings forth of power into the outer world" (p. 493).

60 Augustine, *Concerning the City of God against the Pagans,* trans. Henry Bettenson, introd. John O'Meara (New York: Penguin, 1986), pp. 587, 588.

61 Epictetus, *Discourses,* in *Epictetus: The Discourses as Reported by Arrian, the Manual, and Fragments,* vol. 2, trans. W. A. Oldfather, Loeb Classical Edition (Cambridge: Harvard University Press, 1985), 4. 1. 34, p. 255. For Epictetus's reliance on the illustration of physical movement (even where the overt argument urges a decoupling of freedom from the body), see also vol. 1, bk. I, pp. 15, 19, 21, 27–33, 45.

62 This Swiss passport law has long since been changed; a married woman no longer needs her husband's consent to pass over the country's border.

63 Etymol. Magnum. 329, cited in Maurice Cranston, "The Political and Philosophical Aspects of the Right to Leave and to Return," in *The Right to Leave and to Return: Papers and Recommendations of the International Colloquium Held in Uppsala, Sweden, 19–20 June 1972,* ed. Karel Vasak and Sidney Liskofsky (Ann Arbor, MI: University Microfilms International, 1976), p. 21, 29.

64 Cranston, "The Political and Philosophical Aspects of the Right to Leave and to Return," p. 29. The etymology of "libertas" is by some interpreters seen to stress bodily sexuality rather than bodily movement.

In a fascinating article (one I encountered long after giving this chapter as a lecture for Yale's Whitney Center, November 3, 1986), Hanna Pitkin analyzes Hannah Arendt's claims about the terms "liberty" and "freedom" by tracking in rich detail the etymologies and uses of the two words. Though she sees the emphasis on movement in the Greek and Roman words as attended by some complications, she finds that they are always materially grounded: "For our purposes the many, complexly interrelated theories [of the meaning of "liber"] may be summed into three: one centering on group membership and slavery, one centering on unimpeded motion, and one centering on sexual pleasure and potency" (Hanna Fenichel Pitkin, "Are Freedom and Liberty Twins?", *Political Theory* 16, no. 4 [November 1988]: 523–552).

65 Cranston, "The Political and Philosophical Aspects of the Right to Leave and to Return," p. 21.

66 Socrates usually opens a given argument by making overt his own act of ventriloquism: "Suppose . . . the laws and constitution of Athens were to come and confront us and ask this question," "Then what supposing the laws say, Was there provision for this in the agreement between you and us, Socrates?" "Consider, then, Socrates, the laws would probably continue, whether it is also true." But once any given argument is in full sway, the laws and constitution appear to speak on their own authority unaided by the suppositions of the speaker who animates them and to whom they address themselves: "Now, Socrates," "Never mind our language,

Socrates, but answer our questions" (Plato, *Crito*, trans. Hugh Tredennick, in *The Collected Dialogues of Plato including the Letters,* ed. and introd. Edith Hamilton and Huntington Cairns [Princeton: Princeton University Press Bollingen Series LXXI, 1961], pp. 35, 36, and passim).

67 Emerson, too, sees the laws as an act of ventriloquism: "We must trust infinitely to the beneficent necessity which shines through all laws. Human nature expresses itself in them as characteristically as in statues, or songs, or railroads, and an abstract of the codes of nations would be a transcript of the common conscience" ("Politics" [1844], in *Selected Writings of Ralph Waldo Emerson,* ed. William H. Gilman [New York: Signet-New American, 1965–83], p. 355).

As its title implies, Albert O. Hirschman's *Exit, Voice, and Loyalty* (Cambridge: Harvard University Press, 1970) identifies physical exit and verbal dissent as two ways of reshaping a marketplace, an institution, or a state. His brilliant analysis, throughout as applicable to the political as to the economic sphere, is continually confirmed not only by the historical illustrations he invokes but by events occurring after the book's publication. East Germany in the winter months of 1989–90, for example, provides a graphic instance of the relation between "exit" and "voice" in the crucial interaction among the 2000 persons each day exiting from the country, and the hundreds of thousands voicing their protest each Monday evening on the streets of Leipzig and other cities. Because *Exit, Voice, and Loyalty* makes visible the intimacy of departure and vocalized complaint—and conversely, the intimacy between residing and vocalized consent—it, too, can be read as a treatise about physical-movement-as-ventriloquism.

68 Plato, *Crito,* pp. 37, 38. The laws throughout these cited passages of course address themselves to Socrates rather than to Crito.

69 Plato, *Crito,* p. 38.

70 Plato, *Crito,* p. 35.

71 John Locke, *Second Treatise of Government,* §119, p. 64.

72 Jean-Jacques Rousseau, *The Social Contract, or Principles of Political Right* (1762), trans. and introd. Maurice Cranston (Harmondsworth: Penguin, 1968), bk. IV, ch. 2, p. 153. Rousseau writes this immediately after his claim that "the civil association is the most voluntary act in the world" (p. 152).

73 Rousseau, *The Social Contract,* bk. III, ch. 18, p. 148.

74 Rousseau, *The Social Contract,* bk III, ch. 1, p. 101.

75 Rousseau, *The Social Contract,* bk. II, ch. 10, p. 93.

76 Reproduced in the Cranston edition, p. 44. Rousseau's physical residence in and flight from various countries during the period of publication invites a number of different ways to understand the title page.

77 Cranston, "Introduction," *Social Contract,* p. 22.

78 Hobbes, *On the Citizen,* ed. and trans. Tuck and Silverthorne, p. 101.

79 Locke, *Second Treatise of Government,* "Preface," p. 5.

80 Locke, *Second Treatise of Government,* §99, p. 53 passim.

81 Locke, *Second Treatise of Government*, §95, p. 52.

82 Locke, *Second Treatise of Government*, §112, p. 61.

83 Locke, *Second Treatise of Government*, §104, p. 55; here, as often, Locke's registration of the "peaceful" start is accompanied by the statement that it is a "free" or "voluntary" act.

84 Locke, *Second Treatise of Government*, §134, p. 69; the instrument for maintaining this end is the rule of law.

85 Locke, *Second Treatise of Government*, §163, p. 85.

86 Locke, *Second Treatise of Government*, §101, p. 54; here Locke says that it is when we find ourselves in this midst of this accomplished end that we begin to look for the origins for which there may not be any written record.

87 Locke, *Second Treatise of Government*, §229, p. 115.

88 Locke, *Second Treatise of Government*, §99, p. 53; italics are Locke's.

89 For example, Chapter 2, "Of the State of Nature"; Chapter 3, "Of the State of War"; Chapter 4, "Of Slavery."

90 The decoupling of "political power" from "paternal power" is one of Locke's central goals, and the rejection of patriarchy is the not-construction to which he returns most often throughout the *Second Treatise* (even though he had already dispatched the subject in the *First Treatise* and resummarized it in Chapter 1 of the *Second*). In the *Second Treatise*, it is the subject of "Of Paternal Power" (Chapter 6) and "Of Paternal, Political, and Despotical Power, Considered Together" (Chapter 15) and a central issue in "Of Political or Civil Power" (Chapter 7) where he argues that even the power of adults over children, if it has any reality at all, is "parental" (belonging to both wife and husband and, in fact, originating with the mother and transferring to the father through her) and certainly is not the model of power relations outside the family. It is again a major subject in "Of the Beginning of Political Societies" (Chapter 8), where he places the formation of the social contract in opposition to the founding myth of the father (p. 55, §103; p. 56, §106; p. 60, §112; p. 62, §§115, 116; p. 63, §118). Even when we are in chapters that are not explicitly working to decouple political from paternal power, we encounter frequent single-sentence reminders of the opposition.

91 See Gaines Post, "Chapter IV: A Romano-Canonical Maxim, *Quod Omnes Tangit*, in Bracton and in Early Parliaments," in *Studies in Medieval Legal Thought: Public Law and the State 1100–1322* (Princeton: Princeton University Press, 1964), p. 163–238. For the presence of the word "touch" (*tangere* or *contingere*) as key, see especially pp. 166, 167, 222, 233. Developing into a major principle of due process, *quod omnes tangit* affirmed the idea that "no one should suffer injury because of ignorance of the business that concerns him" (p. 170), and that "all whose rights are touched by an issue should have every opportunity to prepare the defense of their rights" (p. 180).

92 Some problems regularly arising within a hospital between medical staff and patients may be seen as problems arising from the difference between residents

and nonresidents, citizens (physicians) and tourists or resident aliens (patients). Tensions between the resident physicians and the general practitioners with hospital "privileges" are indicative of the sever problems that accompany varying depths of residency.

93 See William L. Prosser and W. Page Keeton, *The Law of Torts*, 5th ed. (St. Paul, MN: West, 1984), pp. 188, 193, on the application of neighborhood standards to doctors, as well as on the displacement of locality rules by a universal standard in a small number of states.

94 Lawrence Stone, *The Family, Sex and Marriage in England 1500–1800*, abridged ed. (New York: Harper Torchbooks, 1979), p. 282. In his anger against the deforming of the body by fashion, Locke was speaking, as H.R.F. Bourne makes clear, in his capacity as physician (*The Life of John Locke*, vol. 1, p. 450).

95 Stone, *The Family, Sex and Marriage*, p. 267.

96 The metaphor of the fence is one of Locke's frequently invoked artifacts. It allows him to move smoothly from tacit consent, to express consent, to legislative restructurings that anticipate and eliminate rebellion. Freedom, he writes, is "the fence" to my preservation. His use of the term is labile: the laws are "fences" to property against the powers of others (*Second Treatise on Government* p. 111); the capacity of the people to "reserve[e] to themselves the choice of their *representatives*" is "the fence to their properties" (p. 112). By transferring the boundary artifact from its literal location in the sphere of individual persons to the sphere of representative acts, Locke shifts over from the arena of tacit consent through residence to express consental acts of voting and choosing officeholders. Finally, the capacity to generate a new legislature if the old too deeply offends the people is, Locke writes, "*the best fence against rebellion*" (p. 114).

97 Rousseau, *The Social Contract*, bk. III, ch. 16, p. 144.

98 Rousseau, *The Social Contract*, bk. IV, ch. 2, p. 152.

99 The citations to Plato and Rousseau are given above at notes 68 and 73. Plato's and Rousseau's statements probably should not be taken as expressing a belief that persons who are paralyzed are less autonomous; they instead suggest that it requires more psychic energy to sustain and express one's powers of consent if one is physically disabled. The restructuring of many American cities in recent decades to ensure the mobility of the physically handicapped (curb and building ramps, lifts on buses) shows the importance of self-authorized movement to persons who are handicapped, if any "evidence" were needed.

Paul Schilder observes that under normal circumstances, the body feels heavier in some parts—bottom of legs, abdomen, base of head—than in others. These locations change once one's posture changes to lying down. In paralysis, the body feels much heavier; even other objects feel heavier when placed on those limbs (*The Image and Appearance of the Human Body: Studies in the Constructive Energies of the Psyche* [New York: International Universities Press, 1950], pp. 51–62). Amartya Sen uses the case of physical disability in his discussion of the difference between positive and negative freedom (*New York Review of Books*, June 14, 1990, p. 49), a reminder of the persistence of its place in philosophic argument.

100 Even apart from the confusion of active and passive it sponsors, consent is often suspected of being fictitious, both by those looking at it from within political philosophy and those within medicine. For example, Kurt Baier writes that "traditionally, the problem of political obligation has been construed as the problem of whether there is any such thing" ("Obligation: Political and Moral," in *Nomos XII: Political and Legal Obligation*, ed. J. R. Pennock and J. W. Chapman [Atherton, 1970], cited in Simmons, *Moral Principles and Political Obligations*, p. 3). Writing on consent in medical contexts, Marcus L. Plante calls informed consent "this unfortunate journalistic expression" ("An Analysis of 'Informed Consent,'" *Fordham Law Review* 36 [1967/68]: 639); and Jay Katz in an article entitled "Informed Consent—A Fairy Tale? Law's Vision" questions whether it spellbinds us into believing that "frog-patients will become autonomous princes" (*University of Pittsburgh Law Review* 39 [Winter 1977]: 137). Consent in marriage—the subject of the third section of this chapter—has also been challenged as a fiction by feminists such as Catherine MacKinnon since marital sex sometimes involves levels of force that are incompatible with the woman's consent.

When consent is looked at across diverse contexts (medicine, political philosophy, marriage) its substantive features—such as its inseparability from the body—come prominently into view. Hence the substantiveness and solidity of consent—its crucial, life-protecting reality—can be more easily grasped than when scrutinizing it within any one isolated sphere. Looking at it in multiple spheres also assists us in comprehending what it is that produces, within any one isolated sphere, the aura of fictiveness.

101 Augustine, *City of God*, p. 585.

102 Augustine, *City of God*, p. 588.

103 Augustine, *City of God*, p. 588.

104 For a more extended description of this mental habit, see Elaine Scarry, "The Merging of Bodies and Artifacts in the Social Contract," in *Culture on the Brink: Ideologies of Technology*, ed. Gretchen Bender and Timothy Druckrey (Bay Press, 1994), pp. 85–97; and Elaine Scarry, "Donne: But Yet the Body is His Booke," in *Literature and the Body* (Baltimore: Johns Hopkins University Press, 1988).

105 Plato, *Crito*, p. 39. See also in note 67 above the account of the throwing of the voice into the public sphere by Ralph Waldo Emerson (who likens the laws to songs) and more recently by Albert O. Hirschman.

106 Hobbes, *Leviathan*, ch. 13, p. 186.

107 Rousseau, *Social Contract*, pp. 64–65. Chapter 8, "Civil Society," is exclusively dedicated to this transformation.

108 Rousseau, *The Social Contract*, bk. I, ch. 9, p. 68.

109 While by the first interpretation, the categories of active and passive cause us to doubt the reality of consent, now by the third interpretation consent causes us to doubt the validity of the categories of active and passive.

110 It would be difficult to overstate the degree to which the first wave of feminist theory and practice was grounded in consent—and more particularly, women's repossession of the powers of consent over their own bodies—even where this overt vocabulary was not used. In the second wave of feminist work, the centrality of "consent" and "contract" continued, became more explicit, and began to take the form of a rigorous critique that (in my view) worked to strengthen the two as conceptual tools in the service of feminist goals. The critique of consent and contract came from multiple spheres, philosophy (see, e.g., Annette Baier, "Trust and Antitrust," *Ethics* 96 [1986]: 231–60, esp. 247ff.), law (Catharine A. MacKinnon, *Towards a Feminist Theory of the State* [Cambridge: Harvard University Press, 1989], pp. 172ff.), political science (Carole Pateman, *The Sexual Contract* [Stanford: Stanford University Press, 1988]), and literature (Susan Staves, "Separate Maintenance Contracts," *Eighteenth-Century Life* 2 [1987]: 78–101).

The overt argument in these writings is sometimes starkly against consent or contract. The charge of the "fictiveness" of contract visible in the spheres of medicine and the nation-state (see note 100 above) resurfaces in the analysis of marriage and sexual relations: Pateman calls contract "an hypothesis, a story, a political fiction" (p. 8) that "justifies subjection by presenting it as freedom" (p. 39) and MacKinnon, arguing that a woman's response to coercion in rape is often called "consent" (p. 168), speaks of "the contract fiction" (p. 174). But in these writings, it is still the vocabulary of consent and contract that permits the unmasking of coercive or patriarchal structures. It can therefore be argued that the writings work not to displace consent (or even to offer an alternative conceptual tool) but to strengthen it by requiring that its claims be made genuine. A third possible reading is that the feminist critique of contract or consent is actually directed not against contract or consent per se but against some associated or overlapping attribute. Reviewing writings by Annette Baier, Virginia Held, Lawrence Blum, Sheila Mullet, and Nel Noddings, David Michael Anderson argues that the second-wave feminist objections to contract are actually directed against "proceduralism" and a distinctly male preoccupation with self-justification ("The Demands of Impartial Justification," an unpublished manuscript, University of Michigan).

111 The centuries of debate over whether the senses are active or passive is one illustration of the body's ability to elude these categories.

112 It may be that the reciprocal, or two-directional, model of consent needs to be examined separately from the one-directional (or asymmetrical) model encountered in medicine and elsewhere. But it is difficult to hold them in wholly distinct spaces. The symmetry or reciprocity of marriage is challengeable, as described below. Conversely, what appear to be asymmetrical acts of consent in medicine

may instead be seen as merely delayed forms of symmetry since the position of the healer and the person healed may be reversed after a passage of time. Although the formal position of physician disguises the exchange, physicians themselves require physicians. More telling, perhaps, are the constant, small "medical" acts of healing (e.g., handing a friend an aspirin) that take place among the population at large and that in their fluidity create an elaborate texture of exchanged consent among friends, colleagues, family, and strangers.

113 Harry D. Krause periodically speaks of the contentlessness of the marriage contract. In *Family Law: Cases, Comments and Questions*, he observes that the marriage contract is analogous to "a *form* contract, with only a few blank lines for the parties to complete, but with most of the content prescribed although usually not disclosed to the parties" (2nd ed. [St. Paul, MN: West, 1983], pp. 79–80; see also Krause, *Family Law in a Nutshell*, 2nd ed. [St. Paul, MN: West, 1986], p. 75).

   A business contract such as one governing a merger and acquisition agreement, in contrast, may have hundreds of pages.

114 Prior to no-fault divorce, the procedures could take several years, and even with no-fault divorce the process can still take time.

115 Locke, *Second Treatise of Government*, p. 53, §99; italics are Locke's.

116 Can. 1801, §§1, 2, cited in H. A. Ayrinhac, *Marriage Legislation in the New Code of Canon Law* (New York: Benziger Brothers, 1918), p. 189. For recent reformulations and the suggested rephrasings of Vatican II, see B. A. Siegle, *Marriage Today: A Commentary on the Code of Canon Law*, 3rd ed. (New York: Alba House, 1979).

117 Pius VI, 1789, cited in Ayrinhac, *Marriage Legislation in the New Code of Canon Law*, p. 190.

118 Ayrinhac, *Marriage Legislation in the New Code of Canon Law*, pp. 190, 191. B. A. Siegle gives the gloss as follows: "The object of this consent is the perpetual and exclusive right over each other's body for the exercise of actions that by their very nature pertain to the procreation of children" (*Marriage Today: A Commentary on the Code of Canon Law*, p. 148).

119 Jean-Baptiste Molin and Protais Mutembe, *Le Rituel du Mariage en France du XII au XVI Siècle* (Paris: Beauchesne, 1973), p. 306. Translated by Michael P. Foley, *Wedding Rites: A Complete Guide to Traditional Vows, Music, Ceremonies, Blessings, and Interfaith Services* (Grand Rapids, MI: William B. Eerdmans, 2008), p. 61. Foley gives the year 1100 but Molin and Mutembe appear to be giving the Barbeau oath from the 1300s.

120 Molin and Mutembe, *Le Rituel du Mariage*, p. 181 ("de mon corps je te fais honneur, et de moi et de tous mes biens que j'ai ou que j'aurai dame je te constitue"). Translated by Foley, *Wedding Rites*, p. 63.

121 Molin and Mutembe, *Le Rituel du Mariage*, pp. 106–7. Translated by Foley, *Wedding Rites*, p. 64.

122 Foley, *Wedding Rites*, p. 68 (citing Ulrich Leupold, *Luther's Works*, vol. 53 (Philadelphia: Fortress Press 1965). Because Luther uses the word "desire" in many

other contexts for wanting or willing, this instance is less corporeal than the other examples given.

123 Foley, *Wedding Rites*, pp. 63, 66, 67. The phrasing with pronouns is from the 1200 CE Paris marriage oath; the phrase without pronouns occurs in the Renaissance Catholic phrasing and in both Catholic and Protestant phrasing thereafter.

124 Joel Foote Bingham, *Christian Marriage: The Ceremony, History, and Significance; Ritual, Practical, and Archaeological Notes; and the Text of the English, Roman, Greek, and Jewish Ceremonies* (New York: E. P. Dutton, 1900), p. 122.

125 The vows of the three religions are given in Foley, *Wedding Rites*, pp. 67, 70, 71.

126 The rejection of other sexual partners is sometimes directly in the promise, as when the man and woman in the Parisian vow of 1200 CE each in turn agreed "that either for better or for worse, thou wilt not replace her (him) with another, nor cast her (him) out, all the days of thy life" (Foley, *Wedding Rites*, p. 63). More often, this specification is not in the vow itself but in closely adjacent parts of the ceremony. Immediately before the giving of vows in the Anglican ceremony, the priest says, "And forsaking all others, keep thee only to her" (Foley, *Wedding Rites*, p. 67). Immediately after the giving of vows in the Lutheran service, the pastor says, "What God hath joined together, let not man put asunder" (Foley, *Wedding Rites*, p. 68). Early in the Byzantine Catholic liturgy, the priest's prayer includes the phrase "Preserve their bed from adulterous snares" (Foley, *Wedding Rites*, p. 110); at the close of that same ceremony, the priest's farewell blessing ends by again asking God's assistance in avoiding sexual contact with others (Foley, *Wedding Rites*, p. 120).

In early centuries, there is a presumption that a promise to make love is made with the intention of having children—hence the many church statements about being fruitful (and even living to see one's offspring down to the "third or fourth generation"). But the vow almost certainly includes the possibility of a shared decision not to have children. In the modern world, the vow continues to give the couple discretion over when and how to protect and love one another's bodies, but includes a wider set of choices, apparently including (as in the "open marriages" in the third-quarter of the twentieth century) intimacy with other partners.

127 Siegle, *Marriage Today: A Commentary on the Code of Canon Law*, p. 147. See also Ayrinhac, *Marriage Legislation in the New Code of Canon Law*, pp. 189, 190.

128 Ayrinhac paraphrasing Petro Cardinal Gasparri in *Marriage Legislation in the New Code of Canon Law*, p. 190.

129 Foley, *Wedding Rites*, p. 128. Many details of the Jewish marriage suggest the reciprocal transfer of rights between man and woman; but the formal written contract is signed only by the man and endorsed by two male witnesses and therefore does not appear to place equality at the heart of the ceremony.

Gender equality also seems to be absent, or obscure, in the Islamic wedding ceremony in which the bride does not even need to be present. The fact of polygamy—with men able to have up to four wives simultaneously but women only a single husband at a time—again makes it hard to discern gender equality. Some have argued that polygamy among "consenting adults" ought to be legalized, just as same-sex marriage has been; but the asymmetries within the Islamic model make it hard to align with two-person marriages (whether same-gender or different-gender). For a review of the arguments on both sides, see Adrienne D. Davis, "Regulating Polygamy: Intimacy, Default Rules, and Bargaining for Equality," *Columbia Law Review* 110 (December 2010): pp. 1955ff.

130 Molin and Mutembe, *Le Rituel du Mariage*, pp. 27, 28, describes "une cérémonie proprement liturgique à la maison des noces"—from the sixth to the sixteenth century—and refers readers to chapter 12 ("La bénédiction de la chamber nuptial"). See also Foley, *Wedding Rites*, pp. 136–38.

131 See Molin and Mutembe, *Le Rituel du Mariage*, p. 44, as well as pp. 77, 105, and passim: "L'essentiel du rite avant la messe est alors constitué par la jonction des deux mains droites des époux, geste accompagné de leur promesses mutuelles, et généralement précédé ou suivi d'une parole du prêtre les invitant ou geste ou bien le ratifiant ou le bénissant." For the joining of hands in the Lutheran service, see Foley, *Wedding Rites*, p. 68.

132 Foley, *Wedding Rites*, p. 67. Between the two acts of enclosing the hands, the Anglican liturgical direction specifies, "*Then they shall loose their hands.*" This brief separation makes the second taking of the hand as visibly performed an event as the first. It is interesting that the woman's hand is placed inside the man's hand by either the priest or her father (he does not just "take" it, perhaps because no vow has yet been spoken) whereas the woman actively takes the man's hand and encloses it in hers (perhaps because his promise has by that moment now been given). As the two vows are spoken, each holds the other person's body inside his or her own.

In addition to literal bodily union through handholding, symbolic affirmation of bodily unity is present in the Jewish *chuppah* or canopy held over the pair, and by the Christian carecloth held over the heads of, or draped upon the shoulders of, the marriage pair, (Foley, *Wedding Rites*, pp. 76–78). Although commentary on the carecloth does not associate it with the interior of the body, two aspects encourage that meaning. First, the cloth is white embroidered with red, suggestive of menstrual blood. Second, an illegitimate child becomes legitimate by bringing him or her under the carecloth during the ceremony; because the child emerges out from under the carecloth once the parents are married, it is as though he or she emerged from the maternal body only once the parents were married.

133 Foley, *Wedding Rites*, p. 71. Foley transcribes a nineteenth-century Quaker service, but the same service today is given by the Philadelphia Yearly Meeting of the Society of Friends, which also enumerates the grounds on which the meeting establishes "clearness" prior to the marriage. Clearness requires the absence of obstacles to marriage and involves matters such as whether the couple each "see themselves and their partner as equal and trusted" (See http://www.pym.org/

content/quaker-marriage-procedure). This website also makes clear the Quaker willingness to oversee the marriages of couples that cannot attain a civil marriage. On same-sex marriage, see notes 140–142, below.

134 See Siegle, *Marriage Today: A Commentary on the Code of Canon Law*, p. 149; and Krause, *Family Law in a Nutshell*, p. 48.

135 The kiss had binding power in a Roman betrothal, according to Mary Brown Pharr: "The interpretation generally accepted by legal scholars...is that this [contractual] kiss was given before witnesses, as part of the betrothal ceremony, and was considered as sealing the betrothal and actually as the initial step in the final consummation of the marriage" ("The Kiss in Roman Law," *The Classical Journal* 42, no. 7 [April 1947], p. 365).

136 Locke, *Second Treatise of Government*, §78, p. 43. Locke is here proceeding to a recitation of the many other elements additionally (though less essentially) entailed in marriage.

137 Immanuel Kant, *The Metaphysics of Morals*, trans. and ed. Mary Gregor, introd. Roger J. Sullivan (Cambridge: Cambridge University Press, 1996), §§24 and 27, pp. 62, 63.

138 William Blackstone, *Commentaries on the Laws of England in Four Books*, incorporating multiple commentaries edited by William Draper Lewis (Philadelphia: Geo. T. Bisel, 1922), bk. I, §434, p. 399.

139 Statute 32 Hen. VIII c. 38, summarized in Blackstone, *Commentaries*, bk. I, §435, p. 400.

140 As of November 2012 the list of countries includes Argentina, Belgium, Canada, Denmark, Iceland, Netherlands, Norway, Portugal, Spain, South Africa, Sweden (Wikipedia, "Same-Sex Marriage," November 17, 2012). Same-sex marriage does not originate with the nation-state. Marriages between two women, for example, took place in at least three regions of precolonial Africa (regions that are today parts of Benin, Nigeria, and South Africa) between 1900 and 1970 (see Beth Greene, "The Institution of Woman-Marriage in Africa: A Cross-Cultural Analysis," *Ethnology* 37, no. 4 [Autumn 1998]: 395–412).

141 As of November 2012, the list of states includes Connecticut, Iowa, Maine, Maryland, Massachusetts, New Hampshire, New York, Vermont, and Washington (Wikipedia, "Same-Sex Marriage in the United States").

142 Quakers have been in the vanguard not only on blessing same-sex civil unions but also in welcoming a church wedding beginning in 1987 in the United States, with marriages following in Canada (1992), Australia (2007), and Britain (2009). Other churches that perform weddings as well as bless same-sex civil marriages include Unitarian Universalist in the United States, the Mennonite Church of Netherlands, the Lutheran Church of Sweden, the Church of Sweden, the Church of Denmark, the Pentacostal Church in the United States, and the Swedenborgian Church of North America (Wikipedia, "Blessing of Same-Sex Unions in Christian Churches," November 17, 2012).

Churches that confer blessings on the civil marriage of same-sex partners (but do not yet conduct the wedding inside the church itself) include the Evangelical Lutheran Church of America; the Evangelical Lutheran Church of Canada; the Evangelical Lutheran Church of the German regions of Brunswick, Hanover, and Oldenburg; the Montreal, Niagara, and Westminister Dioceses of the Anglican Church in Canada; the Episcopal Church in the United States; the Church of Iceland; the Church of God in the Philippines; the Roman Catholic Church in small parts of the German dioceses of Aachen and Limburg; the Old Catholic Church of Netherlands; the Christian Catholic Church of Switzerland; the Catholic Diocese of the Old Catholics in Germany; the Old Catholic Church of Austria; the Eucharist Catholic Church and Old Catholic Church of Sweden; and the Old Catholic Church of USA (Wikipedia, "Blessing of Same-Sex Unions in Christian Churches," November 17, 2012).

143 One formulation occurs in *Bilowit v. Dolitsky* (124 N.J. Super. 101, 304 A.2d 774): "Our courts have long required a more substantial quantum of fraud to entitle a party to an annulment where the marriage has been consummated than where it has not.... Where the marriage has been consummated, the fraud of defendant will entitle plaintiff to an annulment only when the fraud is of an extreme nature, going to one of the essentials" (reprinted in Krause, *Family Law: Cases, Comments and Questions*, p. 473). Even in cases where the level of misrepresentation is profound—such as *Anonymous v. Anonymous*, where a man married a man who presented himself as a woman—the absence of consummation is relevant enough to be cited (67 Misc. 2d 982, 325 N.Y.S. 2d 499, reprinted in Krause, *Family Law: Cases, Comments and Questions*, p. 467).

144 Krause periodically uses the term throughout *Family Law in a Nutshell*; for example, he writes, "Of course, the partners may not ratify a marriage that offends an important policy, *e.g.*, the prohibition on incest" (p. 301; see also p. 46). Some states—for example, New Jersey—use the word "ratify" formally in their state laws; as a result, cases in these states also use the term (e.g., Faustin v. Lewis, 85 N.J. 507, 427 A.2d 1105 reprinted in Krause, *Family Law: Cases, Comments, and Questions*, pp. 45, 47).

145 Krause, *Family Law in a Nutshell*, p. 49.

146 Krause, *Family Law: Cases Comments, and Questions*, p. 474.

147 Kshaiboon v. Kshaiboon, 652 S. W.2d 219 (M. App. 1983) described in Krause, *Family Law in a Nutshell*, pp. 300, 301. Section 208 of the Uniform Marriage and Divorce Act lists among causes of invalidity an inability "to consummate the marriage by sexual intercourse" unknown to the "other party at the time [of] the marriage" (reprinted in Krause, *Family Law: Cases, Comments, and Questions*, p. 471).

148 James Joyce, *Ulysses* (New York: Random House-Vintage, 1986), p. 644.

149 Bingham, *Christian Marriage*, p. 291. The phrase, up to the word "bride," is also found at the opening of the Jewish marriage contract itself (p. 287). The inclusion

of both bride and bridegroom in this phrasing is one of many details that makes the marriage appear reciprocal, despite the fact that the contract itself is made by the bridegroom alone.

150 Bingham, *Christian Marriage*, p. 105.

151 Though lovers and spouses practice the most extreme form of crossing bodily boundaries, friends also open those boundaries to one another, as John Locke's 1659 letter to either his brother Tom or Thomas Westrowe illustrates: "Deare Friend... doe I not grow Stoick apace? me thinkes I finde my self hard and half Iron already and can turne a churlish insensible outside to the world, though my warme affections will still keepe my heart neald soft and pliant to all your commands and ready to receive any impressions from you. tis this tendernesse makes me inquisitive after our affairs" (Letter #82, "Locke to -----, [Thomas Westrowe?]," November 8, [1659?], *The Correspondence of John Locke*, Electronic Edition, vol. 1).

152 On gender inequality in Jewish and Islamic marriage rites, see note 129 above.

153 Jean-Paul Sarte, *Being and Nothingness: A Phenomenological Essay on Ontology*, trans. and introd. Hazel E. Barnes (New York: Washington Square Press, 1956), p. 474ff., but see page 478 restricting the idiom of enslavement, incorporation, and assimilation.

154 Patrick Atiyah in *The Rise and Fall of Freedom of Contract* (Oxford: Clarendon Press, 1979) differentiates contract based on consent from that based on benefits or reliance: that based on benefits moves toward equal distribution; that based on reliance is patriarchal (since responsibilities are transferred to the person relied upon, and the relier is absolved of responsibilities for his or her actions); that based on consent or promise, in contrast, protects our ability to enter very unequal relation. Atiyah calls it a "risk-allocation device," a way of "transferring a risk from one party to another in advance" (p. 5). Such contract often "favour the party who has the better skill and knowledge for assessing future risks" (p. 6); thus they work to increase inequalities.

But it is also possible, in contrast to Atiyah, to see contract as affording the greatest possibility of equality among the three. "Reliance," it can be argued, assumes, accepts, and endorses inequality by building it into its (patriarchal) structure; "benefits," by making a third-party arbiter the patriarch rather than either of the two parties, does not by that solution escape the problem of inequality but only increases the number of subordinates; "contract," while permitting inequality resulting from the greater negotiating skill of one party, at least allows for the possibility of self-authorized equality.

155 Jon Meacham, *Thomas Jefferson: The Art of Power* (New York: Random House, 2012), pp. 217–19. (Drawing on books by Annette Gordon-Reed as well as an edited collection by Jan Ellen Lewis and Peter S. Onuf.)

156 Needless to say, this is a large "if" clause since in many (perhaps most) cases black women gave no consent whatsoever and therefore suffered criminal coercion and rape. At issue here are only those instances where both participants gave consent.

157 Declaration of Helsinki, Principle 9, reprinted in *Law, Science, and Medicine*, ed. Judith Areen, Patricia King, Steven Goldberg, and Alexander Capron (New York: Foundation Press, 1984), p. 928; for all three codes, see pp. 925–26, 927–29, 972 therein.

158 See Chapter 2, note 73 for the ways Patrick S. Atiyah and John Locke distinguish between threshold and perpetual consent.

CHAPTER 6: THINKING IN AN EMERGENCY

1 Clinton L. Rossiter, *Constitutional Dictatorship: Crisis Government in the Modern Democracies* (Princeton: Princeton University Press, 1948).

2 Hans Born, "National Governance of Nuclear Weapons: Opportunities and Constraints," Geneva Center for the Democratic Control of Armed Forces (DCAF), Policy Paper No. 15, 2007. North Korea conducted its first nuclear test in 2006, but according to the Federation of American Scientists, its status as a nuclear state was still unclear at the end of 2012. In their 2013 chart "Status of World Nuclear Forces End 2012," the Federation of American Scientists lists North Korea as having 0 operational/strategic nuclear weapons, and fewer than 10 in its nuclear stockpile (between 0 and 9). The 2013 chart notes: "Despite two North Korean nuclear tests, there is no publicly available evidence that North Korea has operationalized its nuclear weapons capability. A 2009 world survey by the U.S. Air Force National Air and Space Intelligence Center (NASIC) does not credit any of North Korea's ballistic missiles with nuclear capability" (http://www.fas.org/programs/ssp/nukes/nuclearweapons/nukestatus.html).

3 These 2010 weapons figures, as well as those in the next sentence, are reported by SIPRI Yearbook, Bulletin of Atomic Scientists, and the Federation of American Scientists.

4 Born, "National Governance of Nuclear Weapons," pp. 7, 12.

5 Born, "National Governance of Nuclear Weapons," p. 12.

6 For documentation on the U.S. policy of presidential first use, see Chapter 2, note 4. On the joint statement of the U.S. Department of Defense and Department of State defending the legality of U.S. possession, threatened use, use, and first use of nuclear weapons, see "Introduction: The Floor of the World."

7 Born, "National Governance of Nuclear Weapons," pp. 5, 13.

8 Jules Lobel, "Emergency Power and the Decline of Liberalism," *Yale Law Journal* 98 (May 1980): 1401, 1404, 1408, 1418, 1420, 1416.

9 See Chapter 1, section entitled "Authority in a Declaration of War is Transmissible but Not Delegable."

10 Born, "National Governance of Nuclear Weapons," p. 15.

11 Peter Hennessy, *The Secret State: Whitehall and the Cold War* (London: Allen Lane, 2002), p. 105, quoting Public Records Office, DEFE 25/49, "Nuclear Retaliation Procedures," Report from GEN 743/10 (Revise), January 23, 1962. The record does not indicate who appoints the deputies. The use of the word "retaliation" here and

elsewhere in Hennessy's book should not mislead one into thinking that Britain has a second-use policy; what is being "retaliated" against in some of these papers is not an incoming nuclear weapon but a land army marching across Europe. (See the description of Operation VISITATION, p. 186.)

12 On the breaking of national and international law during the administration of George W. Bush, see Elaine Scarry, *Rule of Law, Misrule of Men* (Cambridge, MA: MIT Press, 2010). On the extensive use of a private presidential army during the Bush administration, see Jeremy Scahill's analysis of private contractors in the U.S. wars in Iraq and Afghanistan, as well as in New Orleans following Hurricane Katrina in *Blackwater: The Rise of the World's Most Powerful Mercenary Army* (New York: Nation Books, 2007).

13 Micah Zenko, "Reforming U.S. Drone Strike Policies," Council on Foreign Relations: Center for Preventive Action, Council Special Report no. 65 (January 2013), pp. 3, 13, Table I (giving death figures provided by The Bureau of Investigative Journalism, the New American Foundation, and Long War Journal). The majority of deaths—over 2500—have been in Pakistan. Among the victims are intentionally targeted rescuers attempting to aid those injured in a previous drone strike and participants in funeral processions for persons killed by previous drone strikes (Zenko, p. 14, drawing on Craig Whitlock, "U.S. Airstrike that Killed American Teen in Yemen Raises Legal, Ethical Questions," *Washington Post*, October 22, 2011; Pir Zubair Shah, "25 Militants are Killed in Attack in Pakistan," *New York Times*, May 16, 2009; Scott Shane, "U.S. Said to Target Rescuers at Drone Strike Sites, *New York Times*, February 5, 2012). When the U.S. executive office speaks publicly about drones at all, it invokes Congress's September 18, 2001, "Authorization for the Use of Military Force" as its legal basis (p. 16), and it claims that targets are limited to "high-level al-Qaeda leaders who are planning attacks." But according to Zenko, most of the victims have been "low-level, anonymous suspected militants who were predominantly engaged in insurgent or terrorist operations against their governments, rather than in active international terrorist plots" (p. 10).

14 As I show in *The Body in Pain* (New York: Oxford University Press, 1985, pp. 139–57), nuclear war conforms to the model of torture, not the model of war.

15 Aristotle, *De Anima (On the Soul)*, trans. and introd. Hugh Lawson-Trancred (New York: Penguin, 1986), §434a, p. 216. Tancred sees the distinction between perception and deliberation as the central contribution of Chapter 11 to the doctrines presented earlier in *De Anima*. Bruce Aune states the Aristotelian opposition clearly in "Thinking," *Encyclopedia of Philosophy*, vol. 7, ed. Paul Edwards (New York: Macmillan Publishing, 1967), p. 100.

16 Aesop, "An Unseasonable Reproof," in *Fables of Aesop*, trans. S. A. Handford (New York: Penguin, 1954), p. 197.

17 Charles Baudelaire, "Le Cygne," in Baudelaire, *Selected Verse with an Introduction and Prose Translation by Francis Scarfe* (New York: Penguin, 1961), p. 210.

18 Thucydides, *History of the Peloponnesian War*, trans. Rex Warner (New York: Penguin, 1954), p. 152.

19 Thucydides, *History of the Peloponnesian War*, p. 154.

20 Thucydides, *History of the Peloponnesian War*, p. 155.

21 The laws of most countries accord a special status to dying words. In Anglo-American law, for example, hearsay is ordinarily inadmissible in court, but it becomes admissible if the hearsay is spoken by someone murdered who, before dying, names the murderer; see Karl S. Guthke, *Last Words: Variations on a Theme in Cultural History* (Princeton: Princeton University Press, 1992) p. 28. While dying words permit a loosening of legal constraints, a tightening of constraints may instead arise as illustrated in two other genres of language—whistleblowing (laws protecting whistleblowers suffered a setback in the 2006 Supreme Court decision in *Garcetti v. Ceballos*) and political dissent in wartime (the 1919 case *Schenck v. United States* was the first to address, and then deny, the applicability of First Amendment speech to wartime dissent; writing for a unanimous court, Oliver Wendell Holmes argued that obstructing war conscription, as Schenck had done in a pamphlet urging that "A conscript is little better that a convict," presented a clear danger analogous to "crying fire in a theatre").

22 Sylvain Ayotte, "Emergency Preparedness in Quebec: Co-ordinated Response among Partners," *Emergency Preparedness Digest*, October/December 1991, p. 2.

23 Artaud does not, however, explicitly name Thucydides. Marseilles, the region of France from which Artaud comes, itself has a tradition of plague writing dating back to the 1720 plague in Provence, a set of writings investigated by historian Daniel Gordon in "The City and the Plague in the Age of Enlightenment," *Yale French Studies* 92 (1997), pp. 77–78.

24 Antonin Artaud, *Theatre and its Double*, trans. Mary Caroline Richards (New York: Grove, 1958), p. 92.

25 Artaud, *Theatre and its Double*, p. 82.

26 An everyday habit may in some cases even accelerate an emergency. A study in the 1970s attempted to explain why so many of those raped or robbed were teachers or nurses. The study concluded that the victims were disproportionately people who had habits of serving or helping others. The criminal attack often began with a request for help: the attacker would ask for the time, for a street direction, for a match, or some other form of assistance. People in the habit of helping strangers were therefore at risk. Such a revelation does not mean a librarian should stop helping strangers, but that she should abstain from helping strangers if she is walking alone on a street that is otherwise unpopulated.

27 Donald L. Metz, *Running Hot: Structure and Stress in Ambulance Work* (Cambridge, MA: Abt Books, 1981), p. 145.

28 A. Ocklitz, "Cardiopulmonary resuscitation already in Egypt 5,000 years ago?" *Wiener Klinische Wochenschrift* 109, no. 11 (June 1997): 406–12.

29 Kings 4:34–35, cited in Mickey S. Eisenberg, *Life in the Balance: Emergency Medicine and the Quest to Reverse Sudden Death* (New York: Oxford University Press, 1977), p. 35.

30 Eisenberg, *Life in the Balance,* pp. 55–136.

31 A. Olotu et al., "Characteristics and Outcome of Cardiopulmonary Resuscitation in Hospitalized African Children," *Resuscitation* 80, no. 1 (2009): 69–72.

32 Fifty-two percent of the children were younger than one year; 44 percent were between one and five years old; 18 percent were six to fourteen years old (Olotu, "Characteristics...Hospitalized African Children," p. 70).

33 A 22 percent survival rate (eighteen of eighty-two children) rather than the earlier 15 percent figure (Olotu, "Characteristics...Hospitalized African Children," p. 71).

34 The age would be younger if all patients had been included. Cardiac arrest patients younger than fifteen were eliminated from the study at the outset.

35 I. Desalu and O.T. Kushimo, "An Audit of Perioperative Cardiac Arrest at Lagos University Teaching Hospital," *Nigerian Journal of Clinical Practice* 10, no. 3 (September 2007): 188–93; and I. Desalu, O.T. Kushimo, and O. Akinlaja, "Adherence to CPR Guidelines during Perioperative Cardiac Arrest in a Developing Country," *Resuscitation* 69, no. 3 (2006): pp. 517–20. The second of these two articles focuses exclusively on the need for conformity to guidelines, not introducing the problem of blood loss.

36 Kilifi District Hospital has no equipment for ventilation or defibrillation, so both breathing and compression were done by the physicians and nurses directly. In Lagos Hospital, the breathing part of CPR was given by manual ventilation.

37 Peter Safar and Martin McMahon, *Resuscitation of the Unconscious Victim: A Manual for Rescue Breathing,* pp. 18, 19.

38 A test in which viewers were asked to reproduce the curl of a hand depicted in a photograph, a tracing of a photograph, and a cartoon sketch is described in E. H. Gombrich, Julian Hochberg, and Max Black, *Art, Perception, and Reality* (Baltimore: Johns Hopkins University Press, 1972), pp. 35, 74, 78. Gombrich, Hochberg, and Black argue that cartoon is the opposite of camouflage because it provides an exaggeration of the body that matches the way the body exaggerates inner states, magnifying a small bump into the felt experience of a large one.

39 Safar and McMahon, *Resuscitation,* p. 71. The instruction to "watch the chest" is at least as crucial in giving chest compressions as in assisting the victim's breathing. In its 2010 guidelines, the American Heart Association stresses the importance of compressing the chest of an adult 100 times per minute to a depth of two inches and watching to make sure the chest fully recoils between each compression (co-chairs John M. Field, Mary Fran Hazinski, et al., "2010 American Heart Association Guidelines for Cardiopulmonary Resuscitation and Emergency Cardiovascular Care Science," *Circulation* 122 [November 18, 2010]: 640–56).

40 W. A. Carlo et al., "Educational Impact of the Neonatal Resuscitation Program in Low-Risk Delivery Centers in a Developing Country," *Journal of Pediatrics* 154, no. 4 (April 2009): pp. 504–8.

41 Olotu et al., "Characteristics . . . in Hospitalized African Children," p. 72; italics added. The protocol followed in Kilifi is the Pediatric Advanced Life Support of the Resuscitation Council, U.K. The American Heart Association's November 2010 guidelines acknowledge that the interval for retraining it had earlier recommended—twelve to twenty-four months—is too long, given that "knowledge and skills . . . decline within weeks after initial . . . training." It has not yet arrived at a new recommendation, but it may well approximate the three-to-six-month interval urged by the Zambia study described above (co-chairs Mary Fran Hazinski, Jerry P. Nolan, et al., "2010 International Cardiopulmonary Resuscitation and Emergency Cardiovascular Care Science with Treatment Recommendations," *Circulation* 122 [October 2010]: 250–75).

42 Stephanie Rosborough, MD, conversation, March 11, 2010.

43 American Heart Association, "2002 Heart and Stroke Statistical Update," Dallas, 2002.

44 Safar and McMahon, *Resuscitation*, p. 5. The figures on oxygen loss given here were based on the extensive experiments Safar had conducted. Eisenberg's 1997 book specifies that permanent brain damage begins four minutes after oxygen is cut off (*Life in the Balance*, p. 14).

45 R. Vukmir, "Witnessed Arrest, but Not Delayed Bystander Cardiopulmonary Resuscitation Improves Prehospital Cardiac Arrest Survival," *Emergency Medicine Journal* 21, no. 3 (May 2004): 370–73.

46 Safar and McMahon, *Resuscitation*, p. 12. Safar notes that expired breath actually contains 18 percent oxygen if the rescuer is taking deep breaths, as is urged in the protocol.

47 Eisenberg, *Life in the Balance*, pp. 92, 93, 101.

48 See the copyright page of the handbook.

49 When Safar moved to the University of Pittsburg Hospital in 1968 to establish a Department of Anesthesiology, he set up a paramedic service (called Freedom House) in the city's Hill district, where the greatest number of the city's African American population lived (Eisenberg, *Life in the Balance*, p. 103). It is widely credited as the first advanced medical emergency program in the country, and spread to many other cities.

50 Eisenberg, *Life in the Balance*, p. 127. In fact, there are other points in the story when distribution precedes and assists medical discovery. For example, Elam's initial work on artificial respiration began when he was walking through the polio ward of the University of Minnesota Hospital in 1946, saw a young girl who had turned blue being rushed through the corridor, and interrupted their rush to deliver mouth-to-nose resuscitation which immediately transformed her from

blue to pink. He knew how to do this because he had the night before read a book cataloguing eighty-four historical techniques of resuscitation, and recalled the description of midwives delivering mouth-to-nose breaths to newborns, a procedure scorned as "vulgar" by the medical profession (pp. 85–90).

51 Kouwenhoven cited in Eisenberg, *Life in the Balance*, p. 126.

52 David Segal, "A Reader's Digest that Grandma Never Dreamed Of," *New York Times*, December 19, 2009.

53 Eisenberg, *Life in the Balance*, p. 128.

54 Gary Lombardi, E. John Gallagher, and Paul Gennis, "Outcome of Out-of-Hospital Cardiac Arrest in New York City," *JAMA* 271, no. 9 (March 1994): 678–83.

55 Marc Eckstein, Samuel J. Stratton, and Linda S. Chan, "Cardiac Arrest Resuscitation Evaluation in Los Angeles: CARE-LA," *Annals of Emergency Medicine* 45, no. 5 (2005): 504–9.

56 Mikael Holmberg et al., "Survival After Cardiac Arrest Outside Hospital in Sweden," *Resuscitation* 36 (1998): 29–36.

57 Lombardi et al., "Outcome...in New York City," p. 679.

58 L. B. Becker, "Outcome of CPR in a Large Metropolitan Area—Where Are the Survivors?" *Annals of Emergency Medicine* 20, no. 4 (1991): 355–61.

59 C. Stein, "Out-of-Hospital Cardiac Arrest Cases in Johannesburg, South Africa: A First Glimpse of Short-Term Outcomes from a Paramedic Clinical Learning Base," *Emergency Medicine Journal* 26 (2009): 670–74, esp. 673 comparing Los Angeles and Johannesburg figures for return of spontaneous circulation (ROSC).

60 Stein, "Out-of-Hospital...in Johannesburg," p. 673.

61 Bystanders assisted in 28 percent of the cases in Los Angeles and Sweden, and 32 percent of the cases in New York City.

62 The study of Sweden, for example, cites studies documenting survival rates of between 14 percent and 18 percent in Seattle, Washington, and King County, Washington, and 17 percent in Helsinki. The elapsed time between cardiac arrest and defibrillation in Seattle was three to four minutes (Holmberg et al., "Survival ...in Sweden," pp. 33, 34).

63 Taku Iwami et al., "Continuous Improvements in 'Chain of Survival' Increased Survival after Out-of-Hospital Cardiac Arrests: A Large-Scale Population-Based Study," *Circulation* 119 (2009): pp. 728–34. Prior to the surge of citizen training, Osaka's survival rate had been 5 percent.

64 Tetsuhisa Kitamura et al., "Conventional and Chest-Compression Only Cardiopulmonary Resuscitation by Bystanders for Children Who Have Out-of-Hospital Cardiac Arrests: A Prospective, Nationwide, Population-Based Cohort Study," *Lancet*, March 2010, pp. 1–8.

65 Kitamura, "Resuscitation by Bystanders for Children," pp. 2, 4.

66 Kitamura, "Resuscitation by Bystanders for Children," p. 4.

67 Kitamura, "Resuscitation by Bystanders for Children," pp. 5, 6.

68 Jonathan R. Cole, *The Great American University: Its Rise to Preeminence; Its Indispensable National Role; Why It Must Be Protected* (New York: Public Affairs, 2009), p. 237.

69 American Heart Association, report of the "2005 International Consensus Conference on Cardiopulmonary Resuscitation and Emergency Cardiovascular Care Science with Treatment Recommendations," *Circulation* 112 (2005). The 2010 guidelines make it clear why an untrained bystander can use compression-only when resuscitating adults but should use classic CPR when resuscitating children. While heart attacks in most adults are initiated by ventricular fibrillation, "the majority of pediatric cardiac arrests are asphyxial, with only 5% to 15% attributable to VF [ventricular fibrillation]" (Field, Hazinski, et al., "2010 American Heart Association Guidelines"). Supplying breath is therefore as crucial as compressing the heart, as is also true in cases where an adult's cardiac arrest has been caused by asphyxia (e.g., near-drowning).

70 M. R. Sayre et al., "Hands-Only (Compression-Only) Cardiopulmonary Resuscitation: A Call to Action for Bystander Response to Adults who Experience Out-of-Hospital Sudden Cardiac Arrest. A Science Advisory for the Public from the American Heart Association Emergency Cardiovascular Care Committee," *Circulation* 117 (2008): 2162–67.

71 Amsterdam reported 150 resuscitations in four years (Eisenberg, *Life in the Balance*, pp. 14, 59, 61). Eisenberg is himself a physician and medical researcher. His articles on bystander CPR are cited in the bibliographies of many of the journal articles on bystanders cited above.

72 Eisenberg provides this number, based on sixty beats per minute (*Life in the Balance*, p. 3).

73 Article 2, "Quill Plains (Naicam) Mutual Aid Area" (signed December 1, 1986); and Article 9a, "Battlefords Mutual Aid Area" (Signed August 29, 1988).

74 Each contract lists the population size of the participating regions.

75 Bill 54, "An Act Respecting Emergency" (*Statutes of Saskatchewan, 1989–90*, ch. E-8.1, also called the Emergency Planning Act).

76 Former mayor Dorothy Saunderson, conversation, April 24, 2010. The mayor, who served in that office for twenty-five years, was eighty-five years old at the time of the flood. Some reports place the total rainfall in the area closer to fifteen than to thirteen inches.

77 Fraser Hunter et al., "Interagency Report on the Torrential Rainstorm of July 3, 2000 at Vanguard, Saskatchewan," Canada-Saskatchewan Memorandum of Understanding on Water Committee, July 2003, pp. 3, 11.

78 Saunderson, conversation. As Mayor Saunderson's husband was gravely ill, the declaratory act was carried out by the deputy mayor.

79 Fraser G. Hunter, et al., "The Vanguard Torrential Storm (Meteorology and Hydrology)," *Canadian Water Resources Journal* 27, no. 2 (Summer 2002): 213, 223.

80 Hunter, "Vanguard Torrential Storm," pp. 222–23, 219–20.

81 Carl Friske, emergency management advisor, Saskatchewan Emergency Planning Office, conversations, May 10, 11, 2010. Carl Friske, who arrived by boat on the first day and coordinated public works, social services, and public information for the first twelve days, was the only official present from the Emergency Planning Office. All other labor was carried out by residents and volunteers whose work he describes with quiet amazement.

82 Friske, conversations.

83 D. B. Donald et al., "Mobilization of Pesticides on an Agricultural Landscape Flooded by a Torrential Storm," *Environmental Toxicology & Chemistry* 24, no. 1 (January, 2005): 10.

84 Friske, conversations, May 2010.

85 Saunderson, conversation.

86 Saunderson, conversation.

87 The "Interagency Report on the Torrential Rainstorm" stresses the importance of this form of distributing information on pages 11, 16, and 18 (recommendations 3, quoted above, and 5 on the use of, but nonreliance on, ordinary forms of media).

88 I am grateful to John A. Woltman and Carl Friske of Saskatchewan Community Services for sending me copies of the Battlefords and Quill Plains social contracts and regional maps of "Municipal Mutual Aid Areas" and "Provincial Emergency Planning Districts," as well as for their verbal descriptions by telephone in February 1993 and September 1995.

89 Gary Storey, "Grain Elevators," *The Encyclopedia of Saskatchewan*, www.esask. uregina.ca.

90 Michael Cottrell, "History of Saskatchewan," *The Encyclopedia of Saskatchewan*.

91 Gary Storey, "Grain Elevators." See also Nora Russell's article on "Co-operatives" in that same online volume.

92 "Naicam EMO [Emergency Measures Organization] Co-ordinator Report on Sask Wheat Pool Elevator Fire in Naicam on April 18/19." My thanks to John A. Woltman for sending me the formal report on the 1990 Naicam fire and for speaking with me by phone.

93 Mike Steers, "The Elevator's on Fire," *Emergency Preparedness Digest*, July-September 1990, pp. 10, 11.

94 Steers, "The Elevator's on Fire," p. 11. The name of the lake and the number of trucks is given in the "Naicam EMO Co-ordinator Report," p. 1.

95 "Naicam EMO Co-ordinator Report," p. 1.

96 Steers, "The Elevator's on Fire," p. 11. The after-action report says "the town crew" reported 87,000 gallons (395,500 liters) available at 11:20, 91,000 at 12:10, and 63,000 "on hand" at 3 p.m.

97 John Woltman, conversation, September 25, 1995.

98 Friske, conversations, May 2010.

99 Though the test was three years in the making, it cost the province only $8,000 (Canadian), in part because so much of the labor was volunteer. Mike Theilmann, "The Little Exercise that Grew," *Emergency Preparedness Digest*, July-September 1990, pp. 16–19.

100 1989 Saskatchewan Emergency Planning Act (amended and updated 1992, 1993, 1998, 2002, and 2003). See Sections 15.1.a,b, and c; 18.1.f, j, k; 21.1.1.a.iv, vii, viii, and x, for the potentially problematic provisions, as well as the accompanying provisions that place restrictions on these emergency powers.

101 Following Hurricane Andrew in 1992, the governors of southern states formed a mutual aid plan called EMAC, the Emergency Management Assistance Compact, which the U.S. Congress made a public law in 1996. As EMAC's website notes, it is "the first national disaster compact since the Civil Defense Compact of 1950 to be ratified by Congress." While this is surely an important step, the number of citizens who have heard of EMAC appears to be small. Further, even those who know the term will find a website most of whose categories are unenterable because they are password-protected: "EMAC Operation Manual," "Forms and Checklists," "Notice and Reporting Systems," and many others are off-limits to the public. Some helpful-sounding categories such as "EMAC Mission Ready Package for up to 25 Personnel," "EMAC Mission Ready Package for 50 Personnel" and other mission ready packages for up to 1500 personnel can be opened by anyone, but the mission ready package is only a five-page form with fill-in-the-blanks for items such as "Resource Provider/Agency" and space for projected costs of items such as air travel, per diem food costs, and vehicle costs for state officials traveling to another state. Approximately three-quarters of an inch of space is provided in which to describe the mission purpose and constraints.

102 Robert Pekkanen, *Japan's Dual Civil Society: Members without Advocates* (Stanford: Stanford University Press, 2006), pp. 133, 135.

103 Pekkanen, *Japan's Dual Civil Society*, p. 88.

104 Pekkanen, *Japan's Dual Civil Society*, p. 94.

105 Alexis de Tocqueville, *Democracy in America*, trans. Henry Reeve, Francis Bowen, Phillips Bradley (New York: Vintage, 1960), vol. 1, p. 310.

106 Tocqueville, *Democracy in America*, vol. 2, pp. 114, 115.

107 Pekkanen, *Japan's Dual Civil Society*, pp. 96, 102.

108 Tocqueville, *Democracy in America*, vol. 2, p. 117.

109 Pekkanen, *Japan's Dual Civil Society*, pp. 18, 133.

110 Pekkanen, *Japan's Dual Civil Society*, pp. 133–36.

111 Goran Hyden, *No Shortcuts to Progress: African Development Management in Perspective* (Berkeley, CA: University of California Press, 1983), pp. 6–32.

112 Michael Bratton, "Beyond the State: Civil Society and Associational Life in Africa," *World Politics* 41, no. 3 (1989): 411.

113 Kenneth Little, *West African Urbanization: A Study of Voluntary Associations in Social Change* (Cambridge: Cambridge University Press, 1965), pp. 26, 27, 34, 48.

114 Little, *West African Urbanization*, pp. 26, 27. Those associations that appeared to be based on the former village were often so open to people from other places that Little judges the place name to be quasi-fictional; on the other hand, he shows that migrants often sent money back to the home village.

115 Little, *West African Urbanization*, p. 48.

116 Clifford Geertz, "The Rotating Credit Association: A 'Middle Ring' in Development," *Economic Development and Cultural Change* 10, no. 3, cited in Little, *West African Urbanization*, p. 51.

117 Shirley Ardener, *The Comparative Study of Rotating Credit Associations*, unpublished ms., cited in Little, *West African Urbanization*, p. 51, n. 1. After the publication of Little's book, Ardener's study was published (and is therefore available) in *Journal of the Royal Anthropological Institute of Great Britain and Ireland* 94, no. 2 (July-December 1964): 201–29.

118 Shawn J. McGuire, "Vulnerability in Farmer Seed Systems: Farmer Practices for Coping with Seed Insecurity for Sorghum in Eastern Ethiopia," *Economic Botany* 61, no. 3 (Autumn 2007): 21, 215–16, 219. McGuire explains that the NGOs themselves have limited seed and have to give it to those who have enough wealth to promise that the sowing will be done by a specific date, a promise a farmer who has no oxen cannot make since he must wait to sow until the unscheduled day when a neighboring farmer can provide him with oxen.

119 Michael Bratton, "Drought, Food and the Social Organization of Small Farmers in Zimbabwe," in *Drought and Hunger in Africa: Denying Famine a Future*, ed. Michael H. Glantz (Cambridge: Cambridge University Press, 1987), pp. 224, 225, 239.

120 Bratton, "Drought . . . in Zimbabwe," pp. 231, 232. One year into the drought, 82 percent of the farmers reported their belief that the associations had grown stronger; even three years into the drought, 63 percent still felt they were continuing to strengthen.

121 Bratton, "Drought . . . in Zimbabwe," p. 224.

122 McGuire, "Vulnerability," p. 218.

123 Here I am speaking about the way voluntary associations address the nation-state (and through the nation-state, the large population), rather than about the reverse: the way the nation-state may choose to address the voluntary associations. As became apparent in the description of the Kobai earthquake, a state can encourage or instead discourage civil society by granting or denying legal recognition, tax-exempt status, and low postage rates. More drastically, the state can actively work to suppress civil society, as it did in Ethiopia during the 1974–87 Mengistu regime.

124 Tocqueville, *Democracy in America*, vol. 1, p. 202.

125 Bratton, "Beyond the State," p. 417.

126 Robert D. Putnam with Robert Leonardi and Raffaella Y. Nanetti, *Making Democracy Work: Civic Traditions in Modern Italy* (Princeton: Princeton University Press, 1993), p. 101.

127 Harold Berman, *Law and Revolution: The Formation of the Western Legal Tradition* (Cambridge, MA: Harvard University Press, 1983), p. 366.

128 Statute of the *Spade Compagnia*, cited in Putnam, *Making Democracy Work*, p. 126. Putnam's book shows the startling contemporary relevance of the medieval contracts. Judging the "widening gulf between North and South [to be] the central issue of modern Italian history" (p. 158), he argues that the differences in civic virtue in the two areas correspond precisely with the differences in city contracts in 1300 (Chapter 5) and with mutual aid societies in the 1800s. Not only, then, do mutual aid societies instill habits to address emergencies, but the very predisposition to form associational groups appears itself to be "a habit" that a given region practices across many centuries. In his study of civil society in Japan, Pekkanen cites scholarship showing medieval precedents for the neighborhood associations, though Pekkanen himself rejects these precedents (*Japan's Dual Civil Society*, pp. 102–4).

129 As we saw in Chapter 3 Pirenne tells us that the word "peace" referred both to freedom from war and to freedom from crime: "The peace of the city (*pax villae*) was at the same time the law of the city (*lex villae*)"; "peace" in the twelfth century "designate[d] the criminal law of the city" (*Medieval Cities*, pp. 207, 208).

130 Berman, *Law and Revolution*, p. 396.

131 Putnam, *Making Democracy Work*, p. 125 (citing Kropotkin, *Mutual Aid*, p. 174). Though themselves in need of help, strangers are also helpful: "information may be obtained [from them] about matters which one may like to learn."

132 Federal Office of Civil Defence, *Civil Defence Medical Service*, Bern, n.d., p. 4.

133 Federal Office of Civil Defence, *Civil Defence: Figures, Facts, Data, 1989*, Bern, Spring 1989, 505.1. For the repeated assertion that a fallout shelter makes survivability possible even a short distance from the impact, see additional pamphlets published by the Bern office such as *The 1971 Conception of Swiss Civil Defence*, p. 26.

134 Lecture by David Giri, International Conference on Advanced Electromagnetics, Torino, Italy, September 11, 2011.

135 *Civil Protection Concept: Report of the Federal Council to the Federal Assembly Concerning the New Civil Protection Concept*, Bern, October 17, 2001, pp. v, 23, 24.

136 *Civil Protection Concept*, pp. 5, 28.

137 *The 1971 Conception of Swiss Civil Defence*, Bern, pp. 24, 29; italics added.

138 Federal Law on Civil Protection System and Protection & Support Service, 2003, Article 47, pp. 7, 8; and see *Civil Protection Concept*, p. 24.

139 *Civil Protection Concept*, pp. iii, v, 3, 10, 23.

140 Federal Law on Civil Protection, Articles 11 and 13.

141 Federal Law on Civil Protection, Article 15. See also Constitution of Switzerland, Article 61, Clause 3.

142 For the general requirement for "protection of cultural property" (including cultural property that is privately owned) and for "compulsory service," see *Civil Protection Concept*, pp. ii, 10, 13, 17, 24.

143 The 1998 figure is given in *Civil Protection Concept*, p. 28.

144 Iso Camartine, personal conversation at the Institute for Advanced Study in Berlin, April 1990.

145 See the Federal Office of Civil Protection booklet, *Protection of Cultural Property: A Global Mission*, Bern, 2005, p. 20.

146 *Protection of Cultural Property*, pp. 5, 13, 14, 18, 21.

147 Camartine, conversation.

148 See, for example, *Civil Defence: Figures, Facts, Data, 1989*, p. 103; *The 1971 Conception of Swiss Civil Defence*, p. 17; Federal Office of Civil Defence, *Swiss Civil Defence*, Bern, n.d., pp. 3, 6. Article 2 of the Swiss constitution specifies "safeguard[ing] the independence and security of the country" as a main purpose of the constitution.

149 *The 1971 Conception of Swiss Civil Defence*, p. 47.

150 Paul Hodge, *Washington Post*, January 20, 1977, p. DC1.

151 "FEMA's Focus Found to be on Armageddon," *St. Petersburg Times*, February 22, 1993, p. 1A.

152 These narratives all come from the articles of Ted Gup, listed in note 153, below.

153 Gup has almost single-handedly taken on the task of alerting the public to the existence of these shelters. See, for example, Ted Gup, "Doomsday Hideaway," *Time*, December 9, 1991: 26–29; "Underground Government: A Guide to America's Doomsday Bunkers," *Washington Post [Sunday] Magazine*, May 31, 1992, p. W14; "The Doomsday Blueprints," *Time*, August 10, 1992: 32–39; "How FEMA Learned to Stop Worrying about Civilians and Love the Bomb," *Mother Jones,* January/February 1994: 28–31, 74, 76.

154 Ted Gup, "The Ultimate Congressional Hideaway," *Washington Post [Sunday] Magazine*, May 31, 1992, p. W11. Although Congress was unaware of Greenbrier, it did authorize extravagant funds for the Federal Emergency Management Agency without requiring explanations for how, and on whom, it was being spent.

155 *Civil Defence: Figures, Facts, Data, 1989*, pp. 506, 507.

156 These figures are specified in a July 3, 2009, online report: http://www.swissinfo.ch.

157 *Swiss Civil Defence*, p. 8, and see notes 133, 136, 137 above, for both recent and early iterations of the principle.

158 Between 1981 and 1991, when the $2.9 billion mobile presidential shelter was being built, FEMA spent $243 million on preparation "for natural disasters such as hurricanes, earthquakes, and floods" ("FEMA's Focus Found to Be on Armageddon"). Ted Gup estimates that each year the government spends less than 50 cents per person on civil defense (*Time*, December 9, 1991). The absence of civil defense preparation during Hurricane Katrina in the fall of 2007 was just one particularly vivid illustration of the ongoing exclusion of the population from the country's conception of "national defense." Though I have focused here on the extraordinary discrepancy between executive protection and civilian protection, irrespective of the particular president in office, some presidents have been more concerned about civilian protection than

others. For example, Eisenhower used the need to protect the population as a reason for funding a national highway system; Kennedy wanted civilian fallout shelters but Congress refused to fund them ("Civil Defence: Evacuous," *Economist*, November 18, 1978, p. 20); Carter tried to reactivate civil defense (Richard Burt, "Democrats Back Carter on Nomination Rule," *New York Times*, August 12, 1980, p. A-1); Clinton appointed a FEMA head, James Lee Witt from Arkansas, who sought to steer money toward the population and away from the presidency (Penny Bender, "FEMA Faulted for Not Preparing for Disasters," Gannett News Service, May 18, 1993).

159 Joseph Needham, *Science and Civilization*, vol. 6, pt. 2, pp. 392, 403–4, 407. My thanks to Joe Scarry for directing me to China's granaries.

160 Needham, *Science and Civilization*, p. 407.

161 Needham, *Science and Civilization*, p. 411.

162 Derk Bodde, "Henry A. Wallace and the Ever-Normal Granary, *Far Eastern Quarterly* 5, no. 4 (August 1946): 413.

163 Needham, *Science and Civilization*, p. 417.

164 Pierre-Etienne Will and R. Bin Wong, *Nourish the People: The State Civilian Granary System in China, 1650–1850* (Ann Arbor: University of Michigan Press, 1991), pp. 5, 25.

165 Will and Wong, *Nourish the People*, pp. 12, 528–32.

166 Will and Wong, *Nourish the People*, p. 101.

167 Will and Wong, *Nourish the People*, pp. 14, 26, 33, 36, 57, 72–73.

168 Will and Wong, *Nourish the People*, pp. 104, 125.

169 Will and Wong, *Nourish the People*, pp. 47, 53, 104, 105, 125.

170 Clement Attlee, Public Records Office, CAB 130/41, GEN 253, 1st Meeting, October 10, 1948, cited in Hennessy, *The Secret State*, pp. 124, 127.

171 This Box Hill is distinct from the Box Hill in Surrey where John Keats wrote *Endymion* and Jane Austen situated a key scene in *Emma*.

172 Hennessy, *The Secret State*, pp. 171–77, 184–85. The list of those selected for shelter at Box Hill is contained in the 1963 Ministry of Defence War Book, declassified in 2000.

173 Hennessy, *The Secret State*, p. xvii.

174 Hennessy interview with Sir Frank Cooper, BBC Radio 4, *Top Job*, August 8, 2000, cited in *The Secret State*, pp. 180, 181.

175 Dr. Edgar Anstey of JIGSAW (Joint Inter-Services Group for the Study of All-Out Warfare), "Note on the Concept and Definition of Breakdown," June 1960, cited in Hennessy, *The Secret State*, p. 121. Anstey was a "Principal Scientific Officer from the Home Office" (p. 143).

176 It should also be noted that local communities *within* nuclear states, such as Oakland, California, have sometimes attempted to establish right of exit by creating "nuclear-free zones" that prohibit research, production, or transportation of nuclear weapons within the boundaries of their municipalities. In the case of

Oakland, a federal court ruled that the ordinance violated the U.S. Constitution's War Powers clause and, in effect, jeopardized national defense (*United States v. City of Oakland*, No. C-89-3305 JPV 13–14, Northern District of California, August 20, 1990, invalidating Oakland, California Ordinance 11,062 [December 16, 1988]). See Luis Li, "State Sovereignty and Nuclear Free Zones," *California Law Review* 79, no. 4 (July 1991): 1169–1204.

177 Andrew Mack, *Working Paper 1993/10: Nuclear Free Zones in the 1990s* (Canberra: Department of International Relations, Research School of Pacific Studies, Australian National University, 1993), pp. 17, 19.

178 Mack, *Nuclear Free Zones*, p. 8.

179 Mack, *Nuclear Free Zones*, p. 17.

180 Erik A. Cornellier, "In the Zone: Why the United States Should Sign the Protocol to the Southeast Asia Nuclear-Weapons-Free Zone," *Pacific Rim Law & Policy Journal* 12 (2003): 233, 234.

181 Jozef Goldblat, "Nuclear-Weapon-Free Zones: A History and Assessment," *Nonproliferation Review* (Spring/Summer 1997): 21.

182 See "Treaty on the Prohibition of the Emplacement of Nuclear Weapons and Other Weapons of Mass Destruction on the Sea-Bed and the Ocean Floor and in the Subsoil Thereof (1971 Seabed Treaty)," *Treaty Series* 955 (New York: United Nations, 1974), 117, n. 9, available online at "Oceans in the Nuclear Age: Nuclear Free Zones," Law School, Berkeley, CA: http://www.law.berkeley.edu/centers/ilr/ona/pages/zones2.htm.

183 See "Overview" to "Oceans in the Nuclear Age," Seabed Treaty, p. 9.

184 Cornellier, "In the Zone," pp. 235–36.

185 Goldblat, "Nuclear-Weapon-Free Zones," p. 31. Goldblat enumerates eleven other ways in which the treaties are "deficient." For example, only Africa's Treaty of Pelindaba prohibits research on nuclear explosives (pp. 27, 31).

186 Gerrit Oakes cited in U.S. Navy Release, "Submarine Crew Accomplishes Mission, Earns Quals Doing Extended Patrol," November 16, 2008.

187 Secretary of the Navy Donald Winter cited in States News Service release, "1,000 Trident Patrols: SSBNs the Cornerstone of Strategic Deterrence," February 24, 2009.

188 Hugh Shelton, 14th Chairman, Joint Chiefs of Staff, with Ronald Levinson and Malcolm McConnell, *Without Hesitation: The Odyssey of an American Warrior* (New York: St. Martin's Press, 2010), pp. 174–75.

189 Shelton, *Without Hesitation*, p. 175.

190 Robert S. Norris, Hans M. Kristensen, and Christopher E. Paine, *Nuclear Insecurity: A Critique of the Bush Administration's Nuclear Weapons Policies*, Natural Resources Defense Council, September 2004, p. 9: italics added.

191 Norris, *Nuclear Insecurity*, p. 6. Shelton's book affirms this assessment of the Bush administration: "As of 2008, OPLAN 8010 replaced the SIOP with smaller

and more flexible strike plans that include strike objectives beyond just Russia and China" (*Without Hesitation*, p. 175). See also Hans Kristensen, "White House Guidance Led to New Nuclear Strike Plans Against Proliferators, Document Shows," Federation of American Scientists Strategic Security Blog, November 5, 2007, describing a "United States Strategic Command" report, formerly "Top Secret," but obtained by the Federation of American Scientists through freedom of information (http://blogs.fas.org/security/2007/11/white_house_guidance_led_to_ne).

192 Locke, *Second Treatise of Governmment*, §127, p. 67.

193 See Chapter 2, section entitled "The Right to Bear Arms: An Argument about Distribution."

194 For the relevant constitutional provisions in other countries, see "A Prelude and Summary" to Part Two.

195 As we saw in Chapter 1, neither a Congressional "authorization of force" (e.g. Korea) nor a "conditional declaration of war" (e.g., the Gulf War) has the formal or substantive properties of a declaration of war.

196 Another area where we sometimes debate *whether* to aid rather than *how* to aid is the region of Good Samaritan laws. Many European countries have strict legal requirements for giving aid to strangers, whereas the Anglo-American tradition has (with the exception of a few weak state laws that have never been enforced) virtually none. But the debate centers on the question of legal enforcement, not the question of moral validity. No one questions the moral obligation to help someone in cases where doing so brings no increased risk to oneself. For example, the standard air travel announcement about emergency oxygen begins, "If you are traveling with a child, or seated next to one..." In other words, if you are seated next to a child, you *are* traveling with one.

197 On the two-tiered jury, see Chapter 4, the opening pages of the section entitled "The Brakes Are Material; the Material Is the Human Body."

198 On the double brakes on war making, see all of Chapter 1 (the legislative brake) and Chapter 2 (the citizenry as brake), as well as Chapter 4, the sections entitled "The First Brake on War: The Assembly," "The Second Brake on War: The Soldiers' Referendum," and "The Soldier's Dissent in the Homer of Hobbes."

199 For example, Aristotle, the Stoics, and the Christian fathers addressing spiritual exercises.

200 For example, John Locke, David Hume, and Bertrand Russell in Britain; William James and John Dewey in the United States.

201 For example, Pierre Bourdieu and Maurice Merleau-Ponty.

202 Montaigne, "Of Custom," in *The Complete Essays of Montaigne*, trans. Donald M. Frame (Stanford: Stanford University Press, 1965), pp. 77, 78.

203 The indictment of habit is made by Beckett's Vladimir (late in *Waiting for Godot*), not by Beckett speaking in his own voice.

204 Aristotle, *Nichomachean Ethics*, in *The Complete Works of Aristotle: The Revised Oxford Translation*, ed. Jonathan Barnes, vol. 2, Bollingen Series LXXI (Princeton: Princeton University Press, 1984), p. 1737.

205 William James, *Habit* (New York: Henry Holt, 1914), p. 66. James calculates that only before age twenty can we learn a language without a foreign accent (contemporary research has now pushed that age back to puberty), and between twenty and thirty we learn most professional and intellectual habits. Those, like Montaigne, who believe habit powerfully modifies perception in a negative direction will also be attentive to education, especially its negative outcomes: "I find that our greatest vices take shape from our tenderest childhood, and that our most important training is in the hands of nurses" ("Of Custom," p. 78).

206 Aristotle, *Nichomachean Ethics*, p. 1743.

207 John Dewey, *Human Nature and Conduct: An Introduction to Social Psychology* (New York: Henry Holt, 1922), p. 31. In *How We Think*, Dewey suggests that what makes color particularly hard for a child is that unlike many other sensory events, it does not elicit from him a specific response or adjustment: "By rolling an object, the child makes its roundness appreciable; by bouncing it, he singles out its elasticity; by throwing it, he makes weight its conspicuous distinctive factor.... The redness or greenness or blueness of the object [in contrast] does not tend to call out a reaction that is sufficiently peculiar to give prominence or distinction to the color trait" (*The Middle Works of John Dewey 1899–1924*, vol. 6, ed. Jo Ann Boydston [Carbondale: Southern Illinois University Press, 1985], pp. 275–76).

208 João Manuel Maciel Linhares et al., "The Number of Discernible Colors in Natural Scenes," *Journal of the Optical Society of America* 25, no. 12 (December 2008): 2918–24. My thanks to Bevil Conway for keeping me informed about evolving research on this question.

209 Dewey, *How We Think*, pp. 215, 216.

210 Dewey, *How We Think*, pp. 223, 225, 263.

211 Dewey, *Human Nature and Conduct*, p. 100. So key a matter is sensory perception that James Ostrow, writing about the habitual in Merleau-Ponty and Dewey, titles the book *Sensitivity*. Ostrow sees the overwhelmingly negative connotations of habit for the modern period, and has the utopian hope that by renaming it he can bring about an appropriately positive view. The idea that we might actually begin to use the word "sensitivity" where we yesterday used the word "habit" seems extraordinary (Dewey himself only uses the word once or twice in *How We Think* and *Human Nature and Conduct*). But Ostrow's act of renaming at least reminds us how centrally interested in concrete sensation and sensitivity Dewey and Merleau-Ponty are.

212 Dewey, *How We Think*, pp. 192, 212, 229, 230.

213 See Ronald Melzack, "Gate Control Theory: On the Evolution of Pain Concepts," *Pain Forum* 5, no. 1 (1996): 128–38, esp. 131; and Patrick D. Wall, "Comments After

30 Years of the Gate Control Theory," ibid., 12–22, esp. 19. For preliminary findings suggesting that the neural architecture of pain may eventually have equivalents in other sensory events, see the analogue between phantom-limb pain in those missing a limb and phantom visual objects in those with eye damage (and with no cognitive impairment or psychopathology) in Geoffrey Schultz and Ronald Melzack, "Visual Hallucinations and Mental State: A Study of 14 Charles Bonnet Syndrome Hallucinators," *Journal of Nervous and Mental Disease* 181, no. 10 (1993): 639–43.

214 Edward Jablonski, *Gershwin* (New York: Doubleday, 1987), p. 8; jacket insert to *Gershwin Plays Gershwin: The Piano Rolls* (CD: Electra Nonesuch, 1993). Malcolm Gladwell describes the "10,000 hour rule" according to which great creative achievement in any field, whether music (e.g., the Beatles) or computer design (e.g., Bill Joy, Bill Gates), requires 10,000 hours of practice (*Outliers: The Story of Success* [New York: Little, Brown and Company, 2008], pp. 35–68).

215 Tolstoy writes an instruction to himself in his diary on March 8, 1851: "Keep a journal of my weaknesses (a Franklin journal)"; and his entry for the days following are punctuated with italicized names of weaknesses ("*cowardly*," "*desire to show off*," "*lack of firmness*") followed by a specification of the discredited action. He also enumerates aspirations: "*Rule. Try to form a style: (1) in conversation, (2) in writing.*" See *Tolstoy's Diaries, Volume I: 1847–94*, ed. and trans. R. Christian (London: Athlone Press, 1885), pp. 24, 25. For a rich account of Franklin's huge impact on Tolstoy as well as many other eighteenth- and nineteenth-century Russian writers and scientists, see Eufrosina Dvoichenko-Markov, "Benjamin Franklin and Leo Tolstoy," *Proceedings of the American Philosophical Society* 96, no. 2 (April 21, 1952): 119–28; as well as Boris Eichenbaum's 1922 account of the direct link between Tolstoy's use of virtue charts in his diaries and his eventual achievement as a creative genius in *The Young Tolstoi*, trans. Gary Kern et al. (Ann Arbor: Ardis, 1972), pp. 19–22.

216 D. H. Lawrence, "Benjamin Franklin," *Studies in Classic American Literature* (New York: Viking, 1923, 1964), pp. 13, 14, 16, 19, 21.

217 Lawrence, "Benjamin Franklin," pp. 13, 19, 21.

218 Lawrence, "Benjamin Franklin," pp. 11, 14, 19.

219 Franklin's glass harmonica, merely a curiosity today, was deeply admired in Franklin's own day, as evidenced by Mozart's last work of chamber music, the 1791 *Adagio and Rondo for Glass Armonica, Flute, Oboe, Viola and Cello* (K. 617). Twenty years earlier, Mozart and his father (as we know from a September 21, 1771, letter from Leopold Mozart to his wife) stood on a balcony in Milan and waved to Marianne Davies, the first musician to play the glass harmonica in public and a young woman whose contact with Franklin was extensive enough that she has sometimes been (without sufficient evidence) identified as his niece; the Mozarts continued to meet with her both in Milan and in Venice (Emily Anderson, *Letters of Mozart and*

His Family Chronologically Arranged, Translated, and Edited with Introduction, Notes, and Indexes [New York: Norton, 1985], p. 198). Leopold Mozart's letters to his wife also describe with admiration the glass harmonica owned by Dr. Franz Mesmer ("Wolfgang too has played upon it. How I should like to have one!"), whom he and his son often visited in Vienna during this period (letter of August 12, 1773, in *Letters of Mozart*, p. 236). Mesmer later used the instrument in his medical practice. Though Franklin would eventually be part of a scientific committee that wrote a formal report discrediting Mesmer's claims about the curative powers of magnetism, in 1779 he went to visit Mesmer in Paris because of the famous physician's interest in the glass harmonica (M. E. Grenander, "Reflections on the String Quartet[s] Attributed to Franklin," *American Quarterly* 27, no. 1 [March 1975]: 82). Leopold was also acutely aware of Franklin's nonmusical achievements, as we know from his letter to his wife and son when they were in Paris in April 1778: "Write and tell me whether France has really declared war on England. You will now see the American Minister, Dr. Franklin. France recognizes the independence of the thirteen American provinces and has concluded treaties with them" (*Letters of Mozart*, p. 525).

220 John R. Hale, *Lords of the Sea: The Epic Story of the Athenian Navy and the Birth of Democracy* (New York: Viking, 2009), p. 9. Nonattendance at legislative assemblies has had penalties in widely different eras. Sarah Foot tells us that in tenth-century England, "non-attendance at assemblies" was "deemed an act of insubordination" to country and king (*Æthelstan: The First King of England* [New Haven: Yale University Press, 2011], p. 136). In twenty-first century France, nonattendance at Parliament occasions the levying of fines as the result of a law passed in 2008: as of August 2011, 102 parliamentary members out of a total of 577 have been penalized in fines ranging from 355 euros to 5325 euros ("Une centaine de deputes seraient passibles de sanctions pour absentéisme répété," *Le Monde*, August 2, 2011). According to a July 2010 *Le Monde* story, 93 deputies were sanctioned a year earlier.

221 Barack Obama, Forum with John Shattuck and Bob Herbert, John F. Kennedy Library, Boston, Massachusetts, October 20, 2006.

222 Robert C. Byrd, *Congressional Record-Senate*, 149, February 12, 2003, pp. 3580, 3583.

223 Dick Cheney, *In My Time: A Personal and Political Memoir* (New York: Simon and Schuster, 2011), p. 6. Cheney is here describing a conversation he had with a senator shortly after 9/11 when many members of Congress had evacuated from Washington: "At one point my friend Senator Don Nickles of Oklahoma asked why the executive branch had the right to decide when members of Congress, a coequal branch of government, could come back to Washington. 'Because we've got the helicopters, Don,' I told him."

224 Dan Eggen, "Cheney, Biden Spar in TV Appearances," *The Washington Post*, December 22, 2008 (describing Cheney's interview on "Fox News Sunday," December 21, 2008).

225 Locke, *Second Treatise of Government*, 212, p. 108.

226 Simon Schaffer, "The Glorious Revolution and Medicine in Britain and the Netherlands," *Notes and Records of the Royal Society of London* 43, no. 2, Science and Civilization under William and Mary (July 1989): 170.

227 Bill Clinton, interview with David Frost, *Talking with David Frost*, PBS, October 30, 1992: "Let me say something else. The other lesson of this war [in Vietnam] is if you're going to draft people and put them into combat, you should sell the conflict to the American people. You should get Congress to declare war. So there can be no doubt about what the objective is. And there ought to be clear and achievable objectives that you then put everything you've got behind achieving. None of those things happened in Vietnam. One of the things that it prepared me to do, and I think people who served in our generation—people like Senator John Kerry and Senator Bob Kerrey—I think all of us are determined to see that something like *that* does not happen again."

228 Joseph Story, *Commentaries on the Constitution of the United States: With a Preliminary Review of the Constitutional History of the Colonies and States Before the Adoption of the Constitution*, 4th ed. (Boston: Little, Brown, 1873), vol. 2, p. 87.

229 Locke, *Conduct of the Understanding*, ed. Francis W. Garforth (New York: Columbia University Press, 1966), p. 32.

230 Locke, *Conduct of the Understanding*, pp. 124, 125.

231 Locke, *Conduct of the Understanding*, p. 93.

232 Montaigne, "Of Custom," p. 77.

233 Montaigne, "Of Custom," p. 83.

234 Dewey, *Human Nature and Conduct*, p. 58.

235 Dewey, *Human Nature and Conduct*, p. 25.

236 Montaigne, "Of Custom," p. 83.

237 "The lawmaker of the Thurians ordained that whoever should want either to abolish one of the old laws or to establish a new one should present himself to the people with a rope around his neck; so that if the innovation were not approved by each and every man, he should be promptly strangled" ("Of Custom," p. 86).

238 Aristotle, *Nichomachean Ethics*, p. 1743.

239 Hobbes, *Leviathan*, ed. Macpherson, Pt. I, Ch. 6, p. 127. The alternative (and more widely credited) etymology of deliberation—which locates its root not in the word for "liberty" but the word for "weight"—also illuminates the materiality of the act. Two etymologists—Robert K. Barnhart and Ernest Klein—note that though "deliberation" originates in the root for "weigh," the formation of the word was influenced by the "liberty" root, an important point since scholars sometimes criticize Hobbes for his etymology. (See *The Barnhart Dictionary of Etymology* [New York: H. W. Wilson, 1988] and *A Comprehensive Dictionary of the English Language* [Amsterdam: Elsevier, 1971].)

240 Locke, *Conduct of the Understanding*, pp. 100, 104, 105. Although Locke himself is a brilliant practitioner of similes, he complains that a simile acts as an accelerator

used to trip thinking forward so that it can keep pace with speaking, leaping over ground that instead needs scrutiny.

241 Locke, *Conduct of the Understanding*, p. 87.

242 Locke, *Conduct of the Understanding*, pp. 69, 89.

243 Locke, *Conduct of the Understanding*, pp. 95, 124. Locke did not mean, however, that one should confine oneself to a single field of study. He urges what we today call cross-disciplinary work: "If men are for a long time accustomed only to one sort or method of thoughts, their minds grow stiff in it, and do not readily turn to another. It is therefore to give them this freedom, that I think they should be made to look into all sorts of knowledge, and exercise their understanding in so wide a variety and stock of knowledge. But I do not propose it as a variety and stock of knowledge, but a variety and freedom of thinking, as an increase of the powers and activity of the mind, not as an enlargement of its possessions" (p. 73).

244 Locke, *Conduct of the Understanding*, pp. 86, 87, 106; italics added.

245 Locke, *Conduct of the Understanding*, pp. 74, 75. "Clog" is here a wholly positive word, though it is at one later point used pejoratively (p. 125).

246 Locke, *Conduct of the Understanding*, p. 123.

247 Dewey, *How We Think*, pp. 188, 190.

248 Dewey, *How We Think*, pp. 189, 191.

249 Dewey, *Human Nature and Conduct*, p. 190.

250 Charles S. Peirce, "How to Make Our Ideas Clear," *Popular Science Monthly* (January 1878): 286–302, esp. 292. Though Peirce uses the word "thinking" throughout this essay, he clearly means that part of thinking that Aristotle calls "deliberating" since he repeatedly specifies that its goal is the taking of an action; and he excludes from "thinking" acts like listening to music that have no such action, acts that Aristotle identifies as "contemplation" or "perception" (see earlier in this chapter, the section entitled "The Claim of Emergency").

251 Dewey, *How We Think*, p. 189; Peirce, "How to Make Our Ideas Clear," p. 289.

252 Peirce, "How to Make Our Ideas Clear," p. 293.

253 The term is Peirce's, p. 292.

254 Jon Elster, *Ulysses and the Sirens: Studies in Rationality and Irrationality*, rev. ed. (Cambridge: Cambridge University Press, 1984), esp. pp. 36–111.

255 Dewey, *How We Think*, pp. 193, 194.

256 Elster, *Ulysses and the Sirens*, pp. 43, 111.

257 Aristotle, *Nichomachean Ethics*, p. 1756.

CONCLUSION: AGAINST US ALL

1 General Kevin P. Clinton, quoted by Virginia Senator John Warner in "Hearing: Air Force Nuclear Security," Committee on Armed Services, U.S. Senate, 110th Cong., 2d Sess., February 12, 2008, p. 82.

2 Naveena Kottoor, "IBM Supercomputer Overtakes Fujitsu as World's Fastest," *BBC News Technology*, June 18, 2012. According to IBM, the computer can "calculate[e] in one hour what otherwise would have taken 6.7 billion people using hand calculators 320 years to complete if they had worked non-stop."

3 Peter Linebaugh describes Henry III's Christmas dinner in 1251: "430 red dear, 200 fallow deer, 200 roe deer, 1300 hares, 450 rabbits, 2100 partridges, 290 pheasants, 395 swans, 115 cranes, 400 tame pigs, 70 pork brawns, 7000 hens, 120 peafowl, 80 salmon, and lampreys without number" ("The Secret History of the Magna Carta," *Boston Review*, Summer 2003, p. 12).

4 McKee v. Gratz, 260 US 127 (1922), cited by Linbaugh, *The Magna Carta Manifesto: Liberties and Commons for All* (Berkeley: University of California, 2008), p. 176.

5 1680 printing of *The Great Charter of the Forest, Declaring the Liberties of It. Made at Westminster, the Tenth of February, in the Ninth Year of HENRY the Third, Anno Dom. 1224. and Confirmed in the Eight and Twentieth of EDWARD the First, Anno Dom. 1299 with Some Short Observations taken out of the Lord Chief Justice COKE's Fourth Institutes of the Courts of the FORESTS. Written for the Benefit of the Publick* (London: John Kidgell, 1680), p. 38.

6 James I, "A Proclamation for Preservation of Woods," 1608, Early English Books on Line, Tract Supplement / C7:1[99], pp. 1, 2. At the end of this proclamation, the role of the forest in defending the country is again at issue. Although here the defense of the country is in the hands of the king rather than his loving subjects, interesting is the language of proceduralism both in the choosing of persons and the choosing of trees: the king says he will "appoint and authorize" officers of the Navy who will in turn choose "faitful and expert" persons who will in turn "elect and make choice" of the trees and then mark them as for the special use of the Navy (p. 2). Only woods in counties "assigned for present sale" will be at issue, suggesting a rotation of woodlands from which wood could be sold at any given time. The reign of James I is known as one dedicated to peace.

7 Allen Grossman, "Nuclear Violence, Institutions of Holiness, and the Structures of Poetry," in *The Long Schoolroom: Lessons in the Bitter Logic of the Poetic Principle* (Ann Arbor: University of Michigan Press, 1997), pp. 170, 173.

8 Robert Pogue Harrison, *Forests: The Shadow of Civilization* (Chicago: University of Chicago Press, 1992), pp. 15–17.

9 John Meyer, "Using the Public Trust Doctrine to Ensure the National Forests Protect the Public from Climate Change," *Hastings College of Law West-Northwest Journal of Environmental Law & Policy* 16 (Winter 2010): 212. Meyer writes that the Charter of the Forests was an extremely concrete tool for protecting vassals and serfs, enabling them to get needed food and fuel for warmth; he argues that even though ordinary people today in the United States do not seem to have this direct dependence on the forest, in fact our survival—like the survivor of those earlier people—appears to depend very much on the forests.

10 State constitutions—such as those of Montana, Florida, Hawaii, New York, and North Carolina—explicitly refer to the "beauty" of the state, its availability to and protections by all residing there. The Preamble to the Montana state constitution reads: "We the people of Montana grateful to God for the quiet beauty of our state, the grandeur of our mountains, the vastness of our rolling plains, and desiring to improve the quality of life, equality of opportunity and to secure the blessings of liberty for this and future generations do ordain and establish this constitution." See Bret Adams et al., "Environmental and Natural Resources Provisions in State Constitutions," in *Journal of Land, Resources, and Environmental Law* 22 (2002): 77, 103, 109.

11 For example, Steven Forrest describes the Federal Land Protection and Management Act that Congress enacted in 1976, "mandating that: the public lands be managed in a manner that will protect the quality of scientific, scenic, historical, ecological, environmental, air and atmospheric, water resource, and archaeological values: that, where appropriate, will preserve and protect certain public lands in their natural condition: that will provide food and habitat for fish and wildlife and domestic animals; and that will provide for outdoor recreation and human occupancy and use'" (Steven Forrest, "Creating New Opportunities for Ecosystem Restoration on Public Lands: An Analysis of the Potential for Bureau of Land Management Lands," *Public Land & Resources Law Review* 23 (2002): 29.

12 The beauty of earth and the conviction that it is held in common have been in the past primary inspirations for environmentalists such as Rachel Carson and John Muir, and have led to laws outlawing materials hazardous to other species as well as federal acts securing lands for both humans and other species. In her 1954 lecture "The Real World Around Us," Rachel Carson quotes the British naturalist Richard Jefferies: "The exceeding beauty of the earth . . . yields a new thought with every petal. The hours when the mind is absorbed by beauty are the only hours when we really live. All else is illusion, or mere endurance" (in *Lost Woods: The Discovered Writing of Rachel Carson*, ed. and introd. Linda Lear [Boston: Beacon Press 1998], p. 162).

For an overview of twentieth-century environmental law as inspired by Wesley Newcomb Hohfeld, Rachel Carson, and John Muir (and more recently, Bill McKibben), see Peter Manus, "One Hundred Years of Green: A Legal Perspective on Three Twentieth Century Nature Philosophers," *University of Pittsburgh Law Review* 59 (Spring 1998): 557–675.

13 Thomas Hobbes, *De Mirabilibus Pecci Being the Wonders of the Peak in Darbyshire, Commonly Called the Devil's Arse of Peak: In English and Latine, the Latine Written by Thomas Hobbes of Malmesbury, the English by a Person of Quality* (London: William Crook, 1678): On all four, p. 36; crablike, p. 74; christal water on naked limbs, p. 70; earth's lungs, p. 42; earth's veins, pp. 20, 22, 68; earth's buttocks, p. 30; female genitals, p. 42.

14 Hobbes, *De Mirabilibus Pecci*, pp. 22–24. Like the dead miners, the land itself is "wounded" by the extraction of its leaden ore. The lines in which Hobbes credits the continuity between the miners' bodies and his own reads as follows: "Bodies by bodies in these deeps we sound, / Thus arrows lost, are still by arrows found. / Before our feet, a Corps digg'd up we see, / Which minds us what we are, or ought to be. / Much like the body we about us bring" (pp. 23, 24).

Hobbes also credits nonhuman animals with perceptual acuity, even the knowledge that the ground has been made precarious by mining. See note 18, below.

15 Hobbes, *De Mirabilibus Pecci*, pp. 52–54.

16 Hobbes, *De Mirabilibus Pecci*, pp. 34, 42.

17 His fellow travelers are included only in the collective use of "we" to describe activities such as eating.

18 Hobbes's thoughts in this poem about nonhuman animals enter with acute sympathy into deer but more elaborately into his horse. The horse he rides infers from the "redoubled echo" of its own hoofs that the mined earth beneath it has been hollowed out, and therefore moves skittishly and rapidly over this part of their path (lifting high its legs in "recoil" from the echoing surface). The event lasts for just four lines, but it is one Hobbes describes with acuity (*De Mirabilibus Pecci*, p. 26), as he elsewhere in the poem describes horse motion with great clarity. By the time he wrote *De Mirabilibus Pecci*, Hobbes had already written a Latin treatise on the motion of horses, "Considerations Touching the Facility or Difficulty of the Motions of a Horse on Straight Lines or Circular" (translated and printed by S. Arthur Strong, *A Catalogue of Letters and Other Historical Documents Exhibited in the Library at Welbeck* [London: J. Murray, 1903], Appendix II, pp. 237–240). Hobbes's treatise is a deceptively simple, brilliantly revelatory four-page analysis of horse motion (forward, to the side, backward, straight lined, flexuous, circular, circular with head toward the center, circular with head toward the perimeter, etc.) all from the point of view of the horse's effort, what is easy (straight lines, all body parts moving together, direction forward) versus the three axes of difficulty that emerge when an action requires a single, double, or triple deviation from the three planes of ease.

As an author, reader, and eventually translator of poems, Hobbes surely recognized that humans and horses share a love of meter, as the lines about the counterpoint of echo and recoil above suggest. Throughout *De Mirabilibus Pecci*, Hobbes measures his course sometimes by the sun, sometimes by the stars, but often by the count of the horse's steps—4000 paces, 1000 paces, 2000 paces (pp. 25, 40, 84).

According to Elspeth Graham, Hobbes's writing assisted the Duke of Newcastle in his innovative work on horse dressage in *General System of Horsemanship*, which emphasizes a "participatory sensibility" between rider and horse and a baroque love of spirals (see "The Duke of Newcastle's 'Love . . for Good Horses': An Exploration of Meanings," in Peter Edwards, Karl A. E. Enenkel, and Elspeth

Graham, *The Horse as Cultural Icon: The Real and Symbolic Horse in the Early Modern Period* [Leiden: Brill, 2011], pp. 62, 64).

19 Peter R. Anstey and Stephen A. Harris, "Locke and Botany," in *Studies in History and Philosophy of Science, Part C* 37 (July 2006): 159.

20 M.V.C. Jeffreys, "John Locke," in *British Medical Journal* 4, no. 5935 (October 1974): 34.

21 The first number is given by Jeffreys, the revised count of 973 is given by Anstey and Harris.

22 Anstey and Harris, "Locke and Botany," pp. 159, 160. The specification of the paper is from the card catalogue entry from Oxford University's Bodleian Library where the herbarium is housed, "MS. Locke b. 7."

23 Anstey and Harris, "Locke and Botany," pp. 151, 152.

24 Anstey and Harris, "Locke and Botany," pp. 162, 163, 165.

25 Jean-Jacques Rousseau, "Letters to Mme Delessert" (May 2, 1773; May 24, 1773), in *The Reveries of the Solitary Walker, Botanical Writings, and Letter to Franquières, The Collected Writings of Rousseau*, vol. 8, ed. Christopher Kelly, trans. and annotated Charles E. Butterworth, Alexandra Cook, and Terence E. Marshall (Hanover, NH: Dartmouth College, 2000), pp. 150, 155, 165. (Hereinafter, *Botanical Writings*.)

26 Jean-Jacques Rousseau, "Letter to Margaret Cavendish Bentinck, Duchess of Portland" (September 3, 1766), in *Botanical Writings*, p. 173. Rousseau asks his correspondent to give him not only plants but her instruction: "I would find there that precious Serenity of soul which arises from the contemplation of the marvels that surround us, and, whether or not I became a better botanist, I would thereby become Confident and Wiser and happier.... The more the mind clarifies and instructs Itself, the more peacable the heart remains. The study of nature detaches us from ourselves, and elevates us to its Author. It is in this sense that one truly becomes a philosopher; it is in this way that natural history and botany have a use for Wisdom and for virtue. To put our passions off the track with the taste for beautiful knowledge Is to chain love up with bonds of flowers."

27 William Barclay, *Contra Monarchomachs*, 1.iii.c.16, quoted and translated by John Locke, *Second Treatise of Government*, §237, p. 121.

ACKNOWLEDGMENTS

Nuclear weapons have led to three great untruths: that constitutions don't matter, that centuries of political philosophy don't matter, and that live citizens don't matter. These three untruths are addressed—and corrected—in Part One, Part Two, and Part Three of this book. It is by reanimating our commitment to the three that nuclear weapons can be eliminated.

The way through these materials is—and has to be—highly detailed. The arguments cannot be made casually or in quick assertions. They must be shown to be true. Because the path is long and often intricate, a reader might now and then wish to stand in a place where the overall shape of the whole is visible. A person wishing for that overview—a short, clear book inside the long, complex one—will find it by reading the book's opening, "The Floor of the World," the Preludes to Parts One, Two, and Three, and the book's conclusion, "Against Us All." I am deeply grateful to Amanda Urban, who suggested the inclusion of the three Preludes. Designed to help the reader, her suggestion was also a great help to me. The three archways provided by the Preludes let me walk around the perimeter of the book and feel confident that my reader would be able to do so as well.

Thermonuclear Monarchy (as one of my friends recently observed) is coming out just in time for its own twenty-seventh anniversary. During those intervening years, the book has had an oral life in many public arenas in many countries—primarily the United States, but also England, Scotland, Sweden, Norway, Germany, the former Yugoslavia, and Ethiopia. The assemblies that have listened to and contested its claims have strengthened its arguments. Here I will only mention key pressures in its transformation from a set of oral arguments into a book.

The book had its start at Yale Law School and the Yale Whitney Humanities Center: Chapters 2, 5, and 6 all began there. Over many years, Owen Fiss, Akhil Amar, Bruce Ackerman, and Peter Brooks gave such sweet and brilliant hospitality and help that, when I today remember the quality of their acts, I look up and for a split second expect to see that nuclear weapons have disappeared. If knowledge, intelligence, and kindness could bring an end to harm, the harm would have ended.

In addition to Yale, other law schools have provided an arena for testing the book's claims, either by inviting me to give a single piece of the argument (Berkeley, Northwestern, Georgetown, Stanford, Cornell, Cardozo, and Chicago law schools) or by inviting me to give two, three, or even four parts of the book at spaced intervals (the law schools at Harvard, the University of Southern California, and Columbia). Enduring support and repeated help has come from Noah Feldman, Charles Fried, and Martha Minow at Harvard Law School. My work has also been animated by Hilary Schor, Ariela Gross, Ronald Garet, and Dana Villa at USC Law School; by Julie Stone Peters at Columbia Law School; and by Jeremy Waldron, first at Berkley, later Columbia.

The Introduction, "The Floor of the World," underwent its first trial at the New School of Social Research Lecture Series on Constitutional Law; its second at Trinity College, Cambridge (Center for Research in Arts, Social Sciences, and Humanities); and its third at a UC Santa Barbara 2010 conference on environmentalism. Parts of it were included in an address I gave in Norway to inaugurate the Bergen Lectures in Critical and Political Inquiry; and again in a keynote address I gave to the Bulletin of Atomic Scientists in January 2012 when that group met and reset the doomsday clock to five minutes to midnight. Ongoing conversations with J. T. Scarry during my writing of the piece gave a silver lining to its storm-filled horizon.

Chapter 1, on the incompatibility between nuclear weapons and the constitutional requirement for a Congressional declaration of war, was researched and written at the Wissenschaftskolleg zu Berlin during the year the wall fell. The opportunity to give this piece at Amherst College's Department of Law, Jurisprudence and Social Thought led to discussions with Austin Sarat and to the publication of a preliminary version in his and Thomas Kearn's *Law's Violence*. I have a great debt to historian Marc Trachtenberg for his generous and decisive help with the Eisenhower papers documenting that president's contemplated use of nuclear weapons in the Taiwan Straits crisis and in Berlin. Ongoing conversations with Mark Fisher about historical wars have contributed to this and every chapter.

The year-long research and writing for Chapter 2 on the right to bear arms were made possible by a Guggenheim Fellowship. First given at Yale Law School, this work was also one of my Beckman Lectures at Berkeley; I am grateful to that always-electric intellectual community, especially to Richard Wollheim for his formal response to the lecture and many subsequent conversations; and to John Searle and Steve Knapp for their inquiries and challenges. Three other arenas were helpful: the American Political Science Association Panel on the Second Amendment; a meeting in Stockholm, Sweden, with the Coalition for the Prevention of Accidental Nuclear War (sponsored by all seven political parties and held in their Parliament); and a public symposium, attended by a thousand people, in Addis Ababa on "The Making of a New Ethiopian Constitution." An early version of the chapter appeared in the *University of Pennsylvania Law Review* (whose editorial board shocked and delighted me by insisting on an increase, rather than the usually insisted upon decrease, in footnotes). The 2008 Supreme Court *District of Columbia v. Heller* decision drew me back to this work, and to needed enrichment and revision.

The research on Thomas Hobbes for Chapter 3 ("The Social Contract is a Covenant for Peace") and Chapter 4 ("The Social Contract and the Double Brakes on Injury") began during a 2004 stay at the Center for Advanced Study in the Behavioral Sciences in Palo Alto and continued when I was a 2008 Fellow at Harvard's Safra Center for Ethics, for which I thank Arthur Applbaum. Richard Tuck's revolutionary vision of Hobbes is often cited in these chapters, and I have benefited not only from his writings but from his generous conversation as well. Inspiration, too, came from David Grewal during his years as a junior fellow at Society of Fellows, and from J. T. Scarry. The completed chapters are too recent to have had the oral life enjoyed by Chapters 1, 2, 5, and 6; so I am especially grateful to Noah Feldman and Martha Minow for inviting me to give a part of Chapter 3 at Harvard Law School; and to John Bender for inviting me to give a section of Chapter 4 at Stanford Humanities Center when I was the Marta Sutton Weeks Visitor there in January 2008.

Chapter 5 on "Consent and the Body" was written during a year funded by the University of Pennsylvania (where I then taught) and was first given at Yale's Whitney Humanities Center, and published in an early form in *New Literary History*. My thanks again to Peter Brooks, as well as to Richard Sennett, an ardent supporter of the early version. At Harvard, I have for many years taught a course for both law students and students in the Arts and Sciences on "The Problem of Consent." We scrutinize the medical, legal, and philosophic materials from this chapter during the early weeks of the course, which has continually refreshed and enriched those materials. A 2012 research leave from Harvard University supported me while I carried out extensive research for and revision of this penultimate chapter.

Chapter 6, "Thinking in an Emergency," (like Chapters 2 and 5) had its start at Yale Law School. Invited to be the Leff Fellow there in 1993, I was able to research and write the lecture because of a leave provided by Harvard University. During that summer, Dan McKanan provided inventive research assistance. I have given this lecture in many humanities and social science venues, including a memorable and richly helpful session at Kings College at Cambridge in 1996; Harvard's Program for Ethics and the Professions in 1997; the Institute for Public Affairs and Civic Engagement at Salisbury, Maryland, in 2003; a seminar at the University of Glasgow in 2006, and in Berlin at the Freie Universität Collaborative Research Center and House of World Cultures in 2010. Dennis Thompson has been in the vanguard of inspiration for continuing this research, as have Emma Rothschild, Nancy Cartwright, Kate Medina, and Todd Kelly. Transforming this work from a lecture to a chapter required a full year of work in 2010. I am honored that Norton chose to publish a modified version of the completed chapter separately as the inaugural book in their Global Ethics series, originally undertaken with Amnesty International.

W. W. Norton has enabled me to appreciate the meaning of the phrase "A-team," for Amy, Angela, and Anna always had answers. My editors Amy Cherry and Angela von der Lippe, and their assistant Anna Mageras, solved every problem with an aura of amiability, delight, and angelic wisdom that enacted their names. Their musical voices, affirmative vision, belief in books, and knowledge of how to make books would lift the spirits of any author, and with luck, lift the book into full sail as well. I met their requested manuscript-delivery date of 12-12-12 by sending it in at noon, thereby giving it a 12-12-12-12 arrival. If the 1179 footnotes are correctly attached to their intended sentences, it will be the result of Carol Rose's meticulous copyediting. During the many stages of proofs, project editor Leslie Huang repeatedly amazed me with her patience and precision.

Throughout the writing of this book, Amanda Urban has been a strong, urgent, background force. Known publically for her whirlwind power, Amanda Urban's acts of constant care for her authors and for their readers give her the rarest and most delicate of sensitivities and sensibilities.

From 2006 through 2009 research assistant Matthew Spellberg outpaced every request I could make and provided help whose great benefits (once he deserted Cambridge for Paris, Berlin, and Princeton) outlasted even his own presence.

In the final three years of work, my brother Joe Scarry and my sister Patricia Jones were consulted on a weekly—often a daily—basis about arguments, evidence, and questions of visual design. They are each in their own lives so dedicated to justice and beauty that they probably should not be given any credit here: they made their assistance appear as effortless as it was abundant and decisive.

To describe Philip Fisher's help would require a manuscript as long as the one already here. Early and late, sunrise and sundown, he has tested every argument, touched every hope, turned every page. It is because of him that the book opens, and because of him that it can now at last close.

INDEX